Course	Business Law
Course Number	**BUS 102**
	North Shore Community College

http://create.mheducation.com

ISBN-10: 1121567029   ISBN-13: 9781121567023

Contents

Credits

Preface

The thirteenth edition of *Business Law with UCC Applications* updates many key areas of the law. As in previous editions, a great deal of care has been taken to present business law concepts in the most coherent and accessible way and to provide up-to-date coverage of business law topics that are essential to today's students. All of the chapters for this edition have been updated, and we have continued to enhance our coverage of the important topics of cyber-commerce, international law, identity theft, trade secrets, abandoned property, eminent domain, mortgages, bankruptcy, limited liability companies (LLC), ethics, the Dodd-Frank Act, the revised Uniform Partnership Act, the Health Insurance Portability and Accountability Act, the Genetic Information Nondiscrimination Act, the War Powers Act, changes in state law regarding collective bargaining, the Troubled Asset Relief Program, the Home Affordable Modification Program, the Patient Protection and Affordable Care Act, proposed changes in the court system, the War Powers Act, and alternative dispute resolution.

The popular format of the twelfth edition has been enhanced, with learning objectives identified in the margin where that material appears in the text. Each chapter begins with an outline followed by The Opening Case, with numbered questions and Chapter Objectives. Titles have been given to every example. Major headings and chapter summaries continue to be numbered, following the chapter outline. The popular case illustrations, presenting either hypothetical or actual situations based on well-founded court decisions, have been retained and updated. Our Quick Quiz feature appears in each chapter and allows students to test their knowledge of the chapter topics while they actively study the text. A new Self-Evident Truths feature has been included in many chapters in this edition, giving both the instructor and the students an opportunity to discuss stimulating, provocative, and controversial topics suggested by the content in each chapter.

We also have retained case studies pertaining to each of the nine parts of the book, which summarize an actual litigated case, present a lengthy extract from the judge's decision, and provide follow-up questions that are pertinent to the cases and are appropriate as a review of the legal concepts involved. Activities at the end of each chapter, including Key Terms, Questions for Review and Discussion, and Cases for Analysis, help students self-check their understanding of the terms and concepts presented in the chapter. We also have included the Question of Ethics element throughout the text. The U.S. Constitution appears in Appendix A. Included in Appendix B are four articles of the Uniform Commercial Code. Marginal references within the chapters tie these specific documents to the content. The thirteenth edition of *Business Law with UCC Applications* thus offers a comprehensive package of materials to meet both instructors' and students' needs.

Ethics, Law, and the Judicial System

Part One

Ethics, Law, and the Judicial System

Chapter 1

Ethics, Social Responsibility, and the Law

THE OPENING CASE   WikiLeaks, Secret Documents, and Deception

One of the essential weapons in the diplomatic arsenal is the guarantee of secrecy. If diplomats cannot be certain that their cables, letters, and dispatches will be kept secret, they will not be able to communicate candidly with the decision makers back home. So what happens when a group like WikiLeaks reveals such secrets? Is it ethical for such online groups to reveal the contents of secret dispatches that were obtained illegally in the first place? What happens to the trust that is inherent within the diplomatic process when secrets can be accessed so easily? Does bringing diplomatic activity out into the open help or hinder the public's ability to evaluate the ethical behavior of our diplomats? A case in point can be found among documents disclosed by WikiLeaks that revealed that American diplomats in the former Soviet nation of Georgia may have relied too heavily on the inside reports given to them by Georgian leaders and less on more objective intelligence from outside sources. The secret cables released by WikiLeaks also indicate that the Georgian leaders, with their own agenda aimed at getting United States support for their plan to resist Russian dominance, may have deliberately distorted the information passed onto the Americans. Even more serious, the secret cables reveal that the Georgians probably provoked an encounter with South Ossetia, an enclave that had broken away from Georgia and, in

the process, had sought Russian protection. In fact, it now appears that the Georgians launched a first strike against South Ossetia and then told the Americans that the Ossetians had attacked them. The documents released by WikiLeaks indicate that the Americans relied on the one-sided accounts manufactured by the Georgian government and did not seek any outside verification of the reports. It is clear that the American diplomats made several tactical errors in the management of this incident. However, were they not ethically correct in supporting the democratic Georgian state against the autocratic Russian Federation? Is it not a morally superior position to defend democracy even at the expense of the truth? Or does "truth" occupy a morally superior position in the hierarchy of ethical values? Should the Georgian officials have been more candid with the Americans or did they have a higher responsibility to protect their own people and territory that justified their distortion of the truth? Keep these issues in mind as we explore the nature of ethics in this chapter. (See C. J. Chivers, "Embracing Georgia, U.S. Misread Signs of Region's Rifts, Cables Show," *The New York Times,* December 2, 2010, p. A-15.)

Opening Case Questions

1. Was WikiLeaks justified in obtaining the leaked cables illegally? Explain.

2. Does gaining American support (the end), justify the Georgian first strike against South Ossetia (the means)? Explain.

3. Were the Georgian officials justified in distorting the truth to protect their own citizens and territory? Explain.

4. Does the duty to protect a democracy "trump" the telling of the truth? Explain.

5. Does the morality of a nation-state differ from the morality of an individual? Why or why not?

Learning Objectives

1. Define law and morality.
2. Distinguish among natural law, positive law, negative rights theories.
3. Explain ethical relativism.
4. Describe social contract theory.
5. Outline the steps in applying utilitarianism.
6. Define rational ethics.
7. Explain the dual nature of ethics in government
8. Outline the arguments supporting social responsibility.
9. Explore the need for law in our society.
10. Clarify how the law and ethics are usually in harmony with each other.

1-1 Defining the Law, Morality, and Ethics

In a perfect world, everyone would know what the law is and why the law is an important aspect of our lives. Similarly, in an ideal situation, everyone would know what the term "ethics" means and how it is different from the concept of morality. Of course, a quick glance at any daily newspaper or a brief look at the evening news will reveal that people hold widely diverse views on the difference between right and wrong. If this were not the case, if everyone thought exactly the same about right and wrong, there would have been no conflict over the posting of secret documents by WikiLeaks, no dispute over North Korea's bombing of a South Korean island, no need for the assassination attempts on Iranian nuclear scientists, and no disagreement about the Pope's fluctuating position on birth control. In fact, in a perfect world in which everyone held similar, if not identical, ethical values, there would be no need for secret dispatches, nuclear weapons, or lectures on birth control. Yet in each of these cases, and others like them, many people's opinions clash not only on how to handle each situation but also on the ethical or moral nature of the actions themselves.

It is therefore no surprise that most legal textbooks and many treatises on ethics begin by defining these disciplines. This tradition stands in marked contrast to most other studies. Few physics textbooks pause to tell the reader what physics is. Fewer history books devote space to explaining the term *history*, and almost no math texts begin by defining *math*. However, that is as it should be. These disciplines and others like them are fixed in our minds as implacable fields of study. In history, for example, the fact that Barrack Obama was sworn in as the first African-American president of the United States in 2009 is not open to debate. Nor is our understanding that such an event is historical fact. The same is true of the second law of thermodynamics in physics and the multiplication tables in mathematics. These facts are not debatable, except in the most esoteric way. [See Jeffrie G Murphy and Jules L. Coleman, *The*

Philosophy of Law (Boulder, CO: Westview Press, 1990), p. 6; and John C. Calhoun, "A Disquisition on Government," in *Philosophy in America,* eds. Paul Russell Anderson and Max Harold Fisch (New York: Appleton-Century Crofts, Inc, 1939), pp. 356–357.]

The Law and Morality

This is not the case with morality and the law. People *will* argue about whether the law is a form of civil management or a way to dictate individual behavior, whether it ought to be created by a national government or a regional state system, and whether it should change regularly or stay the same indefinitely. They will even argue about whether the rules made by the government demand absolute, unquestioned obedience or simply ask for occasional recognition as optional guiding principles. People will also argue about moral issues. They will argue about whether schools should censor student newspapers, whether capital punishment should be permitted, and whether waging a preventative war is morally correct. This is why we pause at the beginning of *Business Law with UCC Applications* to define the law and morality and to distinguish between ethics and morals, concepts that many of us usually do not think about on a daily basis.

The law consists of rules of conduct established by the government of a society to maintain harmony, stability, and justice. It accomplishes these objectives by defining the legal rights and duties of the people. The law also provides a way to protect the people by enforcing these rights and duties through the courts, the executive branch, and the legislature. The law is therefore a means of civil management. Certainly, the law usually cannot stop a person from doing wrong. However, the law can punish an individual who chooses to do that wrong, whatever it might be. The law then draws the line between conduct that is permissible and that which is not allowed, so people, at the very least, know that they can be punished if they choose to disobey the law.

In contrast, morals are values that govern a society's attitude toward right and wrong and toward good and evil. As a result, we should see morality as more fundamental than law. Therefore, morality ought to serve as a guide for those bodies within our society, such as the courts, the executive branch, the legislature, and the administrative agencies, that make, interpret, and enforce the law. Most of the time, these law-making, law-interpreting, and law-enforcing bodies will follow the belief that morality and legality ought to match up with each other. Indeed, there are even those philosophers of law who argue that morality is a necessary element of the law. They would say that you cannot have a philosophically valid law that is not grounded in morality.

Values and Ethics

So far we have defined **law** as a set of rules created by the government to establish a means of civil management that directs people to do what is right and avoid what is wrong. The purpose served by the law includes the creation of order, stability, and justice. The assumption is that if these purposes are met, right will be served and wrong defeated. Moreover, we have also defined **morals** as those fundamental values that tell us the difference between right and wrong in the first place. What we have not explained, however, is where those values come from. This is the job of ethics. Ethics is the attempt to develop a means of determining what these values ought to be and for formulating and applying rules that enforce those values.

Natural Law Theory

According to one system of legal thought, morality and the law are united in a common bond based on their intrinsic nature. This system of thought, which is generally known as natural law, sees law as originating from some objective, superior force that stands outside the everyday experience of most people. That superior force might be God, human nature, rational thought, or some other source of universal truth. Thus, according to natural law, there exists an unbreakable link joining morality to the law in a fundamental way. This link exists because a law must, in its most basic form, be moral. Otherwise, it is not lawful. A law with an immoral purpose is not a law at all. Instead it is an anomaly that does not fit into our concept of either law or the legal process. It is, of course, one thing to say that laws must be firmly grounded in morality and quite another to argue that legality and morality are always the same thing. There are, in fact, some laws that have no moral content whatsoever. Thus, a statute that requires a driver to have an operator's license has no intrinsic moral substance, though such a law is not immoral on its face either. The natural law theorist would say that a law must, at the very least, be morally neutral to have any integrity as a law. In a larger sense, a law that says people must be licensed to drive, while not intrinsically moral, contributes to the orderly and stable functioning of society and is therefore moral because of its purpose and effect.

Positive Law Theory

Natural law is sometimes confused with positive law because both depend on an outside force for their understanding of law, morality, and human rights. The difference is that positive law says that the law comes from social institutions rather than from God, from human nature, or from human rationality. Positive law, then, is a legal theory that says that the law originates from an outside source that has emerged from within society. The process works something like this: The people of a society discover their rights as they live and work together. This discovery leads to commonly held rights that are described in a series of documents, such as the Magna Carta and the U.S. Constitution. Exactly why people discover rather than invent universal rights is not clear. One argument says that rights are intuitively understood to exist within the human character. So, when people write documents such as the Constitution, they include certain human rights such as the right to be treated fairly under the law. (See Alan Dershowitz, *Rights from Wrongs: A Secular Theory of the Origin of Rights,* New York: Perseus Books Group, 2004, 39–42.)

Some people say that human decency will ultimately triumph over human cruelty, giving rise to a just and moral society that will eventually abolish the worst sins of humanity. This brand of positive law is sometimes called the *Law of Peoples*. Not everyone agrees with this position, but such agreement is not necessary, so long as principles of decency and social justice can be found in certain universal documents such as the Bill of Rights in the United States Constitution or the United Nations Universal Declaration of Human Rights. Despite the differences between positive law and natural law, they hold one idea in common, namely, the belief that human values apply to all people at all times. Neither theory, however, tells us how to make ethical decisions. For that reason, we now turn to the next topic, ethical decision making. [See John Rawls, *The Law of Peoples* (Cambridge, MA: Harvard University Press, 1999), pp. 6–7.]

Negative Rights Theory

Before moving on to ethical decision making, there is a minority position on human rights that deserves some attention. That opinion argues that "rights" are a human invention designed to help people escape moral law. Thus, the right to privacy is actually a way to hide the truth from the public at large; the right to bear arms is the right to harm, perhaps even kill; the right to free speech is the right to lie and get away with it, and the right to private property is the right to exploit, plunder, and pollute that property. This theory of "negative-rights," as it is sometimes called, admits that the rights themselves do not create the escape from responsibility that they permit. Rather, these so-called rights give people an escape clause when they are caught doing something shameful. Thus, when people are caught with stolen goods or other contraband, they often claim that their privacy was invaded.

THE OPENING CASE *Revisited, Part I*
WikiLeaks, Secret Documents, and Deception, Round 2

A quick review of the opening case at the beginning of this chapter will demonstrate the problems highlighted by the negative rights theory. For example, should the WikiLeaks people be apprehended by the authorities, they will likely defend their posting of the secret papers by arguing that they were merely defending the people's right to know. Moreover, from a more personal perspective, they will also probably argue that they were simply exercising their own right to free speech. On the other hand, the diplomats whose papers were revealed will contend that WikiLeaks invaded their right to privacy by posting the secret papers. Similarly, the governments involved will insist that their property rights were violated when the papers were stolen in the first place. Finally, newspapers like *The New York Times* that published news stories about the secret papers will argue that they had the right to do so based on the First Amendment's guarantee of a right to a free press. A negative rights theorist would argue that every single one of the parties, from the WikiLeaks people to *The New York Times,* has done something wrong and is now trying to escape responsibility by claiming that one of the other parties violated their rights.

Similarly, when media people are sued for libel, they frequently defend their actions by claiming the protection of a free press. Finally, when slumlords fail to repair dilapidated apartment buildings, they claim the right to private property. [See Slavoj Zizek, *The Fragile Absolute* (London and New York: Verso, 2000), pp. 101–102.]

Ethical Decision Making

People make ethical decisions every day. However, how they make those decisions is not always clear. Some people say that they do not think about ethics but instead act instinctively when faced with a moral problem. Others say that they just do what they "believe" is right. Still others say that they follow the rules they learned in school, in their place of worship, or in their family setting. Some professions, businesses, and organizations develop guidelines, usually called rules of conduct or canons of professional responsibility. Such rules generally describe certain levels of behavior. Some behaviors are encouraged; others are discouraged. Punishments are often included in these guidelines.

While such rules are admirable, they are often so long and complex that they end up covering pages of text that require an in-depth study just to understand the basics. A case in point involves the Ohio Rules of Professional Conduct for attorneys. The code consists of eight different subsections, each of which includes from four to eighteen rules. Each rule is then followed by a series of official comments that review, explain, and clarify each of the rules and any amendments that have been made to those rules. In all, the Ohio Rules cover 74 pages of text. Moreover, and more to the point, such rules are aimed at professional conduct alone and often do not even address general moral conduct. Sometimes such codes even go so far as to excuse or ignore immoral conduct. For instance, Official Comment 2 following Rule 8.4 of the Ohio Rules covering the misconduct of an attorney, states that "matters of personal moral fitness, such as adultery and comparable offenses . . . have no specific connection to fitness for the practice of law." Perhaps, most telling, is the fact that these rules frequently supply "loopholes" that permit people to escape culpability even when such culpability is obvious. Again, Official Comment 4 following Ohio Rule 8.4 states that "(a) lawyer may refuse to comply with an obligation imposed by law upon a good faith belief that no valid obligation exists." We can legitimately question the effectiveness of an obligation that can be avoided simply by manufacturing a "good faith belief that no valid obligation exists."

quick quiz 1-1

1. Natural law theory holds that there is no link between morality and law.	true | false
2. Law has nothing to do with civil management.	true | false
3. Ethical decisions are made in a variety of ways.	true | false

1-2 Ethical Theories

Throughout the history of philosophy, many scholars have offered techniques for determining those values that ought to guide all ethical decisions. Although these theories differ in their particulars, they all have one thing in common: Each theory is based on the assumption that people want to live ethical lives. If this were not the case, there would be no need to fashion these theories in the first place. Nevertheless, despite this common assumption, the theories differ greatly in their individual approaches to the problem of determining the nature of the values that underline ethical decision making.

Ethical Relativism

Ethical relativism says that there are no objective or absolute standards of right and wrong. Rather, the standards used to distinguish between right and wrong change from circumstance to circumstance and from person to person. Thus, ethical rules are relative; that is, the rules vary depending upon the actor, the circumstances, and countless other factors that may affect a person's ethical judgments. Because relativism emphasizes the highly individualized nature of ethical decision making, it is also called subjective ethics.

Ethical relativism is a very common position among Americans because the United States is a country of immigrants from a wide variety of cultures, many of which have different social values. Because many Americans want to respect these different cultures and their value systems, they often conclude that each culture is right within its own world, even when the values of those cultures clash with one another. Moreover, the United States was founded on a tradition that allows and even encourages a free exchange of ideas, feelings, and opinions on all subjects, including ethics.

Shortcomings of Ethical Relativism
It should be instantly clear that ethical relativism cannot be reconciled with either natural law or positive law, because both of these two fundamental theories assume the existence of a universal standard of behavior. Natural law says that this universal standard originates on a superior plane of existence, perhaps with God or with human nature, while positive law says that it emerges from within certain documents such as the United Nations Universal Declaration of Human Rights or the Bill of Rights of the United States Constitution. In contrast, ethical relativism denies the existence of any universal standard of behavior. Thus, according to ethical relativism, no one can ever do, say, or think anything wrong. Moreover, no one can disagree

with anyone just because another person holds a different view on the morality of an action. In fact, if we pursue ethical relativism to its logical end, neither natural law nor positive law can exist.

These results are not unlike those that flow from an application of negative rights theory. In both cases the primary objective of the moral actor is to absolve himself or herself of moral responsibility and to shift that moral responsibility to some other moral (or perhaps immoral) actor. Similarly, as noted previously, professional codes of conduct sometimes provide such loopholes. Of course, since everyone else is in the process of using one or more of these strategies for denying moral responsibility, the net result is that no one admits to any moral responsibility at all.

Situational Ethics Still, certain aspects of relativism are appealing, including the
notion that the ethical decisions of other individuals ought not to be judged without taking into consideration the special situation in which those individuals find themselves. This is why some people favor a variation of relativism that takes different situations into consideration but does not necessarily use those different situations to exonerate the actor completely. This theory, which is known as situational ethics, argues that each of us can judge a person's ethical decisions only by initially placing ourselves in the other person's situation. This technique allows us to be aware of the various factors that led to the other person's situation. Such an approach encourages people to look at others with tolerance and patience, an outlook that all of us would like to see practiced by those who might be inclined to judge our ethical decisions. However, it would be more satisfying if we agreed on a single ethical standard for making such moral judgments. Consequently, we must look elsewhere for a more consistent set of ethical values.

Social Contract Theory

Social contract theory holds that right and wrong are measured by the obligations imposed on each individual by an implied agreement among all individuals within a particular social system. At the most fundamental level, the social contract says that for people to live together harmoniously, they must give up certain freedoms to receive certain protections in return. Thus, all individuals give up the freedom to do as they please and in return receive a guarantee that other individuals will curb their behavior, thus protecting everyone else in that society from random and indiscriminate actions. The existence of the implied social contract permits us to live together in peace and harmony. For example, one rule that emerges from the social contract is that people should never make unsupported judgments about one another but should instead always investigate the facts in an effort to uncover the truth about the character of a person or the nature of a situation. Such a rule prevents people from avoiding one another, cheating one another, or, even worse, attacking one another simply because of the way another person looks, speaks, or acts.

Naturally, for the social contract to work, most people must adhere to its rules, and those who do not must be punished. If this were not the case, then the social contract would disintegrate, and the society would return to a "state of nature" in which people must fend for themselves. As is true of ethical relativism, there are problems with social contract theory. One problem is that social contract theory is descriptive rather than prescriptive. A descriptive theory simply describes the values at work within a social system, rather than explaining how the values originated in the first place. In contrast, a prescriptive theory explains how to come up with the values that permit a society to run smoothly. Of course, not everyone believes that social contract theory is descriptive only. Some ethical theorists argue that social contract ethics is a prescriptive theory because it places a value on the obligation itself. Thus, the benefits that people receive by knowing others will not judge them creates the obligation not to judge anyone else. Social contract ethics therefore

THE OPENING CASE *Revisited, Part II*
WikiLeaks, Secret Documents, and Deception, Round 3

If we apply the principles of social contract ethics to the WikiLeaks case, we can see that the decision by the WikiLeak people to post the secret documents on the Web violates the social contract. There is a time-honored principle within the diplomatic social contact that states that the content of diplomatic messages is to remain secret. The principle is designed to assure diplomats that they will be able to communicate openly with the decision makers back home. This process helps government officials make informed decisions based on the assessment of diplomats who have first-hand knowledge of events and personalities in foreign countries. Without the assurance of secrecy, those involved in foreign affairs will be tempted to present a less than candid picture of the conditions present in their assigned areas, thus crippling the decision-making process. The tradition of secrecy works because of the perceived mutual benefit that is gained from the frank nature of diplomatic communication. There is, however, no foolproof way to protect secrecy especially with the Internet, texting, e-mail, and so on. Thus, it is not difficult for the WikiLeaks people or others like them to gain access to and then post secret dispatches. Certainly, there are legal ways to deal with those who violate the principle after the fact. This, however, does not solve the problem once sensitive information has been released and the damage has been done. If the social contract is consistently and regularly violated in this way, the entire social system can unravel.

concentrates on each individual's obligation to everyone else and on the belief that, as long as these obligations are met, social stability will be preserved.

Utilitarianism

Utilitarianism is an ethical theory that says that the morality of an action is determined by its ultimate effects. The more good that results, the more ethical is the action. Conversely, the more bad that results, the less ethical is the action. Unlike ethical relativism, which is constantly shifting, utilitarianism seeks only one stable goal: the greatest good for the greatest number. Determining the greatest good for the greatest number, however, is not as simple as it sounds. For one thing, we must resist the temptation to transform the greatest good for the greatest number principle into the "greatest good for me" principle. One way to avoid mistakes that can result from an improper application of utilitarianism is to follow these steps:

1. The action to be evaluated should be stated in unemotional, general terms. For example, "stealing another person's property" is emotional language; "confiscating property for one's own use" is somewhat less emotional.

2. Every person or class of people that will be affected by the action must be identified.

3. Good and bad consequences in the relation to those people affected must be considered.

4. All alternatives to the action stated in step 1 must be considered.

5. Once step 4 has been carried out, a conclusion must be reached. Whichever alternative creates the greatest good for the greatest number of people affected by the action is the one that ought to be taken.

Despite the systematic approach of the utilitarian theory, many people are uncomfortable with it. One questionable aspect of utilitarianism is that, in business at least, it can be confused with utility thinking. Utility thinking, which is also referred to as cost-benefit thinking, looks only at corporate benefits and problems rather than the benefits and problems that will result for others outside the boardroom.

EXAMPLE 1-1: The Secret America of the Post 9/11 Age

In the aftermath of 9/11 and in a good faith attempt to create an information network among law enforcement agencies across the United States, the Department of Homeland Security, the FBI, and the Department of Defense have enlisted the aid of local law enforcement agencies in a plan designed to create an enormous database that includes information about American citizens on all aspects of their lives. Part of this project, which has poured billions of dollars into state and local law enforcement agencies, is the Nationwide Suspicious Activity Reporting Initiatve, or SAR. Under the SAR strategy, law enforcement agencies are empowered to gather information on American citizens who are suspected of engaging in suspicious activities. The ultimate goal is to create an enormous database of information that can be accessed and shared across the nation at all levels. To aid in this goal, the term *suspicious activity* has been defined by the government as "observed behavior reasonably indicative of pre-operational planning related to terrorism or other criminal activity." The plan and its objectives appear good on paper. However, a closer look might raise some doubts. For example, the definition of suspicious activity seems unduly vague and exceptionally open-ended. What if a tourist, for example, is spotted taking photographs of a town square? So far so good. But what if the local police station or sheriff's office is also located on the square? Could that be grounds for labeling the photographer's activity as "pre-operational planning related to terrorism"? Probably. As a result, the identity of an innocent tourist becomes imbedded within a national database listing suspected terrorists. Now, the utility thinker would argue that the overall security of the United States is worth the cost of the invasion of privacy suffered by one innocent citizen. This might be good utility thinking, but is it pure utilitarian thinking? The utilitarian must always balance the greatest good produced by an action against the effect that the action has on the greatest number of people. (See Dana Priest and William M. Arkin of *The Washington Post*, "Fallout of 9/11: A Secret America," *The Columbus Dispatch*, December 21, 2010, pp. A-1 and A-6.)

Self-Evident Truths

Read the following quotation on the nature of morality. As you read the quotation and reflect on the ideas that the author presents, ask yourself if the position represents your own point of view. Then answer the following questions based on the reading. Make sure that you are prepared to defend each response in a thoughtful manner.

> From the American founding until World War II, there was a widespread belief in this country that there is a moral order in the universe that makes claims on us. This belief was not unique to Americans. It was shared by Europeans since the very beginning of Western civilization, and it is held even today by all the traditional cultures of the world. The basic notion is that morality is external to us and is binding on us. In the past, Americans and Europeans, being for the most part Christian, might disagree with Hindus and Muslims about the exact source of this moral order, its precise content, or how a society should convert its moral beliefs into legal and social practice. But there was little doubt across the civilizations of the world about the existence of such an order. Moreover, the laws and social norms typically reflected this moral consensus. During the first half of the twentieth century, the moral order generated some clear American social norms. . . . The point is not that everyone lived up to the dictates of the moral code, but that it supplied a standard, accepted virtually throughout society, for how one should act.
> —Dinesh D'Souza, *The Enemy at Home* (New York: Doubleday, 2007), p. 19.

Self-Evident Questions

1. The author observes that before World War II people believed in an external morality that binds us all. What sociological, political, and economic events might have worked together to destroy that belief in an external morality? Explain.

2.   Do you agree that Christians, Hindus, and Muslims, all shared in the consent of that universal moral code? Why or why not?

3.   If many people saw fit to completely ignore this common code of conduct, then what was the point of having such a code in the first place? Explain.

4.   What "clear American norms" might have been generated by this universal moral order? Explain.

5.   Given the cosmopolitan world in which we live today, does a universal moral code make any sense at all? Explain.

Thus, in the Secret America-9/11 case, the goals and the techniques of the Nationwide Suspicious Activity Reporting Initiative, seem to benefit a great number of people at a cost that affects only a few innocent citizens. Yet, a closer examination reveals that these activities may actually undermine the long-term stability of the entire American system. If the practice continues, it will inevitably extend to more and more people. Eventually, what appears to be a harmless violation of the rights of one or two people begins to affect us all. Before we know it, children are reporting the "suspicious" activities of their parents; police officers are detaining innocent citizens; business people and politicians are naming names in front of Congressional committees, and the entire social fabric has begun to unravel. Certainly, this is not the intent of utilitarianism nor would well-meaning utilitarian thinkers endorse this kind of social collapse. Nevertheless, because utilitarian thinkers can sometimes be led astray by utility thinking, it is wise for us to look at an additional ethical theory.

Rational Ethics

Rational ethics replaces the shifting standards of relativism, the prescriptive approach of social contract theory, and the result-oriented standard of utilitarianism with a system that is objective, logical, and relatively consistent. Rational ethics is a philosophical theory that says ethical values can be determined by a proper application of human reason. The theory assumes that, because all human beings are rational, all human beings will have the same ethical values. Therefore, rational ethics ought to establish universal rules of behavior that apply to all people at all times. For this reason, rational ethics is often referred to as *objective ethics*. Rational ethics begins with the premise that only human beings are morally responsible for their actions. Animals, plants, and inanimate objects may cause injury or harm, but they are never held morally responsible because they are incapable of making rational decisions. Therefore, we say that they are *amoral*. The only thing that separates moral beings from those that are amoral is the rationality of the moral beings.

The Golden Rule and Rational Ethics   As rational beings, people think for themselves and, in doing so, recognize their own self-worth as individuals. Along with self-worth comes a belief in certain rights. These rights include the right to life, the right to be free from injury, the right to be treated fairly, the right to self-determination, and so on. Rational beings recognize that they do not want to be killed or cheated. They do not want their freedom taken away without just cause and due process. Because they believe in their own rights, they also recognize that all people share these same rights. Thus, each individual has a duty to refrain from violating the rights of all other human beings.

The Logical Premise of Rational Ethics   As rational beings, people also realize that it is logical to establish rules that support the continued existence of society. A rule that destroys a society that tries to follow it would be an illogical rule. Consider the following rule: "False promises are morally correct as long as they are made to gain some advantage." A person who adheres to rational ethics would instantly recognize that such a rule is both illogical and immoral. If everyone in a society were to adopt such a rule, no one could make a promise, and no one would accept a promise, even if it were made. A society without promises would be a society without commerce, diplomacy, credit cards, religion, pizza deliveries, marriage, airline schedules, democracy, and baseball, all of which require promises in one way or another. Such a society would be illogical and therefore immoral.

EXAMPLE 1-2: The Secret America of the Post 9/11 Age Reconsidered

Let's return to the Secret America Case in Example 1-1. Recall that, under the Nationwide Suspicious Activity Reporting Initiative [SAR], law enforcement agencies are empowered to gather information on American citizens who are suspected of engaging in suspicious activities. Recall also that the term *suspicious activity* has been defined by the government as "behavior reasonably indicative of pre-operational planning related to terrorism or other criminal activity." In Example 1-1 we speculated that, under this initiative, an innocent tourist caught taking photographs of a local police station or sheriff's office might be tagged as engaging in "pre-operational planning related to terrorism." The utility thinker argued that the overall security of the United States is worth the cost of invading the privacy of one innocent person. Rational ethics leads to a different conclusion. The Golden Rule of rational ethics states, "Act so that you treat others as you believe you would want to be treated. Be sure to respect others as ends in themselves and not as a means to an end." In this case, any law enforcement officer tempted to tag our tourist as a suspicious person should ask, "Would I want to be tagged as 'suspicious' simply because I stopped to take a photograph in a strange town?" Most of us, including our law enforcement agent, would hopefully answer, "no," to this question. The other question required of rational ethics asks, "Can a society that follows such a rule survive?" In other words in this case, "Can a society that tags an innocent activity such as taking a photograph as a suspicious act survive?" As we saw above, when we endorse this type of conduct (the "tagging," not the picture taking) as the norm, then people become suspicious of even the most innocuous acts and everyone becomes a target of suspicion. Eventually, the concept of trust evaporates, and our orderly society along with it.

quick quiz 1-2

1. Utilitarianism focuses on the consequences of an action.   true | false

2. Rational ethics is a form of ethical relativism.   true | false

3. Utilitarianism and rational ethics always reach the same moral conclusion.   true | false

1-3 Ethics and the Government

So far our study of ethics has focused on individuals. This is natural because ultimately all ethical decisions, even those that drive governmental regulations and corporate policies, are made by individuals. However, the decisions made by individuals affect the policies and procedures carried out by institutions that have the power to affect many parts of our social structure. Probably the most powerful institution that we deal with on a regular basis is the government. Governments run nation-states and, on the international scene, nation-states run the world. This is because nation-states possess territory, raise money through taxation, police their borders, protect their people, and if necessary, use force in a legitimate and responsible way. The government of a nation-state has two objectives that simultaneously justify its power and enable the proper exercise of that power. Those two objectives are (1) to protect its own existence and (2) to protect the lives, health, and well-being of its own citizens.

The Ethic of Ultimate Ends

Many of the misunderstandings about moral decisions within the world today exist because people do not understand the dual nature of international morality. The 20th century philosopher Max Weber explains the problem in his essay, "Politics as a Vocation." In that essay, Weber argues that, often people make the error of assuming that political morality and personal morality are identical. Instead, Weber proposes a dual system of morality represented by the "ethic of ultimate ends" and the "ethic of responsibility." The "ethic of ultimate ends" must be practiced by individuals while the "ethic of responsibility" must be practiced by national leaders. The ethic of ultimate ends must be practiced by individuals because individuals can never completely foresee "the ultimate ends" of their actions. Therefore, individuals must obey absolute moral precepts, such as "turn the other cheek" and "love thy neighbor as thyself" despite the fact that the ultimate consequences of those actions are unclear or uncomfortable.

To express it in even more absolute terms, the ethic of ultimate ends asserts that the action itself is right or wrong in and of itself, regardless of the consequences of the action. From this perspective, we can see why the ethic of ultimate ends is also often referred to as the ethic of benevolence. Under the ethic of benevolence the immediate ends can never justify the means because, even if the immediate ends are foreseeable, the ultimate ends are not. Thus, it does no good to consider those ends. In fact, considering those ends often has the opposite effect. Rather than prompting a moral actor to do the right thing, it gives that actor an excuse for bending or breaking the rules in order to effectuate a "greater good." Under the ethic of ultimate ends, an individual must do the right thing because it is right in and of itself.

The Ethic of Responsibility

On the other hand, the ethic of responsibility demands that the moral actor, in this case a national leader, consider his or her responsibilities to those people who depend on that leader for protection, safety, and sometimes even for their very lives. The ethic of responsibility is the morality of the nation-state and it is not the same as individual morality. The nation-state has a duty that outweighs all other duties and that duty is to promote the civil peace of the nation-state and the value that is rooted in the lives its own people. What this means from the practical perspective of world leaders is that, if a neighboring nation-state is belligerent, aggressive, or determined to fight ancient cultural, religious, and ethnic wars, the leaders of the first nation cannot ignore that threat, as much as they might want to. In short, they are not permitted to "turn the other cheek" because to do so would endanger the innocent people they have the duty to protect.

The threat discussed in the Opening Case Revisited, Part III involves an imminent threat to an individual nation-state that is doing what it needs to do to survive. This justifies its twisting of the truth as reported above. The principle of responsibility might even be stretched to include a regional or a global threat that would indirectly threaten a distant nation-state such as the United States. If a threat is global, as with rogue nations such as Iran or North Korea, a fragmented state such as the Sudan or Somalia, or an autocratic, closed state, such as Cuba or the Russian Federation, then it is unwise for the leaders of the threatened nation-states to act benevolently toward the nation that has initiated the global threat. Moreover, it may also be necessary for a nation that has the power to protect other

THE OPENING CASE Revisited, Part III
WikiLeaks, Secret Documents, and Deception, Round 5

Recall in the Opening Case at the beginning of the chapter that some of the secret cables released by WikiLeaks revealed that Georgian leaders had provoked an encounter with the breakaway province of South Ossetia, in order to garner American support against the Russians who the Georgians believed were planning to reassert control over their newly independent nation. In fact, it now appears that the Georgians actually launched a first strike against South Ossetia and then told the Americans that the Ossetians had attacked them. Under the ethic of responsibility, the Georgian leaders can argue convincingly that they had a duty to protect their people and to preserve their national sovereignty against the threat of a military attack by Russia which had openly declared that it did not recognize Georgia's right to secede from the former Soviet Union. Georgia's responsibility to its own people and territory would take precedence over its duty to tell the truth, even to allies like the United States. (See C. J. Chivers, "Embracing Georgia, U.S. Misread Signs of Region's Rifts, Cables Show," *The New York Times,* December 2, 2010, p. A-15.)

nations to act insofar as it is able, insofar as is necessary to protect innocent people, and insofar as it puts its own people in harm's away no more than necessary. [See Max Weber, "Politics as a Vocation (from Wirtschaft und Gesellschaft)," in *The Great Political Theories: From the French Revolution to Modern Times,* eds. Michael Curtis (New York: Harper, 2008), 426–436; See also: Helene Cooper and Martin Fackler, "U.S. Asking China to Help Rein in North Koreans," *The New York Times,* November 25, 2001, p. A-1.]

EXAMPLE 1-3: The Secret America of the Post 9/11 Age Reconsidered Once Again

At this point it might be a good idea to return once more to the Secret America Case in Example 1-1. Remember, under the Nationwide Suspicious Activity Reporting Initiative [SAR], law enforcement agencies are empowered to gather information about people who are engaged in suspicious activities in order to build a database to help the government fight the threat of terrorism. Utilitarianism suggested that the actions, while basically inoffensive to all but a few in the short run, would, nevertheless, be harmful to the overall security of the social structure. Similarly, the principles of rational ethics would reject SAR as a clear violation of the Golden Rule and the rule of social preservation. However, under the ethics of responsibility, a national leader would endorse the SAR initiative, because that national leader has a duty to ensure the health, safety, well-being, and lives of the nation's citizens.

quick quiz 1-3

1. Political and personal morality are not the same thing.   true | false

2. The ethic of ultimate ends says that the action itself is right or wrong.   true | false

3. The ethic of responsibility is the ethic of the nation-state.   true | false

1-4 Social Responsibility in the Business Sector

Up until now, our examination of ethics has involved only individuals and the government. This is not surprising since many ethics dilemmas entangle politics and the individual. Individuals make the actual day-to-day decisions, and the bureaucracy of the government, often in the form of the courts or law enforcement officers, carry out those decisions. Nevertheless, to make our study complete, we need to add a third element into the equation, the corporation. Corporations carry a great deal of influence over the economy, the community, and the people. There are those who say that a corporation has no social responsibility beyond making a profit for its shareholders. This is, in fact, the traditional view of corporate responsibility. It is a view that has remained so ingrained in our system that, until recently, it was the only view built into statutory and common law. Recently, however, voices have been raised arguing that corporations have a high degree of social responsibility to those people affected by their decisions.

The Traditional Corporate Culture

Although all businesses affect the economy and the community, the greatest force in the American industrial state is the corporation, in general, and the multinational corporation, in particular. The reality of corporate power is revealed by the fact that philosophers on both ends of the political spectrum can point to the corporation as a guiding force in modern civilization. For instance, in his treatise, *Individualism Old and New,* the *pragmatic* American philosopher, John Dewey, notes, "The United States has steadily moved from an earlier pioneer individualism to a condition of corporate dominance." Similarly, the *theoretical* philosopher, Herbert Marcuse, once remarked that no one, not even the former enemies of capitalism, can escape the influence of corporate power. In fact, Marcuse goes so far as to say that in the modern global marketplace, "the socialist and communist systems are linked with capitalism." (See John Dewey, *Individualism: Old and New.* New York: Capricorn Books, 1962; Herbert Marcuse, *Five Lectures: Psychoanalysis, Politics, and Utopia,* trans. Jeremy J. Shapiro and Shierry M. Weber, Boston: Beacon Press, 1970.)

One reason that corporations have such power is that they are legal persons, created under the authority of federal and state statutes. This status as a "legal person" gives the corporation certain rights and abilities that other business entities do not always have. For instance, as legal persons they are accorded certain constitutional rights, such as the right not to be deprived of property without due process of law. They can also own property in their own name and have lawsuits filed to protect them or vindicate their rights. There are, of course, many types of corporations. Our focus will be on those corporations that are privately run to make a profit for their owners, who are referred to as shareholders. The traditional view says that privately owned corporations are created solely to make a profit for their shareholders. Consequently, the foremost job of any manager is to maximize those profits. In fact, under the traditional rule of shareholder dominance, the managers of a corporation could be held liable in a court of law for making decisions that do not guarantee that the shareholders would receive a maximum return on their investment.

As defined previously, the type of thinking promoted by the court in Example 1-4 is referred to as utility thinking or cost-benefit thinking. Using utility thinking, a corporate manager simply looks at the action he or she is about to take and asks whether the benefit to the shareholders will outweigh the cost to the corporation. If the shareholders' benefits offset corporate costs, then the action is taken. If not, the action is abandoned. Proponents of this position justify cost-benefit thinking in three ways. First, the profits to the shareholders must always come first. Second, it would be unfair to divert funds that belong

EXAMPLE 1-4: Corporate Culture and Utility Thinking

When Lynn Cummings discovered that the managers of a corporation in which she owned stock had made a decision that had caused shareholders to lose money in a merger plan, she sued, seeking a reversal of the merger or a suitable payment from the managers that would make up for her losses. Basically, Cummings second-guessed the way that the managers had made their decision, arguing that they had not properly researched the merger and had not placed the shareholders' profits first. The managers argued that they had made their decision based on the long-term benefits of the merger to everyone involved, including the local community and the economy of the nation and state. The court sided with Cummings, noting that the job of the managers was to look out for the shareholders' profits, not the long-term benefits to the community or the economy.

to the shareholders to activities that do not directly benefit the shareholders. Third, a corporation's managers are accountable to the shareholders and to no one else. The problem with utility thinking is that it often results in actions that are clearly unethical and potentially illegal.

EXAMPLE 1-5: Maximum Corporate Irresponsibility

The managers of Taylor-Beechaum Pharmaceuticals, Inc., received a report that the corporation's latest weight loss drug, biomiocin, was having unpredicted side effects that caused problems for several people. The managers of Taylor-Beechaum ordered the accounting department to determine how much it would cost to recall all the biomiocin now on the market, suspend manufacturing, and conduct more tests on the drug's safety. The accountants reported that it would be more cost effective to simply leave the drug on the market and pay off anyone who might be injured and who might bring a lawsuit against Taylor-Beechaum. Keeping the drug on the shelves will allow the corporation to continue to pay dividends to the shareholders. In contrast, if the drug were taken off of the market, the payment of dividends would be suspended pending the outcome of the new testing program. Consequently, the corporate managers decided to leave biomiocin on the shelves. This decision not only violated virtually every ethical standard that we've studied thus far (except ethical relativism) but also evaded the corporation's social responsibility to consumers, to the government, to the shareholders, and to the public at large.

Reasons for Social Responsibility

The fact that corporate officers and directors have made such irresponsible decisions should not be surprising. Nor should it be surprising that, until recently, the law supported such decisions. The idea that a corporation is a legal person did not spring full grown into the law when the first corporations were formed. In fact, it took jurists quite some time to see that corporations were neither partnerships nor miniature democratic states but instead vehicles for making a profit. Once jurists recognized the unique position that corporations hold within the hierarchy of business associations, however, they easily granted certain privileges to corporate entities. Despite this, as the jurists entered the modern age, they began to see that there were a number of reasons that corporations, like Taylor-Beechaum in Example 1-5, should accept social responsibility for their actions. Some of these reasons are built on the legal advantages granted to corporations. Others are based on the idea that many corporations are powerful forces in their communities. Still others focus on the self-interest of the corporation. Whatever the case, these arguments are being voiced more loudly and with more conviction with each passing fiscal year.

Legal Advantages Granted to the Corporation

The first argument supporting corporate social responsibility is based on the premise that corporations are granted certain rights as a result of the incorporation process. For example, the corporate form offers limited liability to those who share in its ownership. This means that the personal assets of the corporate owners cannot be taken if the corporation defaults on a contract or commits a tort or a crime. In addition, under provisions of most incorporation statutes, a corporation is considered an artificially created person. This means that, under provisions of the U.S. Constitution and those of most state constitutions, a corporation, like a natural person, cannot be deprived of life, liberty, or property without due process of law. This also means that a corporation can own property in its own name and bring a lawsuit to vindicate its rights. Because corporations have all these rights, they owe an obligation to the public and to the community at large to act responsibly. In practical terms, this means that the decisions of corporate managers must not be narrowly focused on the profits of the shareholders.

EXAMPLE 1-6: The Andrean-Harrison Donation

As part of a downsizing campaign, the Andrean-Harrison Corporation was about to close down operations in Tulsa. The company owned an office building and a small laboratory on the outskirts of Tulsa that are adjacent to 30 acres of undeveloped land. The corporation had a chance to sell the land at a price that would have made a profit for the shareholders of the company. Rather than take advantage of this offer, Andrean-Harrison decided to donate the land to the city. The fact that the corporation was a legal person meant that it owned the land and could donate it to the city. Corporate officials acted responsibly in this case, taking advantage of the corporation's right to own land in its own name.

The Impact of Corporate Decision Making

A second reason for demanding social responsibility from corporations is that corporate decision making clearly has an impact on more people than just the shareholders and the managers. Those who support corporate social responsibility often argue that many corporate decisions, such as the decision to open or close a factory, will affect everyone in the local community. Those affected by such decisions include suppliers, consumers, employees, support businesses, and community members. Consequently, the argument goes, all of these groups should be taken into consideration when corporate managers make decisions. Some individuals who support this form of extreme corporate social responsibility would like to see representatives from the employees' union, from consumer protection groups, from environmental protection groups, and from the local chamber of commerce on every corporation's board of directors. Others, however, argue that because corporate decisions affect more individuals and groups than just the shareholders and managers, those decisions should be made by an impartial group of corporate outsiders. Often the corporate outsiders named are governmental officials.

EXAMPLE 1-7: Corporate Cooperation and Compromise

When the directors of Igar International Corporation were working on plans to diversify their operation, they considered opening a chemical plant in Santa Ana. Before making the decision, they sent a team of experts to Santa Ana to investigate the possibility of establishing an operation just within the city limits. Although the city officials promised Igar a tax abatement plan and agreed to donate several acres of land to the corporation, citizens' groups were against the plant because of environmental and health concerns. The corporation could have simply found a more receptive or, perhaps, a less vocal city in which to locate. However, instead of simply discarding their consideration of Santa Ana, they worked with the citizens' groups to meet their concerns. Ultimately the two sides agreed on modifications to the project and moved forward. The willingness of the company to discuss the proposed changes in its operation reflected an understanding of the corporation's social responsibility based on the fact that corporate decisions have a far-ranging impact.

Enlightened Corporate Self-Interest Finally, there are those who argue, rather convincingly, that accepting social responsibility is actually in the long-term best interests of the corporation. This argument, which is generally referred to as enlightened self-interest, is based on the notion that socially responsible corporations benefit by creating goodwill for themselves, thus motivating consumers to purchase their products, investors to buy their stock, and lawmakers to grant them further legal advantages. In addition, the corporation benefits because the community at large gains from such decisions. If the community at large is healthy, the argument goes, then the corporation that relies on that community will be healthy also.

EXAMPLE 1-8: Failed Negotiations Lead to Problems

The president of Pilder and Wesselkamper International, Inc., decided to suspend negotiations with union representatives when he learned that they were about to demand a salary increase that he believed was untenable given the corporation's financial health, or lack thereof. The union threatened to file a complaint with the National Labor Relations Board, charging that the president and his staff were not cooperating with the collective bargaining process. The union also indicated that it was considering publishing an advertisement in *The New York Times* denouncing the president's decision and eventually would authorize a strike. The president continued to resist further negotiations and simply shut down operations. Eventually, the company filed for bankruptcy and dissolved its operation. Neither of the parties involved in this case opted to pursue a course of enlightened self-interest, which resulted in the worst possible conclusion for all those involved.

Efforts to Promote Social Responsibility

As noted previously, the traditional view of a corporation says that its primary role is to make a profit for its shareholders. This means that corporate managers are obligated to make decisions that maximize those profits. Moreover, under the traditional role of corporate managers, those managers could be sued for making a decision that hurt the corporation's profits and thereby reduced or eliminated dividends. However, recent amendments to many corporate statutes have been designed to encourage corporate managers to make broader-based decisions. Thus, some statutes now permit managers to consider factors beyond profit in making corporate decisions. These factors include the economic well-being of the nation, the state, and the local community; the interests of employees, consumers, and suppliers; and the betterment of the environment, the economy, and the overall social structure. These statutes generally hold managers immune from shareholder lawsuits, which claim that the managers did not put the shareholders' profits first.

EXAMPLE 1-9: Corporate Trade-Offs Mean Corporate Survival

The directors of Chindi-Mowry Enterprises, Inc., were under fire because of a takeover bid against Chindi-Mowry engineered by an alien corporation known as Rixensart Industries. To stave off the assault, the directors invited a friendly bid from Sandoff, Inc., a firm that promised not to dismantle Chindi-Mowry after the deal was entered. The final amount of the offer from Sandoff was less than that offered by Rixensart, and so those shareholders who sold their stock received less on the sale to Sandoff than they would have received had the directors endorsed the Rixensart plan. However, in making their decision, the directors were persuaded that the deal offered by Sandoff would save jobs, help the community, boost the national and state economy, and eventually result in a long-term gain for the corporation and for those shareholders who remained with the company.

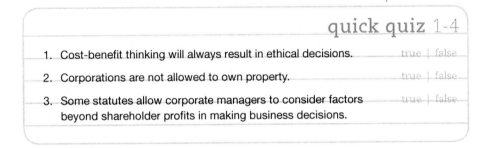

quick quiz 1-4

1. Cost-benefit thinking will always result in ethical decisions.   true | false

2. Corporations are not allowed to own property.   true | false

3. Some statutes allow corporate managers to consider factors beyond shareholder profits in making business decisions.   true | false

1-5 The Relationship between Law and Ethics

Thus far, we have seen that ethics and morals can be distinguished from one another. We have defined values, examined the causes of unethical conduct, and determined how to develop an ethical lifestyle. Some people determine an ethical lifestyle as simply doing what is legal. Such a course of action may often result in ethical conduct. However, that is not always the case. Even when most people know that a particular type of conduct is illegal, that does not prevent some people from engaging in that conduct. For example, everyone knows that killing is illegal. Yet that knowledge does not stop the national murder rate from remaining disturbingly high. Similarly, everyone knows that child abuse, spousal abuse, and elder abuse are immoral, but that consensus has not eliminated the problem of abuse from our society.

The Need for Law in Our Society

The law is needed because, though people know better, they do not always follow ethical principles. As noted previously, the law consists of rules of conduct established by the government of a society to maintain harmony, stability, and justice in that society. It does so by defining the legal rights and duties of the people. It also provides a way to protect the people by enforcing these rights and duties through the courts and the legislature. Ethical principles can tell us what is right, but they cannot stop us from doing that which is wrong. The law also cannot stop us from doing wrong. However, the law can punish us if we choose to do wrong. The law draws the line between permissible and impermissible conduct, so that people, at the very least, are punished if they hurt or cheat one another or threaten society as a whole.

Of course the law also has other functions. For instance, the law serves as the ultimate rule maker, providing a sense of stability and harmony when order breaks down in any other area of society, from our schools and universities to the family itself. This is why each state has established a system of juvenile courts and a network of domestic relations courts to handle such disputes when they arise. The law also promotes economic growth by granting tax abatements, by rezoning certain urban areas for the establishment of stores and businesses, and by exercising the power of *eminent domain* to confiscate privately owned land for community purposes. In addition, the law guards property rights by enforcing contracts and other similar agreements and providing a forum for tort victims and their families. The law also protects the environment by regulating those industries that might overdevelop the land and those that dump waste materials and other pollutants on to the land and into the waterways. Finally, as noted, the law is responsible for advancing social justice and guaranteeing personal freedom by granting all people due process and equal protection and providing a system by which legitimate grievances can be resolved in an orderly and timely fashion.

Is the law perfect? Does the law always succeed in its goals and objectives? Certainly not. As is true of all institutions, the law is flawed. It is filled with loopholes, foolishness, red tape, and, at times, absolute idiocy, much of which is unintentional and most of which could be avoided if people just take the time to think coolly and rationally. For example, it makes very little sense for Congress to pass legislation to punish flag burners when it is quite clear that the Supreme Court will declare that legislation unconstitutional. Or, in a similar vein, it makes no sense for Congress to pass unfunded mandates that force the state governments to raise money to perform tasks that the federal government should have taken care of in the first place. Yet this type of thing happens all of the time. Nevertheless, having an imperfect but functioning legal system is always preferable to the alternative—anarchy and all the unpleasantness that would surround a descent into chaos.

Ethical and Legal Harmony

In a utopian society, ethics and the law would always coincide. Our society is not perfect however, and it is not likely to become perfect in the foreseeable future. Therefore, our society needs the law and the legal system to give it structure, harmony, predictability, and justice. However, ethical considerations should always form the foundation of law and the legal system. If the law is not founded on ethics, it will rarely succeed in reaching its objectives. Ethics can lead the way in difficult situations or in areas of the social structure into which the law has yet to venture.

quick quiz 1-5

1. The law cannot stop us from doing wrong, but it can punish us if we choose to do wrong.   true | false

2. In a perfect society, ethics and law would always coincide.   true | false

3. The law and the legal system need not be founded on ethical considerations.   true | false

Summary

1.1   The law consists of rules of conduct established by the government of a society to maintain harmony, stability, and justice. Morals involve the values that govern a society's attitude toward right and wrong. Ethics, in contrast, attempt to develop a means for determining what those values ought to be and for formulating and applying rules in line with those values.

1.2   Ethical relativism holds that there are no fixed or stable standards of right and wrong. Social contract theory holds that right and wrong are measured by the obligations imposed on each individual by an implied social agreement. Utilitarianism determines right and wrong by looking at the consequences of a person's actions. According to rational ethics, actions are either right or wrong, regardless of the circumstances and regardless of the consequences.

1.3   The government of a nation-state has two objectives that simultaneously justify its power and enable the proper exercise of that power. Those two objectives are (1) to protect its own existence and (2) to protect the lives, health, safety, and well-being of its

own citizens. In order to meet those two objectives, national leaders must recognize the conflict that emerges from (a) the exercise of individual morality, represented by the ethic of ultimate ends, and (b) the exercise of national morality, represented by the ethic of responsibility.

1.4   Corporations owe society a level of responsibility because the government has granted certain legal advantages to corporations. Another reason for expecting socially responsible decisions from corporate executives is that corporations have a great deal of power in the economic structure, and with power comes responsibility. Finally, corporations should act responsibly because it is in their own best interest to do so.

1.5   In a perfect society, ethics and the law would always coincide. Our society is not perfect and is not likely to become so in the foreseeable future. Therefore, our society needs the law and the legal system to give it structure, harmony, predictability, and justice.

Key Terms

cost-benefit thinking, 9
descriptive theory, 8
ethic of responsibility, 13
ethic of ultimate ends, 13
ethical relativism, 7
law, 4

morals, 4
natural law, 4
negative rights theory, 6
positive law theory, 5
prescriptive theory, 8

rational ethics, 11
situational ethics, 8
social contract theory, 8
utilitarianism, 9
utility thinking, 9

Questions for Review and Discussion

1. What is the difference between law and morality?
2. What are the differences among positive law, natural law, and negative rights?
3. What is ethical relativism?
4. What is social contract theory?
5. What are the steps in applying utilitarianism?
6. What is rational ethics?
7. What is the dual nature of ethics in government?
8. What are the arguments supporting social responsibility?
9. Why is law needed in our society?
10. How is harmony established between the law and ethics?

Cases for Analysis

1. The Oklahoma state constitution was amended by a vote of the people to prohibit judges in the state courts from considering any law other than state or federal law in their cases. The new constitutional amendment read, "Courts shall not look to the legal precepts of other nations or cultures. Specifically, the Court shall not consider International law or Sharia law." A federal judge issued an injunction nullifying the vote because, according to the judge, the amendment is an unconstitutional violation of the Supremacy Clause and of the First Amendment of the U.S. Constitution. The main target of the amendment appears to be the Islamic legal tradition of Sharia. The Islamic legal tradition is an interesting one because it requires Islamic judges to use a specific methodology that helps them to examine and interpret religious texts in an attempt to determine the will of God. Which of the three major ethical theories that we have examined in this chapter would support the action of the federal judge? Explain. Which of these ethical theories would support the position of the Oklahoma voters? Explain. (See Abed Awad, "Oklahoma Amendment Is Unconstitutional: Barring Courts form Considering Sharia Law violates the Supremacy Clause and the First Amendment," *The National Law Journal*, November 15, 2010, p. 39.)

2. When former Illinois Governor Rod Blagojevich was on trial, the judge was asked to keep the identities of the jurors hidden from the community. The request was unusual because it violates the legal practice of permitting the public to have access to information about jurors in order to build public faith in the objectivity of the legal system. Despite this principle, the judge ordered that the identities of the jury members be kept secret to prevent the jurors from being influenced by e-mail, blogging, texting, Facebook, tweats, and other electronic media. The appeals court urged the judge to reconsider the ban, arguing that denying the public access to the identity of the jury flies in the face of the long-standing legal tradition of accessibility and candor. Using utilitarianism, construct an argument that supports the appeals court. Now use rational ethics to construct an argument that upholds the judges' original ruling. Explain each argument and determine which of the two positions you prefer. Explain that preference. (See David J. Bird and Jeffrey

M. Weimer, "Keep Jurors' Identities Public," *The National Law Journal*, August 23, 2010, p. 50.)

3. Under provisions of the Alien Tort Statute, the federal courts are permitted to hear civil cases involving international law. Following the dictates of that statute, a group of Somali citizens brought a lawsuit against a former government official of the Somali government alleging that defense forces under his command illegally detained, tortured, and murdered their family members. The trial court dismissed the case under the Federal Sovereign Immunity Act which prevents foreign governments from being sued in U.S. Courts unless the foreign government agrees to the action. The U.S. Court of Appeals for the Fourth Circuit and the U.S. Supreme Court both overturned the decision of the trial court. The two higher courts ruled that the immunity act protected foreign governments but not foreign individuals. Using the ethic of responsibility and the ethic of ultimate ends, defend the ruling that was made by the two higher courts in this case. Explain your defense. (See John B. Bellinger III, "Ruling Burdens State Department," *The National Law Journal*, June 28, 2010, p. 47.)

4. Some political commentators have argued convincingly that in recent years the United States Supreme Court has shifted from a liberal to a conservative interpretation of the United States Constitution. These commentators have characterized the court as a battleground between two ways of interpreting the rights guaranteed under the Constitution: the conservative position represented by Chief Justice John Roberts, Justice Clarence Thomas, Justice Samuel Alito, and Justice Antonin Scalia; and the liberal position represented by Justice William Brennan and Justice Ruth Bader Ginsburg. Some decisions made by the court have limited the ability of plaintiffs to bring civil rights actions, while others have limited the right to privacy and the rights of criminal defendants. Using the negative rights theory, defend the court's limitation of such rights. Now using rational ethics show how such limitation might be considered unethical. (See Erwin Chemerinsky, "Constitutional Protections Under Attack," *The National Law Journal*, September 13, 2010, p. 43.)

5. Ethical codes of conduct are helpful standards that develop general guidelines for the conduct of professionals. However, they are frequently limited in their application because of their length, their complexity, and their ambiguity. A case in point is Rule 8.5 of the Ohio Rules of Professional Conduct for Attorneys. This rule dictates that the rules themselves will apply in multijurisdictional cases to the jurisdiction in which the lawyer "*reasonably believes* the predominant effect of the lawyer's conduct will occur." Of course, the complexity of multijurisdictional transactions and the ambiguity of the phrase "reasonably believes" leave the rule open to a wide variety of interpretations. Consequently, the jurisdiction with the "predominant effect" may not be immediately self-evident. Explain how the theory of utilitarianism might help clear up the ambiguity inherent in this situation. Now explain how utilitarian principles might deteriorate into utility thinking in this situation. (See "Ohio Professional Conduct Rule 8.5 Discipline Authority; Choice of Law." See also: Deborah L. Rhode, "Legal Ethics on a Global Scale," *The National Law Journal*, September 20, 2010, p. 38.)

6. William Yurchak, vice president of production for Dragonfly Enterprises, was passed over for what he believed was a much deserved promotion to the presidency. Instead of promoting Yurchak, the board of directors of Dragonfly, a firm that specializes in the development and production of recreational aircraft, decided to hire an outsider. Clyde Kellor, the chair of the board of Vostok Incorporated, one of Dragonfly's chief competitors, offers Yurchak the presidency of Vostok. Although Yurchak still has three years to run on his contract with Dragonfly, he is tempted to take Kellor's offer because he feels that he has been badly treated by Dragonfly and because he could use the 50 percent raise that Kellor has offered him. Kellor has added one stipulation: He wants Yurchak to bring with him the plans for Dragonfly Six, the corporation's latest revolutionary aircraft. Was it ethical for the board of Dragonfly to hire an outsider as president? Is Kellor's offer to Yurchak ethical? Would the offer be ethical if Kellor had not added the request for the Dragonfly Six plans? What is the ethical course of action for Yurchak? Explain all of your answers.

7. Barbara McMahon is a reporter for *The Lake County Press*. McMahon is approached by Julie Bryant, a research scientist for the International Chemical Corporation. Bryant, who asks for and receives a promise of confidentiality from McMahon, informs the reporter that International Chemical has been disposing of its chemical waste product by illegally dumping it in the Lake County River. On the strength of Bryant's word alone, *The Lake County Press* runs a series of articles on the illegal dumping. The district attorney of Lake County elects to prosecute the president and board members of International. At the trial, McMahon is called as a witness and asked to reveal her confidential news source. The state in which Lake County is located does not recognize any journalist–news source privilege. The judge tells McMahon that if she does not reveal her source, she will be placed in jail until she does so. Was it ethical for Bryant to go to McMahon with her confidential story in the first place? Was it ethical for McMahon to print the news stories on the basis of Bryant's word alone? Would it be ethical for the judge to place McMahon in jail? What is the ethical course of action for McMahon? What is the ethical course of action for Bryant? Defend all of your responses.

quick quiz Answers

1-1	1-2	1-3	1-4	1-5
1. F	1. T	1. T	1. F	1. T
2. F	2. F	2. T	2. F	2. T
3. T	3. T	3. T	3. T	3. F

Chapter 2   Sources of the Law

THE OPENING CASE   When the States Challenge Federal Authority

In an attempt to deal with the problems associated with illegal immigration, the state of Arizona passed a new statute that empowered local law enforcement officials to inspect the identification papers of anyone who might be in the country illegally. The law caused a wave of protests across the nation, mostly from people who saw the statute as racially biased. Arizona state officials argued that they had been forced to act because the federal government had done a terrible job of policing the borders and that, as a result of this neglect, there had been an unprecedented rise in violence associated with illegal border crossings. Many American citizens supported the Arizona law and encouraged their state governments to pass similar legislation. Despite the support for the state immigration statute, the federal government sued the State of Arizona in an attempt to block the administration of the law. The Justice Department, under the control of Attorney General Eric Holder, argued that federal law trumped state law in this case because the Constitution gave the power to control immigration to the national government. The Supremacy Clause of the U.S. Constitution does in fact state that, "(t)his Constitution and the Laws of the United States . . . shall be the supreme Law of the Land." Thus, it would seem that the federal government had a solid argument. Still it

is strange that the government avoided the discrimination claim and chose, instead, to rely on the technical argument of federal supremacy. In essence, the Justice Department chose to challenge the law based on a minor "technicality," rather than on a more substantive civil rights claim. As you read the chapter, see if you can determine if the federal government is right in its claim. Also, see if you can offer a few counter arguments to support Arizona's position. Finally, try to determine why the Justice Department decided to fight the law based on a technicality, rather than something more substantial. (See "Immigration: Why Did Obama Sue Arizona?" *The Week*, July 23, 2010, p. 6.)

Opening Case Questions

1. What powers regarding citizenship were given to the federal government in the U.S. Constitution? Explain.

2. What powers regarding citizenship were given to the state governments in the U.S. Constitution? Explain.

3. In what article and section is the Supremacy Clause of the U.S. Constitution located and why did the Framers include such a clause? Explain.

4. What clause in the U.S. Constitution gives the executive branch of the federal government the power to make certain that the laws of the United States are faithfully executed? Explain.

5. If Arizona (or any other state for that matter) wanted to shift the power to regulate immigration to the states, what would it have to do and how can that be accomplished? Explain.

 Learning Objectives

1. List the objectives of the law.
2. Clarify the duality of the law.
3. Outline the content of the U.S. Constitution.
4. Explain several central constitutional principles and powers.
5. Explain the role of statutory law in the legal system.
6. Defend the need to set up a system of uniform laws.
7. State the role of common law in the legal system.
8. Describe how the principle of *stare decisis* provides stability within the law.
9. Differentiate between statutory interpretation and judicial review.
10. Account for the legislature's need to establish administrative agencies.

2-1 The Purpose and Operation of the Law

As explained in Chapter 1, the law consists of rules of conduct established by the government to maintain harmony, stability, and justice within a society. Ideally, the primary objectives of the law should be balanced equally at all times. Unfortunately, in "real life," this balance is not easy to maintain. Often justice must be sacrificed for harmony and stability. Sometimes the opposite is true.

The Law as a Balancing Act

The law should be viewed as a delicate balancing act. One person's rights are enforced while another's are not. One group is allowed to act while another group is limited in what it is permitted to do. One person is allowed to go free while another is imprisoned, fined, and forced to forfeit his property. One corporation's contracts are upheld while another's are struck down. Trade-offs like this occur within the law on a regular basis. Generally, the objectives of order, stability, and justice are kept in mind when such decisions are made. Because the law is made by people, however, it is not perfect. Legislators, judges, and administrators bring their own limitations into the process. Still, most of them do their best to be as objective and fair as possible. The law is made even more complex because it involves a series of competing dualities.

The Dualities within the Law

What is often *not* clear is that the need to balance rights and duties within the law is not unusual. Rather, this balancing act is part of the law's fundamental nature. As Anthony Chase explains in his study, *Law and History*, the legal system is shaped by several dualities, each of which is essential to the law's success. These dualities include the balance between the spirit and the letter of the law, between legal words and their interpretation, and between abstract principles and concrete situations. This balancing act also comes into play in the application of the Uncertainty Principle to the law. [See Anthony Chase,

"Historical Jurisprudence: I. Inside/Outside," *Law and History: The Evolution of the American Legal System* (New York: The New Press, 1997), pp. 12–19.]

The Spirit and the Letter of the Law

According to Chase, one of the most obvious dualities in the law is the balance between the **spirit** and the **letter of the law.** Generally, a person who follows the spirit of the law has found its actual intent, while one who is tied to the letter of the law has missed its true meaning. However, this is not always the case. Sometimes, following the letter of the law to avoid the spirit of the law can be a good thing. Thus, a shop owner who is discouraged by the complexity and intrusiveness of the law might avoid a prohibition against the sale of alcohol on Sunday by "giving away" bottles of wine to his customers who come in the next day and "give" the shop owner cash which just happens to be equivalent to the cost of their Sunday "gift." The shop owner has met the letter of the law by not "selling" alcohol on Sunday, but he and his customers have clearly violated the spirit of the law. Is this a good thing? We'll leave that to your imagination. (See Chase, pp. 12–14.)

Words versus Interpretation

Chase explains that much of the confusion over the spirit of the law emerges when the law is written down. Because words are often ambiguous, the language of the law can become a hindrance rather than a help in the execution of the law. This is why it is sometimes necessary to manipulate the language in order to uncover the actual intent of the lawmakers and to apply that intent in a consistent and fair fashion. Certainly, this oddity opens the law to adjustments that are sometimes good and sometimes bad. However, to view this particular brand of duality, **words** versus **interpretation**, as either a strength or a weakness would be an error because it is neither. Instead, it is merely how the law works. (See Chase, pp. 14–15.)

The Abstract and the Concrete

According to Chase, duality in the law is also seen in the work of judges, legislators, and administrators. In one way or another, all three are involved in the law-making process, and as a result, all three must tackle a third type of duality, that which exists between *abstract* principles and *concrete* situations (Chase, p. 15.) Thus, at times, legislators must take a principle, such as the idea that the government should be fair and equitable whenever it enacts a new tax bill, and apply that abstraction to a concrete piece of legislation. Similarly, a judge must take an abstract principle, such as the notion that all physicians must act with due care in performing their duties, and apply that principle in a case in which Dr. Jones's fails to properly diagnose Mr. Smith's ailment. In all such cases, it is not possible to eliminate the tension that exists between the duality of the abstract and the concrete. The only thing that can be done is for lawmakers to deal with the concrete incident without violating the abstract principle. This is not the end to the duality issue, however. In another study of the law, Gerald Turkel points out that this duality (Turkel calls is bipolarity) exists in the very nature of a lawsuit when the plaintiff and the defendant face off against one another. This bipolarity, is the essence of the adversarial system. [See Gerald Turkel, *Law and Society: Critical Approaches* (Boston: Allyn and Bacon, 1996), p. 13.]

EXAMPLE 2-1: Attempting a Fair and Equitable Tax

Sometimes lawmakers must apply an abstract principle, such as the idea that the government should be fair when it taxes the people, to a concrete piece of legislation. This is exactly what happened at the end of President Obama's first two years in office when Republicans and Democrats negotiated a tax plan that addressed the concerns of taxpayers, businesses, and unemployed workers. In brief, here is what resulted when the *abstract* met the *concrete*. Every taxpayer saw a two-year continuation of the tax rates that were in place under the old law. Lower income workers received an increase in the child tax credit of $1000. Upper income taxpayers saw a favorable alteration in the estate tax rate and middle income workers received an extension of a tax credit for students. Businesses received a continuation of research and development tax credits and unemployed workers continued to receive the same benefits in place under the old law. Was the bill completely fair? Probably not. Was everyone satisfied? Certainly not. Did the system and everyone in it survive? Of course. Why? Simple. The legislature took an abstract principle ("let's be fair to everyone when we develop a new tax law") and applied that abstract principle to the concrete reality of competing constituencies (taxpayers, businesses, and the unemployed). In the ultimate mix everybody gets something and everybody loses something, and in the final analysis, that is the way a well-balanced legal system works. (See Jonathan Weisman, John D. McKinnon, and Janet Hook, "Deal Struck on Tax Package: Grand Bargain Includes One-Year Drop in Wage Levy, Estate Tax of 35%" *The Wall Street Journal,* December 7, 2010, pp. A-1-A-2).

The Uncertainty Principle Duality also exists in the way a decision is intended and the way it is actually executed. The two, intent and result, almost never coincide, and when they do it is generally a matter of luck, nothing more. This principle, which is generally referred to as the *uncertainty principle,* exists in physics, in politics, and in economics. John Maynard Keynes recognized the uncertainty principle in economics and made it one of the lynch pins of his economic theory. Uncertainty between intentions and results in the law is very common. It occurs when legislators pass statutes that are vetoed by the chief executive; when a trial judge rules on a case that gets overturned by an appellate court; and when the chief executive makes an appointment that is nullified by the legislature. (See Chase, p. 19; See also Robert Skidelsky, "Keynes's Economics: Uncertainty," *Keynes: The Return of the Master* (New York: Public Affairs, 2010), pp. 83–85.) Moreover, the legal scholar Richard Posner tells us that this inclination toward uncertainty, especially as it relates to economics, is exacerbated by the fact that some

THE OPENING CASE *Revisited, Part I*
When the States Challenge Federal Authority, Round 2

In the Opening Case at the beginning of this chapter, we learned that Arizona passed a statute that enabled the police to inspect the identification papers of anyone who might be in the country illegally. The intended goal of the new law was to solve the problems associated with illegal immigration. However, instead of solving those problems, the new law unexpectedly ignited a series of unintended consequences. First, the new law sparked a wave of protests across the nation, mostly from people who saw it as a racially biased statute that victimized minorities. Second, the federal government, which the Arizona state officials argued was doing a terrible job of policing the borders, did not address the border problem but instead sued the state of Arizona in an attempt to block the administration of the new law. Third, the federal government's suit did nothing to address the issue of immigration or the problems associated with illegal immigration. Instead, the Attorney General and his entourage simply used

the much safer technical argument of federal supremacy. Thus, nothing intended by the state came to pass, and much that was unintended emerged, demonstrating the unavoidable operation of the uncertainty principle. (See "Immigration: Why Did Obama Sue Arizona?" *The Week,* July 23, 2010, p. 6.)

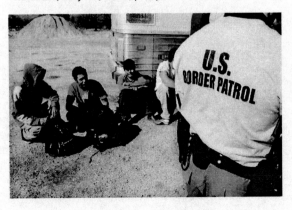

people act in unpredictable ways on a regular basis, while others react to what their neighbors have done. What is true in economics is equally true in the law. (See Richard Posner, *A Failure of Capitalism* (Cambridge; Harvard UP, 2009), pp. 83–84).

quick quiz 2-1

1. The law consists of rules of conduct established by the government   true | false
   to maintain harmony, stability, and justice within a society.

2. Often justice must be sacrificed for harmony and stability, but   true | false
   the opposite is never true.

3. Legislators and judges bring their own personal prejudices and   true | false
   biases into the process.

2-2 Constitutional Law

The law has been defined as rules of conduct created by the government to maintain harmony, stability, and justice within a society. This definition is adequate, but it is also somewhat limited. It does not explain where the government comes from or who gives it the power to make those rules.

In some societies, the government is represented by a hereditary monarchy. In others, the establishment of a government depends on which political faction can muster the necessary power to take control of that nation's resources. In the United States, the government was established by a constitution.

A constitution is the basic law of a nation or state. The United States Constitution provides the organization of the national government. Each state also has a constitution that establishes the state's governmental structure. The body of law that makes up a constitution and its interpretation is known as constitutional law.

EXAMPLE 2-2: Constitutional Law in the UK

Unlike the United States Constitution, the British Constitution has never been reduced to a single document. However, contrary to popular opinion, including the views offered by Jon Stewart on *The Daily Show*, this does not mean that the British government has no constitution. On the contrary, the principles that make up the British Constitution are found in many documents including the *Magna Carta*, an endless series of court cases, and a complex mix of statutory law. There are of course problems with this fragmented approach. First, the amalgam of legal precedents that makes up the British constitution plays right into the problems associated with the uncertainty principle. This occurs because it is difficult to know what precedent will be called upon to support or to attack a particular legal position. Second, the absence of a written failsafe system like that found in the American Constitution opens the door to power abuse in the British system. Third, while the British constitutional method avoids the ambiguities associated with the need to determine the difference between the words and the interpretation of those words, the British must still deal with this duality whenever statutes and cases are interpreted by the courts. Finally, when interpreting the British constitution, there is no need to distinguish between the letter of the law and the spirit of the law since, at least in relation to constitutional law, in the British system, there simply is no letter of the law. (See Sarah Lyall, "As a New Government Goes to Work, the Constitution Offers Britain Few Guides," *The New York Times,* May 25, 2010, p. A6.)

The Articles of Confederation

The Constitution of the United States, as it exists today, is not the nation's first constitution. The first constitution was known as the Articles of Confederation. The Articles of Confederation were created to hold together a fragile coalition of states, each of which was determined to maintain its own independent existence. Although the Articles of Confederation fulfilled a much needed function during the first years in the life of the United States, they contained certain weaknesses.

One of the primary weaknesses was the fact that the United States in Congress, as the national legislature was known under the Articles, could not impose taxes or tariffs. Although a common treasury was supposed to be supplied by the states in proportion to the value of the land within each state, the states retained the power to levy and collect taxes. In essence, this rule meant that the United States in Congress had to rely on the goodwill of the states to obtain money. Such revenues were rarely forthcoming. Some states paid nothing at all; others turned over a portion of what they owed but rarely by the date the payments were due. Part of this problem was caused by the fact that the states were not about to trade one dictatorial central government for another and, therefore, simply ignored the national government.

Moreover, the desire to prevent the type of tyranny that the colonies had experienced under the rule of King George and the British Parliament led the framers of the Articles to include other limitations on the national government. For instance, all delegates to the Congress were appointed by the state legislatures and served at their pleasure. Several times, the national government found itself powerless to act, because some of the legislatures did not even bother to send delegates to Congress. In addition, whereas the United States in Congress had the authority to regulate the value of any money created under its own authority or under the authority of a state, the states retained the power to issue their own currency.

This is not to say that the Articles did not have some strong points. The Articles did, in fact, establish a few principles that became part of the U.S Constitution and a few others that we arguably should have kept. For example, under both the Articles and the U.S. Constitution, members of Congress are guaranteed that they will not be arrested while on the way to or returning from a session of Congress, except for treason, a felony, or breach of the peace. Both documents also contain a full faith and credit clause under which each state is required to honor the public acts, records, and judicial proceedings of all the other states. The Articles also contain a clause that limits the terms of congressional delegates and one that limits the term of the president, something that should have been retained from the outset under the U.S. Constitution.

Despite these strong points, the weaknesses of the Articles far outweighed its strengths and so, in the summer of 1787, 12 of the 13 states sent delegates to a Constitutional Convention in Philadelphia. The purpose of the convention was to revise the Articles. However, the Articles were so weak and the nation was in such disarray that the delegates decided to write a new constitution, the result of which is the present U.S. Constitution. In writing this new constitution, the delegates must have done something right because their document has lasted for more than two centuries. Still, some legal scholars and several historians argue that the action taken by the delegates at the convention was illegal. Moreover, there is some merit to this position. Article XIII of the original Articles states that the only way to amend the Articles is by a vote taken by "a Congress of the United States." Did the Constitutional Convention act as "a Congress of the United States" or were the delegates acting on their own and outside the authority of the Articles? It is an interesting question, one that might merit further attention at some time in the future. For now, however, we turn to an examination of the U.S. Constitution.

The Principles of the United States Constitution

The Constitution of the United States is based on two fundamental principles that were supported by many of the delegates to the convention in Philadelphia. Those two principles promote, first, a separation of national powers among three distinct branches of government

30   Part One   Ethics, Law, and the Judicial System

THE OPENING CASE *Revisited, Part II*
When the States Challenge Federal Authority, Round 3

In the Opening Case, Arizona passed a statute that enabled the police to demand identification papers from anyone suspected of being an illegal alien. Also recall that, in reaction to this law, the federal government sued Arizona in an attempt to block the administration of that law. In its brief, the Justice Department argued that federal law trumps state law in this case because, under Article I, section 8, clause 4, of the U.S. Constitution, Congress alone has power to control the naturalization of citizens. To further cement their position the Justice Department also called upon the Supremacy Clause which says that, "(t)his Constitution and the Laws of the United States . . . shall be the supreme Law of the Land." Thus, it would seem that the Justice Department has a solid argument in this case. Interestingly enough, under the Articles of Confederation, the results would have been different. When we examine the Articles we would find that, under Article II, "(e)ach state retains its sovereignty, freedom, and independence, and right, which is not by this Confederation expressly delegated to the United States, in Congress assembled." Moreover, a lengthy and detailed search of the Articles reveals that the naturalization of citizens is not mentioned anywhere. The Articles do explain that, in most situations, only Congress can negotiate treaties, send and receive

ambassadors, and declare war, but the Articles make no mention of immigration or naturalization, indicating that, under Article II, such matters are left to the states. Now remember that there are reputable legal scholars and historians who believe that the Articles of Confederation were violated when the delegates to the Philadelphia convention created a new constitution. Consequently, if Arizona wanted to play hard ball with the feds, it could argue (1) that the Articles of Confederation could only be amended by a "Congress of the United States"; (2) that the Constitutional Convention held in Philadelphia did not qualify as "a Congress of the United States" and could not, therefore, amend the Articles; (3) that, even if the Convention was "a Congress of the United States," it did not have the power to simply "tear up the original Articles" and "start from scratch"; (4) that, in either case, the Articles of Confederation are still in effect and that, under those Articles, the states retain the power to control the naturalization process, which means that the Arizona statute cannot be subject to a nonexistent supremacy clause and, therefore, is constitutionally sound under Article II of the Articles of Confederation. This argument would not work, of course, because it would require any federal court that so rules to recognize that it also has no right to exist, something that is unlikely to happen ever.

and, second, a system of checks and balances that allows each branch to oversee the operation of the other two branches. The principle of the separation of powers set up the now familiar three branches of the national government: the executive branch, the legislative branch, and the judicial branch. The principle of checks and balances allows each branch to share in the power of the other two.

The Structure of the United States Constitution

The U.S. Constitution is divided into two parts: the articles and the amendments. The articles establish the organization of the national government. The amendments change provisions in the original articles and add ideas that the framers did not include in those articles.

U.S. Const. Articles
I–VII (see pages
807–811)

The Articles The first three of the seven articles distribute the power of the government among the legislative, executive, and judicial branches. Article I establishes Congress as the legislative (statute-making) branch of the government. Article II gives executive power to the president, and Article III gives judicial power to the Supreme Court and other courts established by Congress. Article IV explains the relationships among the states and the relationship between the federal government and the states, while Article V outlines the methods for amending the Constitution. Article VI establishes the U.S. Constitution, federal

Table 2-1	Articles of the U.S. Constitution

Articles	Content
Article I	Establishes the legislative branch of the federal government (the Congress) Defines the duties and powers of each house Outlines how Congress must conduct its business Lists legislative powers granted to Congress Lists powers denied to Congress Lists powers denied to the states
Article II	Gives executive power and responsibilities to the president Outlines the president's term of office, qualifications, and manner of election Identifies the president as commander in chief Gives the president power to make treaties
Article III	Establishes the Supreme Court and authorizes the establishment of other federal courts Provides for trial by jury for crimes Defines treason against the United States
Article IV	Defines interstate relations Sets up the full faith and credit clause obligating each state to recognize the public acts and proceedings of other states Provides for extradition of those accused of crimes in other states
Article V	Outlines the method of amending the Constitution
Article VI	Establishes the Constitution, federal laws, and federal treaties as the supreme law of the land
Article VII	Provides for the original ratification of the Constitution

laws, and treaties as the supreme law of the land. Finally, Article VII outlines how the original 13 states would go about ratifying the new Constitution. Table 2-1 outlines the content of each article in the Constitution.

The Amendments The amendments to the Constitution establish the rights that belong to the people, change some of the provisions in the original articles, and add ideas that the Framers did not include in those articles. Thus, the amendments are attempts to fine-tune the Constitution and update its provisions to meet the demands of a changing socioeconomic structure. The first 10 amendments of the Constitution compose the Bill of Rights. They were added soon after the ratification of the Constitution by the original 13 states. Other amendments that secure the rights of the people include the Thirteenth, which prohibits slavery; the Fourteenth, which guarantees equal protection of the law and due process; the Fifteenth, which guarantees voting rights; the Nineteenth, which extends voting rights to women; the Twenty-Fourth, which prohibits poll taxes; and the Twenty-Sixth, which extends the right to vote to eighteen-year-old citizens. Table 2-2 provides a more detailed look at the amendments.

States Rights, Democracy, and the Amendment Process

The Articles of Confederation did not set up a democracy. From the very first statement to the very last sentence, the Articles expressly support state supremacy. Article II, for instance, explicitly establishes that each state retains its sovereignty, while Article V requires each state to keep a well-armed militia and empowers those states to launch a preemptive strike in the event

Did You Know?
Roman law was first codified into The Law of the Twelve Tables in 450 BC. The Twelve Tables declared that all free citizens had certain fundamental rights.

U.S. Const. Amendments I–XXVII (see pages 811–815)

Table 2-2 Amendments to the U.S. Constitution

The Bill of Rights	Pre–Civil War Amendments	Civil War Amendments	Progressive Amendments	Depression-Era Amendments	Modern Amendments
Amendment I Freedom of religion, speech, press, assembly	*Amendment XI* Lawsuits against the states	*Amendment XIII* Slavery is abolished	*Amendment XVI* The income tax is established	*Amendment XX* Terms of president, vice president, senators and representatives altered	*Amendment XXII* President's terms limited to two
Amendment II The right to bear arms and set up a militia	*Amendment XII** President and vice president elected together	*Amendment XIV* Equal protection of the law, due process, citizenship	*Amendment XVII* Senators elected by direct election	*Amendment XXI* Prohibition repealed	*Amendment XXIII* Washington, DC gets electors
Amendment III The quartering of soldiers in homes is prohibited		*Amendment XV* Voting rights guaranteed	*Amendment XVIII‡* Prohibition established		*Amendment XXIV* Poll taxes outlawed
Amendment IV Search and seizure by probable cause			*Amendment XIX* Women given right to vote		*Amendment XXV* Disability of the president; vacancies in the vice presidency
Amendment V Grand juries, double jeopardy, self-incrimination, due process, and eminent domain					*Amendment XXVI* Vote extended to 18-year-olds
Amendment VI Procedures allowed in criminal cases					*Amendment XXVII* Congress prevented from voting itself instant pay raises
Amendment VII Jury trials in common law cases guaranteed					
Amendment VIII Bill of Rights guaranteed, cruel and unusual punishment prohibited					
Amendment IX People retain other rights					
Amendment X Powers reserved to states					

*Altered somewhat by the Twentieth Amendment. †Voting age changed by Twenty-sixth Amendment. ‡Repealed by Twenty-first Amendment.

of an imminent attack. Moreover, under the Articles, each state had only one vote in Congress and all Congressional delegates were chosen by the state legislatures and served at their pleasure. When the U.S. Constitution was written, many but not all of these provisions were lost. States no longer have the right to launch preemptive military strikes on their own, for example, and the members of the House of Representatives are now chosen by a vote of the people. Under the original Constitution, however, Senators were still chosen by the state legislatures, much as the delegates to Congress were chosen under the original Articles. This changed with the Seventeenth Amendment when the people were empowered to vote directly for senators.

There are some people who would like to see the Seventeenth Amendment repealed, or replaced with a new amendment that returns the process of electing senators back to the state legislatures. At first blush this idea may seem strange. After all, we have always been taught that the power of the government originates in the hands of the people. So why should the people not vote for senators in the same way that they vote for representatives. Those commentators who support the repeal of the Seventeenth Amendment are not anti-democracy as much as they are pro-states' rights. Like the delegates who wrote the original Articles, they believe that the states should have a voice in national politics. The federal government, or so the argument goes, would not be as powerful, as intrusive, as debt ridden, or as willing to spend tax dollars on pointless projects if the senators had to periodically answer to their state legislatures.

In fact, these commentators argue that the Seventeenth Amendment (along with the Sixteenth Amendment which led to our present income tax system) opened the way to a powerful central government which, despite the direct voting power of the people, is extremely undemocratic, at least in the way it responds to (or perhaps does not respond to) the will of the people. In contrast, those commentators who favor keeping the Seventeenth Amendment intact, argue, rather convincingly, that the amendment was part of a progressive trend that gave the vote to women (the Nineteenth Amendment), provided electors for the District of Columbia (the Twenty-Third Amendment), eliminated the poll tax (the Twenty-Fourth Amendment), and gave the right to vote to 18-year-olds (the Twenty-Sixth Amendment). Therefore, repealing the amendment would be a step backward, at least in terms of individual political rights. Moreover, one of the main purposes of the Seventeenth Amendment is to insulate the election of senators from the influence of corporations which, before the amendment, often provided monetary incentives for state legislatures to elect senators who favored big business. (See Tony Mauro, "The 17th Amendment Under Fire," *The National Law Journal*, November 22, 2010, pp. 1 and 8.)

State Constitutions

Each state in the union adopts its own constitution. A state constitution establishes the state's government. It also sets down principles to guide the state government in making state laws and conducting state business. Most state constitutions are patterned after the U.S. Constitution. However, state constitutions tend to be longer and more detailed than the U.S. Constitution, because they must deal with local as well as statewide matters.

The Principle of Supremacy

A basic principle of constitutional law is that the U.S. Constitution is the supreme law of the land. This principle of constitutional supremacy means that all other laws must be in line with constitutional principles. If a law somehow conflicts with the Constitution, that law is said to be unconstitutional. If it does not conflict, it will be upheld by the court as constitutional.

U.S. Const. Article VI
(see page 811)

The Principle of Preemption

The Constitution also says that all federal laws that are made in line with constitutional principles are to be considered the supreme law of the land. Cases that involve such conflicts, however, are not always as clear cut as those that involve state statutes that conflict with the Constitution. Preemption is the process by which the courts decide that a federal statute must take precedence over a state statute. The preemption of a state statute can occur in three situations. First, Congress can be very clear about its intent and explicitly state that the federal statute preempts any state statute that covers the same issues. If that is the case, then all that remains for the courts is to determine which statutes are covered by the preemption clause. Second, state statutes can be preempted by federal statutes when they conflict with the objectives of federal legislation. Third, the courts will preempt a state statute that has entered an area of the law that is traditionally an area that the federal government handles, such as foreign affairs or banking.

The Doctrine of Devolution

Devolution occurs when the courts redefine a right and shift the obligation to enforce a right from an upper level authority to a lower one. For instance, a court may decide that a state agency, rather than a federal one, can control what governmental employees, in the course of performing their duties, are permitted to talk or write about in relation to official policies, procedures, and programs. Such a prohibition might appear to violate the employee's Constitutional right of free speech as a U.S. citizen. However, in such cases, the court has decided that the duty and the power to define and enforce that right belongs to the state rather than to the federal government. It is important to note that the devolution of a right does not destroy that right. Rather, devolution simply redistributes the authority to define the nature of that right in certain situations. (See Isidore Silver, "Recent Supreme Court Opinions: A Devolving Constitution," *The National Law Journal*, March 12, 2007, p. 22; Robert Tannenwald, "Devolution: The New Federalism—An Overview," *New England Economic Review*, May/June 1998, 1–7.)

A QUESTION OF ETHICS

Federal Supremacy, Discrimination, and a Lesson in Ethics

A quick review of the Opening Case at the beginning of this chapter will remind us that Arizona passed a statute that empowered the local police to demand identification papers from anyone suspected of being in the country illegally. In response, the federal government sued the state of Arizona in an attempt to block the administration of the law arguing that federal law trumped state law in this situation because the Constitution gave the power to control immigration to the national government alone. Recall that the federal government could have argued that the law was discriminatory because it had a disparate impact on people of a particular color and a certain national origin. The question we pose here is not the relatively easy one of whether the Arizona statute is unethical. Rather, the question we ask is whether it is ethical for the Justice Department to use the relatively safe argument of federal supremacy while ignoring the far greater legal and moral transgression of deliberate, unapologetic, legislative discrimination?

The Commerce Clause

The states have the power to regulate business under their inherent police power, a power that the federal government does not have. In contrast, the federal government's power to regulate business has emerged over the years out of the Commerce Clause of the U.S. Constitution. The Commerce Clause is found in Article I, Section 8, Clause 3. The wording of the clause is a study in simplicity; the interpretation is not. In fact, the clause and its long history clearly demonstrate the duality that exists in the law at all three levels: spirit versus letter, words versus interpretation, and abstract principle versus concrete situation. The clause reads, "Congress shall have Power To . . . regulate Commerce with foreign Nations and among the several states." The U.S. Supreme Court has held that the phrase "commerce power" means "the power to . . . prescribe the rules by which commerce is to be governed." This ruling sounds reasonable enough and, had the Court stopped at that point, many future problems might have been avoided.

The Court, however, did not stop. Nor was it obliged to. Over the years, as case piled upon case, the Supreme Court further refined its position, gradually broadening the federal government's power to regulate business. The power to regulate is so broad today that the federal government can regulate any business activity that affects interstate commerce, even if that activity takes place solely within the borders of a single state. Just about the only thing that the U.S. Supreme Court has not yet allowed the government to do is to force citizens, or anyone else for that matter, to participate in an activity whether they want to or not. In contrast, the states do sometimes order their citizens to engage in some forms of commerce, as when they require automobile owners to buy insurance. Such legislation, however, is permitted under the state's police power. On the other hand, even that power is limited. The state can require insurance, but only if a citizen actually wants to own a car. It is unlikely that a state can order a person to engage in a business activity merely because that person exists. Moreover, it is even more unlikely that the federal government has that power.

The First Amendment

The First Amendment of the U.S. Constitution has been the source of much power over the last two centuries. However, it has also been the source of much controversy. This is to be expected because the First Amendment contains some of the most important rights in the Bill of Rights. These include freedom of the press, freedom of speech, freedom of assembly, and freedom of religion. Freedom of speech has always been a source of controversy because, by its very nature, speech has a political dimension that must be balanced with the actions that might be sparked by that speech. The limits that are placed on speech are easy to articulate but difficult to implement. One of these limits states that one person's freedom of speech is limited by next person's rights. Thus, if a person lies about someone and that lie hurts the other person's reputation, the speaker may find himself or herself liable for the tort of defamation. Similarly, people have the right to free speech including the right to criticize political candidates, but they do not have the right to incite violence.

---

quick quiz 2-2

1. The present U.S. Constitution is the only constitution that the United States has ever had.   true | false

2. The principle of separation of powers was never adopted by the framers of the U.S. Constitution.   true | false

3. A basic principle of constitutional law is that state law is the supreme law of the land.   true | false

---

2-3 Statutory Law

Laws passed by a legislature are known as statutes. At the federal level, statutes are the laws made by Congress and signed by the president. At the state level, statutes are enacted by state legislatures, such as the Ohio General Assembly or the Oregon Legislative Assembly. Many statutes prohibit certain activities. Most criminal statutes are prohibitive statutes. For instance, Ohio criminal law prohibits hazing, which is defined as coercing someone into doing an act of initiation that has a substantial risk of causing mental or physical harm. Other statutes demand the performance of some action. For instance, Ohio statutory law requires all motor vehicle drivers and passengers to wear safety belts. Some statutes, such as those that create governmental holidays or name state flowers, simply declare something.

Codes and Titles

Statutes must be arranged, cataloged, and indexed for easy reference. This is done by compiling state and federal codes. A code is a compilation of all the statutes of a particular state or the federal government. All federal statutes, for instance, are gathered in the United States Code (USC), while all Ohio statutory law is collected in the Ohio Revised Code (ORC). In general, codes are subdivided into titles, which are groupings of statutes that deal with a particular area of the law. Title 17 of the Ohio Revised Code, for example, covers corporations and partnerships. Often titles are subdivided into chapters, and chapters subdivided into sections. Thus, ORC 1701.03, *Purposes of a Corporation,* can be read from right to left as the third section of the first chapter of Title 17 of the ORC.

Uniform Laws

Because many different statutes are passed each year by the 50 state legislatures, statutory law differs from state to state. This lack of consistency can cause problems when legal matters cross state boundaries. One solution to the problem of inconsistent statutory law is for all the state legislatures to adopt the same statutes. The National Conference of Commissioners on Uniform State Laws (NCCUSL) was founded to write these uniform laws. The NCCUSL is composed of commissioners that come from every state, the District of Columbia, Puerto Rico, and the Virgin Islands. These commissioners are usually selected by the governor. Most of the commissioners serve for a term of years set by the state. Some however have no set term and therefore can be replaced by the governor at any time. The number of commissioners from each jurisdiction is established by that jurisdiction. Some jurisdictions decide to have a lot of commissioners, while others decide to send only a few. California, for example, appoints 14, while New Hampshire limits its number to 3. The states are also responsible for sending money to the NCCUSL to support its activities. The more populated states generally pay more than the smaller states.

Just about anybody can submit a suggestion for a uniform law. However, most often, such suggestions come from the states, the American Bar Association, and those people in a particular profession or activity who have a specific interest in that area of the law. Recent topics that have been considered for uniform laws include genetic engineering, organ donation procedures, and the electronic discovery of evidence during lawsuits. Once a suggestion has been made, the NCCUSL's Committee on Scope and Program will appoint a committee to study the advisability of working on that uniform law. If the committee decides that such a law would be useful and appropriate, the committee members send the proposal back to the Scope and Program Committee, which then transmits the proposal to the executive committee and, eventually, to all of the commissioners. If everyone approves the proposal, they set up a drafting committee. As the name suggests, the job of the drafting committee is to write the actual uniform law, point by point. After the draft is written, it must be reviewed and voted upon. This can be a long and involved process that includes input from the states, legal experts, and those people, businesses, organizations, and institutions directly affected by a newly proposed law. Once the entire group of commissioners has voted to endorse a law, the state delegations must then vote to confirm it also. After a proposed uniform law is accepted by the state delegations within the NCCUSL, it is recommended to the state legislatures for adoption. Some states may adopt it, others may not. Remember that a uniform law does not become a binding statute until it has been officially passed by a state legislature.

A QUESTION OF ETHICS

The NCCUSL and a Lesson in Ethics

Very few people, even those commentators who are concerned with the injustice associated with the Arizona immigration law, the inequities within the new tax law, or the attack on states' rights symbolized by the Seventeenth Amendment, care, discuss, or even notice the vast power that has been placed in the hands of a group of unelected legal experts who write uniform laws and then pass those laws onto state legislators, many of whom simply enact those uniform codes into law, sometimes without changing a single word. The NCCUSL manufactures literally dozens of these uniform codes covering such diverse topics as tort law, corporate law, family law, and surrogate parenting law, just to name a few. Is it ethical for legislators to abdicate their responsibility for the state's legislative agenda by turning it over to these unelected, private "experts"?

The Uniform Commercial Code

The most significant development in uniform state legislation has been the Uniform Commerical Code. The Uniform Commercial Code (UCC) is a unified set of statutes designed to govern almost all commercial transactions. The basic principles of commercial law were not changed by the UCC provisions. By defining and clarifying often misunderstood business and legal terms, the UCC helps parties involved in commercial transactions prepare their contracts. Even the famed UCC, however, has been adjusted by various states, and not all states decide to the accept suggested amendments that come from the NCCUSL from time to time. Some states have even decided to eliminate some of the chapters and articles in the UCC that they have found obsolete or irrelevant or that do not fit within their established legal traditions. Louisiana, for example, which still uses the Napoleonic Code, has adopted only four of the nine articles. Nevertheless, the UCC remains one of the most successful achievements of the NCCUSL. The National Conference of Commissioners on Uniform State Laws maintains a Web site that includes the final drafts of all uniform acts that have been approved and recommended for adoption by the state legislatures.

Cyber-Law Statutes

The advent of the Information Age has sparked the need for specific cyber-law statutes that address the problems associated with cyber-commerce. Cyber-commerce is the term applied to all cyber-transactions. The NCCUSL has responded to this challenge by creating several new uniform laws. For example, the Uniform Computer Information Transactions Act (UCITA) is designed to deal directly with cyber-contracts that involve the sale or licensing of digital information. Another uniform cyber-law approved by the commissioners for enactment by state legislatures is the Uniform Electronic Transactions Act (UETA). This uniform cyber-law points out those principles that should be used in every state to make certain that cyber-contracts are enforceable.

quick quiz 2-3

1. Laws passed by a legislature are known as amendments.   true | false

2. Once the NCCUSL adopts a uniform law, it becomes binding in   true | false
   all states.

3. Cyber-commerce is the term that is applied to all   true | false
   cyber-transactions.

2-4 Court Decisions

When most people think of the law, they think of the Constitution or of statutes passed by Congress and the state legislatures. Although these two sources are important, they are not the only two sources of law in this country. The courts also make law in the following ways:

- Common law
- Interpretation of statutes
- Judicial review

Common Law

The term *common law* comes from the attempts of early English kings to establish a body of law that all the courts in the kingdom would hold in common. At that time, judges in towns and villages had instructions to settle all disputes in as consistent a manner as possible. The judges maintained this consistency by relying on previous legal decisions whenever they faced a similar set of circumstances. In this way, they established a body of common law. As the process continued, judges began to record their decisions and share them with other judges. Common law is the body of previously recorded legal decisions made by the courts in specific cases. The process of relying on these previously recorded legal decisions is called *stare decisis* (let the decision stand). The previously recorded legal decisions themselves are referred to as precedents.

The legal system of the United States, except Louisiana, is rooted in the common law of England. These roots derive from the early American colonists who came from England and were governed by the English monarchy. Over time, English common law has been eroded in the United States by the passing of state statutes and court decisions that better meet the needs of today's society. Nevertheless, parts of the common law as practiced in England still exist in the laws of the United States today. Courts still apply the common law when there are no modern court decisions or statutes dealing with an issue in dispute.

Today's judges make decisions in the same way as their counterparts from the Middle Ages. They rely on precedent according to the principle of *stare decisis*. A precedent is a model case that a court can follow when facing a similar situation.

There are two types of precedent: binding and persuasive. Binding precedent is precedent that a court must follow. Persuasive precedent is precedent that a court is free to follow or ignore. Generally, whether a precedent is binding or persuasive is determined by the court's location. For instance, decisions made by the Florida Supreme Court would be binding in all Florida state courts but persuasive in all other states' courts.

The U.S. Supreme Court has frequently emphasized the crucial role that precedent plays in the American legal system. In emphasizing the importance of precedent, the Court has outlined a series of questions that judges should ask as they contemplate whether to overturn a rule of law established in an earlier case. These questions include the following:

- Is the established rule still practical?
- Have so many people relied upon the rule that overturning it would cause difficulty and injustice?
- Is the rule still legally viable, or has it become merely a relic of an outdated and deserted legal doctrine?
- Is the rule still up to date, or has it become obsolete because of changes in society?

Precedents, past decisions, form the basis of common law.

Only if judges can answer these questions satisfactorily should they consider overturning an established precedent.

Statutory Interpretation

A second way that court decisions make law is in the interpretation of statutes. Statutory interpretation is the process by which the courts analyze those aspects of a statute that are unclear or ambiguous or that were not anticipated at the time the legislature passed the statute. When legislators enact a new statute, they cannot predict how people will react to the new law. Nor can they foresee all of its future ramifications and implications. Thus, when two or more parties have a dispute that challenges the statute, they may differ as to what the legislature had in mind when it wrote the statute. Also, legislators may have purposely made the language of a statute general. The job of reacting to unforeseen circumstances and making generalities fit specific circumstances falls to the courts. As a result, a judge may be called upon to determine how a certain statute should be interpreted.

Courts are not, however, free to interpret a statute at random. A court cannot interpret a statute unless it is faced with a case involving that statute. In interpreting a statute, a court looks to a variety of sources, including the legislative history of the statute and the old statute that the new statute replaced, if any. Naturally, the court also must review any binding precedent that interprets that statute. This requirement exists because the court must still rely upon previous cases when engaged in statutory interpretation, just as it does when deciding questions of common law.

Judicial Review

A third way that courts make law is through judicial review, which is the process of determining the constitutionality of various legislative statutes, administrative regulations, or executive actions. In exercising the power of judicial review, a court will look at the statute, regulation, or action and compare it with the Constitution. If the two are compatible, no problem exists. However, if they are contradictory, one of the two must be declared void. Because the Constitution is the supreme law of the land, the Constitution always rules, and the statute, regulation, or action is ruled unconstitutional.

Naturally, in exercising the power of judicial review, the court also must review any binding precedent involved in the constitutional issue, because the court still must rely upon previous cases in judicial review, just as it does in common law and statutory interpretation. The lower courts in this country have the capacity to review issues of constitutionality and interpret the meaning of provisions within the U.S. Constitution. However, the ultimate authority, and therefore the final word, on such issues rests with the United States Supreme Court.

quick quiz 2-4

1. The process of relying on previous decisions is called *stare decisis*.	true | false
2. Common law originated in France.	true | false
3. Judicial review is another name for statutory interpretation.	true | false

40   Part One   Ethics, Law, and the Judicial System

2-5 Administrative Regulations

Neither legislators nor judges can administer to all aspects of today's society. Moreover, legislators are generalists; they are rarely experts in all areas over which they have power. Because legislators are generalists and today's problems are so complex, statutory law, created by legislators, is very limited in what it can do. To broaden the power of statutory law, legislators delegate their power to others. They do this when they create administrative agencies.

Administrative Agencies

Federal administrative agencies administer statutes enacted by Congress in specific areas, such as communication, aviation, labor relations, working conditions, and so on. Similarly, agencies have been designated by the states to supervise intrastate activities. These agencies create rules, regulate and supervise, and render decisions that have the force of law. Their decrees and decisions are known as administrative law.

Administrative Procedures Act

Problems sometimes occur because administrative agencies have the power to make the rules, enforce the rules, and interpret the rules. To help prevent any conflict of interest that could arise from these overlapping responsibilities, Congress passed the federal Administrative Procedures Act. Similarly, most states have adopted a uniform law known as the Model State Administrative Procedures Act. Under these two acts, an administrative agency planning new regulations must notify the affected parties and hold hearings to allow those parties to express their views. These acts also allow the courts to review agency decisions and rulings.

Fuel economy standards are rising, increasing the need for more fuel efficient vehicles to be produced.

The Federal Register and the Code of Federal Regulations

The Federal Register is a publication that produces a daily compilation of new regulations issued by federal administrative agencies. The Federal Register operates within the National Archives and Records Administration under the authority of the Office of the Federal Register. The Government Printing Office is reponsible for actually printing the document, though today it is also available online. Most of the documents included within the Federal Register are directly related to the agencies. Those subdivisions devoted to the agencies include a section on rules and regulations, one on proposed rules, and one on notices of hearings, meetings, application deadlines, and administrative orders. There is also a section devoted to presidential orders and proclamations. Once a rule is finalized, it is included in the Code of Federal Regulations (CFR), which is updated each year.

quick quiz 2-5

1. Together, legislators and judges can administer all aspects of today's society.   true | false

2. Most legislators are specialists.   true | false

3. The decrees and decisions made by administrative agencies are known as administrative law.   true | false

Summary

2.1 The law consists of rules of conduct established by the government to maintain harmony, stability, and justice within a society. Ideally, the primary objectives of the law are to promote harmony, stability, and justice. In everyday life, the balance is not easy to maintain. The law or, more properly, the entire legal framework consists of a series of dualities that must be resolved somehow.

2.2 A constitution is the basic law of a nation or state. The United States Constitution provides the organization of the national government. Each state also has a constitution that determines the state's governmental structure. The body of law that forms a constitution and its interpretation is known as constitutional law.

2.3 The laws passed by a legislature are known as statutes. At the federal level, these are the laws made by Congress and signed by the president. At the state level, statutes are enacted by state legislatures. Statutes must be arranged, cataloged, and indexed for easy reference by compiling state and federal codes. Because many different statutes are passed each year by the 50 state legislatures, there are important differences in state statutory law throughout the nation. One solution to the problem of inconsistent statutory law is for the legislatures of all the states to adopt the same statutes.

The National Conference of Commissioners on Uniform State Laws (NCCUSL) was founded to write these uniform laws.

2.4 Courts make law through common law, the interpretation of statutes, and judicial review. Common law is the body of previously recorded legal decisions made by the courts in specific cases. Statutory interpretation is the process by which the courts analyze those aspects of a statute that are unclear or ambiguous or that were not anticipated at the time that the legislature passed the statute, and judicial review is the process by which the courts determine the constitutionality of various legislative statutes, administrative regulations, or executive actions.

2.5 Federal administrative agencies administer statutes enacted by Congress in specific areas, such as commerce, communication, aviation, labor relations, and working conditions. Similar agencies have been designated by the states to supervise intrastate activities. These agencies create rules, regulate and supervise, and render decisions. To help prevent any conflict of interest that could arise from these overlapping responsibilities, Congress passed the federal Administrative Procedures Act. Similarly, most states have adopted a uniform law known as the Model State Administrative Procedures Act.

Key Terms

administrative law, 40
Articles of Confederation, 29
binding precedent, 38
code, 36
Code of Federal Regulations (CFR), 40
common law, 38
constitution, 28

constitutional law, 28
cyber-commerce, 37
devolution, 34
Federal Register, 40
judicial review, 39
law, 25
persuasive precedent, 38
precedent, 38

preemption, 34
statutes, 35
statutory interpretation, 39
titles, 36
Uniform Commercial Code (UCC), 37

Questions for Review and Discussion

1. What are the objectives of the law?
2. How does the law reflect a series of complex dualities?
3. What are the functions of the articles and the amendments of the U.S. Constitution?
4. What is the difference between the principle of preemption and the doctrine of devolution?
5. What is the role of statutory law in the legal system?

6. Why does this country need to set up a system of uniform state laws?

7. What is the role of common law in the legal system?

8. How does the principle of *stare decisis* provide stability to our legal system?

9. What is the difference between statutory interpretation and judicial review?

10. Why does the legislature need to establish administrative agencies?

Cases for Analysis

1. On the very day that President Obama signed the 2010 Health Care bill into law, the attorney general of Virginia filed a lawsuit in federal district court arguing that parts of the statute were unconstitutional. Specifically, the attorney general argued that the new statute was unconstitutional because it required people to buy health insurance, which amounts to an unconstitutional extension of the Commerce Clause of the U.S. Constitution. The federal government argued that the Supreme Court has upheld federal laws regulating commercial activity even when that activity takes place solely within a single state, if the activity has an effect on interstate commerce. Clearly the failure to purchase health insualrance affects interstate commerce because, when one person does not purchase health insurance, the cost of treating that person will fall on the rest of society in one way or another. The Virginia attorney general disagreed, arguing that the cases that have upheld this principle have always involved commercial activities already taking place. They have never approved a mandate that forces someone to begin an activity that they would not have entered (in this case buying health insurance) absent the federal mandate. Therefore, the attorney general concluded, the health care law is unconstitutional. Should the statute be upheld or overturned given these arguments? Explain. (See Kevin Sacks, "Lying Ahead for Health Law, Years of Constitutional Wrangling," *The New York Times*, December 14, 2010, p. A22; See also: Kevin Sack, "Core of Health Care Law," *The New York Times*, December 14, 2010, pp. A1 and A22.)

2. Karen Silkwood was an employee at the Kerr—McGee Nuclear Power Plant in Oklahoma. During her employment there, she was apparently contaminated by exposure to plutonium. The contamination was so severe that she had to be sent to a special facility for an examination, and her personal belongings at her home had to be destroyed. After Silkwood died in an unrelated car accident, her father, as administrator of her estate, brought a lawsuit against

the Kerr-McGee power plant. Under state tort law, Silkwood's estate was awarded actual damages of $505,000 ($500,000 for personal injuries, and $5,000 for property loss), and $10 million in punitive damages, that is, damages designed to punish the defendant for its wanton misbehavior. The power plant argued that when Congress passed the Atomic Energy Act, it intended to completely outlaw any state regulation of nuclear power plants. Permitting the plaintiff to receive punitive damages in this case would destroy that intent. Silkwood's father, as the plaintiff in the case, argued that there was no intent expressed by Congress to preempt tort law in the area of nuclear regulation. In fact, when the plaintiff searched the Congressional Record, he could find no evidence that Congress intended to replace state tort law by passing the Atomic Energy Act. He also found that whenever Congress passed statutes similar to the Atomic Energy Act, there was never any intention to replace state tort law. Therefore, the plaintiff concluded, Congress did not intend to preempt state tort law in this case either. Is the plaintiff correct? Explain. *Silkwood v. Kerr-McGee Corporation*, 464 U.S. 238 (U.S. Supreme Court).

3. Richard Ceballos worked as a deputy district attorney for the city of Los Angeles. Ceballos wrote a memo in which he criticized the accuracy of an affidavit in a case that he had been assigned to handle. In the memo, he expressed doubt about the truthfulness of another employee in the department. Ceballos also testified in court about his doubts in relation to the affidavit. Afterward, Ceballos was victimized by reassignments, transfers, and the loss of a promotion. He argued that the actions of his superiors violated his right to speak freely about this problem in his department. The district attorney's office argued that a public employee's right to free speech could be limited by a state agency when that speech was made in the exercise of his or her official duties. Ceballos argued that his free speech rights, as guaranteed by the First Amendment to the U.S.

Constitution, trumped any state action. The district attorney argued that the power to control the right of free speech in relation to public employees had devolved to the states. Is the district attorney correct? Explain. *Garcetti, et al. v. Ceballos,* 126 S. Ct. 1951 (U.S. Supreme Court).

4. Barbara Rome entered Flower Memorial Hospital to undergo a series of X-rays. When she was ready for the X-rays, she was assisted by a student radiological intern. The intern placed Rome on the X-ray table and strapped her onto the table correctly. However, the intern did not properly fasten the footboard, which was located at the foot of the table. As a result of this error, Rome fell and was hurt when the table was raised. As a consequence, Rome brought a lawsuit against Flower Memorial Hospital alleging that the ordinary negligence of the intern had caused her injury. In contrast, the hospital argued that the lawsuit involved a medical claim, as defined under the state's medical malpractice statute. Whether a case involves ordinary negligence or a medical claim would determine whether the state's two-year statute of limitations for negligence or the state's one-year statute of limitations for medical claims would apply. This case clearly involves a difference of opinion on the interpretation of a statute. What sources might the court consider when interpreting the statute in question? *Rome v. Flower Memorial Hospital,* 635 N.E.2d 1239 (OH).

5. The Heart of Atlanta Hotel brought an action against the United States seeking a judgment that would declare Title II of the Civil Rights Act of 1964 unconstitutional. Congress's power to enact the Civil Rights Act is based upon Article I, Section 8, Clause 3, which gives Congress the power to regulate commerce among the states. The Heart of Atlanta Hotel argued that the statute was an unconstitutional extension of congressional power. The hotel also contended that the unconstitutional nature of the act especially applied to establishments like itself, which are incorporated and do business in only one state. However, because at any given time, three-fourths of the hotel's registered guests came from other states, the hotel clearly had an impact on interstate commerce. Do the lower federal courts have the authority to determine the constitutionality of Title II of the Civil Rights Act? What court has the ultimate authority to determine the constitutionality of the Civil Rights Act? Speculate on the outcome of this case. Do you think that the court should uphold the act? Explain. *Heart of Atlanta Hotel v. United States,* 370 U.S. 241 (U.S. Sup. Ct.).

quick quiz Answers

2-1	2-2	2-3	2-4	2-5
1. T	1. F	1. F	1. T	1. F
2. F	2. F	2. F	2. F	2. F
3. T	3. F	3. T	3. F	3. T

Chapter 3

The Judicial Process and Cyber-procedure

THE OPENING CASE   When Is a Citizen Not a Citizen?

One of the most perplexing problems that litigators often face is where to bring a lawsuit. In the federal courts jurisdiction can be established either by demonstrating the case involves an issue directly related to federal law (federal question) or by demonstrating diversity jurisdiction. In most cases of diversity, the parties, the plaintiff and the defendant, must be citizens of different states. Again the problem is not difficult when dealing with flesh and blood people. However, when one of the parties is a corporation, the problems begin. This is because federal law defines the corporate citizenship as a duality. A corporation is a citizen (1) in the state in which it is incorporated and (2) where it has its principal place of business. Unfortunately, the concept of "principal place of business" is vague at best. In the case of *Hertz Corporation v. Friend* the United States Supreme Court directly addressed the issue of corporate duality. Of course, whether the court improved or aggravated the situation is still open to debate. In that case the Hertz Corporation was sued by a group of California citizens in a state court. Hertz, sensing the probable hostility of a California jury, asked that the case be removed to federal court, arguing that the proper forum would be in New Jersey where its corporate headquarters was located. The plaintiffs disagreed. In the alternative, they maintained that Hertz's "principal place of business" was really located in California because it was in California that Hertz did

the vast majority of its business. The trial court agreed, ruling that California was the corporation's principal place of business. The appeals court followed suit, but the U.S. Supreme Court did not. The Supreme Court ruled that a corporation has its "principal place of business" where its nerve center is located, that is, the state in which the activities of the corporation are controlled by corporate management. New Jersey, then, was the proper forum for Hertz, not California. Ironically, although in this case Hertz, the corporate defendant, won the battle, their victory may prove to be a mixed blessing. It is a victory because it will help corporations get into federal court by making diversity a more straightforward proposition. However, the decision will also increase the number plaintiffs that can sue the corporation in federal court, especially in class action cases. Why does limiting a corporation's principal place of business increase the number of potential plaintiffs? Think about that question when diversity jurisdiction is covered later in the chapter. [See *Hertz Corporation v. Friend,* No. 08-1107, slip. op. (February 23, 2010); and Michael McNamara and Christine Henge, "'Hertz' Expands Companies Access to Federal Court," *The National Law Journal,* April 12, 2010, pp. 16–17.]

Opening Case Questions

1. Is this case a civil lawsuit or a criminal action? Explain.

2. Why does this case begin in the state court? Explain.

3. Why would the defendant corporation want to move the case into the federal court system? Explain.

4. Under what circumstances can a case be held in the federal court system? Explain.

5. What Article in the U.S. Constitution established the federal court system and what branch actually establishes the courts? Explain.

Learning Objectives

1. Explain the fundamental nature of the American courts.
2. Determine when a case can be brought in federal court.
3. Recognize those cases that can be heard by the U.S. Supreme Court.
4. Identify the structure of most state court systems.
5. Define civil litigation.
6. List the most common discovery techniques.
7. Detail the nature of an appeal.
8. Determine the extent of cyber-jurisdiction.
9. Explain the nature of electronically stored information (ESI).
10. Describe the steps in a criminal prosecution.

3-1 The Court System

The laws of the American government are interpreted and implemented by a system of courts authorized by either the federal or state constitutions and generally established by legislative authority. Courts are judicial tribunals that meet in a regular place and apply the law in an attempt to settle disputes by weighing the arguments presented by advocates for each party. Each of these official bodies is a forum for the party who presents a complaint, the party who responds to the complaint, and the jury and/or judge who settles the dispute. As noted in the previous chapter, the law involves a set of competing dualities including the spirit of the law versus the letter of the law, the words of the law versus the interpretation of those words, and the abstract principles of the law versus the concrete situations to which those principles are applied. Nowhere in the law are these dualities more obvious on a daily basis than in the court system. The same is true of the uncertainly principle which is played out every time a plaintiff and defendant place their case in the hands of a judge and jury.

The Federal Court System

The federal court system is authorized by Article III of the U.S. Constitution, which states, "The Judicial Power of the United States shall be vested in one supreme court, and in such inferior courts as Congress may from time to time ordain and establish." The present federal court system includes the Supreme Court, courts of appeals, and federal district courts.

U.S. Const. Article III (see page 810)

Court Jurisdiction

The authority of a court to hear and decide cases is called the court's jurisdiction. It is set by law and limited as to territory and type of case. A court of original jurisdiction has the authority to hear a case when it is first brought to court. Those courts that have the power to review a case for errors are courts of appellate jurisdiction. Most of the time courts with appellate jurisdiction will be empowered to determine whether the lower courts have made errors of law. This process is referred to as plenary review. Sometimes an appellate court will review the factual decisions made by the judge or the jury in lower courts. Such a review, however, only occurs when the appeals court determines that the decision made in the lower court was undeniably wrong, given the facts and evidence in the case. This determination relies on the clearly erroneous standard. Appellate courts also have the ability to determine whether the judge in the lower court has in some way misused his or her authority. This type of review is referred to as abuse of discretion.

Courts with the power to hear any type of case are said to exercise general jurisdiction. Those with the power to hear only certain types of cases have special jurisdiction. Examples of courts with special jurisdiction are probate courts and courts of claims. Courts also exercise subject matter jurisdiction and personal jurisdiction. Subject matter jurisdiction is the court's power to hear a particular type of case. Personal jurisdiction is the court's authority over the parties to a lawsuit.

Federal District Courts
Each state and territory in the United States has at least one federal district court. These courts are also known as *U.S. district courts.* The district courts are the courts of general jurisdiction in the federal system. Most federal cases begin in the federal district court. Not all cases belong there, however. The federal courts have subject matter jurisdiction over two types of cases: those involving federal law and those involving diversity.

Federal district courts have subject matter jurisdiction over cases that pertain to a federal question. A federal question could involve the U.S. Constitution, a federal statute or statutes, or a treaty. A state law issue can be included in a suit involving a federal question if the state claim is part of the same situation that created the federal question. If the federal claim is thrown out by the federal court, the state law issue usually cannot stand by itself. The people bringing the lawsuit would have to take their case to a state court.

Subject matter jurisdiction in federal court also arises in cases of diversity, even when no federal law is involved. Diversity cases include lawsuits that are (1) between citizens of different states, (2) between citizens of a state or different states and citizens of a foreign nation, and (3) between citizens of a state and a foreign government as the plaintiff. This last method of establishing jurisdiction usually applies only when a foreign government sues a citizen of a state. Congress has, however, provided an exception to this rule: Federal law now permits lawsuits in the federal courts against a foreign state when that state supports terrorism. The lawsuit must involve a request for damages arising from terrorist acts related to that support and as those acts are defined by law.

In diversity cases, and for other legal purposes, corporations are considered citizens of the state in which they are incorporated and the state where they have their principal place of business. In federal court, if even one defendant is a citizen of the same state as one of the plaintiffs, diversity cannot be established. In such a case, the law says that "diversity is not complete." Diversity cases also must involve an amount over $75,000.

Sometimes a case that begins in a state court can be transferred to the federal court. The process of moving a case from a state court to a U.S. District Court is called removal. Such requests are not granted on a whim. A defendant who wants to move a case from state court to federal court must have proper grounds for that removal. To convince the court to remove a case, a defendant must show that the case actually belonged in the federal court in the first case. This requirement means that the defendant will have to show that diversity exists or that a federal question was involved from the start. The defendant must file a motion to remove the case within 30 days of being served. It is also possible to remove a case to federal court even after the case has started, if circumstances change in the middle of a case, creating grounds for the removal. The statute of limitations on this type of move, however, is one year from the time that the case began, with the filing of the complaint.

THE OPENING CASE *Revisited, Part I*
When Is a Citizen Not a Citizen? Round 2

Recall that in the Opening Case, that the Hertz Corporation was sued by a group of California citizens who brought the case in a state court. Recall also that Hertz filed a motion asking that the case be removed from the California state court to the federal district court in New Jersey, where its corporate headquarters was located. In order to succeed in such a motion, Hertz would have to demonstrate that it had proper grounds for that removal. In this case, proper grounds would involve establishing diversity. That was the point of dispute in the case. The defendant argued that New Jersey was the proper pace for the case because New Jersey was where its "principal place of business" was located. On the other side, the plaintiffs contended that Hertz's "principal place of business" was California because Hertz did the vast majority of its business in that state. The trial court agreed with plaintiffs and dismissed the motion. The appeals court agreed and upheld the dismissal. The U.S. Supreme Court, however, disagreed and ruled that a corporation has its "principal place of business" where the activities of the corporation are controlled by corporate management. In this case that turned out to be New Jersey. Ironically, although in this case Hertz, the corporate defendant, won the battle, the victory may be a mixed blessing. It is a

victory because it will help corporations get into federal court by making diversity a more straightforward proposition. However, the decision will also increase the number plaintiffs that can sue the corporation in federal court, especially in class action cases. Limiting a corporation's principal place of business increases the number of potential plaintiffs because it extends diversity jurisdiction to at least one additional state. Thus, before the *Hertz* case, if California actually were the corporation's principal place of business and if New Jersey were the state of incorporation, both the federal courts in California and those in New Jersey would have jurisdiction over the corporation. However, that also means that citizens of California and citizens of New Jersey cannot sue the corporation in federal court in their home states because there would be no diversity. After the *Hertz* case, with California eliminated as a "citizenship state," the citizens of California could sue the corporation in federal court in California under diversity. Of course, the citizens of California would also have to invoke the California "long arm" statute and either the doctrine of "minimum contacts" or the newer "stream of commerce" test, but at least they would have an initial forum for their case (See Example 3-1).

Establishing subject matter jurisdiction will not be enough to get a case into federal court if the federal court does not have personal jurisdiction over a party. To establish personal jurisdiction, the court must look at the long-arm statute in the state in which the federal court is physically located. The court must then look to see if an appropriate level of contact has been made with the home state. A long-arm statute lists circumstances in which a court can exercise personal jurisdiction over an out-of-state defendant. Typically, these circumstances include the following:

- Owning real property in the state.
- Soliciting business in the state.
- Having an office or a store in the state.
- Committing a tort within the state.
- Transacting business in the state.

Some of the circumstances listed in the long-arm statute are relatively clear. Committing a tort in a state, for instance, leaves little room for misunderstanding. Other circumstances, however, such as "transacting business in the state," are not as precise. Therefore, personal jurisdiction under a state long-arm statute also requires meeting the required minimum contacts with the state. The concept of minimum contacts identifies the fewest number of contacts needed to allow the court to exercise jurisdiction over the out-of-state defendant. For example, let's say that a state allows the court to establish personal jurisdiction over any person who transacts business in the state. Now suppose a person buys a newspaper at an airport during a layover in the state. Does the purchase of that single newspaper constitute "transacting business" in the state?

The question turns on whether the purchase establishes a minimum contact with the state. In this case, the answer is probably "no." In general, the courts exclude contacts that are passive or that do not rise to a level that would permit the person transacting the business to reasonably foresee that he or she would come under the court's jurisdiction as a result of that transaction. It is difficult to conclude that the casual purchase of a newspaper at an airport kiosk would lead a person to foresee that he or she has voluntarily submitted to the jurisdictional power of a state. Something more would have to be involved. For instance, if the person in question specifically targeted the airport layover time to conduct negotiations with a client, and if a contract resulted from those negotiations, then the minimum contacts requirement would have been met and jurisdiction established.

Most of the time a court will determine subject matter jurisdiction before turning to the question of personal jurisdiction. Determining subject matter jurisdiction first, however, is not absolutely necessary. If the issue of personal jurisdiction is very obvious to the court, the court is free to dismiss the case before considering the question of subject matter jurisdiction. For example, this dismissal might happen if the defendant meets none of the categories in the long-arm statute or clearly does not meet the minimum contacts required by the case law of a state. In fact, if determining subject matter jurisdiction is especially difficult, the court is free to look at personal jurisdiction first, without even considering the question of subject matter jurisdiction.

EXAMPLE 3-1: The Stream of Commerce Theory

When attempting to establish personal jurisdiction over an out-of-state defendant, the plaintiff must convince the judge that the defendant had a set of "minimum contacts" with the state. Generally, the establishment of "minimum contacts" requires some kind of proactive strategy on the part of the defendant. This proactive strategy might involve opening a store, an office, a manufacturing plant, or a service center in the state. However, in some jurisdictions this is not always true. In the case of *Nicastro v. McIntyre,* for example, the Supreme Court of New Jersey established a standard called the *stream of commerce theory.* In this case, the plaintiff was injured by a product made by a British manufacturer. The plaintiff sued the manufacturer for failing to warn the ultimate user of a danger involved in the operation of the product, a metal press, and for a manufacturing defect related to the absence of an appropriate safety guard. The trial court dismissed the case because the plaintiff had failed to demonstrate the needed minimum contacts. The Supreme Court of New Jersey agreed that the plaintiff had not met the minimum contact test. Oddly, this did not stop the court from establishing personal jurisdiction over the manufacturer. To establish personal jurisdiction, the New Jersey court embraced a new theory of jurisdiction, the stream of commerce test. Under the stream of commerce test, the plaintiff must demonstrate that the defendant, in this case a foreign manufacturer, sent one of its products into "the stream of commerce" using a plan of national distribution that the manufacturer knew or at least reasonably should have known would in some way impact New Jersey. The New Jersey Supreme Court was satisfied that this was what had happened in the *Nicastro v. McIntyre* case. However, the New Jersey court *did limit* the stream of commerce standard to *product liability cases,* that is, cases in which the plaintiff claims to have been injured by a product manufactured or sold by the defendant. [See *Nicastro v. McIntyre,* 2010 N.J. Lexis 19 (N.J. Feb. 2, 2010); and J. Russell Jackson "Buy Globally, Sue Locally for Products Liability," *The National Law Journal,* March 22, 2010, p. 10.]

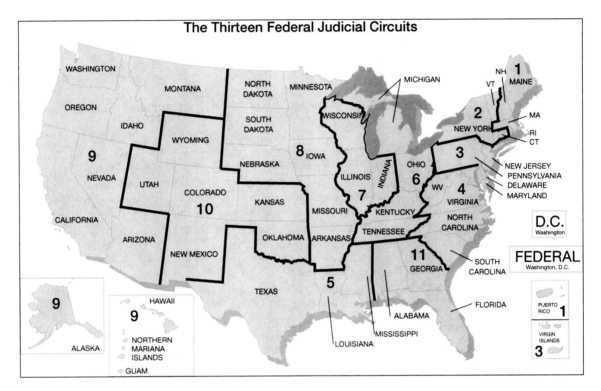

The Thirteen Federal Judicial Circuits

Figure 3-1 The U.S. federal court system is divided into 13 circuits, including the Washington, D.C., and federal circuits. Each circuit has several district courts.

U.S. Courts of Appeals

The judges at the appellate level must be guided by the standard of review that is appropriate to each case. The standard of review tells the appellate-level judges the degree to which they must remain faithful to the decision of the lower court judge. As noted previously, the three standards of review are *plenary, clearly erroneous,* and *abuse of discretion.* Although they do not hear as many cases each year as the district courts, there are fewer U.S. courts of appeals and therefore fewer judges to hear those cases. The U.S. Courts of Appeals hear appeals from the district courts, the U.S. Tax Court, and from many of the administrative agencies. At present, there are 13 U.S. courts of appeals within the federal court system (see Figure 3-1). Eleven of these appellate courts cover geographical groupings of states. For example, the Sixth Circuit Court of Appeals includes Michigan, Ohio, Kentucky, and Tennessee. The Fifth Circuit includes Texas, Louisiana, and Mississippi. There is also a special appellate court for the District of Columbia called the U.S. Court of Appeals for the District of Columbia.

In addition to 12 appellate courts, organized on a geographical basis, there is a thirteenth appellate court that has special jurisdiction over certain types of cases. This court is known as the U.S. Court of Appeals for the Federal Circuit. The Federal Circuit was established by Congress primarily to streamline and unify patent law. However, the Federal Circuit was also given the power to hear appeals in cases that entail government contracts, trademark disputes, federal workers, veterans' benefits, and international trade, among others. Still, more than one-third of the appeals that end up in the Federal Circuit are patent cases that come either from the U.S. district courts or the U.S. Patent and Trademark Office. Critics of the Federal Circuit have argued that the court's approach to patent law has become too narrow and too formalistic. (See Marcia Cole, "Critics Target Federal Circuit," *The National Law Journal,* October 16, 2006, pp. 1, 20–21.)

The United States Supreme Court Established by the Constitution, the U.S. Supreme Court is the court of final jurisdiction in all cases appealed from the lower federal courts and in cases coming from state supreme courts. It has original jurisdiction in cases affecting ambassadors or other public ministers and consuls and in cases in which a state is a party. The Supreme Court is composed of a chief justice and eight associate justices. They are appointed by the president with the consent of the Senate and hold office during good behavior.

U.S. Const. Article III (see page 810)

In many situations, a case will reach the U.S. Supreme Court only if the court agrees to issue a writ of certiorari. A writ of certiorari is an order from the Supreme Court to a lower court to deliver its records to the U.S. Supreme Court for review. The Court will issue a writ of certiorari if several lower courts have dealt with an issue but cannot agree on how it should be handled. If the case involves an issue that affects a large segment of society, the Court is likely to grant a writ. Finally, the Court may also hear a case if it involves a constitutional issue.

Applicable Law When a federal court hears a case involving only federal law or the U.S. Constitution, it must follow that federal law, the Constitution, and/or any line of federal precedent that can be used to interpret the situation. Circumstances are different in diversity cases or federal law cases that also concern issues of state law. For instance, if a federal judge in Minnesota hears a diversity case between a Minnesota citizen and an Iowa citizen, would that judge use federal law, Minnesota law, or Iowa law? As a general rule, a federal court hearing a diversity case will apply the law of the state in which it is physically located.

EXAMPLE 3-2: The "Foreign-Cubed" Theory

Often, the question of what law to apply in a case is crucial to the management of a lawsuit. The law of one jurisdiction may favor the plaintiff while another may support the defendant. Often whoever wins the battle of jurisdictions also wins the battle of the law and, ultimately, the war itself. Such was the situation in the case of *Morrison v. Australian National Bank*. In that case, Morrison, the plaintiff, and the Australian National Bank, the defendant, were foreign citizens and the alleged fraud was carried out in a foreign country. Despite all of this, the case ended up in the United States District Court and eventually in the United States Supreme Court. The class action lawsuit was filed by the investors who argued that the bank had defrauded them by overvaluing the bank's mortgage portfolio. The suit was filed in federal court in the United States because much of the original data used to create the overvalued portfolio was compiled in the United States. When a foreign plaintiff files a case against a foreign defendant alleging fraud committed in a foreign country, that plaintiff has filed a "foreign-cubed" lawsuit. What makes a foreign-cubed case so complicated, besides the obvious jurisdictional problems, is the fact that often the alien plaintiffs file in the United States because their own home jurisdictions do not consider the behavior of the bank to be fraudulent. Thus, the questions of jurisdiction and choice of law become more than simply legal issues. They become ethical issues as well. Should the United States become the "world police" guarding against investment fraud anywhere on the planet, or should the American courts stay out of the dispute, thus respecting foreign traditions? (See Tony Mauro, "A Border Battle Over Lawsuits: High Court Challenges the Use of American Courts by Foreign Plaintiffs," *The National Law Journal*, March 29, 2010, pp. 1 and 26.)

State Court Systems

The courts of each state are organized according to the provisions of the state constitution. Despite differences from state to state, such as the names for similar types of courts, there are basic similarities. For example, each state has an arrangement of inferior, or lower-level,

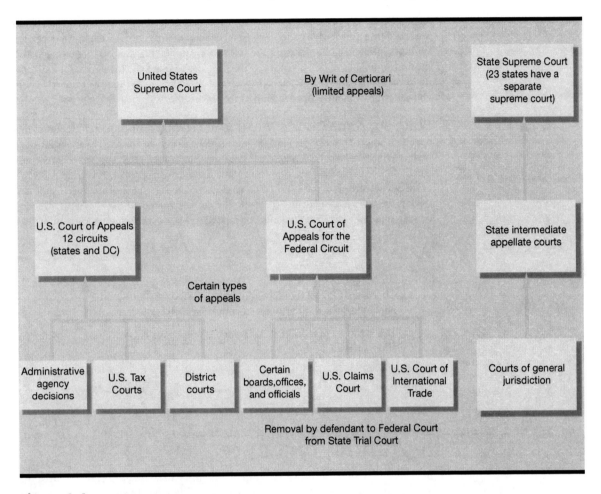

Figure 3-2 Federal and state court systems.

courts that serve as limited jurisdiction trial courts. Higher-level trial courts with broader jurisdiction are also provided. In addition, each state has appellate courts to which questions of law (not questions of fact) may be appealed. Figure 3-2 provides a general outline of the federal and the state court systems.

State Trial Courts   The state trial courts, also known as general jurisdiction courts, have the power to hear any type of case. They are often called superior courts, circuit courts, or courts of common pleas. Some states, notably New York, refer to them as supreme courts. These courts are usually organized around the counties of the state, so that each county has its own trial court of general jurisdiction. Most states also have other trial courts that are lower than the general jurisdiction courts. These limited jurisdiction courts usually hear only certain types of cases. For instance, a municipal court may be empowered to hear only those cases that involve municipal ordinances, criminal cases involving crimes within the city limits, and other cases that involve monetary claims of less than $10,000. Many localities have small-claims courts that hear civil cases involving small dollar amounts, ranging from $500 to $5,000, depending on state law.

State Intermediate Appellate Courts   State court systems provide for a variety of appellate court structures. Still, the purpose of the appellate courts remains the same, that is, to hear appeals on questions of law from the lower courts. Usually, appeals are heard by a three-judge panel. The panel examines the records of the lower court, reads the written arguments submitted by the attorneys, studies the law on its own, and listens to the oral arguments of the attorneys. If the panel agrees with the lower court, it will affirm the decision of that court. However, if the panel disagrees with the lower court's decision, it can set aside or modify the decision of that court.

State Supreme Courts Twenty-seven states rely on their supreme court as their only appellate court. These states have no intermediate appellate courts. The other 23 states have both intermediate appellate courts and state supreme courts. Most supreme courts consist of a panel of three to nine judges. As is true at the intermediate appellate level, the panel of judges examines the records of the lower court, reads the written arguments submitted by the attorneys, studies the law on its own, and listens to the oral arguments of the attorneys. The decisions of state supreme courts are final unless a federal issue or a constitutional right is involved.

---

quick quiz 3-1

1. Courts are judicial tribunals that meet in a regular place and apply the laws in an attempt to settle disputes fairly.   true | false

2. The authority of a court to hear and decide cases is called the court's jurisdiction.   true | false

3. A writ of certiorari is an order from the Supreme Court to a lower court to deliver its records to the U.S Supreme Court for review.   true | false

---

3-2 Civil Procedure

In a civil lawsuit, one individual, organization, or corporation brings an action against another individual, organization, or corporation. The objective of a civil suit is usually to obtain money to compensate the victim. Civil litigation is another name for the process of bringing a case to court to enforce a right.

Commencement of the Action

The principal parties to a lawsuit are the plaintiff and the defendant. The plaintiff is the person who begins the lawsuit by filing a complaint in the appropriate trial court of general jurisdiction. The defendant is the person against whom the lawsuit has been brought and from whom a recovery is sought.

Filing the Complaint The complaint sets forth the names of the parties to the lawsuit, identifying them as plaintiffs or defendants. Generally, the complaint includes the addresses of all parties. The complaint also sets forth the following:

- The facts in the case from the plaintiff's perspective.
- The alleged legal violations by the defendant.
- The injuries that the plaintiff suffered.
- The plaintiff's request for relief.

If the plaintiff wants a jury trial, this information must also be specified in the complaint. In federal court, the complaint must also include a statement of jurisdiction, which will tell the court whether the case has been brought in federal court because of a federal question or because of diversity among the plaintiffs and the defendants.

Class Action Lawsuits

At times filing a complaint is pointless because the amount of recovery for one plaintiff would be so low that it would not be worth the effort, energy, and expense a lawsuit. Sometimes, however, the extent of the harmful conduct is so pervasive and the number of plaintiffs so high that the cost of conducting the lawsuit is justified. This was the motivation that led to the creation of the class action lawsuit. A class action is a lawsuit in which one (or a small number) of the potential plaintiffs file a lawsuit on behalf of the entire class. The courts will permit a class action lawsuit provided that (1) it is not feasible for the members of the group to bring the action on their own; (2) the members of the group share common questions of law that can be tried together; and (3) the class action approach is far better than forcing the plaintiffs to file separate actions.

Unfortunately, class action lawsuits are easy to abuse. One of the most common abuses is forum shopping. Forum shopping occurs when a plaintiff searches for a jurisdiction with law that is favorable to its case, and then files the case in that jurisdiction. The defendant can do something similar by filing a motion to remove a case filed in state court to federal court. When a case features multiple plaintiffs, as in a class action lawsuit, forum shopping becomes easier because the number of possible jurisdictions increases as the number of plaintiffs from different states increases. In order to counteract abuses, Congress enacted the Class Action Fairness Act (CAFA). The act included a number of innovations designed to limit forum shopping and to counteract some of the other abuses associated with class actions.

For example, CAFA requires that the amount in controversy for a class action in federal court exceed $5 million. Second, CAFA also requires that the class bringing the actual class action lawsuit number at least 100 plaintiffs. Third, CAFA offers what is called the "home state exception" to personal jurisdiction. The exception limits federal jurisdiction by declaring that if two-thirds of the class action plaintiffs and the corporate defendants are from the same state there will be no federal jurisdiction. The net effect of all three of these provisions is to limit the tactic of filing in federal court, thus effectively limiting the forum shopping option. (See Archis Parasharami and Kevin Ranlett, "The Class Action Fairness Act, Five Years Later," *The National Law Journal*, April 12, 2010, pp. 14 and 18; and Michael McNamara and Christine Henge, "'Hertz' Expands Companies Access to Federal Court," *The National Law Journal*, April 12, 2010, pp. 16–17.)

THE OPENING CASE *Revisited, Part II*
When Is a Citizen Not a Citizen? Round 3

Recall that in the Opening Case of *Hertz Corporation v. Friend* the Hertz Corporation was sued by a group of California citizens who brought the case in a state court. Hertz, knowing that it would find little sympathy in a California court, filed a motion to remove the case to the federal court in New Jersey, arguing that the proper forum would be the site of its corporate headquarters. The plaintiffs disagreed, claiming that Hertz's "principal place of business" was California because it did most of its business there. The Supreme Court decided that a corporation has its "principal place of business" where its decision-making body is headquartered. For Hertz that would be New Jersey, not California. The Supreme Court's ruling is going to have an effect on class action cases. In essence what the court has done is limit the citizenship of corporate defendants to fewer, perhaps even, in some situations, to a single state. Explain why this decision will probably increase the number of class action cases that end up in federal court.

Service of Process

The complaint is presented to the appropriate court officer, usually the clerk of courts. The clerk will then see that the defendant is served with a copy of the complaint and a summons. The *summons* names the court of jurisdiction, describes the nature of the action, and demands that the defendant answer the complaint within a specified period of time, usually between 20 and 30 days, depending on the state rules of civil procedure. Giving the summons and the complaint to the defendant is called service of process.

The Pre-Answer Stage

As noted, once the defendant has been served, he or she has 20 to 30 days to file an answer. Usually, however, the defendant will ask for and receive an extension of that time period. The time between service and the answer is termed the *pre-answer stage.* During this stage, the defendant will take some time to examine the nature of the claim that has been filed by the plaintiff. The defendant may, as a result of this initial examination, decide to file one or more pre-answer motions. A *motion* is a request for the court to rule on a particular issue. One possible motion is a motion for dismissal of the case for failure to state a claim for which relief can be granted. Some states call this a demurrer. Other motions to dismiss may be based on the grounds that the court lacks subject matter jurisdiction, that the court lacks personal jurisdiction, or that the court cannot hear the case because the statute of limitations has passed.

EXAMPLE 3-3: To Demurrer or Not to Demurrer

Lauren Jensen agreed to purchase a desk for $295 from the Stephens Sisters Furniture Store. During a management change at Stephens, Jensen's order was lost, and the furniture was never delivered. Jensen never contacted Stephens but instead purchased a similar desk for $495 at another store. Five years later, Jensen decided to bring suit against Stephens for breach of contract. She wants to recover the extra $200 that she paid to the second store. Stephens' attorney realizes that the state statute of limitations for such contracts is four years. As a result, she files a motion to dismiss for failure to state a claim for which relief can be granted. Some states call this motion a demurrer. If Stephens's attorney is correct, the suit will be dismissed.

The Answer

The answer is the defendant's official response to the complaint. In the answer, the defendant admits or denies the allegations in the complaint. The defendant's answer can also include affirmative defenses. An affirmative defense is a set of circumstances that indicate that the defendant should not be held liable, even if the plaintiff proves all of the facts in the complaint. One affirmative defense is *assumption of the risk.*

EXAMPLE 3-4: Assessing the Risk of a Risky Business

Carol Jennings took a cruise of the Mediterranean on the Underwood Cruise Line, a firm incorporated and doing business in the United States. While the cruise ship *Principia* was docked at a Greek island, Jennings joined a tour group. She was cautioned numerous times to remain with the tour group and not to wander off by herself because of the danger of being attacked and robbed. Nevertheless, Jennings ignored the warnings and left the tour group. While on her own, she wandered into a particularly dangerous part of the city where she was beaten and robbed. She later brought a lawsuit against the Underwood Cruise Line. In its answer to Jennings' complaint, the cruise line may wish to use the defense of assumption of the risk. Such a defense would argue that Jennings was aware of danger when she chose to abandon the tour group and wander off by herself. As a result, the cruise line might argue, she assumed the risk of being attacked and robbed.

The defendant's answer may also contain counterclaims and cross-claims. A *counter-claim* is a claim that a defendant has against a plaintiff. A *cross-claim* is a claim filed by a defendant against another defendant in the same case. At this time, a defendant may also wish to file a *third-party complaint,* which is a complaint filed by the defendant against a third party not yet named in the lawsuit.

The Pretrial Stage

After the answer has been filed, the parties must await trial. During this waiting period, cleverly dubbed the pretrial stage, several activities can be carried out, including the pretrial conference, discovery, and the filing of pretrial motions.

Pretrial Conference
Some courts require cases to go to a pretrial conference after the complaint and the answer have been filed. A pretrial conference usually has two purposes. One is to discuss the possibility of settling the case without the need for a trial. Another is to decide on the details involved in bringing the case to trial. Such a conference is generally called a *case management conference.* Issues that might be discussed at a case management conference include the way that the parties will conduct discovery or the need to place a limit on the number of expert witnesses that will be called at trial.

Pretrial Motions
Several motions may be filed during the pretrial stage. One motion available at this time is a motion for summary judgment. A summary judgment motion is a motion that asks the court for an immediate judgment for the party filing the motion. This motion is filed when there is no genuine issue as to any material fact, and the party filing the motion is entitled by law to a favorable judgment. The motion cannot be filed without supporting legal arguments written out in a brief and accompanied by applicable supporting evidence.

Discovery
Discovery is the process by which the parties to a civil action search for information that is relevant to the case. The objective is to simplify the issues and avoid unnecessary arguments and surprises in the subsequent trial. Discovery techniques and tools include the following:

Depositions are oral statements made out of court under oath by witnesses or parties to the action in response to questions from the opposing attorneys. The answers are recorded by a court stenographer and can be used for later reference.

Interrogatories are written questions that must be answered in writing under oath by the opposite party. Interrogatories cannot be given to witnesses. Only plaintiffs and defendants can be required to answer interrogatories.

Requests for real evidence ask a party to produce documents, records, accounts, correspondence, photographs, or other tangible evidence. The request may also seek permission to inspect land.

Requests for physical or mental examination ask a party to undergo a physical or a mental examination. Such requests can be made only if the physical or the mental condition of the party is in controversy; it must be a central concern to the lawsuit.

Requests for admissions are made to secure a statement from a party that a particular fact is true or that a document or set of documents is genuine. An admission eliminates the need to demonstrate the truthfulness of the fact or the genuineness of the documents at trial.

The discovery process cannot be taken lightly by the litigants. The rules of court provide severe penalties for those who fail to cooperate with discovery. Should a litigant withhold his or her cooperation, the other litigant can ask the court to compel the uncooperative party to respond to the discovery request. If the uncooperative party has a reason for not complying, then he or she may try to persuade the court of the validity of the refusal. If, for instance, the discovery request seeks information protected by the attorney–client privilege, the judge may refuse to compel the litigant to comply with the request.

If, however, the litigant cannot persuade the judge that the refusal is legally justified, the judge may impose severe penalties on the litigant. For example, the judge may elect to dismiss the lawsuit completely. The judge may also decide to render a default judgment against the uncooperative party. Reasonable expenses caused by the refusal to comply with discovery may also be assessed against the uncooperative party. These expenses may include attorney's fees. In many states, the rules allow the expenses to be assessed against either the attorney or the litigant.

The Civil Trial

Upon completion of discovery, the pretrial conference, and any hearings held on pretrial motions, the case is ready for trial. A trial by jury is an adversarial proceeding in which the judge's role is secondary to that of the jury's. Competition between attorneys permits the jury to sort out the truth and arrive at a just solution to the dispute.

Jury Selection   Once it is decided that the case will involve a jury, the process of *voir dire* (to speak the truth) begins. In this process, the lawyers for both parties question prospective jurors to determine whether they will be allowed to sit on the jury. Prospective jurors may be rejected if they are unable to render an impartial judgment. One reason for rejecting a prospective juror is if he or she had a personal relationship with the litigant or with a witness.

Prospective jurors may also be rejected if they have a financial interest in the outcome of the trial. However, the financial interest must be a direct, substantial interest. Remote financial interests in a trial will not disqualify a juror. Thus, the fact that the outcome of a trial may result in higher insurance rates would not disqualify a juror who has an insurance policy.

Prospective jurors may be selected or rejected based on their ability to render an impartial judgment.

Another reason might be if the prospective juror has had past experience that would prevent him or her from being impartial in the present case. Thus, a juror who has had a bad experience with a psychologist, for instance, might be unable to judge impartially the actions of a psychologist who has been sued for malpractice.

In most lawsuits, *voir dire* is conducted in the open, which means that the process is generally accessible to the press and the mass media. However, in cases that have attracted a lot of public attention, the judge may order that the media's access to the *voir dire* process be limited. Often news reporters will be limited to reading abridged copies of the transcript of the *voir dire* process after the process has been completed. The names of the jurors may also be censored, along with personal data about those jurors. This limit on the access to *voir dire* usually occurs in notorious criminal trials, but it could also happen in high-profile civil lawsuits.

Opening Statements
At the beginning of the trial, both attorneys have the opportunity to make an opening statement. In the *opening statement,* an attorney presents the facts in the case and explains what he or she intends to show during the trial. Attorneys are not permitted to argue their case in the opening statement. There is widespread disagreement, however, as to what constitutes "arguing the case" during the opening statement. Consequently, the degree of argument permitted during the opening statement often depends on what the judge will allow.

The Plaintiff's Case in Chief
The plaintiff's case in chief is the plaintiff's opportunity to present evidence that will prove his or her version of the case to the jury. The plaintiff's attorney calls witnesses and immediately subjects those witnesses to direct examination. Direct examination is designed to present the facts that will support the plaintiff's version of those facts. Opposing attorneys then have the chance to challenge the truthfulness of each piece of evidence presented. In this process of cross-examination, the witnesses answer questions of the defense attorney.

The Defendant's Case in Chief
After the plaintiff has ended the presentation of his or her case in chief, the defendant has the opportunity to present his or her case in chief. The defendant's attorney calls witnesses for direct examination, and the plaintiff's attorney has an opportunity to cross-examine the defendant's witnesses.

The Rebuttal and the Surrebuttal
Once the plaintiff and the defendant have presented their cases in chief, each attorney may present evidence to discredit the evidence presented by the opposition and reestablish the credibility of his or her own evidence. This step is called the rebuttal. The term surrebuttal is used in some states when referring to the defendant's rebuttal.

Closing Statements
After the rebuttals are completed, each attorney makes a closing statement. In this statement, the attorneys emphasize aspects of the testimony and other evidence they believe will best persuade the judge or jury.

Jury Instructions
Because juries comprise many people who are not familiar with particular aspects of the law, someone must explain the law to the jury. This is one of the duties of the judge. Although the attorneys may suggest to the judge what instructions ought to be used, the judge makes the decision. The judge's instructions explain the rules of law that the jurors are to apply to the facts in reaching their decision.

Verdict and Judgment
After receiving the judge's instructions, the members of the jury retire to a private room, where they apply the rules stated by the judge to the evidence presented by the witnesses. The jury eventually reaches a verdict. A verdict is a finding of fact. The verdict may be limited to the question of liability, or it can be extended to include the issue of damages. Liability means that the defendant is held legally responsible for his or her actions. The term damages refers to the money recovered by the plaintiff for the injury or loss caused by the defendant. The verdict is entered by the judge in the court records, and the case is said to be decided. According to the terms of the judgment, the defeated party either is required to pay the amount specified or do a specific thing, such as perform the terms of the contract. Court costs are usually paid by the losing party.

In some cases, money will not be adequate to satisfy the plaintiff. In such cases, the plaintiff may seek an equitable remedy. An equitable remedy requires a party to do something or to refrain from doing something beyond the payment of money. One equitable remedy is specific performance, which would require a party to a contract to go through with the terms of the contract. Usually, specific performance is permitted only in cases involving real estate or unique, one-of-a-kind goods such as art objects or rare antiques. Another equitable remedy is an injunction. An injunction stops a party from doing something. For instance, an employer may seek an injunction against a former employee to prevent that employee from using a trade secret on his or her new job if that trade secret is the property of the original employer.

A QUESTION OF ETHICS

Televised Trials: Threat or Transformation

In California, Proposition 8 was placed on the ballot in order to outlaw same sex marriages. The legality of the proposition was challenged in the federal trial court in the Northern District of California. Noting the great interest in the case and recognizing its social and political significance, the presiding judge suggested televising the trial at least within the courthouse in San Francisco where the trial was located. Later the judge, in consultation with the Chief Judge of the 9th Circuit, suggested widening the broadcast field to include all courthouses in the 9th Circuit. Those who supported the proposition opposed the plan to televise the trial and attempted to get a *writ of mandamus* to prevent the broadcast. The 9th Circuit denied the *writ*, but the United States Supreme Court reversed the decision and stopped the broadcast indefinitely. The Supreme Court stated that it suspended the broadcast to protect witnesses who might otherwise be threatened or harassed. The ethical issue here is not the morality of Proposition 8. Rather the question is whether a trial of this transformative significance should be broadcast, or "gagged" as the Supreme Court ruled. Using both utilitarianism and rational ethics (See Chapter 1-Ethics, Social Responsibility, and the Law), analyze the decision made by the U.S. Supreme Court and decide whether the Supreme Court's decision can be defended using either theory. Explain your rationale using each theory. (See David R. Fine, "Television Trials," *The National Law Journal*, January 25, 2010, p. 38.)

The Appeal

An appeal is the referral of a case to a higher court for review. For an appeal to be successful, it must be shown that some legal error occurred. For example, a party could argue that some of the evidence that was admitted should have been excluded or that evidence that was not allowed should have been allowed. A party could also argue that the judge's instructions were erroneous or were stated in an inappropriate manner. Generally, an appeal is filed by the party that lost the case in the trial court. However, it is also possible that the party that prevailed at trial may wish to file an appeal. This step is referred to as a cross-appeal. For instance, if the trial court upheld most of the claims made by the plaintiff but denied one or two key claims, the plaintiff may wish to file a cross-appeal. It may also be advisable to file a cross-appeal if the trial court did not award the appropriate amount in damages, if it refused to grant attorney's fees, or if it allowed money damages but refused to permit equitable relief. (See Aaron S. Bayer, "Appellate Law: The Cross-Appeal," *The National Law Journal*, February 9, 2004, p. 13.)

Execution of the Judgment

In civil cases, if the judgment is not paid, the court will order the loser's property to be sold by the sheriff to satisfy the judgment. This order by the court is known as a writ of execution. Any excess from the sale must be returned to the loser. Execution of the judgment also may be issued against any income due to the loser, such as wages, salaries, or dividends. This process is known as execution against income, or garnishment, and the proceedings are known as garnishee proceedings. Checking accounts are also subject to garnishment.

quick quiz 3-2

1. In state court, a complaint must include a statement of jurisdiction.   true | false

2. The defendants' answer must not include either counterclaims   true | false
   or cross-claims.

3. *Voir dire* must always be open to the press.   true | false

3-3 Cyber-procedure

The world of litigation has changed dramatically because of the electronic revolution. Gone are the days when litigators could wait until the last minute to conduct discovery prior to trial because they could see the limited number of paper documents sitting in a neat pile on their desks. Also gone are the days when attorney-client privilege could be protected by simply closing the office door. Electronically stored data comes in so many different formats (e-mail, texting, Facebook, Linked-In, voice mail, spreadsheets, instant messages, databases, and so on) and is stored in so many different electronic devises (laptops, mobile phones, iPods, Kindles, GPS units, PDAs, desktop PCs, fax machines, scanners, smartphones, and so on) that litigators have to get the jump on the process from the first moment that a lawsuit is threatened. Add to that the fact that many courts now expect and some even require the electronic filing of documents, and it becomes obvious that lawyers, paralegals, and business people cannot ignore the electronic age even if they want to.

Cyber-jurisdiction

Whether courts have jurisdiction over out-of-state defendants has been complicated by the electronic age. Previously, back in the age of face-to-face, U.S. Mail, and over-the-phone transactions, it was fairly obvious where a corporation or an institution had its principal place of business. Of course, exactly what was meant by "principal place of business" might be at issue, but at least everyone knew the alternative sites available. Doing business on the Internet complicates all of this. Using the Internet, sellers can solicit business on their Web site, negotiate and enter a contract using "the point and click method," receive payment using PayPal, and deliver goods via FedEx or UPS without leaving the comfort of their home office and without revealing where they, the sellers, are located, how the goods were obtained, where they were stored, and how they were transported and delivered to the seller before being loaded on a FedEx or UPS truck.

Does the type of activity described above reach the level of minimum contacts needed to establish personal jurisdiction? Should the minimum contacts standard be replaced by the New Jersey stream of commerce standard for electronic buying and selling? Cyber-jurisdiction, (AKA electronic jurisdiction and e-jurisdiction) is the power of the court to hear a case based on Internet-related transactions. While this area of the law is still in its adolescence, we can, nevertheless, extract at least one general principle:

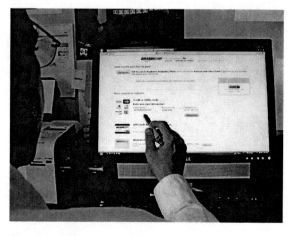

Cyber-transactions must be handled on a case-by-case basis.

because of its complex nature, cyber-jurisdiction is a moving target. To help attorneys, paralegals, and business people, hit this moving target, the courts have established a sliding scale on which several types of jurisdiction can be measured.

On one side of the scale are business transactions that are carried out from beginning to end using the Internet. These would include operations that are run like those engineered by Amazon.com and e-Bay. Transactions that involve solicitation, negotiation, finalization, payment, and shipping arrangements exclusively on the Internet, establish the minimum contacts needed for the state of the buyer. Moreover, if a case involves product liability, the type of transaction described above would satisfy New Jersey's stream of commerce standard. Of course, it is possible for the seller to specify the state that will serve as the forum for settling any dispute that arises from the contract. Still, such stipulations can always be challenged if the matter actually gets to court.

On the other side of the sliding scale, are those cases in which the defendant simply placed an inactive advertisement on the Internet. Such inactive advertisements will not usually establish jurisdiction under the minimum contacts test or the New Jersey stream of commerce test. The final type of transaction falls in between the two extremes. These cases include cyber-transactions that involve more than simply placing an advertisement on the Internet. The courts have not established any single normative approach to such transactions and so the matter must be handled on a case-by-case basis.

Cyber-filing

The federal court system officially joined the 21st century when it added a provision to the Federal Rules of Civil Procedure that permits lawyers to file court documents electronically. Moreover, under Rule 5 (3) the courts can even go so far as to require that documents be filed electronically, as long as the court also accepts reasonable exceptions from those unable to comply with the new provision. Those federal courts that have adopted the new procedure have found that cyber-filing (electronic filing or e-filing) is more cost effective and efficient than paper filing. Because some of the electronic systems used to keep track of court documents are accessible on the Internet, papers are no longer lost or misplaced as often as they once were. The Internet filing network also permits people to access the papers at their own convenience. This is an important feature of the electronic system because, once a party has been served properly, that party is sent a notice whenever a new document is filed electronically with the court. This eliminates the old-fashioned and time-consuming process of filing a formal notice with each party.

Still, cyber-filing does have its disadvantages. Not every law firm is properly equipped for cyber-filing and so the courts must maintain a dual filing system to accommodate "cyber-challenged" firms. Moreover, just because a firm is electronically up to date does not guarantee that its attorneys are cyber-savvy. Consequently, many courts have been forced to provide training and ongoing assistance to these attorneys at the court's expense. Also, from the attorney's perspective, since cyber-filing process is controlled by local rules, learning one set of electronic rules is rarely enough. Instead, the attorney must learn the rules for every court in which he or she does regular business. Fortunately, however, there are consistent features in these rules from one court to the next and so a diligent and conscientious attorney can survive as long as he or she is willing to be flexible.

Cyber-discovery

That part of the litigation process that has been affected the most by the cyber-revolution is the discovery process. Part of this is due to the actual changes caused by the cyber-revolution itself and part of it has been caused by extensive changes made in the rules of discovery by the federal courts to accommodate the revolution. There was a time when the federal courts were satisfied to look at electronic evidence as if it were just another way to produce paper documents. To deal with data stored in or produced by computers, they simply used the catchphrase *data compilations* to cover all such evidence, whether produced by hand or by the computer. Unfortunately, this shortcut no longer works. The Federal Rules now refer to cyber-evidence as electronically stored information (ESI). Moreover, the rule makers have officially recognized that ESI can cause many difficulties that cannot be solved by the old rules. For example, as noted above, computers produce and store so much ESI in so many different formats that it is difficult for the average lawyer to keep current. This complexity makes coming up with an effective discovery a difficult challenge. Another problem is caused by the unavoidable fact that electronic devices delete some material automatically and hold on to material that the user believes has been deleted months earlier.

The courts have made several changes in the federal rules to deal with these difficulties. These changes were designed to alter the behavior of attorneys so that they adjust to the peculiar characteristics of ESI. First, the rules now force attorneys to get an early start on all discovery plans or they will be unable to comply with the time limits built into the rules. Second, attorneys must now deal with the question of which electronic format will be used to request and deliver data. Third, attorneys can rest assured that the rules provide several ways to deal with those problems that arise with ESI and privilege. Fourth, attorneys can use the rules to help in the recovery of ESI that might otherwise be difficult to find. Fifth, to deal with the expenses that are involved in the identification and collection of ESI, attorneys can now refer to provisions in the rules that guarantee a fair apportionment of these expenses. Finally, attorneys can also be certain that everyone will cooperate with the new electronic discovery process, because the rules have provided severe penalties for those who ignore or disobey the new ESI discovery rules.

quick quiz 3-3

1. Cyber-jurisdiction is the power of the court to hear a case based on Internet-related transactions.　true | false

2. The Federal Rules of Civil Procedure do not permit lawyers to file court documents electronically.　true | false

3. The Federal Rules now refer to cyber-evidence as data compilations.　true | false

3-4 Criminal Procedure

The objectives of a criminal prosecution are to protect society and to punish the wrongdoer by a fine or imprisonment. The steps in a criminal prosecution include the following:

- Arrest and initial appearance.
- Preliminary hearing.
- Formal charges.
- Arraignment.
- Trial.

62   Part One   Ethics, Law, and the Judicial System

The Arrest and Initial Appearance

A crime is an offense against the people. Once a law enforcement agency learns that a crime has been committed, the agency begins a criminal prosecution. The first step in a criminal prosecution is to gather evidence of the crime and identify all possible suspects. When the law enforcement agency is convinced that it has ample evidence of both the crime and the identity of the suspect, an arrest warrant is issued, and the suspect is arrested. At the time of arrest, the defendant must be informed of his or her rights. One of the principal rights of the accused is the right to be represented by counsel. This right is guaranteed by the Sixth Amendment to the Constitution. Another important right is the right to remain silent, which is protected under the Fifth Amendment, which states that a criminal defendant cannot be compelled to be a witness against him- or herself. The U.S. Supreme Court has ruled that the Fourteenth Amendment to the Constitution requires that both the right to remain silent and the right to representation by counsel must also be protected by state governments. The defendant is then brought before a judge or a magistrate for an initial appearance, where once again the defendant is reminded of his or her rights. At this time, a preliminary hearing is also scheduled.

Defendants must be informed of their rights at the time of arrest. Two important rights are the right to representation by counsel and the right to remain silent.

The Preliminary Hearing

A preliminary hearing is a court procedure during which the judge decides whether probable cause exists to continue holding the defendant for the crime. The government is represented by an attorney called the prosecutor. In some states, this government official is called the district attorney. During the preliminary hearing, the prosecution and the defendant are permitted to make arguments and call witnesses. The case will move on to the next step if there is probable cause to hold the defendant. If not, the defendant is set free.

The Formal Charges

In the United States, formal charges against the defendant may be brought either by indictment or by information. Some states do not have a grand jury system and therefore can bring formal charges only by an information. In those states that use both, the indictment is usually used to bring formal charges for serious crimes.

A QUESTION OF ETHICS

Reading Rights: What is Right and What Is Wrong?

Edward McDonough, assistant district attorney for the city of Middletown, has just left a session with Harold Harrison, a criminal defendant accused of armed robbery. During the session, acting under the advice of Jennifer Miller, his attorney, Harrison confessed to the crime and entered a plea bargain agreement that will place him in prison for 10 years. On his way back across the city square to his office, ADA McDonough is stopped by Sgt. Anne Wade, who confesses to him that neither she nor her partner, Sgt. Sam Newton, read Harrison his rights. McDonough knows that this admission means that the confession he just obtained is tainted and would be thrown out of court if it were challenged by Miller on behalf of Harrison. From an ethical point of view, what action should McDonough take now?

An Indictment The federal courts and many state courts bring formal charges against the defendant by issuing an indictment. An indictment is a set of formal charges against a defendant issued by a grand jury. A *grand jury* consists of citizens who serve as jurors for a specified period of time to review a variety of criminal cases. The objective of a grand jury review is to determine whether probable cause exists to believe that a crime has been committed and that this particular defendant may have committed the crime. Grand jury proceedings are held in secret and are directed by the prosecutor or district attorney. If the grand jury finds probable cause exists, an indictment is issued.

An Information An information is a set of formal charges against a defendant drawn up and issued by the prosecutor or district attorney. No grand jury is involved in this process. Nevertheless, an information does the same thing that an indictment does. If the prosecutor has found that probable cause exists to indicate that a crime has been committed and that this particular defendant committed the crime, an information is issued.

The Arraignment

The arraignment is a formal court proceeding, during which the defendant, after hearing the indictment or information read, pleads either guilty or not guilty. Should the defendant enter a guilty plea, a sentence may be imposed immediately. If the defendant enters a plea of not guilty, the case moves on to the trial.

The Criminal Trial

If the defendant has requested a jury trial, a jury is selected. After the jury has been seated, each side makes its opening statement. Opening statements are followed by the production of evidence by both the prosecution and the defendant. One very significant difference between a criminal trial and a civil trial is the burden of proof. In a civil trial, the plaintiff must prove his or her case by a preponderance of evidence. In contrast, in a criminal case, the prosecution must prove the defendant's guilt beyond a reasonable doubt. As is the case with civil procedure, the criminal trial is completed by the attorneys' closing statements and the judge's instructions to the jury. The jury members are then allowed to retire to deliberate and decide on a verdict. In most states, a defendant can be found guilty only by the unanimous agreement of all of the jurors. A defendant who is found not guilty is released. One who has been found guilty is sentenced by the judge.

quick quiz 3-4

1. The objectives of a criminal prosecution are to protect society and to punish the wrongdoer by a fine or imprisonment.   true | false

2. The steps in a criminal prosecution include the arrest and initial appearance, the preliminary hearing, the formal charges, the arraignment, and the trial.   true | false

3. A crime is an offense against a single individual.   true | false

Summary

3.1 Courts are judicial tribunals that meet in a regular place and apply the laws in an attempt to settle disputes fairly. The federal court system is divided into three levels: the district courts, the courts of appeals, and the U.S. Supreme Court. State systems vary in structure but often consist of several levels, including lower-level limited jurisdiction trial courts, higher-level trial courts, intermediate appellate courts, and state supreme courts.

3.2 Litigation begins when the plaintiff files a complaint with the appropriate trial court. The defendant must then be given a copy of the complaint and a summons. During the pre-answer stage, the defendant may attempt to dismiss the lawsuit by filing certain pre-answer motions. In the answer stage, the defendant will file an answer, which may contain affirmative defenses, counterclaims, and/or cross-claims. The defendant at this time may also file third-party complaints. During the pretrial stage, conferences may be held, motions may be made, and discovery conducted. The trial includes the opening statement, each side's case in chief, the opportunity for rebuttal and surrebuttal, the closing arguments, and the jury instructions. The jury then renders a verdict. Either party may appeal the case if that party believes that a legal error was made during the trial that influenced the verdict unfavorably. If a judgment is not paid, the court may issue a writ of execution.

3.3 Cyber-jurisdiction (AKA electronic jurisdiction and e-jurisdiction) is the power of the court to hear a case based on Internet-related transactions. The Federal Rules of Civil Procedure now permit federal courts to allow, and at times even require, lawyers to file court documents electronically. The Federal Rules now refer to cyber-evidence as electronically stored information (ESI). The rules also now deal with special situations involving ESI and discovery.

3.4 The steps in a criminal prosecution include the arrest and initial appearance, the preliminary hearing, the formal charges, the arraignment, and the trial. At the time of the arrest, the defendant must be informed of his or her rights. Immediately following the arrest, the defendant is brought before a judge or a magistrate for an initial appearance, at which time the defendant is again reminded of his or her rights. A preliminary hearing is also scheduled. A preliminary hearing is a court procedure during which the judge will decide whether probable cause exists to continue to hold the defendant pending formal charges. Formal charges against the defendant may be brought either by indictment or by information. The arraignment is a formal court proceeding, during which the defendant pleads guilty or not guilty. The trial includes the opening statement, each side's case, the closing arguments, and the jury instructions. The jury then renders a verdict.

Key Terms

abuse of discretion, 46

affirmative defense, 54

answer, 54

appeal, 58

appellate jurisdiction, 45

arraignment, 63

case in chief, 57

civil litigation, 52

class action, 53

clearly erroneous standard, 46

complaint, 52

courts, 45

cross-appeal, 58

cross-examination, 57

cyber-jurisdiction, 59

damages, 57

defendant, 52

demurrer, 54

deposition, 55

direct examination, 57

discovery, 55

diversity cases, 46

electronic/e-jurisdiction, 59

electronically stored information (ESI), 61

equitable remedy, 57

federal question, 46

forum shopping, 53

general jurisdiction, 46

indictment, 63

information, 63

injunction, 58

interrogatories, 55

jurisdiction, 45

liability, 57

minimum contacts, 47

original jurisdiction, 45

personal jurisdiction, 46

plaintiff, 52

Questions for Review and Discussion

1. What is the fundamental nature of the American court system?
2. Under what circumstances might a federal court have jurisdiction to hear a case?
3. Under what circumstances might the U.S. Supreme Court hear a case?
4. What is the structure of a typical state court systems?
5. What is civil litigation?
6. What are the most common discovery techniques?
7. What is involved in an appeal?
8. How is cyber-jurisdiction determined?
9. What is electronically stored information?
10. What are the steps in a criminal prosecution?

Cases for Analysis

1. William Stevenson offered to help Rayford Le-Blanc remove his truck from the mud. At first, LeBlanc refused. However, later, when the towing company that LeBlanc had called proved to be unavailable, he accepted Stevenson's offer of assistance. LeBlanc then bought a towing strap from a nearby store to help in the removal of his truck from the mud. The first two attempts at removing the truck failed. On the third attempt, while LeBlanc was still in the process of connecting the straps to his truck, Stevenson, apparently without warning, pulled his vehicle forward. This movement caught LeBlanc by surprise. His hand was still wrapped up in the strap, and therefore, as Stevenson's vehicle moved forward, LeBlanc's hand was severely injured. LeBlanc sued Stevenson for damages related to the injuries to his hand. The jury decided that Stevenson was not at fault, and LeBlanc found himself on the losing end of the lawsuit. Accordingly, he appealed the case. The appellate court threw out the jury's factual finding and awarded LeBlanc over $190,000 in damages. Stevenson hollered "foul" and asked the Supreme Court of Louisiana to hear his request to have the decision reversed. The high court accepted the case. One of the central issues involved the question of whether, and under what circumstances, an appellate court can overturn decisions of fact made by a jury. Should the supreme court uphold the appellate court's decision? What standard of review should be involved here? Explain. *LeBlanc v. Stevenson*, 770 So.2d 766 (Sup. Ct. LA).

2. On October 12, 2000, an American naval vessel, the U.S.S. *Cole*, was bombed while it was berthed in Aden Harbor in Yemen in the Middle East. The bombing, which killed 17 American sailors, was planned and executed by Al-Qaeda. Relatives of those 17 sailors brought a lawsuit in U.S. District Court against the foreign state of the Republic of Sudan, alleging that Sudan was responsible for the bombing because that government supported al-Qaeda in general and the terrorists who carried off this assault in particular. The government of the Republic of Sudan moved to dismiss the case, arguing that the court lacked subject matter jurisdiction. The argument was based on the fact that the case involved citizens of states of the United States in an attempt to sue a foreign government, something not permitted under federal law. Is the government of Sudan correct in this case? Explain. *Rux v. Republic of Sudan*, 461 F.3d. 461 (4th Cir. 2006).

3. The state of Alabama was required under the provisions of its own constitution to reapportion its electoral districts every 10 years. However, the state had failed to reapportion districts for more than half a century. Since then, the population of Alabama had grown to such an extent that severe inequalities existed among the electoral districts. The inequalities were so great in some cases that the votes of citizens in some parts of the state carried as much as 10 times the weight of the votes of citizens in other parts of the state. A suit was brought in federal court on the grounds that the inequalities in voting power violated certain guarantees found in the U.S. Constitution. The defendants argued that the federal court should not interfere in what is essentially a state matter and that by doing so, it would upset the delicate balance between the states and the federal government. Nevertheless, the federal district court struck down the apportionment scheme as unconstitutional. Does this case belong in the U.S. Supreme Court? Explain the reasons for your response. Should the Supreme Court uphold or overturn the federal district court's decision? Explain. *Reynolds v. Sims,* 377 U.S. 533 (U.S. Sup. Ct.).

4. Speculate on which of the following cases the U.S. Supreme Court might decide to review: a case involving a dispute over whether computer software can be copyrighted; a case involving an appeal of a zoning board's decision to limit the number of adult book stores on any single city block; a case involving the constitutionality of an abortion statute; a case involving an antitrust suit based on a violation of a federal antitrust statute between the National Football League and a former seller of NFL sports gear; a libel case against a small town newspaper involving allegations of the mayor's dishonesty; a case involving the placement of a religious scene on city property; a case brought by a steel company to enjoin employees from going on strike; a case involving the distribution of antiwar flyers at a private shopping mall; and a case involving the search of a high school student's locker without her permission. In each case, give reasons for your answer.

5. Eight limited partners filed a lawsuit in the Lucas County Court of Common Pleas, alleging that the general partners in 10 different limited partnerships had engaged in an extensive pattern of self-dealing that had involved converting partnership property for their own personal use. Also named in the lawsuit was the accounting firm of Donald J. Goldstein, CPA, a resident of Florida, and Goldstein, Lewis, and Company, a professional corporation located in Florida. The plaintiffs claimed that the accountant and the accounting firm had known of the general partners' misconduct and were therefore liable to the plaintiff for that malpractice. The accountant and the accounting firm decided to end the suit as quickly as possible. Consequently, they filed a motion for dismissal. The motion stated that the courts of Ohio lacked personal jurisdiction over them because they were from Florida. They further stated that they did not solicit business in Ohio, maintained no place of business in Ohio, had no license to act as accountants in Ohio, owned no property in Ohio, provided all services from Florida, and filed no documents with the state of Ohio. Thus, they concluded that they fell outside the power of Ohio's long-arm statute. Conversely, the plaintiffs argued that the defendants transacted business in the state of Ohio on a continuing and ongoing basis by regularly submitting financial statements to the limited partners in Ohio and by being actively involved in the decisions of the general partnership. Did the activities of the accountant and the accounting firm place them under the jurisdiction of the Ohio court, according to the state "long-arm" statute? Explain. *Goldstein v. Christiansen,* 638 N.E.2d 541 (OH).

6. The criminal defendant in this case, a man named Gideon, broke into a pool room in Florida with the objective of committing a minor crime. Because Gideon was without any means of financial support, he could not afford an attorney. He asked for but was denied representation by a court-appointed attorney. Consequently, he represented himself at trial. Ultimately, he was found guilty and sentenced to five years in prison. Gideon later challenged his conviction on the grounds that he had been deprived of his constitutional right to representation by an attorney. In opposition, Florida argued that, though all fundamental rights guaranteed by the federal government through the Bill of Rights should also be guaranteed by state governments, the right to legal representation was not such a fundamental right. In fact, the right to a court-appointed attorney arose only when the criminal defendant had been accused of a very

serious crime. The U.S. Supreme Court agreed to hear the case. How should the Supreme Court rule in this case? Is the right to an attorney a fundamental right that should be guaranteed to criminal defendants by the states, regardless of the seriousness of the crime? Explain. Examine the Constitution and find the Amendment that guarantees the right to representation by an attorney. Examine the Constitution and find the Amendment that extends that right to defendants in state criminal actions. *Gideon v. Wainwright*, 372 U.S. 355 (U.S. Sup. Ct.).

7. Ernesto Miranda was arrested in his own home for a serious crime and held in an interrogation room. He was not informed of his right to remain silent, nor was he informed that he could be represented by an attorney. Eventually, after a two-hour interrogation conducted by two police officers, Miranda signed a statement that indicated he had voluntarily confessed to the crime of which he was accused. On the basis of the confession, Miranda was found guilty. He appealed to the Arizona Supreme Court, which affirmed the guilty verdict. Miranda asked the U.S. Supreme Court to hear his appeal. Is this the type of case that belongs in the U.S. Supreme Court? Explain the reasons for your response. Should the Supreme Court uphold or overturn the state court's conviction of Miranda? Explain the Constitution and find the Amendment that guarantees the right to remain silent when arrested for a criminal action. Examine the Constitution and find the Amendment that extends that right to defendants in state criminal actions. *Miranda v. Arizona*, 384 U.S. 436 (U.S. Sup. Ct.).

quick quiz Answers

3-1	3-2	3-3	3-4
1. T	1. F	1. T	1. T
2. T	2. F	2. F	2. T
3. T	3. F	3. F	3. F

Chapter 4

Alternative Dispute Resolution

THE OPENING CASE Mediation, Arbitration, and the Science Court

One of the most difficult questions that faces anyone who has initiated a lawsuit is whether to continue down the rigorous and expensive route of litigation or to take a detour down the road of alternative dispute resolution (ADR). ADR is not the same as negotiation. Every lawsuit involves some negotiation, no matter how brief or pointless that process might seem at the time. The decision to enter ADR is different. That decision involves taking an uncommon route, the road less traveled as it were. Sometimes ADR is the best path to take and sometimes it does not work. Consider the following case. Two power co-ops, the Cooperative Power Association and the United Power Association, announced their intention to construct high-voltage power lines across Minnesota farmland. The owners of the farms involved in the plan challenged the project, arguing that the planned route of the lines would destroy their ability to use their own farmland appropriately. The governor of Minnesota called for the creation of a science court to resolve the issue. The science court would be made up of scientists, engineers, and other experts educated in the discipline and the industry involved in the dispute, thus allowing them to use their expertise in deciding the case. The science court would also permit the parties to avoid the long and involved process of litigation. Other ways of solving this problem might

be to submit the dispute to mediation or arbitration. In mediation, the parties to the dispute invite an impartial third party, the mediator, to assist them in solving the problem. In arbitration, the parties invite a third party, the arbitrator, to actually settle the dispute. In the Minnesota Powerline Case any one of these processes might have been used to develop a compromise that would have satisfied everyone involved, at least to some extent. As you read the chapter, ask yourself which of these methods would have been used most effectively in this case. [See Barry Casper and Paul Wellstone, *Powerline: The First Battle of America's Energy War* (Amherst: University of Massachusetts Press, 1981); and Barry Casper and Paul Wellstone, "Science Court on Trial in Minnesota," *Science in Context: Readings in the Sociology of Science,* ed. Barry Barnes and David Edge (Cambridge, MA: MIT Press, 1982).]

Opening Case Questions

1. Is this case a civil lawsuit or a criminal action? Explain.

2. Why would the parties want to avoid a trial in this case? Explain.

3. What advantages and disadvantages might arise in the establishment of a science court? Explain.

4. Under what circumstances would mediation be a proper route to take in the settlement of a dispute? Explain.

5. Under what circumstances would arbitration be a proper route to take in the settlement of a dispute? Explain.

Learning Objectives

1. Examine the shortcomings of litigation.
2. List the advantages and the disadvantages of ADR.
3. Identify the advantages of mediation.
4. Explain the nature of an arbitration hearing.
5. Outline the med-arb process.
6. Relate the role of the early neutral evaluator.
7. Describe the process of running a summary judgment trial.
8. Clarify the private options available under proactive ADR.
9. Specify the governmental options available under proactive ADR.
10. Discuss the advantages and disadvantages of the science court proposal.

4-1 A Primer on ADR

As we have seen at various points throughout the text, the law is often reflected in a series of dualities. These dualities include the symmetry sought between the spirit and the letter of the law, between legal words and their interpretation, and between abstract principles and concrete situations. This synchronization is also involved in the application of the uncertainty principle to legal disputes. Thus far we have focused on the dispute-solving process known as litigation. Litigation has always been part of the American legal system. Lately, however, things have begun to change. The complexity, the expense, and the time involved in litigation have discouraged many potential litigants who have decided to sidestep the regular court system in favor of pursuing more efficient, effective, and economical methods of settling their disputes. These unconventional methods are referred to as the alternative dispute resolution process, or simply as ADR. Alternative dispute resolution (ADR) occurs whenever people move outside the traditional adversarial system and try to solve their legal dispute by using creative settlement techniques many of which have fact finding and truth as their goals rather than simply achieving a final victory. Thus, we have a fourth duality in the law: the duality that exists between the traditional litigation system and the unorthodox ADR process.

Problems with Litigation

Many people choose a dispute resolution process that sidesteps the adversarial approach of civil litigation because they believe that it is the best way to achieve justice. Part of this belief is based on the suspicion that, with an adversarial approach, victory often depends not on who is in the right but on which advocate is the better tactician. Watching assistant district attorney Jack McCoy outwit hapless defense attorneys in a decade's worth of *Law and Order* reruns has probably contributed to this image. Unfortunately, the best tactician is often one of the most expensive advocates available, which can mean that justice often goes to those who can afford it. For this reason, many people seek an alternative that is less costly to both sides.

Litigation can also be expensive because of the initial steps that lead to the filing of a lawsuit. For instance, before an attorney can file a medical malpractice lawsuit, he or she must obtain the client's medical records, which means paying an initial copying fee that can amount to hundreds or even thousands of dollars. The attorney must then hire an expert to evaluate the records to determine whether the information in the records indicates that the client has a viable claim. Again this expense can run into hundreds or thousands of dollars. All these expenses are encountered before the attorney even knows that a claim actually exists.

In addition to being expensive, litigation can be time consuming. The initial steps after the filing of a complaint can delay progress on a lawsuit for many months. For instance, should the defendant's motion for dismissal be granted by the court, a lengthy and time-consuming appeal process may ensue. In some cases, the appeal could even find its way to the highest court in the jurisdiction. In such a case, if the highest court reverses the lower court's dismissal of the action, the case quite literally returns to the starting line. Another time-consuming step in litigation is the process of discovery. Taking depositions, answering interrogatories, filing, and responding to requests for real evidence and handling requests for mental or physical examinations can tie up a lawsuit for months.

Moreover, some jurisdictions require litigants to submit to case management hearings and settlement hearings before they can secure a trial date. Even when a court date is secured, many court dockets, especially those in large urban areas, are backed up for months, or even years, which often means that the parties to a lawsuit must wait for long periods of time before having their day in court. Even once a trial has occurred and a decision rendered, recovery can be delayed as the parties enter a second phase of the lawsuit, the execution of the judgment phase. This process involves its own complex set of procedures which, like the actual lawsuit, can cause expensive and time-consuming delays.

The ADR Option

However, ADR can provide an economical and efficient alternative to litigation. Depending on the ADR technique employed, the time involved in settling a dispute can be shortened considerably and the expenses lowered significantly. Arbitration and mediation, for example, can be scheduled quickly, even before a lawsuit is filed. When scheduling either a mediation or an arbitration session, the parties need not consult the court's dockets or worry about any preliminary requirements, such as a case management conference. Moreover, even if the arbitration or mediation session does not end the dispute, it can save time by narrowing the issues or providing an evaluation of the strength of each side's case. The arbitration or mediation session may also, in some cases, provide a shortcut to discovery, thus saving time and lowering expenses.

Other ADR approaches, such as early neutral evaluation (ENE), can save money and time by providing an assessment of the issues at stake and the range of damages available, should the outcome of the case demand a remedy of some sort. Summary jury trials, private trials, and mini-trials can all be inexpensive and quick because they can be scheduled without regard to the court's docket and can be held without the expenses involved in hiring expert witnesses and providing travel and hotel accommodations for those witnesses. The cost and time involved in lengthy discovery processes can also be avoided by selecting any one of these ADR techniques.

Private proactive ADR techniques such as drafting contract clauses and entering partnering agreements can help to make litigation unnecessary from the outset. The idea behind the proactive ADR approach is to anticipate

ADR options provide a timely, cost-efficient method for resolving legal issues.

and deal with disputes before they occur. By providing a solution to problems before those problems arise, proactive ADR eliminates the uncertainty and risk inherent within the litigation process.

Shortcomings of ADR

Yet ADR is not without problems. On the contrary, some critics of the alternative dispute resolution process have pointed out that the private administration of justice hampers the development of the law. Because many ADR techniques completely sidestep the courts, many critical social issues may never reach the judicial system, causing gaps in the evolution of case law and the progression of legislation. Another criticism of ADR involves its limited scope. Some legal conflicts, notably employment, contract, and tort cases, are especially well suited for ADR. However, other legal problems, primarily those involving constitutional law, civil rights, and criminal law, could never be brought before an ADR panel.

EXAMPLE 4-1: Contract, Property, or Civil Rights?

Some cases are perfectly well suited for easy transfer from the regular court system to the ADR forum. Others are not. Still others may appear to be a good fit for ADR, but on further examination, turn out to be ill suited for any of the alternative approaches to the law. Such is the case of *State v. Bontrager.* The facts in the case are simple. Adam Bontrager, the defendant, purchased a piece of land. Before the sale, the previous owner had been notified by the Department of Health that the current septic system on the property was not up to specs. Consequently, the Health Department ordered a systems upgrade. Once Bontrager bought the property the obligation to upgrade the system passed to him.

Bontrager began the process of upgrading the system and then stopped. Without the system upgrade, untreated sewage was flowing into a local stream causing a health hazard. As a result, the defendant was cited for a violation of the administrative code and fined accordingly. Nevertheless, he still refused to build the upgrade that had been ordered by the Health Department, which then brought the current suit. Now on the surface this does not appear to be a complicated case. Nor does it appear to involve any significant matter of law. After all, we're talking about septic tanks and sewage here, not issues of constitutional law. Or are we? Just what is the issue at stake here?

If the case had turned out to be a contract dispute, perhaps between Bontrager and the original owner, then ADR might have been pursued before the Health Department, was forced to bring this action. Or if Bontrager had disputed the need for a new system because he had found another way to deal with the sewage problem, then arbitration or mediation might have been appropriate. That was not the case, however. Instead, Bontrager argued that, since he was Amish and since his religion forbid him to use electricity, which the upgrade required, the Health Department order was a violation of his religious rights under the U.S. Constitution. Unlike contract disagreements or property utilization disputes, a civil right action like this one is not appropriate for ADR. (See *State v. Bontrager,* 149 Ohio Misc.2d 33 (Newton Falls Municipal Court).)

Other difficulties associated with ADR have also appeared in recent years. One problem is that ADR does not always save time and money the way it is supposed to. Typically, two of the advantages that supporters of ADR promote are the ideas that ADR is less expensive and less time consuming because such procedures do not get tangled up in the red tape of the court system. Unfortunately, this is not always the case. Sometimes even cases that are decided by arbitration end up in the court system. Most often this happens when one or more of the parties decide to challenge the decision of the arbitrator. When such challenges occur, there is only one place for the parties to go: to court.

Two additional advantages of ADR are that little discovery and very few motions are involved in the process, thus saving the litigants a lot of money. Although this argument sounds good in theory, it does not always play out in reality. Unfortunately, sometimes a case may actually take longer to resolve because there is no discovery or motion practice involved. Part of the delay is due to the fact that discovery and motion practice often help attorneys focus on the most crucial issues in a case. Also, discovery will sometimes reveal that it is necessary to settle a case rather than proceeding to trial. When there is no discovery or motion practice, the issues remain wide open. This gap means that attorneys must anticipate all the possible moves that their opponents might make. The lack of discovery also means that the small flaws in an argument may not be revealed, and a case that would have been settled during a conventional lawsuit might drag on in arbitration.

Admittedly, ADR is not intended as a replacement for the legal system. Rather, it is intended to provide potential litigants with a wider variety of choices when they are facing a legal dispute. As noted previously, because of the delays and the expense involved in litigation, many people would like to avoid that route altogether. Others would like to find a way to streamline the litigation process, so that, should the need for a trial finally present itself, the preliminary steps can be administered as painlessly as possible. With these facts in mind, we will proceed with an examination of ADR techniques.

quick quiz 4-1

1. Adversarial litigation has only recently become a part of the American legal system.   true | false

2. Two of the advantages that supporters of ADR promote are the ideas that ADR is less expensive and less time consuming than litigation.   true | false

3. ADR is not intended as a replacement for the legal system.   true | false

4-2 ADR Techniques

There are numerous ADR techniques that can be invoked once a dispute has arisen between parties. These include but are not limited to mediation, arbitration, med-arb, early neutral evaluation, summary jury trials, and private civil trials.

Mediation

According to the American Arbitration Association, mediation is "a non-binding process where a neutral third party works with the parties to reach a mutually agreeable settlement." The neutral third party is referred to as a mediator. Some people erroneously confuse mediation with negotiation. Negotiation is the usual way that attorneys handle disputes before they end up in litigation. Such negotiation is part, or at least should be a part, of every dispute that might possibly lead to litigation. In fact, negotiation is something that can take place before a lawsuit is filed, after it has been filed, before trial, and even during trial. There is no specially designated neutral third party "negotiator" during negotiation as there is during mediation. The job of the mediator is to convince parties to adjust or settle their dispute. The mediator will try to persuade the parties to reach some sort of compromise but cannot decide what the parties will do. (See American Arbitration Association, FAQ's. Retrieved on June 28, 2010, from http://www.aamediation.com/FAQ.)

Like the timing of a negotiation conference, the timing of a mediation session can vary. Sometimes mediation follows the filing of a lawsuit but sometimes it occurs to prevent a lawsuit from being filed. Mediation can occur before a conflict, during a conflict, after a conflict, or when a settlement following a conflict is not being followed properly. (See The JAMS Foundation, retrieved on July 28, 2010 from http://ww.jamsdr.com.) Mediation is often more successful than litigation, because in mediation the parties remain involved in the settlement of the dispute. Unlike litigation, which is decided by a judge or jury, a mediation session is in the hands of the parties. The mediator does not decide the disagreement. Rather, he or she serves as an intermediary who attempts to understand what brought the parties into disagreement and what issues lay at the heart of the disagreement. The mediator does not act as a therapist, a judge, or an advocate. Rather, he or she acts as an impartial outsider who can suggest solutions that will please all the parties involved in the dispute. Often the mediator can cut to the center of a dispute in objective ways that are unavailable to the parties themselves.

EXAMPLE 4-2: Mediation: Practical Solutions to Practical Problems

Bruce Langton brought suit against David Winchester in small claims court after Winchester's daughter, Jackie, backed her car into Langton's truck, causing extensive damage to the front end of the vehicle. Langton wanted damages in the amount of $4,000. Langton's sister-in-law, Wendy Miller, suggested that the parties hire a mediator to try to reach a settlement. During the mediation session, the mediator saw that the real issue was the fact that Langton's truck was still damaged. Winchester's brother, who owned and operated an auto body shop, agreed to fix Langton's truck at no cost. This solution satisfied both parties. Langton had his truck fixed, and Winchester suffered no out-of-pocket expenses.

Arbitration

Arbitration is the process by which the parties invite a third party, called an arbitrator, to settle their dispute. The procedures involved in arbitration are generally more flexible than those followed in a lawsuit. The rules are either set by law or agreed to by an arbitration agreement. The hearing may be relaxed, with the arbitrator or arbitrators receiving informal testimony from the parties, or it may be rigidly controlled, with the arbitrator or arbitrators following strict rules of evidence and requiring lengthy explanations. The parties may agree in advance to be bound by the arbitrator's decision. If they do not so agree, the arbitrator's decision can be appealed in court. There is a common misconception that arbitration, and mediation for that matter, are carried out exclusively by non-lawyers. Sometimes arbitrators are lawyers and sometimes they are not. This is made clear by the American Arbitration Association which states that arbitrators must have, "senior level experience in law, business, industry or another profession." (See American Arbitration Association, FAQ's. Retrieved on June 28, 2010, from http://www.aamediation.com/FAQ.)

Some states require arbitration prior to trial in certain cases. Required arbitration is called *mandatory arbitration*. Some litigants have challenged government-imposed mandatory arbitration as an unconstitutional deprivation of their right to a trial by jury and equal protection under the law. Most states faced with this question have disagreed with these arguments as long as the arbitration requirement does not replace the jury trial and as long as the motives for requiring arbitration are reasonable.

An arbitration hearing can be planned and executed by the parties themselves. Generally, this step means that the parties set the ground rules for choosing the arbitrator or arbitrators, for conducting discovery, for presenting evidence, for determining the outcome, and for enforcing the reward. In addition, details such as setting the time and the place of the hearing, filling vacancies on the arbitration panel, recording the proceedings, handling objections, granting time extensions, and so on, must also be agreed upon. Because of the intricacies of such a process, many individuals who select arbitration prefer to use professional arbitration organizations such as the American Arbitration Association to handle the details of their arbitration proceeding.

Like most forms of ADR, arbitration is not without its difficulties. One shortcoming is that an arbitration hearing is run like a trial but without the safeguards that come with the rules of civil procedure, discovery, and motion practice. This characteristic may actually extend the time involved in arbitration because attorneys and negotiators must prepare a wide variety of legal arguments, some of which might have been eliminated during motion practice. Discovery also sometimes reveals facts that lead the parties into settlement negotiations that might not otherwise take place. Moreover, the wide discretion that is usually granted to arbitrators has, in some cases, led to unreasonable decisions and unjustifiable awards. Sometimes the decision made by an arbitrator comes under the review of the courts, which may result in a reversal of the arbitration order and thus frustrate the whole object of entering arbitration in the first place. Some of these difficulties can be overcome by stipulating that an arbitration award cannot be reversed by the courts except to correct a violation of the arbitration agreement itself.

EXAMPLE 4-3: Is Arbitration Worth the Effort?

In the case of *Natare v. D.S.I. Duraplastec Systems, Inc.,* the arbitrator agreed that D.S.I. had violated the non-disparagement contract that had been negotiated between the two companies. Consequently, he ordered D.S.I. to pay Natare $5,000. However, the arbitrator did not order D.S.I. to pay Natare attorney's fees, something that the managers of Natare felt was due to them under the agreement. Natare then brought a claim in state court asking the court to overturn the decision of the arbitrator. The case went to the trial court, then to the appellate court, and finally to the Supreme Court of Indiana. The Indiana Supreme Court found no abuse of discretion on the part of the arbitrator, and the ruling stood. This ruling meant that Natare, which had hoped to use the arbitration clause to avoid the delays and the expense of the state court system, may have actually spent more time and money than it would have had the case started in the court system in the first place.

The difficulties associated with discovery can be solved by streamlining the discovery process in arbitration, without going to the extremes represented by the way that discovery is conducted in litigation. Other problems can be solved by making sure that arbitrators follow the same rules in all hearings and insisting that they write down the reasons behind their decisions.

Med-Arb

Med-arb is an ADR process that combines mediation with arbitration. Under med-arb procedures, the parties first submit their dispute to a mediation session. If the dispute is settled via mediation, then all of the parties can leave satisfied. If, however, some matters are left undecided, the parties can move on to an arbitration hearing. During the hearing, the undecided issues would be placed before an arbitrator for final deliberation.

Early Neutral Evaluation

Early neutral evaluation (ENE) is an ADR process in which the parties permit a referee to assess their case on the basis of the facts and legal arguments alone. At the outset of an ENE process, an independent, objective referee is provided with an overview of the facts involved in the dispute and a summary of the legal arguments on which each side has built his or her case. The evaluator, after examining the facts and the law, renders an impartial assessment of the legal rights of each party and a determination of the amount of the award that should be rendered, if any. The parties can use this impartial evaluation to either settle the case or proceed to trial. Even if the ENE does not result in a final decision, it can be used to shape the issues, plan discovery, and guide any research that the attorneys must conduct as the case proceeds to trial.

Summary Jury Trials

A summary jury trial is a shortened version of a trial conducted in less than a day before an actual jury that then renders an advisory verdict in the case. The summary jury process offers litigants a chance to see how a jury would react to the facts of the case, as well as to the legal arguments that will be made by both sides at trial. On the day of the summary jury trial, lawyers from both sides present an abbreviated version of the case to an actual jury. The presentations are simplified, focusing on the essential facts and law. In this way, the summary jury trial eliminates much of the redundancy that occurs during a "real" trial and allows the judge and jury to focus on the essentials of the case.

As noted previously, the ultimate objective of a summary jury trial is to help both sides evaluate the effectiveness of their arguments in front of a judge and jury. This effort in turn helps the attorneys shape the issues and select the positions that are most advantageous to their case. This knowledge is enhanced by the fact that, after the trial, each side has the chance to interview the jurors to see why they reacted as they did.

The success or failure of a summary jury trial depends on several factors. First, only those cases that involve a *bona fide* dispute as to the facts or authentic questions of law should be considered for a summary jury trial. Second, advanced planning is necessary to ensure a successful summary jury trial. The judge must be consulted, issues should be settled, the facts should be composed properly, the jury instructions should be determined, and a date and time established before the trial begins.

Third, during the process, strict controls and ironclad time limits must be imposed on the parties. For instance, opening statements should last no more than 20 minutes. Both sides should have no more than one hour for the presentation of their case in chief and 30 minutes for their rebuttal. The closing arguments should also be limited to no more than 20 minutes. Finally, a conference should be held after the trial, during which the parties have the opportunity to discuss an immediate settlement. Such a conference should be held after the jury has been polled so that their input can be factored into the settlement discussion.

EXAMPLE 4-4: Summary Jury Trials: A Posttrial, Pretrial Settlement

When Ashley Utalizar was discharged from her job with Solarpower Industries Inc., she was certain that the dismissal had been in direct violation of an implied contract that had been created by Solarpower's employee policy manual. When she brought a lawsuit against Solarpower, both parties decided to hold a summary jury trial. After the trial was held, both sides participated in a posttrial settlement conference. The results of the jury poll indicated that, though the jury had decided in favor of Utalizar, they were unable to agree on the amount of damages that should be awarded to her. As a result, both Solarpower and Utalizar decided that it would be in their best interests to settle the case immediately. The attorneys for Solarpower agreed to the settlement because they saw that the jury was sympathetic to Utalizar, while Utalizar's attorneys agreed that they could not be certain that Utalizar would receive an adequate award if the jury were permitted to decide the amount of damages.

Because one reason for holding a summary jury trial is to determine how the judge and jury will react to the facts and the arguments, it is helpful to have observers gauge how the judge and the jurors react to the points made by both sides. The observers, who are often students recruited from local law schools and paralegal institutes, will record the reactions of the judge and the jurors during the trial. As an alternative, the entire process can be recorded, so that reactions can be observed later.

Private Civil Trials

A private civil trial is an ADR technique by which the parties hire a retired judge or magistrate to hear their dispute, following the same rules used in an official trial. Many states now permit the parties to a lawsuit to have their cases tried in a private civil trial rather than an official court. One advantage of a private trial is that the parties can hold the trial at a time and a place of their own choosing. In addition, the parties have the opportunity to choose their own judge. Decisions rendered by a judge in a private civil trial are just as binding as those made by judges on the official court docket. Moreover, private trial decisions can be appealed in the same way that public decisions are appealed.

Private civil trials are not postponed nor are they interrupted because the court has more pressing duties to perform. In addition, a private trial receives the undivided attention of the judge, who is not sidetracked by the need to attend to other matters such as the sentencing of criminal defendants. Intricate, lengthy civil cases are ideally suited for private civil trials because, in such cases, time is money. Consequently, the shorter the trial, the less expensive the final bill facing the client.

In recent years, some private firms have appeared that specialize in setting up private civil trials. Such firms will make most of the arrangements for the litigants. These arrangements include securing a judge, providing the place for the trial, and providing all necessary administrative support. These firms can also provide a jury for the trial. Jurors for private trials are generally selected from a pool of individuals who have recently served on a jury in an official trial. Therefore, the jurors at the private civil trial are well acquainted with the trial procedures.

quick quiz 4-2

1. The job of a mediator is to convince the contending parties to adjust or settle their dispute.   true | false

2. Some states require arbitration prior to trial in certain cases.   true | false

3. The early neutral evaluator process is similar to that of a settlement hearing.   true | false

4-3 Proactive ADR

All of the ADR techniques discussed thus far are invoked after a dispute has arisen. Since ADR has become so popular in recent years, some business people are taking a proactive approach to the situation by agreeing in advance to submit to one of the alternative dispute resolution tools should a disagreement between the parties arise at a later date. These proactive ADR techniques include, but are not limited to, partnering, ADR contract clauses, settlement week, negotiated rule making, post-appellate procedures, international arbitration agreements, and the science court proposal.

Partnering

Partnering is a process that establishes supportive relationships among the parties to a contract to head off disputes before they occur. Generally, partnering is best used when a contract involves complex interrelationships among a wide variety of different parties. Construction agreements are ideally suited to partnering arrangements, because construction contracts involve contractors and subcontractors, all of whom must perform in a cooperative manner to fulfill a contract that often takes a long period of time to complete.

Partnering attempts to deter the disorder that can arise during a dispute by drawing up certain ground rules that all the parties agree to observe. The entire process begins with a meeting held after the contract has been finalized but before the project has begun. The meeting is held at a location that is unrelated to the business of any party to the contract. In this way, the process can procede in an uninterrupted fashion.

Moreover, the meeting should be directed by an objective third party, whose job it is to help create an atmosphere of trust among the parties to the contract. The parties attempt to anticipate problems that may arise during the project as well as potential solutions to those problems. The parties agree to address all problems when they arise and to look for solutions that will mutually benefit all those involved in the project. Ultimately, the goal is to improve efficiency, ensure safety, and maximize profit by minimizing expenses, especially those that arise from cost overruns.

The parties agree to handle problems according to some ADR technique rather than by litigation. Finally, they agree to deal with one another in a fair manner within the confines of their legal relationships.

A QUESTION OF ETHICS

When Breaking Your Word is Easy to Do

Andrew Zapior, the president and CEO of Zapior Industries, and Oliver McMurray, the president of Georgetown Construction, have just finalized a contract for the construction of Zapior's new research facility in Cincinnati, Ohio. To minimize the problems that may arise, they agree to enter a partnering arrangement. At the end of a three-day meeting, the parties draw up an agreement, one clause of which states that they will submit any claim to mediation. In the third month of the contract, one of Georgetown's suppliers goes on strike, delaying an important shipment of material to the construction site. Zapior demands that McMurray and Georgetown find a different supplier. McMurray, who has done business with this supplier for 20 years, resists the suggestion and calls for a mediation session. Zapior refuses to comply, stating that there is no need to delay the project to maintain a contractual relationship with a supplier that can easily be replaced. Analyze the ethical stand taken by McMurray. Now do the same for Zapior. Which stand do you find easier to support? Explain.

ADR Contract Clauses

An ADR contract clause will specify that the parties to the agreement have promised to use an alternative dispute resolution technique when a disagreement arises rather than litigating the issue. Like partnering, the drafting of ADR contract clauses is a proactive attempt to ensure that litigation will be avoided should a dispute arise. Unlike partnering, which is best suited to long-term construction contracts, ADR clauses can be included in just about any contract.

These ADR clauses can take many shapes and forms. It is possible, for instance, to insert a clause that states merely that the parties have the option of using an ADR technique. Such a clause is weak, at best, serving only to remind the parties that they do not have to sue one another to gain satisfaction. One step beyond the optional clause is a compulsory clause. This clause states that the parties are required to submit all claims that arise under the contract to an ADR technique, most often mediation or arbitration, before filing a lawsuit. The final type of clause would require the parties to submit any claim to binding arbitration. This strictest type ADR clause forces the parties to abide by the decision of the arbitrator.

Regardless of the type of clause used by the parties, the language should include certain standard provisions. For instance, the clause should specify the types of disagreements that will be submitted to ADR, the ADR technique or techniques that can be used, the scope of discovery allowed, the substantive law and the procedural rules that will be followed in the proceeding, the remedies that will be authorized, the grounds for and the procedure to follow in an appeal, and the methods of enforcing an award. The failure to follow provisions specified in an ADR clause may be grounds for the court to revoke a ruling made by an arbitrator.

Such ADR clauses have several advantages. They are especially helpful when two or more parties have embarked on an extended affiliation that may involve numerous contracts, because ADR clauses clearly establish a reliable and predictable method of dealing with the disputes that will inevitably arise whenever two parties are involved in a lengthy association with each other. In addition, ADR clauses are very beneficial to those parties with the weakest position within a contractual relationship. Often, when a dispute does arise, the more powerful party will threaten litigation, secure in the knowledge that he or she can afford a lawsuit more easily than the weaker party. An ADR clause eliminates this leverage point.

EXAMPLE 4-5: ADR Clause: Power to the Powerless

Audrey Kemmelman, a freelance photographer, entered a work-for-hire agreement with The Daily Montgomery Central Times Corporation. During the negotiation stages, Kemmelman asked that an ADR clause be added to the contract that would compel the signatories to submit any claim to ADR. The clause stated that, in the event of any dispute, the signatories to the contract would first discuss the points of conflict informally. If after 30 days, no satisfactory solution had been reached, the signatories agreed to submit the problem to the American Arbitration Association, which would assist in selecting an objective moderator who would help the signatories decide on an appropriate ADR method. This ADR clause would benefit Kemmelman because, as the weaker party, she might not have the resources to finance a lengthy and expensive lawsuit.

Because the parties to an ADR clause are agreeing, at least initially, to forgo the right to litigate any claims that arise among them, the courts prefer that such clauses be clear and precise. Clauses that are drafted in imprecise and ambiguous language may be invalidated by the court. If the parties intend to submit all the claims arising out of their contractual relationship to ADR, they should spell that out as precisely and completely as possible. Otherwise a party that, at a later date, wishes to invoke the clause, may find that the court is reluctant to support that position. When writing an ADR contract clause, it is best to use standard expressions that the court will recognize. Clauses that say that the parties agree to use ADR for "any controversy or claim arising out of or relating to the agreement" will convince the court to enforce the clause for most disputes between the parties. Anything less may meet with judicial resistance.

Settlement Week

Settlement week is a five-day period during which a court's docket is cleared of all business, except for settlement hearings. Prior to the opening of settlement week, all attorneys with cases pending before the court are asked to choose which of those cases might be best handled by a mediator. Judges are also permitted to nominate cases for mediation during settlement week. Also before the opening of settlement week, a list of volunteer mediators is compiled. Cases are then matched with mediators, and a schedule is established. Attorneys are required to be present for the mediation session.

A mediation session is then held for each case. Following each session, the mediator is required to file a report with the court, stipulating the results of the session and asking for the judge's approval. Occasionally, some cases, chiefly those that do not involve determining liability, are submitted to an arbitration panel rather than to a single mediator. In such a situation, the plaintiff chooses one of the arbitrators, the defendant chooses one, and the court names the final one. Not all cases scheduled for settlement week are actually resolved during that time. However, the technique is an effective way to lighten the court's docket and is becoming more and more popular.

Negotiated Rule Making

Negotiated rule making (reg-neg) is a process by which an agency invites the people and the organizations to be affected by a new rule to have input into the writing of that rule. A working team is established that consists of representatives of the affected groups, including the agency issuing the rule. One member of the team is an objective outsider trained in the art of facilitating such discussions. The objective of negotiated rule making, of course, is to avoid disputes before they have a chance to blossom.

All representatives have the opportunity to present their point of view in relation to the proposed rule. Discussions follow, during which all of these issues are examined. Eventually, the team is expected to formulate a rule that reflects a consensus of the representatives. This consensus does not necessarily mean that all parts of the rule are enthusiastically embraced by all of the representatives. Rather, it means that all of the parties agree that they have fashioned a rule that everyone on the rule-making team can live with. The text of the proposed rule is then submitted to the rule-making agency. The success of the process depends on the willingness of the members of the team to work in a cooperative fashion and the willingness of the agency to accept the results of the team's deliberations.

Despite its advantages, negotiated rule making cannot be used in all situations. Certain subject areas are more fitting than others. A suitable subject area for reg-neg would be one that will ultimately affect a wide range of individuals and institutions, is both complicated and controversial, and would meet with resistance if those individuals and institutions affected did not have a hand in shaping the rule. Reg-neg is also a wise course of action when the subject area affected involves nuances that fall outside the expertise of the agency representatives.

EXAMPLE 4-6: Reg-Neg: The Great Lakes Initiative

The Ohio Environmental Protection Agency (OEPA) was charged with the task of drafting a series of rules to implement the Great Lakes Initiative. Rather than simply writing the rules and placing them before the affected parties, the OEPA decided to take a negotiated rule-making approach. Consequently, it created the Great Lakes Initiative External Advisory Group (EAG). The EAG was composed of representatives from the agency itself, from the regulated industry, and from environmental groups. The team engaged in eight months of intense negotiations. These negotiations followed a precisely planned series of steps carried out under the watchful eyes of professional facilitators. The EAG reached a firm consensus on most of the issues that arose during the negotiations. Consequently, the Joint Committee on Agency Rule Review of the Ohio General Assembly adopted a set of rules to implement the Great Lakes Initiative in a relatively harmonious atmosphere and with almost no conflict. This is an extremely successful example of reg-neg in action.

Post-Appellate Procedures

Post-appellate procedures involve taking a case that has been rejected or dismissed by a domestic court to an international organization such as the Inter-American Commission on Human Rights of the Organization of American States. In such a situation, a party that has exhausted all domestic remedies available, up to and including the United States Supreme Court, might ask such a non-governmental organization (NGO) to hear its case. The post-appellate case is brought against the government of the aggrieved party for allegedly failing to provide an appropriate legal remedy to redress the grievances of the victim. The claim generally involves the violation of some fundamental right, generally a due process or an equal protection right that is guaranteed by an international document such as the American Declaration of the Rights and Duties of Man or the United Nations Universal Declaration of Human Rights. The NGO then hears the case, considers the evidence, and determines whether the party's claim is justified. The NGO may demand that the government of the aggrieved party provide compensation for the injuries visited upon the victim. The NGO may also suggest actions beyond that compensation, including needed reforms in the governmental and/or judicial system to prevent such problems from occurring in the future. Whether the NGOs actually have jurisdiction over such claims is open to debate. Moreover, even if they have jurisdiction, whether their findings are actually enforceable against the government in question is problematic.

International Arbitration Agreements

An international arbitration agreement involves a pledge to use arbitration should the parties find themselves in disagreement as to the enforcement rights under the original contract. Generally, the agreement permits the parties to agree on a forum in which the arbitration will be held that is different from the home forum of either party. The parties also can agree to use the rules and procedures promulgated by an independent institution, such as the International Bar Association's Rules of International Commercial Arbitration.

There are several clear advantages to entering an international arbitration agreement. First, because the parties to the agreement are incorporated in different nation-states, they are free to specify whatever forum they can agree upon as the place to hold an arbitration hearing, should that become necessary. This agreement is in contrast to a litigation clause that might specify that the law of one or the other nation would apply to any legal dispute between the parties. Ultimately, such a clause can become very restrictive. The law of a particular nation-state might, for instance, specify that a dispute that arises within the borders of that nation-state would have to be tried within that nation-state. This rule can put one of the two corporations at a distinct disadvantage that may not become evident until the lawsuit has begun. Arbitration agreements can avoid this problem because the arbitration hearing can be held on neutral ground.

Second, when negotiating an arbitration agreement, the parties are also free to specify the identity of the arbitrators or leave open the option to choose the arbitrators at the time of the dispute from a large pool of potential experts. The arbitrators can thus reside in any location that satisfies all of the parties. Third, the same option is open to the parties in relation to their choice of legal representation. Rather than being limited to the forum in which the dispute is to be heard, the parties can bring in representation from any point on the globe. Fourth, using an international arbitration agreement avoids one of the most troublesome problems linked to international litigation: enforcement. Often a party that has won a favorable decree in one nation will find it challenging to execute that decree in any other nation. International arbitration eliminates this problem because the original arbitration contract will include the terms of enforcement.

Of course, as is often the case, the best laid plans of mice and CEOs often go astray. Thus, sometimes a corporation will find that the jurisdiction that it has chosen for an arbitration hearing has different ideas about whether certain arbitrators and/or attorneys will be permitted to practice within its borders. If a country decides that certain legal representatives and certain arbitrators are not welcome in its jurisdiction, then the parties may find themselves using local attorneys and/or arbitrators, something that not only defeats the objective of the international arbitration agreement but also places the validity and acceptability of the entire arbitration process at risk. This possibility also delays the process further because when an arbitrator is dismissed, the entire action usually must begin again.

Nor are these risks trivial. The danger is especially acute in Latin America, where some nation-states still apply a nineteenth century legal principle that says that foreign corporations doing business in a Latin American country or involved in an international legal dispute within the borders of such a country must apply the law of that country, regardless of any agreement made by the parties to the contrary. Sometimes this agreement means simply securing local legal assistance, but it can also mean that the foreign attorneys operating within that jurisdiction are subject to local law, which sometimes includes criminal penalties for not following the procedural rules of that jurisdiction. (Note: For a more detailed look at the problems associated with international arbitration agreements see Lawrence W. Newman and David Zaslowsky, "International Litigation/International Arbitration—Pitfalls for Participants," *International Litigation and Arbitration Newsletter* November 2006, pp. 3–7 retrieved from http://www.bakernet.com. The article first appeared in *The New York Law Journal,* September 29, 2006).

The Science Court Proposal

A science court acts as a forum for disputes involving scientific and technological controversies. Individuals and institutions with concerns about certain scientific activities, such as genetic engineering, nuclear energy research, and so on, might ask the court to act as an impartial arbitrator in the evaluation of those concerns. The judges on the science court would be scientists educated in the areas under investigation, thus allowing them to use their expertise in deciding cases.

Supporters of the establishment of a science court argue that a panel of objective judges with scientific backgrounds provides a neutral body capable of making unbiased, well-informed decisions. Moreover, the science court would not necessarily provide the last word in any case held under its jurisdiction. An appeal stage would be a part of the process. Finally, the decision-making process involved in science-related controversies would be centralized by the science court, thus providing a forum that many individuals could use to their advantage.

Critics of the science court proposal argue that a panel made up of objective judges with scientific backgrounds would be almost impossible to convene. Moreover, critics point out that

THE OPENING CASE *Revisited, Part I*
Mediation, Arbitration, and the Science Court, Round 2

Recall that in the Opening Case at the beginning of the chapter, two power co-ops, the Cooperative Power Association and the United Power Association, planned to construct a system of high-voltage power lines across farmland located in Minnesota. The farm owners objected to the way in which their land was appropriated for the project by the government and the co-ops. The farmers also objected to the planned location of the power lines because they would interfere with their ability to farm the land properly. The governor of Minnesota called for the creation of a science court to resolve the dispute. Unfortunately, the situation rapidly became politicized. The co-ops, which had received a green light for the project from conventional authorities, refused to cooperate with the science court unless they were allowed to continue building the power lines during the science court's deliberations. The farmers argued that the purpose for calling the science court in the first place would be undermined if the construction of the power lines was allowed to continue. Moreover, the farmers wanted an extended set of issues placed before the court, including the possible rerouting of the lines and the consideration of alternative power sources. The co-ops, in contrast, wanted the issues narrowed to an examination of any health problems associated with the power lines. Ultimately, the governor was compelled to withdraw his science court proposal because it caused more political problems than it had solved.

the science court would represent an additional level of bureaucratic red tape. In addition, such a forum could rapidly become buried under an avalanche of claims, many of which would be a frivolous waste of the court's time. Finally, some critics argue that because the issues placed before a science court would be highly controversial, the entire process could be plagued with political considerations that would threaten the legitimacy of the entire process.

The Minnesota experience taught certain valuable lessons about the establishment of a science court. First, a science court will not succeed unless it has the power to compel the parties to submit to its authority. In the Minnesota case, for instance, the co-ops saw no reason to cooperate with a voluntary court because their project had already been approved by conventional authorities. Second, a successful science court must have the power to halt work done on any project that is the focus of the court's investigation. Otherwise, the court's entire process becomes an exercise in futility. Third, a successful science court will ensure that all sides have the opportunity to present their views on all issues facing the court. Permitting certain parties to speak on certain issues while denying the same right to others can destroy the credibility of the court and of those involved in its creation and operation.

quick quiz 4-3

1. The partnering process begins with a meeting held after a contract has been finalized but before the project has begun.   true | false

2. In negotiated rule making, a government agency creates a new set of regulations without the troublesome, time-consuming, expensive, and difficult step of getting input from its constituency, thus streamlining the process, saving money, and eliminating controversy.   true | false

3. The proposed science court would act as a forum for disputes involving scientific and technological controversies.   true | false

Summary

4.1   Litigation has always been a part of the American legal system. Lately, however, things have begun to change. The extensive backlog in many court systems and the perceived injustice of many verdicts have led many people to seek other methods to redress their grievances. These other methods are often grouped under the heading of alternative dispute resolutions (ADR). Alternative dispute resolution occurs whenever individuals attempt to resolve a disagreement by stepping outside the usual adversarial system and applying certain creative settlement techniques, many of which have fact finding and the discovery of truth as their goal.

4.2   There are many different ADR techniques that can be invoked once a dispute has arisen between parties. These include but are not limited to mediation, arbitration, med-arb, early neutral evaluation, summary jury trials, and private civil trials.

4.3   Since ADR has become so popular in recent years, some business people are taking a proactive approach to the situation by agreeing in advance to submit to one of the alternative dispute resolution tools should a disagreement between the parties arise at a later date. These proactive ADR techniques include, but are not limited to, partnering, ADR contract clauses, settlement week, negotiated rule making, international arbitration agreements, the post-appellate option, and the science court proposal.

Key Terms

ADR contract clause, 77

alternative dispute resolution (ADR), 69

arbitration, 73

arbitrator, 73

early neutral evaluation (ENE), 75

international arbitration agreement, 80

med-arb, 74

mediation, 72

mediator, 72

negotiated rule making (reg-neg), 79

non-governmental organization (NGO), 80

partnering, 77

post-appellate procedures, 80

private civil trial, 76

science court, 81

settlement week, 79

summary jury trial, 75

Questions for Review and Discussion

1. What are the shortcomings of litigation?
2. What are the advantages and disadvantages of ADR?
3. What are the advantages of mediation?
4. What is the nature of an arbitration hearing?
5. What happens during the med-arb process?
6. What is the role of an early neutral evaluator?
7. What happens in the running of a summary judgment trial?
8. What are the private options available under proactive ADR?
9. What are the governmental options available under proactive ADR?
10. What are the advantages and disadvantages of the science court proposal?

Cases for Analysis

1. Turner Pte. Ltd. was the main contractor in the building of *Gateway*, a long-term project to be constructed in the heart of Singapore. One of Turner's subcontractors was a company called Builders Federal Ltd. (BFL). As part of the overall contract, the two companies signed an arbitration

agreement, which was designated as Clause 22 in the main contract. When the two parties found themselves in the middle of several serious disputes, they invoked Clause 22 and began arbitration. Turner asked that Mr. David Gardam be appointed as the arbitrator, and BFL asked for Mr. Douglas Smith. The court appointed Smith. From the outset there was bad blood between Turner and Smith, which was revealed in a series of letters that went back and forth between the parties and Smith. At one point in the process, Turner realized that Clause 22 actually had no legal effect until each party activated it by giving their permission to proceed with arbitration. Smith denied that this was the case and ordered the arbitration process to continue. Turner objected, and Smith, who admitted that Turner had made a fairly convincing case, agreed to submit that argument to the High Court of Singapore. Nevertheless, Smith pushed the arbitration process forward. BFL was delighted, but Turner objected. Still the action went forward despite the precarious nature of Smith's position as arbitrator. Can the high court of Singapore dismiss Smith even though BFL is quite satisfied with his work as arbitrator? What grounds might be used to dismiss Smith? If Smith is dismissed, will the arbitration process continue or start over? *Turner (East Asia) Pte. Ltd. v. Builders Federal (Hong Kong) Ltd.* SLR 532 SGHC 47 (Singapore High Court).

2. Jessica Gonzales obtained an official restraining order from a Colorado court that prevented her estranged husband from approaching either her or her children any closer than 100 yards. The order, however, did not stop her husband, who kidnapped their three children. Mrs. Gonzales went to the police and asked for their help. The police did very little to help her, despite the restraining order. Early the next morning, Mr. Gonzales arrived at the police station and began shooting at police officers, who shot back and eventually killed him. After the shooting was over, the police found the bodies of the three young daughters in Mr. Gonzales' truck. Mrs. Gonzales brought suit against the police department, arguing that her due process rights had been violated when the police did not enforce the restraining order. The case went from trial court to the appellate court to the United States Supreme Court, with no result other than a dismissal of the suit. Mrs. Gonzales, with the assistance of the American Civil Liberties Union, filed a post-appellate complaint against the United States with the Inter-American Commission on Human Rights. In her complaint, Mrs. Gonzales argued that she had been deprived of due process and equal protection under the American Declaration of the Rights and Duties of Man, an agreement that the United States was legally bound to follow. Mrs. Gonzales and her attorneys hoped that the commission would issue a judgment in her favor and against the United States. What two initial questions must be answered first before this post-appellate case can begin? Explain. *Jessica Ruth Gonzales v. The United States of America,* Petition No. P-1490-05, The Inter-American Commission on Human Rights of the Organization of American States.

3. In a case involving an ADR clause, the parties to a contract disagreed as to whether the clause required them to submit a dispute over a trade secret problem to arbitration. The clause required the parties to submit "any controversy or claim arising out of the agreement" to arbitration. Strictly speaking, the trade secret controversy did not arise "out of" the agreement. However, it was clear that the trade secret dispute was related to the agreement. The trial court held that the language of the ADR clause was too narrow and that because the trade secret dispute did not arise out of the controversy, the parties were not required to send it to arbitration. Should the appellate court overrule the trial court's decision rejecting the requirement that the parties arbitrate the trade secret dispute? Explain your response. *Tracer Research Corp. v. National Environmental Services, Co.,* 42 F.3d 1292 (9th Cir.).

4. In the early 1990s, serious concerns about the dangers associated with genetic engineering arose after an incident pertaining to the use of certain genetically altered mice in experiments involving a highly infectious disease. In the wake of these concerns, the National Institute of Allergy and Infectious Diseases held a conference to discuss the level of safety that should be followed in laboratories involved in such research. Those involved in the conference included the researchers themselves, certain biosafety experts, representives from organizations involved in or planning to be involved in similar research, and governmental representatives from the Centers for Disease

Control, the National Institutes of Health, and the Food and Drug Administration. Would this type of situation be appropriate for a reg-neg approach? Explain. Might a science court handle this type of situation even better than an agency's reg-neg procedure? Explain.

5. Andrei Kerensky, CEO of the Malenkov Electronic Surveillance Corporation, entered negotiations with Thomas John King, president and chair of the board for Beckett Industries, Inc., the purpose of which was to develop a new security system for Beckett. The system would use a newly designed security system based on a new laser electronic coding system developed by engineers at Malenkov. King and Kerensky finalized the deal, and the security system was installed at Beckett. After Malenkov's engineers installed the system, security personnel and engineering technicians at Beckett made some subtle alterations in the system's computerized control system. Shortly thereafter, the entire system crashed. When Malenkov's bill was not paid, Kerensky went to see King at Beckett's corporate headquarters. During a short encounter, King informed Kerensky that Beckett was not going to pay Kerensky and Malenkov because the system had crashed. King argued that Malenkov's engineers were responsible for the breakdown, while Kerensky insisted that the modifications made by the engineers at Beckett were at fault because of their unauthorized and incompetently rendered modifications to the system. Kerensky wants to sue King and Beckett but is hesitant to do so because the primary factual issues in the case focus on the engineering modifications. Consequently, he is apprehensive that a judge and jury will be lost by the technical jargon that may be used at trial. What alternatives are available to Kerensky?

quick quiz Answers

4-1	4-2	4-3
1. F	1. T	1. T
2. T	2. T	2. F
3. T	3. T	3. T

Chapter 5

Criminal Law and Cybercrimes

THE OPENING CASE The Gulf Spill Vendetta and Corporate Criminal Liability

Judges and legislators are often faced with making decisions that make no sense or, rather, that make sense only after the fact. A case in point involves the explosion of the Deepwater Horizon drilling rig that led to a massive oil spill in the Gulf of Mexico. The destruction that followed the explosion of the rig left many people demanding that someone be punished for what happened to the workers on the rig, to the wildlife in the Gulf, and to the lives of the people living in the area.

Such action is not as easy as it sounds. Had the rig been destroyed by a terror attack or by a criminal cartel, everyone would know what to do. The FBI and local law enforcement departments would investigate the crime scene, collect the evidence, hunt down the perpetrators, and make their arrests. The Justice Department would then prosecute the defendants to the fullest extent of the law. That, however, is not what happened. Instead of career criminals or radical fundamentalists, the Justice Department had to deal with business people and with corporations. Is it possible to prosecute the people involved in the incident? Certainly. What is more, there are specific laws under which such action can be taken. Laws such as the Clean Water Act, the Refuse Act, and the Migratory Bird Treaty Act could be used to prosecute the offenders. But what about the corporations themselves?

What about British Petroleum, and Halliburton, and Transocean? How do we hold a corporation liable?

As you will learn in this chapter, criminal liability requires that the prosecutor prove that the defendant possessed a particular mental state when the criminal act was committed. Corporations, however, do not have mental states let alone mental states that can demonstrate criminal liability, so how do we prove corporate criminal liability? What about punishment? How is a corporation punished and just who is actually punished when a corporation is fined? Is it the board of directors and the officers? One would hope so, but often that punishment is shared by the stockholders, the employees, the customers, the community, pensioners, and the public-at-large, most of whom had nothing to do with the actual wrongs committed. Keep all this in mind as you read this chapter. The results of your reading may surprise you. (See David M. Uhlmann, "Prosecuting Crimes Against the Earth," *The New York Times,* June 4, 2010, p. A-23.)

Opening Case Questions

1. Would the case against British Petroleum be a civil lawsuit or a criminal action? Explain.

2. Would a case against British Petroleum be brought in state or federal court or could it be brought in both? Explain.

3. What legal theory or theories might be used to hold a corporation liable for the torts of an employee? Explain.

4. How is a corporation punished in a case like this? Explain.

5. Since shareholders, employees, and customers end up paying for the corporation's wrongdoing, does it really make any sense to pursue such prosecutions? Explain.

Learning Objectives

1. Explain the purpose of criminal law.
2. Enumeate the various categories and classes of crimes.
3. Describe the nature of an act within the concept of criminal liabiliy.
4. Identify the four mental states to be found in the criminal code.
5. Explain the nature of corporate criminal liability.
6. Explain the various theories of punishment within criminal law.
7. Enumerate and explain the elements of several key crimes.
8. Define and explain the nature of cybercrimes.
9. Explain the three standards for the insanity defense in criminal law.
10. Outline the requirements of entrapment as a defense in criminal law.

5-1 Definition and Classes of Crimes

Perhaps one of the most discussed and least understood areas of the law is criminal law. Most people think they know a lot about criminal law, because they read about it frequently in the newspaper and view programs about it on television. In fact, there is a lot of misinformation spread in the media about criminal law and procedure. This section of the chapter attempts to rectify some of these misconceptions by defining crime and explaining the various classes of crimes.

Definition of a Crime

A crime is an offense against the public at large. As such, a crime threatens the peace, safety, and well-being of the entire community. For this reason, crimes are punishable by the official governing body of a nation or state. Also for this reason, the state or federal government, representing the public at large, is the prosecution, that is, the one who brings the criminal action. The person accused of the crime is called the defendant. No act can be considered criminal unless it is prohibited by the law of the place where it is committed, and the law provides for the punishment of the offenders. These laws are created by the federal government and the governments of the 50 states.

The Objectives of Criminal Law The primary objectives of criminal law are to protect the public at large, to preserve order and stability within society, to punish those who commit criminal acts, and to discourage future criminal activity. In contrast, as we shall see, tort law is concerned with private wrongs that have caused injury to an individual's physical well-being, property, business, or reputation. Because tort law involves private wrongs rather than public ones, it focuses on the victim. Because criminal law protects the public, it seeks to eliminate crime by punishing wrongdoers and removing them from society. When a tort is committed, the victim has a cause of action against the person who has committed the tort, which may permit the victim to recover money as compensation for any injuries that he or she has suffered. In contrast, when a crime is committed the government may prosecute the accused.

Prosecutions and Lawsuits
A single act can be both a crime and a tort. Thus, when a criminal battery is committed against a victim, the criminal defendant will be prosecuted for that battery in a criminal case, the results of which can include imprisonment, a fine, or both. However, the defendant can also be sued by the victim in tort law. The victim will seek damages from the defendant which can include money for hospital bills, lost wages, pain and suffering, and so on. The standard of proof required in a criminal case differs from that required in a tort case. In a criminal case the prosecutor or district attorney is required to prove that the criminal defendant is guilty of the crime *beyond a reasonable doubt*. In a tort case the plaintiff's attorney must prove that the defendant is liable for the tort *by a preponderance of the evidence*. Because criminal defendants can lose their freedom, be fined, and sometimes, in capital cases, even lose their lives, the level of proof needed for a conviction is higher than what is needed to demonstrate liability in a tort case.

Double Jeopardy
The United States Constitution protects people from being tried twice for the same crime. This principle is called the rule of double jeopardy. Double jeopardy, however, does not protect a defendant from being tried for a criminal offense and then being sued under tort law for that same wrongful act. This is what happened in the case of O.J. Simpson. After being found not guilty for the crime of murder, he was sued by his children for the wrongful death of their mother. This did not violate the rule of double jeopardy. Note that the Simpson case also illustrates the difference between the standard of proof in a criminal case and the standard in a tort case. Thus, although the prosecutors failed to prove Simpson guilty *beyond a reasonable doubt*, he was found liable for wrongful death *by a preponderance of the evidence*. It is also interesting to note that a single offense may trigger two prosecutions if the offense can be designated as two different crimes and can be tried in two different courts. Thus, it is possible, for example, for a police officer to be tried in a state court for assaulting a suspect and be tried in federal court for depriving that same suspect of his civil rights.

Victim's Rights
Under common law, criminal law did not focus on the victim. The theory was that, if the victim needed some sort of compensation for the actions of the defendant, it was up to the victim to pursue that case in tort law. This has been altered somewhat by the legislatures that have enacted statutes that create a series of victim's rights. These rights often include notice to the victim that an offender has been arrested, the name of the criminal defendant, the defendant's eligibility for pretrial release, the telephone number of the law enforcement agency responsible for the defendant, and the date, time, and place of the defendant's release, if that occurs. Later in the legal process the victim is also generally notified of the defendant's acquittal or conviction, the defendant's incarceration, the defendant's appeal, and the defendant's release date. Victims are also permitted to provide the prosecutor with a written description of his or her injuries. In addition, in many states the victim is permitted to be present at the defendant's trial, is entitled to the return of his or her property, is empowered to give the court a victim's impact statement before sentencing and another statement when the defendant's possible release is pending. In most cases, it is the prosecutor or the district attorney who is charged by law with enforcing the rights of victims.

Criminal Law in the American System

The American legal structure consists of the federal and the state systems. Both make and enforce criminal law. However, because there are 50 states and the District of Columbia, it is actually more accurate to say that the American system is made up of 52 systems. Nevertheless, it is helpful to limit any discussion of the law to an examination of federal and state systems. We simply must remember that each state has its own code and its own procedures, which, though similar in most respects to all other states, may have its own peculiarities.

Federal Criminal Law Another peculiarity about the American system is that the federal government has no express power in the Constitution that allows it to enact criminal law statutes or establish a national police force. Yet the federal government does enact criminal law and has set up the Federal Bureau of Investigation (FBI) as a national police force. The federal government also has a cabinet-level criminal law enforcement official called the attorney general who has the power to conduct federal criminal investigations. The existence of the federal criminal law system and the various national law enforcement agencies is made possible by the adaptive processes at work within the legal system itself.

Criminal Law as Adaptation The way Congress has assumed powers never granted to it by the Framers of the Constitution demonstrates how the law is a balancing act. The process works something like this: The Framers of the Constitution intended that Congress have only those powers enumerated in Article I, Section 8, of the Constitution. Because the term "police power" is not mentioned anywhere in the Constitution, the Framers did not give that power to the federal government but instead expected the states to exercise all police power. Consequently, Congress can create criminal law statutes only in those areas over which it has jurisdiction. For instance, Congress has the power to coin money, so it can set up laws against counterfeiting. Yet, as we've seen, Congress has created criminal law statutes in areas beyond counterfeiting. If there has been no constitutional amendment explicitly handing Congress police power, how did Congress get the power to create a set of criminal law statutes and a national police force?

The answer is that Congress balanced the actual *words* of the Constitution against the need to *interpret* those words to protect the people from criminal activity. The balance occurred when Congress extended its power through a generous interpretation of the Commerce Clause. The Commerce Clause, found in Article I, Section 8, Clause 3, permits Congress to pass laws that regulate commerce "among the several States." Congress used this clause to regulate interstate criminal activities, which impact "commerce." Although the ultimate results were a long time coming, eventually the courts, through a series of cases, culminating in the case of *Wickard v. Filburn* (63 S.Ct. 82), gave their "stamp of approval" to the legislature's creative balancing act. In a sense then, Congress and the courts cooperated to give the federal governmnent police power, a power it did not have under the Constitution. That power includes the authority to create federal criminal law.

Classes of Crimes

Under common law, crimes were dealt with in the order of their seriousness: treason, felonies, and misdemeanors. Most states now divide offenses into felonies and misdemeanors. A felony is a crime punishable by death or imprisonment in a federal or a state prison for a term exceeding one year. Some felonies are also punishable by fines. Some states define a felony as a crime subject to "punishment by hard labor," as an "infamous

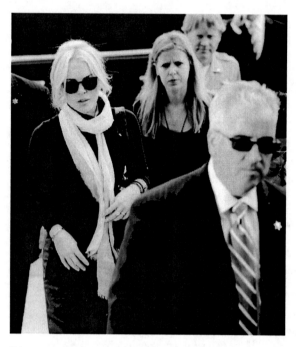

Following her arrest for driving under the influence, Lindsay Lohan was charged with a misdemeanor and sentenced to 23 days in jail.

crime," or as a "crime subject to infamous punishment." Manslaughter, armed robbery, and arson are examples of felonies.

Some states also have separate categories for their most serious crimes. For instance, a state might classify premeditated murder and murder as *special felonies* or *capital felonies* if these are the only two offenses that might result in a death sentence or life imprisonment. States may also have a separate category for violent offenses. Sometimes these violent offenses are termed *aggravated felonies*. Assault with a deadly weapon might be an example of an aggravated felony.

A misdemeanor is a less serious crime, generally punishable by a prison sentence of not more than one year. Included in this category are offenses such as disorderly conduct. Some states also have a separate category for their least serious offenses. The label for these least serious offenses varies, but two of the most common are *petty offenses* and *minor misdemeanors*. Traffic violations and building code violations are usually within this classification.

quick quiz 5-1

1. A misdemeanor is a crime punishable by death or imprisonment in a federal or a state prison for a term exceeding one year.   true | false

2. The primary objective of criminal law is to protect victims.   true | false

3. It is impossible for a single act to be both a tort and a crime.   true | false

5-2 Elements of a Crime

The two elements necessary to create criminal liability are a criminal act and the required state of mind. Although it is difficult to generalize about both of these concepts, certain characteristics are common to each, regardless of jurisdiction. Nevertheless, keep in mind that criminal law is largely statutory in nature. Consequently, specific statutory definitions may vary from state to state.

A Criminal Act

Under American law, a crime cannot be committed unless some act has occurred. An individual cannot be accused of a crime for merely thinking of a criminal act. However, even a small act that appears by itself to be innocent can, in the proper context, become an illegal act. For example, even something as simple as inserting a key into the ignition of a vehicle can constitute an act under the law, if the driver is intoxicated at the time. The act is such an important element to criminal liability that convictions may be avoided or overturned if defendants can show that the statute under which they were prosecuted is ambiguous in its description of the act. Often, such ambiguity will occur when the legislature passes a statute that creates a new offense, when the statute outlaws an activity that may be protected by the U.S. Constitution, or when the statute seeks to outlaw statutes or behavior that cause no imminent negative effect but may eventually lead to great public harm. For instance, the courts have frequently held statutes that outlaw a status, such as drug addiction or vagrancy, to be void for vagueness. The courts have also struck down statutes that are overbroad. The language of a criminal statute is overbroad if the courts cannot determine what specific activity the legislature intended to outlaw.

Omissions and Refusals to Act

At times, the failure to act, an omission, or the outright refusal to act may be considered criminal. Generally, however, an omission must be coupled with a legally imposed duty. An air traffic controller who sees two planes on a collision course, yet fails to warn the pilots, would be held criminally liable for this omission. This liability exists even though the controller did not act but instead failed to act.

Involuntary Movement or Behavior

Many states specifically exclude involuntary movement and behavior from their general definition of a criminal act. Convulsions, reflexes, movements during sleep or unconsciousness, or behavior during a seizure are all considered involuntary movement or behavior falling outside the limits of criminal liability. However, the mere fact that someone is unconscious during a seizure may not absolve that individual of criminal liability if that person knew that he or she might suffer the seizure, yet took no precautions to avoid harming people or property. A person who decides to drive an automobile knowing that she or he is subject to sudden, unpredictable epileptic seizures may be criminally liable if a seizure causes that person to lose control of the vehicle and kill or injure someone.

The Required State of Mind

In general, a crime cannot be committed unless the criminal act named in the statute is performed with the required state of mind. Many state criminal codes include the following four states of mind:

- Purpose
- Knowledge
- Recklessness
- Negligence

Purpose

Individuals act with purpose when they intend to cause the result that in fact occurs. For example, if a person were to point a loaded gun at another person with the intention of shooting that second person, and if shots are actually fired, the person with the gun would have acted with purpose. Some states choose to call this mental state *intent*. Intent or purpose should not be confused with *premeditation,* which is often an added condition in the case of aggravated or first-degree murder. Some states specifically define premeditation as an action that results from the criminal defendant's "prior calculation and design." If, in the previous example, the person with the gun had also planned to shoot the victim, and then actually carried out this plan, the shooting would have been premeditated.

Knowledge

When people act with an awareness that a particular result will probably occur, they act with knowledge. For instance, if the person with the gun in the preceding example took that loaded gun to a crowded shopping mall and began to fire at random, not aiming at anyone in particular, that person would be acting with the knowledge that a lot of people would be either wounded or killed. This awareness would be true even if the person with the gun were to yell, "I really don't want to shoot anyone. I hope I don't hit anybody!"

Recklessnes

Recklessness involves a perverse disregard of a known risk of negative consequences. People act recklessly when they are indifferent to a serious risk they know to exist. Two drivers who challenge each other to an illegal drag race on a public highway are acting recklessly. In other words, they have disregarded the possible serious consequences of their decision to engage in an illegal drag race.

Negligence

People act with negligence when they fail to see the possible negative consequences of their actions. A person who cleans a hunting rifle without checking to see if it is loaded is acting with negligence, because that person has not bothered to look for any possible negative consequences that could result from those actions. Criminal negligence should not be confused with negligence in tort law. Negligence in tort law is concerned with the compensation of accident victims (see Chapter 6). In contrast, negligence in criminal law is concerned with punishing the wrongdoer and protecting the public at large.

The Matter of Motive

Motive in criminal law is the wrongdoer's reason for committing the crime. One common misconception about criminal law, which is perpetuated by countless television programs and films, is that motive is an element of criminal liability. Such is not the case. Establishing motive may help the prosecution persuade the jury that the accused is guilty, but proving an evil motive is not necessary for a criminal conviction.

The Matter of Corporate Liability

Criminal liability requires that the prosecutor prove that the defendant possessed a particular mental state when the criminal act was committed. Such mental states are generally stated quite clearly in the statute that creates the criminal offense. In fact, since criminal liability requires only two elements, the act and the mental state, legislators are very careful in drafting criminal law statutes to make certain that they explain both elements stating booth with great specificity. It is not always easy for a prosecutor to prove that a defendant possessed the required mental state. Still, when the criminal defendant is an individual, at least the prosecutor knows how to proceed. The prosecutor must produce evidence, generally consisting of actions and words, that demonstrate what was in the mind of the defendant at the time that the criminal act was committed. This is hard enough with a flesh and blood defendant. Corporations, on the other hand, do not have mental states, let alone mental states that can demonstrate criminal liability. Nor do they act or speak, except through their corporate officers and employees. How, then, does a prosecutor go about proving criminal liability when the criminal defendant is a corporation?

Corporate Personality

The law provides a fairly complete picture of a corporate identity. The law has established that corporations are "legal people." As a corporate person, a corporation possesses an identity, a corporate self, if you will, that maintains an existence that is separate from those who formed it in the first place. The upside to this is that the corporation will exist long after its founders. The downside is that corporations are taxed directly for what they earn as part of the marketplace. The courts have also decided that corporations have just enough "personhood" to qualify for constitutional protections. Thus, under the Fourteenth Amendment, a corporation has the right to life, liberty, and property, rights that cannot be violated by the government either at the state or the federal levels. In addition, as a legal person, a corporation can institute a lawsuit or can be the target of a lawsuit.

Corporate Liability Theories Despite popular opinion, corporations are not modern inventions developed in the 19th century. In fact, we know that corporate-like organizations existed in the Middle Ages. At that time, however, common law judges could not conceive of corporate liability because corporations did not possess a mind with which to form a mental state. The modern age changed all of that. Once the courts decided that a corporation was person enough to sue or be sued, it was not a huge leap for them to conclude that a corporation could be held criminally liable as well. One of the earliest theories on corporate criminal liability emerged from within the doctrine of *strict liability*. Strict liability was an appropriate theory at the time, because it did not require intent, something that was difficult to prove in the case of a corporation. By the beginning of the 20th century, however, the courts began to hold corporations liable for the criminal acts of their employees using the doctrine of vicarious liability, a theory which is also called *respondeat superior*. Under this approach, the courts decided that a corporation could be declared criminally responsible if one of its employees committed a crime while on the job, working for the benefit of the corporation. The doctrine has been liberalized to such an extent that today, even if a worker is expressly prohibited from doing anything outside the law, the corporation might still be declared liable for a crime committed by that worker.

THE OPENING CASE *Revisited, Part I*
The Gulf Spill Vendetta and Corporate Criminal Liability, Round 2

Recall that, in the Opening Case at the beginning of this chapter, many people called for the prosecution of British Petroleum, Halliburton, and Transocean because they were believed to be responsible for the explosion of the Deepwater Horizon drilling rig and the massive oil spill in the Gulf of Mexico. In response, the federal government set up a special panel to investigate the incident. More than six months after the accident, the panel reported that the problems aboard the drilling rig resulted from a substandard level performance *common throughout the entire oil industry.*

This finding could be a problem for prosecutors who, under the *respondeat superior* test, must demonstrate, first and foremost, that a corporate agent committed a crime. This may not sound difficult at first blush, but the more we consider the situation, the darker it becomes. The problem plays out like this: If a crime requires intent or knowledge, then the prosecutor will have to prove, beyond a reasonable doubt, that the corporate agent purposely or knowingly performed the wrongful act outlined in the statute. So, for example, suppose the prosecutor wants to target one of the corporations by using an aggravated arson statute to prosecute a rig operator, who was acting as a corporate agent at the time of the

explosion. Aggravated arson would require the prosecutor to demonstrate that the defendant, by fire or explosion, knowingly created a risk of serious physical harm to another person or to an occupied structure. So far, this sounds like an open and shut case. But remember the explosion was not set off by the rig operator throwing a bomb. It resulted from the day-to-day operation of the rig. If the day-to-day operation of the rig was well within industry standards (okay, substandards, but standards, nonetheless), then how can the prosecutor show that the defendant "knowingly" created a "substantial risk"? How do I knowingly create a substantial risk if I am just doing what everyone in the entire industry does as a matter of day-to-day operational conduct? The answer is that I can't and if I can't be held responsible, neither can the corporation. Of course, the prosecutor may have a case against the agent and, therefore, the corporation, for a lesser offense, perhaps one like criminal damaging, which requires only recklessness or negligence as the appropriate state of mind. However, convictions under these lesser offenses may not satisfy those victims of the oil spill who want the prosecutor to "throw the book" at the defendants, especially the defendant corporations.

THE OPENING CASE *Revisited, Part II*
The Gulf Spill Vendetta and Corporate Criminal Liability, Round 3

As noted above, many people were outraged by the oil spill that resulted in the Gulf of Mexico from the explosion of British Petroleum's Deepwater Horizon drilling rig. Much of this anger was directed, in general, at British Petroleum and, in particular, at BP's CEO, Tony Hayward. In hearings held in Washington, D.C., the CEO testified that he did not directly participate in any of the decisions made in relation to that particular rig. Under the Model Penal Code, corporate criminal liability requires the authorization, the approval, or the reckless toleration of criminal activity by the board of directors or by a managing officer who is clearly responsible for establishing corporate policy, especially in relation to the incident under investigation. If, in fact,

the CEO did not know what was going on at the Deepwater Horizon drilling rug then, under the Model Penal Code, neither he nor the corporation can be held liable. By distancing himself from the decision-making process, the CEO had clearly adopted a defense of plausible deniability. In engineering this defense, he was undeniably acting in the corporation's best interests, as well as his own. However, he was not acting in the best interests of the shareholders, other employees, the community, and so on. Still, under the Model Penal Code, there was nothing wrong with his conduct. In fact, his conduct was perfectly understandable and eminently reasonable. What does that tell us about the Model Penal Code?

The Model Penal Code The Model Penal Code offers a third theory of corporate liability. Under this theory, a corporation might be held criminally liable if the directors or officers of a corporation authorize, approve, or recklessly tolerate the criminal actions of their employees. Like the doctrine of *respondeat superior*, the directors or the officers must be acting on the job when the crimes occur. On the surface, this policy looks like an effective tool for stopping corporate criminal activity. However, in practice, the Model Penal Code may simply encourage directors and officers to remain ignorant of the actions of their employees in order to develop a defense of "plausible deniability." The defense of plausible deniability allows corporate managers to "honestly" testify that they knew nothing about the criminal activity of which they, their employees, and the corporation are accused.

The Matter of Punishment

The ultimate purpose of criminal law is to protect the public. This purpose means that criminal law must outline not only the offenses that are prohibited but also the negative consequences that result when an individual has committed one of those offenses. Many legal experts disagree however about what that punishment ought to be. Still, these experts have narrowed the debate to two approaches to the sentencing of convicted criminals: (1) consequences that are designed to protect the public at large and (2) those that are tailored to fit the individual offense or the individual offender.

Protecting the Public at Large Consequences that have been created to protect the public send a message not just to the convicted felon but also to all potential offenders. These techniques include deterrance, education, and retribution. Those experts who believe in *deterrence* advocate long and difficult prison sentences so that other people in society are dissuaded from committing similar offenses and thus suffering the same fate. Those who support the theory of *education* say that the criminal process should be presented in a public way so that the public will learn the difference between acceptable and unacceptable bevhavior. Finally, those who believe in *retribution* are convinced that it does society good to seek revenge against those who have disrupted the smooth running of the social system.

This theory probably has the fewest supporters today. Still, some experts argue that obtaining retribution against those who seek to gratify themselves at the expense of others will prevent many potential offenders from committing similar misdeeds in the future.

Individual Offenses and Punishment Consequences that have been created to fit a particular offense or to punish a specific offender are designed to make certain that the individual offender will no longer engage in criminal activity in the future. The techniques for promoting this approach are prevention, restraint, and rehabilitation. Those experts who believe in *prevention* support long sentences in unpleasant prisons so that criminal defendants will abandon their criminal careers. Those who support *restraint* believe that criminal defendants should be incarcerated or even executed for capital offenses to prevent them from ever committing that crime—or any crime, for that matter—ever again. Finally, those who support the theory of *rehabilitation* say that convicted defendants ought to be given the opportunity to reform their conduct, restructure their lives, and start over.

The Death Penalty The use of the death penalty in criminal cases has been subject to a series of controls designed to limit the imposition of this punishment to those cases in which the criminal defendant truly deserves to be put to death. Generally, these limits are built into the criminal code and are applied by the court which is responsible for sentencing the convicted criminal defendant. The safeguards come in the form of aggravating and mitigating circumstances, which must be taken into consideration by the court at the time of sentencing.

Aggravating circumstances are those that involve offenses so appalling that the death penalty is clearly warranted. In most jurisdictions the list of aggravating circumstances looks like this: (a) the assassination of the president, the vice president, the governor, or the lieutenant governor of the state; (b) a murder for hire; (c) a murder committed to escape detection, apprehension, trial, or punishment; (d) a murder committed while the offender was in detention; (e) a murder by a convicted murderer; (f) a murder of a law enforcement officer; (g) a murder of a witness against the offender; (h) a murder of a child under 13 years of age; or (i) a murder during the commission of a felony. Usually, the death penalty cannot be imposed without the presence of at least one of these aggravating circumstances.

Moreover, even if aggravating circumstances are present, the death penalty might still be avoided, if the mitigating circumstances outweigh the aggravating circumstances. Mitigating circumstances include: (a) the victim somehow induced the offense; (b) the offender was coerced or provoked; (c) the offender was suffering from a mental impairment of some sort; (d) the offender is very young; (e) the offender has no past criminal record; (f) the offender was not the principal actor in the offense; (g) or the offense was subject to other factors that might be relevant to a reduced sentence. It is also extremely important for the judge who administers the death penalty to be fair and impartial and to be free from undue pressure, conflict of interest, and any other external influence. Generally, the appellate court that reviews the application of the death penalty is required by the rules to evaluate the conduct of the sentencing judge for any hint of partiality, impropriety, or outside pressure.

quick quiz 5-2

1. The two elements needed to create criminal liability are a criminal act and the requisite state of mind.	true | false
2. Individuals act with negligence when they act with the intention to cause the result that does in fact occur.	true | false
3. Motive is an element of criminal liability.	true | false

5-3 Specific Crimes

Statutory definitions and classifications of crimes vary from jurisdiction to jurisdiction. Nevertheless, several generalities can be drawn to simplify an examination of specific crimes. Crimes can be classified as crimes against people, crimes against property, crimes involving business, and crimes against justice.

Crimes against People

Crimes against people include, but are certainly not limited to, first-degree murder, second-degree murder, manslaughter, battery, and assault. A more recent addition to this list involves hate speech.

First-Degree Murder   Any killing of one human being by another is labeled as a homicide. Criminal homicide is either murder or manslaughter. When the unlawful killing is done with premeditation and deliberate intent, it is labeled first-degree murder, aggravated murder, or premeditated murder, depending on the jurisdiction. The definition of first-degree murder differs from state to state. However, some of the elements are consistent. In general, most states define first-degree murder to include one of the following circumstances: killing someone with premeditation (thinking about it and planning the homicide in advance with "prior calculation and design") and/or killing someone while committing a major crime, such as rape, robbery, or kidnapping. Moreover, several jurisdictions have added other circumstances to the definition of first-degree murder, including causing the death of a victim under 13 years of age; causing the death of a law enforcement officer, when the offender knows or has reasonable cause to know that the victim is a police officer; causing the death of another while the offender is escaping detention for a felony; and killing someone in a cruel way such as with torture. Some states have added most or all of these to their statutory definition of first-degree murder, while others have added a combination of these new factors. It should also be obvious that these states have included some of the aggravating circumstances related to the death sentence within the definition of first-degree murder. The inclusion of these circumstance within the core definition of first-degree murder makes the application of the death penalty more likely.

Second-Degree Murder and Manslaughter   If none of the conditions for first-degree murder apply, the crime is known as second-degree murder or, in some states, murder. In many jurisdictions, the difference between first- and second-degree murder is important because first-degree murder usually carries the death penalty, whereas second-degree murder does not. In contrast to murder, manslaughter is an unlawful killing of a person without the intent to kill. A killing that results when a person is in a state of extreme fright, terror, anger, or blind rage that destroys the ability to reason is known as voluntary manslaughter. When the killing results from negligence, it is usually called involuntary manslaughter.

Did You Know?

In 1999, SabreTech, Inc., was indicted by a grand jury in Miami for the 110 deaths that resulted from the crash of ValuJet Flight 592. In the case, the corporation faced 110 counts of murder.

EXAMPLE 5-1: First Degree Murder and Voluntary Manslaughter

Brent Haywood entered a convenience store and robbed the clerk at gunpoint. As he was leaving the store, the clerk pulled a revolver from under the counter and ordered Haywood to stop. In response, Haywood fired his weapon at the clerk, who returned fire. In the exchange of gunshots, an innocent bystander, nine-year-old Teddy Newman, was shot and killed. Haywood was convicted of first-degree murder and sentenced to death by lethal injection. However, the judge, who opposed the death penalty, gave Haywood a life sentence. Teddy's father was in the courtroom when this sentence was announced. In a state of extreme rage, Teddy's father attacked and killed Haywood. Even though Teddy's father's actions were clearly intentional, they were performed in a state of extreme rage as a result of a reasonable provocation. Consequently, he was charged with voluntary manslaughter.

Battery and Assault Throughout most of English and American history, the term battery has been used to describe a crime in which the offender causes actual physical harm to the victim. In contrast, assault has generally been taken to include the threat of harm to the victim. Today, however, this simple distinction is no longer applicable because many states have created a wide variety of levels and degrees of battery and assault. Some states have even altered the actual language of the law. Ohio, for example, has completely eliminated the term battery and replaced it with the word assault. In Ohio, then, the term assault is used to describe various crimes involving the infliction of physical harm on the victim. To describe offenses that should be identified with the word assault, Ohio uses the terms *aggravated menacing* and *menacing*. Moreover, Ohio has added a few new offenses to the criminal code that are related to, but are not exactly the same as, assault and battery. These include stalking, hazing, and abuse. Given these subtle distinctions, it is always best to check the criminal code in your own jurisdiction before discussing assault and battery.

Hate Speech In recent years, many legislative bodies have attempted to criminalize the use of certain symbols, writings, and speech intended to provoke outrage or fear on the basis of race, religion, color, or gender. These statutes and ordinances are frequently referred to as laws against *hate speech*. Such statutes are constitutional only if they are not content specific. Therefore, though it may be acceptable to draft a statute that outlaws any speech designed to rouse fear or outrage, regardless of the content of that speech, it would be impermissible to outlaw speech aimed at inciting outrage or fear based solely on race, religion, color, gender, or any similar category.

Has 9/11 increased hate speech focused on Muslim women?

Crimes against Property

Crimes against property include but are not limited to: burglary; breaking and entering; trespass; aggravated arson; arson; aggravated robbery; robbery; theft; fraud, and related offenses.

Burglary, Breaking and Entering, and Trespass The crime of burglary has evolved since the Middle Ages. It was once limited to the unlawful entry into a dwelling place at night. Modern legislatures have extended the definition of burglary to include using force, deceit, or cunning to trespass into an occupied structure with the intent to commit a crime. A more serious form of burglary is generally referred to as aggravated burglary. Aggravated burglary includes everything that burglary includes but adds the use of a deadly weapon, the infliction of harm, the threat of harm, or the attempt to harm another person. A third related offense is breaking and entering, which generally includes using force, deceit, or cunning to trespass into an unoccupied structure with the intent to commit any theft or any felony. Breaking and entering can also involve trespassing on land with the intent to commit a felony. The last offense that is related to these three offenses is trespass, which involves knowingly entering land without permission to do so. Some, but not all, forms of trespass include entry onto the land with the intent to commit a misdemeanor.

Aggravated Arson and Arson

Under common law rules, arson involved the burning of another person's home. Legislatures have expanded this definition so that arson now includes more than one offense. Aggravated arson includes using fire or explosives to create a substantial risk of physical harm to an individual or to an occupied building. Often also included in this offense is the hiring of another person to carry out the burning or the use of the explosives. A lesser offense is ordinary arson, which involves using fire or explosives to harm or cause a substantial risk of harm to the property of another or to do the same to another's property or to the offender's own property in order to carry out fraud. Again also included in this is the hiring another to actually burn the property or use the explosives. Some states have expanded the arson statutes even further to specifically include the burning or use of explosives against government owned buildings, government parklands, government wildlife preserves, and so on.

Aggravated Robbery and Robbery

Like many of the criminal offenses already discussed in this chapter, robbery involves more than one offense. Unlike many of the others, however, the definition of robbery has not changed much over the years. The more serious offense is generally known as aggravated robbery. Aggravated robbery involves attempting to commit or actually committing a theft using a deadly weapon or a dangerous ordnance or doing the same by inflicting physical harm on the victim. Robbery involves essentially the same elements as aggravated robbery. However, in ordinary robbery the offender possesses a deadly weapon but neither uses nor shows the weapon. Robbery can also involve attempting to commit or actually committing a theft by inflicting or attempting to inflict physical harm on another person.

Theft, Fraud, and Related Offenses

Today many jurisdictions will place theft, fraud, and a series of related offenses, such as receiving stolen goods or passing bad checks, together under a single heading. What each of these offenses has in common is the attempt to separate the rightful owner of property from that property or to somehow profit from that separation once it has taken place. Theft, the simplest, and arguably the oldest of these offenses is defined in many jurisdictions as knowingly taking or obtaining control over the property of another individual without that individual's consent using deceit, threats, or coercion. Fraud covers a wide variety of crimes today including such diverse activities as identity fraud, Medicaid fraud, worker's compensation fraud, telecommunications fraud, insurance fraud, defrauding a rental agency, and defrauding creditors. What each type of fraud has in common, however, is a deliberately engineered deception that the offender uses to obtain property or services that belong to another. The offenses that are related to theft and fraud cover a wide variety of situations including motion picture piracy, misuse of credit cards, trademark counterfeiting, receiving stolen property, and tampering with records.

Crimes Involving Business

Nonviolent in nature, business crimes are those carried out by a business or individual in the course of doing business to obtain a business related advantage. Covering a wide range of illegal business practices, business crimes are directed against individuals, other businesses, the government, or the public. The business crimes discussed here include embezzlement, forgery, criminal simulation, passing bad checks, and defrauding creditors.

Embezzlement

In many jurisdictions, embezzlement is defined as wrongfully taking property or funds that have been entrusted to the care of the offender. Unlike similar offenses such as theft, robbery, and burglary, a fundamental element of embezzlement is that the embezzler had control over the property or the funds that were wrongfully taken. Thus, embezzlement often occurs in a business setting and frequently involves the employees of the victim.

Forgery, Criminal Simulation, and Passing Bad Checks

The crime of forgery involves the false making or changing of a writing (without proper authorization) with the intent to defraud. It is also forgery to possess or sell an altered or false writing with the intent to defraud. Some states have expressly added identity cards to their forgery statutes to emphasize the criminal nature of forged IDs. These states generally make it a crime to create, sell, use, or possess a false ID. Criminal simulation is analogous to forgery because it also involves the alteration or falsification of an object or a document with intent to defraud. However, criminal simulation involves altering or falsifying art objects, antiques, photographs, films, tapes, recordings, and/or antiquities with the intent to defraud. Passing bad checks includes issuing or transferring a check or other negotiable instrument knowing it will be dishonored and with the intent to defraud.

Defrauding Creditors

Many jurisdictions have statutes that are specifically designed to protect the rights of creditors. The statute against defrauding creditors is the crime of removing, hiding, destroying, giving away, or transferring any person's property with the intent to defraud creditors. Under these statutes it is also criminal to hide, misrepresent, or refuse to disclose information about the existence, amount, or location of a person's property to a fiduciary who has been appointed to administer that person's affairs or estate. The crime of defrauding creditors can be either a felony or a misdemeanor depending on the amount of the property involved in the fraud.

Racketeer Influenced and Corrupt Organizations Act

To prevent a criminal invasion of legitimate businesses, Congress enacted the Racketeer Influenced and Corrupt Organizations (RICO) Act. Under provisions of this statute, conducting a legitimate business with the funds acquired from a "pattern of racketeering activities" can give rise to criminal liability. Many of the offenses that fall within the scope of "racketeering activity"—such as arson and robbery—are serious crimes. Others, however, are less sinister. For example, both mail fraud and wire fraud fall within the definition of racketeering activities. The provisions of RICO can give rise not only to criminal charges but also to civil liability. Thus, it is not uncommon for individuals to seek damages in lawsuits filed against corporations that have violated RICO.

Crimes against Justice

Crimes against justice involve offenses committed by or with the cooperation of a public servant or a public official. Such crimes include bribery, theft in office, and dereliction of duty. Others, such as intimidation, are committed against a public official or public servant. Still others, such as obstruction of justice, resisting arrest, perjury, and tampering with evidence are committed against the justice system itself.

Bribery and Theft in Office

In most states, bribery involves offering, promising, or actually giving something of value to a public official with the goal of influencing that official in the discharge of his or her public duties. It is also bribery when the public official solicits or accepts a thing of value in exchange for that public official's influence in whatever capacity. Many states have further expanded the crime of bribery to include witnesses who are offered or given something of value in exchange for their testimony. The bribery can be committed by the person who offers the bribe and by the witness who solicits or accepts the bribe. Another offense that involves public servants is theft in office. Most jurisdictions define theft in office to include any theft offense in the criminal code that is committed by a public official or a party official. The theft must involve the use of that official's governmental or party power to obtain unlawful control over governmental or party property or services.

Dereliction of Duty

In most states the crime of dereliction of duty can involve law enforcement officers and public servants. In relation to *law enforcement officers,* dereliction of duty is any activity that involves the officer's failure to carry out his or her lawful duties. These duties include, but are not limited to, serving lawful warrants; preventing the commission of a crime; controlling unruly prisoners; preventing the escape of prisoners; carrying out criminal proceedings; providing persons confined in a detention facility with food, shelter, and medical assistance; preserving sanitary conditions in detention facilities, and, in general, properly managing those detention facilities. *Public servants* are charged with carrying out those duties that are specifically related to the proper operation of their governmental office. In addition, many dereliction of duty statutes also expressly state that public servants have an affirmative duty to keep their department or agency within the budget set for it by the state legislature.

Intimidation

The crime of intimidation involves threats of harm to the person or property of a public servant, party official, or witness with the intention of coercing that individual into some violation of his or her public duty. Some jurisdictions have expanded the definition of intimidation to include threats of harm to the public servant's reputation by the publication of false information. This would seem to include not only the publication of false statements in newspapers and magazines and on television, but also the posting of such false information on the Internet via the various social media outlets, such as Facebook, Linked-In, and so on.

Obstruction of Justice and Resisting Arrest

Most jurisdictions define obstruction of justice as any activity designed to prevent the discovery, apprehension, arrest, prosecution, conviction, or punishment of a criminal defendant. Each jurisdiction also specifies those activities that qualify as obstruction of justice. These activities include but are not necessarily limited to: hiding a criminal defendant; providing that defendant with money, transportation, weapons, disguises, and so on; warning that person of possible discovery or arrest; destroying or concealing evidence; and communicating false information to law enforcement officials about the defendant. Resisting arrest is defined as interfering in the lawful arrest of a criminal defendant. Most statutes defining this offense also penalize the resister for any harm that comes to a law enforcement officer involved in the arrest.

Perjury and Tampering with Evidence

Under the laws of most states, perjury is defined as making a false statement under oath. However, many jurisdictions also add that the false statement must be material to the proceeding. A statement is material if it can have an impact on the final disposition of the case. Interestingly enough, in most cases, the fact that the perjured testimony is inadmissible as evidence makes no difference; the false statement is still perjury. However, a person cannot be convicted of perjury by a single witness. Tampering with evidence means altering, destroying, or removing any piece of evidence with the intent to somehow lessen the probative value of that evidence. In addition, tampering with evidence includes presenting false evidence to a public official in order to somehow destroy the effectiveness of an official investigation.

quick quiz 5-3

1. In most states, the distinction between first- and second-degree   true | false
    murder is important because first-degree murder usually carries
    the death penalty while second-degree murder does not.

2. It is acceptable to draft a statute that outlaws speech aimed at   true | false
    inciting outrage or fear based solely on race, religion, color, gen-
    der, or any similar category.

3. Passing bad checks includes issuing or transferring a check or   true | false
    other negotiable instrument knowing it will be dishonored and
    with the intent to defraud.

5-4 Cybercrimes

As is true of most other crimes, statutory definitions and classifications of cybercrimes (electronic crimes and e-crimes) vary from state to state. Moreover, in the case of cybercrimes, the definitions are even more varied because there is no agreement on what constitutes a cybercrime. One approach is to state that cybercrimes involve any criminal act that includes a computer. This strategy, which is often referred to as cyber-trespass, computer trespass, or e-trespass, can solve many of the problems associated with cybercrime, if only by an indirect treatment of such crimes. Another way to classify cybercrimes is to distinguish between crimes committed with a computer and crimes committed against a computer.

Cyber-trespass

A problem arises when crimes that are already on the books are committed with a computer. As noted previously, one way to deal with this situation is to create a single generic offense called cyber-trespass, electronic trespass, or e-trespass. Cyber-trespass is the process of gaining access to a computer with the intent to commit a crime. In effect, in one single stroke, this strategy incorporates the rest of the criminal code into this one crime, making it an offense to use a computer to commit any other crime in the code. In a state that takes this approach, all criminal statutes, especially those pertaining to fraud, embezzlement, blackmail, and theft, become part of this one crime known as cyber-trespass.

Crimes Committed with a Computer

Another approach to dealing with cybercrime is to distinguish between using a computer to commit a crime and committing an offense against a computer. Naturally some of these crimes will overlap. Nevertheless, enough of a distinction exists between the two to make this a viable approach to the subject. Cybercrimes that focus on the use of a computer include cyber-extortion, cyber-stalking, cyber-harassment, cyber-assault, cyber-bullying, cyber-spoofing, phishing, smishing, and vishing.

Cyber-extortion *Cyber-extortion, electronic extortion,* or *e-extortion* can occur when an experienced hacker gains access to the computer records of a corporation or other institution and discovers some sort of illegal, negligent, unethical, or embarrassing conduct that might damage the reputation of the target organization. Using the computer, the hacker can then contact the organization to threaten exposure unless he or she is rewarded financially.

Cyber-stalking *Cyber-stalking, e-stalking,* or *electronic stalking* involves targeting individuals for exploitation using computer connections. Cyber-stalkers usually target vulnerable individuals who may be searching for a genuine connection on the Internet. Minors are often targeted by cyber-stalkers. After gaining the trust of the minor or other innocent victim, the cyber-stalker arranges a meeting so that he or she can take advantage of the innocent party.

Cyber-harassment *Cyber-harassment, electronic harassment* or *e-harassment* involves using computer connections, often via e-mail or some other social media, to blanket the target with offensive sexual, racial, religious, or political comments, photographs, videos, and so on aimed at disrupting the victim's peace of mind. The psychological impact of cyber-harassment is severe, but often difficult to prove, thus making cyber-harassment an especially vicious crime.

Cyber-assault *Cyber-assault, electronic assault,* or *e-assault* has several definitions depending on the jurisdiction. Cyber-assault can involve using social media to threaten to inflict immediate and severe bodily harm on the target victim. In this sense of the term, it is simply an extension of common law assault. However, cyber-assault can also mean a direct attack on a computer system with the intent to disrupt that system.

Cyber-bullying *Cyber-bullying, electronic bullying,* or *e-bullying* involves intentional, aggressive, upsetting activities by a single individual or a group of individuals aimed at destroying the mental well-being of a peer. Generally, cyber-bullies use a variety of cyber-social media, including chatrooms, discussion groups, blogs, Web pages, texting, instant messaging, and so on to disrupt the life of the target. The term cyber-bullying is generally used to describe the cyber-activities of students against one another. In most jurisdictions it is not yet a crime.

Cyber-spoofing To commit *cyber-spoofing, electronic spoofing,* or *e-spoofing,* a cyber-criminal must falsely adopt the identity of another computer user or create a false identity on a Web site to commit fraud. A simple form of cyber-spoofing involves adopting the identity of an e-mailer to defraud the recipients of the original e-mail. Another type of cyber-spoofing involves creating phony Web sites or diverting users from legitimate Web sites to obtain credit card numbers, debit card numbers, PINs, passwords, or other confidential information to commit a wide variety of fraudulent activities.

Phishing and Spear Phishing Phishing and spear phishing are two forms of cyber-spoofing. *Phishing* involves sending out phony e-mails that solicit buyers and, in the process, obtain credit card information, account numbers, PINs, account balances, and so on. When the e-mail has been customized to such an extent that the recipient believes the e-mail comes from a co-worker, a friend, or a relative, the offense is called *spear phishing.* (See "Briefing Cyberwar: War in the Fifth Domain," *The Economist,* July 3, 2010, p. 26.)

Smishing and Vishing *Smishing* links SMS (short message service) texting with phishing. *Vishing* connects phishing to voice messaging. In both situations, cyber-criminals send out messages at random, sometimes targeting a particular city, profession, or exchange number, and sometimes using a particular phone list purchased or obtained illegally from an institution like a savings and loan, a credit card company, or a department store. The messages will warn the recipients that their credit card information needs to be updated, or that their account is overdrawn, prompting the victims to contact a number or to access an Internet site. The victims then provide private information such as account numbers, PINs, passwords, and so on. These confidential numbers and passwords are used to infiltrate the victim's financial records, credit card accounts, debit card records, and so on. (See "Smishing and Vishing and Other Cyber Scams to Watch Out for this Holiday," *The FBI-Federal Bureau of Investigation,* November 2010, http:www.fbi.gov/news/ stories/2010/ november/cyber_112410/cyber_112410.)

Crimes that Target Computers

Cybercrimes that target computers attempt tp disable the computer itself, to disable the system that it operates, or to confiscate and use the information stored in the computer, sometimes after erasing the original data. Crimes that target computers include cyber-terrorism, identity theft, cyber-vandalism, and cyber-germ warfare.

Cyber-terrorism
Cyber-terrorism, electronic terrorism, or *e-terrorism* involve using a computer to disrupt or destroy one of the critical elements of the nation's cyber-infrastructure, such as the power grid, the air traffic control system, water and sanitation plants, the ground transportation system, a harbor traffic-control network, a cell tower network, the nation's stock exchange, the banking system, hospital back-up generator systems, or the national defense system.

Identity Theft
Another cybercrime that targets computers and computer information is identity theft. In identity theft, a perpetrator uses one of the techniques noted previously to steal credit card information, PINs, financial data, access codes, passwords, or debit card information. The perpetrator then passes himself or herself off as the victim. Using this technique, the identity thief can clean out bank accounts, run up credit card debt, divert cash transfers, buy and sell stocks, enter electronic auction networks, approve or cancel shipments, make or revoke hotel and travel reservations, and disrupt the financial and the personal life of the victim.

Cyber-vandalism
Sometimes expert vandals can attack a computer system so that a Web site is completely destroyed or paralyzed to the extent that legitimate business can no longer be conducted on that site. This type of attack is known as *cyber-vandalism, electronic vandalism,* or *e-vandalism.* Often cyber-vandalism is used to cripple a business as a form of revenge for real or imagined wrongs, to exercise power over a business, or to hurt the owner of a business just for "fun."

A QUESTION OF ETHICS

Ronald King, who was recently elected mayor of a fairly large Midwestern city, has learned that an underground organization, named the Kesselmen Group, has infected the city's computer system with a virus that threatens to disrupt the city's safety forces' communication system and the city's water supply. If the virus is activated, it will prevent the police and the fire department from receiving emergency calls. The virus will also cause the city's sewer system to contaminate the city's main reservoir. The Kesselmen Group makes one demand: that Mayor King resign so that the deputy mayor, Diane Robertson, can become mayor. As the mayor's chief of staff, what would you advise him to do? Explain the reason for your response using one of the ethical theories identified in Chapter 1 of this textbook.

Cyber-germ Warfare
When cyber-criminals use viruses to attack a computer system, they are engaged in cyber-warfare, cyber-germ warfare, electronic germ warfare. Clearly, viruses can be used to enter computer systems for many of the crimes listed previously. Thus, a cyber-extortionist can threaten to unleash a virus into a computer system unless

he or she is paid a certain amount of money. In effect, the cyber-extortionist is using the virus to extract ransom money from the business. Similarly, the cyber-terrorist or cyber-vandal can use a virus to disrupt a computer system for political or psychological reasons.

Federal Cybercrimes

Many states have enacted legislation to combat these cybercrimes and other cyber-offenses. The federal government has also attempted to deal with the issue by passing a number of anti-cybercrime statutes. The statutes of primary importance as determined by the Computer Crime and Intellectual Property Section of the United States Department of Justice include the Computer Fraud and Abuse Act (CFAA), the Electronic Communications Privacy Act (ECPA), the Communications Assistance for Law Enforcement Act (CALEA), the Economic Espionage Act (EEA), the National Stolen Property Act (NSPA), the Identity Theft and Assumption Deterrence Act (ITADA).

The Computer Fraud and Abuse Act (CFAA) Congress first specifically addressed the subject of cybercrime over two decades ago when, as a part of a comprehensive crime control statute, it passed the Computer Fraud and Abuse Act (CFAA). Currently, this act outlaws the following activities: obtaining national security information, compromising the confidentiality of a computer, trespassing in a government computer, accessing a computer to defraud, damaging a computer, damaging computer information, trafficking in passwords, and threatening to damage a computer.

The Electronic Communications Privacy Act (ECPA) Originally the Federal Wiretap Act was designed to cover only wire and oral communications. The Electronic Communications Privacy Act (ECPA) amended the original wiretap act to cover communication by computer. The purpose of the amendment was to protect the privacy of electronic communication in the same way that wire and oral communication are protected. To do this, the act prohibits the intentional interception of electronic communication.

The Communications Assistance for Law Enforcement Act (CALEA) The ECPA was later amended to help law enforcement officials keep pace with modern advances in electronic communication. The Communications Assistance for Law Enforcement Act (CALEA) amended the earlier law by requiring communication companies to update their electronic equipment in order to make certain that such law enforcement officers could carry out their surveillance duties properly.

The Economic Espionage Act (EEA) The Economic Espionage Act (EEA) is designed to protect trade secrets. A trade secret is a plan, process, or device that is used in a business and is known only to those employees who need to know the secret to carry out their work. Examples of trade secrets include customer lists, chemical formulas, manufacturing processes, marketing techniques, pricing methods, and food or beverage recipes (think *Coca-Cola*). The EEA outlaws the downloading of trade secrets.

The National Stolen Property Act (NSPA) Under the National Stolen Property Act (NSPA), it is a federal crime to use interstate or foreign commerce to transport personal property, currency, or securities that an individual is aware were stolen, were secured by fraud, or were taken by some other illegal method including an unauthorized electronic transfer.

The Identity Theft and Assumption Deterrence Act (ITADA) The Identity Theft and Assumption Deterrence Act (ITADA), which was amended by the Identity Theft Penalty Enhancement Act, outlaws the unauthorized transfer, possession, or use of a means of identifying another person to violate federal law. The amendment adds a new crime, called *aggravated identity theft* to the original statute. The section on aggravated identity theft makes it clear that identity theft is much worse when it involves certain very serious felonies, including terrorism.

The CAN SPAM Act   Spam is the nickname for all of those pop-up advertisements that appear on computer screens while users are tapped into the Internet. The CAN SPAM Act is designed to deal with this problem, as well as the problem of unsolicited commercial e-mail.

The Global Cyber-crisis

The U.S. government, U.S. corporations, and the U.S. military have become increasingly aware of both the power and the vulnerability of the Internet. National and global computer networks tie together a wide variety of systems that are used to make the global infrastructure more manageable, more efficient, and more affordable than ever before. Moreover, given the chance, very few of us would return to the days of manually controlled banking, line-of-sight air traffic control, in-person stock market trading, three-channel television, land-line rotary phones, and manually operated passenger rail service. Nevertheless, with efficiency and convenience comes a tradeoff. That tradeoff is vulnerability. The computer network is susceptible to collapse. A solar storm, a shift in the earth's magnetic field, a volcanic eruption, poorly written software, an incorrect file number, or inadequately maintained hardware can disrupt even the best computer system. Human operators can enter an outdated password, an inaccurate code, or the wrong person's PIN. Most of these errors are predictable and can be handled with a minimal amount of inconvenience. Other problems, those that are deliberate and knowingly target a computer system, are less easily solved.

For example, an enemy nation, a drug cartel, a crime syndicate, a gang of cyber-pirates, or a team of terrorists can, with a minimal amount of effort, send an e-mail with an attached PDF file that, when opened, will install a deadly software program in a computer system. The software might command the system to shut down, delete data, or, perhaps worse, transfer control of the system to the attacker. Generally, when this type of terror attack occurs, no one knows what happened until the damage is done. Thus, without warning, the nation's air traffic control system might be shut down, a city's water supply might be contaminated, a hospital's blood bank could lose refrigeration, or a banking system might be wiped clean of all transactions. Constructing a plan for dealing with a deliberate computer attack is difficult at best. Nevertheless, steps must be taken to deal with such attacks. (See "Briefing Cyberwar: War in the Fifth Domain," *The Economist*, July 3, 2010, p. 25.)

Cyber-Strategies and Cyber-Solutions   One step might be to split up data and send it along a series of different routes so that, if one data stream is compromised, the others continue on their way unimpeded. This strategy is effective most of the time. However, even this tactic does not always work. One weakness in the submerged fiber-optic cable system, along which many data streams travel, is a network of bottlenecks, sites at which these streams intersect and fall under the control of a limited number of domain-name servers, making them tempting targets for cyber-criminals and cyber-terrorists. These bottlenecks appear in the Middle East, in South East Asia, and along the Eastern seaboard of the United States, any one of which is a tempting target. (See "Briefing Cyberwar: War in the Fifth Domain," p. 25.)

Cyber-Command (Cybercom)   The federal government has responded to these threats in a number of ways. First, the Pentagon has established a new cyber-command center which is charged with the job of protecting the military's computer command system. This new agency, which is officially referred to as Cyber Command or Cybercom, is under the control of the National Security Agency. It has been charged not only with protecting the American cyber-system from attack, but also with developing plans to undermine the computer systems of enemy nations. One of its goals might be to protect the "chokepoints" in the submerged fiber-optic system, but also to uncover effective ways to use the system in a way that benefits the American military (See "Briefing Cyberwar: War in the Fifth Domain," p. 25.)

Internet Crime Complaint Center (IC3) On the homefront, the federal government has taken steps to combat domestic cybercrime by establishing the Internet Crime Complaint Center (AKA IC3). The IC3 operates as a joint venture between the National White Collar Crime Center (NW3C) and the Federal Bureau of Investigation (FBI). The IC3 handles complaints involving cybercrimes such as hacking, trade secret infringement, identity theft, cyber-extortion, and internet fraud. Individuals and businesses can file complaints with the IC3 by accessing their Web site online. The IC3 also works closely with administrative agencies as well as with local, state, and federal law enforcement agencies. (See *Internet Crime Complaint Center,* http://www.ic3.gov)

Domestic Strategies The battle against cyber-abuse can now be fought in the home. Using a variety of computer software programs, parents can filter e-mails, text messages, and social site contacts on the Internet to prevent their children from receiving messages that are symptomatic of cyber-bullying and similar unwanted cyber-contacts. One popular weapon in this battle is the MouseMail software package developed by Safe Communications. The MouseMail stystem permits a parents to have e-mails, text messages, and other cyber-contacts heading to their children to be intercepted and filtered by a rapid comparison between the content of the message and a list of improper words. Unfamiliar senders are also tagged. The tagged messages are sent to the parents first who handle them from that point on. Other similar software packages include Cyber/Bully/Alert.com and Social Shield.com. (See Mike Snyder, "MouseMail Traps Kids' Cyberbullies," *USA Today,* January 5, 2011), 1A; see also *Welcome to Mouse Mail,* http://mousemail.com.)

---

quick quiz 5-4

1. Statutory definitions and classifications of cybercrimes have become uniform within all jurisdictions in the United States. true | false

2. Cyber-trespass is defined as gaining access to a computer with the intent to commit a crime. true | false

3. The federal government has passed several cybercrime statutes. true | false

---

5-5 Defenses to Criminal Liability

Because criminal liability lies within the elements of an act and the required mental state, a logical defense would be aimed at eliminating one or both of those elements. Most defenses attempt to do just that. The most common defenses are insanity, entrapment, justifiable force, and mistake. (See Table 5-1.)

The Insanity Defense

Although the insanity defense has been around for a long time, many people do not understand the nature of the defense. One of the key points of confusion is the difference between *competency to stand trial* and the *insanity defense* itself.

Table 5-1 Criminal Liability and Defenses	
Criminal Liability	**Criminal Defenses**

The act:
  Criminal behavior specifically
    outlined by statute
	Defenses to the act:
	  Act as defined is "status" only
	  Act as defined is ambiguous
	  Act as defined is overbroad

The mental state:
  Mental state specifically
    outlined by statute
  Purpose
  Knowledge
  Recklessness
  Negligence
	Defenses to the mental state:
	  Insanity
	  Entrapment
	  Justifiable force
	  Mistake

Competency to Stand Trial Criminal defendants are generally presumed to be mentally competent to stand trial. However, the issue of competency to stand trial can be raised if the court, the defense attorney, or the prosecutor suspects that the defendant is not competent. If the issue of competency is raised, the defendant will undergo psychiatric examinations to determine his or her level of competency. Generally, defendants are considered competent to stand trial if they understand the nature and the purpose of the charges against them, and if they are capable of aiding their attorneys in their defense. When defendants are found to be incompetent, they are usually given treatment to improve their competency level so that they can understand what is going on and can assist in their case.

EXAMPLE 5-2: Competency and the Ability to Assist

The question of competency to stand trial was a key factor in a case in which Harold Gunther was prosecuted for the murder of one person and the attempted murder of two others. Listening at the door of an apartment, Gunther believed he heard three co-workers plotting against him. Convinced that he was about to be attacked, Gunther entered the apartment and assaulted his three co-workers, killing one and severely injuring the other two. Gunther consistently maintained that he was the intended target of a plot to destroy him. No evidence was ever presented that such a plot existed. In contrast, expert testimony indicated that Gunther was paranoid and delusional. Consequently, his defense attorney moved for a competency hearing. Despite the expert testimony, the judge in the case found Gunther competent to stand trial. The competency ruling was based on the fact that, despite Gunther's mental problems, he was capable of understanding the charges against him and was able to assist in his defense. Under state law, these were the only qualifications needed for a competency finding by the court. Gunther met these qualifications and was found competent to stand trial.

Not Guilty by Reason of Insanity (NGRI) American law recognizes that individuals cannot be held responsible for their actions if they do not know what they are doing. In addition, it serves no practical purpose to imprison someone who needs the care of mental health professionals. For these reasons, insanity is recognized as a valid defense to criminal conduct.

The oldest test of insanity is the M'Naughten Rule. Under this rule, a defendant can be found NGRI if, at the time the criminal act was committed, he or she was suffering from a mental disease that was so serious that the defendant did not know the nature of the act or did not know that act was wrong. Another test of insanity is the irresistible impulse test. This test holds that criminal defendants can be found NGRI if, at the time of the offense, they were stricken with a mental disease that prevented them from knowing right from wrong or that compelled them to commit the crime.

Under the American Law Institute (ALI) test, a person is not responsible if "as a result of mental disease or defect he lacks substantial capacity either to appreciate the criminality of his conduct or to conform his conduct to the requirements of law." The ALI test is plainly a relaxation of the usual insanity standard, as expressed in M'Naughten and the irresistible impulse test, because both of the older tests require "total" rather than "substantial" impairment. M'Naughten requires an inability to appreciate the wrongfulness of an action, and the irresistible impulse test requires a thorough loss of self-control.

It is important to understand that people found not guilty by reason of insanity do not automatically go free. Instead, they are committed to institutions and must undergo periodic psychiatric examinations. Once they are found to be sane, they may be released. Many people object to the fact that these individuals can look forward to release without serving any time in prison.

Entrapment

If a law enforcement officer induces a law-abiding citizen to commit a crime, entrapment may be used as a defense. The person using the defense must show that the crime would not have been committed had it not been for the inducement of the officer. The defense of entrapment is not available to a defendant who would have committed the crime even without the involvement of the officer. This factor is referred to as the propensity to commit the crime. The entrapment defense can be used in many different types of criminal cases. However, it occurs most often when the police have engineered a sting operation designed to tempt individuals who already have the propensity to commit the crime in question. Often in a sting operation, the main players are undercover law enforcement officers. However, sometimes they can be informants or reformed crminals who are used by the police to tempt individuals who are known by the police to be presently involved in a pattern of criminal activity. The fact that the police have used informants rather than undercover agents will not negate the entrapment defense, as long as all of the other elements are present.

Justifiable Force

In general, the law will not condone the use of force to solve problems. Still, special circumstances may arise that justify the use of force. Three of these situations lead to the following defenses: self-defense, defense of others, and battered spouse syndrome.

Self-Defense
When individuals have good reason to believe that they are in danger of death or serious injury, they can use force to protect themselves. This action is known as self-defense. In some states, the person claiming self-defense must retreat, if possible, before resorting to force. However, a person does not have a duty to retreat before using force if the attack occurs in his or her own home. When self-defense is used in a criminal case, the defendant must show that he or she was not the one who started the altercation in the

first place. Moreover, in all cases, the person claiming self-defense must not have used more force than necessary to stop the unprovoked attack.

Defense of Others

Defense of Others If a person uses force to rescue another person who is the victim of an apparent attack, most states will allow the rescuer to escape criminal liability. This exception is known as the defense of others. As in the case of self-defense, the rescuer must have good reason to believe that the victim was in danger of severe bodily injury or even death.

Battered Spouse Syndrome

Battered Spouse Syndrome The law also protects a married individual from being abused by his or her spouse. In most cases of spouse abuse, the wife is victimized by the violent outbursts of her husband. Many communities have established shelters where abused and battered wives can seek safety and receive counseling and legal services for themselves and their children. Wives who wish to protect themselves from the continual abuse caused by their husbands may seek legal help from the courts.

One such remedy is a *protective order.* Protective orders bar the abusing spouse from maintaining any contact with the victim. Such orders are enforced by the local police. Unfortunately, protective orders are not always effective. In some very severe cases, the victimized spouse has taken the law into her own hands and killed her tormentor. The set of circumstances that leads a woman to believe that the only way that she can escape death or severe bodily injury is to use force against her tormentor is called battered spouse syndrome. These circumstances are also known as *battered woman* or *battered wife syndrome.* Because the spouse had good reason to believe that she was in danger of death or severe bodily injury, battered spouse syndrome is considered a form of self-defense in some courts.

Mistake

Mistake is a defense to charges of criminal liability, as long as the mistake destroys one of the elements necessary to that crime. If the mistake does not destroy an element, it is not a valid defense. To be a successful defense, the mistake must be based on a reasonable belief. It would be no defense for a defendant to say that he shot his wife because he believed she was an invader from Mars. Note also that it is not a defense for an accused to say that she did not know that this particular conduct was prohibited by law. Nor is it a defense to a gambling charge for the defendant to argue that she did not know that the gambling law applied to her. Finally, the mistake must destroy the criminal nature of the act in the mind of the accused. It would be no defense, for example, if a defendant argued that he injured an individual by mistake when he was actually trying to injure someone else.

---

quick quiz 5-5

1. Most defendants who are found NGRI are released immediately.   true | false

2. A person does not have to retreat to his or her own home before resorting to force to repel an attack.   true | false

3. Mistake is never a defense to a charge of criminal liability.   true | false

Summary

5.1 A crime is an offense against the public at large. As such, a crime threatens the peace, safety, and well-being of the entire community. For this reason, crimes are punishable by the official governing body of a nation or state. A felony is a crime punishable by death or imprisonment in a federal or a state prison for a term exceeding one year. Some felonies are also punishable by fines. A misdemeanor is a less serious crime that is generally punishable by a prison sentence of not more than one year.

5.2 The two elements necessary to create criminal liability are (a) an act and (b) the requisite state of mind. Generally speaking, a crime cannot be committed unless the criminal act named in the statute is performed with the requisite state of mind. Many state criminal codes include four possible states of mind: (a) purpose, (b) knowledge, (c) recklessness, and (d) negligence. Establishing motive may help investigators pinpoint the guilty party, but proving an evil motive is not necessary for a criminal conviction. Conversely, establishing the existence of a good motive will rarely absolve a defendant of criminal liability.

5.3 Crimes against people include but are certainly not limited to first-degree murder, second-degree murder, manslaughter, battery, and assault. A more recent addition to this list involves hate speech. Crimes against property include but are not limited to burglary; breaking and entering; trespass; aggravated arson; arson; aggravated robbery; robbery; theft; fraud, and related offenses. Crimes involving business include embezzlement, forgery, criminal simulation, passing bad checks, and defrauding creditors. RICO offenses also involve business crime. Crimes against justice include bribery, theft in office, and dereliction of duty. Others, such as intimidation, are committed against a public official or public servant. Still others, such as obstruction of justice, resisting arrest, perjury, and tampering with evidence are committed against the justice system itself.

5.4 Cybercrimes include cyber-trespass, which involves any conventional crime committed with a computer. Cybercrimes that focus on the use of a computer include cyber-extortion, cyber-stalking, cyber-harassment, cyber-assault, cyber-bullying, cyber-spoofing, phishing, smishing, and vishing. Crimes that target computers include cyber-terrorism, identity theft, cyber-vandalism, and cyber-germ warfare. Federal cybercrimes include Computer Fraud and Abuse Act (CFAA), the Electronic Communications Privacy Act (ECPA), the Communications Assistance for Law Enforcement Act (CALEA), the Economic Espionage Act (EEA), the National Stolen Property Act (NSPA), the Identity Theft and Assumption Deterrence Act ((ITADA).

5.5 Because criminal liability relies on the two essential elements of act and requisite mental state, a logical defense aims at eliminating one or both of those elements. Most defenses attempt to do just that. The most common defenses are insanity, entrapment, justifiable force, and mistake.

Key Terms

aggravated arson, 98

aggravated burglary, 97

aggravated murder, 96

aggravated robbery, 98

American Law Institute (ALI) test, 108

arson, 98

assault, 97

battered spouse syndrome, 109

battery, 97

breaking and entering, 97

bribery, 99

burglary, 97

crime, 87

criminal simulation, 99

cyber-trespass, 101

cyber-extortion, 101

defense of others, 109

defrauding creditors, 99

dereliction of duty, 100

double jeopardy, 88

embezzlement, 98

entrapment, 100

felony, 89

first-degree murder, 96

forgery, 99

fraud, 98

homicide, 96

intimidation, 100

involuntary manslaughter, 96

irresistible impulse test, 108	perjury, 100	self-defense, 108
knowledge, 91	premeditated murder, 96	tampering with evidence, 100
misdemeanor, 90	purpose, 91	theft, 98
M'Naughten Rule, 108	recklessness, 92	theft in office, 100
negligence, 92	resisting arrest, 100	trespass, 97
obstruction of justice, 100	robbery, 98	voluntary manslaughter, 96
passing bad checks, 99	second-degree murder, 96	

Questions for Review and Discussion

1. What is the purpose of criminal law?
2. What are the various categories and classes of crimes?
3. What is the nature of an act according to the meaning of criminal liability?
4. What are the four mental states that can be found in the criminal code?
5. What is motive, and how does it differ from the elements of criminal liability?
6. What are the various crimes against people?
7. What are the various theories involved in criminal punishment?
8. What are the various ways that the federal government has dealt with cybercrime?
9. What are the three standards for the insanity defense found in criminal law?
10. What are the requirements of entrapment as a defense against criminal liability?

Cases for Analysis

1. Fred Pomeroy was an assistant traffic manager for the New York Central and Hudson River Railroad Company. In that capacity, he handed out "rebates" to the American Sugar Refining Company in New York and New Jersey and to W. H. Edgar & Son in Detroit. The goal of the rebates was to convince the sugar refiner and the sugar dealer, to use the railroad for their shipments rather than some other method. The problem with this arrangement was that the shipping rates were fixed by federal law and, thus, the rebates amounted to a bribe. Pomeroy and New York Central were prosecuted under the Elkins Act and were found guilty. On an appeal that went all the way to the U.S. Supreme Court, New York Central argued that, while Pomeroy could be prosecuted under the criminal statute, the corporation could not. Can the corporation be prosecuted? What theory would you advise the court to use in this case? Explain. What will the outcome be? (See *New York Central & Hudson River Railroad v. United States,* 212 U.S. 481 (U.S. Supreme Court).)

2. The hospitality industry in Portland, Oregon, instituted an organization that was designed to bring

convention business to the city. Association members made fixed contributions to the organization and companies in the supply business were expected to donate funds based on a percentage of their sales. Supply companies that did not contribute were boycotted by the membership. This boycott was a clear violation of the federal Sherman Antitrust Act. Both the president of Hilton Hotels Corporation and the manager of the Portland Hilton ordered the purchasing agent of the Portland Hotel to ignore the boycott entirely and to make purchases based only on the quality of the products and service from suppliers. The purchasing agent for the Portland Hilton, however, out of personal resentment toward the sales rep of a particular supplier, enforced the boycott. After being found guilty of violating federal law, Hilton appealed, arguing that the trial court misinterpreted the law because the corporation could only be held liable if the purchasing agent committed a crime within the scope of employment with the intention that the corporation gain some benefit from that crime. In this case, it was clear that the agent had committed a crime but the acts were not within the scope of employment because he had been expressly forbidden to continue the boycott. What was the result on appeal? Explain. *United States v. Hilton Hotels Corporation*, 467 F. 2d 1000 (9th Circuit).

3. After Charles Hood was convicted of murder, he was sentenced to death in accordance with Texas law. It was later revealed, however, that the judge who presided at Hood's trial had been involved in a lengthy affair with the prosecutor in the case. Neither the judge nor the prosecutor had revealed this relationship during the trial. Moreover, after the trial, they denied the relationship until they were compelled to tell the truth under oath. The Texas Court of Criminal Appeals later agreed to a new sentencing hearing for Hood. However, the hearing was limited to questions concerning the jury instructions and, therefore, did not involve the conflict of interest problem caused by the affair. Hood filed a petition for certiorari with the United States Supreme Court. Should the U.S. Supreme Court hear the case? Explain. See Mark White, "Death Penalty Must Be Fair," *The National Law Journal*, March 29, 2010, p. 43.)

4. Antonio Martinez, also known as Muhammad Hussain, discussed the killing of American soldiers with an unnamed individual who, unknown to Martinez, was actually an FBI informant. The informant passed that information to FBI agents who arranged a sting operation during which Martinez helped build a phony car bomb. Martinez was arrested as he attempted to set off the phony car bomb in front of a recruiting center in suburban Baltimore. Martinez claimed that he was entrapped by the federal agents. Martinez's attorney argued that the defendant was not capable of developing the plan to make the bomb on his own. The federal attorney also argued that Martinez had clearly been making plans to attack U.S. soldiers before the informant contacted him. The federal attorney also argued that whether Martinez was capable of actually building a bomb on his own did not matter since, he not only believed that he could do it, but also actually tried to do it, and would have done it had the bomb not been a fake. The prosecuting attorney also had a tape of Martinez arming the bomb. The video shows that Martinez enjoyed the prospect of killing the soldiers. Was Martinez entrapped? Explain by outlining the elements of entrapment. "Lawyer

Argues Entrapment in Bomb Plot," *The New York Times*, December 14, 2010, p. 18.)

5. Katie Roberts was wasting away from the effects of an incurable disease. She asked her husband Frank to help her commit suicide. In response to her request, Mr. Roberts mixed poison and water and placed the mixture on a chair within her reach. She took the poison and died several hours later. Mr. Roberts admitted placing the poison within her reach but denied having the required mental state for first-degree murder because he was responding to his wife's request and was motivated by love and mercy. Will he prevail? Explain. *People v. Roberts,* 178 N.W.690 (MI).

6. Several teenagers taped the broken legs of a chair together to create a cross, which they then ignited and placed on the lawn of an African-American family in the neighborhood. One of the teenagers, a minor, was charged with a misdemeanor under the St. Paul Bias-Motivated Crime Ordinance. The St. Paul ordinance criminalized the placing on private property of any "symbol, object, appellation, characterization or graffiti . . . which one knows or has reasonable grounds to know arouses anger, alarm, or resentment in others on the basis of race, color, creed, religion or gender." The defendant argued that the ordinance was an unconstitutional violation of the First Amendment. The city contended that the statute was constitutional because it was necessary for the preservation of a compelling state interest, namely, the right of group members who have been discriminated against in the past "to live in peace where they wish." Is the St. Paul ordinance constitutional? Explain. *R.A.V. v. St. Paul,* 505 U.S. 1992 (U.S. Sup. Ct.).

7. Tomas Reese entered a fast-food restaurant before the restaurant had opened for business through an unlocked rear entrance. The door had been left unlocked by an accomplice who was an employee of the restaurant. After entering the restaurant, Reese pushed one employee against a soda machine and, while holding a gun to the neck of the manager, forced her to open the safe. Reese then locked the employees in a cooler and fled the scene with over $5,000. Has Reese committed burglary, robbery, or larceny? Explain. *State v. Reese,* 113 Ohio App. 3d. 642 (OH).

8. Cuttiford and Banks lived in the same duplex; Banks lived upstairs and Cuttiford lived down-

stairs. The two apartments shared a common internal stairway at the back of the duplex. A confrontation began between Banks and Cuttiford in the rear stairway of the duplex. Banks became rather violent and threatened Cuttiford and Cuttiford's wife. Cuttiford went to his apartment on the bottom floor and retrieved two guns from his bedroom. When he returned to the back door near the stairway, Banks told him, "You don't have the guts to use that, because you're going to have to use it because I'm going to kill you!" Banks then came at Cuttiford, lunging from the common stairway into the kitchen of the Cuttiford's apartment. Cuttiford then shot and killed Banks. At trial, Cuttiford argued that he shot Banks in self-defense. The trial court refused to instruct the jury that Cuttiford did not have to retreat into his own home before acting to repel an attacker. The court apparently believed the prosecution, which had argued that because Banks and Cuttiford occupied the same duplex, Cuttiford had the duty to retreat before repelling Banks's attack. Was the trial court judge correct in his instruction to the jury regarding self-defense? Explain. *State v. Cuttiford,* 639 N.E.2d 472 (OH).

9. Cowen had on many occasions operated as a paid drug informant for the FBI and the Ventura Police Department. The Ventura police asked Cowen to keep in touch with them, should he become involved in any deals. Subsequently, Cowen asked Busby to introduce him to any drug dealers he knew. Busby introduced Cowen to Mandell, who sold Cowen several samples of cocaine in anticipation of a $41,500 deal. Cowen then contacted the Ventura police. A police officer posed as Cowen's buyer, and both Busby and Mandell were arrested and eventually turned over to the federal authorities. Busby was convicted of possession of cocaine with the intent to distribute it. He appealed this conviction, claiming that he had been entrapped by Cowen. Will Busby's entrapment defense succeed on appeal? Explain. *United States v. Busby,* 780 F.2d 804 (9th Cir.).

quick quiz Answers

5-1	5-2	5-3	5-4	5-5
1. F	1. T	1. T	1. F	1. F
2. F	2. F	2. F	2. T	2. T
3. F	3. F	3. T	3. T	3. F

Chapter 6   Tort Law and Cybertorts

THE OPENING CASE   Jurisicience and Tort Law: *Daubert v. Merrell Dow Pharmaceuticals, Inc.*

The law is a balancing act that struggles to assimilate new ideas while maintaining useful and effective traditions. Sometimes this balancing act works well; and sometimes it just falls apart. A case in point is *Daubert v. Merrell Dow Pharmaceuticals, Inc.,* a United States Supreme Court case in which the frontiers of science and the cultural paradigms of the law collide. The case involves a lawsuit filed by the Dauberts against Merrell Dow in which the plaintiffs argue that Bendectin, a drug produced by Merrell Dow, and taken by Mrs. Daubert for nausea during her pregnancy, had caused birth defects in their children. The case depends on the issue of causation, a traditional tort law principle that says that, to succeed in a negligence lawsuit, a plaintiff must prove that the defendant's action caused the plaintiff's injury. However, because of the scientific nature of the case, the court needed expert testimony to determine causation. This point in the case, the point at which science and the law intersect, is referred to as *jusriscience.*

The judges at each level, from the trial court, through the appellate court, up to the Supreme Court, and then back down to the appellate court, had to weigh the scientific evidence on causation leading from the development of the drug Bendectin to the birth defects. The judges were faced with two competing lines of evidence, one presented by the plaintiffs, the other by the defendants. The defendants' evidence included peer-reviewed articles published in scientific journals and studies issued by the Federal Drug Administration (FDA). None of these reports or articles could find a link between Bendectin and birth defects. In response, the plaintiff's scientific experts offered a reanalysis of the accepted data. This reanalysis demonstrated that the original data had been badly misinterpreted by previous scientists.

To determine which line of evidence should be followed, the court had to interpret Rule 702 of the Federal Rules of Evidence and *Frye v. United States,* a case that predated Rule 702, but that had, nevertheless, set up a standard that the federal courts had used for decades to evaluate expert testimony. Ultimately, the Supreme Court decided that expert evidence did not have to be "generally accepted" as *Frye* had suggested, because some scientific discoveries may be "too particular, too new, or of too limited interest to be published." The court thus emphasized that the Rules had to be interpreted liberally rather than narrowly in determining the use of expert testimony. Still, the Supreme Court concluded that such testimony did have to "rest on a reliable foundation and (be) relevant to the task at hand." Since the lower courts had used only the *Frye* standard, the case was sent back to the appeals court, which still supported Merrell Dow because the evidence produced by the plaintiffs did not demonstrate a definite causation link between Bendictin and birth defects. [See *Daubert v. Merrell Dow Pharmaceuticals, Inc.,* (509 U.S. 579) (U.S.S.Ct.); see also *Daubert v. Merrell Dow Pharmaceuticals, Inc.,* 43 F.3d 1311 (Ninth Circuit)]

Opening Case Questions

1. Would *Daubert v. Merrell Dow Pharmaceuticals, Inc.* be a civil lawsuit or a criminal action? Explain.

2. Was *Daubert v. Merrell Dow Pharmaceuticals, Inc.,* heard in state or federal court? Explain.

3. What legal theory or theories might be used to hold a corporation liable for the torts of an employee? Explain.

4. How does causation fit into a case like this? Explain.

5. Could a case be constructed based on strict liability in the *Daubert* case? Why or why not?

Learning Objectives

1. Differentiate between the objectives of tort law and those of criminal law.
2. Outline the nature of *respondeat superior.*
3. Describe the element of duty.
4. Identify the principal intentional torts and outline the elements of each.
5. Explain the four elements of negligence.
6. Contrast contributory negligence, comparative negligence, and assumption of the risk.
7. Judge when the doctrine of strict liability applies.
8. Discuss the emerging trends in cybertort law.
9. Outline the various remedies available in tort law.
10. Point out some developments in tort reform.

6-1 Tort Law Defined

A tort is a private wrong that injures another person's physical well-being, emotional health, business, property, or reputation. The English word "tort" comes from the Latin word *tortus,* which can be translated as "twisted." A person who commits a tort and has thus engaged in "twisted" behavior is called a tortfeasor. The other party is alternately referred to as the injured party, the innocent party, the victim, or the plaintiff if a lawsuit has been filed. In the case of a lawsuit, the tortfeasor would be called a defendant.

Tort Law versus Criminal Law

One purpose of tort law is to compensate the injured party for his or her loss. Another objective is to protect potential victims by deterring future tortious behavior. In contrast as noted in the previous chapter, criminal law involves a public wrong, that is, a wrong that affects the entire society. When a crime is committed, the government authorities begin a legal procedure that is designed to remove the offender from society, and to punish that offender to the fullest extent allowed by the law. As noted in the last chapter, however, it is possible for a single act to be both a crime and a tort. As noted in the chapter on criminal law, the U.S. Constitution protects people from being tried twice for the same crime. This rule is known as the principle of *double jeopardy*. Double jeopardy does not protect a defendant from being sued under tort law for the consequences of an action, even if that defendant has already been tried for the same wrongdoing in a criminal court using criminal law.

Respondeat Superior

About the Law

The doctrine of *respondeat superior* is also known as vicarious liability.

In criminal law the courts will hold a corporation liable when an employee commits a crime on the job to benefit the corporation. In like fashion, in tort law the courts use *respondeat superior* to hold a business or organization liable for the torts of an employee whenever an employee commits a tort while working for that business or organization. Later in the book, when we reach the chapter on agency law, this concept will be examined in depth and the proper legal terms of *master* and *servant* will be explained at length. For now it is enough to remember that employers are at risk in tort law when their employees commit torts, and for that reason alone, both employers and employees must have some working knowledge of tort law.

The Element of Duty

One approach to the law is to think of legal liability in terms of elements. This approach emphasizes that no liability can be imposed against an individual unless all the elements are present. In tort law, the first element is duty. A duty is an obligation placed on individuals because of the law. The second element is a violation of that duty. A duty can be violated intentionally, through negligence, or under the theory of strict liability.

Causation and Juriscience

A negligence case requires the plaintiffs to prove that the defendants caused their injuries. In negligence cases there are two kinds of causation, actual cause and proximate cause. These two types of causation will be examined at length later in the chapter. However, for now it is enough to point out that actual cause is cause "in fact" or "real" cause. Real cause exists in the physical universe and is thus subject to experiments, tests, measurements, and other forms of proof. This means that the plaintiff will often have to use scientific evidence to demonstrate how action "A" led to effect "B." Moreover, because of the scientific nature of a case, the court generally needs to hear the testimony of an expert to determine causation. This stage in a case, where science and the law intersect, is referred to as juriscience.

THE OPENING CASE *Revisited, Part I*

Juriscience and Tort Law: *Daubert v. Merrell Dow Pharmaceuticals, Inc.* Round 2

In the *Daubert v. Merrell Dow Pharmaceuticals, Inc.,* the Dauberts sued Merrill Dow in tort law. The Dauberts argued that Merrell Dow had produced and marketed a dangerous drug named Bendectin. Mrs. Daubert took that drug for nausea during her pregnancy which caused birth defects in her children, or so the argument goes. The case is grounded in negligence which requires the plaintiff to prove the existence of four elements: (a) duty, (b) breach of duty, (c) proximate cause, and (d) actual harm or injury. Duty exists when one party has a responsibility not to harm another party. Since the idea of duty is at the center of tort law it is rarely, if ever, at issue. In the *Daubert* case, it would be nothing short of ludicrous for Merrell Dow to argue that it has no duty to the people who take their drugs.

THE OPENING CASE *Revisited, Part II*
Juriscience and Tort Law: *Daubert v. Merrell Dow Pharmaceuticals, Inc.* Round 3

In *Daubert v. Merrell Dow Pharmaceuticals, Inc.*, the Dauberts sued Merrell Dow because Bendectin, a drug produced by Merrell Dow, caused birth defects in their children. The case revolved around the issue of causation. In a negligence case, the plaintiff must prove that the defendant's action caused the plaintiff's injury. The corporation, however, cannot act on its own. It can only act through its employees. This is why, in a case like *Daubert v. Merrell Dow Pharmaceuticals*, the plaintiffs must be aware of the doctrine of *respondeat superior*. The doctrine of *respondeat superior* requires that (a) the defendants (those who committed the tort) were actually employed by Merrell Dow and (b) those employees were on the job when they developed Bendectin. None of this seems to have been at issue in this case. The real issue was the alleged negligence of Merrell Dow in placing a dangerous drug on the market. As we will see later, this is why expert testimony was required in the case.

Judges at all levels, but especially those in the trial courts, must determine the validity of scientific evidence. Unfortunately, because the law is an adversarial process, judges will frequently be forced to choose between two or more competing lines of scientific proof. Judges, however, are educated in the law not science, and so they need help unraveling the intricacies of scientific evidence beyond simply listening to the experts, many of whom may have hidden agendas.

The Federal Rules of Evidence provide some help. After *Daubert v. Merrell Dow*, the federal rule on expert testimony was amended to help judges make this determination. The rule states that an expert may testify on a scientific matter as long as, "(1) testimony is based upon sufficient facts or data, (2) the testimony is the product of reliable scientific principles and methods, and (3) the witness has applied the principles and methods reliably to the facts in the case." Still, even this standard is somewhat vague and ambiguous. Many questions remain unanswered. Who is to determine when testimony has reached a level of "sufficient facts or data"? What makes a scientific principle or method "reliable"? How will the judge know when a witness has applied a principle in a reliable way? Some states have tried to be more specific in the formulation of this rule. Ohio, for example, as gone so far as to say that, if an expert witness bases an opinion on a test or an experiment, that test or experiment is reliable *only* if *all* of the following apply: "(1) the theory upon which the procedure, test, or experiment is based is objectively verifiable or validly derived from widely accepted knowledge, facts, or principles; (2) the design of the procedure, test, experiment reliably implements the theory; and (3) the particular procedure, test, or experiment was conducted in a way that will yield an accurate result."

quick quiz 6-1

1. A person who commits a tort is engaged in "twisted" behavior.   true | false

2. The purpose of tort law is to protect the public at large.   true | false

3. Employers are never liable for the torts of their employees because such a move would violate the constitutional prohibition against double jeopardy.   true | false

6-2 Intentional Torts

Intentional violations of duty include a vast variety of intentional torts, all of which have their own individual elements. Table 6-1 summarizes the primary intentional torts.

Assault and Battery

Under U.S. tort law, assault and battery, though often closely associated with each other, are separate torts. An assault occurs when the victim is placed in fear or apprehension of immediate bodily harm by a tortfeasor who has the present apparent ability to inflict that harm. No actual physical contact is needed for an assault. The essence of the tort lies in the fear or apprehension that is created in the victim.

EXAMPLE 6-1: Assault with a Deadly Dart

Terry Kline and Patrick Fisher were playing a friendly game of darts at the Wood Street Tavern one evening when they invited Fred Feeney and David Ballentine to join them. Unknown to either Kline or Feeney, Ballentine was intoxicated. After losing several games, Ballentine became enraged and tried to hit Kline by throwing several darts at him. In his intoxicated state, Ballentine's aim was poor, and he did not hit Kline. Nevertheless, Ballentine has committed an assault.

Table 6-1 Intentional Torts	
Tort	**Definition**
Assault	An assault occurs when the victim is placed in fear or apprehension of immediate bodily harm by tortfeasor who has the present apparent ability to inflict that harm.
Battery	A battery involves an offensive or harmful, unprivileged touching.
False imprisonment	When one party prevents another party from moving about freely, the first party has committed the intentional tort of false imprisonment.
Defamation	Any false statement communicated to others that harms a person's good name or reputation may constitute the tort of defamation.
Invasion of privacy	Invasion of privacy occurs when one person unreasonably denies another person the right to be left alone.
Misuse of legal procedure	Misuse of legal procedure occurs when one person brings a legal procedure action with malice and without probable cause.
Intentional infliction of emotional distress	Intentional or reckless infliction of emotional distress occurs when an individual causes another to undergo emotional or mental suffering, even without an accompanying physical injury.
Disparagement	Disparagement involves any false statement communicated to others that somehow questions the quality of an item of property or that raises uncertainty as to who actually has legal ownership rights to the property in question.
Fraud	Fraud involves false statements or actions, or a combination thereof, that misrepresent facts so that an innocent party relies on those misrepresentations and suffers an injury or loss as a result.

A battery involves an offensive or harmful, unprivileged touching. Naturally, if in Example 6-1, Ballentine had actually managed to hit Kline, he would have committed a battery. However, as the definition points out, a touching need not be harmful to be a battery. Moreover, a battery does not always require the touching of the actual person of the victim, if the tortfeasor touches something closely associated with that victim. So, if a prankster pulls a chair out from under someone before that person sits down, and the person falls to the floor, the joker has committed a battery. Or if he or she knocks a cafeteria tray out of a diner's hands, again he or she has committed a battery, despite the fact that the actual person or the victim has not been contacted.

EXAMPLE 6-2: Battery by Antibody

Lucy Pickett works as a nurse at Garner County Hospital. Because she knows that her patient, Jim Luger, is afraid of needles, she sneaked up behind him and injected him with an antibiotic that had been ordered by his primary physician. Despite her desire to help Luger, and her wish to save him from feeling unnecessary fear, Pickett has committed a battery.

False Imprisonment

When one party prevents another party from moving about freely, the first party has committed the intentional tort of false imprisonment. This tort is called false arrest in some states. The victim of false imprisonment need not be locked in a prison or a jail cell. All that is required is that the person's freedom of movement be restricted. For example, a physician who refuses to return a patient's clothing until a partial payment is received for a long overdue bill has committed false imprisonment.

Store owners must be very careful about detaining suspected shoplifters, because such a detention could result in a false imprisonment lawsuit if not handled properly. Still, because of the growing problem of shoplifting in society today, most states have laws that allow storekeepers to detain a suspected shoplifter if they have reasonable grounds to suspect that a shoplifting incident has occurred. However, the storekeeper must detain the suspect in a reasonable manner and for no longer than a reasonable length of time.

Defamation and Disparagement

Intentional torts such as battery, assault, and false imprisonment involve direct physical and psychological injury to an individual. These injuries are not the only type of harm, however, that can be imposed on individuals in tort law. Sometimes the injury results from words that damage a reputation and lead to monetary loss. Two of these word-oriented torts are defamation and disparagement.

Defamation   Any false statement communicated to others that harms a person's good name or reputation may constitute the tort of defamation. To be defamatory, the statement must hold the victim up to ridicule, contempt, or hatred. Defamation in a temporary form, such as speech, is slander; in a permanent form, such as writing, movies, videocassettes, or DVDs, it is libel.

People can usually bring a libel suit whenever the permanent statement is damaging to their reputation, is false, and is communicated to a third party. However, under common law, individuals can bring slander lawsuits even if they have suffered no actual loss if the false statements fall into one of the following categories:

1.   An accusation that the victim of the slanderous statements has committed a very serious crime, such as murder or rape.

2.   An accusation that the victim has a communicable disease, such as venereal disease.

3.   An accusation that the victim has engaged in improprieties in a business, trade, or profession.

4.   An accusation that an unmarried female victim has been unchaste.

Individuals may speak the truth without being sued successfully for defamation as long as it is done without spite or ill will. In addition, statements made by senators and representatives on the floor of Congress and statements made in a court of law are privileged. Privileged statements are not the proper subject of a defamation lawsuit. The idea behind creating these privileges is to promote the open debate of legislative and judicial matters.

The U.S. Supreme Court has given journalists the extra protection of the actual malice test when they write about public officials. Under the actual malice test, a public official must prove not only that the statement made or printed was false but also that it was made with actual malice. Actual malice means that the statement was made or printed either with the knowledge that it was false or with a reckless disregard for its truth or falsity. Later decisions expanded the actual malice test to cover public figures. Public figures are people like television actors, sports figures, and rock stars who seek out public fame and are readily recognizable by the public at large.

Temporary public figures are people who are placed against their will into the public view by some event beyond their control. Disaster victims, hostages, and rescuers are examples of temporary public figures. Generally, such people are held to the actual malice test as long as their notoriety lasts.

Disparagement

Disparagement involves any false statement communicated to others that somehow questions the quality of property or raises uncertainty as to who has legal ownership of that property. Generally, to recover for disparagement, the plaintiff must show monetary loss. Such losses may include the loss of sales, money spent to correct the public's image of a product, or expenses spent on litigation due to the disparagement. The difference between defamation and disparagement is that in defamation, the false charge is made about the victim's reputation, whereas with disparagement, the falsehood is made about a person's property or product. The falsehood usually casts doubt on the value of the product or on the property rights of the owner.

EXAMPLE 6-3: Toys, Tots, and Tall Tales

Warren Barrington owned and operated Toys and Tots—From Two to Twelve, a toy store that specialized in educational toys for children between two and twelve years of age. Barrington and his wife, who operated the store as a partnership, did their best to market only original toys made of natural materials. Electronic toys, computers, and toys made of plastic were never sold in the store. During the National Toy and Model Association of America convention, Raymond Matthews, who owned a competitive shop, started several rumors, most of which suggested that many of the toys that were being shown by the Barringtons at the convention were not made of natural materials as advertised. He also suggested that those toys that were made of natural materials involved ideas stolen from him and that the Barringtons did not have the right to market them as they were doing at the convention. Matthews has clearly committed disparagement here. He has planted false reports about both the value of the Barrington's products and about the Barrington's property rights to the toys.

Fraudulent Misrepresentation

Another word-oriented tort is fraudulent misrepresentation. Fraudulent misrepresentation, or fraud as it is known in some states, occurs when false statements or actions, or a combination thereof, are made by one party in a way that causes another party to rely on those misrepresentations and then to suffer an injury or loss as a result. Frequently, fraud involves a business relationship and works to destroy the mutual assent that ought to exist between the parties that are involved in a contract. For that reason, it is discussed at length in Chapter 9. However, fraud is also a tort and need not involve a contract.

Invasion of Privacy

The courts in the United States have consistently held that people have a right to privacy. Consequently, a violation of that right would involve the tort of invasion of privacy. The right to privacy can be violated in several ways:

1. Revelation of confidential records
2. Intrusion
3. Creating a false light
4. Exploitation

Revelation of Confidential Records
Individuals who, because of their jobs, work with confidential records containing private information must ensure that those records remain private. A failure to protect such confidential matters could result in an invasion of privacy lawsuit. Although it is not a violation of privacy for individuals to discuss confidential matters for professional reasons, it could be an invasion of privacy to discuss those same records for non-professional reasons. The motive of the person who releases the information does not matter. Moreover, whether there has been an invasion of privacy depends on the level of privacy expected by that person in that situation. For instance, an employee would expect privacy involving his or her employment record but not concerning the information that is printed on his or her identification badge.

Public officials and public figures, such as the President of the United States and his family, have little or no expectation of privacy when they are on stage at a political event. Therefore, they can not claim intrusion, when their photos end up on the front page of most every newspaper in the country.

Intrusion
An individual's privacy can also be violated if there is an unwarranted intrusion into the person's expectation of privacy. Such an intrusion might occur if a person's photograph is taken and then published on the front page of a local newspaper. The issue at the heart of such case is the question of whether the plaintiff had a high expectation of privacy. Recall that the expectation of privacy depends on the situation. A person walking across a college campus has a very low expectation of privacy, whereas a person who is in his or

her own home has a very high expectation of privacy. Thus, the publication of a photo of a person walking across campus would *not* be actionable as an invasion of privacy, but taking a similar photo while that person was in his or her home would be.

Creating a False Light

Creating a false light is closely akin to defamation because it involves the publication of information about a person that paints him or her in a way that the majority of the population would see as unfavorable. A fashion model who poses for photographs for a bathing suit catalog and finds her image printed in a sexually explicit magazine would have a cause of action for being placed in a false light.

Exploitation

The courts have held that an individual holds the rights to his or her own likeness to make money. An invasion of privacy can occur when one party uses an individual's photo, likeness, or name without permission for advertising, marketing, or publicity. Some courts treat the misappropriation of a person's likeness as a separate tort, calling it an invasion of the right to publicity.

Intentional Infliction of Emotional Distress

In recent years, the courts have recognized a tort called the intentional or reckless infliction of emotional distress. Before these more enlightened court decisions were handed down, victims who were injured emotionally by the wrongful acts of others could not recover damages without proving some sort of bodily injury. Today, in many states, someone who intentionally or recklessly causes another individual to undergo emotional or mental suffering will be responsible, even without an accompanying physical injury. The actions complained of must be extreme and outrageous and cause severe emotional suffering.

EXAMPLE 6-4: Extreme and Outrageous Silence

Marc Christian, who gained notoriety as the live-in boyfriend of Rock Hudson, sued the estate of the late actor for the intentional infliction of emotional distress. Christian argued that he had been induced to continue having "high-risk" sexual relations with the late screen star because Hudson had remained silent and failed to inform him that he had contracted AIDS. As a result of Hudson's misrepresentations, Christian contended that he suffered extreme emotional distress when he learned that Hudson was ill. This was true, Christian argued, despite the fact that he was not HIV positive himself. Although Hudson did not attempt deliberately to transfer the virus to Christian and did not plan to cause Christian emotional distress, the inherent harmfulness of Hudson's actions could easily amount to extreme and outrageous conduct.

Misuse of Legal Procedure

The intentional tort known as the misuse of legal procedure occurs when one person brings a legal action with malice and without probable cause. When the misuse of the legal procedure involves the filing of a false civil lawsuit, it is called wrongful civil proceedings. In contrast, when the misuse involves bringing false criminal charges, it is labeled malicious prosecution. Some states use only the term "malicious prosecution" to refer to both forms of the tort. All of the following conditions must be present for a lawsuit based on misuse of legal procedure to succeed:

1. The defendant (the person against whom the misuse of legal procedure suit has been filed) must have brought civil or criminal charges against the plaintiff at an earlier time.

2. The earlier case must have been resolved favorably for the plaintiff.

3. The plaintiff must prove that the earlier case was brought by the defendant with malice and without probable cause.

When these conditions are present, an individual may be able to recover damages from the defendant for making the innocent party the target of a legal action without a good cause.

A related cause of action, which can easily be confused with malicious prosecution, is abuse of process. Abuse of process occurs when a legal procedure is used for a purpose other than that for which it is intended. It differs from malicious prosecution in that there is no requirement that the earlier case be brought without probable cause or be resolved favorably for the plaintiff. The tort can involve either a criminal or a civil case. Typically, abuse of process happens when a perfectly legal process is used as a pressure tactic to convince someone to do something he or she would not be inclined to do under ordinary circumstances.

EXAMPLE 6-5: Misuse and Abuse: Crossing the Legal Line

Janice Franklin and Karen Yalta were involved in a very difficult dissolution of their partnership. As a result of this problematic dissolution, as well as many other factors, the two young women did not like each other. Accordingly, Franklin filed a lawsuit against Yalta for defamation. The lawsuit was resolved in Yalta's favor. Yalta then sued Franklin for wrongful civil proceedings. Yalta won the case because she was able to prove that the original defamation suit against her was fabricated by Franklin, who was motivated by hatred and ill will. This suit is an example of the misuse of legal proceedings. If Franklin had filed a defamation suit to force Yalta to agree to Franklin's terms in the dissolution, she would be involved in abuse of process. This involvement would be true even if Franklin had legitimate reasons for filing the defamation suit.

quick quiz 6-2

1. Assault and battery never exist simultaneously.   true | false

2. To be defamatory, a statement need not be communicated to a   true | false
   third party.

3. The intentional infliction of emotional distress has yet to be   true | false
   recognized as a tort in any state jurisdiction.

6-3 Negligence

People and property are sometimes injured even when no one intends that the injury occur. Such an occurrence is usually labeled an accident. Although no one acted with intent, someone was injured. The victim has experienced pain and suffering, lost wages, or incurred medical or repair bills. Justice demands that the injured party be compensated. The part of tort law that is concerned with the compensation of accident victims is called negligence.

Elements of Negligence

The issue before the court in a negligence action is as follows: Under what circumstances can the actions of an alleged tortfeasor be labeled negligent so that the victim can be compensated? Four elements must be present to establish negligence: legal duty, breach of duty, proximate cause, and actual harm. Table 6-2 gives an overview of these four elements.

Legal Duty
A determination that a legal duty exists between the parties must be made to establish liability through negligence. This issue is solely a question of whether the tortfeasor should have reasonably foreseen a risk of harm to the injured party. Often today, the element of duty is not at issue in a lawsuit. However, there are some instances, often when a novel case comes before a court, that the legal duty of the defendant may be placed at issue. The phrase "at issue" refers to a legal question that must be answered for the case to be decided.

Breach of Duty
The judge or the jury must determine whether the person accused of negligence has breached the duty owed to the victim. A breach of duty occurs if the alleged tortfeasor has not met the appropriate standard of care. To determine if the alleged tortfeasor has met the appropriate standard of care, the court uses the reasonable person test. This test compares the actions of the tortfeasor with those of a reasonable person in a similar situation. If a reasonable person would not have done what the tortfeasor actually did, then the tortfeasor is liable. The reasonable person standard is an objective test. Circumstances may change, but the standard of care applied by a reasonable person does not. How a reasonable person would behave in one set of circumstances may not be the same in another set of circumstances.

Table 6-2   The Elements of Negligence

Element	Definition
Legal duty	A determination that a legal duty exists between the parties must be made to establish liability through negligence. This is solely a question of whether the tortfeasor should have reasonably foreseen a risk of harm to the injured party.
Breach of duty	The judge or the jury must determine whether the person accused of negligence has breached the duty owed to the victim. To determine if the alleged tortfeasor has met the appropriate standard of care, the court uses the reasonable person test.
Proximate cause	For the tortfeasor to be held liable, the unreasonable conduct must be the proximate cause of the victim's injuries. Proximate cause is the legal connection between the unreasonable conduct and the resulting harm.
Actual harm	The injured party in a lawsuit for negligence must show that actual harm was suffered.

EXAMPLE 6-6: The Case of the Unreasonable Limo Service

Luigi Tarentino hired a limousine from Highland Limo Service so that he and his wife, Maybeth, could attend their high school reunion in style. When the limousine arrived, Tarentino told the driver to take them to the Regency Hotel. Once they were on the freeway, it became clear that the driver did not know how to reach the hotel. Every time the driver took a wrong turn, Tarentino attempted to correct him. The driver continued to ignore Tarentino's instructions. Eventually, the driver, who later said he was aggravated by Tarentino's frequent interruptions, stopped the limousine and told Tarentino and his wife to walk to their reunion. He then drove off and left his passengers several miles from the hotel in the middle of an ice storm. While walking to the hotel, Tarentino slipped on a patch of ice and fell and broke his arm. Later the Tarentinos learned that the driver had a long history of similar conduct and that the limousine company had not done a proper search into the driver's work history before hiring him. The question to the jury was, "Would a reasonable person hire an employee who will be responsible for the safety of paying passengers without checking the work history of that potential employee?" The jury said no, and Highland was held liable for the injuries that befell Tarentino from this breach of duty to protect paying passengers from harm.

If the defendant in a particular case is a professional, such as a physician or an engineer, the circumstances—not the test—change. To determine whether the defendant acted reasonably, the jury would have to know how the reasonable professional would act under similar circumstances. Determining this point may require the use of expert witnesses to testify as to a reasonable professional's conduct under the circumstances.

Actual and Proximate Cause

It is not enough to simply show that the tortfeasor's actions were unreasonable. For the tortfeasor to be held liable, the unreasonable conduct must be tied to actual and proximate cause. Actual cause, or cause in fact, demonstrates that the cause (the unreasonable conduct) led to the effect (the injury to the plaintiff). The question can be viewed like a problem in physics. We look at the plaintiff's injury (the effect) and deconstruct the events that preceded it, ending with the original unreasonable behavior (the cause). Imagine a set of dominoes falling one after the other and you'll have an accurate image of this process. So, let's say that a driver is texting while driving and that inattentiveness causes him to run a red light and collide with another vehicle, injuring the other driver and totaling the other car. To find actual cause we deconstruct events from the crash and, working backwards, see that, if the driver had not been texting, then the second vehicle would not have been hit. This is called the "but for" test. Using the "but for" test, the judge tells the jury to ask themselves, "Would there have been no accident, 'but for' the unreasonable conduct of the defendant?" In this case, it is clear that the accident would not have happened "but for" the unreasonable conduct (texting while driving). This gives us actual cause.

The problem with actual cause is that there is no end to the consequences that flow from the defendant's unreasonable conduct. Thus, in the car accident mentioned above, negative effects can flow from the accident for days and weeks afterwards, events that would not have occurred "but for" the original unreasonable conduct (the texting while driving). Thus, our innocent victim may lose work, may have to pay medical bills, may have to buy new clothing, may have to cancel a dinner date, may lose the services of a baby sitter, may miss her favorite television show, might be unable to attend a Rotary luncheon, may be fined for an overdue library book because she has no car, may fail to defrost her refrigerator because she is distraught or has a broken arm, and so on. The law must place a limit on these effects. This policy is referred to as proximate cause or legal cause. The law

THE OPENING CASE *Revisited, Part III*
Juriscience and Tort Law: Daubert v. Merrell Dow Pharmaceuticals, Inc. Round 4

Recall in the Opening Case, *Daubert v. Merrell Dow Pharmaceuticals, Inc.,* the Dauberts brought a lawsuit against Merrell Dow in which the plaintiffs argued that Bendectin, a drug produced by Merrell Dow and taken by Mrs. Daubert during her pregnancy, had caused birth defects in their children. The case is grounded in negligence which requires the plaintiff to prove the existence of four elements: (a) duty, (b) breach of duty, (c) proximate cause, and (d) actual harm or injury. The case turned on the issue of causation, which means that the plaintiffs had to prove that the defendant's action caused the plaintiff's injury. Recall, however, that causation involves two parts, actual cause, which is also known as cause in fact, and proximate cause, which is also referred to as legal cause. In this case the initial issue was the existence of actual cause. The issue before the court was the question of whether the Bendectin actually led to the birth defects. Because of the scientific nature of the case, the court needed expert testimony to determine causation. The judges at each level, from the trial court to the Supreme Court, had to weigh the scientific evidence on causation leading from the development of the drug Bendectin to the birth defects. After the standard was reformulated by the Supreme Court, the case was handed back to the appellate court which had to make a judgment as to whether actual cause existed in the case. The court, after considering the scientific evidence from both sides, concluded that the Dauberts had not proven actual cause. The court formulated its conclusion in the following way: "But what the plaintiffs would have to prove is not that Bendectin causes some defects but that it caused *their* defects. To show this, the plaintiffs' experts would have to testify either that Bendectin actually caused plaintiff's injuries (which they could not say) or that Bendectin doubled the likelihood of limb reduction birth defects (which they did not say). As the district court properly found below, 'the strongest inference to be drawn for the plaintiffs based on the epidemiological evidence is that Bendectin could *possibly* have caused the plaintiff's injuries.'" 727 F. Supp. At 576. Since the plaintiffs had not proven the existence of actual cause there was no need to go on the issue of proximate cause. *Daubert v. Merrell Dow Pharmaceuticals, Inc.,* 43 F.3d 1311 (Ninth Circuit).

says there must be a final effect for which we will hold the defendant liable. The test used to determine this "last effect" is referred to as the foreseeability test. In determining proximate cause, the court asks whether the harm that resulted from the original unreasonable conduct was foreseeable at the time of the original action. If the effect was foreseeable at the time of the unreasonable conduct, the defendant is liable for the damages that flow from that effect. If the effect was not foreseeable, the defendant cannot be held liable for it. In this case the driver's injuries, the damage to the car, the medical bills, and the lost wages were all foreseeable. The overdue library fines, the undefrosted refrigerator, the lost babysitter, and so on, were not.

Actual Harm
The injured party in a lawsuit for negligence must show that actual harm was suffered. In most cases, the harm suffered is a physical injury and is therefore visible. Harm suffered due to fright or humiliation is difficult to demonstrate. Courts often deny damages in actions for negligence unless they can see an actual physical injury. Actual harm can also come in the form of property damage.

Defenses to Negligence
Several defenses can be used by the defendant in a negligence case. These defenses include contributory negligence, comparative negligence, and assumption of the risk.

Contributory Negligence

The defense of contributory negligence involves the failure of the injured party to be careful enough to ensure his or her personal safety. Contributory negligence completely prevents the injured party from recovering damages. In other words, if the injured party's negligence contributed to personal injury, the tortfeasor wins. Last clear chance is the injured party's defense to a charge of contributory negligence. Under this doctrine, a tortfeasor may be held liable if the injured party can show that the tortfeasor had the last clear chance to avoid injury.

Comparative Negligence

To soften the harsh effects of contributory negligence, many states have adopted comparative negligence statutes that require courts to assign damages according to the degree of fault of each party. Rather than deny all recovery, the court weighs the relative degree of wrongdoing in awarding damages. If the tortfeasor was 80 percent negligent, the injured party may be allowed to recover 80 percent of the losses suffered. Some states have adopted the "50 percent rule." Under this rule, an injured party who was found to be more than 50 percent negligent cannot recover any damages from the tortfeasor.

Assumption of the Risk

Another defense to negligence is assumption of the risk, which involves the voluntary exposure of the victim to a known risk. If the injured party was aware of the danger involved in a situation, and by his or her actions indicated a willingness to be exposed to the danger, then he or she has assumed that risk. An awareness of the extent of the danger is the court's primary consideration in awarding or denying damages. It is important that the victim's decision to enter the risky situation be voluntary. If he or she is forced to enter the risky situation because no other choice is available, it is not an assumption of the risk.

---

quick quiz 6-3

1. Legal duty is never at issue in any lawsuit today.   true | false

2. Proximate cause is sometimes referred to as legal cause.   true | false

3. Under the defense of comparative negligence, the plaintiff   true | false
   always loses all the damages that he or she might have been
   awarded, absent the defense.

6-4 Strict Liability

Under certain circumstances, the courts may judge a person liable for harm even though that person was not negligent and did not commit an intentional tort. This doctrine is known as strict liability or absolute liability. In recent years, strict liability has also been applied to product liability cases.

Grounds for Strict Liability

Under strict liability, the court will hold a tortfeasor liable for injuries to a victim even though the tortfeasor did not intend the harm and was not in any way negligent. Strict liability is generally applied when the harm results from an ultrahazardous or very dangerous activity. Such activities include using explosives and keeping wild animals. A number of dangerous activities, such as flying an airplane, operating X-ray equipment, and laying public gas lines, are not subject to liability without fault. These activities are recognized as essential to the economic health and welfare of the public.

128

Counterfeit Colgate toothpaste was recently imported from China and sold in dollar stores across the United States How does this affect Colgate's reputation?

Product Liability

Product liability is a legal theory that imposes liability on the manufacturer and seller of a product produced and sold in a defective condition. A product in defective condition is unreasonably dangerous to the user, to the consumer, or to property. Anyone who produces or sells a product in defective condition is subject to liability for the physical or emotional injury to the ultimate consumer and for any physical harm to the user's property. The courts have regularly held that liability for a defective product extends to the producer of the product, the wholesaler, and the retailer. The seller or producer must be engaged in the business of selling such products. In addition, the product manufactured or sold must be expected to reach the ultimate consumer without substantial change in the conditions under which it was originally manufactured or sold.

Product liability is not without its limits. In most states, product liability also is not available as a cause of action if the only property damaged is the defective property itself. In such a situation, the product owner must seek a remedy in sales law for breach of warranty. (Note: People who are injured by faulty products might also be able to bring a product liability lawsuit in sales law. This issue is discussed at length in Chapter 15.)

quick quiz 6-4

1. Keeping wild animals is an ultrahazardous activity.   true | false
2. Strict liability is also known as absolute liability.   true | false
3. Product liability is completely unrelated to strict liability, and the   true | false
   two torts should never be confused with each other.

6-5 Cybertorts

Computers have provided unscrupulous individuals with new ways to commit crimes and torts. In the previous chapter, we examined several cybercrimes. In this chapter, we focus on another group of legal problems, cybertorts. We look first at the nature of cybertorts and then at the problems associated with defining, describing, and preventing cybertorts.

The Nature of Cybertorts

A cybertort involves the invasion, distortion, theft, falsification, misuse, destruction, or exploitation of information stored in or related to electronic devices, including but not limited to desktop PCs, laptops, mobile phones, mainframe computers, phonecams, PDAs, mobile phones, and home computers that stand alone or are part of a computer network. Cybertorts rarely, if ever, involve any physical harm to a victim. Instead, the victim's reputation has been hurt because a false statement has been posted on FaceBook; the victim's emotional state has been disturbed because a his or her privacy has been invaded by a photograph passed from cell phone to cell phone; the victim has suffered extensive financial loss due to identity theft; or the victim has been terrified by repeated threats from cyberbullies sending text messages in a relentless, ruthless fashion.

Cyber-defamation

Cyber-defamation is the communication of false and destructive information about an individual through the use of electronic devices. Most legal moves in cyber-defamation have been designed to limit, rather than extend liability for defamatory comments disseminated electronically. For example, when the courts were first involved in cyber-defamation, they easily extended liability for defamation from the party who posted the defamation on the Internet to the Internet Service Provider (ISP), such as America Online, that provided the vehicle for the posting. Thus, for example, it was not difficult in one case for a court in New York to decide that the Prodigy Service Company was responsible when an investment banking firm sued for defamation after false statements were posted on a cyber-bulletin board that was under Prodigy's control.

After the Prodigy case, however, the Communications Decency Act was enacted by Congress to protect ISPs from future defamation lawsuits for false statements posted by other individuals on the net. Despite the passage of the law, many cases have been filed attempting to hold ISPs liable for defamatory postings. Few have succeeded, but they remain a nuisance to the providers. Still, the greater nuisance, that to the innocent victims, has not been handled adequately. In one case, AOL was found not liable for defamation even though the provider had been informed of the defamatory content of a posting and still delayed its removal. Moreover, the protection granted to ISPs has gone far beyond protection for defamatory postings. The courts have found that ISPs are not liable when hackers place a virus into a system, when piracy is involved on the Net, or when an invasion of privacy takes place via a provider's link.

Cyber-disparagement

Disparagement involves false statements communicated to others that in some way casts doubt upon the ownership or the quality of an item of property or a product offered for sale. Cyber-disparagement involves the same activity on the Internet. The FaceBook phenomenon has opened an avenue for the relatively new tort of cyber-disparagement. Businesses now solicit videos from their consumers for postings on their own Web sites. These businesses often go so far as to run games and contests in which clients and customers can submit homemade advertisements or videos that will be added to the Web site of the business. Unfortunately, this process is filled with legal risks, not the least of which is the possibility of a cyber-disparagement lawsuit. Such homemade videos typically target the product of a company's competitor. Thus, a company that posts such videos must make certain that the competitor's product is not subject to false statements and descriptions. This assurance requires an enormous effort aimed at monitoring the content of such submissions. Legal activity in this area has not been heavy as of yet, but that is because the tort is so new. As time goes on and competitors find themselves injured by such postings the activity will increase and more cyber-disparagement lawsuits will be filed.

Cyber-invasion of Privacy

A cyber-invasion of privacy is the unwelcome intrusion into private matters initiated or maintained by an electronic device. Because the development of computer technology is in a constant state of flux, it is not surprising that the law is still uncertain about just what constitutes a cyber-invasion of privacy. One area that has been expanded recently involves computer-related privacy in the workplace. As the result of at least one federal case, workers employed by businesses that keep a close eye on their workers' time on the Internet have no expectation of privacy, at least in relation to their Fourth Amendment rights, provided that the employer has openly informed the workers of the surveillance.

When employees know that their employer monitors their Internet use, those employees have no expectation of privacy.

Privacy and Employees   The low expectation of privacy has long been a part of the law in relation to governmental employees. Thus, it has been clear that the Fourth Amendment Right against unreasonable searches and seizures does not protect a governmental employee who knows that the government regularly monitors its employees' Internet use. The same standard now extends to employees within the private sector. How this ruling relates to the tortious invasion of privacy is problematic. However, because the standard for the invasion of privacy is based on the level of privacy expected, the fact that a worker knows that the company monitors computer use means that the expectation is low. The moral of the story is twofold: (1) Employers should routinely remind their workers that all computer use is monitored by the information technology department, and (2) workers should use computers for work-related tasks only.

Privacy and Clients   Businesses and other organizations, such as educational institutions, health care facilities, and financial institutions must also deal with the privacy of their customers, students, patients, and clients. Most invasions of privacy affect private records that pertain to employees who, because of their jobs, work closely with confidential files, such as educational, medical, and financial records. The failure to protect such records, whether they are on paper or in a computer, can result in an invasion of privacy lawsuit. Nevertheless, some courts have held that records that are stored in a computer require a degree of protection that is greater than the protection given to paper records because paper records can be kept hidden away or locked in a filing cabinet or a safe, whereas computer records are easy to retrieve, compile, and disseminate. Still, not every claim of a computer-related invasion of privacy automatically translates into a successful lawsuit. The laws is still unsettled in several key areas, not the least of which is the question of whether ISPs are permitted to protect the privacy rights of their subscribers.

Private Privacy and Public Privacy   Most of the time, private information, or private private information, as it is sometimes called, includes reports on personal matters, family relationships, sexual habits, employment records, medical data, and financial records. However, the law also recognizes a fundamental difference between *private privacy* and *public privacy*. The law is familiar with private privacy concerns about matters such as health concerns, sexual preferences, family matters, and so on. However, the computer age has given rise to another privacy issue, that is, the concern over the publication of what is essentially public information, or what has been termed public-privacy matters. As noted above, many people believe that computer records deserve a higher degree of protection because, unlike paper documents, they are more readily vulnerable to hacking from remote sites.

Data Mining of Public Private Data   The process of data mining takes place when a hacker links multiple strings of data together and develops a data package that the target considers a compilation of private information, despite the public sources from which the hacker composed the package. The issue here is whether the hacker's mining of public databases to construct a private data portrait violates the target's privacy. Some commentators argue that an individual's right to privacy is invaded if, in the process of gathering the data, the hacker ignores or bypasses the target's consent to produce a data portrait that embarrasses, disturbs, ridicules, bullies, exploits, or financially harms the innocent target. To the extent that the victim is harmed, he or she ought to have a cause of action against the hacker.

EXAMPLE 6-7: ATMs, Digital Cameras, and Data Mining

Frank Vilnius, a dedicated health enthusiast and avid cyclist, rode his recumbent bike into town each week to do his errands. One of the errands involved a stop at the ATM at the local branch of Superior Savings. Unknown to Vilnius, the ATM contained a digital camera that photographed the bank's customers when they used the machine. Vilnius suddenly found himself the target of spam, telemarketing calls, text messages, and snail mail ads, selling products for cyclists. After some investigative work of his own, Vilnius discovered that one of Superior's subsidiaries, "B-A-Cyclist" was a sports equipment chain with an active Internet presence. "B-A" regularly tapped into Superior's data bank and used the photos and other customer data to target potential customers. Vilnius was not financially hurt by the intrusion, but he was annoyed enough to remove his savings from Superior Savings and move his business to the St. Georges Savings across town.

In the Vilnius case in Example 6-7, the various pieces of data that Superior Savings mined included Vilnius's address, phone number, e-mail address, mobile phone number, bank account balance, and his hobby as a cyclist. Arguably, all this data is public when looked at in isolation. Nevertheless, privacy rights emerge because the public pieces of data have been mined to produce a valuable public private data portrait that was exploited by Superior and its subsidiary, "B-A," without Vilnius's consent and in a manner that annoyed him enough to lead him to move his business to St. Georges. Unfortunately, there is still little case law on the issue of public private data portraits. Moreover, the law that does exist militates against the firm establishment of a public privacy right, despite the convincing case that can be made for its acceptance.

quick quiz 6-5

1. Cybertorts always involve information that has been invaded, distorted, stolen, falsified, or destroyed by an electronic device.   true | false

2. Most legal moves in cyber-defamation have been designed to extend liability.   true | false

3. Government employees have a high expectation of privacy in the workplace.   true | false

6-6 Remedies for Torts

When a wrongdoer has injured another person by committing a tort, the victim can usually be compensated with monetary damages. However, at times, the equitable remedy of an injunction is more appropriate.

The Right to Damages

The compensation paid to the victims of a tort is known as damages. Damages can come in several forms. Economic compensatory damages are those that are directly quantifiable. These include damages awarded for lost wages, medical expenses, and expenses incurred in the repair or replacement of property. Noneconomic compensatory damages are those that result from injuries that are intangible and therefore not directly quantifiable. For example, damages resulting from pain and suffering, mental anguish, and loss of companionship are considered noneconomic. If the tortfeasor's acts are notoriously willful and malicious, a court may also impose punitive damages. These are damages above and beyond those needed to compensate the injured party. Punitive damages are designed to punish the tortfeasor so that similar malicious actions are avoided by others. For this reason, they are also referred to as exemplary damages. Some courts say that another purpose of punitive damages is to comfort the victim.

The Right to an Injunction

If a tort involves a continuing problem, such as the dumping of chemical waste into a river, the injured party may ask the court for an injunction. An injunction is a court order preventing someone from performing a particular act. If a tort involves some permanent fixture that harms the interests of the injured party, the court may order the wrongdoer to take positive steps to alleviate the problem. Thus, the court might order a company to clean up a landfill that has become a nuisance to neighborhood homes. If the company failed to complete the cleanup, it would be in contempt of court. Contempt of court is a deliberate violation of the order of a judge that can result in a fine or in jail time for the wrongdoer.

---

quick quiz 6-6

1. Economic and noneconomic compensatory damages are essentially the same thing.	true | false
2. Punitive damages are designed to compensate the victim of a tort.	true | false
3. An injunction is never granted by the court in any kind of tort case.	true | false

---

6-7 Developments in Tort Law

Tort law is in an unsettled stage of development. Much of tort law is still common law, but public dissatisfaction with the high number of tort-based lawsuits has caused some legislatures to pass statutes aimed at tort reform. Some of these moves make sense, as with the passage of wrongful death and survival statutes. The advisability of others is not quite as clear. Nevertheless, this evolutionary surge in tort law is part of the legal culture's ongoing attempt to create a balanced system. The balance this time is between the rights that victims have to be compensated for injuries caused by tortious conduct and the right that society has to be spared the heavy cost of unjustified and expensive litigation.

Survival Statutes and Wrongful Death

Under common law, if someone died from another's wrongful act, then the right to bring a lawsuit also died. This rule originated because the king would execute the wrongdoer and then take his or her property. As a result, there was no property left for the next of kin to recover in a tort suit. In the modern world, this practice makes no sense, and so the state legislatures have nullified the rule with legislation. The two statutes that deal with this problem are survival statutes and statutes that deal with wrongful death.

Survival Statutes
Many state legislatures have revised common law by passing survival statues. Survival statutes allow a lawsuit to be brought even if the plaintiff, or the defendant, or both are deceased. Many states also have survival statutes that preserve the right to bring a lawsuit no matter what caused the death or deaths. Most states also allow such suits if the tort involves damage to real or personal property. However, there are some limitations placed on survival statutes. For example, suits cannot be brought for libel or slander after the death of a defamed person, because such a suit is for injury to a live person's reputation. Survival suits are brought or defended by the lawful representative of the estate of the deceased.

Wrongful Death Statutes
Unlike survival statutes, wrongful death statutes preserve the right to bring a lawsuit only if the death is caused by the negligence or the intentional conduct of the person who caused the death. Generally, only those family members who have lost the support of the deceased have the right to bring a wrongful death suit. The definition of family members generally includes husbands, wives, children, and parents. Under wrongful death statutes, creditors, business partners, and the like have no right to bring lawsuit.

The Tort Reform Movement

Other suggestions for tort reform include the introduction of statutes of repose in product liability and medical malpractice cases, the use of comparative negligence in product liability cases, and alterations in the availability of wrongful death lawsuits

Statutes of Repose
One suggested tort reform would introduce a statute of repose into product liability lawsuits. Statutes of repose establish a limit in years, usually but not necessarily 15 years, beyond which an injured party could not bring a lawsuit for an injury caused by a product. The limitation would be placed on end users. An *end user* is a purchaser or a user who is not involved in the production or the assembly of the product. A statute of respose differs from a statute of limitations in that the statute of limitations begins to run when the injury occurs, while the statute of repose begins to run when the product is sold. Often such statutes carry limitations and exceptions. Thus, if the manufacturer fraudulently represented the condition of the product and that fraud led to the harm caused by the product, the statute of repose would not apply. Extremely dangerous products might also fall outside the protective zone of the statute of repose.

Statutes of respose have been suggested also as tort reform measure in medical malpractice lawsuits. Time limits for such statutes vary from four to six years and usually begin to run when the professional services have been rendered. As is the case with statutes of repose for product liability lawsuits, the statute of respose for medical malpractice would include exceptions under which the statute would not apply. For instance, the statute would not apply if the defendant in such a lawsuit engaged in fraud in relation to the relevant facts pertaining to the professional services that form the basis of the suit.

Comparative Negligence and Product Liability
Another reform that has been suggested in some states is the application of comparative negligence as an affirmative defense in some product liability cases. Under this standard, the responsibility of the manufacturer in a product liability case can be lessened by the degree to which the plaintiff's own negligence contributed to his or her injury. Some statutes even say that the manufacturer can escape liability altogether if the plaintiff's share in the responsibility exceeds 50 percent.

Wrongful Death Reform   Some states have introduced a reform measure aimed at eliminating any chance of a double recovery under wrongful death statutes. Such reform provisions generally maintain that a wrongful death action cannot be instituted by family members if the deceased recovered damages from the defendant in a prior lawsuit. Thus, if during his or her lifetime, the deceased recovered damages from the defendant in a negligence action, the family cannot bring a subsequent wrongful death action based on the same facts that gave rise to the original negligence lawsuit. In essence, under such a provision, the deceased is said to have waived all rights to bring the wrongful death action when he or she recovered under the original negligence action.

Cultural Paradigms and Balance in Tort Law

There is a great deal of opposition to tort reform within the legal community, especially among attorneys who represent plaintiffs. The most fundamental complaint is that tort reform threatens the very paradigm upon which tort law is based. Fundamental to this argument is the belief that the tort law paradigm establishes a delicately balanced legal system that is threatened by the well-intentioned, but essentially clueless, supporters of tort reform.

Cultural Paradigms   A paradigm is an unchallenged world view that establishes the rules by which everyone in a particular culture thinks, speaks, and acts. This is true whether we are dealing with a national cultural, a religious culture, a political culture, or a professional culture. The problem with tort reform is that it challenges the assumptions of the legal paradigm without offering an alternative paradigm. Instead, it offers a piecemeal, patchwork approach that borrows concepts and principles from other areas of the law and applies them in ways that are inappropriate at best. This approach to reform reveals a fundamental misunderstanding of the tort law paradigm.

Balance in Tort Law   As noted above, the delicately balanced system of tort law is threatened by legislators and reformers who mean well, but who seem unable or unwilling to understand and appreciate the intricacies and the complexities of the tort law paradigm. In his treatise, *Law's Empire*, the legal philosopher Ronald Dworkin, argues that two very strong reasons exist for preserving the current tort law paradigm. Dworkin explains it this way: "Our law as a whole recognizes two principles as pertinent to the loss people should be permitted to suffer through accidents. The first is the principle of collective sympathy. It holds that the state should try to protect people from being ruined by accidents even when the accident is their own fault. The principle is most apparent in regulative safety programs of different sorts, in workmen's compensation statutes and in state-subsidized schemes of insurance for risks to property and person not adequately covered in the private insurance market. The second is the principle of apportioning the costs of an accident among the private actors in the drama that produced it. It holds that accidental loss should be bourne by the person at fault, not the innocent victim. This principle is most evidently at work in negligence law, including legislative amendments or supplements to common law of negligence." The second principle is the one that concerns us the most here. In a succinct and direct way, Dworkin has restated the fundamental rule of the tort law paradigm: people have a duty not to harm one another and when they do cause harm, whether intentionally, through carelessness, or by engaging in a dangerous activity, they pay. The principle is both logical and fair because it rehabilitates the innocent victim at the expense of the wrongdoer. It's just that simple. (See Ronald Dworkin, *Law's Empire*, Cambridge: The Belknap Press of Harvard University, 1986, p. 269.)

quick quiz 6-7

1. Survival statutes allow a lawsuit to be brought even if both the plaintiff and the defendant are deceased.   true | false

2. Statutes of repose establish a limit in years beyond which an injured party could not bring a lawsuit for an injury caused by a product.   true | false

3. A paradigm is an unchallenged world view that establishes the rules by which everyone in a particular culture thinks, speaks, and acts.   true | false

Summary

6.1 A tort is a private wrong that injures another person's physical well-being, emotional health, property, or reputation. A person who commits a tort is called a tortfeasor. The other party is alternatively referred to as the injured party, the innocent party, or the victim. The primary purpose of tort law is to compensate the innocent party by making up for any loss suffered by that victim. The doctrine of *respondeat superior* may impose legal liability on employers and make them pay for the torts committed by their employees within the scope of the employer's business.

6.2 The principal intentional torts include assault, battery, false imprisonment, defamation, disparagement, fraudulent misrepresentation, invasion of privacy, intentional infliction of emotional distress, and malicious prosecution.

6.3 Negligence is the failure to exercise the degree of care that a reasonable person would have exercised in the same circumstances. Negligence includes four elements: duty of care, breach of duty through a failure to exercise the appropriate standard of care, proximate cause, and actual harm. Three defenses to negligence are contributory negligence, comparative negligence, and assumption of risk.

6.4 Under the doctrine of strict liability, when people engage in ultrahazardous activities, they will be liable for any harm that occurs because of that activity, regardless of intent and regardless of care.

6.5 Cybertorts involve computer data that has been invaded, distorted, falsified, misused, destroyed, or exploited financially by an electronic devise. Therefore, cybertorts rarely involve any harm to a party's physical well-being. Instead, the victim's reputation has been hurt because a false statement has been placed on the Internet, the victim's emotional state has been disturbed, because his or her privacy has been invaded by a posting on Facebook, or the victim has suffered monetary harm because of identity theft.

6.6 Tort remedies include monetary damages and injunctions.

6.7 Survival statutes allow a lawsuit to be brought even if both the plaintiff and the defendant are deceased. Wrongful death statutes preserve the rights of third parties affected by the death of the deceased to bring a lawsuit. Statutes of repose establish a limit in years beyond which an injured party could not bring a lawsuit for an injury caused by a product or by medical malpractice. Another reform that has been suggested in some states is the application of comparative negligence as an affirmative defense in some product liability cases.

Key Terms

abuse of process, 123

actual cause, 125

actual malice, 120

actual malice test, 120

assault, 118

assumption of the risk, 127

Questions for Review and Discussion

1. What is the difference between a tort and a crime?
2. What is *respondeat superior?*
3. What is meant by the legal term "duty"?
4. What are the principal intentional torts?
5. What are the elements of negligence?
6. What are the differences among contributory negligence, comparative negligence, and assumption of the risk?
7. When does strict liability apply?
8. What is a cybertort?
9. What remedies are available in tort law?
10. What innovations have been suggested for contemporary state tort reform?

Cases for Analysis

1. Patrick Clawson was described by reporter Karen Branch-Brioso in a newspaper story as a "1970s era St. Louis journalist turned private eye turned FBI informant." The story was published in the *St. Louis Post-Dispatch*. The fact that he had been characterized as an "informant" bothered Clawson, who saw it as damaging to his reputation. Accordingly, he brought a libel case against the *Post-Dispatch*. Recall that to be libelous, a statement must be false and "hold the victim up to ridicule, contempt, or hatred." Clawson would have preferred the term "whistleblower" rather than "informant," because that term commands more respect. Why is the use of the term "informant" to describe Clawson not libelous? Explain. *Clawson v. St. Louis Post-Dispatch*, No. 04-CV-486; see also "Media Law: Label of 'Informer' Is Found Not Defamatory," *The National Law Journal*, September 11, 2006.

2. Curtis Ellison was riding as a passenger in his own vehicle when it was pulled over by the police for a parking violation. The vehicle had actually been targeted because the police had routinely checked the license plate through the department's database. This routine check had revealed that the owner of the vehicle had an outstanding warrant pending against him. When the police searched the van, they found two firearms hidden in the vehicle. As a result, Ellison was charged with felonious possession of a firearm. He argued that the search had violated his Fourth Amendment rights and that his right to privacy had been infringed. The trial

court agreed and dismissed the case. The case went to the appellate court. The issue before the appellate court was whether Ellison had a high expectation of privacy about the number on his license plate. Although this is a criminal case, it is still interesting to speculate on how the court would rule on the expectation of privacy in relation to a license plate. Why should the appeals court reverse the ruling by the trial court that there is a high expectation of privacy in relation to a license plate? Explain. *United States v. Ellison*, No. 04-1925; see also "Criminal Practice: No Privacy Expectation on License Plate Numbers," *The National Law Journal*, September 18, 2006, p. 16.

3. A St. Louis police officer was speeding the wrong way down a one-way street when he collided with a vehicle being driven by Ann Martin. Martin was seriously injured in the crash and brought a lawsuit against the police officer, the City of St. Louis, and the board of police commissioners. The board of commissioners is an agency of the state of Missouri. Martin passed away, and her daughter, Kimberly Hodges, took over as the plaintiff in the case. The case was settled in relation to the board and the officer but not the city. The City of St Louis argued that the officer could not be employed by both the board and the city at the same time. The city further argued that the officer's real employer was the board, so it, the city, could not be held liable under the doctrine of vicarious liability. Why should the city be held liable under the doctirne of vicarious liability? Explain. *Hodges v. City of St. Louis*, No. SC87513; see also "Torts: Officer Is City Agent Even if Working for State Board," *The National Law Journal*, March 12, 2007, p. 15.

4. At the height of the modern civil rights movement, *The New York Times* ran a full-page advertisement entitled "Heed Their Rising Voices." The advertisement detailed police efforts in Montgomery, Ala., to suppress the nonviolent civil rights demonstrations being carried on there by thousands of college students. The police commissioner of Montgomery, L.B. Sullivan, filed a lawsuit against *The New York Times*, alleging that he had been libeled by information carried in the advertisement, even though he was never mentioned by name. Should the Court use the actual malice test in this case to determine whether the newspaper libeled the commissioner? Explain. *New York Times Co. v. Sullivan*, 376 U.S. 254 (U.S. Sup. Ct.).

5. Five Commerce City police officers were summoned to break up a disturbance at a local party of teenagers. At the party, Ralph Crowe, who had consumed eight cups of beer and three cups of alcoholic punch, became rowdy and had to be detained by the officers. The police released Ralph after receiving the assurances of his brother Eddie that he would drive Ralph home. After leaving the party, Eddie Crowe allowed Ralph to take the wheel. Instead of going home, Ralph drove to the site of another party, where he lost control of the car and ran down six people. The police officers were sued for negligence in releasing Ralph. Did the five officers owe a duty to the six victims of Ralph's drunk-driving accident? Explain. *Leake v. Cain*, 720 P.2d 152 (CO).

6. Seventy-four years of age at the time, Ramona Booker entered a drugstore by pushing her way through one door and then through a second. Both doors were extremely heavy, so Booker was compelled to use both hands, causing her cane to drag on the ground. As she entered the second door, the tip of her cane caught on the exposed coil of a security device, causing her to fall and injure herself. Booker brought a lawsuit against Revco DS, Inc., to recover for her injuries. Did the drugstore owe a duty to Booker and other customers to maintain a safe environment? Explain. Is Booker's lawsuit based on allegations that the store owners committed an intentional tort or that they were negligent? Explain. What test would be used to judge whether the drugstore owners should be held liable for Booker's injuries? Explain. *Booker v. Revco DS, Inc.* 681 N.E.2d 499 (OH).

7. Queenway Tankers, Inc., Kingsway Tankers, Inc., the East River Steamship Corporation, and Richmond Tankers, Inc., all chartered supertankers designed by Transamerican Delaval, Inc. Under the terms of the charters, each shipping company was financially responsible for many repairs to the tankers. From the start, there were problems with the tankers' turbines, which needed extensive and costly repairs. The plaintiffs brought a product liability suit against Delaval. The suit alleged that the manufacturing defects caused the damage. Should the shipping companies have prevailed in product liability against the manufacturer? Explain. *East River Steamship Corporation v. Transamerican Delaval, Inc.*, 106 S. Ct. 2305 (U.S. Sup. Ct.).

8. Myers was injured when she slipped and fell on an ice patch on the front walkway of the Canton Centre Mall. The mall is owned and operated by Forest City Enterprises. Forest City had employees who were responsible for clearing the ice off of the mall walkways every morning. On this particular morning, they had cleared the ice from the walkway a short time before Myers took her tumble. Nevertheless, an ice patch had formed, and Myers did fall, sustaining injuries. Cooper, one of the employees charged with the ice-removal task, theorized that water may have been splashed up onto the sidewalk by passing cars where it froze sometime after their initial cleaning of the day. According to Cooper, "the vehicles could have splashed this back up on there . . . we're constantly moving around the building at all times, so anything can be going on in this half of the building while you're over here doing this half coming around." Was Forest City negligent in failing to keep the sidewalk clear of ice at all times that winter? What test would be used to judge Forest City's conduct? Explain. *Myers v. Forest City Enterprises, Inc.* 635 N.E.2d 1268 (OH).

9. Michelle Wightman was driving toward a railroad crossing at which the gates were down and the lights flashing. Wightman noted a stopped train a short distance from the gate. Believing the stopped train to be the cause of the closed gate, she drove around the gate and was struck and killed by a train that suddenly appeared from behind the stopped train. The stopped train had blocked her view of the oncoming train. Both trains were owned and operated by Consolidated Rail Corporation (CRC). Wightman's mother brought a wrongful death lawsuit and a survivorship action against CRC. In response, CRC claimed that Wightman's action of driving around the gates, in violation of both state and city law regarding the operation of a motor vehicle at a railroad crossing, constituted negligence on her part. Furthermore, CRC argued that if Wightman had not crossed the tracks, she would not have been struck by the train. Therefore, her actions were the sole cause of the accident, and the railroad corporation should not be held liable for her death. The attorney for the plaintiff argued that the placement of the first train, blocking the view of the other track, contributed to the accident and that CRC should be held liable for Wightman's death. Should Wightman's own negligence be a complete bar to the plaintiff's recovery of damages in this case? Explain. *Wightman v. Consolidated Railroad Corporation,* 640 N.E.2d 1160 (OH).

quick quiz Answers

6-1	6-2	6-3	6-4	6-5	6-6	6-7
1. T	1. F	1. F	1. T	1. T	1. F	1. T
2. F	2. F	2. T	2. T	2. F	2. F	2. T
3. F	3. F	3. F	3. F	3. F	3. F	3. T

Part 1 Case Study

United Citizens v. Federal Election Commission
United States Supreme Court
130 S. Ct. 876 (2010)

Summary

During the 2004 presidential campaign, Michael Moore promoted the film, *Fahrenheit 9/11*, which was critical of the Bush presidency and which expressly urged the removal of Bush from the presidency. The film was released, promoted, distributed, and shown using funds supplied by Moore and other entities, all of which had made contributions to a series of political candidates of a clearly identifiable political persuasion. A conservative nonprofit political group named Citizens United, also with a clearly identifiable political agenda, filed a complaint with the Federal Election Commission asking that the film be censored under provisions of the Bipartisan Campaign Reform Act of 2002. The federal reform law, which is popularly known as the McCain-Feingold Act, forbids all "electioneering communications" by all unions, and by all profit and nonprofit corporations, 60 days before an election and 30 days before a primary. The McCain-Feingold law did allow some political advertisements during that same period of time, just as long as those advertisements were funded by the candidate's campaign. For clarity, McCain-Feingold defined "electioneering communications" as speech that is intended to promote a candidate's election or, in the alternative, the defeat of a candidate. In response to the complaint, the Federal Election Commission ruled that the activities of Moore and his associates in the release, promotion, distribution, and showing of the film had not in any way violated the law. The commission decided that the money spent on the promotion and release of the film including the film's Web site and trailers were, in fact, simply commercial activities and not political speech as defined within the act. As a result, the complaint was dismissed. (It is interesting to note that at this point neither Citizens United nor the Federal Election Commission had presented any arguments regarding the law's constitutionality. That was about to change.)

Taking its cue from this decision, in the 2008 election campaign, Citizens United fought back by producing its own film entitled *Hillary: The Movie*. The film, which was admittedly critical of Senator Hillary Clinton, was scheduled to be promoted in television commercials and ultimately broadcast on Direct TV. As a preemptive strike, Citizens United brought an action in Federal District Court, arguing that McCain-Feingold, at least to the extent that it might be applied to *Hillary: The Movie*, was unconstitutional and asking for an injunction to prevent the Federal Election Commission from using the law to interfere with the promotion and presentation of the film. The Federal Election Commission argued that both the film and the commercials advertising the film violated both the spirit and the letter of the McCain-Feingold Act. Therefore, the commission was entitled to a summary judgment in the case. Citizens United opposed the summary judgment motion, arguing that the film was a documentary that was plainly nonpartisan, that the film was not "publically distributed," and that, as a result, the film was not "electioneering communication." Therefore, they concluded that none of their activities violated McCain-Feingold. Moreover, Citizens United also contended that, even on the remote chance that their actions did violate McCain-Feingold, the law itself was unconstitutional. Specifically, Citizens United believed that the section of McCain-Feingold that censored political films like *Hillary: The Movie* and the section that mandated certain disclosure and reporting requirements were both unconstitutional. The court did not agree with Citizens United and ruled that the film, which had been financed by Citizens United, was a deliberate, unapologetic attempt to malign the reputation of Senator Clinton and, as such, violated the statute's prohibition against "independent expenditures" for "electioneering communications" within 30 days of a primary. Also, following a previous case, *Austin v. Michigan Chamber of Commerce*, in which the U.S. Supreme Court ruled that corporate political speech could be censored by law without violating the First Amendment, the district court in the Citizens United case ruled McCain-Feingold to be constitutional. As a result, two interesting and obviously contradictory rulings were now caught within the legal system: the *Fahrenheit 9/11* ruling, permitting the promotion and release of a corporately financed, obviously political film, and the ruling in *Hillary: The Movie,* outlawing what was essentially the same thing. As you would expect, the case ended up in the United States Supreme Court.

The Supreme Court was actually faced with a dispute that consisted of two levels of inquiry. The first level is the issue of whether the activities of Citizens United in relation to the distribution, promotion, and presentation of *Hillary: the Movie* violated the provisions of the McCain-Feingold Act. Generally, if a court can decide a case on the narrower issue of strict legality rather than the broader issue of constitutionality, the court will do so. Such a decision has a much more limited and, therefore, much less disruptive effect on the legal system outside of the current case, thus promoting two of the three purposes of the law, order and stability. Deciding a case in this way is also part of the balancing function of the law. One of the most obvious dualities in the law is the balance between the spirit and the letter of the law. Generally, a person who follows the "spirit" of the law has found its actual intent, while one who is tied to the letter of the law has missed its true meaning. In this case, the Court could have followed the letter of the law and ruled that the activities of Citizen's United violated McCain-Feingold. This would have ended the case right then and there. However, such a decision on the part of the Court would have violated the spirit of the law, represented by the U.S. Constitution, in general, and the First Amendment, in particular. For these reasons it makes sense to defend the Supreme Court's decision to move on to the issue of McCain-Feingold's constitutionality. This

means that the Court elected to immerse itself within the process of *judicial review,* that is, it decided to determine the constitutionality of a portion of McCain-Feingold. The Citizens United case revolved around the First Amendment's guarantee of free speech, especially as it relates to politics and corporations.

Whenever rights become the focus of a legal discussion, it is informative to look first at the *theory of negative rights.* The theory of negative rights argues that "rights" are a human invention designed to help people escape moral law. Thus, under this theory, the right to free speech is actually the right to lie and get away with it or, stated another way, it is the right to say what one wants, without legal consequences. The courts rarely follow this line of reasoning. Nevertheless, judges sometimes limit the right of free speech perhaps because, intuitively or subconsciously, they perceive the truth of the negative rights theory. Thus, it is not impossible for the law to impose some limits on free speech. The law can limit free speech, for example, to protect individuals from slander and libel, to protect an author's copyright and, thus, to preserve his nor her right to receive royalties, or to limit what a governmental agent might say in carrying out his or her duties as a representative of the government. Despite these limitations, in most instances, speech is protected from prior restraint (read "censorship" here) by the Federal government under the First Amendment, and by the states under the First and the Fourteenth Amendments.

The Court then goes on to explain that there are two clearly delineated situations in which the government cannot limit free speech. First, the government is not permitted to prohibit or punish speech simply based on the content of that speech. Second, the government is not permitted to prohibit or punish speech based on the identity of a speaker. Thus the government cannot let one speaker speak while prohibiting another speaker from taking the same podium. The only exception to this rule involves government employees. Here the courts says that the government, in exercising its duty to see that the government itself runs smoothly and fairly, may prohibit what its own employees may say in a governmental capacity. Applying these standards to the present case, the Supreme Court could not condone the censorship of corporations and unions under the provisions of the McCain-Feingold Act based on the content of the speech and on the identity of the speaker. Thus, the Court declared unconstitutional that part of the McCain-Feingold Act that prohibited the release, promotion, and airing of *Hillary: The Movie.* The Court concluded that Congress could not censor political speech simply because it was supported by the "independent expenditures" of a nonprofit corporation. Such censorship was clearly aimed at prohibiting the political content spoken by a particular speaker, a nonprofit corporation, and as such was a violation of free speech as guaranteed by the First Amendment. In making this decision, the Court was also compelled to overturn the line of precedent that followed and supported the case of *Austin v. Michigan Chamber of Commerce.*

Justice Kennedy delivered the opinion of the Court.

Federal law prohibits corporations and unions from using their general treasury funds to make independent expenditures for speech defined as "electioneering communication" or for speech expressly advocating the election or the defeat of a candidate . . . limits on electioneering communications were upheld in *McConnell v. Federal Election Comm'n,* 540 U.S. 93, 203–209 (2003). The holding in McConnell rested to a large extent on an earlier case, *Austin v. Michigan Chamber of Commerce,* 494 U.S. 652 (1990). *Austin* held that political speech may be banned based on the speaker's corporate identity.

In this case we are asked to reconsider *Austin* and, in effect, *McConnell.* It has been noted that *"Austin* was a significant departure from ancient First Amendment principles" . . . We agree with that conclusion and hold that *stare decisis* does not compel the continued acceptance of *Austin.* The Government may regulate corporate political speech through disclaimer and disclosure requirements, but it may not suppress that speech altogether. We turn to the case now before us.

I

Citizens United is a nonprofit corporation. It brought this action in the United States District Court for the District of Columbia. A three-judge court later convened to hear the cause. The resulting judgment gives rise to this appeal.

Citizens United has an annual budget of about $12 million. Most of its funds are from donations by individuals; but in addition, it accepts a small portion of its funds from for-profit corporations.

In January 2008, Citizens United released a film entitled *Hillary: The Movie.* We refer to the film as *Hillary.* It is a 90-minute documentary about then-Senator Hillary Clinton, who was a candidate in the Democratic Party's 2008 Presidential primary elections. *Hillary* mentions Senator Clinton by name and depicts interviews with political commentators and other persons, most of them quite critical of Senator Clinton. *Hillary* was released in theaters and on DVD, but

Citizens United wanted to increase distribution by making it available through video-on-demand.

Video-on-demand allows digital cable subscribers to select programming from various menus, including movies, television shows, sports, news, and music. The viewer can watch the program at any time and can elect to rewind or pause the program. In December 2007, a cable company offered, for payment of $1,2 million, to make *Hillary* available on video-on-demand channel called "Election'08.". . . . Some video-on-demand services require viewers to pay a small fee to view a selected program, but here the proposal was to make *Hillary* available to viewers free of charge.

To implement the proposal, Citizens United was prepared to pay for the video-on-demand; and to promote the film, it produced two 10-second ads and one 30-second ad for *Hillary.* Each ad includes a short (and, in our view, pejorative) statement about Senator Clinton, followed by the name of the movie and the movie's Web site address . . . Citizens United desired to promote the video-on-demand offering by running advertisements on broadcast and cable television.

Before the Bipartisan Campaign Reform Act of 2002 (BCRA), federal law prohibited—and still does prohibit—corporations and unions from using general treasury funds to make direct contributions to candidates or independent expenditures that expressly advocate the election or defeat of a candidate, through any form of media, in connection with certain qualified federal elections . . . An electioneering communication is defined as "any broadcast, cable or satellite communication" that refers to a clearly identified candidate for Federal office" and is made within 30 days of a primary or 60 days of a general election . . . The Federal Election Commission's (FEC) regulations further define an electioneering communication as a communication that is "publicly distributed. . . .Corporations and unions are barred from using general treasury funds for express advocacy of electioneering communications . . .

II

Before considering whether *Austin* should be overruled, we first address whether Citizen's United's claim that section 441b cannot be applied to *Hillary* may be resolved on other narrower grounds. (Note: After an extensive, in-depth examination of this issue covering fifteen pages, the court decided that the case could not be decided by using the statute alone and moves on to the constitutional issue of First Amendment free speech guarantees.)

III

The First Amendment provides that "Congress shall make no law . . . abridging the freedom of speech." Laws enacted to control or suppress speech may operate at different points in the speech process. The following are just a few examples of restrictions that have been attempted at different stages of the speech process—all laws found to be invalid: restrictions requiring a permit at the outset . . . imposing a burden by impounding proceeds on receipts or royalties . . . seeking to exact accost after the speech occurs . . . and subjecting the speaker to criminal penalties.

The law before us is an outright ban, backed by criminal sanctions. Section 441b makes it a felony for all corporations—including nonprofit advocacy corporations—either to expressly advocate the election or defeat of candidates or to broadcast electioneering communications within 30 days of a primary election and 60 days of a general election. Thus, the following acts would be felonies under 441b: The Sierra Club runs an ad, within the crucial phase of 60 days before the general election, that exhorts the public to disapprove of a Congressman who favors logging in national forest; the National Rifle Association publishes a book urging the public to vote for the challenger because an incumbent U.S. Senator supports a handgun ban; and the American Civil Liberties Union creates a Web site telling the public to vote for a presidential candidate in light of that candidate's defense of free speech. These prohibitions are classic examples of censorship. . . .

Premised on a distrust of governmental power, the First Amendment stands against attempts to disfavor certain subjects or viewpoints. . . . Prohibited too are restrictions distinguishing among different speakers, allowing speech by some but not others . . . As instruments to censor, these categories are interrelated: Speech restrictions based on the identity of the speaker are too often simply a means to control content.

Quite apart from the purpose or effect of regulating content, moreover, the Government may commit a constitutional wrong when by law it identifies certain preferred speakers. By taking the right to speak from some and giving it to others, the Government deprives the disadvantaged person or class of the right to use speech to strive to establish worth, standing, and respect for the speaker's voice. The Government may not by these means deprive the public of the right and privilege to determine for itself what speech and speakers are worthy of consideration. The First Amendment protects speech and speaker, and the ideas that flow from each . . .

The Court has recognized that First Amendment protection extends to corporations . . . This protection has been extended by explicit holdings to the context of political speech . . . Corporations and other associations, like individuals, contribute to the discussion, debate, and the dissemination of information and ideas that the First Amendment seeks to foster . . . The Court has thus rejected the argument that political speech of corporations or other associations should be treated differently under the First Amendment simply because such associations are not "natural persons." . . .

Less than two years after *Buckley, Bellotti,* 435 U.S. 765, reaffirmed the First Amendment principle that the Government cannot restrict political speech based on the speaker's corporate identity. *Bellotti* could not have ben clearer when it struck down a state-law prohibition on corporate independent expenditures related to referenda issues . . .

Thus, the law stood until *Austin. Austin* upheld a direct restriction on the independent expenditure of funds for political speech for the first time . . . There, the Michigan Chamber of Commerce sought to use general treasury funds to run a newspaper ad supporting a specific candidate. Michigan law, however, prohibited corporate independent expenditures that supported or opposed any candidate for stew office. A violation of the law was punishable as a felony. The Court sustained the speech prohibition. . . .

Our precedent is to be respected unless the most convincing of reasons demonstrates that adherence to it puts us on a course that is sure error. "Beyond workability, the relevant factors in deciding whether to adhere to the principle of *stare decisis* include the antiquity of the precedent, the reliance of interests at stake, and of course whether the decision was well reasoned. . . . We have also examined whether "experience has pointed up the precedent's shortcomings . . . These considerations counsel in favor of rejecting *Austin,* which itself contravened this court's earlier precedent in *Buckley* and *Bellotti.* "This Court has not hesitated to overrule decisions offensive to the First Amendment." . . . *Stare decisis* is a principle of policy not a mechanical formula of adherence to the latest decision." For the reasons above, it, must be concluded that *Austin* was not well reasoned. . . .

Some members of the public might consider Hillary to be insightful and instructive; some might find it to be neither high art nor a fair discussion on how to set the Nation's course; still others simply might suspend judgment on the points but decide to think more about issues and candidates. These choices and assessments, however, are not the Government's to make. "The First Amendment underwrites the freedom to experiment and to create in the realm of thought and speech. Citizens must be free to use new forums, for expression of ideas. The civic discourse belongs to the people, and the Government may not prescribe the means used to conduct it . . .

The judgment of the District Court is reversed with respect to the constitutionality of 2 U.S.C. 441b's restrictions on corporate independent expenditures . . .

It is so ordered.

Questions for Analysis

1. The Federal Elections Commission filed a summary judgment motion with the District Court to have the case brought by Citizens United dismissed. What is a summary judgment motion and why is it appropriate in this case? Explain.

2. Citizens United filed a request for an injunction in the same case. What is an injunction and why is it appropriate in this case? Explain.

3. What is at stake in the balancing act generally involved in the law-making process in a case like this? Explain.

4. What is the negative rights theory of ethics and just how does it impact this case? Explain.

5. The court stipulates that there are some very specific situations in which the government is permitted to censor free speech. What are they?

6. The court explains that there are two situations in which the government cannot limit free speech. What are they?

7. Which of these two situations would explain why the courts have outlawed hate speech crimes? Explain.

8. In this case, the Supreme Court must engage in both statutory interpretation and in judicial review. Explain the difference between the two.

9. Explain how *stare decisis* is at the heart of this case. What case is overturned and why is it overturned? Explain.

10. In the Supreme Court's opinion, Justice Kennedy outlines three situations that will permit a case to be overturned. List those three situations.

Contract Law

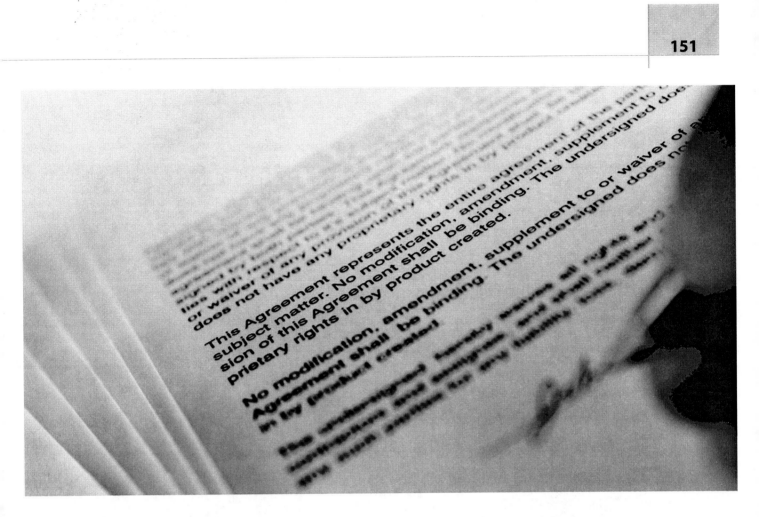

Part Two

Contract Law

THE OPENING CASE   Multidimensional Contract Law: *Tubelite Co., Inc. v. Original Sign Studio*

In the balancing act that is the law, judges and attorneys must often weave their way through a series of overlapping and inconsistent legal dimensions before arriving at a solution to their problems. Unfortunately, even that does not always work. Such was the case in a multidimensional lawsuit entitled *Tubelite Co., Inc. v. Original Sign Studio.* The lawsuit concerns two agreements between Tubelite, the seller, and Original Sign Studio, the buyer. The first agreement was an application for credit, in which Original Sign agreed to pay for all materials shipped by Tubelite and to remit an 18 percent finance charge for overdue payments. In the second agreement, Tubelite agreed to be Original Sign's exclusive supplier. The terms of the contract were reduced to writing in a letter written by an agent of Original Sign but never signed by anyone from Tubelite. The agreement stated that Tubelite would supply Original Sign with all the material that it requested but that it would bill Original Sign only for the materials that the sign company actually used and then, in exchange for being Original Sign's exclusive supplier, it would charge a discounted rate of somewhere between 10 and 25 percent. Tubelite also agreed to install shelving at Original Sign's warehouse for proper storing of the materials. Tubelite shipped the materials that Original requested and installed the shelving as per the agreement. So far so good. Then the trouble started.

Tubelite billed Original for all the material it shipped, not just the material used. Moreover, the bill that Tubelite sent to Original ignored the discounts promised under agreement number two. Original ignored the bill as written by Tubelite and, instead, paid only for the materials it had used at a 25 percent discount rate. Tubelite insisted that, under agreement one, Original still owed money for the unused portion of the material. In addition, since that payment was now late, Tubelite tacked on its 18 percent penalty (remember the "finance charge"). Original argued that agreement two, the discount agreement, superseded, agreement one, the credit agreement. Tubelite argued that agreement one, the credit application, was still in effect because agreement two, was never signed by anyone from Tubelite. Therefore, the agreement failed to meet Statute of Frauds requirements (the statute that tells us what contracts must be written), and was unenforceable. Besides, Tubelite added, agreement number two was too vague to be enforced, even if the writing were okay. It should be clear that, if any dispute is multidimensional, this one is. Look at all the questions in these two contacts that remain. What law applies here? Common law or the Uniform Commercial Code (UCC)? Which contract rules? Did Original err in not getting a Tubelite agent to sign the agreement? Is the writing really too vague or is Tubelite pulling a fast one? These and other similar questions will be addressed in the Unit called Contract Law. [See *Tubelite Co., Inc. v. Original Sign Studio*, 176 Ohio App.3d 241 (Tenth District).]

Opening Case Questions

1. Would *Tubelite Co., Inc. v. Original Sign Studio* be a civil lawsuit or a criminal action? Explain.

2. What law will the court apply in this case to answer the questions noted above? Will the court use common law or the Uniform Commercial Code (UCC)? Explain.

3. What is the legal status of a contract that is supposed to be in writing under the law, but is never reduced to writing? Explain.

4. What legal exceptions exist to the rule that says that certain contracts must be in writing? Explain.

5. When an agent fails to perform one of the many duties imposed on agents by law, what are the legal consequences for that agent? Explain.

Learning Objectives

1. Define contract.
2. Explain the origin of the law merchant.
3. Discuss the relationship between common law and the law merchant.
4. Identify the four elements of a contract.
5. Explain the objectives of contract law.
6. Explain the place of the UCC in contract law.
7. Distinguish contracts from other agreements.
8. Explain the role of privity and agency in contract law.
9. List the contracts that must be in writing to be enfoceable.
10. List the characteristics of a contract.

7-1 The History of Contract Law

A contract is an agreement between two or more competent parties based on mutual promises and an exchange of things of value, to do or refrain from doing some particular thing that is neither illegal nor impossible. The agreement results in an obligation or a duty that can be enforced in a court of law. Most people understand the basic nature of a contract as a process of give and take. There are rules, however, that govern how those agreements are made, how they are carried out, how they end, and how disputes are resolved when someone yells, "foul." Before delving into these basic principles, however, we will pause for a moment to consider how these rules originated.

Mercantile Law, Ancient Rome, Capitalism, and the Church

The history of contract law is intertwined with the parallel development of Western mercantile law, often referred to alternately as the law merchant and *lex mercatoria*. The law merchant outlines the laws and the procedures followed by merchants in commercial transactions. As Harold J. Berman explains in his landmark study, *Law and Revolution: The Formation of the Western Legal Tradition*, mercantile law originated among the merchants themselves who needed a formalized way to deal with one another when disputes arose. According to Berman, the law merchant saw a sudden and unprecedented burst of development between the 11th and the 13th centuries in Western Europe, both on the continent and across the channel in England. This is not to say that there was no commercial law before the 11th century. Between the fall of Rome and the rise of the mercantile city states of the late Middle Ages, which is to say during the second half of the first millennium, commercial transactions were limited to seasonal festivals, small town marketplaces, and coastal cities. The law that governed these transactions emerged from rules within the ancient traditions of the Justinian Code of the old Roman Empire. All of this began to change with a series of agricultural innovations and a sudden European population explosion. [See Harold J. Berman, *Law and Revolution: The Formation of the Western Legal Tradition,* (Cambridge: Harvard UP, 1983), pp. 333–341.]

Agriculture, Technology, and Population

Ancient Roman law was adequate at the time because commerce itself was limited during that era. The population of Europe barely topped 20 million at the end of the first millennium and most people lived out their lives in the small villages and manors that dotted the countryside. Several irresistible driving forces changed all of that in the 11th century. Technological developments in agriculture (including a number of important inventions such as a new type of horse collar, a heavy plow, horse shoes, fish farming, three-field crop rotation, the overshot waterwheel, and the wind powered post mill) led to crop surpluses that could be sold for a profit; changes in manor law freed many peasants who turned to selling as a livelihood; and Europe saw an unprecedented population explosion. This all led to a new group of professional sellers who developed their own system of laws over a relatively short time. That system came to be called *mercantile law* or the *law merchant.* [See Berman, 333–341; see also Rodney Stark, *The Victory of Reason: How Christianity Led to Freedom, Capitalism, and Western Science* (New York: Random House, 2005), pp. 38–44.] In his book, *The Victory of Reason,* Rodney Stark notes that, despite popular views to the contrary, an enormous amount of progress occurred during the Muddle Ages, including the inventions listed above. [See Stark, pp. 38–44.]

The Development of the Law Merchant

Mercantile law is also closely associated with the development of capitalism. Capitalism is an economic system that operates on the basis of competition and a free market that responds to the movement of supply and demand. Contrary to the thesis proposed by Max Weber in *The Protestant Ethic: The Spirit of Capitalism,* European capitalism did not begin with the Protestant Reformation in the 16th century, but in the 11th and 12th centuries, some 400 years before Martin Luther nailed his famous 95 theses on the cathedral door in Wittenberg. Moreover, one of the driving forces behind the growth of capitalism was the Roman Catholic Church which helped provide a rational and moral foundation for the principles and procedures that guided the activities of merchants in their communities, their courts, and in the making of their contracts. The Church refused to condemn commercial activity. Instead, the Church monitored how those activities were carried out. In short, the Church encouraged this new class of sellers to establish guilds that followed the law of the Church, a legal tradition that is generally referred to as canon law. The Church also insisted that these emerging businessmen never engage in deceit or dishonesty and always follow a good faith approach to contract development. As long as they followed these basic precepts, the Church reassured the members of the new and expanding class of professional sellers that there was nothing inherently wrong with their chosen profession. [See Berman, pp. 336–341; and Stark, xi. See also Henri Sée, *Modern Capitalism: Its Origin and Evolutions,* trans. Homer B. Vanderblue and Georges F. Doriot (New York: Adelphi Co. 1928), pp. 7–13.]

A QUESTION OF ETHICS

Of course, the Roman Catholic Church was not always as supportive of capitalism as it eventually became. In fact, both Henri Sée in a study entitled *Modern Capitalism* and Harold Berman in his book *Law and Revolution* refer to the work of the French historian, Henri Pirenne, who wrote extensively about the development of capitalism in Europe in the Middle Ages. According to Berman, Pirenne points out that the Church often took a decidedly anti-capitalist position, especially in relation to such things as moneylending and placing an unfair value on goods. On the other hand, See points out that, when circumstances were right, in certain areas of Europe, notably the Low Countries of Holland and Zeeland, the Church was willing to support those emerging businessmen who worked diligently to create an authentic form of modern capitalism that included moneylending. Even Max Weber does not deny that certain theologians in the Medieval Church managed to support the growth of capitalism. (Specifically, he refers to Anthony of Florence and Bernhard of Siena, although, to be fair, Weber does hide this reference in a lengthy footnote at the back of his book.) The question before us is this: What religious values would operate to oppose capitalism? What is it about the very nature of religious doctrine that places it in opposition to making a profit? On the other hand, what arguments can overcome this religious opposition to making a profit? Explain all your answers. (See Berman, pp. 336–337; Sée, pp.12–13; and Max Weber, *The Protestant Ethic: The Spirit of Capitalism* (Mineola, NY: Dover, 2003), p. 197.)

The Characteristics of the Law Merchant

With the Roman Catholic Church supplying political and social support, with canon law providing a moral framework, and with practicality guiding their activities over a 300-year period, the this new class of businessmen developed a body of effective commercial law. Berman tells us that this legal system was distinguished by six characteristics: neutrality, universality, mutuality, involvement, integration, and evolution.

Neutrality of the Law Merchant   The law merchant was made up of fairly neutral system of laws and procedures. *Neutrality* characterizes any system of laws that is consistently applied in the same evenhanded way, no matter who the antagonists might be. The law developed in the festivals, marketplaces, and coastal cities of Europe by practical men who saw the value of recording their procedures and principles in writing so that commercial activities, financial transactions, and dispute settlements could be carried out in a customary, predictable, and even-handed way. The legal treatises and codebooks that resulted covered the making of negotiable instruments, the execution of contracts, and the procedures used in the mercantile courts. The actual process of writing these things down was authorized and supported by the ruling classes, especially those in the merchant cities of Genoa, Milan, and Pisa, and by the birth of a class of professional notaries, whose job it was to write down contracts and draft negotiable instruments which, by virtue of this process, were lawful, valid, and enforceable. (See Berman, pp. 341 and 355.)

Universality and the Law Merchant   *Universal* laws are those that apply to everyone regardless of their social status or their place of origin. The universal applicability of the law merchant was made necessary by the global nature of trade in the late Middle Ages. The city-states of Europe hosted international fairs and the coastal cities became permanent centers for international trade. Towns and coastal cities began to adhere to the law merchant rather than their local laws which tended to be prejudiced against foreigners. In *Law and Revolution*, Berman tells us that, as the influence of the central government began to grow, some rulers agreed to incorporate the law merchant into their national documents, such as the *Magna Carta* in 1215 which contains a clause that specifically grants safe passage to foreign merchants in England. Other rulers, notably those in Italy, entered formal agreements that guaranteed that the law merchant would be used in settling any contract disagreements that might involve their people. (See Berman, pp. 342–344.). Weber agrees with Berman that a successful capitalist system depends upon the establishment of a legal system with formal rules that emerge from a rational process (Weber, p. 25). Moreover, Henri Sée concurs that the international character of trade gave birth to modern capitalism (Sée Henri See, pp. 25, 29–30).

Mutuality and the Law Merchant

The concept of *mutuality* or *reciprocity* in the law merchant is the notion that commercial arrangements always involve a process of evenhanded cooperation between the parties. Mutuality in the law merchant emerged organically from within the commercial culture which had at its foundation a belief in reciprocity. Moreover, Berman tells us that the principle of reciprocity insisted on mutuality at two levels. First, parties to any commercial transaction were expressly forbidden to cheat, lie, or trick one another. Second, all commercial transactions had to be fair to each party. This principle outlawed contracts that involved outrageous prices and those that took advantage of a party's weakened position (See Berman, pp. 344–346). Of course, Weber reminds us that there is a practical foundation for the principle of reciprocity as there are for all such virtues. Honesty, he reports, has its value, if only because it will earn good credit for trustworthy merchants. (Weber, p. 52). Does the utilitarian nature of reciprocity make it wrong? No. However, it does make the pursuit of reciprocity a bit less romantic.

Involvement and Law Merchant

Involvement requires that those affected by the law participate in its making and its execution. According to Berman, from the outset merchants were involved in the establishment and the operation of the courts that adjudicated disputes involving contracts and other commercial disagreements such as those that might question the authenticity of negotiable instruments. Specifically, the courts held in European markets and fairs were run by businessmen who were elected to act as judges. The courts established by the guilds were run by the elected guild leaders who often hand picked guild members to assist in deciding certain disputes. Some territories also developed staple courts that dealt with cases involving the primary product or "staple" of a certain town or village. The courts in the Italian city-states such as Milan also elected merchants to hear disputes involving contract and other commercial transactions. Many of the coastal cities created their own local courts, sometimes referred to as admiralty courts, to handle commercial disputes involving goods carried as cargo by the ships that docked at those ports. (See Berman, pp. 346–348.) Berman, however, is careful to remind us that this exclusive control of the courts by the business class also had its down side. Berman argues that when people have the power to control their own legal system they can use that power to protect themselves, which is exactly what happened to the new business class in Europe during the Middle Ages (See Berman, p. 348). Another legal scholar, Gerald Turkel, agrees with Berman arguing that it is generally best for the legal system to stand on its own, free from the outside influences of other institutions within the social structure. This permits the legal system to develop its own cultural identity, something that can help legal practitioners to resist outside pressure. (See Gerald Turkel, *Law and Society: Critical Approaches* (Boston: Allyn and Bacon, 1996), p. 133).

The Law Merchant and the Common Law

The integration of mercantile law into the diverse legal traditions in Europe was especially difficult in England where a strong common law tradition had developed during the late Middle Ages. As noted in Chapter 2, The Sources of the Law, common law was established in England as a way to bring all English law together into a single, consistent, comprehensive system. This program put the law merchant and the merchants who administered that law on a collision course with common law and with common law lawyers and judges. Such collisions did occur from time to time, but ultimately the law merchant evolved and was integrated into common law.

Fair Courts and Staples Courts   The first merchant courts in England were established in the 11th century as part of every royal charter that legalized a local fair. These fair courts (also known as pie powder courts because of the dusty feet ["pie poudre"] of the merchants who took part in the proceedings) were empowered to hear cases involving commercial disputes, and since the juries were inevitably made up of merchants, the law merchant was used to adjudicate the cases. The fair courts lost their power with the creation of staple courts under the Ordinance of the Staple of 1353. Staple courts heard cases that involved certain set commodities. They were run by mayors who were forced to learn and apply mercantile law. This worked well for about two centuries. Then in the 16th century the staples courts were taken over by the judges of the King's Court and common law dominated that court [See E. Allan Farnsworth and John Honnold, *Commercial Law: Cases and Materials* (Mineola, NY: The Foundation Press, 1976), pp. 3–4; Berman pp. 348–350.]

Admiralty Courts, Arbitration, and Statutory Law   Admiralty courts were tribunals set up in seaport towns to handle disputes involving maritime law, shipping contracts, contests over docking rights, collisions at sea, and the like. When the common law judges took over the staples courts, the merchants took their cases to the admiralty courts to ensure that the law merchant would be used to settle their disputes. This tactic became ineffective when the common law courts were given jurisdiction over most commercial cases throughout England, including those that had been handled by the admiralty courts. The merchants fought back by establishing their own arbitration groups to avoid common law altogether. The common law courts finally began to see the wisdom of integrating common law with the law merchant and this integration practice became more accepted by the beginning of the 18th century. When Lord Mansfield became the Chief Justice, the program kicked into high gear and for more than three decades the Chief Justice worked to integrate the law merchant into common law. His work continued for the next century. Then late in the 19th century, Parliament passed the Bills of Exchange Act and the Sale of Goods Act both of which codified common law principles which by that time had successfully absorbed most law merchant principles. When the National Conference of Commissioners was established in 1895 in the United States, they developed two model laws, the Uniform Negotiable Instruments Act which followed the Bills of Exchange Act

quick quiz 7-1

1. A valid contract results in an obligation that can be enforced in a court of law.   true | false

2. Mercantile law, the law merchant, and *lex mercatoria* are all different names for the same area of law.   true | false

3. The six characteristics of the law merchant are neutrality, universality, mutuality, involvement, integration, and evolution.   true | false

Table 7-1 Law Merchant Principles in Modern Law

CONTRACT LAW

The division between a law that focuses only on goods and one that centers on real property

The development of the rights of a good faith purchaser in goods

The transfer of ownership of goods based on the transfer of documents.

The development of the concept of warranties of fitness and warranties of merchantability.

NEGOTIABLE INSTRUMENTS

The development of negotiable bills of exchange and promissory notes.

BUSINESS ORGANIZATIONS

The invention of limited joint stock companies and the "company under a collective name"—forefathers of the modern corporation

Development of joint property ownership in partnerships

The development of survivorship rights among partners in a partnership

SECURED TRANSACTIONS

The invention of the chattel mortgage

CREDIT AND BANKING

Development of credit institutions at the great monasteries in Europe

The banking and lending operations of the Teutonic Knights and the Templars lead to modern banking procedures

INSURANCE CONTRACTS

The development of maritime insurance

The appearance of "private" insurance in the Middle Ages

The development of insurance companies in the 17th century

INTERNATIONAL LAW

Increased international trade leads to the need to develop international agreements

INTELLECTUAL PROPERTY

The creation of patents and trademarks

Sources: Table adapted from information in Harold J. Berman, *Law and Revolution: The Formation of the Western Legal Tradition.* (Cambridge: Harvard UP, 1983), 349–350 and Henri Sée, *Modern Capitalism: Its Origin and Evolution* (New York: Adelphi Company, 1928), 20–24.

and the Uniform Sales Act which was patterned after the Sale of Goods Act. (See Farnsworth and Honnold, pp. 4–5) Despite this tangled power struggle between common law and the law merchant, the two traditions were merged, with the principles of the law merchant dominating the law governing commercial transactions. Some of these principles are charted in Table 7-1. (See Berman, pp. 348–350 and Henri Sée, pp. 20–24.)

7-2 The Multidimensional Nature of Contract Law

Contract law forms the basis of all other law in the corporate capitalist setting. Without contract law there could be no buying and selling, no transfer of property rights, no properly planned and executed deliveries, no hiring of agents, no partnership agreements, no stock transfers, and so on. Like many other areas of the law, contract law is based on safeguarding people's rights. We saw this in criminal law and in tort law, and we see it now in contract law. The difference is that in criminal law and tort law, most of the time, human rights are inherent within the social setting. In other words, people have rights just because they are a part of our social structure. In contract law, people adopt new rights and duties as part of their contractual relationships which are entered voluntarily. For this reason among a few others, contract law is a multidimensional area of the law, laying out not only what our rights and duties are, but also whether we have actually undertaken those duties and been given those rights. To explore this in more detail, we will first look at the elements of a contract and then at several additional multidimensional aspects of contract law, including the objectives of contract law, remedies in contract law, contracts and the UCC, contracts and other agreements, contracts and agency law, and contracts that must be written.

The Elements of a Contract

In order for a contract to be legally binding on all parties, each element must be present. There are four elements that make up a contract. If even one of these elements is missing, there is no contract. This does not mean that there is no agreement. It simply means that there is no contract and no contractual relationship that can be vindicated in a court of law. The four elements are mutual assent, consideration, capacity, and legality. (Note: Before reading about these elements you might want to study Table 7-2 on page 155.)

Mutual Assent   A valid *offer* requires that the *offeror* make a definite expression of the desire to enter a contract in terms that are clear and unambiguous and that are communicated to the *offeree*. An *acceptance* occurs when, without changing the essential terms of the offer, the offeree communicates an acceptance to the offeror. Once the offer has been properly made by the offeror and accepted properly by the offeree, then *mutual assent* exists between them. Often the courts will say that mutual assent exists when there has been a *meeting of the minds* among the parties to the agreement. If mutual assent has been destroyed, the relationship that results is said to be defective. Those situations that might destroy assent include: *fraud* (both active and passive), *misrepresentation, mistake, duress,* and *undue influence.*

Contracts create binding legal obligations that each party may enforce against the other.

Consideration   *Consideration* is the thing of value promised to the other party in exchange for something else of value promised by the other party. Each side in a contract must give up something, their legal detriment, and must gain something, their legal benefit. The courts are generally not concerned with the adequacy of consideration. This means that the courts avoid determining "how much" consideration is enough consideration. That determination is up to the parties to the contract. However, if the consideration

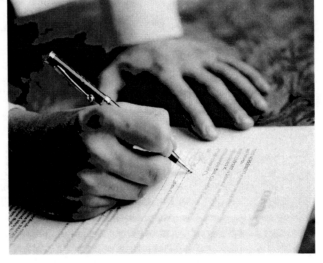

is *unconscionable* (ridiculously out of line with the nature of the contract), the court might intervene. The parties can settle value-related disputes on their own through a process of *accord and satisfaction*. Some things that might at first appear to be consideration are not consideration. These things include: *past consideration, pre-existing duties, illusory promises,* and *future gifts*. On the other hand, those situations involving *promissory estoppel* will not eliminate a party's responsibility to compensate an innocent party, even in the absence of real consideration.

Capacity   The third contractual element is *capacity,* that is, the legal ability to make a contract. All the parties to a contract are legally permitted to assume that the other parties possess capacity. This assumption, however, is a *rebuttable presumption* which means that any one of the parties to the contract can attack or rebut that presumption. Many, perhaps most, capacity questions involve minors. The law permits a minor to rescind his or her contracts. This means that minors actually have "extra-capacity," that is, the capacity to enter and the capacity to leave a contract. There are limits to this privilege, however. Minors must provide the reasonable value for *necessaries,* that is, materials that are needed for the minor's health, safety, and welfare that are not provided by a parent or a guardian. Minors must also abide by certain contracts required by law, such as insurance contracts, contracts for educational loans, agency contracts, valid marriage contracts, enlistment contracts, contracts concerning child support, and those for pregnancy care, among others. Capacity also appears as a question in cases involving a party with a mental impairment. Some mental impairments result from physical injuries; others are genetic; some are health-related illnesses; and others are psychological in nature. Whatever the source of the difficulty, a person's mental impairment may also eliminate contractual capacity, but only if the party claiming the impairment can demonstrate that the impairment was so severe at the time the contract was made that he or she could not understand the nature, the purpose, or the effect of the agreement. If that is the case, then the contract will be voidable by the party lacking capacity. In contrast, if a person has been declared incompetent by a court, then that person's contracts are absolutely void.

Legality   The final element of a binding contract is *legality*. Parties cannot be permitted to enforce a contract that involves something that the law says cannot be done. Clearly, any contract to commit a crime or a tort would be illegal and, therefore, void. Some contracts are also made illegal by statutory law. These include usurious contracts, gambling contracts, unlicensed agreements, unconscionable agreements, and some Sunday agreements. There are also some contracts that have been made illegal by the courts based on the doctrine of *public policy*. These include agreements to obstruct justice, agreements interfering with public safety, agreements to defraud creditors, agreements to escape liability (AKA exculpatory clauses), agreements in restraint of trade, and agreements to suppress competition. In some states, several of these contracts, agreements to obstruct justice, for instance, are also made illegal by statutory law.

The Objectives of Contract Law

In general the law is designed to promote order, stability, and justice. All the subdivisions within the law are charged with these same goals. Criminal law does this by defining criminal behavior with great specificity and then by providing a set of procedures that are followed fairly and consistently in order to make certain that those who threaten order, stability, and justice no longer walk among us. Tort law does the same thing by providing a system of compensation for the innocent victims of deliberate and accidental torts. Contract law is much more complicated and multidimensional than other areas

Table 7-2	The Four Elements of a Contract
Element	**Explanation**
Mutual Assent	Once the offer has been properly made by the offeror and accepted properly by the offeree, then mutual assent exists between them. Often the courts will say that mutual assent exists when there has been a meeting of the minds among the parties to the agreement Those situations that might destroy assent include: fraud (both active and passive), misrepresentation, mistake, duress, and undue influence.
Consideration	Consideration is the thing of value promised to the other party in exchange for something else of value promised by the other party. Each side in a contract must give up something, their legal detriment, and must gain something, their legal benefit. The courts are generally not concerned with the adequacy of consideration.
Capacity	The third contractual element is capacity, that is, the legal ability to make a contract. All the parties to a contract are legally permitted to assume that the other parties possess capacity. This assumption, however, is a rebuttable presumption which means that any of the parties can attack or rebut that presumption. Many, perhaps most, capacity questions involve minors. Capacity also appears as a question in cases involving some sort of mental impairment.
Legality	The final element of a binding contract is legality. Clearly, any contract to commit a crime or a tort would be illegal and, therefore, void. Some contracts are also made illegal by statutory law. These include usurious contracts, gambling contracts, unlicensed agreements, unconscionable agreements, and some Sunday agreements. There are also some contracts that have been made illegal by the courts based on the doctrine of public policy.

of the law because it must not only provide the mechanism for punishment or compensation but also explain why that mechanism is used and not some other simpler and more effective method.

Rehabilitation in Contract Law The underlying objective of contract law is to determine whether the parties to the contract entered the agreement freely. If the court determines that the parties willingly entered the agreement, then the contract is valid. Then, if the court finds that one of the parties breached the contract, that party will have to rehabilitate the innocent party by compensating that party for any loss that results from the breach. Usually the courts will not force a party to go through with the terms of a contract, even when a breach has been proven. This is especially true of service contracts. However, the courts will compel the breaching party to rehabilitate the innocent party for any loss that resulted from the breach. The courts say that the objective of this rehabilitation is to place the innocent party in as good a position as he or she would have been had the contract been performed.

The Payment of Damages In contract law the victims are compensated by the payment of money damages to make up for their losses. Generally, these damages are equal to the real financial loss suffered by the innocent victim. These damages are called *actual* or *compensatory damages*. Sometimes victims are entitled to damages for indirect losses. *Incidental damages* are those that are paid by the breaching party to make up for any expenses paid by the victim to prevent any additional loss. *Consequential damages* are indirect damages that result because of special circumstances that exist with a particular contract. Punitive damages are designed to punish the wrongdoer for his or her outrageous conduct. As a general rule, the courts do not award punitive damages in contract cases. Such damages are generally more appropriate in tort law cases. Nevertheless, there are exceptions to this rule. For instance, in cases of fraud, a court may approve punitive damages, because a party who commits fraud has attempted to undermine the entire contract system, something the court will not abide.

Recovery Limits and Equitable Relief
There are built-in limits to the measure of the damages awarded in a contract case. For example, the innocent party cannot take advantage of the breach by deliberately raising the amount of damages that the other party must pay. This principle is called the duty to mitigate the damages or just the *duty to mitigate*. Also, there is an exception to the rule that says that the courts cannot force a party to go through with a contract. The court may force a party to perform the terms of an agreement if the contract involves land or some other unique item, such as an original work of art or a family heirloom. This is an equitable remedy called *specific performance*. *Equitable remedies* are those that are imposed by the courts when the payment of money would not compensate for the loss suffered by the innocent party. Another equitable remedy is injunction. In contract law, an *injunction* is a court order issued by a court directing a party to refrain from some activity that represents a breach of contract. Injunctions can be temporary or permanent. A temporary injunction is issued as a way to delay further activity until the court can decide whether to make the injunction permanent. A party who disobeys an injunction does so under threat of a contempt of court.

Multidimensional Principles of Contract Law

Stacked on top of the elements of a contract, the objectives of contract law, and the remedies offered in contract law are a series of additional aspects that must be examined to set the stage before entering a more detailed study of contract law. We have referred to these additional areas of the law as the multidimensional principles of contract law. These multidimensional principles include contracts and the Uniform Commercial Code, contracts and other agreements, contracts and privity, contracts and agency law, and contracts and the Statute of Frauds.

Contracts and the Uniform Commercial Code
The Uniform Commercial Code (UCC) is a model set of laws designed to govern almost all commercial transactions. The UCC is organized in the following way: sale of goods contracts (Article 2); commercial paper (Article 3); bank deposits and collections (Article 4); letters of credit (Article 5); bulk transfers (Article 6); warehouse receipts, bills of lading, and other documents of title (Article 7); investment securities (Article 8); secured transactions, sales of accounts, contract rights and chattel paper (Article 9); effective date and repealer (Article 10); and transition provisions (Article 11). All other types of contracts, such as employment contracts and real property (land) contracts, are covered by common law and by special statutes dedicated to some aspect of those contracts. Thus, employment contracts will be affected by labor law and minimum wage statutes; real property contracts will be covered by zoning laws and property tax laws; while both employment and real property contracts will be affected by civil rights legislation.

Contracts and Other Agreements

All contracts are agreements, but not all agreements are contracts. An agreement may or may not be legally enforceable. To be enforceable, an agreement must conform to the law of contracts. This means at the very least that to be a legally recognized contract, an agreement must possess the four elements

THE OPENING CASE *Revisited, Part I*
Multidimensional Contract Law: *Tubelite Co., Inc. v.*
Original Sign Studio, Round 2

Recall that the Opening Case at the beginning of this chapter involved a dispute over two agreements between the Tubelite Co., the seller, and Original Sign Studio, the buyer. The first agreement was an application for credit, in which Original Sign agreed to pay for all materials shipped by Tubelite and to remit an 18 percent finance charge for overdue payments. In the second agreement, Tubelite agreed to be Original Sign's exclusive supplier. The terms of the agreement were written in a letter by an agent of Original Sign but never signed by anyone from Tubelite. The agreement stated that Tubelite would supply Original Sign with all the material that it requested but that it would bill Original Sign only for the materials that the sign company actually used and then, in exchange for being Original Sign's exclusive supplier, it would charge a discounted rate of somewhere between 10 and 25 percent.

Tubelite also agreed to install shelving at Original Sign's warehouse for proper storing of the materials. Both agreements, the one for credit and the one for the actual shipment of construction materials concern goods and, therefore, fall within Article 2 of the Uniform Commercial Code. Although this might seem obvious, the appellate court felt compelled to make certain that both parties understood this. Thus, the court writes, "Goods are 'all things (including specially manufactured goods) which are movable at the time of identification to the contract for sale other than the money in which the price is to be paid, investment securities, and things in action.' R.C. 1302.01(A)(8). Here Tubelite seeks to recover payment for signage materials that it sold to Sign Studio. As these materials are 'movable' the Ohio Uniform Commercial Code applies to the transactions at issue."

of a contract: mutual assent, consideration, capacity, and legality. The courts have never been inclined to enforce social agreements such as dates, dinner engagements and so on. Many states have extended this concept to agreements to marry and agreements to live together without the benefit of a marriage contract.

Contracts and Privity   The general rule of contract law is that the parties must stand in privity to one another. Privity means that all parties must have a legally recognized interest in the subject of the contract if they are to be bound by it. Parties who do not have such an interest in the subject matter of the contract may not be bound by it. Their right to bring a lawsuit in the event of a breach of contract would also be in question. Despite the privity rule, it is possible for two or more parties to provide benefits to a third party under the terms of a contract. However, the law still makes a distinction between third parties who are *intended beneficiaries* and third parties who are *incidental beneficiaries*. For example, in a life insurance contract, the parties who are named as those who will receive payment on the death of the insured would be intended beneficiaries. Given a breach of that contract, those intended beneficiaries would have a cause of action against the defaulting life insurance company. Moreover, an exception to the general rule of privity exists in cases involving warranties and product liability.

UCC 1-201(11) and (21) (see pages 817 and 818)

Contracts and Agency Law   An *agent* is a party who has been hired or appointed by a *principal* to perform some sort of work, usually of a business nature, for the principal. Agents owe several levels of duty to the principal. For example, the agent must obey the instructions of the principal, must be loyal to the principal, must exercise due care in doing work for the principal, must perform the work for the principal personally, must account for all money and property that is entrusted to his or her care by the principal, and must communicate all relevant agency information to the principal. The agent has all of these duties because, in effect, when the agent acts the principal acts. Agents can, therefore, bind the principal to a contract, even if the principal is not present. If the agent creates a contract for the principal and there is a breach of contract suit filed by the third party, the principal will be the initial target of that lawsuit. If the principal loses the lawsuit, and the fault lies with the agent, the agent will be liable to the principal for the losses he or she incurred because of that lawsuit.

Contracts and the Statute of Frauds The *Statute of Frauds* is a law that outlines those contracts that must be in writing to be enforceable in court. The original Statute of Frauds was passed by Parliament in 1677 and was officially named the Act for the Prevention of Frauds and Perjuries. The statute was part of colonial law in New England and was, thus, assimilated into American law by the states after the Revolution. It is still part of the statutory law covering contracts in every state and in the District of Columbia. Six types of contracts must be in writing to be enforceable. These six include (1) contracts that cannot be completed within one year; (2) contracts involving land; (3) contracts in consideration of marriage; (4) contracts made by executors to pay a debt of the estate out of his or her own finances; (5) a promise to pay the debt of another; and (6) contracts for the sale of goods valued at $500 or more. If the statute of frauds demands a written contract

THE OPENING CASE *Revisited, Part II*
Multidimensional Contract Law: *Tubelite Co., Inc. v. Original Sign Studio*, Round 3

Recall that the lawsuit entitled *Tubelite Co., Inc. v. Original Sign Studio* involved two agreements. The first agreement was an application for credit, in which Original Sign agreed to pay for all materials shipped by Tubelite and to remit an 18 percent finance charge for overdue payments. In the second agreement, Tubelite agreed to be Original Sign's exclusive supplier. The terms of the agreement were in a letter written by an agent of Original Sign and presented to an agent of Tubelite. The letter read in part, "The purpose of this document reflects the agreements reached between the parties . . . The parties agreed to a full consignment program, as described by the participants from, Tubelite Co., Inc., to the participants representing, The Original Sign Studio, Inc." This letter, however, was never signed by anyone from Tubelite.

In an effort to jettison the second agreement, Tubelite argues that the second agreement was never placed in writing, as the Statute of Frauds demands, and should, therefore, be disregarded in favor of the first agreement. The people from Tubelite are correct when they argue that the contract was not in writing as it should be under the Statute of Frauds. However, one of the

exceptions provided under the UCC applies in this case, removing the need for a writing. The exception tracks this way. First, the contract was presented to agents of Tubelite. Second, those agents had 10 days to reject that version of the contract. Third, Tubelite agents never took advantage of that grace period and did not reject the writing. This means that, under the Statute of Frauds, the letter created by the Original Sign agent becomes a writing that satisfies the statute's rules. This is, in fact, how the appellate court ruled in the lawsuit.

Another issue emerges in this case. The Tubelite agent who did not reject the letter from Original Sign within the 10-day period will be liable to Tubelite should it lose the case. The agent breached his duty of due care when he did not reject the letter. It is that failure to act that makes the second contract enforceable and opens the door to a likely loss for Tubelite. If Tubelite does lose the case, it would have the right to bring a separate cause of action against that agent. Such a move is unlikely, however. Companies like Tubelite rarely bring such lawsuits. As you can imagine, they are very bad for corporate morale.

and, for some reason, the parties never reduce that contract to writing, the contract remains valid but is unenforceable, which means that the court will probably dismiss the action.

Exceptions to the Statutory Rule Several interesting exceptions apply to the rules imposed by the Statute of Frauds in relation to sale of goods contracts. The statute says that a contract for the sale of goods valued at $500 or more must be in writing unless the contract is for specially manufactured goods. The writing also becomes unnecessary with a sale of goods contract if the goods have already been shipped and accepted or a payment has been received and accepted. Also, if one of the parties reduces the contract to writing and sends that writing to the other party, that unsigned paper will be sufficient as a writing under the statute unless the receiving party objects in writing within 10 days. Finally, in a court action if the party that has invoked the Statute of Frauds to escape enforcement has also admitted under oath that the contract exists, no writing is needed.

Rules of Interpretation Despite the careful precision with which the Statute of Frauds was written, whenever contracts are reduced to writing, someone is going to disagree on what was meant by the written terms. To deal with this problem, the courts have developed rules of construction to guide judges as they interpret the written word. The first rule is the *standard construction rule* which tells judges that their primary objective in the interpretation of a written contract is to uncover the goals that the parties had when they entered the contract in the first place. As a corollary of that rule, the courts must also interpret any ambiguous clause against the party who actually wrote the contract. The goal of this rule is to encourage those parties who actually put pen to paper (or fingers to keyboard) to be as clear

THE OPENING CASE *Revisited, Part III*
Multidimensional Contract Law: *Tubelite Co., Inc. v. Original Sign Studio*, Round 4

As noted above, *Tubelite Co., Inc. v. Original Sign Studio* involved two agreements. The first agreement was an application for credit, in which Original Sign agreed to pay for all materials shipped by Tubelite and to remit an 18 percent finance charge for overdue payments. In the second agreement, Tubelite agreed to be Original Sign's exclusive supplier. The terms of the agreement were reduced to writing in a letter written by an agent of Original Sign and presented to an agent of Tubelite. Although the letter was never signed by anyone at Tubelite, under the Uniform Commercial Code, inaction by Tubelite transformed the letter into a written version of a consignment agreement between the two companies. It is important to understand that, while the court ruled that the letter satisfies the Statute of Frauds requirements for a writing, it did not say that the letter is a contract. So the court has decided that the case can be heard in court, but it has not decided who will

win. This requires determining which agreement, the credit application or the consignment letter, was valid. To determine this the court must look at two things, the words themselves and the conduct of the parties. The words of the credit application are by themselves too incomplete to create a valid contract. There is no way to identify subject matter, quantity, or price. In contrast, the second agreement, the consignment letter, describes the goods ordered, sets out the quantity that Original Sign has requisitioned, establishes the price of the items, and outlines a payment plan. Thus, between the two agreements, the odds-on favorite to be declared the actual contract between the parties is the consignment letter. Of course the court is free to also consider the conduct between the parties to establish which of these documents is the actual contract and so the final resolution is still up in the air. (See UCC 2-204 (1).)

and straightforward as humanly possible. Otherwise, if a question of interpretation comes up later, they risk having the judge rule against them. A different problem arises when some of the terms are not just vague or ambiguous, but are actually missing from the contract. Terms such as the subject matter, the quantity, and the price to be paid are essential to a binding contractual relationship. On the other hand, at least under the UCC, it is not always necessary to have all of the terms just as long as the judge has enough information to determine a "reasonably certain basis for giving an appropriate remedy." (See UCC 2-204 (3).

---

quick quiz 7-2

1. The four elements are mutual assent, consideration, capacity, and legality.   true | false

2. The courts says that the objective of rehabilitation is to place the innocent party in as good a position as he or she would have been had the contract been performed.   true | false

3. All contracts must be in writing to be enforced in a court of law.   true | false

---

7-3 Contractual Characteristics

Contractual characteristics fall into five different categories: valid, void, voidable, and unenforceable; unilateral and bilateral; express and implied; informal and formal; and executory and executed. Any given contract can be classifiable in all five ways. Thus, for example, a single contract could be said to be valid, bilateral, express, formal, and executed, or any other acceptable combination of characteristics.

Valid, Void, Voidable, and Unenforceable Contracts

A valid contract is one that is legally binding and fully enforceable by the court. In contrast, a void contract is one that has no legal effect whatsoever. For example, a contract to perform an illegal act would be void. A voidable contract is one that may be avoided or canceled by one of the parties. Contracts made by minors or induced by fraud or misrepresentation are examples of voidable contracts. An unenforceable contract is one that, because of some rule of law, cannot be upheld by a court of law. An unenforceable contract may have all the elements of a complete contract and still be unenforceable.

Unilateral and Bilateral Contracts

A unilateral contract is an agreement in which one party makes a promise to do something in return for an act of some sort. The classic example of a unilateral contract is a reward contract. A person who promises to pay $5 to the finder of a lost driver's license does not expect a promise in return. Rather, the person expects the return of the lost license. When the license is returned, the contract arises and the promisor owes the finder $5.

In contrast, a bilateral contract is one in which both parties make promises. Bilateral contracts come into existence at the moment the two promises are made. A breach of contract occurs when one of the two parties fails to keep the promise. When there is a breach of contract, the injured party has the right to ask a court of law to somehow remedy the situation. (Breach of contract and remedies are discussed in detail in Chapter 12.)

Express and Implied Contracts

A contract can be either express or implied. An express contract requires some sort of written or spoken expression indicating a desire to enter the contractual relationship. An implied contract is created by the actions or gestures of the parties involved in the transaction.

Express Contracts When contracting parties accept mutual obligations, either through oral discussion or written communication, they have created an express contract. Oral negotiations in many cases will be reduced to writing, but this is not always necessary.

A written contract does not have to be a long, formal preprinted agreement. Although such lengthy, preprinted forms are common in some businesses, other, less formal written documents are frequently used to show that a contract exists. For example, a written contract may take the form of a letter, sales slip and receipt, notation, or memorandum. A written contract may be typed, printed, keystroked, scrawled, or written in beautiful penmanship. In some situations, state laws require certain types of contracts to be in writing. (See Chapter 11.)

A QUESTION OF ETHICS

Suppose you posted a reward notice that read, "Reward: $50 for the return of my lost college class ring." Suppose further that someone who did not know of the reward offer found your ring and returned it. Legally you would not have to pay the reward money to the person who found your ring because he or she did not know about your offer. However, would it be ethical not to pay the reward to the finder? Explain.

When a contract is placed in writing, it is essential that the content be as clear and unambiguous as possible. When faced with a dispute over an ambiguous clause, the court may be compelled to look at factual evidence to determine the actual intent of the parties. This review may mean that a case that could have been dismissed early will have to go to trial so that the court can make a factual determination of intent by looking at evidence beyond the terms in the writing.

When the law does not require a written agreement, an *oral contract* resulting from the spoken words of the parties will be enough. Parties to such an agreement, however, should anticipate the difficulty of proving the contractual relationship, should disputes arise later. Nevertheless, expressing every agreement in writing, in anticipation of a future need of proof, is impractical in the fast-paced modern world of business.

Implied Contracts One who knowingly accepts benefits from another person may be obligated for their payment, even though no express agreement has been made. An agreement of this type can be either implied-in-fact or implied-in-law. A contract implied by the direct or indirect acts of the parties is known as an implied-in-fact contract. Pumping gas into a car at a self-service gas station is an example of an implied-in-fact contract. Because the parties to a contract enter that contract by an exercise of free will, the court follows the objective concept rule in interpreting the acts and gestures of a party. Under this rule, the meaning of one's actions is determined by the impression those actions would make upon any reasonable person who might have witnessed them, not by a party's self-serving claim of what was meant or intended by the actions.

About the Law

The law that declares which contracts must be in writing is called the Statute of Frauds. In its original form when it was passed by Parliament in 1677, it was known as the Act for the Prevention of Fraud and Perjuries.

EXAMPLE 7-1: Implied-in-Fact Deals: Can Inaction Create a Contract?

Herbert Ward watched workers employed by the Rice Lawn and Garden Greenhouse as they chemically treated his front lawn. In fact, Ward had no contract with Rice and had not ordered any chemical treatments of his property. The treatment should have been performed on another house at 750 Maple Street, instead of at Ward's, which had an address of 570 Maple St. Ward never stopped the work crew, even though he knew that a mistake had been made. Rice would be within its rights to believe that the work was being done with Ward's consent. In assessing damages for the cost of the improvement, the court would apply the objective concept rule. A reasonable person who might have watched Rice treat the front lawn would conclude that Ward had freely consented to the work.

An implied-in-law contract is imposed by a court when someone is unjustly enriched. It is used when a contract cannot be enforced or there is no actual written, oral, or implied-in-fact agreement. Applying reasons of justice and fairness, a court may obligate one who has unfairly benefited at the innocent expense of another. An implied-in-law contract is also called a quasi-contract.

EXAMPLE 7-2: Implied-in-Law Deals: Can Injustice Be Prevented?

Karl Rapp was found unconscious in his hotel room by Jan Stevens, the third-floor maid. She immediately called 911 and then notified Ken Kramer, the hotel manager. Kramer arranged to have Rapp placed in a hospital for emergency treatment. When Rapp regained consciousness, he refused to pay for the treatment, claiming that he was not aware of what was going on and had not agreed to what had been done to him. The case illustrates a quasi-contractual situation, wherein it would be unfair to allow the injured person to benefit at the expense of the hospital. In any suit that might arise over this expense, a court would require Rapp to pay the fair value of the services rendered.

The quasi-contract concept cannot apply, however, to obtain payment for an act that a party simply feels should be done. The concept also cannot be applied when one party bestows a benefit on another unnecessarily or through misconduct or negligence. A quasi-contract is not a contract in the true sense of the word, because it is created by the court. It does not result from the mutual assent of the parties, as do express or implied-in-fact contracts.

Informal and Formal Contracts

The law sometimes requires that contracts follow formalities prescribed by statute or common law. These are called formal contracts. All others are classified as informal.

Informal Contracts

Any oral or written contract that is not under seal or is not a contract of record is considered an informal contract. An informal contract is also known as a *simple contract*. An informal contract generally has no requirements as to language, form, or construction. It comprises obligations entered into by parties whose promises are expressed in the simplest and usually most ordinary, nonlegal language.

UCC 2-203 (see page 823)

Formal Contracts

Under common law principles, a formal contract differs from other types of contracts in that it has to be (1) written; (2) signed, witnessed, and placed under the seal of the parties; and (3) delivered. A *seal* is a mark or an impression placed on a written contract indicating that the instrument was executed and accepted in a formal manner. The UCC removed the requirement for a seal in sale-of-goods contracts. Some states, however, still require the use of the seal in agreements related to the sale and transfer of real property.

Today, a person's seal may be any mark or sign placed after the signature intended to be the signer's seal. In states still requiring the seal or formal contract, it is sufficient to write the word *seal* after the signature.

EXAMPLE 7-3: Formal Contracts: Is a Seal Still Needed?

Audrey Kimmel signed an agreement with Corey Baumberger to buy seven acres of farmland owned by Baumberger just outside Bellville. Later that day, Baumberger found another interested buyer who was willing to pay seven times as much as Kimmel had offered for the land. Kimmel had signed the sales agreement without including any representation of the seal. In any state that required such formality in all real property contracts, Kimmel would now be helpless in attempting to enforce the original contract that she had made with Baumberger.

Contracts of Record   A special type of formal contract is known as a contract of record. Often, such a contract is confirmed by the court with an accompanying judgment issued in favor of one of the parties. The judgment is recorded, giving the successful litigant the right to demand satisfaction of the judgment. A contract of record is not a contract in the true sense of the word, because it is court created. Although it does not have all of the elements of a valid contract, it is enforced for public policy reasons.

EXAMPLE 7-4: Contracts of Record: When Can Litigants Demand Their Money?

Mortimer Byrne installed a new roof on Alexander Harper's house in Lakeside for the agreed-upon price of $7,500. Harper paid Byrne $4,000 so that he could secure materials. After the job was completed, Byrne sent Harper a bill for $3,500. Harper sent Byrne a check for $2,500, on which was written "in full payment of all money owed." These words were in very fine print and not seen by Byrne. Byrne sued Harper in the small claims division of the Ottawa County Court of Common Pleas for the amount still owed. The court ruled in favor of Byrne and entered a judgment against Harper for the money owed. Entry of the judgment created a contract of record, which was enforceable against Harper.

Executory and Executed Contracts

A contract that has not yet been fully performed by the parties is called an executory contract. Such a contract may be completely executory, in which case nothing has been done, or it may be partly executory, in which case the contract is partially complete. When a contract's terms have been completely and satisfactorily carried out by both parties, it is an executed contract. Such contracts are no longer active agreements and are valuable only if a dispute about the agreement occurs.

quick quiz 7-3

1. A void contract is one that can be avoided by one or more of the parties. true | false

2. A formal contract is also known as a simple contract. true | false

3. A contract that has not yet been fully performed by the parties is called an executory contract. true | false

Summary

7.1 With the Roman law providing a model, with the Roman Catholic Church supplying political and social support, with canon law supplying a moral framework, and with practicality guiding their activities over a 300-year period, the merchants of the late Middle Ages developed a body of active law that was characterized by neutrality, universality, mutuality, involvement, integration, and evolution. The law merchant was developed by the merchants themselves. The law merchant also successfully integrated itself into other legal tradition such English common law. Many of its provisions still exist in today's court decisions and statutes.

7.2 Contract law is a multidimensional area of the law, laying out not only what our rights and duties are, but also whether we have actually undertaken those duties and been given those rights. To explore this in more detail, we looked at the elements of a contract and at several additional multidimensional aspects of contract law including the objectives of contract law, remedies in contract law, contracts and the UCC, contracts and other agreements, contracts and agency law, and contracts that must be written.

7.3 Contractual characteristics fall into five different categories. These categories are valid, void, voidable, or unenforceable; unilateral or bilateral; express or implied; informal or formal; and executory or executed.

Key Terms

admiralty court, 151
bilateral contract, 160
breach of contract, 160
canon law, 148
capitalism, 148
contract, 147
contract of record, 163
executed contract, 163
executory contract, 163
express contract, 161

fair court, 151
formal contract, 162
implied contract, 161
implied-in-fact contract, 161
implied-in-law contract, 162
informal contract, 162
law merchant, 147
objective concept rule, 161
pie powder court, 151
privity, 157

punitive damages, 156
quasi-contract, 162
rehabilitate, 155
staple court, 151
unenforceable contract, 160
unilateral contract, 160
valid contract, 160
void contract, 160
voidable contract, 160

Questions for Review and Discussion

1. What is a contract?
2. How did the law merchant develop?

3. How did the law merchant merge with common law?
4. What are the four elements of a contract?

5. What is the objective of contract law?
6. What is the role of the UCC in contract law?
7. How do contracts differ from other agreements?
8. What are the roles of privity and agency in contract law?

9. What contracts must be in writing to be enfocrceable?
10. What are the characteristics of a contract?

Cases for Analysis

1. Several businesspeople secured a contract with the state of Massachusetts that permitted them to construct a bridge spanning the Charles River. The businesspeople intended to charge a toll for passage over the bridge to recover the expense of building the bridge and make a sizable profit off its operation. Later, another group of businesspeople made a similar contract. They too were permitted to build a bridge and charge a toll. There was, however, a six-year limit on the tolls that would be charged on the second bridge, transforming it into a free bridge after the end of the six-year period. The first group of businesspeople realized that the existence of a free bridge would make their bridge worthless. Accordingly, they sued to prevent the second bridge from being constructed. They argued that the original contract that they had negotiated with the state implied that no other bridge would be built. The second group argued that because there was no explicit agreement in the first contract preventing a second bridge from being built, the court, under the Contracts Clause of the Constitution, could not impair the rights they had freely negotiated under the new contract to build a second bridge. The case ended up in the United States Supreme Court. How did the Supreme Court decide the case? Explain. *Proprietors of the Charles River Bridge v. Proprietors of the Warren Bridge,* 11 Pet. 420 (USSCt. 1837). See also L. Friedman, "Economy and Law in the Nineteenth Century," *Law in America* (New York: The Modern Library, 2002), pp. 49–54.

2. The Borg-Warner Protective Services Corporation and Burns International Security Services contracted to provide security for the Cleveland Institute of Art (CIA). Robert Adelman was struck by an object thrown by a CIA student from the roof of one of the Institute's buildings. Adelman sued both the CIA and the security corporations. The security corporations moved for summary judgment, arguing that they had contracted with CIA to protect the faculty and the students and that

they therefore had no duty to protect pedestrians outside the buildings. Adelman argued that the contract specifically obligated the security corporations to control the activities of CIA students within the Institute's buildings. The disputed clause read that the security corporations agreed "to control the movement and activities of students within the buildings at all hours." The trial court granted the summary judgment motion, and Adelman appealed. Should the appellate court reverse the decision of the lower court? Explain. If the case goes to trial, how will the court determine the meaning of the ambiguous clause? Explain. *Adelman v. Timman,* 690 N.E.2d 1332 (OH).

3. One of Stewart's clients gave him a check for $185.48. The check had been drawn up by the client's corporate employer and properly endorsed by the client. Nevertheless, the bank refused to cash the check for Stewart, even though there was enough money in the account to cover the $185.48. Could Stewart sue the bank for not cashing the check as he requested? Explain. *J.E.B. Stewart v. Citizens and Southern National Bank,* 225 S.E.2d 761 (GA).

4. Vokes was told that she would become a professional dancer if she took a very expensive dancing course offered by Arthur Murray, Inc. She was also continually told that she had great talent. The contract called for payments amounting to a total of $31,000. As it turned out, she never became a professional dancer and, in fact, had little or no talent. She sued Arthur Murray, claiming that the Arthur Murray people misrepresented the facts to entice her to enter the contract. The court agreed and found in her favor. Would Vokes have the right to void the contract? Explain. *Vokes v. Arthur Murray, Inc.,* 212 So.2d 906 (FL).

5. Anderson, a farmer, orally agreed to buy a used tractor from the Copeland Equipment Company for $475. Copeland delivered the tractor to Anderson, who used it for 11 days. During this period, Anderson could not borrow enough funds to cover

the purchase price. Anderson therefore returned the tractor to Copeland. Both parties agreed that their sales contract was canceled when the tractor was returned. However, Copeland later claimed that under the doctrine of quasi-contract, Anderson was required to pay for the 11-days' use of the tractor. Do you agree with Copeland? Explain your answer. *Anderson v. Copeland*, 378 P.2d 1006 (OK).

6. B.L. Nelson & Associates, Inc., entered into a contract with the city of Argyle to design and construct a sanitary sewer collection and treatment facility for the city. The city attempted to get out of the contract by citing certain provisions of the state constitution. These provisions made it illegal for the city to enter a contract for services if it did not have the money to pay for these services. Because the city did not

have the funds to pay Nelson, it argued that the contract was illegal and therefore void. Was the city correct? Explain. *B.L. Nelson & Associates, Inc. v. City of Argyle*, 535 S.W.2d 906 (TX).

7. Peters entered into a contract to purchase Dowling's business. The following terms were agreed to: (a) Peters would take over all of Dowling's executory contracts, (b) Peters would purchase Dowling's tools at an agreed-to price, (c) Peters would accept full responsibility for all warranties made by Dowling on previous contracts, and (d) Dowling would remain as a consultant to the new firm for a period of five years. Analyze each part of this contract and classify each term according to whether it is executed or executory. *Wagstaff v. Peters*, 453 P.2d 120 (KS).

quick quiz Answers

7-1	7-2	7-3
1. T	1. T	1. F
2. T	2. T	2. F
3. T	3. F	3. T

Chapter 8

Offer, Acceptance, and Mutual Assent

THE OPENING CASE   Mutual Assent and Its Destruction: *Urbanek v. All State Home Mortgage Company*

The success or the failure of a contractual relationship is frequently a matter of faith. The buyers trust the sellers (or their agents) to play fair with them by providing a full and accurate account of the condition and the value of the subject matter of the contract. Does it always work out that way? Certainly not. Sometimes the seller makes a mistake. Sometimes the buyer fails to hear or to understand what is said. Often there are things that interfere with the arrangement that no one notices until it is too late to undo the contract. It is at that point that the courts must get involved. A situation on point is the case of *Urbanek v. All state Home Mortgage Company*. The plaintiff in the case, Edward Urbanek, was a landscaper who, at the urging of an agent of All State Mortgage, decided to get into the housing market as a way to compile an investment portfolio and improve his credit. At the prompting of two All State agents, Urbanek purchase three houses in Cleveland. The houses had been appraised, but there was no evidence that Urbanek ever received, read, or considered the appraisal, which was made some time before Urbanek visited or made an offer for the three houses. Evidently Urbanek trusted the All State agents implicitly because, once he was told the asking prices of the three houses, he made his offer to purchase without challenging those figures.

It was at this point that Urbanek's problems began in earnest. Urbanek had been told that the houses were being rented. Yet, after the sale, he found he could not collect any rent. In fact, he began to suspect that the renters were fictitious. Later, he was asked for and, without hesitation, turned over $14,186.34 for repairs on one of the houses. As it turned out the house was never repaired and he never received a refund of that money. Perhaps even more telling, he never received keys for any of the houses at the closing.

Without the rental income, Urbanek could not keep up the payments and he tried to sell the houses. It was at that time that he learned from local realtors that the value of each property was overinflated. As a result, the houses sold in foreclosure, for prices that were appreciably under the original prices. The plaintiff sued All state and its agents along with Ace Home Loans, Inc., and its agents, and the appraiser. Who was the offeror in this case? Who was the offeree? At what point did the acceptance go into effect? Did the actions of the agents disrupt the assent? Was fraud or mistake an issue here? What about undue influence? Any hint of that or duress? See if you can answer these questions as you read through this chapter on offer, acceptance, and mutual assent. (See *Urbanek v. All State Home Mortgage Company,* 178 Ohio App.3d 493 (2008-Ohio-4871)).

Opening Case Questions

1. Would *Urbanek v. All State Home Mortgage Company* be a civil lawsuit or a criminal action? Explain

2. What law will the court apply in this case to answer the questions noted above? Will the court use common law or the Uniform Commercial Code (UCC)? Explain.

3. Who is the offeror in the sale of the houses and who is the offeree? Explain.

4. At what point is there a "meeting of the minds" in this case, if at all? Explain.

5. Does Urbanek have a case based on fraud in this situation? Explain.

Learning Objectives

1. Define mutual assent.
2. Identify the elements of an offer.
3. Explain the UCC's concept of offer in contract law.
4. Explain the nature of acceptance.
5. Define the mirror image rule
6. Explain the process of revocation.
7. Identify those statutes that affect mutual assent in cyberspace.
8. Explain the elements of fraud and misrepresentation.
9. Identify the effects of mistake on mutual assent.
10. Describe duress and undue influence.

8-1 Mutual Assent and the Offer

Contractual relationships are, to a large extent, unique relationships that people enter voluntarily. Nevertheless, once a party has agreed to the terms of a contract, he or she has assumed a set of duties that are just as binding as those that are imposed automatically by law. This is why the courts and the legislatures have been very careful about spelling out the details involved in forming a contract. Many of these rules have evolved as part of the law merchant and common law. Others have been adopted by the legislature in response to social and economic changes such as the cyberspace revolution. Whatever the case, the objective of the law is to provide a proper balance between the duties of each party and their rights, both of which emerge in the contract-making process. To understand how this works we will first examine the nature of mutual assent and the method for creating that assent through the process of offer and acceptance.

The Nature of Mutual Assent

A contract is an agreement between two or more competent parties based on mutual promises and an exchange of things of value, to do or refrain from doing some particular thing that is neither illegal nor impossible. The agreement results in a set of duties that can be enforced in a court of law. The power of the courts to enforce these duties comes from the fact that both parties have agreed to accept those duties. This is mutual assent. It is the first of the four elements of a valid contract. The courts are fond of saying that mutual assent emerges when the parties to the contract have a "meeting of the minds." In other words, both parties know what the terms of the agreement are and both willingly agree to be bound by those terms. Mutual assent can be reached quickly as in buying a Kindle on Amazon.com, or it may result from a long and involved series of negotiations as in the purchase of a house. Whatever

Table 8-1 Requirements of an Offer	
Requirement	**Explanation**
Serious intent	The offeror's words must give the offeree assurance that a binding agreement is intended.
Clarity and reasonably definite terms	The terms of an offer must be sufficiently clear to remove any doubt about the contractual intentions of the offeror. Most courts require reasonable rather than absolute definiteness.
Communication to the offeree	The proposed offer must be communicated to the offeree by whatever means are convenient and desirable. The communication of the offer can be express or implied. Public offers are made through the media but are intended for one party whose identity or address is unknown. Invitations to trade are not offers.

the case, the assent that emerges comes from a communication of an open offer by an offeror that is authentically accepted by the offeree. The twin keys to mutual assent then are an "open offer" and "authentically accepted." Remember those key terms.

Requirements of an Offer

An offer is a proposal freely made by one party to another indicating a willingness to enter a contract. The person who makes the offer is the offeror and the person to whom it is made is the offeree. If certain requirements are met, the court concludes that the parties intended to make and accept an offer. In the case of an open offer, the courts have established three elements that must exist: (1) serious intent; (2) clear and reasonably definite terms; and (3) communication to the offeree. We now turn to a discussion of these requirements.

Serious Intent An offeror's offer is invalid if that offeror makes the alleged offer as a joke, during an emotional outburst of rage or anger, or under circumstances that convey a lack of seriousness. The offeror's words and actions must give the offeree assurance that a binding agreement is intended. This is what makes an offer an open offer, that is, it is open to acceptance by the offeree. Serious intent will be present within the actions and the words of the offeror. (see Table 8-1)

Clear and Reasonably Definite Terms The communicated terms of an offer must be sufficiently clear to remove all doubt about the contractual intentions of the offeror. No valid offer will exist when terms are indefinite, inadequate, vague, contradictory, or confusing. To determine whether the terms in the alleged offer are clear and definite enough ask whether the terms are so clear that, if there were a breach, the court would know how to assess a remedy. If the answer is yes, the terms are probably definite enough. If the answer is no, then some critical term in the alleged offer is missing or too obscure to create a contract.

EXAMPLE 8-1: When Is it Possible to Assess a Remedy?

The Lindbergh-Sikorsky Aircraft Corporation e-mailed an offer to Kenneth Hiebel, the owner of the Triple R-Bar Ranch in Idaho. The e-mail stated, "Please consider this our offer to purchase 20,000 acres of your 61,200-acre ranch land near Harrington, Idaho. Our offering price is between $60,000 and $65,000 per acre. Please respond soon." If we apply the suggested test, we can easily see that this e-mail is not a legally effective offer. The terms are much too indefinite. The e-mail does not specify which of Triple R-Bar's acres Lindbergh-Sikorsky wants to purchase. Nor does it specify a set price per acre. If there were a breach of contract, the court would not know how to set damages. Would it use the $60,000 figure, the $65,000 figure, or something in between? If Lindbergh-Sikorsky asked for specific performance of the contract, the court would not know which acres to transfer to the aircraft company. All in all, the terms lack an appropriate level of clarity and definiteness to constitute an offer.

Degree of Definiteness In general, an offer should include points similar to those covered in a newspaper story—who, what, when, where, and how much—if it is to be clear, definite, and certain. This requirement means that the offer should identify (1) the parties involved in the contract, (2) the goods or services that will be the subject matter of the contract, (3) the price the offeror is willing to pay or receive, and (4) the time required for the performance of the contract. Most courts require reasonable rather than absolute definiteness. Offers will be upheld as long as the language is reasonably definite enough to enable the court to establish what the parties intended the terms to be so that, should there be a breach, a remedy can be set.

Offers and the UCC The UCC permits offers to omit certain information. It states that "even though one or more terms are left open, a contract for sale does not fail for indefiniteness if the parties have intended to make a contract and there is a reasonably certain basis for giving an appropriate remedy." Under this section of the UCC, cost-plus contracts, output contracts, requirement contracts, and current market price contracts are enforceable even though they are not complete in certain matters. A cost-plus contract does not include a final price; rather, the contract price is determined by the cost of labor and materials, plus an agreed-to percentage or dollar markup. A requirements contract is an agreement in which one party agrees to buy all of the goods it needs from the second party. The terms of a requirements contract must be carefully worded. If the agreement allows the buyer to purchase only those goods that the buyer desires or wishes, the agreement is unenforceable, because it is illusory in that the buyer is not really obligated to do anything. An output contract is an agreement in which one party consents to sell to a second party all of the goods that party makes in a given period of time. Finally, a current market price contract is one in which prices are determined by reference to the market price of the goods as of a specified date.

UCC 2-204 (3) (see page 823)

Communication to the Offeree To be valid an offer must be freely communicated to the offeree. The offeror's intent may be communicated by whatever means are convenient and desirable. For example, the offer may be communicated orally, by mail, by fax, by e-mail, by text, or by any other capable means. It may be implied. The proposing party's acts and conduct in many cases are successful in communicating he intention to make an offer to another party that witnesses them. When acts and conduct are sufficient to convey an offeror's intentions, an implied offer results.

Public Offers At times, an offer must be communicated to a party whose name, identity, or address is unknown. In such cases, the public offer is made. A public offer is one that is made through the public media but is intended for only one person whose identity or address is unknown to the offeror. A classic example of a public offer is an advertisement in a lost-and-found notice on an electronic bulletin board. Although it is a public offer, it is legally no different from other types of offers.

Invitations to Trade By contrast, invitations to trade are not offers. An invitation to trade is an announcement published to reach many persons for the purpose of creating

THE OPENING CASE *Revisited, Part I*
Mutual Assent and Its Destruction: *Urbanek v. All State Home Mortgage*, Round 2

Recall that in the Opening Case at the beginning of this chapter, the plaintiff in the case, Edward Urbanek, decided to get into the housing market as a way to compile an investment portfolio and improve his credit. At the prompting of two All State agents, Urbanek purchased three houses in Cleveland. The houses had been appraised but there was no evidence that Urbanek ever received, read, or considered the appraisal, which was made some time before Urbanek visited or made an offer for the three houses. Apparently, Urbanek trusted the All State agents completely because, once

he was told the list price, he agreed to purchase them at that price. In the housing market such a move is highly unusual. The price named by the seller is almost never intended as an offer, but as an invitation to trade or an invitation to which Urbanek would make his own offer. When Urbanek agreed to purchase the houses at the list price, he actually made an offer that the owner then accepted, creating the contract. Generally, however, it would have been expected for him to make an offer at a lower price, which the seller would have responded to with a counteroffer.

interest and attracting responses. Newspaper and magazine advertisements, radio and television commercials, store window displays, price tags on merchandise, for rent signs, and prices in catalogs fall within this definition. In the case of an invitation to trade, no binding agreement develops until a responding party makes an offer that the advertiser accepts. Probably one of the most common invitations to trade is the listing price for real property. A list price for real property is the price that the seller asks initially when the property is placed on the market. The price is an invitation to the buyer to make an offer. Traditionally, there is little expectation that the buyer will actually make an offer based on that price. The expectation is that the buyer will make an offer at a price under the list price which the seller will then respond to with a counteroffer. Counteroffers are discussed below.

In very rare circumstances, advertisements may be held to be offers. However, such advertisements would have to contain very particular promises, use phrases like "first-come, first-served," or limit the number of items to be sold. Because the number of people who can buy the product is very limited, the advertisement becomes an offer.

Auctions An auction is a sale that is open to the public, during which potential buyers compete for the right to purchase certain items by placing higher and higher bids until the highest bid is reached and the auctioneer accepts on behalf of the seller. Many people have the mistaken belief that in an auction the original property owner, that is, the seller, is the offeror and that the bidder is the offeree. These roles are true only if the auction has been expressly labeled as an auction without reserve. If the auction has not been so designated, it is considered an auction with reserve, which means that the bidders are the offerors and the seller is the offeree. Consequently, the seller can stop the bidding at any time that he or she wants, up to the time that the auctioneer declares a winner, generally by striking the podium with the gavel. A seller can also control the bidding somewhat if he or she establishes the lowest acceptable bid. In such a case, should the auctioneer *not* hear a bid that meets the least possible bid, he or she can reject all of those bids, and the seller retains the property.

Bait-and-Switch Confidence Games The bait-and-switch confidence game is a deliberately deceptive practice that entices buyers into a place of business when the seller actually has no intention of selling the item at the price stated in the advertisement. The practice has been outlawed by the Federal Trade Commission. In addition, many, and perhaps most, states have similar laws prohibiting bait-and-switch confidence games.

quick quiz 8-1

1. The person who freely makes an offer is called an offeree.   true | false

2. An offer is valid only if it has (a) serious intent, (b) clear and reasonably definite terms, and (c) communication to the offeree.   true | false

3. No valid offer will exist when terms are indefinite, inadequate, vague, or confusing.   true | false

8-2 Acceptance of an Offer

The second major element in a binding contract is acceptance of the offer. As previously stated, acceptance means that the offeree agrees to be bound by the terms set up by the offeror. Only the offeree, the one to whom the offer is made, has the right to accept the offer. If another party attempts to accept, that attempt would actually be a new and independent offer.

Unilateral contracts do not usually require oral or written communication of an acceptance. When the offeror makes a promise in a unilateral contract, the offeror expects an action, not another promise in return. Performance of the action requested within the time allowed by the offeror and with the offeror's knowledge creates the contract.

EXAMPLE 8-2: When Is a Unilateral Offer Accepted?

Patrick Barnes and George Layton were employed by the Sailors' Maritime Service. When they expressed dissatisfaction with their jobs, their employer offered them a new contract whereby they would receive a 10 percent bonus on company profits if they remained with the firm. Several times they discussed the terms of the new agreement with an official of Sailors' Maritime. Eventually, they decided that the offer was a good one, and they continued on the job as usual. Sailors' Maritime later refused to pay the 10 percent bonus, claiming that its offer had never been accepted. The court ruled this scenario to be a unilateral agreement and that their performance in remaining with Sailors' Maritime constituted acceptance.

In bilateral contracts, unlike unilateral ones, the offeree must communicate acceptance to the offeror. Bilateral contracts consist of a promise by one party in return for a promise by the other. Until the offeree communicates a willingness to be bound by a promise, there is no valid acceptance.

EXAMPLE 8-3: When Does a Bilateral Agreement Go into Effect?

Suppose in the previous example, Sailors' Maritime had said to Barnes and Layton, "We will consider your written acceptance of this new proposal as binding us to the payment of the 10 percent bonus." This statement would indicate the intent to create a bilateral contract, supported by mutual promises by both Sailors' Maritime on the one hand and Barnes and Layton on the other.

Communication of Acceptance

The communication of the acceptance of an offer may be either express or implied. In an express acceptance, the offeree chooses any method of acceptance, unless the offer states that the acceptance must be made in a particular manner. A stipulation such as "reply by fax" or "reply by e-mail" included in the offer must be carried out to achieve acceptance.

The offer can dictate the form of acceptance required. If using an e-mail or text message to accept an offer, always follow up with a written and signed correspondence to create a permanent record.

Face-to-Face and Telephone Communication No special problem as to the timing of acceptance usually arises if the parties are dealing face-to-face. The acceptance becomes complete and effective as soon as the offeror hears the words of acceptance spoken by the offeree. In a similar vein, if the parties are negotiating over the telephone, the acceptance becomes effective when the offeree speaks the words of acceptance into the telephone receiver (see Table 8-2). When the parties negotiate by mail, telegram, private courier, e-mail, or fax, problems may arise, and the law provides certain rules as to when acceptance occurs.

Long-Distance Communication Under traditional common law principles, if a long-distance acceptance is made by an authorized method of communication, the acceptance is effective when it is sent. An authorized means of communication is one that has been endorsed by the offeror. The endorsement can be made either expressly or by implication. An acceptance is expressly endorsed by the offeror if he or she specifies the means of acceptance to be used by the offeror. Under traditional common law rules, an authorization of an acceptance is implied when the offeree accepts by the same means or by a means that is faster than that used to make the offer. Thus, an offer made through the mail is accepted when the acceptance is mailed or sent by a faster means such as a private courier (DHL, FedEx, or UPS), a fax, a phone call, an e-mail, or an in-person visit.

Text Messages Text-messages have become an integral, accepted method of communicating in many people's daily routine. It is quite common for people to "text" one another about informal, personal matters. However, texting business colleagues is another matter entirely. While text messages are efficient and fast, they are also, by nature and

Table 8-2 Communication of Acceptance	
Method Used	**Legal Effect**
Face-to-face communication	Acceptance is complete and effective when offeror hears the words of acceptance.
Telephone communication	Acceptance is complete and effective when offeror hears the words of acceptance.
Text messages	Acceptance is complete when text message is sent, if offeror has asked for a text response. If not, the acceptance is complete when sent, only if a text message is faster than the requested method.
Authorized means of communication	Acceptance is complete and effective when given by that same medium (e.g., mailed offer is accepted when acceptance is dropped in the mail).
Acceptance improperly dispatched	Acceptance is complete and effective when it actually reaches offeror.

design, without detailed content. These shortcomings probably explain why texting is still not the usual way to communicate in the business world. Nevertheless, should an offeror ask for a text message acceptance, the offeree should not hesitate to respond as requested. An acceptance will be valid when sent if the offeree uses a technique requested or endorsed by the offeror. However, it is also good practice to follow up such an acceptance with something more detailed and more permanent, such as a confirmation letter.

The Uniform Commercial Code   The Uniform Commercial Code asserts that a contract comes into existence if any reasonable means is used to communicate the acceptance. The UCC is quite explicit in noting that to establish a contract for the sale of goods, unless otherwise indicated by the offeror or by the circumstances, the offeree may accept the offer in any manner and by any medium that is reasonable. A contract for the sale of goods then comes into existence when the acceptance is sent, as long as the method used to send is reasonable. The actual text of this rule is found in UCC 2-206 (1) (a).

Unequivocal Acceptance

To be effective, an acceptance must be *unequivocal*, which means that the acceptance must not change any of the terms stated in the offer. Under common law, this requirement is known as the mirror image rule.

The Mirror Image Rule   Under the mirror image rule, the terms as stated in the acceptance must exactly "mirror" the terms in the offer. If the acceptance changes or qualifies the terms in the offer, it is not an acceptance. A qualified acceptance is actually a counteroffer. A counteroffer is a response to an offer in which the terms of the original offer are changed. No agreement is reached unless the counteroffer is accepted by the original offeror.

Counteroffers under the UCC   The UCC has changed the mirror image rule for sale-of-goods contracts. Under the UCC, as long as there is a definite expression of

UCC 2-207 (see page 823)

Take another look at the Opening Case at the beginning of this chapter. In that case, the plaintiff, Urbanek, had entered the housing market to compile an investment portfolio and improve his credit. At the prompting of two All State agents, Urbanek purchase three houses in Cleveland. Recall that the All State agents introduced Urbanek to three houses and told him the list price. Once Urbanek knew the list price of the three houses, he agreed to purchase them at that price. In the real estate game this type of a move is very unusual. The price named by the seller is never (rarely?) intended as an offer. Instead, that price is considered as an invitation to trade or an invitation to make an offer to which Urbanek would respond with his own offer.

When Urbanek agreed to purchase the houses at the list price, he actually made an offer that the owner then accepted, creating the contract. Generally, however, it would have been expected for him to make an offer at a lower price, which the seller would have responded to with a counteroffer. The next move would then belong to the buyer who would make his own counteroffer (a counter-counteroffer, if you will). The exchanging of counteroffers would continue until both the buyer and the seller agree on a final price, or in the poetic words of the courts, "the battle of the counteroffers continues until the acceptance *mirrors* the offer." Of course, it is always possible that one of the two parties will pull out of the battle. This happens if the price goes too low for the seller or stays too high for the buyer.

acceptance, a contract will come into existence, even if an acceptance has different or additional terms. If the parties are not both merchants, the different or additional terms are treated as proposals for additions to the contract. If both parties are merchants however, the different or additional terms become part of the contract unless (1) they make an important difference to the contract, (2) the offeror objects, or (3) the offer limits acceptance to its terms. This exception is discussed further in Chapter 13.

Implied Acceptance

Acceptance may result from the conduct of the offeree. Actions and gestures may indicate the offeree's willingness to enter into a binding agreement.

Unordered merchandise delivered by mail can be treated as a gift by the recipient. If a package is delivered by an agency other than the post office, the disposition of the merchandise is determined by state law.

Unordered Merchandise According to the Postal Reorganization Act, the recipient of unordered merchandise through the mail may treat such goods as a gift. The receiver has no obligation to pay for or return the goods or to communicate with the sender in any way. When unordered merchandise is delivered by agencies other than the post office, the common law rule is usually followed. Under the common law rule, the receiver is not obligated to contact the sender or to pay for the goods. There is, however, an implied obligation to retain the good and give them reasonable care over a reasonable period of time. After that time, the receiver may consider that the sender no longer claims the goods and may use or dispose of them as desired. Some states, however, have laws similar to the postal law that allows recipients of unordered goods to consider them as gifts no matter who delivers them.

Silence as Acceptance

As a general rule, in most situations, the offeror cannot bind the offeree just by declaring that the offeree's silence will signal an acceptance. However, should both parties agree that silence on the part of the offeree will be regarded as an acceptance, then the offeree's silence would operate as a valid acceptance.

EXAMPLE 8-4: When Will Silence Be Acceptance?

Sarah Jameson read an advertisement in *The Independent* inviting her to become a member of the New Era DVD Club. Jameson chose several DVDs that were listed in the advertisement. She paid only $1 for those DVDs and became a member of the DVD club. In doing so, she also agreed to purchase four more DVDs in a year's time. Under terms clearly specified in the advertisement, Jameson knew she would receive a brochure 12 times a year listing selections. The brochure would also identify the main selections, which would be sent to her automatically unless she sent a reply form to stop the shipment. In effect, Jameson agreed that whenever she did not return the reply card, her silence would amount to acceptance of the main selections.

A QUESTION OF ETHICS

Suppose, after conducting a survey that revealed most people did not know about their rights under the Postal Reorganization Act, a company began a mailing campaign that sent unordered merchandise to certain targeted groups. Would such a move be ethical? Explain.

Another exception to the general rule occurs when the offeree has allowed silence to act as an acceptance. The offeror cannot force the offeree into a contract by saying silence will mean acceptance. The offeree, however, can force the offeror into a contract if the offeror set up the silence condition.

Jason Riley wanted to sell his 1962 Volkswagen. He wrote a letter to Rita Tenpenny offering to sell the Volkswagen to Tenpenny for $25,000. Riley ended the letter by stating, "If I don't hear from you by December 3 of this year, I will take your silence to mean you accept my offer." Tenpenny received the letter and did not reply. Although Riley could not bind Tenpenny to this contract, Tenpenny could hold Riley to his offer because Riley set up the silence condition himself.

Rejection and Revocation

A rejection comes about when an offeree expresses or implies a refusal to accept an offer. Rejection terminates an offer and all negotiations associated with it. Further negotiations could commence with a new offer by either party or a renewal of the original offer by the offeror. Rejection is usually achieved when communicated by the offeree. A revocation is the calling back of the offer by the offeror. With the exception of an option contract and a firm offer, an offer may be revoked any time before it is accepted. The offeror has this right, despite what might appear to be a strong moral obligation to continue the offer. An offer may be revoked by the following methods and circumstances: communication, death or insanity of the offeror, automatic revocation, destruction of the subject matter, passage of time, and the subsequent illegality of the contract.

Option Contracts

An option contract is an agreement that binds an offeror to a promise to hold open an offer for a predetermined or a reasonable length of time. In return for this agreement, the offeror receives money or something else of value from the offeree. Parties to an option contract often agree that the consideration may be credited toward any indebtedness incurred by the offeree in the event that the offer is accepted. Should the offeree fail to take up the option, however, the offeror is under no legal obligation to return the consideration. An option contract removes the possibility of revocation through death or insanity of the offeror. The offeree who holds the option contract may demand acceptance by giving written notice of acceptance to the executor or administrator of the deceased offeror's estate or to the offeror's legally appointed guardian.

About the Law

Although the Ch'ing Dynasty, which ruled China from 1644 to 1911, codified the law of criminal offenses, it left civil law, for the most part, in the hands of the family and clan.

Takashi Osaka offered to sell Andras Galai a collection of rare Japanese prints for $755,000. Galai requested time to consider the offer, and Osaka agreed to hold the collection for Galai for one week in return for Galai's payment of $755. Osaka died several days later. When Galai tendered the $755,000, the executor refused to deliver the collection, claiming that death had revoked the offer. The court ruled otherwise, with judgment given to the offeree based on the option agreement between Galai and the deceased.

Firm Offers and Sale of Goods Contracts A special rule that involves the creation of a firm offer has been developed under the Uniform Commercial Code. A firm offer is created when a merchant agrees in writing to hold an offer open. Under this condition, no consideration is needed to hold the offer open. A firm offer may be made for a specified period of time. If no time limit is specified, then the offer may remain open for a reasonable amount of time. However, the upper limit for a firm offer is three months. Remember that a firm offer under the UCC involves only sale-of-goods contracts.

UCC 2-205 (see page 823)

Lease Options and Real Property A lease option is a contract that permits a party to lease real property while at the same time holding an option to purchase that property. Generally, to hold open the option to purchase the leased property, the person leasing the property will make an additional deposit beyond the amount that an ordinary renter would make, so that he or she retains the opportunity to purchase that property at a later time. Because a lease option involves two separate contracts, the lease contract and the option contract, it is often divided into two documents. The lease contract will detail the terms of the lease, whereas the option contract will outline the terms under which the renter can exercise the option to purchase the property.

---

quick quiz 8-2

1. An acceptance means that the offeree agrees to be bound by the terms set up by the offeror.   true | false

2. According to the Postal Reorganization Act, the recipient of unordered merchandise through the mail may treat such goods as a gift.   true | false

3. A rejection comes about when an offeree expresses or implies a refusal to accept an offer.   true | false

---

8-3 Mutual Assent in Cyberspace

As is true of most areas of the law, contract law, in general, and the law of offer and acceptance, in particular, have been affected by the use of computers in commercial settings. In many situations, the courts have taken orthodox laws that govern contracts and applied them to cyber-contracts, electronic contracts or e-contracts, that is, to contracts that are made using computers either via e-mail or the Internet or contracts that involve computer-related products such as databases and software. This application is true of the law as represented in the Uniform Commercial Code and the Restatement (Second) of Contracts. In addition, the courts must also be aware of several new approaches to cyber-contract law as represented by federal law and by the model codes written by the National Conference of Commissioners on Uniform State Laws. The new rules are found in the federal Electronic Signatures in Global and National Commerce Act (E-Sign Act), the Uniform Electronic Transactions Act, and the Uniform Computer Information Transactions Act.

The E-Sign Act

The E-Sign Act was passed by Congress several years ago and represents an effort by the national legislature to make certain that commercial cyber-documents are given the same credence as their paper counterparts. Simply stated, the act provides that cyber-contracts that are entered into over the Internet or via e-mail will be valid, provided that the parties to the e-contract have agreed that electronic signatures will be used. As long as the cyber-contract can be duplicated and stored, it will have the same validity as a paper contract. The act expressly applies to Article 2 (Sale of Goods Contracts) and Article 2A (Leases) of the UCC.

The Uniform Electronic Transactions Act

The Uniform Electronic Transactions Act (UETA) was written by the NCCUSL to ensure that cyber-contracts are given the same legal effect as their paper equivalents. The act does not create any new rules applying to mutual assent, consideration, capacity, and legality but instead makes certain that the laws that govern these elements apply to cyber-contracts just as they apply to paper contracts. There are three basic elements under the UETA. First, the participants must concur on the use of an electronic medium to create their contractual relationship. This agreement is usually not a problem, because the parties to an cyber-contract are generally aware of the nature of their relationship when they sit down at a computer. Second, once the first requirement is met, the act says that the electronic record generated by the computerized transaction will have the same weight that a paper document would have in a traditional transaction. Third, once the first requirement is met, the act acknowledges that an cyber-signature is just as effective as a written signature on a paper document.

The Uniform Computer Information Transactions Act

The Uniform Computer Information Transactions Act (UCITA) arose when the NCCUSL and the ALI attempted to revise Article 2 (Sale of Goods Contracts) and Article 2A (Leases) of the UCC. Revising these articles to meet the demands of cyber-commerce and cyber-contractual relationships proved very difficult. In fact, the attempt was so difficult that the ALI dropped out of the process altogether, leaving the NCCUSL on its own. The NCCUSL then elected to write an entirely new act that came to be known as UCITA. One of the problems encountered by the NCCUSL in the writing of the new act was that many of the contracts that are entered into in cyberspace are more akin to licensing agreements than sale-of-goods contracts. The UCITA therefore covers such diverse areas as database contracts, software licensing agreements, customized software formulation, and the rights to multimedia commodities.

Many of the legal questions associated with Internet-made cyber-contracts are answered by the new act. For example, Section 102 of UCITA makes it clear that a license is to be considered "a contract that authorizes access to, or use, distribution, performance, modification, or reproduction of, information or information rights, but expressly limits the access or uses authorized or expressly grants fewer than all rights in the information, whether or not the transferee has title to a licensed copy." The UCITA has unified, streamlined, and refined the legal principles regarding such diverse areas as reverse engineering, consumer protection, shrinkwrap licenses, fair use, and consumer warranties. Despite all of this effort, the UCITA has been an extremely controversial act because many groups see it as increasing the rights and protections of software manufacturers rather than those of consumers.

Offer and Acceptance in Cyberspace

In addition to the terms included in most other offers, an cyber-offeror should insert the following terms in his or her offer: (1) payment criteria, (2) remedies that can be used by the offeree, (3) refund policies, (4) return procedures, (5) dispute settlement instructions, (6) the applicability of cyber-signatures, (7) liability disclaimers if needed, and (8) provisions relating to the offeree's manner of acceptance. In general, the offeree's acceptance in an cyber-contract is referred to as a "click-on" acceptance or a "click-on" agreement. A click-on acceptance or a click-on agreement is one that is created by having a party click on a box on the computer screen that states he or she agrees to be bound by the terms of the contract. Otherwise, it is important to recall that, as explained previously, when the agreement deals with goods, the provisions of Article 2 of the UCC will apply.

---

quick quiz 8-3

1. The Uniform Electronic Transactions Act (UETA) was passed by Congress as a federal law.   true | false

2. The Electronic Signatures in Global and National Commerce Act was written by the National Conference of Commissioners on Uniform State Laws.   true | false

3. The process of accepting an online offer is often referred to as a "click-on" agreement.   true | false

---

8-4 The Destruction of Mutual Assent

As is true of most other parts of the legal system, contract law seeks to balance the rights and the duties of two or more parties. In contract law those two parties are the offeror and the offeree and the rights and the duties are assumed voluntarily. The balance emerges from a dialectic that pairs the offer with the acceptance and sets the stage for the development of a synthesis between the two. That synthesis is referred to as mutual assent. As the first element of a contract, mutual assent must stand on its own, without being propped up by artificial supports. Mutual assent, however, can be elusive. Unfortunately, some emergent agreements that appear to be correctly constructed at first glance are, in fact, substantively false, despite the pretty picture that they might create. Those forces that destroy assent come in five flavors: fraud, misrepresentation, mistake, duress, and undue influence.

Fraud and Misrepresentation

Both fraud and misrepresentation disrupt mutual assent. They do so by sabotaging the essential component of trust upon which all agreements, but especially contracts, are based. This is what makes both fraud and misrepresentation so insidious. They are based on deceitful practice that makes a mockery of the entire commercial process. Of the two, fraud is the more serious and the more despicable because it is deliberate. It is also the more difficult of the two to prove. This may be why many cases that should be litigated as fraud, end up in court as misrepresentation lawsuits.

Fraud To destroy mutual assent through a claim of fraud, the complaining or innocent party must prove the existence of five elements.

1. The complaining party will have to prove that the other party made a false representation about some material fact (i.e., an important fact, a fact of substance) involved in the contract. A material fact is one that is very crucial to the terms of the contract.

2. The plaintiff must demonstrate convincingly that the other party made the representation knowing that it was false.

3. The plaintiff must show that the false representations were made with the intent that they be relied upon by the innocent party.

THE OPENING CASE *Revisited, Part III*
Mutual Assent and Its Destruction: *Urbanek v. All State Home Mortgage*, Round 4

A situation that appears to involve several levels of fraud can be found in the Opening Case at the beginning of this chapter. Recall that in the case, the plaintiff, at the prompting of two All State agents, purchased three houses. Now with fraud in mind, consider the following allegations. According to the judge's opinion in the case, the houses had been appraised but there was no evidence that Urbanek ever received, read, or considered the appraisal, which was made some time before Urbanek visited or made an offer for the three houses. Nevertheless, as it turned out when the plaintiff tried to sell the houses he discovered that the value of each property was overinflated. The plaintiff argued that he had been defrauded by the overinflated appraisal of the houses.

If we look at the elements of fraud, we should be able to unravel this claim. First, in any fraud claim, the plaintiff must prove that the other party made a false representation about some material fact involved in the contract. The appraisal of the property would clearly involve a series of material facts. No one could argue that the value of the property was

not material. Second, the plaintiff must prove that the other party made the representation knowing that it was false. This is more difficult to prove but, given the fact that the houses were, in fact, overinflated, added to the other alleged deceptions involved in the case, the plaintiff might be able to pass that hurdle successfully. Third, the plaintiff must show that the false representations were made with the intent that they be relied upon by the innocent party. This should not be difficult, since the point of an appraisal is to provide the buyer with evidence of value so that the buyer . . . buys. Fourth and fifth, the plaintiff must establish that he actually relied on the false representations and suffered a loss as a result. These last two points are the ones the judge found difficult to believe. She stated that the plaintiff offered "no evidence that he relied on the appraisal when making his decision to purchase the property. Therefore, she concluded that the plaintiff "failed as a matter of law to establish the reliance element of fraud." (See *Urbanek v. All State Home Mortgage Company*, 178 Ohio App.3d 493, at 499 (2008-Ohio-4871)).

4. The complaining party must establish that there was a reasonable reliance on the false representations.

5. The plaintiff must verify that he or she actually suffered some loss by relying on the false representation after entering the contract.

A case involving either active or passive fraud must be based on these five elements.

Types of Fraud There is more than one way to commit fraud. The law distinguishes between fraud in the inception and fraud in the inducement. Fraud in the inception occurs when one party tricks another party into a contract by lying to the innocent party about the actual nature of the contract. In effect, because of false representations made by one party, the innocent party believes that he or she is doing "A" when he or she is actually doing "B." For example, if an insurance agent were to tell an accident victim that the paper she was signing was a privacy waiver, when it was actually an agreement releasing the insurance company from all liability, it would be fraud in the inception. Fraud in the inducement occurs when one party tricks another into a contract by lying about the terms of the agreement to get the innocent party to enter the contract under false pretenses. In this case, because of the false representations made by one party, the innocent party believes that he or she is doing "A," but "A" turns out to be actually "A−" or "A+" or "a" rather than simply "A." If, for instance, a loan officer at a bank were to tell a borrower that the interest rate on the loan would be 8 percent when it was actually 18 percent, that officer would have committed fraud in the inducement.

About the Law

While the Common law courts of England were quite willing to acknowledge fraud in tort law, they were not as willing to see its application in contract law.

EXAMPLE 8-7: *Rhodes v. Hayden*

Gabriel Hayden owned a motorboat that was docked at the Butler Reservoir. Hayden, however, was about to move to the city and so was anxious to get rid of a boat for which he would have no use in the city. Kelly Rhodes, who was new in town, wanted to purchase a motorboat quickly so that she would have several weeks of summer weather left to enjoy the boat. Sensing that he could make a real killing on the deal, Hayden told Rhodes about the boat. Rhodes was impressed by Hayden's sales pitch, but she wanted to see the boat first and take it for a test run on the reservoir. Hayden agreed. Before Rhodes arrived the next day for the test run, Hayden patched up several obvious holes in the bottom of the boat with putty and poster board. Hayden knew the repairs would not make the boat seaworthy for longer than 15 minutes, but he figured that would be enough time to fool Rhodes into thinking that the boat was in good condition. Deceived by the apparently good condition of the boat, Rhodes purchased it. The next time she took it out on the reservoir, the boat quickly sank. Even though Hayden never actually told any verbal lies to Rhodes, he would still have committed fraud.

To be fraudulent, statements must involve facts. Opinions and sales puffery consist of the persuasive words and exaggerated claims made by salespeople to induce a customer to buy their product. As long as the comments are reserved to opinion and do not misstate facts, they cannot be considered fraud in a lawsuit, even if they turn out to be grossly wrong.

EXAMPLE 8-8: *Oldacker v. Kellog Formal Wear Shoppe*

Fran Holiday, a sales clerk representing the Kellog Formal Wear Shoppe, was trying to sell a tuxedo to Ken Oldacker. During the sales discussion, Holiday told Oldacker that the tux (1) came with two pairs of pants, (2) was made of 100 percent wool, (3) had a very rich texture, (4) looked very good on Oldacker, and (5) would make him look like James Bond. The first two statements are statements of material fact and could be the basis of a lawsuit for fraud if they are proven false. The others are either opinions expressed by the seller or the persuasive puffery that might induce Oldacker to buy the tux and therefore could not be used as the basis of a lawsuit for fraud.

Fraud can occur in many ways. A consumer's best defense is to be knowledgeable, listen, and ask questions

Active and Passive Fraud As noted previously, active fraud occurs when one party actually makes a false statement intended to deceive the other party in a contract. In contrast, passive fraud, which is generally called concealment or nondisclosure, occurs when one party does not say something about certain facts that he or she is under an obligation to reveal. If this passive conduct is intended to deceive and does in fact deceive the other party, fraud results. In general, a party is not required to reveal every known fact related to the subject matter of a contract. Certain facts may be confidential and personal. However, if the problem or defect is hidden and the other party cannot reasonably be expected to discover the defect, provided the problem involves some material fact, the offeror may be obliged to reveal it. Some states have held that sellers are legally bound to reveal only problems so hidden that even an expert would not be able to uncover them. In these states, problems such as insect or rodent infestation would not be hidden problems because an expert could easily uncover them.

EXAMPLE 8-9: *Bernstein v. Crowley*

Franklin Bernstein had decided to purchase an apartment building in lower Manhattan near the World Financial Center, which he intended to convert into condominiums. Before finalizing the deal, he visited the building several times with the real estate agent representing the seller, Keyfitz Management, Inc. Each time, Bernstein examined a different aspect of the building, concentrating first on the plumbing, then on the electrical system, then on the heating and air conditioning system, and so on. He also hired Guftanson Contractors Ltd. to make a thorough inspection of the entire building. What Bernstein did not know and could not reasonably be expected to discover was that the foundation had been damaged when the World Trade Center collapsed in 2001. Max Crowley, the actual owner, knew of the damage. However, he did not reveal the problem to Bernstein. Crowley had committed passive fraud or concealment because he did not reveal a serious hidden problem that Bernstein could not reasonably be expected to discover on his own.

A fiduciary relationship is a relationship based on trust. Such relationships exist, for example, between attorneys and clients, guardians and wards, trustees and beneficiaries, and boards of directors and corporations. If one party is in a fiduciary relationship with another party, then an obligation arises to reveal what otherwise might be withheld when the two parties enter an agreement.

A QUESTION OF ETHICS

Suppose that you are showing your car to Tim Jorgenson, a potential buyer. You know that if Jorgenson takes your car out for a ride, he will notice that the front end rattles at speeds in excess of 35 miles per hour and that the brakes grind badly. Jorgenson, however, does not take the car on a test drive and therefore fails to detect any defects. Would you have an ethical duty to tell Jorgenson about the car's problems? Explain.

Table 8-3   Agreements Made Defective by Falsehood

Falsehood	Definition	Remedy
Active fraud	Active fraud occurs when one party to a contract makes a false statement intended to deceive the other party and thus leads that party into a deceptively based agreement.	Damages Rescission
Passive fraud	Passive fraud occurs when one party says or does not say something about certain facts that he or she is obligated to reveal. Obligations arise in situations involving hidden problems and fiduciary relationships.	Damages Rescission
Misrepresentation	Misrepresentation occurs when a false statement is innocently made.	Rescission

EXAMPLE 8-10: *San Rafael Motor Corporation v. Groza*

Otto Groza was vice president of business and finance for the San Rafael Motor Corporation when he learned that Toth Properties Ltd. wanted to buy 12,000 acres of ranch land owned by San Rafael. Groza was the only one at San Rafael who knew that a new extension of the interstate was going to be located on the acreage owned by the company. Moreover, Groza knew that Toth wanted the land for an outlet mall and an adjoining hotel and was willing to pay $19,000 per acre. Groza made a deal with Toth agreeing to sell the land at that price. He then went to the CEO and the board of San Rafael and offered to buy the farmland without revealing anything about the Toth deal. As a result, he purchased the acreage for $1,000 per acre and made an $18,000 profit on each acre he resold to Toth. Groza will be liable to San Rafael because he concealed a material fact that he was obligated to reveal because of his fiduciary relationship with the company.

Misrepresentation A false statement made innocently with no intent to deceive is misrepresentation. Innocent misrepresentation makes an existing agreement voidable, and the complaining party may demand rescission. Rescission means that both parties are returned to their original positions, before they entered into the contract. Unlike cases based on fraud, which allow rescission and damages, cases based on innocent misrepresentation allow only rescission, not monetary damages. If a party to an agreement makes an innocent misrepresentation and then later discovers that it is false, that party must reveal the truth. If the party does not reveal the truth, the innocent misrepresentation becomes fraud.

EXAMPLE 8-11: *Sanderson v. Straus*

Anthony Sanderson was browsing on eBay when he located what was labeled as a 1932 edition of *Brave New World* by Aldous Huxley, produced by Chatto and Windus, the London publisher that had printed the first edition of that landmark novel. The book was advertised as coming along with a companion book by Julian Huxley, entitled *If I Were Dictator,* published in 1934 by the London publishing house of Methuen. The seller was Juliette Straus, who set the minimum bid for the two volumes at GBP 8,700. Sanderson, who quickly bid on the two books, eventually won the auction with a successful bid of GBP 9,800. Later, after receiving the two books, Sanderson discovered that the copy of *If I Were Dictator* was actually a 1948 reprint of the original work. Without any indication of wrongdoing, Straus would be liable for nothing more than an innocent misrepresentation. In cases of this kind, the parties often renegotiate the purchase price if the agreement is affirmed.

Mistake, Duress, and Undue Influence

When there has been no real meeting of the minds because of a mistake, mutual assent was never achieved, and the agreement may be rescinded. As in misrepresentation, mistake permits rescission. Both duress and undue influence rob a person of the ability to make an independent, well-reasoned decision to enter a contractual relationship freely. Both of these conditions therefore strike at the heart of contract law.

The Nature of Mistake A mistake made by only one of the contracting parties is a unilateral mistake and does not offer sufficient grounds for rescission or renegotiation.

Table 8-4 Agreements Made Defective by Mutual Mistake	
Mistake	**Legal Effect**
Mistake as to description	Rescission will be granted.
Mistake as to existence	Proof that subject matter was destroyed *before* the agreement was made gives grounds for rescission.
Mistake as to value	Rescission will not be granted since value is a matter of opinion, not fact.

When both parties are mistaken, it is a bilateral mistake. A bilateral mistake, which is also called a mutual mistake, may permit a rescission by either the offeror or the offeree. Mutual mistakes are of several kinds. Some are universally accepted as grounds for rescission. Others are not grounds for rescission. Still others can give rise to lawsuits, but not in all courts or in all states. When both parties are mistaken in the identification and description of subject matter, there is a real mutual mistake, and rescission will be granted.

Proof that the subject matter had been destroyed before the agreement was made gives grounds for rescission. Thus, if one party accepted an offer to purchase a boat that both parties mistakenly believed to be berthed at a specified marina, the agreement would be voidable if it were proved that moments before acceptance, the boat had been destroyed. Had the boat been destroyed after final acceptance, there would have been no mutual mistake, and an enforceable contract would have resulted. When two parties agree on the value of the subject matter and later find they were both mistaken, it is a mutual mistake of opinion, not of fact. Mutual mistakes of opinion are not grounds for rescinding a contract.

The Nature of Duress In general, duress may be viewed as an action by one party that forces another party to do what need not otherwise be done. Duress forces a person into a contract through the use of physical, emotional, or economic threats. In contrast, undue influence merely involves the use of excessive pressure. Moreover, undue influence requires the existence of a special relationship, generally of a confidential or fiduciary nature. Physical duress involves either violence or the threat of violence against an individual or against that person's family, household, or property. If only threats are used, they must be so intense and serious that a person of ordinary prudence would be forced into the contract without any real consent. Threats of physical duress are relatively rare today. Perhaps more common are threats that create emotional duress. Emotional duress arises from acts or threats that would create emotional distress in the one on whom they are inflicted. It is generally necessary that the action threatened be either illegal or illicit.

Economic duress, also known as business compulsion, consists of threats of a business nature that force another party without real consent to enter a commercial agreement. To establish economic duress, the complaining party must demonstrate the existence of three elements:

1. The plaintiff must prove that the other party wrongfully placed the plaintiff in a precarious economic situation.
2. The plaintiff must show that he or she had no alternative other than to submit to the contractual demands of the wrongful party.
3. The plaintiff must demonstrate that he or she acted reasonably in entering the contract.

If the plaintiff can prove the existence of these three elements, the court will rule the contract voidable on grounds of economic duress.

EXAMPLE 8-12: *National Air Races Inc. v. Macon City Airport*

The owners and operators of National Air Races negotiated a seven-year lease with the city of Macon for use of the Macon City Airport. Each summer, during the Fourth of July weekend celebration, the National Air Races were held at the Macon City Airport. One week before the first race of the fourth year under the contract, Macon City officials informed the owners and operators of the National Air Races that they would no longer be able to use the Macon City Airport for the Fourth of July races unless they paid a substantial rent increase. The owners and operators of the Air Races, who had already sold at least 5,000 tickets per race, accepted entry fees from 95 pilots, and had contracts with 20 concessionaires, could not find any other suitable airport within 120 miles of Macon. As a result, they agreed to the terms. Later, the owners of the Air Races sued Macon to have the rent increase rescinded. The court ruled that the rent increase was voidable due to economic duress.

Did You Know?

It is possible for a party to ratify a contract made under duress if, after the duress has ended, the party makes a new promise to abide by the terms of the original agreement. In such a situation, the party ratifying the contract need not supply any new consideration.

The Nature of Undue Influence

The problem of undue influence occurs when the dominant party in a special relationship uses excessive pressure to convince the weaker party to enter a contract that greatly benefits the dominant party. A plaintiff who wants to demonstrate that he or she was enticed into a contract by undue influence must prove the existence of two elements.

1. The plaintiff must show that a special relationship existed between the parties. A special relationship can generally be characterized as one that is fiduciary in nature or one that involves domination. Examples of fiduciary relationships include the relationships of parent to child, guardian to ward, attorney to client, physician to patient, pastor to parishioner, and so forth. Relationships that involve dominance frequently occur when the stronger of the two parties is acting as a caretaker of the weaker party.

2. Second, the plaintiff must show that the other party used excessive pressure to take advantage of him or her to enter a contract that greatly benefits the party applying the pressure.

In most cases involving undue influence, one party in the special relationship has enough strength and leadership to dominate the other party, who is obviously weaker and dependent.

Table 8-5 Agreements Made Defective by Force or Pressure	
Type of Force or Pressure	**Explanation**
Physical duress	Violence or threat of violence to person, family, household, or property.
Emotional duress	Acts or threats that create emotional distress in the one on whom they are inflicted.
Economic duress	Threats of a business nature that force another party without real consent to enter a commercial agreement.
Undue influence	Dominant party in a special relationship uses excessive pressure to convince the weaker party to enter a contract.

quick quiz 8-4

1. Misrepresentation is a false statement made with no intent to deceive.   true | false

2. Mutual mistake is grounds for rescinding a contract.   true | false

3. Economic duress is also known as business compulsion.   true | false

Summary

8.1 If certain requirements are met, the court will conclude that the parties intended to make and accept an offer. Mutual assent is created when an offer is made by one party and accepted by the other party. An offer is valid if it is made with serious intent, displays clear and definite terms, and is communicated to the offeree.

8.2 The second major part of mutual assent is the acceptance of the offer. Communication of the acceptance may be either express or implied. Under the mirror image rule, an acceptance must not change any of the terms of the offer. The UCC has altered the mirror image rule. At any time prior to acceptance, the offeror can withdraw the offer. Still, some types of offers cannot be revoked by the offeror. These involve option contracts, firm offers, and lease option contracts.

8.3 The principal rules concerning the interpretation of the enforcement of cyber-contracts are found in the E-Sign Act, the Uniform Electronic Transactions Act (UETA), and the Uniform Computer Information Transactions Act (UCITA).

8.4 Fraud involves deliberate deception about some material fact that leads a party into an agreement that is damaging to that party. Misrepresentation is a false statement innocently made with no intent to deceive. A mutual mistake may allow for rescission by either party. Duress and undue influence rob a person of the ability to make an independent, well-reasoned decision to enter freely into a contract.

Key Terms

acceptance, 173
active fraud, 182
auction, 172
auction with reserve, 172
auction without reserve, 172
bait-and-switch confidence game, 172
bilateral mistake, 185
business compulsion, 185
click-on acceptance or agreement, 179
concealment, 182
contract, 169
cost-plus contract, 171

counteroffer, 175
current market price contract, 171
cyber-contract, 178
duress, 185
economic duress, 185
electronic contracts or e-contracts, 178
emotional duress, 185
fiduciary relationship, 183
firm offer, 178
fraud, 180
fraud in the inception, 181
fraud in the inducement, 181
invitation to trade, 171

lease option, 178
list price, 172
material fact, 180
mirror image rule, 175
misrepresentation, 184
mutual assent, 169
mutual mistake, 185
nondisclosure, 182
offer, 170
offeree, 170
offeror, 170
option contract, 177
output contract, 171

Questions for Review and Discussion

1. What is mutual assent?
2. What are the elements of an offer?
3. What is the UCC's concept of an offer?
4. How does an acceptance come about?
5. What is the mirror image rule?
6. What is revocation?
7. What statutes affect mutual assent in cyberspace?
8. What are the elements of fraud and misrepresention?
9. What are the effects of mistake on mutual assent?
10. What are duress and undue influence?

Cases for Analysis

1. An advertisement appeared in the *Chicago Sun-Times* for the sale of a Volvo station wagon at Lee Calan Imports, Inc., for $1,095. The advertisement had been misprinted by the *Sun-Times*. The actual price of the automobile was $1,795. O'Keefe showed up at Lee Calan and said he would buy the Volvo for $1,095. Lee Calan refused to sell the car for $1,095. O'Keefe sued, claiming that the advertisement was an offer that he accepted, creating a binding agreement. Was O'Keefe correct? Explain. *O'Keefe v. Lee Calan Imports,* 262 N.E.2d 758 (IL).

2. The Great Minneapolis Surplus Store published the following advertisement in a Minneapolis newspaper: "Saturday 9 A.M. 2 Brand New Pastel Mink 3-Skin Scarfs selling for $89.50—Out they go Saturday. Each . . . $1.00. 1 Black Lapin Stole. Beautiful, Worth $139.50 . . . $1.00. First Come, First Served." Leftkowitz, the first customer admitted to the store on Saturday, tried to buy the Lapin stole. The store refused to sell, stating that the offer was for women only. Leftkowitz sued. Was the offer definite enough to allow Leftkowitz to tender a valid acceptance? Explain. *Leftkowitz v. Great Minneapolis Surplus Store,* 86 N.W.2d 689 (MN).

3. Morrison wanted to sell a certain parcel of land to Thoelke. He decided to make an offer by sending Thoelke a letter. When Thoelke received the letter, he decided to accept. He wrote a letter to Morrison saying that he would buy the land at the price quoted in the letter. Thoelke then mailed the letter. Before he received the letter from Thoelke, Morrison changed his mind and withdrew the offer to Thoelke. When Thoelke found out Morrison would not sell the land to him, he sued. Was Thoelke's letter a valid acceptance, binding Morrison to the sale? Explain. *Morrison v. Thoelke,* 155 So.2d 889 (FL).

4. Wholesale Coal Company ordered 25 carloads of coal from Guyan Coal and Coke Company. Guyan could not come up with 25 carloads. However, it did have 7 carloads available. Before shipping the coal, Guyan wrote back to Wholesale stating, "You can be sure that if it is possible to ship the entire twenty-five carloads, we will do so. But under the circumstances, this is the best we can promise you." When Guyan heard nothing from Wholesale, it shipped the 7 carloads. When Wholesale did not pay for the 7 carloads, Guyan brought suit to compel payment. Wholesale countersued, claiming Guyan had not yet delivered the remaining 18 carloads. Was Wholesale correct? Explain. *Guyan Coal and Coke Company v. Wholesale Coal Company,* 201 N.W. 194 (MI).

5. Tockstein wrote an offer to purchase a house owned by Rothenbeucher. Tockstein signed the offer and personally delivered it to Rothenbeucher. The offer included a condition that acceptance must be made within 24 hours. At the end of that 24-hour period, the offer would be automatically revoked if Rothenbeucher had not accepted. Rothenbeucher signed the agreement within the 24-hour period. However, he did not deliver the acceptance to Tockstein personally, as Tockstein had done with the offer. Instead, Rothenbeucher delivered the acceptance to his own real estate agent, who delivered it to Tockstein after the

automatic revocation time. Tockstein claimed that the offer was automatically revoked when Rothenbeucher did not deliver it within the specified time period. Was Tockstein correct? Explain. *Rothenbeucher v. Tockstein,* 411 N.E.2d 92 (IL).

6. Walker and Cousineau were both in the gravel business. Walker placed an advertisement for a tract of land, claiming that he had an engineer's report that indicated the land held at least 80,000 cubic yards of gravel. In fact, Walker knew the land\contained much less gravel. Cousineau purchased the land and began to excavate it. After 6,000 cubic yards of gravel had been removed, the supply ran out. Cousineau sued Walker, asking the court to rescind the contract. Did Cousineau win the case? Explain. *Cousineau v. Walker,* 613 P.2d 608 (AL).

7. Young sold a residential lot to Sorrell without revealing that the lot had been filled. The landfill was not obvious, and Sorrell could not have been reasonably expected to detect it. When Sorrell discovered the landfill, he sued Young and asked the court to rescind the agreement. Young claimed he was under no obligation to reveal the fill to Sorrell. Was Young correct? Explain. *Sorrell v. Young,* 491 P.2d 1312 (WA).

8. Boskett offered to sell a 1916 dime to Beachcomber Coins, Inc. Beachcomber examined the coin carefully and agreed to pay Boskett $500 for it. Later, Beachcomber asked a representative from the American Numismatic Society to examine the coin. The coin turned out to be counterfeit. No evidence existed to indicate fraud on Boskett's part. Beachcomber sued Boskett for rescission and a return of the $500. Beachcomber claimed this bilateral mistake of fact created grounds for a rescission. Was Beachcomber correct? Explain. *Beachcomber Coins, Inc. v. Boskett,* 400 A.2d 78 (NJ).

9. Prisoners rioted at the Iowa State Penitentiary and held prison staff members as hostages. The warden agreed in writing that no reprisals would be levied against the rioting inmates. In exchange, the prisoners released the hostages. After the hostages were released, several of the prisoners were punished for the riot. One prisoner, Wagner, was placed in solitary confinement for 30 days. He also received 180 days of administrative segregation and the loss of 1,283 days of goodtime earned. On what legal grounds could the warden refuse to keep his promise to the inmates? Explain. *Wagner v. State,* 364 N.W.2d 246 (IA).

10. Loral Corporation had a contract with the U.S. government to manufacture radar sets. Loral subcontracted with Austin Instrument for the production of precision parts to be used in the radar sets. In the middle of production, Austin told Loral that it would deliver no more parts unless Loral agreed to pay Austin a good deal more than originally agreed upon. Loral could not obtain the same parts in time from any other company. As a result, Loral agreed to the price increase. After delivering the radar sets, Loral sued Austin and asked the court to rescind the price increase. Did the court grant Loral's request? Explain. *Austin Instrument, Inc. v. Loral Corporation,* 272 N.E.2d 533 (NY).

quick quiz Answers

8-1	8-2	8-3	8-4
1. F	1. T	1. F	1. T
2. T	2. T	2. F	2. T
3. T	3. T	3. T	3. T

Chapter 9

Consideration and Cyber-payments

THE OPENING CASE   Benefits and Detriments:
Hamer v. Sidway

Literature instructors are fond of saying that a poem, a play, a novel, or a short story is considered good, sometimes even great, if it has stood the "test of time." The same is true of many legal cases. Such is the situation with the long-standing case of *Hamer v. Sidway,* a lawsuit that most law students and paralegals encounter at some time in their academic careers. *Hamer and Sidway* begins at a golden wedding anniversary celebration. At the party, Uncle William promised his nephew and namesake, William, that if he, the nephew, would give up a long list of vices that included smoking and swearing, until his 21st birthday, he, the uncle, would pay his nephew, William, $5,000. The challenge was made in front of a room full of family members and close friends, and so, William agreed to the arrangement. Following this and in compliance with the agreement, William embarked on an extensive period of abstinence that lasted several years. Soon after his 21st birthday, William wrote to his Uncle telling him of his accomplishments and asking for the $5,000 due to him under the contract. Uncle William wrote a lengthy letter back to young William in which he praised his nephew for his perseverance. He also promised to pay the money that was due. Unfortunately, Uncle William passed away before sending the money to his nephew. Undeterred, the nephew petitioned the executor of Uncle William's estate for payment.

The executor refused to pay and William brought this lawsuit. William argued that he had performed as promised and was, therefore, entitled to the money. The executor recognized that William had, indeed, refrained from smoking and swearing, but argued that, in contract law, both sides must suffer a detriment for consideration to be valid and for a contract to exist. In this case, the executor said, young William had not suffered a detriment. In fact, the opposite was true. He was much healthier than he would have been, absent the promise, and he had, therefore, benefited greatly from giving up his bad habits for such an extended period of time. In the absence of consideration, no contract ever existed and, as a result, the estate did not owe young William a single cent. The court in the case referred to a standard treatise on contract law and noted that, consideration "means not so much that one party is profiting as that the other abandons some legal right in the present, or limits his legal freedom of action in the future, as an inducement for the promise of the first." How would you predict the court will rule in this case? Did the nephew give up enough under the law, or is his promise to Uncle William a cleverly constructed illusion? See if you can answer these questions as you read through this chapter on consideration. [See *Hamer v. Sidway,* 124 N.Y. 538, 27 N.E. 256 (Court of Appeals of New York).]

Opening Case Questions

1. Would *Hamer v. Sidway* be a civil lawsuit or a criminal action? Explain

2. What law will the court apply in this case to answer the questions noted above? Will the court use common law or the Uniform Commercial Code (UCC)? Explain.

3. What is the nature of the consideration that passed from the nephew to the uncle? Explain.

4. What is the nature of the consideration that passed from the uncle to the nephew? Explain.

5. Can the court determine the value of the nephew's detriment in this case? Explain.

Learning Objectives

1. Define the term *consideration*.
2. Identify the different types of detriment.
3. Explain the characteristics necessary for valid consideration.
4. Define the term *unconscionable*.
5. Explain whether a promise not to sue can be consideration.
6. Explain whether a charitable pledge can be consideration.
7. Define accord and satisfaction.
8. Identify those enforceable contracts that lack consideration.
9. Explain *promissory estoppel*.
10. Describe the issues involved in cyber-payments.

9-1 Requirements of Consideration

In Chapter 8, we explored the nature of mutual assent, the first of the four elements of a contract. The second element is the mutual promise to exchange benefits and sacrifices among the parties. This exchange of things of value is called consideration. If an agreement has no consideration, it is not a binding contract. For example, a promise to give someone a ride to the campus in the morning is not a contract. Instead, it is simply a social arrangement because the rider has given nothing in exchange for the ride. In contrast, if the rider decides to take the bus, call a cab, or rent a vehicle to get to campus then a contract will exist. This is because, in the second case, the rider will have to transfer consideration in the form of a fare or a rental price in exchange for the ride to class.

The Nature of Consideration

Consideration consists of a mutual exchange of gains and losses between contracting parties. In the exchange, a gain by the offeree is at the same time a loss to the offeror. Likewise, the gain bargained for by the offeror will result in a loss or sacrifice by the offeree. The legal term used to designate the gain that each party experiences is that party's legal benefit. Similarly, the legal term used to describe the sacrifice that each party must experience is that party's legal detriment. A legal detriment can be any of the following: (1) doing something (or promising to do something) that one has a legal right not to do; (2) giving up something (or promising to give up something) that one has a legal right to keep; and (3) refraining from doing something (or promising not

THE OPENING CASE *Revisited, Part I*
Benefits and Detriments: *Hamer v. Sidway*, Round 2

Recall that in the Opening Case at the beginning of this chapter, Uncle William promised his nephew and namesake, William, that if he, the nephew, would give up a long list of vices that included smoking and swearing, until his 21st birthday, he, the uncle, would pay his nephew, William, $5,000. Young William agreed and embarked on an extended period of abstinence that lasted several years. Soon after his 21st birthday, William wrote to his Uncle telling him of his accomplishments and asking for the $5,000 due to him under their contract. Unfortunately, Uncle William passed away before sending the money to his nephew. Undeterred, the nephew petitioned the executor of Uncle

William's estate for payment. The executor refused to pay and William sued. In court, the executor argued, rather convincingly, that consideration requires that both parties suffer a detriment and reap a benefit. In this case, young William had not suffered a detriment. In fact, the executor said, the opposite was true. William was actually much healthier than he would have been, absent the contract. The court disagreed with this analysis. The court noted that, when William gave up something that he had a legal right to do, he had suffered a detriment sufficient to provide the consideration needed to make the agreement into a *bona fide* contract. End of story—period.

to do something) that one has a legal right to do. This last type of detriment is known as forbearance.

It is likely that William improved his health by giving up smoking. However, the fact that William gained a medical benefit does not eliminate his sacrifice. The simple reality here is that he stopped doing something that he had the legal right to do. This "non-act" by itself is consideration. William has suffered what the courts call a legal detriment, so giving up smoking has legal value, and the contract is valid.

The Characteristics of Consideration

Consideration has three characteristics: (1) The agreement must involve a bargained-for exchange; (2) the contract must involve adequate consideration; and (3) the benefits and detriments promised must themselves be legal.

Bargained-for Exchange The law will not enforce an agreement that has not been bargained for. An agreement involves a bargained-for exchange when (1) a promise is made in exchange for another promise, (2) a promise is made in exchange for an act, or (3) a promise is made for forbearance of an act. The concept of bargaining means that each party will be hurt in some way if the other party fails to keep a promise. Conversely, each party gains something when the promises are kept and the exchange is made.

EXAMPLE 9-1: When Is a Contract not a Contract?

David Sable agreed to loan Carla Laszlo his car so that Laszlo could drive across country to attend a literary workshop on Ralph Waldo Emerson and the Transcendentalists planned for a week in June in Concord, Massachusetts. There was no understanding that Laszlo would pay for the use of the vehicle. Sable then refused to allow Laszlo to drive his car. Although Sable might have an ethical duty to lend Laszlo the car, their agreement was not an enforceable one, because it contained no bargained-for promise.

Adequacy of Consideration
The fact that a contract has legal value is not the same as saying that it has adequate consideration. However, there are no specific requirements, other than being legal, regarding what one party may promise the other party in return for a pledge to deliver goods and services. The promise itself is adequate consideration when it represents something of value. Thus, the promise to assist another to repair an automobile would be something of value promised. The value placed on goods and services need not be street or market value. It is important only that the parties freely agreed on the value and the price. In general, the courts do not look into the adequacy of consideration; that is, they do not look to see whether the value of the consideration was fair to both parties. Ever since industrial capitalism became the primary economic system in the West, the courts no longer looked to see if the things exchanged in a contract are of equal value. Such a move would violate the profit-making principle of capitalism. Therefore, the courts let people make their own agreements, placing their own values on the goods or services exchanged. The court then enforces those agreements.

The price and value of the goods exchanged need not be equal as long as the agreement is voluntary.

There are, however, exceptions to this general rule. In one exception, the courts give a party relief when the consideration is so outrageous that it shocks the conscience of the court. A court may refuse to enforce a contract or any clause of a contract if it considers the contract or clause unconscionable, that is, the consideration is so ridiculously inadequate that it shocks the court's conscience. This designation usually happens when there is a great inequality in bargaining power between the two parties. In very specific matters, usually related to taxes, some states have adopted statutes dealing with adequacy. In general though, courts remain reluctant to disturb the promises made by parties to an enforceable contract.

THE OPENING CASE Revisited, Part II
Benefits and Detriments: Hamer v. Sidway, Round 3

In the Opening Case at the beginning of the chapter, Uncle William promised his nephew, William, $5,000 if the nephew would give up smoking, until he turned 21. Young William agreed and did so. Sadly, Uncle William passed away before sending the money to his nephew. Undaunted, the nephew asked the executor of the estate for the money. The executor refused, arguing that consideration requires that both parties suffer a detriment and reap a benefit, and William had suffered no detriment. The court disagreed and said that, when William gave up something that he had a legal right to do, he had suffered a detriment sufficient to provide consideration. But what about *Uncle* William? Certainly he suffered a detriment in parting with his $5,000. However, what benefit did he receive in the contract? Can the court place a value on a healthy nephew? The court did not set a value on what Uncle William received. However, it did not have to set any value on it, as long as it was clear to the court that the uncle did, in fact, value the actions and the results that he had requested. The adequacy of the consideration is of no concern to the court. To demonstrate this point, the courts said, "we see nothing in this record that would permit a determination that the uncle was not benefited in a legal way." And that, as they say in the law, was that.

Self-Evident Truths

Although he does not necessarily endorse the position himself, in his book, *Public Goods, Private Goods,* Raymond Geuss of Cambridge University notes that some people have suggested that there ought to be two ways to determine the value of consideration, one for contracts made with private individuals and another for contracts made with the government. Geuss explains it this way: "What is judged to be 'good,' 'right,' 'valuable' (and alternatively, 'bad,' 'wrong,' 'nuisance') in the public sphere is to be evaluated by different standards from what is 'good' in the private sphere. The standards and procedures for justifying a particular course of action or choice, and the audience in whose eyes the justification must be convincing, are often thought to differ depending on whether what is at issue is a 'private' act (e.g., individual purchase of food for one's own consumption) or a public one (procurement of new trains for the municipal underground or new submarines for the navy)." This position sounds remarkably similar to the ethic of responsibility which we discussed in Chapter 1. Recall that the ethic of responsibility demands that the moral actor, in this case a national leader, consider his or her responsibilities to those people who depend on that leader for protection, safety, and sometimes even for their very lives. The ethic of responsibility is the morality of the nation-state and it is not the same as individual morality. The nation-state has a duty that outweighs all other duties and that duty is to promote the civil peace of the nation-state so that the lives its own people remain undisturbed. What this means from the practical perspective of governmental leaders is that, if the military needs a new weapons system to protect its people from a belligerent, aggressive, or suicidal rogue state, then the cost of that weapons system must be evaluated by a process that is divorced from the methods used to determine value in the private sector. In short, national leaders are not permitted to turn down a contract for this weapons system simply because it would "cost too much" in terms of money because doing so would endanger the innocent people they are duty-bound to protect.

Self-Evident Questions

1. Do you agree or disagree with the premise that two different rules should apply to consideration, based on whether the transaction is private or public? Explain,

2. Regardless of your answer to the first question, which of the two realms, private or public, should be valued higher? Explain.

3. How should this differentiation be determined? Is it up to governmental officials or should private citizens be consulted? Explain.

4. Should there be a different standard for military procurements, such as a weapons system, than for an administrative project, such as a new bridge, dam, highway, or hospital? Explain.

5. What if the cost of doing business includes an illegal action such as bribing the military personnel of a foreign nation to obtain permission for our bombers and fighters to fly through their airspace? Should such illegal payments be sanctioned under the ethic of responsibility? Explain.

See Raymond Geuss, *Public Goods, Private Goods* (Princeton: Princeton University Press, 2001), p. 5. See also Max Weber, "Politics as a Vocation (from Wirtschaft und Gesellschaft)," in *The Great Political Theories: From the French Revolution to Modern Times,* eds. Michael Curtis (New York: Harper, 2008), pp. 426–433.

Legality of Consideration Consideration requires that the benefits and sacrifices promised between the parties be legal. Absence of legality renders the consideration invalid. Thus, a party cannot agree to do something that he or she does not have the legal right to do. Similarly, a party cannot promise not to do something that he or she has no legal right to do. Also, a party cannot make valid consideration out of a promise to stop doing something that was illegal to do in the first place.

quick quiz 9-1

1. The fact that each party has received a benefit and suffered a detriment means that the consideration has legal value.   true | false

2. The legal term used to designate the gain that each party experiences is the party's legal benefit.   true | false

3. Consideration does not require that the benefits and sacrifices promised between the parties be legal.   true | false

9-2 Types of Consideration

Generally, consideration takes the form of money, property, or services. In certain special kinds of agreements and promises, however, the benefits and sacrifices are in some manner unique and not immediately obvious to the casual observer. Significant among these agreements are promises not to sue and charitable pledges.

Money as Consideration

Money is so closely connected with global commerce that we forget that it was not always part of the marketplace. The shift from a barter to a cash economy occurred when transporting goods to the market became difficult and hazardous. By the ninth century, the use of cash as a medium of exchange had become prevalent in medieval Europe. This shift to a cash economy was also accelerated by the need for credit. Because goods are perishable and the quality of goods can vary from transaction to transaction, contracts that required future payments were more attractive to merchants when coins rather than goods were involved. Thus, agreements based on credit backed up by coins had become commonplace throughout Europe by the eleventh century, as had the practice of lending coins in exchange for interest. By the thirteenth century, the use of mortgage agreements based on transferring the right to receive all of the cash income from a tract of land had become routine. Today, we are once again in an era of change as we move from a cash/credit economy to one based almost totally on electronic transfers. Nevertheless, when electronic transfers are involved, people still tend to think in terms of cash, even those who have not actually handled coins or currency for some time. For this reason, it is best to always remember that hidden at the foundation of all contracts is the idea of cash equivalency. (See Rodney Stark, *The Victory of Reason: How Christianity Led to Freedom, Capitalism, and Western Success*, New York: Random House, 2005, pp. 60–61.)

Property and Services as Consideration

Before money in the form of cash was accepted as a medium of exchange, consideration consisted of property and services. Sometimes, even today during recessionary or inflationary cycles, parties find it more beneficial to enter into barter agreements than to base their promises on cash payments. The courts have held that barter agreements contain valid consideration. For example, the exchange of services in return for the use of another's car or a promise to trade a DVD player for a cell phone represent benefits and sacrifices that constitute valid consideration to support a legally binding contract.

Did You Know?

Common law judges would rarely entertain arguments regarding the adequacy of consideration, even in unconscionable situations. One exception involved the promise to repay immediately a greater sum of money than that originally transferred. This is what happened in the case of *Schnell v. Nell*, an 1861 case, in which a man promised to pay $600 in return for the loan of one penny.

Promises Not to Sue

A promise not to sue, when there is the right, or at least the apparent right, to sue, is enforceable when it is supported by consideration. Promising not to sue is a forbearance. A promise not to sue in exchange for an amount of money is a customary way to settle or prevent a pending lawsuit. Settlements of this type often are preferred to expensive and time-consuming litigation. Such settlements are also better than submitting a claim to alternate dispute resolution procedures, such as arbitration or mediation.

EXAMPLE 9-2: Releases and Promises Not to Sue

Danny Hollinger was injured when a delivery van ran a red light and collided with his vehicle. Hollinger discussed his legal rights with an attorney, who suggested that he might receive compensation from the delivery company if he brought suit against the driver and the company. When faced with the suit, the delivery company's insurance company elected to offer Hollinger $250,000 if he would agree not to bring suit against the company. Hollinger agreed to these terms and signed a release in exchange for the money. The "thing of value" that Hollinger transferred to the insurance company was his right to bring a lawsuit. A court would uphold this agreement on the basis of the promise between the parties.

Acceptance of an agreement not to sue, supported by consideration, terminates one's right to continue any lawsuit, presently or in the future, on grounds described in the agreement. A promise not to sue is commonly called a release. Agreements of this kind are usually negotiated and agreed upon before a suit is even filed. However, occasionally they are negotiated between attorneys after a lawsuit has been filed and sometimes even after a trial has begun. In such an event, the settlement is arranged in cooperation with the court and presiding judge. Interestingly enough, some states will uphold a promise not to sue exchanged for consideration, even if circumstances later indicate that the party granting the release did not have the right to sue in the first place, as long as at the time of the agreement, the exchange was made in good faith and fraud was not involved.

Charitable Pledges

Courts today enforce charitable pledges by applying promissory estoppel and public policy.

Under traditional rules, charitable pledges are not enforceable as contractual obligations because they are not supported by consideration. The dependence of charitable institutions and nonprofit organizations on the solicitation of contributions has encouraged the courts to enforce charitable pledges as though they were contractual obligations. Basically, there are three ways that the courts can seek to uphold charitable pledges. The first way involves actual consideration, which occurs when charitable contributions are made on the condition that the promisor be remembered for the gift by having his or her name inscribed in some way on a memorial associated with the project. Some courts see this promise to install a memorial to the pledgor as consideration.

A more contemporary approach is to use either promissory estoppel or public policy to support the claim. Promissory estoppel involves the detrimental reliance on a promise made by another party. If in reliance on a pledge or a series of pledges, a charity goes forward

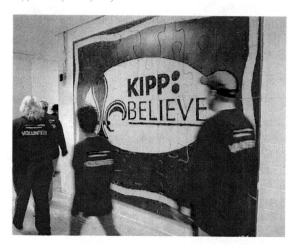

with a project, such as building an addition to the church hall or adding a wing to the syna-gogue, the courts will see the commencement of the project as evidence that the charity relied on the promises and will stop the promisors from denying the effects of the promise. At times pledges are used for the general operation and maintenance of a charitable or nonprofit organization rather than for a specific project.

When there is no promise to carry out a specific project, the courts have held that each pledge made is supported by the pledges of all others who have made similar pledges. This concept of consideration is used in support of all promises of money for undefined causes. The ultimate argument in this situation is that it would violate public policy to allow one pledgor to get away with denying his or her pledge when the other promisors relied on one another in making their individual pledges.

quick quiz 9-2

1. Today contractual parties never find it beneficial to enter barter agreements.   true | false

2. If a party promises not to sue another party, and it is later dis-covered that the first party never really had the right to sue, the original promise not to sue is invalid in every state, and the consideration must be returned.   true | false

3. Even though charities depend on the solicitation of contributions, the courts have refused to enforce charitable pledges.   true | false

9-3 Problems with Consideration

Problems sometimes arise when the consideration involved in a contract is money and the parties disagree as to the amount of money that the debtor owes the creditor. How such problems are resolved depends on whether the transaction involves a genuine dispute as to the amount owed. One way such disputes can be settled is by an agreement known as ac-cord and satisfaction.

Disputed Amounts

A disputed amount is one on which the parties never reached mutual agreement. It may be difficult at first to see how the amount due under a contract can end up as the focal point of a dispute, until we recall that the law permits a certain degree of incompleteness in the final terms of an agreement, provided there is a way to settle on the eventual amount owed. For instance, when a contractor is hired to do work on a home or an accountant is retained to figure out a client's taxes, the final amount owed is never laid out in absolute terms. In-stead, the custom is to settle on an amount per hour, estimate the number of hours that will be spent on the job, and then settle on the final amount once the job is finished.

If a creditor accepts as full payment an amount that is less than the amount due, the dispute has been settled by an accord and satisfaction. Accord is the implied or expressed acceptance of less than what has been billed the debtor. Satisfaction is the agreed-to settle-ment contained in the accord. Only if the dispute is honest, and the offer to settle made in good faith, and not superficial or trivial will the courts entertain arguments based on accord and satisfaction.

EXAMPLE 9-3: Accord and Satisfaction in Action

Jon Delaware, a freelance writer of magazine articles and short stories, hired Monica Mather to figure out his income tax for last year. During the initial consultation with Delaware, Mather told him that her rate was $250 per hour. Mather estimated that the job would take 10 to 20 hours of intensive work. (The fact that Delaware turned all of her records over to Mather in a paper bag may have had something to do with this relatively high estimate, even though Mather used a software package to do all her clients' returns.) When Mather completed the work, he sent a bill to Delaware for 20 hours of work at $250 per hour for a total of $5,000. The number of hours included a five-hour seminar that Mather took at the local college. When questioned about this, Mather said that she had attended the seminar to learn how to deal with a problem that had cropped up in Delaware's return in relation to Delaware's royalties. Delaware balked at the added expense for Mather's seminar and subtracted $1,250 from the bill and sent Mather a check for $3,750. Delaware wrote the following notation on the check: "In full payment for all services involved in making out my tax return for last year." Mather cashed the check and later sued Delaware in small claims court for the balance. Mather is doomed. She will lose the suit because she had already accepted a lesser amount, which had been offered by Delaware in good faith, in full payment of the amount in dispute. As an accountant, Mather should have known better.

Undisputed Amounts

An undisputed amount is one on which the parties have mutually agreed. Although a party may have second thoughts about the amount promised for goods or services rendered, the amount that was agreed to by the parties when they made their contract remains an undisputed amount. A part payment in lieu of full payment when accepted by a creditor will not cancel an undisputed debt.

EXAMPLE 9-4: An Undisguised Undisputed Amount

Bonnie Findley had new shingles placed on the roof of her summer home, agreeing to pay the Rollins Roofing Company $2,625 for parts and labor. A week later, before paying the $2,625, Findley saw the same shingles at the Sandusky Home and Garden Show. She talked to the representative at the show, who told her that he would have been able to sell her the shingles and have them installed for only $2,125. Findley sent a check to Rollins for $2,125 with the notation "In full payment for the shingles applied to the roof of my house at 765 Pine Street in Lakeside." Rollins deposited the check and demanded payment of the balance of $500. Findley would still be obligated to pay that balance. In this situation, there was no good faith dispute over what Findley owed to Rollins.

quick quiz 9-3

1. A disputed amount is one on which the parties never reached mutual agreement.   true | false

2. If a creditor accepts as full payment an amount that is less than the amount due, the dispute has been settled by promissory estoppel.   true | false

3. An undisputed amount is one on which the parties have mutually agreed.   true | false

9-4 Agreements without Consideration

As a general rule, an agreement without consideration will not be an enforceable contract, because consideration is so important as the binding element within a contractual relationship. Nevertheless, some states eliminate the requirement of consideration in specific types of agreements. In contrast, there are certain promises that the courts always refuse to enforce because they lack even the rudimentary qualities of valid consideration, even though on the surface they may appear to offer that much-needed element.

Enforceable Agreements

As noted previously, some states have chosen to eliminate the element of consideration in a few specifically named contracts. Unfortunately, as is frequently the case in such matters, there is no uniformity among jurisdictions as to the types of agreements subject to such laws. Still, some typical agreements falling into this category include promises under seal, promises after discharge in bankruptcy, debts barred by the statute of limitations, promises enforced by promissory estoppel, and options governed by the UCC (see Table 9-1).

Promises under Seal A seal is a mark or an impression placed on a written contract indicating that the instrument was executed and accepted in a formal manner. Today a seal is usually indicated by the addition of the word "seal" or the letters "L.S." (*locus sigilli*, meaning "place of the seal") following a party's signature. Years ago, contracts under seal required no consideration. Some states still honor a promise under seal, but most have abolished this concept especially in relation to sale of goods contracts. In fact, the UCC has eliminated the use of the seal in all sale of goods contracts. However, a few states still require the use of the seal in real property and certain other types of transactions. Because there is no uniformity in this regard, it is advisable to research and consult the specific requirements in your jurisdiction.

UCC 2-203 (see page 823)

Table 9-1 Agreements without Consideration

Agreement	Legal Status
Promises under seal	Enforceable in some states for contracts not involving goods; unenforceable under the UCC for contracts involving goods
Promises after discharge in bankruptcy	Enforceable in most states
Promise to pay debts barred by statute of limitations	Enforceable
Promises enforced by promissory estoppel	Enforceable only if offeror knew that offeree would rely on the promise and offeree places himself or herself in a different and difficult position as a result of that promise
Option	Enforceable under the UCC if made by a merchant, in writing, stating the time period over which the offer will remain open
Illusory promises	Unenforceable
Promise of a gift	Unenforceable
Past considerations	Unenforceable
Preexisting duties	Unenforceable as a consideration in a new contract

Promises after Discharge in Bankruptcy

Persons discharged from indebtedness through bankruptcy may reaffirm their obligations, prompted perhaps by moral compulsion. In the past, reaffirmation has been the subject of abuse by creditors who used pressure against those whose debts have been excused. In response, Congress passed a bankruptcy reform act that makes it more difficult for creditors to extract such promises. The bankruptcy court must now hold a hearing when a reaffirmation is intended, informing the debtor that reaffirmation is optional, not required, and of the legal consequences of reactivating a debt. It is also up to the court to approve such reaffirmations. State laws, in most cases, provide that no new consideration need be provided in support of reaffirmation. Most states require that a reaffirmation be supported by contractual intent. Some states require the new promise to be in writing. However, when there is no such provision, an oral promise or reaffirmation is usually sufficient.

Debts Barred by Statutes of Limitations

State laws known as statutes of limitations limit the time within which a party is allowed to bring suit. The time allowed for the collection of a debt varies from state to state, usually from three to ten years. Some states allow more time for collection when the document of indebtedness is under seal, as in the case of a promissory note containing the seal of the maker. Debtors may revive and reaffirm debts barred by the statutes of limitations without the necessity of new consideration. Affirmation will result from the part payment of the debt. When a debt is revived, the creditor again is permitted the full term, provided by the statute of limitations, to make collection. Some states require a written reaffirmation when a debt made unenforceable by the statute of limitations is reactivated. Consequently, it would be best to check the rule in your jurisdiction.

Promises Enforced by Promissory Estoppel

The doctrine of estoppel denies rights to complaining parties that are shown to be the cause of their own injury. Promissory estoppel is a legal doctrine that restricts a party from denying that a promise was made under certain conditions, even though consideration has not been exchanged to bind an agreement. To be effective, promissory estoppel requires that the party making the promise know, or be presumed to know, that the other party might otherwise make a definite and decided change of position in contemplation of those promises. In reaching this doctrine, courts have accepted the principles of justice and fairness in protecting the party receiving the promise from otherwise unrecoverable losses.

EXAMPLE 9-5: Raymond and Remington and Promissory Estoppel

Rachel Raymond was arrested for a crime she did not commit. Rick Remington, her supervisor at Anwar Enterprises, told her that he had to suspend her. However, he also told her that if she were later found not guilty and released, she would have her old job back with the same seniority and pay grade that she had when she left. Two months later, the charges were dropped, when another person confessed to the crime, and Raymond tried to get her job back. Remington refused to let her return to work. It took Remington six months to secure suitable employment. In a suit brought by Raymond against Anwar to recover the pay she lost during those four months, the court ruled in her favor. Remington and Anwar were stopped from denying the promise they'd made to Raymond despite the absence of consideration from her because she had relied on that promise and had not looked for other work while suspended.

Option   An option is the giving of consideration to support an offeror's promise to hold open an offer for a stated or a reasonable length of time. The UCC has made an exception to the rule requiring consideration when the offer is made by a merchant. In such cases, an offer in writing by a merchant, stating the time period during which the offer will remain open, is enforceable without consideration. The offer, which is called a firm offer or an irrevocable offer, must be signed by the offeror, and the time allowed for acceptance may not exceed three months. When the time allowed is more than three months, firm offers by merchants must be supported by consideration to be enforceable.

UCC 2-205 (see page 623)

Unenforceable Agreements

The promises just described are exceptions to the general rule that consideration must support a valid contract. The exceptions are allowed by state statute or because the courts, in the interest of fairness or justice, find it inappropriate to require consideration. There are certain promises, however, that the courts will not enforce because they lack even the rudimentary qualities of valid consideration. Included in this category are promises based on preexisting duties, promises based on past consideration, illusory promises, and promises of future gifts and legacies.

Preexisting Duties   A promise to do something that one is already obligated to do by law or by some other promise or agreement cannot be made consideration in a new contract. Such obligations are called preexisting duties. The same rule of consideration applies to police officers, firefighters, and other public servants and officials who may pledge what appears to be some special service in exchange for a monetary reward, when all they have actually promised is to execute the duties they are already obligated to perform. Suppose, for instance, that the local fire chief, in exchange for a monetary reward, promises an apartment owner that he or she will provide protection should a fire break out in the owner's building. Neither the fire chief nor the apartment owner could enforce such an agreement in court. The promise is based on the chief's empty guarantee to do what is already his or her job.

Past Consideration   A promise to give another something of value in return for goods or services rendered and delivered in the past, without expectation or reward, is past consideration. Only when goods or services are provided as the result of bargained-for present or future promises is an agreement enforceable.

EXAMPLE 9-6: Past Consideration Is No Consideration

Gale Hansen wanted to have her hair dyed before her college graduation party but could not afford to pay the $120 fee that was expected by the local hairdresser. Without any mention of payment, her friend Marianne Everett helped Hansen dye her hair. After seeing what a good job Everett did on her hair, Hansen told Everett that she'd give her $35 for helping. Hansen's promise to Everett is not enforceable because Everett has already completed the work. Her consideration is therefore in the past.

A QUESTION OF ETHICS

In Example 9-6, legally Hansen does not have to pay Everett a single penny, despite her promise to do so. However, is she ethically bound to keep her pledge and deliver to Everett the $35 that she promised to give her? Explain.

202   Part Two   Contract Law

Illusory Promises An illusory promise is one that seems genuine but that on close examination actually fails to obligate the promissor to do anything. A party who makes an illusory promise is the only one with any right to determine whether the other party will benefit in any way. Illusory promises fail to provide the mutuality of promises required in establishing consideration.

EXAMPLE 9-7: As Many Illusory Promises as You Might Desire

Pemberton Grocery agreed to buy such fruits and vegetables as it "might desire" for one summer season from Enchanted Farms, Inc. In return for this promise, Enchanted negotiated terms whereby it would give Pemberton a special schedule of discounts for the fruits and vegetables. The promise to buy as much as it "might desire" had actually obligated Pemberton to do nothing. Its promise was illusory because Pemberton might desire absolutely no fruits and vegetables and still keep its promise. The benefits that Pemberton were to derive from the schedule of discounts were not supported by a real or enforceable promise on Pemberton's part. A suit brought by either party to enforce this agreement would fail for want of consideration.

Future Gifts and Legacies The promise of a gift to be given at some future time or in a will is not enforceable if no consideration is given for the promise. Included here are promises to provide gratuitous services or to lend one's property without expectation of any benefits in return.

---

quick quiz 9-4

1. An option is the giving of consideration to support an offeror's promise to hold an offer open for a stated length of time.   true | false

2. Although illusory promises provide the mutuality of promises required in establishing consideration, the courts will not enforce them due to the doctrine of unconscionability.   true | false

3. The promise of a gift to be given at some future time or in a will is completely enforceable even if no consideration is given for the promise.   true | false

---

9-5 Cyber-Payment Tactics and Concerns

Cyber-buying and cyber-selling has become second nature to most American consumers. Part of this process involves setting prices that are attractive to the buyer and profitable for the seller. Since the price involved in a contract is a major part of the consideration equation, and since the online marketplace has affected the pricing process, it is appropriate that we pause at this point to consider the legal ramifications of this new approach to the making of a contract. We will examine two aspects of the online pricing process (1) cyber-price and competition and (2) cyber-payments. As these ideas develop, we will also cover several pieces of cyber-legislation.

Cyber-Price and Competition

Businesses that buy products, supplies, and services from one another have always held an advantage over the average consumer. In the commercial network of market competition, businesses could frequently negotiate with one another over the value of the consideration involved in their contracts. The same was not true of consumers who were generally paralyzed by the price set by the other party. Oddly, this was true whether the offeror was the buyer or the seller. Certainly, there have always been consumers who would comparison shop as they sought the best prices available to them. Most consumers, however, were not that ambitious. The Internet has helped improve the pricing process. Consumers can now use the Internet to seek out competitive prices, thus improving their ability to set the consideration at a level with which they are comfortable.

Cyber-Price Shopping
Consumers have a wide variety of ways to comparison shop when it comes to establishing consideration in online contracts. Some online cyber-consumers now make regular use of electronic agents, referred to as a *bot* (*robot, shopping bot, cyber-bot or e-bot*) to comb the vast reaches of cyberspace to find the lowest price available on an item or a service. Cyber-consumers must be aware of the legal ramifications of this process. Two model acts that cover this process are the Uniform Computer Information Transactions Act (UCITA) and the Uniform Electronic Transactions Act (UETA).

Cyber-Shopping Costs
Cyber-shopping is not without its drawbacks. One such drawback involves the danger of hidden costs. One hidden cost is the Internet access fee. Most of the time, however, Internet users can track the number of minutes, or more often the number of megabytes, that they have utilized under the contract so that they can pace their time on the net, and either cut back or renegotiate a new contract with their internet service provider (ISP). Another "hidden" cost comes in the form of shipping and handling fees. Most sellers provide shipping and handling data at the outset or at least as the contract is finalized so that the consumer enters the contract knowing the full value of the consideration paid for the goods purchased on line. Some shippers, however, will over estimate the shipping costs just to make certain that they are not caught paying more for shipping than they are prepared to spend. Buyers should be aware of this unavoidable and often untraceable hidden cost, and be ready to absorb the extra cost if they really want the merchandise.

Cyber-Shopping and the Law
Cyber-shopping is not without its legal entanglements and its illegal practices. Cyber-buyers and cyber-sellers must both be attuned to the difficulties lying in wait when when the enter the online cyber-commerce arena. Some traditional and reccuring illegal practices, such as discriminatory price-setting and credit card fraud, are still prevalent in cyberspace. Others, such as the bait-and-switch schemes that we discussed in the previous chapter, are almost impossible to detect online until the damage is done. While both buyers and sellers can be targeted, it is the sellers who are especially vulnerable to credit card fraud and identity fraud. This is because it is much easier for buyers to use stolen credit cards and identity information online. To protect consumers, Congress passed the Identity Theft and Assumption Deterrence Act (ITADA). Later, ITADA was amended by the Identity Theft Penalty Enhancement Act (ITPEA), which outlaws the unauthorized transfer, possession, or use of a means of identifying another person to violate federal law. The amendment adds a new crime, called *aggravated identity theft,* to the original statute.

Cyber-Payments and Cyber-Contracts

Shopping online has many advantages that make it one of the fastest-growing market places on record. Most people shop online because it is quick and efficient. In addition, as noted above, shopping online also permits consumers to compare prices and to settle on the amount of consideration that they can afford. Additionally, some products that are not available in stores, are accessible online. Hard-to-get products available online include out-of-print books, antiques, vintage clothing, rare works of art, hi-fi speaker systems, Polaroid cameras, obsolete auto parts, black and white TV's, rotary dial phones, turntables and vinyl records, out-dated appliances, old license plates, carbon paper, old-fashioned audio tapes, vacuum tubes, pulp magazines, out-of date VHS and Beta cassettes, Golden and Silver Age comics, and other vintage products. Still, despite these advantages online shopping still has many difficulties, not the least of which is selecting a payment method.

Cyber-Payment Options Online consumers can choose from several payment methods. One of the most popular methods is by credit card or debit card. It would be very rare today for an online seller to refuse to accept credit or debit card payments. Most online sellers will accept the major credit cards such as Visa, Master Card, Discover, and so on. Many online cyber-sellers also moving toward the use of direct on-line payment systems such as PayPay. This type of system protects both the buyer and the seller. The system is so effective that at some time in the future this may be the only way permissible to buy and sell in cyberspace. This process may become the most acceptable process because most of the time when people buy and sell in cyberspace they are they are dealing with strangers. The issue is especially acute in the cyber-auction industry, involving firms such as eBay. The on-line payment process elimnates (well, almost nearly eliminates) the identity verification problem. This is important because one of the biggest concerns about online shopping is security. Once a buyer and a seller have agreed on consideration, they both want to make certain that the contract is fulfilled as promised.

Cyber-Payment Security Issues Consumers who shop online must provide the seller with a means of payment. As we have seen, the most popular method of making payment online is through the use of credit and debit cards. Unfortunately, the ease and efficiency of using such cards is frequently offset by the security concerns associated with their use. Oddly, the United States is not as up-to-date as the European Union in providing data and privacy protection to its consumers. The EU Data Protection Directive along with the EU E-Privacy Directive guarantee the rights of European citizens while, at the same time, ensuring the smooth exchange of data among those nation-states that honor the privacy and data protection standards themselves. U.S. corporations that are involved with EU corporations must demonstrate that, despite the lack of legislation in the United States, the companies themselves will promise to honor the same degree of protection to data and to privacy as guaranteed by the EU. These guarantees have been labeled the Safe Harbor Principles. They are enforced by the U.S. Department of Commerce. Ironically, this means that U.S. consumers who deal with European companies or with U.S. companies that follow the EU standards will have more security protection than those who deal with purely U.S. companies. Unfortunately not all companies who claim to follow the safe harbor provisions actually do so. It is best for a consumer to check directly with the United States Department of Commerce to determine the true status of a company rather than just relying on the company's blanket assertion that they follow the safe harbor standards. Exactly when the United States will officially adopt more protective privacy rights is anybody's guess at the present time.

quick quiz 9-5

1. The Internet has helped to improve the transparency of the pricing process.   true | false

2. Bait and switch are almost impossible to detect online until the damage is done.   true | false

3. The European Union has provided greater protection for cyber-shoppers than the United States.   true | false

Summary

9.1 The fifth element necessary to any valid contract is consideration. Consideration is the mutual exchange or promise to exchange benefits and sacrifices between contracting parties. Consideration has three requirements: (1) promises made during bargaining depend on the consideration to be received, (2) the consideration must involve something of value, and (3) the benefits and detriments promised must be legal.

9.2 Generally, consideration takes the form of money, property, or services. There are certain special kinds of agreements and promises to which the benefits and sacrifices are unique. Among these are promises not to sue and charitable pledges.

9.3 Problems sometimes arise when the consideration involved in a contract is money and the parties do not agree on the amount of money owed. If there is a genuine dispute, a creditor can accept an amount as full payment even though it is less than the amount claimed. Once the creditor has accepted the lesser amount, the dispute is settled by an act of accord and satisfaction. If the dispute is not genuine, accord and satisfaction do not apply.

9.4 As a general rule, contracts are not enforceable without consideration. However, some states eliminate the need for consideration in some agreements. These agreements include promises bearing a seal, promises after discharge in bankruptcy, debts barred by the statute of limitations, promises enforced by promissory estoppel, and options governed by the UCC. There are other agreements that seem to involve consideration but that the courts will not enforce. These agreements involve preexisting duties, past consideration, illusory promises, and gifts.

9.5 The measurement of consideration has become an issue when consumers buy and sell online. Consumers can comparison shop online using shopping search engines, patronizing user-friendly industries, and shopping with companies that provide price comparison rates on their Web sites. Cyber-shopping hidden costs include Internet access fees and shipping and handling costs. Some illegal practices involved in online shopping include: discriminatory price-setting, credit card fraud, and bait-and-switch schemes. Online consumers can choose from several payment methods including credit cards, debit cards, smart cards, and alternative cyber-payment systems such as PayPal. Privacy protection and security, however, are limited.

Key Terms

accord, 197	consideration, 191	EU Data Protection Directive, 204
accord and satisfaction, 197	disputed amount, 197	EU E-Privacy Directive, 204
bargained-for exchange, 192	estoppel, 200	firm offer, 201

forbearance, 192	past consideration, 201	seal, 199
illusory promise, 202	preexisting duties, 201	statutes of limitations, 200
irrevocable offer, 201	promissory estoppel, 200	unconscionable, 193
legal detriment, 193	release, 196	undisputed amount, 198
locus sigilli, 199	Safe Harbor Principles, 204	
option, 201	satisfaction, 197	

Questions for Review and Discussion

1. What is consideration?
2. What are the different types of detriment?
3. What characteristics are necessary for consideration to be valid?
4. What is meant by the term "unconscionable"?
5. Can a promise not to sue be consideration?
6. How can a charitable pledge be consideration?
7. What is the procedure that a debtor and creditor may use to settle a claim by means of accord and satisfaction?
8. What agreements may be enforceable by a court of law even though they lack consideration?
9. What is the doctrine of promissory estoppel?
10. What issues are involved in the cyber-payment process?

Cases for Analysis

1. Twenty-two congressional representatives proposed a bill that would permit corporate shareholders to review the consideration packages that had been granted to key corporate executives of public corporations. The bill, which was named the Shareholder Vote on Executive Compensation Act, would empower the shareholders of public corporations to evaluate and vote on the appropriateness of the compensation packages that had been granted to the corporation's top five officers. The vote, however, would not obligate the corporation to change the compensation package if the shareholders disapproved of its terms. Would such a bill, if enacted into law, conflict with established contract law principles that permit parties to negotiate their own level of consideration? Explain. See Donna Block, "Proposal Seeks Shareholder OK on Executive Pay," *The National Law Journal,* March 12, 2007, p. 9.

2. Consideration can serve as a strong motivator. At least this is what a newly founded shareholder forum believes. The forum was formed to monitor the salaries of top corporate executives, especially CEOs, by matching those salaries with the executive's incentive package, which includes the corporation's latest list of objectives and the number or the percentage of those objectives that the executive must meet to receive incentive pay. The goal of incentive pay is to motivate top executives to do more than sit in the CEO's office from 9:00 to 5:00 each day. Is incentive pay a violation of the principle that says that preexisting duties cannot be used as consideration in a new contract? Explain. See Gretchen Morgenson, "Hear Ye, Hear Ye: Coralling Executive Pay," *The New York Times,* June 17, 2007, sec 3, pp. 1 and 8.

3. General Motors decided to move a car producing operation to Arlington, Texas, from a plant located in Ypsilanti, Michigan. As a result, the township of Ypsilanti brought a lawsuit to stop General Motors from making the move. Ypsilanti argued that GM had promised to keep the plant in Ypsilanti in exchange for certain tax privileges. The township argued further that it had relied on those promises when it granted that tax abatement to the corporation. Therefore, GM should be forced to keep its promise to maintain the Ypsilanti plant. Should the court stop this move based on the doctrine of promissory estoppel? Explain. *Charter Township of Ypsilanti v.*

General Motors, 508 N.W.2d 556 (Michigan Court of Appeals).

4. Aviation Electronics entered a contract with Sky Train Institute of Montana in which Aviation agreed to supply the institute with 17,000 component parts for the development of the institute's remote control bomber. The bomber had to be operational by December 3; otherwise, the institute would lose a research grant from the Department of Defense. After delivering 5,000 parts, Aviation told Sky Train that it wanted an additional $4 million beyond the original price agreed upon to deliver the remaining parts. Sky Train attempted to obtain the parts from other firms, none of which could fill the order in the time limit required by the DOD contract specifications. To make the deadline stipulated in the government contract, Sky Train reluctantly agreed to the new price demanded by Aviation. What "thing of value," if any, has Aviation transferred to the institute that it did not already owe the institute under the original contract? Explain.

5. Savaretti offered to pay his niece, Wilma, $2,000 if she would agree to give up eating meat and pastries and drinking caffeinated beverages for six months. Wilma agreed and gave up these activities for six months. At the end of those six months, Savaretti refused to give Wilma the $2,000, arguing that because giving up caffeine, meat, and pastries was beneficial to her health, she suffered no detriment and was owed nothing. Wilma took Savaretti to small claims court and demanded payment of the $2,000. She argued that because she had the legal right to consume the caffeine, meat, and pastries, she suffered a legal detriment and was entitled to her money. How should the referee rule in this case? Explain.

6. Daniel Davidson told Velma Evans that he would hire her to work on an architectural job. He gave her a date to show up for work and told her to leave her present job. Relying on Davidson's statements, Evans left her job. Davidson never let Evans begin work, and as a result, she was out of work for six months. Evans sued Davidson for the wages she lost during those six months. Davidson argued that because they'd never decided on the final terms of employment, no contract ever existed between the two of

them. Evans argued that the principle of promissory estoppel should apply here. Is Evans correct? Explain.

7. Mers was arrested and charged with a felony. Dispatch Printing, his employer, told him that he had to be suspended. However, Mers was also told that he could return to work if the case against him was resolved in his favor. Relying on this promise, Mers did not seek other employment. The case ended in a hung jury, and Mers reported back to work. Dispatch Printing, however, refused to let him work or pay him any back pay. In a suit against Dispatch Printing, what legal argument might Mers use to compel Dispatch Printing to pay him for any losses due to his reliance on the promise to let him return to work when the case ended in his favor? Explain. *Mers v. Dispatch Printing*, 483 N.E.2d 150 (OH).

8. The Mighty Fine Food Emporium agreed to buy such fruits and vegetables as it "might desire" for one summer season from Kennelsworth Farms and Vineyards. In return for this promise, Kennelsworth negotiated terms whereby it would give Mighty Fine a special schedule of discounts for the fruits and vegetables. Did the promise to buy as much as it "might desire" obligate Kennelsworth in any way? Are the benefits that Kennelsworth was to derive from the schedule of discounts supported by an enforceable promise on Kennelsworth's part? Would a suit brought by either party to enforce this agreement succeed? Explain each answer.

9. Graham O'Hanlon, without any mention of payment, helped his friend, Patricia Tippon, move from Westerville to Pepper Pike. The entire move took 48 hours to complete. At the end of the day, after she was in her new house, Tippon told O'Hanlon that she'd give him $200 for helping her move. Is Tippon's promise to O'Hanlon enforceable? Why or why not?

10. Vanoni Biological Supplies, Inc., contracted with the Hayden Institute to supply the Institute with 24,000 biological specimens for a series of experiments that the Institute has agreed to perform for the Maritime University of Columbia. The Institute must have the specimens by September 9 to meet the University's schedule. After delivering 12,000 of the specimens,

Vanoni told the Institute that it wanted an additional $1,600 to deliver the remaining 12,000 specimens. Can Vanoni make the delivery of the remaining 12,000 specimens consideration in a new agreement with the Institute? Explain.

11. Seier agreed to pay $10,000 to Peek in exchange for all the stock in a corporation. The agreement was placed in writing. Nevertheless, when the time came for payment, Seier refused to live up to his end of the deal. His argument was that the stock was not worth the $10,000 that he had agreed to pay for it. Did the court listen to Seier's argument and attempt to determine the value of the consideration? Explain. *Seier v. Peek,* 456 So.2d 1079 (AL).

12. N.B. West Contracting Co., Inc., agreed to repave Koedding's parking lot. When the repaving work was done, Koedding was unsatisfied with the quality of the work. Consequently, he informed West of his intention to bring suit. West told Koedding that the lot would be resealed and that the job would be guaranteed for two years if Koedding agreed not to pursue the lawsuit, which had already commenced. Koedding agreed. After the repaving was completed a second time, Koedding was still not satisfied. Would the agreement not to sue stop Koedding's lawsuit? Explain. *Koedding v. N.B. West Contracting Co., Inc.,* 596 S.W.2d 744 (MO).

13. Evans used his credit card to run up a $98.75 bill with the Rosen Department Store. When Rosen tried to collect, Evans wrote a check for $79.00. He wrote on the check that he meant it to be "full payment of all accounts to date." Rosen cashed the check. When Rosen sued Evans for $19.75 balance, Evans argued that under accord and satisfaction, the fact that Rosen cashed the $79.00 check meant that it had accepted that amount as full payment. Was Evans correct? Explain.

14. Jill Anderson agreed to purchase William and Teresa Dawson's flower shop for $75,000. Anderson paid the Dawsons $20,000 when the contract was signed. She also agreed to pay the balance of $55,000 at an interest rate of 8.5 percent per year for five years. This agreement meant that she would be making monthly installments of $1,128.41 to the Dawsons. During the

negotiation stages of the contract, Anderson was told that all of the equipment in the store was in perfect condition. Moreover, the Dawsons told Anderson that she could expect a profit of $75,000 per year. Anderson discovered that the equipment needed extensive repairs and that the financial condition of the business had been misrepresented so that she made considerably less than the $75,000 that the Dawsons had cited. Accordingly, Anderson sent a check to the Dawsons for $6,560.21. On the reverse side of the check she wrote, "Payment in full for University Flower Shop." This final check would mean that after making installment payments for more than a year and a half, she had paid a total of $50,000 for the flower shop. In a letter that accompanied the check, Anderson indicated that because she had been misled by the Dawsons about the condition of the equipment and the financial state of the business, the store had actually been worth only $50,000 at the time she purchased it. The Dawsons disagreed but deposited the check and then brought suit against Anderson for breach of contract. Anderson argued that when the Dawsons negotiated her check, the debt was discharged under accord and satisfaction. Is Anderson correct here? Explain. *Dawson v. Anderson,* 698 N.E.2d 1014 (OH).

15. Tim W. Koerner and Associates, Inc., was a distributor for electrosurgical products for Aspen Labs, Inc. Zimmer U.S.A., Inc., purchased Aspen and replaced Aspen's distribution system with its own. Aspen remained in business as a subsidiary. Koerner sued Aspen and Zimmer, joined as defendants, trying to force them to honor a contract that Aspen and Zimmer had made compensating former Aspen dealers for their past efforts. Zimmer refused to honor the agreement. For whom did the court find and why? *Tim W. Koerner & Assocs., Inc. v. Aspen Labs, Inc.,* 492 F. Supp. 294 (S.W. TX).

16. Trisko purchased a loveseat from the Vignola Furniture Company. The loveseat arrived at Trisko's home in a damaged condition. Vignola agreed to repair the loveseat if Trisko agreed not to sue. Trisko agreed but then later brought suit. Vignola argued that Trisko could not bring suit because he had promised not to sue them in exchange for the repair of the loveseat. Trisko

argued that Vignola had a preexisting duty to deliver an undamaged love-seat. This preexisting duty could not therefore be consideration in a

new agreement. Was Trisko correct? Explain. *Trisko v. Vignola Furniture Company,* 299 N.E.2d 421 (IL).

quick quiz Answers

9-1	9-2	9-3	9-4
1. F	1. F	1. T	1. T
2. T	2. F	2. F	2. F
3. T	3. F	3. T	3. F

Chapter 10

Capacity and Legality: The Final Elements

THE OPENING CASE   Public Policy, Statutory Law, and Contract Validity: *R.R. v. M.H. & Another*

New England Surrogate Parenting Advisors (NESPA) is a nonprofit organization the purpose of which is to match potential surrogate mothers with couples who are unable to have children of their own. In this case, a surrogate mother candidate was matched up with a couple who wanted to have a baby but could not do so on their own. The couple and the surrogate mother entered an agreement that stipulated that the father would pay for all pregnancy expenses plus a $10,000 fee to the mother for "conceiving, carrying and giving birth to the child." The fee was to be transferred to the surrogate mother in installments based on a structured payment plan. The final $3,500 was to be paid to the surrogate mother when the child was born. All three parties to the agreement—the surrogate mother, the father, and the father's wife—underwent psychological screening by a psychologist. The psychologist reported that the surrogate mother was a stable, considerate, and knowledgeable woman who was aware of what she was doing and would be emotionally and psychologically capable of transferring custody to the child's biological father. For a while everything went according to the contract. The surrogate mother conceived a child by the father. The first two payments were sent and accepted by the mother. However, at the end of the sixth month, after receiving the third payment, the

mother changed her mind, returned that third payment, and told the father's attorney that the contract was ended. That was the only money returned. She kept the first two payments and the expense money she had received under the agreement. The father sued for custody, arguing that the surrogate mother had breached the contract. The judge agreed and transferred custody to the father based on the contract and because she believed such a move would ultimately be in the child's best interests. The surrogate mother appealed. The state supreme judicial court noted that, since the state had no statute covering this type of agreement, it would apply an adoption statute that was roughly analogous to the situation. Under that statute, a mother could not give up her child for adoption until four days after the child's birth. The statute also outlawed the payment of money to the mother for an adoption, although she could be paid pregnancy expenses. If the court applies this statute to this case, the contract is illegal and, therefore, void. Can the court apply an adoption statute to a contract claim? If so, should the court apply that statute in this case? Moreover, if it does apply the statute, what is the net effect of that application in this case? In other words, who wins? (See *R.R. v. M.H. and Another*, 426 N.E.2d 790 (Supreme Court of Massachusetts).)

Opening Case Questions

1. Can the judge apply adoption law to a contract case or should she confine her ruling to contract law? Explain

2. Sometimes a judge will apply the public policy doctrine in this type of a case. What is public policy? Explain.

3. Does public policy apply here? Explain. If public policy applies, what would the result be? Explain.

4. Could the surrogate mother argue that the contract is void because she was suffering from a mental impairment when she entered the agreement? If so, would she win? Why or why not?

5. Should the court consider the best interests of the child in a contract case like this? Explain.

Learning Objectives

1. Identify the age of minority and the age of majority.
2. Explain the legal status of a contract made by a minor.
3. Differentiate between ratification and disaffirmance.
4. Identify the effects of mental impairment on a contract.
5. Discuss the contractual capacity of a drugged or intoxicated person.
6. Explain the legality of agreements to commit torts and crimes.
7. Identify those agreements made illegal under statutory law.
8. Enumerate those agreements contrary to public policy.
9. Explain what happens under the doctrine of *in pari delicto.*
10. Explain the effects of illegality.

10-1 The Final Elements

The final two elements of a contract are capacity and legality. A contract can have a valid offer, an effective acceptance, mutual assent, valid consideration, and still be void if it involves doing something illegal. An illegal agreement is one that violates criminal law or tort law, a statute, and/or public policy as established by the court. In general, the law will aid neither party involved in an illegal agreement. Capacity is the legal ability to enter a valid contract. Generally, a person has the ability to enter a contract if he or she possesses free will, displays a certain degree of self-knowledge and is informed about the nature, purpose, and

effect of the agreement. The chapter here is designed to first explore the various factors that affect capacity and then the take a look at what makes a contract illegal and what happens as a result of that illegality.

Minors are able to rescind most contracts. However, adults that contract with minors generally cannot.

The Nature of Capacity and Minority

Capacity is considered to be a rebuttable presumption; that is, a defending party has the right to attack that presumption to rescind the contract. Under the current state of the law, for instance, contracts entered by minors are voidable by the minor. The law allows minors the privilege to disaffirm (negate) a contract to protect them

212   Part Two   Contract Law

from unscrupulous adults (or unscrupulous minors for that matter) who might take advantage of the young people who might not fully comprehend the responsibilities that they are assuming. When a minor indicates by a statement or act an intent not to live up to a contract, that minor is entitled to a return of everything given to the other party. This right exists even when the property transferred to the minor under the contract has been damaged or destroyed. A few states will deduct something from the amount due back to the minor if the goods are damaged. Most states, however, deduct nothing.

U.S. Const. Amend-
ment 26 (see page 953).

Definition of Minority

Under common law, minority, was a term that described persons who had not yet reached the age of 21 years. Upon reaching that age, a person was said to have reached majority. Ratification and adoption of the Twenty-Sixth Amendment to the U.S. Constitution in 1971 lowered the voting age in federal elections from 21 to 18 years. To avoid the confusion that would result from having two voting ages, the states started to enact new laws that enabled 18-year-olds to vote in state and local elections. Then states began to lower the age of majority to 18 years for certain types of contracts. Still, there are other age requirements that differ from state to state in relation to matters such as the legal ability to purchase alcoholic beverages, enter a marriage, buy tobacco products, purchase firearms, and operate motor vehicles. Recently, for instance, in response to outside influences from a variety of social organizations and governmental institutions, many states have raised the legal age for purchasing and consuming alcohol to 21 years.

Emancipation and Abandonment

In some jurisdictions, minors who become emancipated, that is, no longer under the control of their parents, are responsible for their contracts. This responsibility means that they cannot void a contract, despite their apparent minority. Emancipated minors include those who are married, those in the armed forces, and those who leave home and, in the process, give up all right to parental support. In certain states, minors are even allowed to ask the court for a legally sanctioned emancipation. In all these cases, emancipated minor are said to have abandoned the usual protective shield given them. Although minors in these categories are no longer protected from liability on their contracts, merchants are still reluctant to deal with them on a credit basis, fearing that they may still attempt to disaffirm, or repudiate, their contracted debts. Again, for practical, not legal, reasons, merchants often require that minors get the signature of a responsible adult who will agree to guarantee payment of money owed.

Moreover, the hesitancy felt by some merchants in relation to emancipated minors is justified because a few states still hold to the opposite rule, that is, that emancipated minors do not give up the legal advantages associated with minority simply because they leave home or become married. To support this position, the courts in these jurisdictions note that the rule that allows minors to rescind contracts is based on the idea that minors are less experienced and less knowledgeable than adults about the consequences of their actions. It is therefore difficult to see why getting married or leaving home somehow bestows more common sense on a minor who does so. In fact, one court remarked that getting married and leaving home may actually indicate that a minor has less good sense than another minor who does neither. Because this rule differs from state to state, it would be a good idea to check on the rule of law in your jurisdiction.

Misrepresentation of Age

Minors sometimes lie about their age when making a contract. Despite this misrepresentation of age, most states will allow the minor to disaffirm or get out of the contract. Some jurisdictions, however, do not permit the minor to get away with the lie. Some states require the minor to place the adult party to the contract in the same situation that he or she was in before the contract. Others allow the adult to use tort law, rather than contract law, to sue the minor for fraud. Some states have also enacted statutes that allow recovery against a minor who is engaged in business and who misrepresents his or her age in a commercial contract. A number of states, for example, have statutes that deny disaffirmance if the minor has signed a written statement falsely asserting adult status. Without such a statute, the minor would be allowed to get out of the primary contract despite her or his signature on that primary contract or the contract asserting adult status.

Contractual Capacity of Minors

Executory contracts, those that have not been fully performed by both parties, may be repudiated by a minor at any time. A promise to deliver goods or render services at some future time need not be carried out by the minor who decides not to do so. This privilege is not available to an adult who contracts with a minor. If goods delivered to a repudiating minor are still in the minor's possession, it is the minor's duty to return them to the other party.

EXAMPLE 10-1: Cancellation of an Executory Contract

Gina Scott, who was 16 years old, purchased a new flat screen TV from the Planetary Electronics Supply Store. Scott paid $50 down and agreed to pay the balance in six monthly installments. Two weeks later, after she had used the TV, Scott decided she didn't want it any longer. When Planetary refused to take back the computer, Scott sued the company in small claims court for the return of her down payment and the cancellation of the balance she still owed. In most states, Planetary would be required to make the refund and cancel the debt. Scott would have to return the computer.

Contracts for Necessaries
Goods and services that are essential to a minor's health and welfare are called necessaries. Thus, necessaries can include clothing, food, shelter, medical and dental services, tools and equipment needed for the minor to carry out his or her business, and even, in some cases, educational expenses. If a minor makes a contract for necessaries, he or she will be liable for the fair value of those necessaries. Despite the general tenor of this principle, if the necessaries have already been provided to the minor by parents or others, the rule does not apply. In addition, not everything that a party claims as a necessary will actually be a necessary. To determine whether goods and services qualify as genuine necessaries, the court will inquire into the minor's family status, financial strength, and social standing or station in life. Necessaries, then, are not the same to all persons.

Did You Know?

Despite being designated as "necessaries," such things are not always needed to preserve or protect life. In fact, in one case the court held that funeral expenses were necessaries.

EXAMPLE 10-2: Necessaries as an Exception to the Rule

Rachel Kennedy had lived in Hawaii her entire life. Because she had "skipped" third and fifth grades, she was 16 when she entered college. The college she attended was in Buffalo, New York. She had never owned a winter coat, so she purchased one in October from the Jacob Brothers Department Store, while she was still 16. This coat would be a necessary, and any attempt to repudiate the purchase would probably fail.

Technically, a minor's contract covering necessaries is not enforceable against the minor in the truest sense of the term. Instead, the minor is required to pay the fair value of the necessaries that have been provided by the adult. The fair value is determined by the court.

This approach to the law is an extension of the concept of quasi-contract. Remember that when applying the concept of quasi-contract, the court will require the parties to act as if there were a contract, even though a true contract does not exist. The point of requiring the minor to pay the fair value of the item is to play it straight with adults who carry the risk of dealing with minors in relation to necessaries. Allowing the minor to get away with completely rescinding such contracts would amount to unfair enrichment of the minor. The concept of quasi-contract is aimed at preventing this type of unjust enrichment.

There is an interesting corollary related to the concept of necessaries that many people, including minors and the adults who deal with them, overlook. This corollary is the standard that states that the rules related to necessaries apply only to executed contracts. An executed contract is one whose terms have been completely and satisfactorily carried out by both parties. In contrast, an executory contract is one that has not yet been fully performed by the parties. Wholly executory contracts calling for a future delivery or rendering of services may be repudiated by the minor. Thus, in the foregoing example, had Kennedy's coat been ordered but not delivered or paid for, she could have repudiated her agreement with no damages or monetary loss being assessed against her.

Technically, parents are liable for a contract executed by a minor, even a contract for necessaries, *only* when they cosign the agreements. When a parent, or anyone else for that matter, cosigns for a loan or for a contract involving installment payments, the cosigner becomes a guarantor. A guarantor promises to pay the other party's debts if that party does not settle those debts personally. This promise is known as a guaranty of payment. In contrast, if parents do not cosign a contract, they are *not liable* for that contract, even though the contract was made by their minor child. As might be expected, there is an exception to this general rule. If a parent has neglected or deserted the minor, the parent may be held liable to a third person for the fair value of the necessaries supplied by the third party to the minor.

Other Contracts not Voidable

 By statute and court decision, certain other types of contracts have been excepted from the general rule that the contracts of minors are voidable at the minor's option. For public policy reasons, minors may not at their option disaffirm a valid marriage or repudiate an enlistment contract in the armed forces based on a claim of incapacity to contract. Neither may a minor repudiate a contract for goods and services required by law; for example, minors may not repudiate payments for inoculations and vaccinations required for attendance at a university or college or required in securing a visa for travel in certain foreign lands. They may also be prevented from terminating contracts with banks and other financial institutions for educational loans. Some states bar minors from repudiating agency contracts and insurance contracts. Others prevent them from voiding contracts for psychological care, pregnancy care, the transfer of stocks and bonds, and contracts involving child support. These exceptions are state-by-state issues, so it is wise to check your own state statutes to determine which of these contracts are not voidable by minors in your jurisdiction.

Shield or Sword Doctrine

If tempted to see the rescission rights of minors as unfair, we must keep in mind the original intent of the court in granting this power. As noted previously, the right to rescind contracts was given to minors as a protective device or "shield" against those unscrupulous adults who might try to take unfair advantage of the immaturity and inexperience of minors. This type of situation is precisely what the law envisioned when it granted minors the "shield" that allows them to rescind contracts.

The problem with this protective device is that it can be exploited by minors who use it to rescind legitimate contracts. In effect, an unprincipled minor can take this safeguard, which is meant as a protective shield, and transform it into a sword that violates the rights of the other party. Fortunately, the courts are not oblivious to this type of abuse. Because the doctrine was never meant to allow minors to take advantage of innocent people, the courts have no difficulty denying rescission rights to minors when they use it as a weapon against another contracting party.

EXAMPLE 10-3: The Shield and Sword Doctrine

Amber Sampson, who was 16 years of age, purchased a round-trip ticket on New England Airlines for a trip from Portland, Maine, to San Diego, California, for spring break. When spring break was over, Sampson returned to Portland and, on arrival, demanded the return of all the money that she had paid for the round-trip ticket. Her demands were based on her rescission rights as a minor. Clearly, Sampson was using her right to rescind to take advantage of New England Airlines. She was not using her rights as a minor as a protective shield, as the law intended. It is doubtful that Sampson will be permitted to recover money for her ticket.

Voidable Contracts and Innocent Third Parties

Another curb on a minor's right to rescind contracts appears in the provisions of the UCC. These provisions protect the rights of an innocent third party who purchases goods from an individual who originally purchased those same goods from a minor. Although individuals who buy goods from minors have voidable ownership rights, under the UCC, those same individuals can transfer valid ownership rights to an innocent third-party purchaser of those goods. Thus, rescission by a minor will not require the innocent purchaser to return the goods.

EXAMPLE 10-4: Protecting the Innocent

David Wittmer, age 17 years, sold his laptop to Lustbader Electronics, LLC. Lustbader refurbished the ancient laptop and then sold it to Alex Myers, an innocent third-party buyer. Before Wittmer became an adult, he decided to get back his laptop from Myers by disaffirming his contract with Lustbader. Wittmer is out of luck here. He will not be able to recover the laptop by disaffirming his contract with Lustbader. Myers is an innocent third party and is thus protected by the UCC.

The UCC rule refers to the sale of personal property. In cases in which a minor has sold real estate to one who subsequently sells it to an innocent third party, the minor, on reaching adulthood, may disaffirm the sale and recover the real property.

Ratification and Disaffirmance

People may ratify their contracts made during minority only after reaching their majority or within a reasonable time thereafter. Ratification or affirmance is the willingness to abide by contractual obligations. It may be implied by using the item purchased, making an installment payment, paying off the balance of money owed on a previously voidable contract, continuing to accept goods and services being provided under a contract, or just doing nothing about the contract after reaching majority. Affirmation may also result from the person's oral or written declaration to abide by the contract. These acts, as well as others, ratify an existing agreement and elevate it to the status of one that is enforceable against an adult.

An individual may disaffirm an agreement made during minority before or within a reasonable time after reaching adulthood. The exact period of time will vary depending on the nature of the contract and on applicable state and local laws. Failure to disaffirm within a reasonable period of time would imply that the contract had been ratified. The method of disaffirmance is fundamentally the same as the method of ratification. Disaffirmance may be implied by the acts of the individual after achieving majority, such as by a failure to make an installment payment. Similarly, an oral or written declaration of disaffirmance would achieve the same end. In general, there are no particular protocols attached to the act of disaffirmance by a minor. However, it is generally a good idea to make the disaffirmance in writing so that there is a record of the transaction should questions arise at a later time. This recommendation is especially true if the contract is disaffirmed after the minor has reached the age of majority.

quick quiz 10-1

1. Executory contracts, those which have not been fully performed by both parties, may be repudiated by a minor at any time.   true | false

2. Ratification is the willingness to abide by contractual obligations.   true | false

3. Necessaries are the same for all persons.   true | false

10-2 Other Capacity Problems

Persons deprived of the mental ability to comprehend contractual obligations have the right to disaffirm their contracts. Their rights are, in many respects, the same as the rights of minors. Agreements of mentally impaired persons are valid, voidable, or void, depending on the seriousness of their disability and whether they have been declared insane.

Persons Mentally Impaired

Under the orthodox rule of competency in contract law, a contract made by a person who is mentally infirm, has brain damage, is suffering from a physical illness such as Alzheimer's disease, or suffers from a psychological disorder may be voidable if the person's impairment is severe enough to rob that person of the ability to understand the nature, purpose, and effect of that contract. The question will be whether the mental problem existed at the time the contract was made and was so serious that the person did not understand the nature of the contract. If that is the case, the mentally impaired person may disaffirm any contract made under the influence of that mental impairment. The incompetent person must return all consideration received. This rule is true especially when the other party had no knowledge of the person's mental impairment. If, however, the other party knew about the person's mental impairment and took advantage of that knowledge, there is no requirement to return the other party to the identical place that he or she was in before the original agreement was established.

A second rule is also recognized by the Restatement of Contracts and by some states. That rule says that a person's contractual obligations may be voidable if that person suffers from a mental impairment that prevents him or her from acting in a reasonable manner. Under this version of the rule, a person may understand the nature of the contract but, because of his or her impairment, be unable to stop himself or herself from entering the contract. In such a situation, as long as the contract has yet to be executed or, if executed,

THE OPENING CASE *Revisited, Part I*
Public Policy, Statutory Law, and Contract Validity:
R.R. v. M.H. & Another, Round 2

Recall that in the Opening Case at the beginning of this chapter a married couple and a surrogate mother entered an agreement that stipulated that the father would pay for all pregnancy expenses plus a $10,000 fee to the mother for "conceiving, carrying and giving birth to the child." The fee was to be transferred to the surrogate mother in installments based on a structured payment plan. As part of the screening process, the surrogate mother, the father and the father's wife each underwent a psychological session orchestrated by a psychologist. The psychologist reported that the surrogate mother was a stable, reasonable, and knowledgeable woman who was aware of what she was doing and would be emotionally and psychologically capable of transferring custody to the child's biological father.

For a while everything went according to the contract. However, at the end of the sixth month, after receiving the third payment, the mother changed her mind, returned that third payment, and told the father's attorney that the contract was ended. That was the only money returned. She kept the first two payments and the expense money she had received under the agreement.

If the surrogate mother defended her decision to rescind the contract by saying that she lacked capacity due to a mental impairment, she would have difficulty making her case. The first standard would require her to demonstrate that the mental impairment prevented her from truly appreciating the nature the purpose and the effect of the agreement. This would be unlikely to happen given the psychologist's report. If the state adhered to the second standard her chances would be a bit better. That standard would require her to demonstrate that the mental impairment prevented her from acting in a reasonable manner. Still, even using this standard, she would have to counteract the psychologist's report that stated she was a stable, considerate, and knowledgeable woman. In either case, she would be required to return all of the money that she received from the couple.

can be shown to be very unjust, the impaired person may void the contract. If the contract is executed or fair, the impaired party may still void the contract but also must return the other party to the place he or she was in before the contract was entered. If returning the other party to his or her precontract condition cannot be done, the court will decide on a fair alternative.

A person declared to be insane by competent legal authority is denied the right to enter contracts. Such persons will be under the care of a guardian who acts on behalf of the impaired person, who has in effect become a ward of the court. Any contractual relationship with others results is nothing more than a void agreement. In most states, persons who knowingly take advantage of one declared insane are subject to criminal indictment and prosecution.

Persons Drugged or Intoxicated

A contract agreed to by someone under the influence of alcohol or drugs may be voidable. Incompetence related to either alcohol or drugs must be of such a degree that a contracting party would have lost the ability to comprehend or be aware of obligations being accepted under the contract. A person who enters into a contract while in this condition may either affirm or disaffirm the agreement at a later time. Disaffirmance in such cases requires the return to the other party of all consideration that had been received. However, such a return may be refused when evidence indicates that the other party took advantage of the person's drunken or otherwise weakened condition.

EXAMPLE 10-5: Involuntary Intoxication Invalidates a Contract

Samuel K. Richardson III attended a reception at the Yakuza Gallery on Madison Avenue at 75th Street in Manhattan. Unknown to Richardson, the punch at the reception had been laced with alcohol. After drinking several glasses, Richardson became highly intoxicated. While intoxicated, he agreed to sell the original manuscript of the novel, *The Bay Tree*, to an antiquarian book dealer named Maynard Posner, who was also at the reception and who was quite sure that Richardson was "tipsy" at the time of the sale. When Richardson recovered, he sought to disaffirm the contract. Because his involuntary state of intoxication had robbed Richardson of his ability to comprehend the contract he was making with Posner, he would be allowed to get out of the agreement.

---

quick quiz 10-2

1. For a contract to be voidable by a person with a mental impairment, the mental problem must exist at the time the contract was made.   true | false

2. A person declared to be insane by competent legal authority cannot be denied the right to enter contracts.   true | false

3. A contract made by a person who is intoxicated is completely void.   true | false

---

10-3 Agreements to Engage in Unlawful Activity

The final element of a valid contract is legality. Ordinarily, the court will leave the parties to an illegal agreement where they placed themselves. If an illegal agreement is still executory, the court will not order it performed or award damages for breach of contract. If the illegal agreement has been executed, the court will not award damages or assist in having it annulled. The most obvious type of illegal contract is one in which parties agree to perform some sort of unlawful activity. This activity could be a crime or a tort, depending on the circumstances. However, when we use the term "unlawful activity" in this context, we are referring to activities that are clearly wrong in and of themselves. These unlawful activities include crimes and torts that most people would recognize as wrong, even if there were no statute, regulation, or court decision to tell them it was wrong.

Agreements to Commit Torts and Crimes

The law will not uphold any contract that obligates one of the parties to commit a tort. For example, a network television reporter who agrees to defame several politicians in return for a position as their opponent's press secretary would find no remedy in the law should her benefactor fail to follow through after the libelous story was printed. The agreement to commit a tort would be void in the eyes of the law. This approach only makes good sense. The law cannot lend its approval to a contract that breaks the law, no matter how complete it is in relation to the other five elements.

In like manner, the law cannot honor any agreement if the purpose of the agreement is to commit a crime. If, for example, a storekeeper would pay a known criminal to vandalize the shop of a competitor, that storekeeper would not be able to sue the criminal for breach of contract should the criminal take the money and run. As strange as it may seem, the nature of criminality is not always as clear as might be imagined. Because criminal law involves serious offenses that can result in the loss of a person's freedom or, more seriously, the loss of a person's life, all criminal statutes must be drawn as precisely and as clearly as possible. A statute that is obscure or outlines conduct that is ambiguous may be struck down by the court as void for vagueness. This ruling would mean that a contract that involves the conduct that is allegedly outlawed by a vague statute might not be void.

Agreements Illegal under Statutory Law

Most people of good faith would know, even in the absence of any statute, regulation, ordinance, rule, or court decision, that the behavior outlined in the previous examples would be wrong. It is difficult to imagine, for instance, that the shopkeeper would be surprised to discover that it is wrong to hire someone to destroy his competitor's property. Similarly, it is not easy to believe that the television reporter who agreed to lie in a television broadcast thought that her behavior was in any way admirable. In contrast, some activities that do not seem wrong on the surface may have been made wrong by specific statutory enactments. Therefore, the fact that some of these activities are illegal may catch us by surprise. For example, the shopkeeper knows vandalism is illegal but may be confused to learn that he cannot hold a garage sale without a license. Or the reporter who knows that libel is wrong may be amazed to learn that her Wednesday evening poker game is not legal. For this reason, we will examine those activities that are wrong because a statute says they are wrong. These activities include usurious agreements, wagering agreements, unlicensed agreements, unconscionable agreements, and Sunday (Sabbath) agreements.

Usurious Agreements The illegal practice of charging more than the amount of interest allowed by law is called usury. To protect borrowers from excessive interest charges, each state has passed laws that specify the rate of interest that may be charged in lending money. These interest rates vary from state to state. Agreements to charge more than is allowed by law are illegal. Special statutes, however, allow small loan companies, pawn shops, and other lending agencies that accept high-risk applicants for credit to charge a higher rate of interest.

Wagering Agreements Any agreement or promise concerning a wager or some other form of gambling is invalid and may not be enforced. States make exceptions when bets are placed in accordance with laws that permit horse racing, state lotteries, church related or charitable games of bingo, and gambling casinos regulated by state authority. However, even in states in which gambling is legal, borrowing money to gamble it is frequently still illegal.

Unlicensed Agreements Certain businesses and professions must be licensed before they are allowed to operate legally. One reason for requiring a license is to provide a source of revenue, part of which is used to supervise the business or profession being licensed. A city ordinance requiring all residents to obtain a license before holding a yard or garage sale would fall into this category. Another purpose that the government has in licensing individuals is to provide supervision and regulation of businesses and professions that might inflict harm on the public if they were allowed to operate without such controls. Physicians, nurses, dentists, attorneys, engineers, architects, public school teachers, and others in public service must be supervised for the protection of the public. The law distinguishes between licenses purely for revenue and licenses for protection of the public. If a license is required simply to raise revenue, the lack of a license will not necessarily make a contract void; if a licensing requirement is designed to protect the public, unlicensed persons will not be able to enforce their contracts.

Unconscionable Agreements

A court will not enforce a contract or any part of a contract that it regards as unconscionable. An agreement is considered unconscionable if its terms are so grossly unfair that they shock the court's conscience. When the court so desires, it will limit how the unconscionable clause in an agreement is carried out, provided it can do so without causing any unfair consequences.

Sunday Agreements

State statutes and local ordinances that regulate the making and performing of contracts on Sunday are called blue laws because one of the first laws banning Sunday or Sabbath contracts was written on blue paper. Today, the enforcement of restrictive blue laws varies in different geographical areas. Certain states have eliminated uniform statewide laws regulating Sunday activities but permit counties and incorporated cities, towns, and villages to adopt their own ordinances under a concept known as local option. Other states have rolled back these laws almost entirely, permitting most contracts while prohibiting or limiting only a few select Sunday contracts, such as those involving the sale of alcohol. Where laws do restrict Sunday business, two rules are usually observed. First, agreements made on Sunday or any other day requiring performance on Sunday may be ruled invalid. Exceptions to this rule are those agreements necessary to the health, welfare, and safety of the community and its residents. Second, agreements made on Sunday for work to be done or goods to be delivered on a business day are valid and enforceable. However, some states still require that there be an affirmation of such agreements on a day other than Sunday if such agreements are to be enforceable. The enforcement of blue laws varies widely from state to state, county to county, and village to village.

Agreements Contrary to Public Policy

The general legal principle of public policy says no one should be allowed to do anything that injures the public at large. Agreements most commonly invalidated as contrary to public policy are those to obstruct justice, interfere with public service, defraud creditors, escape liability, and restrain trade. Some of these agreements are prohibited by statute, such as those that suppress competition and those that interfere with public service. Consequently, they could have been listed and explained in the last section. Instead, these contracts are listed here with the other public policy–related contracts, because they share one thing in common, though such contracts are made between private individuals, they would hurt the entire social structure if the law enforced them in any way.

Agreements to Obstruct Justice

Agreements to obstruct justice include agreements to protect someone from arrest, to suppress evidence, to encourage lawsuits, to give false testimony, and to bribe a juror. The category also includes a promise not to prosecute someone or not to serve as a witness in a trial. Any agreement promising to perform any of these activities would be void.

Agreements Interfering with Public Service

Agreements interfering with public service are illegal and void. Contracts in this group include agreements to bribe or interfere with public officials, to obtain political preference in appointments to office, to pay an officer for signing a pardon, or to illegally influence a legislature for personal gain.

THE OPENING CASE Revisited, Part II
Public Policy, Statutory Law, and Contract Validity:
R.R. v. M.H. & Another, Round 3

In the Opening Case at the beginning of this chapter we learned that a married couple and a surrogate mother entered an agreement that stipulated that, in exchange for expenses and a $10,000 fee, the mother agreed to conceive, carry, and give birth to a child for the infertile couple. The fee was to be transferred to the surrogate mother in installments based on a structured payment plan. The contract went forward as planned until the sixth month when the mother changed her mind, returned that third payment, and told the father's attorney that the contract was ended. The father sued for custody of the baby, arguing that the surrogate mother had breached the contract. The judge agreed with the father and awarded him custody. The judge also believed such a move would ultimately be in the child's best interests. The surrogate mother appealed. The state supreme court decided that, since the state had no statute covering this type of agreement, it would apply an adoption statute that covered

situations that were roughly analogous to the surrogacy situation. Under the adoption statute, a mother could not give up her child for adoption until four days after the child's birth. The statute also outlawed the payment of money to the mother for an adoption, although she could be paid pregnancy expenses. The state supreme court recognized that the legislature had a good reason for requiring a four-day waiting period before a mother could give up her child for adoption. The court took judicial notice of the fact that a mother comprehends the power of the connection between mother and child after the fourth day and is, therefore, in a better position to be fully aware what she is surrendering in an adoption. Using public policy, the court applied those same principles to the surrogate mother contract. In doing so, it concluded that, since the surrogate mother contract did not include a four-day waiting period, it was an illegal contract and was, therefore, void as a matter of law.

A QUESTION OF ETHICS

In February 2011, the Egyptian people displayed their dissatisfaction with the government of Hosni Mubarak by demonstrating in Tahrir Square in Cairo and in the port city of Alexandria. The demonstrations led to Mubarak's abdication and to a military takeover of the government. The military leaders pledged to develop a new constitution and to turn the government over to civilian control as soon as possible. Nevertheless, despite the movement's victory over Mubarak and his government, many protestors continued to disrupt the peaceful transition to domestic peace. Chief among these demonstrators were members of the labor movement who had created a tightly knit network of agreements under which striking textile employees, airport workers, ambulance drivers, electrical engineers, and journalists continued to cause economic disruption. All of this continued to occur despite warnings by the military government that such actions should cease. Clearly the strikers believe that their cause is moral and their actions ethical despite their dubious legality. Under American law, agreements to strike illegally would violate public policy. Should the ethical motivation of the strikers trump the illegality of their actions? Defend your response using one of the ethical theories discussed in Chapter One of the text.

Agreements to Defraud Creditors An agreement that tends to remove or weaken the rights of creditors is referred to as an agreement to defraud creditors. Such agreements are void as contrary to public policy. Thus a debtor's agreement to sell and transfer personal and real property to a friend or relative for far less than actual value would be void if done for the purpose of hiding the debtor's assets from creditors with a legal claim to them.

Agreements to Escape Liability

A basic policy of the law is that all parties should be liable for their own wrongdoing. Consequently, the law looks with disfavor on any agreement that allows a party to escape this responsibility. One device frequently used in the attempt to escape legal responsibility is the exculpatory agreement. Such an agreement is usually found as a clause in a longer, more complex contract or on the back of tickets and parking stubs. The exculpatory clause will state that one of the parties, generally the one who wrote the contract, will not be liable for any economic loss of physical injury even if that party caused the loss or injury.

EXAMPLE 10-6: *Newsome v. Tibbs*

Pat Newsome, who worked for Van Sloane, Wentworth, and Michelson, was the chief architect on a project that involved building a new community center on the west side of Baltimore. Before the center could be built, a set of four high-rise apartment buildings, the Towers, had to come down. That job went to Tibbs TNT, LLC, an expert in razing ancient buildings. When Newsome arrived at the job, he was told by Elizabeth Tibbs, the owner of Tibbs TNT that he had to sign an additional contract with Tibbs. One of the clauses in the additional contract included an exculpatory clause that stated that Newsome would hold Tibbs blameless should Newsome be injured during the tear down of the Towers. The actual implosion of the Towers went without incident. However, afterwards, Newsome was injured when the brakes on a Tibbs-owned truck failed and ran over Newsome. Newsome sued Tibbs. Tibbs pointed to the exculpatory clause and said she was not liable. The court disagreed, saying that the exculpatory clause could not protect Tibbs from liability for injuries that result from negligence on the part of Tibbs or her employees.

This exculpatory clause is an example of the type that the courts have found to be a violation of public policy. Such exculpatory clauses are not favored by the law because they permit behavior to fall below acceptable standards, which was what happened in the Newsome case. A clause simply disclaiming liability in general terms is often insufficient to release a party from his or her own negligence. Still, some courts will enforce exculpatory clauses if they do not offend public policy and there is no inequality of bargaining power between the parties. However, whenever an exculpatory provision is ambiguous, confusing, vague, incomplete, or can be interpreted in different ways, the court will construe the clause against the party it was designed to protect.

Sale of Business

When a business is sold, it is common practice for the agreement to contain covenants that restrict the seller from entering the same type of business. Such restrictive covenants in a contract for the sale of a business will be upheld by the court if they are reasonable in time and geographical area. What is reasonable is determined by a careful examination of the business being sold. For example, an agreement by the seller of a barbershop not to open a similar shop in the same community for the next year would seem to be reasonable. In contrast, the opening of a different business, over a wider geographical area, or for a longer period of time might not be allowed by the court.

Restrictive Employment Covenants

A restrictive employment covenant, or noncompete agreement as it is often called, limits a worker's employment options after leaving his or her present job. The idea is to protect the present employer from an employee who might take trade secrets, customer lists, or other confidential material to a competitor. In a typical restrictive employment covenant, an employee promises not to work for a competitor in the same field for a specified time period and within a specified geographical area after leaving the current job. Restrictive employment covenants must be reasonable in the type of work they prohibit, the length of time involved in the prohibition, and the geographical area covered by the prohibition.

Nondisclosure Agreements A nondisclosure agreement requires employees to promise that, should they leave their present place of employment, they will not reveal any confidential trade secrets that they might learn while on their current job. Because the limitation is placed on the use of confidential information rather than actual employment of the worker, such agreements do not deprive people of their employment and therefore do not constitute an extensive limit on competition. Although helpful, nondisclosure agreements are often not needed to protect trade secrets. The court will generally issue an injunction to prevent the revelation or the utilization of trade secrets if the employer can convince the court that (1) the information revealed by the former employee was actually a trade secret, (2) the secret information was crucial to the running of the employer's business, (3) the employer had the right to use the trade secret, and (4) the former employee came into possession of the trade secret while in a position of trust and confidence and in such a way that it would be unfair for the former employee to disclose that trade secret in a way that would hurt his or her former employer.

---

quick quiz 10-3

1. The illegal practice of charging more than the amount of interest allowed by law is called usury.   true | false

2. If a license is required simply to raise revenue, the lack of a license will make a contract void.   true | false

3. A restrictive employment covenant limits a worker's employment options after leaving his or her present job.   true | false

---

10-4 Consequences of Illegality

Illegality of contract, as in promises to commit criminal acts, not only serves to void existing agreements but may also lead to indictment and prosecution when sufficient evidence warrants such an action. Persons who agree to commit criminal acts for a promised consideration are involved in what criminal law defines as a conspiracy. Agreements that do not violate criminal laws may still be invalid. Thus, many agreements considered contrary to public policy have been declared invalid as against the public good but not illegal in terms of criminal liability. Both types of agreements fail to have the characteristics that permit legal enforcement.

In Pari Delicto Contracts

When both parties to an illegal agreement are equally wrong in the knowledge of the operation and effect of their contract, they are said to be *in pari delicto* (in equal fault). In such cases, the court will give no aid to either party in an action against the other and will award no damages to either. When the parties are not *in pari delicto*, relief will often be allowed if sought by the more innocent of the two. Although this rule is not applicable when one may be less guilty of premeditation (plotting or planning an illegal act) and intent to achieve a gain through known illegal acts, it may be applied when one party is not aware that a law is being broken and there is no intent to do a wrong.

Partial Illegality in an Agreement

Sometimes an agreement will be partly legal and partly illegal. If the legal part of a contract can be removed from the illegal part, without changing the essential nature of the contract, then the agreement is said to be divisible. The court will enforce the legal part but not the illegal part. As long as the main purpose of the agreement can be reached without enforcing the illegal part, the courts are likely to uphold the agreement.

quick quiz 10-4

1. Persons who agree to commit criminal acts for a promised consideration are involved in a conspiracy.   true | false

2. When both parties to an illegal agreement are equally wrong in the knowledge of the operation and effect of their contract, they are said to be *in pari delicto*.   true | false

3. If the legal part of a contract can be removed from the illegal part, without changing the essential nature of the contract, the court will enforce both parts.   true | false

Summary

10.1 The third element essential to a legally effective contract is the legal ability to enter into a contractual relationship. This legal ability is known as capacity. Under the law, there is a rebuttable presumption that anyone entering a contract has the legal capacity to do so. Because the presumption is rebuttable, a party can attack it. Minors are allowed this privilege. Minority means that an individual has not yet attained the age of majority. An exception to the rule about minors and contracts involves necessaries. By statute and court decision, certain other types of contracts have been excepted from the general rule that the contracts of minors are voidable at the minor's option.

10.2 Contracts of persons who are mentally infirm or mentally ill, but not legally declared insane, may be valid or voidable, depending on the seriousness of the mental problem. Persons declared to be insane by competent legal authority are denied the right to enter into contracts, and contracts entered into may be declared

void. Incompetence related to alcohol or drugs must be of such a degree that the contracting party has lost the ability to comprehend or be aware of the obligations being accepted under the contract.

10.3 An agreement might have offer, acceptance, mutual assent, competent parties, and consideration and still be invalid if the objective of the agreement is to do something that is illegal. These contracts include those to commit crimes, to commit torts, or to violate statutory law. Public policy is a general legal principle that says no one should be allowed to do anything that tends to hurt the public at large. Agreements found void for a violation of public policy include agreements to obstruct justice, agreements interfering with public service, agreements to defraud creditors, exculpatory agreements, and agreements in restraint of trade.

10.4 Contracts that involve illegal agreements are invalid. Moreover, promises to commit illegal acts may lead to indictment and prosecution. If an entire agreement is illegal, no binding contract results. If only part of an agreement is illegal, the court may rescind only those parts found to be illegal. When both parties are equally at fault in creating an illegal agreement, the court will award no damages to either. When the parties are not in equal fault, relief will often be granted if sought by the innocent party.

Key Terms

abandoned, 212	illegal agreement, 211	public policy, 220
affirmance, 215	in pari delicto, 223	ratification, 215
blue laws, 220	local option, 220	rebuttable presumption, 211
capacity, 211	majority, 212	restrictive covenants, 222
conspiracy, 223	minority, 212	restrictive employment
disaffirm, 211	necessaries, 213	covenant, 222
emancipated, 212	noncompete agreement, 222	usury, 219
exculpatory clause, 222	nondisclosure agreement, 223	

Questions for Review and Discussion

1. What is the age of minority and what is the age of majority?
2. What is the legal status of a contract made by a minor?
3. What is the difference between ratification and disaffirmance?
4. What are the effects of mental impairment on a contract?
5. What is the contractual capacity of a drugged or intoxicated person?
6. What is the legal status of an agreement to commit a tort or a crime?
7. What agreements are illegal under statutory law?
8. What agreements are contrary to public policy?
9. What happens under the doctrine of *in pari delicto?*
10. What are the effects of illegality?

Cases for Analysis

1. After she was married, Sherri Mitchell, a young woman of 17 years of age, was in an automobile accident in which she was hurt enough to require medical treatment. She was later approached by an insurance agent who offered her $2,500 as a settlement. All she had to do was sign a release that would absolve the insurance company of any complaint that she might have against it in regard to the accident. She agreed to accept the $2,500 and signed a release to that effect. However, she then changed her mind and decided to void the agreement. She argued that since she was 17 at the time she signed the release, she was a minor and could therefore void the contract. Is Mrs. Mitchell correct? Explain. *Mitchell v. State Farm Mutual Automobile Insurance Co.,* 963 S.W.2d (Ky. Ct. App.).

2. Sperry Ford sold a car to Bowling when Bowling was only 16 years old. Once Bowling had paid the full purchase price in cash, Sperry turned over the car and the certificate of title. After driving the car for only a week, Bowling discovered that the main bearing was burned out. When Bowling found out that repair costs would almost equal the price he'd paid for the car, he left the car on Sperry's lot and asked for his money back. Sperry Ford refused to give Bowling his money. Was Sperry justified in this refusal? Explain. *Bowling vs. Sperry,* 184 N.E.2d 901 (IN).

3. Quality Motors, Inc., refused to sell a car to Hays because he was only 16 years old. However, Quality told Hays that they would sell the car to an adult and then show Hays how to transfer the title to his name. Hays agreed with the scheme and came back with a friend who was 23. Quality sold the car to Hays's friend. Quality then gave Hays the name of a notary public who would transfer

the title to Hays. After the transfer was accomplished, Hays's father found out about the deal and tried to get Quality Motors to take the car back. Quality replied that the car had been sold to an adult, so Hays could not disaffirm the contract. Is Quality correct? Explain. *Quality Motors v. Hays*, 225 S.W.2d 326 (AR).

4. Lonchyna enlisted in the U.S. Air Force while he was still a minor. Three times he applied for and received educational delays that put off the beginning of his tour of duty. The last time, he claimed he could void the contract, because he'd entered into it when he was a minor. Was Lonchyna correct? Explain. *Lonchyna v. Brown, Secretary of Defense*, 491 F. Supp. 1352 (N.D. IL).

5. Darwin Kruse was a construction worker. He was injured while working for the Coos Head Timber Company. Subsequent to the accident, Kruse signed an agreement with his employer that granted Kruse compensation in exchange for his promise not to sue. Kruse is now trying to have the agreement voided. Evidence introduced proved that Kruse had an IQ of 83 and that he dropped out of school at age 18. When he dropped out of school, he was in the eighth grade but was doing less than sixth grade–level work. Will Kruse's "slowness" necessarily invalidate the contract? Explain. *Kruse v. Coos Head Timber Co.*, 432 P.2d 1009 (OR).

6. Clear Channel Broadcasting, Inc., required Diane Ignazio to sign a new contract that included an arbitration clause under which she agreed that all grievances that she might have with Clear Channel would be settled by arbitration. As part of the agreement, Ignazio gave up any right to bring a lawsuit against Clear Channel. When Ignazio was discharged, instead of moving to arbitration, she sued Clear Channel for discrimination and wrongful discharge. Clear Channel filed a motion to dismiss the case, arguing that Ignazio was bound by the arbitration agreement. Ignazio pointed to a clause in the agreement that rendered the entire agreement illegal. The clause allowed the arbitration award to be reviewed by a court based on the same broad standards used by an appeals court in reviewing a trial court's decision. This provision contradicts state law, which states that if an appeals court reviews an arbitration decision, it can only use a very limited approach to the appeal, including only such things as clerical error or misconduct. Clear Channel argued that even if the clause was illegal, it could be severed from the agreement, and the rest of the agreement could be enforced. In fact, the contract even included a clause that stated that any clause found illegal ought to be removed from the contract, so that the rest of the contract could be upheld. The question before the court was whether the illegal clause could be removed from the agreement without changing the essential nature of the contract. Is it legally permissible to remove the illegal part of a contract so that the court can uphold the legal part? Should the court sever the illegal clause in this case? Explain. *Ignazio v. Clear Channel*, 113 Ohio St.3d 276 (Ohio Supreme Court).

7. Cyberian Enterprises and BrandAid Marketing Corporation entered a deal under which Cyberian was supposed to purchase $21 million in Brand-Aid's stock. Cyberian, however, did not have the funds available to make the actual purchase, a fact that was concealed by Cyberian representatives. When BrandAid discovered the lie, it filed a lawsuit against Cyberian for fraud, breach of contract, and breaking federal securities law. Cyberian brought a countersuit against BrandAid for fraud because BrandAid had apparently failed to tell Cyberian about its own financial difficulties. However, BrandAid's financial problems were on file with the Securities and Exchange Commission (SEC). When the case went to District Court, the judge dismissed the case because, citing the doctrine of *in pari delicto*, he stated that both parties were at equal fault in concealing their financial difficulties. The case then went to the Second Circuit Court of Appeals, which decided that the trial court had made a mistake in dismissing the case. Why did the appeals court overturn the decision of the trial court? Explain. *BrandAid Marketing Corp. v. Biss*, 05-5243-cv (2d U.S. Cir. Ct. of App.). (See also Beth Bar, "Civil Practice: Finding of Equal Fault Is Overturned," *The National Law Journal*, September 11, 2006, p. 13.)

8. Shannon Audley, a professional model, signed an agreement before starting work on a photo shoot at Bill Melton's studio. The agreement stated: "I, Shannon Audley, realize that working with wild and potentially dangerous animals (i.e., lion, white tiger, hawk) can create a hazardous situation resulting in loss of life or limb. I take all responsibility upon myself for any event as described above that may

take place. I hold Bill Melton and T.I.G.E.R.S. or any of their agents free of any or all liability. I am signing this of my own free will." During the photo shoot, Audley was bitten on the head by the adult male lion with which she had been posing. Audley brought suit against Melton. Would the exculpatory clause be upheld by the courts? Explain. *Audley v. Melton*, 640 A.2d 777 NH).

9. Judy Myers and the Terminix International Company entered a contract in which Terminix agreed to inspect Myers's home and eliminate any termite problem found there. The service cost Myers an initial payment of $1,300 plus annual renewal fees of $85. Terminix failed to eradicate the termite infestation, causing more than $41,000 in damage to Myers's home. The contract contained a clause that required the parties to submit any disputes to arbitration under the American Arbitration Association (AAA). What the contract did not disclose was that Myers would be required to pay a filing fee to submit a claim to AAA. In this case, the filing fee amounted to $7,000. In a lawsuit filed for breach of contract, Myers asserted that the undisclosed filing fee requirement was unconscionable. Is Myers correct? Explain. *Myers v. Terminix*, 697 N.E.2d 277 (OH).

quick quiz Answers

10-1	10-2	10-3	10-4
1. T	1. T	1. T	1. T
2. T	2. F	2. F	2. T
3. F	3. F	3. T	3. F

<table>
</table>

Chapter 11

Written Contracts and Cyber-Commerce

THE OPENING CASE Written Contracts and The New Frontier: *Wilcox v. Trautz*

The Statute of Frauds was first introduced into the legal system in 1677 when Parliament created the Act for the Prevention of Frauds and Perjuries. The act outlined those contracts that had to be in writing to be enforced by the courts. One of those contracts was an agreement made in consideration of marriage. This did not include the marriage contract itself, but only those ancillary agreements to distribute property if the marriage broke up. Today, we call such contracts prenuptial agreements. The members of Parliament were quite progressive in adding "pre-nups" to the statute. However, even with the benefit of their combined wisdom, they never foresaw the strange case of *Wilcox v. Trautz*. Carol Wilcox and John Trautz lived together as an unmarried couple for 25 years, beginning when they were both youngsters in their twenties. During those two and a half decades, Wilcox managed to contribute only $25 each week for household expenses. However, she also performed all the household duties, and she used her own money to buy food and clothing. Unfortunately, all good things must come to an end, and so, when Trautz discovered that Wilcox had become involved in another relationship, he sought legal advice regarding his rights with respect to the assets acquired during their relationship. At that point, the two parties negotiated, wrote, and signed an agreement providing, among other things that "each party's earnings and

property is his or hers alone, and the other party shall have no interest in the property of the other." The assets, all in Trautz's name, included a house, valued at $180,000; an amphibious airplane, valued at $55,000; various bank accounts totaling $1,300; individual retirement accounts; and a one-half share in some real estate in Maine, valued at $15,000. Wilcox had no assets other than a small bank account, the other one-half share of the Maine real estate, household furniture, clothing, and jewelry. Had the written contract been a genuine prenuptial agreement, it would have been fine. It did exactly what a "pre-nup" is supposed to do, that is, it explained the terms of the agreement in specific, understandable language. However, it was not really a pre-nup, and that single fact gave the court pause. As a result, after due deliberation, the judge ruled that the agreement could not be enforced. In addition, the judge also decided that, to prevent unjust enrichment, Trautz would have to pay Wilcox damages amounting to approximately $30,000. Trautz appealed the decision. Read on to see what happened. (See *Wilcox v. Trautz*, 693 N.E.2d 141(Supreme Judicial Court of Massachusetts).)

Opening Case Questions

1. Can the court use the Statute of Frauds to decide this case? Explain.

2. Does the actual written agreement satisfy all the requirements of the Statute of Frauds? Explain.

3. Does public policy apply here? Explain. If public policy applies, what should the result be? Explain.

4. If the court follows a strict interpretation of the law here, it will have to dismiss the contract as unenforceable, not because it does not meet the Statute of Frauds, but because it encourages the cohabitation of unmarried couples. Does this principle make sense in the modern world or is it simply an outdated, old-fashioned notion that should not influence the court today? Explain.

5. Should the courts try to reshape social norms this way or should that job be left to the legislature? Explain.

 ## Learning Objectives

1. Identify the goals of the Statute of Frauds.
2. Identify those contracts that must be in writing.
3. List the information that must be in the writing.
4. Explain the Standard Construction Rule.
5. Discuss the Parol Evidence Rule.
6. Explain the exceptions to the Parol Evidence Rule.
7. Explain the Best Evidence Rule.
8. Discuss the Equal Dignities Rule.
9. Explain the problems associated with cyber-commerce.
10. Outline the latest cyber-commerce statutes.

11-1 The Statute of Frauds

Often when people hear the word *contract*, they immediately think of a piece of paper. Instead, they should think of an agreement, which may or may not be in writing. Many contracts do not have to be in writing to be enforceable. Most oral contracts are valid and upheld by the court. Although it may be desirable to put a contract in writing so that its terms are clear, only certain kinds of contracts are required to be in writing. This chapter discusses the Statute of Frauds, which is the law that requires certain contracts to be in writing to be enforceable.

Contracts that Must Be in Writing

According to the Statute of Frauds, applicable in most states, six types of contracts must be in writing to be enforceable:

1. Contracts that cannot be completed within one year.

2. Contracts transferring real property rights.

3. Contracts for the sale of goods of $500 or more.

4. Certain contracts entered into by executors and administrators.

5. Contracts by one party to pay a debt of another party.

6. Contracts in consideration of marriage.

The third contract on the list, contracts for the sale of goods of $500 or more, is actually included in the Uniform Commercial Code rather than the Statute of Frauds. This point is covered in depth in Chapter 13.

Contracts that Cannot Be Completed Within One Year If the terms of a contract make it impossible to complete the agreement within one year, the contract must be in writing.

EXAMPLE 11-1: *Strachan v. Wright Weber Construction*

Frank Strachan entered a contract with Wright Weber Construction for the building of an addition to his new home in Lakeside. The construction firm was to begin building the addition on April 2. Wright Weber agreed that the addition might be finished by March 1 of the following year, but also stipulated that May 1 of the following year was a more reasonable estimate. The details of the agreement were never reduced to writing. When Wright Weber ran into labor problems in August, it had to put the construction of the addition on hold. One month later, unable to resolve the labor dispute, Wright Weber shut the company down and abandoned the Strachan work site. As a result, Strachan had to negotiate a new contract with a new construction firm. The new contract cost $12,900 more than it would have had Weber completed the job as promised. In addition, because the Lakeside house could not be used during construction, Strachan incurred storage costs for his furniture because he had to move out of the home he was living in to accommodate the new owners. He also had to live in a hotel for four months while the Lakeside addition was completed. Strachan sued Wright Weber. Wright Weber moved for a dismissal because the contract was not in writing. Strachan argued that the contract could have been completed within one year and was therefore outside of the statute. As a result, he correctly concluded that the writing was not needed.

About the Law

In addition to those mentioned here, states have enacted various statutes requiring other types of contracts to be in writing, such as promises to leave something to someone in a will, promises to pay debts that have been discharged in bankruptcy, and certain types of assignments.

Although the marriage agreement itself does not have to be written, some contracts associated with marriage do.

Contracts Transferring Real Property Rights

Under the Statute of Frauds, conveyances of real property must be in writing to be enforceable. This provision covers the sale of land; however, it also covers trusts that are created by one party, the trustor, that permit a second party, the trustee, to possess and control the land for the advantage of a third party, the beneficiary. Whether the provision includes leases is problematic, because some jurisdictions permit short leases, generally those that last less than a year, to be oral. Most states, however, are relatively clear that leases that are designed to last longer than one year must be in writing to be enforceable. Moreover, it is not enough that the lease actually be in writing; the writing must also be presented to the court for it to be enforceable.

When a party owns land, he or she owns a bundle of rights that can be distributed among various other parties. Thus, it is possible, for example, for

231

EXAMPLE 11-2: *Nicklesworth v. Marblehead Properties*

Walt Nicklesworth entered a lease agreement with Marblehead Properties, under which Nicklesworth used the property located at 5293 Lake Shore Boulevard as a used bookstore. The terms of the lease included a right of first refusal, such that Nicklesworth could purchase the property if Marblehead ever decided to sell. Two years into the five-year lease, Marblehead sold the property to Daniel O'Donnell. Nicklesworth brought suit for breach of contract. At trial, no one could produce a written copy of the lease for the judge. The judge dismissed the case because the Statute of Frauds required a writing, and none could be produced at court.

the owner of a parcel of land to divide the rights to that land among several different parties. One party might hold a lease to a house on the land allowing her to live there, a second could have an easement that permits him to cross the land, a third might own the right to mine the land, and so on. The Statute of Frauds requires a writing for each of these different transactions. The object of this requirement is to make certain that there is a way to follow the trail of each of these rights to determine who owns them, should a dispute arise concerning them.

EXAMPLE 11-3: *Xavier v. Brookhaven*

In 1919, Pasha Patel owned several acres of land in the Upper Peninsula of the state of Michigan. Half a pond was located on Patel's land. The other half of the pond was located on land owned by Brooke Brookhaven. For a small consideration, Patel transferred the right to cut ice on her side of the pond each winter to Fred Xavier. The contract was oral and supposed to last for the next five winters. Each day from early October to late March, Xavier would cut the ice and remove it. He would carefully carve the ice into large cubes that fit perfectly into the ice boxes located in the rental cabins dotting the upper peninsula. (This was 1919, remember.) He then sold the ice to the cabin renters. One summer Brookhaven drained her part of the pond. In October, this action meant that ice was sparse, and what was available was sunk into the mud at the bottom of the lake and thus unusable for carving and sale. Xavier brought suit against Brookhaven, arguing that her action in draining the lake made his interest in the property worthless. The court asked for a copy of the written contract transferring the right to cut the ice to Xavier. When Xavier could not produce one, the judge dismissed the case.

An exception to the rule that contracts for the sale of land must be in writing is called part performance or equitable estoppel. The exception applies when a person relies on an owner's oral promise to sell real property and then makes improvements on the property or changes his or her position in an important way. The plaintiff in such a case must prove three elements to succeed in a lawsuit. First, the plaintiff must show that he or she made the improvement relying on the original promise and without suspecting that the other party intended to renege on the agreement. Second, the plaintiff must show that any other remedy, such as restitution for the amount spent, is not enough to satisfy his or her effort or outlay of funds. Third, the plaintiff must show that the part performance itself is evidence of the existence of the contract.

EXAMPLE 11-4: *Zuer v. Iafigliola*

Jake Iafigliola agreed in an oral contract to sell Dwight Zuer a run-down parcel of storefront property for $50,000. The storefront was located across the street from the site of a new Target that was about to be established in the neighborhood. Relying on Iafigliola's agreement, Zuer spent $20,000 improving the premises so that he could move his DVD rental business into the storefront. Iafigliola then backed out of the deal. Zuer sued, asking the court to order Iafigliola to go through with the contract. Iafigliola argued this was a real property contract and it had to be in writing to be enforceable. Zuer asked the court to apply the part performance doctrine. Zuer made the following case: First, he had made the improvements relying on the original promise. Second, he pointed out that any other remedy, such as restitution for the amount spent, would not be enough, because he clearly wanted the storefront in the lot across from the new Target. Third, Zuer argued that the fact that he spent $20,000 to improve the storefront could not be explained in any other way other than his reliance on the contract. The court agreed and allowed the lawsuit even without the writing.

The courts do not require a writing for a contract in which the owner of land agrees to improve the land for the use of another party who has already received a partial interest in the land. In such a situation, the courts believe that once the real interest in the land has been transferred, the contract to improve the land does not create a new interest. Instead, the new contract is solely a promise to provide labor and make changes in the land. It therefore falls outside the statute, and no writing is required.

EXAMPLE 11-5: *Dewey v. Collins*

Rene Collins owned a piece of land in rural Pennsylvania, just outside Streetsboro. Frederick Dewey received an easement across Collins's land. The easement, which was supposed to last for five years, was executed in a written document. After the first year, Dewey asked Collins to lay gravel on the small road that constituted the easement. Collins said that she would not lay the gravel herself but would permit Dewey to do so and reimburse him for the expense. Dewey laid the gravel and presented Collins with the bill. Collins refused to reimburse Dewey as agreed. Collins argued that because there was no writing, the contract, which involved land, was unenforceable. The referee disagreed, concluding that the agreement to lay gravel did not create a new interest. Instead, it simply involved a commitment to pay for improvements to land in which Dewey already owned an interest.

UCC 2-201 (see pages 622–623)

Contracts for the Sale of Goods of $500 or More Under the UCC, contracts for the sale of goods (moveable items) for $500 or more must be in writing to be enforceable. However, there are four exceptions to this rule. Oral contracts for the sale of goods of $500 or more will be enforced in situations involving the following:

1. Oral contracts between merchants when a written confirmation has been received by one party and not objected to by the other party.
2. Specially manufactured goods that cannot be resold easily.
3. Admissions in court.
4. Executed agreements.

Certain Contracts Entered by Executors and Administrators

An *executor* is a person who is named in a will to oversee the distribution of the estate of a deceased according to the provisions outlined in the will. An *administrator* is a person named by the court to do the work of an executor if none is named in the will or if the executor cannot or will not perform those duties. As a general principle of law, neither an executor nor an administrator is personally liable for the debts of the decedent's estate. Executors and administrators must pay the debts of the estate, to be sure, but out of the assets of the estate, not out of their own pockets. Thus, any promise to pay the debts of the estate using the executor's or the administrator's own funds is unenforceable without a writing.

EXAMPLE 11-6: *Trautman v. Quinn*

Max Quinn was named the executor of his sister's estate. One of his sister's creditors, Nancy Trautman, demanded immediate payment of a debt of $6,600 owed by the deceased. To protect his sister's good name, Quinn promised Trautman that he would pay her the amount owed out of his own funds if the estate could not cover that amount. Trautman refused to agree unless Quinn placed the agreement in writing. Quinn agreed. After things calmed down, Trautman tried to collect the debt. Quinn refused to pay. Trautman was able to enforce the promise because she had written evidence of Quinn's agreement to pay the debt.

Contracts by One Party to Pay a Debt Incurred by Another

Party A promise made by one party to pay another person's debts, if that person fails to pay the debt, falls within the statute and must be in writing to be enforceable. Several terms have been used to describe these types of transactions. They are alternately referred to as a guaranty of payment, a guaranty contract, or a collateral contract. The promisor is usually called a guarantor. Often in a commercial setting, the guarantor is referred to as a cosigner. The person to whom the promise is made is the obligee, and the person who owes the original debt is referred to as the obligor. It is crucial to distinguish between guaranty contracts and original contracts.

An exception to this rule is known as the primary objective test. Under the primary objective test (also referred to as the leading objective test and the main purpose test), if the promise to pay another party's debt is actually made to obtain a gain for the guarantor, there is no need for a writing to enforce the promise. Suppose, for instance, that Hans McKnight, the owner of Scottish Inn, depends on the Hometown Bakery for the inn's sub buns for its lunch trade. Suppose further that McKnight knows that the Hometown Bakery has had some financial trouble and may have to shut down its operations if it cannot pay Jakub's Supply for its regular flour shipment. If McKnight promises Jakub's that, if it continues to supply Hometown with flour, he will pay the bill, that promise falls under the primary objective test and need not be in writing to be enforceable.

Contracts in Consideration of Marriage

Agreements made in consideration of marriage must be in writing to be enforceable. This part of the statute does not refer to the marriage contract itself or to engagement promises to marry, which are almost always oral. Rather, it refers to promises made by parties before marriage, in which they accept additional obligations not usually covered in the marriage vows. A prenuptial agreement (also referred to as a premarriage agreement and an antenuptial agreement) involves two people who are planning marriage and who agree to change the property

THE OPENING CASE *Revisited, Part I*
Written Contracts and The New Frontier:
Wilcox v. Trautz, Round 2

The Statute of Frauds was first introduced into the legal system in 1677 when Parliament enacted a bill entitled the Act for the Prevention of Frauds and Perjuries. The members of Parliament were quite forward looking in adding prenuptial agreements to the statute. Still, even with the benefit of their foresight, they never imagined that the rules would be applied to a contract like the one that existed between Carol Wilcox and John Trautz. Recall that Wilcox and John Trautz lived together as an unmarried couple for 25 years, until Trautz discovered that Wilcox had become involved in another relationship. At that point, after Trautz consulted his lawyer, the two parties negotiated, wrote, and signed an agreement providing, among other things that "each party's earnings and property is his or hers alone, and the other party shall have no interest in the property of the other." The assets, all in Trautz's name, included a house, valued at $180,000; an amphibious airplane, valued at $55,000; various bank accounts totaling $1,300; individual retirement accounts; and a one-half share of real estate in Maine, valued at $15,000. Wilcox had no assets other than a small bank account, the other one-half share of the Maine real estate, household furniture, clothing, and jewelry. Had the written contract been a genuine prenuptial agreement, it would have been an exemplary model. After all, it did exactly what a pre-nup is supposed to do. It proved the parties had made an agreement and it outlined the terms of that agreement in specific, understandable language.

rights they possess by law in a marriage. Such promises are enforceable only if they are in writing and agreed upon prior to the marriage. Many state legislatures, as well as the District of Columbia, have enacted the Uniform Premarital Ageement Act (UPAA). The UPAA supports the use of prenuptial agreements and provides for their enforcement.

Other Contracts Each state has enacted special statutes outlining other agreements that must be in writing. Other contracts that are usually required by special statutes to be in writing include the release of a party from debt (general release) and the resumption of obligations after bankruptcy. In addition, some states require real estate listing contracts and insurance binders to be in writing. Other contracts that require a writing under the UCC are contracts for the sale of securities (stocks and bonds) and agreements creating security interests.

The Contents of a Writing

The Statute of Frauds requires that the agreement be in writing—nothing more. The purpose of the writing is twofold. First, it proves that the parties entered an agreement. Second, it provides detailed information about the terms of that agreement. To accomplish these goals, the writing must be intelligible, but it need not follow any preset format. It can be found in letters, memos, documents, invoices, packing slips, and purchase orders that have been mailed, privately delivered, faxed, or sent electronically between the parties. It may be written on any surface suitable for the purpose of recording the intention of the parties, as long as all the required elements are present. A writing can even be placed in an e-mail, in a text message, or on a Web site, as long as it is possible to store and reproduce the electronic record of the agreement, and as long as the cyber-record includes an electronic signature as defined by the appropriate cyber-commerce statute.

THE OPENING CASE *Revisited, Part II*
Written Contracts and The New Frontier:
Wilcox v. Trautz, Round 3

The written agreement between Wilcox and Trautz does what all written agreements are supposed to do. First, it provides evidence of the agreement itself. Second, it identifies the terms of the agreement. These terms include the subject matter (the house, the airplane, the bank accounts, the IRAs, the Maine real estate, the furniture, the clothing, and the jewelry), the consideration that passed from one to the other (a release from any future obligations in exchange for the property outlined in the agreement), and the names and signatures of both parties. As such, we have a perfectly enforceable written agreement that satisfies the Statute of Frauds. It was made by competent parties, who had the capacity to contract, who understood the terms, who had an opportunity to seek legal advice, and who entered the agreement with full mutual assent. This, by the way, is exactly how the appeals court ruled when it overturned the decision of the lower court.

Elements of a Writing   To be absolutely complete, a written agreement, or memo-randum, as it is often called, should contain the following elements:

- Terms of the agreement.
- Identification of the subject matter.
- Statement of the consideration promised.
- Names and identities of the persons to be obligated.
- Signature of the party sought to be bound to the agreement.

quick quiz 11-1

1. A contract is said to be outside the statute if it must be in writing to show that the two objectives of the Statute of Frauds have been met.   true | false

2. An administrator is a person who is named in a will to oversee the distribution of the estate of a deceased person according to the provisions outlined in the will.   true | false

3. Agreements made in consideration of marriage must be in writing to be enforceable.   true | false

11-2 Legal Rules for Written Contracts

The legal system has developed certain basic criteria that make the construction and interpretation of written contracts as flawless as possible. These criteria act very much the way basic axioms or rules work in mathematics. Therefore, we could characterize these rules as unquestioned assumptions about the text of a writing that must be followed when an attorney, a magistrate, or a judge interprets a writing that claims to contain the terms of a contract. These four rules are: (1) the standard construction rule, (2) the parol evidence rule, (3) the best evidence rule, and (4) the equal dignities rule. The first two rules cover the interpretation of contracts, whereas the latter two govern their enforcement.

The Standard Construction Rule

Appropriately, the first of the interpretation rules is the most critical and the most fundamental of the four. The standard construction rule guides the entire interpretation process by directing the interpreter of a contract to determine the principal objective of the parties in the making of the contract. The *principal objective* is the primary or main goal that the parties hoped to accomplish by entering the agreement in the first place. Once this principal objective is stated, everything else must be interpreted to promote that principal objective. In line with this rule, the law also says that common words used in the contract are given their expected, everyday definition, and technical terms or professional slang will be given their technical or professional definitions. The standard construction rule also says that any standard operating procedures that are used in the parties' professions or trades should be followed whenever there is any doubt about what procedure should be used in the contract.

Because the standard construction rule is the most fundamental guideline involved in the interpretation of written contracts, it also guides the interpreter on matters of ambiguity and misinterpretation. The rule says that whenever an ambiguous term, clause, or line is found in a prewritten or preprinted contract, that ambiguity is interpreted against the party who wrote the contract. This approach should encourage those people who draft contracts to do so in clear and unambiguous terms, because if they draft a clause that is ambiguous, it will be interpreted against them. Thus, there is no profit in making things difficult to understand in any written contract.

The Parol Evidence Rule

Under the parol evidence rule, evidence of oral statements made before signing a written agreement is usually not admissible in court to change or contradict the terms of a written agreement. Following oral discussion and negotiation, parties may reduce their agreements to some written form. When this is done, only the terms, conditions, and promises included in the writing will be allowed as evidence in court. This provision is enforced because the court presumes that the parties will have put everything they agreed to in the writing.

EXAMPLE 11-7: *Twaine v. Krell, Inc.*

Emily Twaine purchased a $1,250 desktop computer from Krell, Inc. Before all of the documents of sale were signed, the salesperson promised that she would get round-the-clock tech support from Krell technicians whenever she had a problem with her computer or any of the software associated with the computer. Krell subsequently refused to take care of any problems that Twaine had with the computer. The court ruled that the salesperson's oral warranty statements were not admissible in court because they were not contained with the other conditions in the written sales agreement.

Exceptions to the Parol Evidence Rule The parol evidence rule will not apply when unfair and unjust decisions might result from its application. In cases in which a written agreement is incomplete, oral evidence may be used to supply the missing terms. Similarly, when a written contract is obscure or indistinct in certain of its terms, oral evidence may be used to clarify those terms. Also, if a written agreement contains a typographical or clerical error of some sort, the court will allow oral evidence as to the true intent of the parties.

EXAMPLE 11-8: *Bulwark v. Greene*

Edgar Bulwark was hired as an independent contractor to produce a series of magazine and journal articles that would appear under the name of a famous, and very busy, newspaper columnist named Arnold Greene. The written agreement had an error that indicated that Bulwark would receive $500 per article. The actual amount of consideration was supposed to be $5,000. The court would likely allow oral evidence to correct this obvious error.

In general, the courts allow a party to a written agreement to introduce oral testimony to show that the contract is void or voidable due to a lack of mutual assent or contractual capacity. The courts are willing to allow such testimony because it does not affect the terms of the agreement. Rather, it seeks to discredit the entire transaction. Thus, it is permissible to introduce oral evidence as to fraud, duress, misrepresentation, mistake, and undue influence. Similarly, it is appropriate to offer oral testimony as to a party's minority or mental incompetence.

EXAMPLE 11-9: *Staniland v. Morris*

James Staniland contracted with Richard Morris to purchase an original painting by Henrietta Stein, an artist who was part of the Dadaist movement in Paris during the 1920s. After signing the written contract, Staniland took the painting and had it placed in the lobby of his business office. After one week, a customer spotted the painting and told Staniland that it was a forgery and that he had been defrauded by Morris. When Staniland took the witness stand during the trial, he was permitted to introduce evidence of the oral statements made by Morris that led him to the fraudulent conclusion that the painting was a genuine work by Stein. The court allowed the testimony because it did not affect the terms of the agreement. Rather, it sought to discredit the entire transaction.

If a written agreement depends on some event before it becomes enforceable, oral evidence may be offered regarding that condition precedent. A condition precedent is an act or promise that must take place or be fulfilled before the other party is obligated to perform his or her part of the agreement. The courts allow this type of oral evidence because, like the oral evidence involving assent and capacity, it does not have an impact on the terms of the agreement, but it does affect the enforceability of the entire contract.

EXAMPLE 11-10: *Lauretig v. Pierce*

Asa Pierce agreed to lease Jay Lauretig's warehouse. The terms of the lease were laid out in a lengthy, detailed written agreement. However, as a condition precedent, a credit history and background check by Lauretig on Pierce would have to come back flawless; otherwise, the deal would be canceled. When the Search and Discover Detective Agency reported that Pierce had both a bad credit rating and two criminal convictions on drug charges, Lauretig refused to go through with the contract. At court, the judge permitted oral testimony about the credit check and the criminal background search because they were precedent conditions that had to be met before the contract went into effect.

Oral evidence may be used to prove that the parties orally agreed to rescind or modify the terms of a written contract after entering into it. Subsequent negotiations to change or rescind the agreement are permitted, and evidence to that effect does not undermine the spirit of the parol evidence rule. However, if the change in the contract involves an agreement that would have to be in writing under the Statute of Frauds, then a writing would be required. Similarly, if the original written contract requires later modifications to be in writing, then that written requirement will rule.

EXAMPLE 11-11: *George Laurie Construction v. Popson*

George Laurie Construction entered into a contract with Terry and Sherrie Popson, the terms of which indicated that Laurie Construction was to place aluminum siding, downspouts, and gutters on the Popson vacation house on Kelley's Island. The agreement was written out in a long, preprinted contract with blanks for the pertinent individual information. All of the appropriate blanks were filled in, the contract was signed by all the parties, and the job began on schedule. Once Laurie was on the job for three days, Sherrie Popson decided that she wanted a window placed on the house. She discussed the cost of the additional work with George Laurie, who agreed to make the change indicated. The additional terms were not put in writing. After the job was completed, the Popsons paid the original amount but did not pay the added cost of the new window. The small claims court allowed testimony as to the terms involving the window because those terms represented negotiations subsequent to the original agreement to change the original terms.

UCC 1-205, 2-202, 2-208 (see pages 820 and 823)

As a final exception to the parol evidence rule, the UCC allows oral testimony about how the parties have done business together over a long time period. The UCC makes allowance for this type of testimony because, from a practical point of view, parties often get so used to dealing with each other in a particular way that they neglect to include certain terms in their written agreements. Similarly, some practices are so universal in a particular trade, business, or industry that the parties feel no need to include such universal practices in their written contracts. Accordingly, the UCC allows oral testimony to supplement a written agreement as to these practices.

EXAMPLE 11-12: *Commonwealth Chemical Company v. St. Clair Printing, Inc.*

St. Clair Printing, Inc., and the Commonwealth Chemical Company have been doing business for 20 years. St. Clair prints all labels, business cards, letterheads, invoices, and purchase orders for Commonwealth. During their long time working together, St. Clair has always delivered orders to Commonwealth. When a new foreman took over the bindery and delivery operation for St. Clair, he decided that there would be no deliveries to any customers outside a five-mile radius of the print shop. As a result, Commonwealth did not receive an important order of labels and lost several big orders. When Commonwealth sued St. Clair for breach of contract, St. Clair pointed out that there was nothing mentioned in the written contract about delivery responsibilities falling to St. Clair. However, because of their 20-year history of consistently dealing with each other, the court allowed oral testimony about past practices to supplement the written contract.

The Best Evidence Rule

Under the best evidence rule, the courts generally accept into evidence only the original of a writing, not a copy. Under this rule, a written instrument is regarded as the primary or best possible evidence. Thus, the best evidence rule concurs with and supports the parol evidence rule.

The Equal Dignities Rule

The equal dignities rule, which is followed in some states, provides that when a party appoints an agent to negotiate an agreement that must be in writing, the appointment of the agent must also be in writing. In contrast, the appointment of an agent to negotiate an agreement that the law does not require to be in writing may be accomplished through an oral agreement.

quick quiz 11-2

1. Whenever an ambiguous term is found in a preprinted contract, that ambiguity is interpreted in favor of the party who wrote the contract.   true | false

2. The principal objective is the main goal that the parties hope to accomplish by entering an agreement.   true | false

3. Parol evidence is another term for written evidence.   true | false

11-3 Formalities of Construction

Certain formalities are usually followed in the formation of anything other than the simplest kinds of written agreements. Although the Statute of Frauds may necessitate nothing more than the briefest written disclosure of promises, conditions, and terms, plus the signature(s) of the obligated party or parties, usually contracts in general commercial and consumer use are carefully written, researched for legal compliance, and signed. Furthermore, leases and contracts for the sale of real property may have additional requirements of content and formality that extend beyond these demands.

Signature Requirements

Written agreements should be, but need not be, signed by both parties. If signed by only one party, any obligation in the agreement would be limited to that party alone. Parties should use their usual signatures, that is, the signatures used in other matters in the regular course of business. However, any mark that the signer intends to be a signature will be the legal signature of that person. Although it is unusual, a party may adopt any name desired in creating a contractual obligation, as long as the party intends to be bound by that signature.

Facsimile Signatures With the increased use of facsimile (fax) machines, methods have been adopted to bypass the best evidence rule by giving authentication to signatures sent by way of facsimile machines. A facsimile signature will be acceptable on a contract if the contract states that facsimile signatures are valid. More commonly, however, people fax copies of signed documents to other parties, and follow it up by sending the original signed documents by overnight mail or express delivery. Some states have enacted statutes allowing certain facsimile signatures.

EXAMPLE 11-13: Massachusetts General Laws Chapter 92

Massachusetts has enacted the following statute relative to residence insurance agents: "A facsimile of a signature of any such resident agent imprinted on any property or casualty insurance policy issued by mail, computer modem or facsimile machine, so-called, shall have the same validity as a written signature." (Mass. Gen. Laws Chapter 92, s. 43.)

In addition, some states have adopted the Uniform Facsimile Signatures of Public Officials Act. This law allows the use of facsimile signatures of public officials when certain requirements are followed.

In cases in which a party cannot sign the written agreement due to illness, physical disability, or some other physical reason, another person may sign for that person. The signature should be followed by a statement indicating that the contracting party was physically unable to sign the document and that a signature was placed on the document by another person in the contracting party's presence and at the request of the contracting party. The person who has signed for the contracting party then signs the document (see Figure 11-1). Persons who lack the ability to read or write are often obliged to sign contracts. In such situations, the law accepts the person's mark, usually an X, properly witnessed, as a valid signature (see Figure 11-2).

Witnesses and Acknowledgments

Witnesses are required in the signing of a will and sometimes a deed, but in most other documents, their signatures are at the option of the contracting parties. To ensure that no misunderstanding will arise as to the acceptance and signing of a written agreement, the use of witnesses is advised. Certain official documents, such as a certificate of title to a motor vehicle and a deed to real property, require the owner's signature and an acknowledgment by a notary public that the signature was the person's free act and deed. The notary

signature: *Daniel Colletti*

WITNESS: I hereby attest that Daniel Colletti was physically
           unable to sign his name and that his name was signed
           by me in his presence and at his request.

Jonas Abraham

Figure 11-1   The signature for an incapacitated person bears a witness's name.

Her

Samantha X Cunningham

Mark

WITNESS: I hereby attest that Samantha Cunningham made her
mark as her signature and that, at her request, I
added her name to her mark.

Lindsay Quartermain

Figure 11-2   The signature (*X*) of a person who does not know how to write has been witnessed.

witnesses the signing of the document and then acknowledges this act by signing the document and adding the official seal to it. A notary is not authorized to read the document being signed and may be prevented from doing so.

quick quiz 11-3

1. Written agreements must always be signed by both parties to the contract.   true | false

2. Facsimile signatures are not acceptable in any state.   true | false

3. A notary is required by law to read and understand all documents that he or she has witnessed.   true | false

11-4 Cyber-Commerce and the Law

Cyber-commerce (computer commerce, electronic commerce, or e-commerce) involves transacting business by computer. One of the most common cyber-commerce techniques involves buying and selling directly on the Internet by accessing a company's Web site. Some companies, such as Amazon.com, have made a name for themselves by perfecting this e-commerce technique. Other enterprises, such as eBay, have made a business of providing a marketplace for putting buyers and sellers together in an electronic auction setting. Others, such as Orbitz and Priceline, have found a niche in the marketplace by providing bargain prices for airlines and hotels. There are, of course, problems associated with buying and selling on the Internet, one of which involves the difficulty of verifying the identity of the party on the other side of an Internet connection. Another problem involves how to make up for the lack of paper documents in cyber-commerce. In both cases, the law has provided a solution. We will look at the problems associated with verification first.

Online shopping is fast, easy, and convenient. Utilizing digital signatures is an effective method used by businesses to verify the legitimacy of the transaction.

Verification Problems

Verification problems can be solved in a number of ways. In fact, the parties can avoid the problem altogether by adding a term that delays the creation of the contract until the identities of the parties can be verified by some means other than computers. Or a business might elect to use its Web site only as an advertisement site. These solutions are unsatisfactory to most businesspeople, however, because they eliminate the advantages of doing business on the Internet. Another technique is for the parties to an Internet transaction to customize the verification process for each contract individually. However, in the interests of efficiency and cost, it would be preferable to have a process that applies to all contracts. A possible solution to this problem is the use of digital signatures. As we shall see, the Uniform Electronics Transactions Act defines a **digital signature** as "an electronic sound, symbol, or process attached to or logically associated with a record and executed or adopted by a person with the intent to sign the record." A digital signature is also referred to as a *cyber-signature*, an *electronic signature,* and an *e-signature.* Those businesses and legal practitioners who promote the use of digital signatures hope that the courts and/or the legislatures will institute a principle that states the use of a digital signature creates a rebuttable presumption that the signature is authentic and that the terms of the transaction have not been altered in transmission.

Offer and Acceptance Online   An electronic party should always ensure that a copy of the contract is available on a hyperlink that will display the actual language of the agreement. The following terms should appear in any online agreement package: (1) payment procedures; (2) a limitation on the remedies that can be used by the parties; (3) refund policies; (4) the return process; (5) dispute settlement, forum selection, and choice-of-law provisions; (6) the applicability of cyber-signatures; (7) liability disclaimers; and (8) provisions relating to the offeree's manner of acceptance. In general, the other party accepts by clicking on a box on the computer screen that states that the party agrees to be bound by the terms of the contract. Sometimes this process is referred to as a *click-on acceptance* or *click-on agreement.* In a sense then, the *click* amounts to the party's signature. It is also critical to remember that when a cyber-agreement deals with goods, the provisions of Article 2 of the Uniform Commercial Code apply.

Online Advertisement "Click" Fraud   One problem that arises in this area is verifying the identity of the "clicker." When companies are actually creating contracts, they police the process of verification rather closely. However, the click-on process functions not only in online contracts but also for online advertisements. Companies that advertise on the Internet often make contracts with search engines like Bing, Google, Yahoo, or America Online. The terms of these contracts generally include a provision that states that the company that places the advertisement online will pay the search engine on the basis of the number of clicks detected on that advertisement. The clicks are supposed to be a foolproof way to gauge interest in the advertiser's service or product. However, policing the exact nature of each click has proven difficult. Thus, hundreds of thousands of phony clicks have occurred in advertisements, inflating the bills of the advertisers which pay per click. The problem arises because the search engines often farm out the actual posting of the ads to intermediary companies, called *domain parkers,* that get paid on the basis of the number of clicks on the ads for which they are responsible. The domain parkers then transfer the ads to subsidiary Web sites. Some of these Web sites display advertisements and nothing more. This scenario provides a fertile ground in which the phony click campaigns grow. Some owners of these subsidiary Web sites pay fraudulent clickers a small amount to click on the ads, thus driving up the cost for the advertisers and increasing the Web site owner's split of the proceeds. Some even use "clickbot" software, capable of mechanically clicking on certain advertisements at programmed intervals. All of the major search engines have found themselves in litigation because of this new *cyber-confidence game*. (See Brian Grow and Ben Elgin, "Click Fraud: The Dark Side of Online Advertising," *BusinessWeek,* October 2, 2006, pp. 46–57.)

Cyber-Commerce Legislation

Cyber-commerce legislation has taken many forms over the past decade. However, the three most influential acts have been the E-Sign Act, the Uniform Electronic Transactions Act (UETA), and the Uniform Computer Information Transactions Act (UCITA). A fourth new law that deals with a slightly different but no less serious problem, that of credit cards and identity theft, is the Fair and Accurate Credit Transactions Act (FACT).

Self-Evident Truths

The cyber-revolution cannot be ignored by anyone who wants to succeed in business today. Manufacturers and sellers regularly use the Internet to advertise, to negotiate, and to send payments across the globe. Business people, however, are not the only ones who have discovered the power of the net. Political activists have also learned how to use the Internet to make governments pay attention to their demands. In his book *The Lexus and the Olive Tree,* Thomas L. Friedman predicted this revolution years ago when wrote, "In such a world, activists (will) learn how to use globalization to their advantage. They (will) learn how to compel companies to behave better by mobilizing global consumers through the Internet. I call this the 'network solution for human rights,' and it's the future of social advocacy. It is bottom up regulation, or side by side regulation—not top down regulation. You empower the bottom, instead of waiting for the top, by shaping a coalition that produces better governance without global government." What Friedman predicted in 2005 has come to pass. Populist movements have used the net to topple governments in Tunisia and Egypt and they threaten other governments the world over. So far this strategy seems to have worked fairly well for the protestors, but can you spot any dangers that might be hidden within the cyber-politics revolution? Think about that as you answer the following questions.

Self-Evident Questions

1. Do you agree with Friedman's premise that the electronic "network solution for human rights" is beneficial? Explain.

2. Regardless of your answer to the first question, do you see the growth of populist movements, such as the Muslim Brotherhood and the Kefaya, as a good thing? Explain.

3. Play devil's advocate for a moment. How might an autocrat like Qaddafi in Libya use the World Wide Web to keep himself in power? Explain.

4. Are electronic populist movements the wave of the future or just a temporary tactic that the autocrats will soon learn to suppress? Explain.

5. What if the net is used to coordinate violent populist movements? Is violence avoidable or does it always result from political advocacy? Explain

(*Source:* Thomas L. Friedman, *The Lexus and The Olive Tree,* Random House, 2000, p. 207.)

THE OPENING CASE *Revisited, Part III*
Written Contracts and The New Frontier:
Wilcox v. Trautz, Round 4

Recall that in the Opening Case at the beginning of this chapter, when Carol Wilcox and John Trautz broke up, they negotiated, wrote, and signed an agreement providing, among other things, that "each party's earnings and property is his or hers alone, and the other party shall have no interest in the property of the other." The written agreement did what all written agreements are supposed to do. It provided evidence of the agreement itself, along with evidence of the terms to which the parties agreed. As such, it was a perfectly enforceable written agreement that satisfied the Statute of Frauds. Nevertheless, if the parties had negotiated the contract today and had used an electronic method to record the agreement, it would still have to be reduced to a paper format and duplicate originals of that paper format would have to be distributed to both parties. This limitation results because the E-Sign Act excludes prenuptial agreements from those that can be produced electronically. While the Trautz-Wilcox agreement is not, strictly speaking a "pre-nup," it is close enough to that kind of an agreement to demand that the parties follow the E-Sign rules, just in case it becomes an issue later. After all, as they say, it is better to be safe than sorry.

The E-Sign Act The E-Sign Act is a federal act designed to deal with problems associated with cyber-commerce, especially those related to the recognition of electronic contracts and electronic signatures. Basically the act states that if the parties to a contract have voluntarily agreed to transact business electronically, the cyber-contract that results will be just as legally acceptable as a paper contract. The act also notes that the parties must be able to store and reproduce the cyber-record of the contract; otherwise, the cyber-record will not be legally sufficient under the act. The final word here is that under the provisions of the E-Sign Act, cyber-contracts and cyber-signatures are just as legitimate as their ink counterparts. There are a few documents that are not covered by this statute, including court records, eviction notices, health insurance cancellations, wills, foreclosure notices, prenuptial contracts, and divorce papers. However, sale and lease of goods contracts as covered by the Uniform Commercial Code are included in the E-Sign Act.

The Uniform Electronic Transactions Act (UETA) The Uniform Electronic Transactions Act establishes the same type of legal parity between electronic records and paper records as does the E-Sign Act. It does not establish any new guidelines governing contracts just because they are entered electronically. The approach therefore is not to establish the differences between electronic contracts and paper agreements but instead to focus on the similarities. As a result, once the parties to a contract have voluntarily agreed to enter a transaction using an electronic medium, the agreement that results in electronic form, including the cyber-signatures, will be just as valid as a paper agreement. The UETA applies only to transactions that involve some sort of commercial, business, or governmental matter. The law also states that if an act, such as the Statute of Frauds, requires a writing and a signature, then a cyber-record and a cyber-signature will fulfill that requirement. Also, under provisions of the E-Sign Act, the UETA will trump the E-Sign Act provided that the state that has adopted the UETA has not altered its content. Most states, 48 at last count, have adopted the UETA. However, some states have altered provisions in the act and so it is best to check the version that has been enacted by your state. This is also why it would be smart to check the forum selection clause in any cyber-contract that you are about to enter. (See The E-Sign Act, 15 USC Section 7002 9 (2) (A) (I))

The Uniform Computer Information Transactions Act (UCITA)

The Uniform Computer Information Transactions Act (UCITA) focuses on contracts that involve the sale or lease of computer software, computer databases, interactive products, multimedia products, and any other type of computer information. The UCITA is in line with the basic provisions of the E-Sign Act and the UETA, in that it also declares that any transaction entered into using an electronic medium is just as valid as a paper agreement. Not all states have adopted the UCITA, so it is important to check on the applicability of the statute in your jurisdiction.

The Fair and Accurate Credit Transactions Act (The FACT Act)

The Fair and Accurate Credit Transactions Act (The FACT Act) is Congress's antidote to one manifestation of the identity theft epidemic. The new law, which is actually an amendment to the Fair Credit Reporting Act (FCRA), is designed to cut down on identity theft related to the use of credit cards. The act prohibits merchants from using credit card receipts that show anything other than the last five credit card numbers. Receipts also cannot display credit card expiration dates. In effect, because the act outlaws such numerical displays, identity thieves will no longer be able to assume the identity of a consumer by obtaining a copy of a credit card receipt and using the credit card number and expiration date on the receipt to "verify their identity" over the phone or online.

quick quiz 11-4

1. The E-Sign Act is a model act designed to deal with problems associated with cyber-commerce.   true | false

2. The Uniform Electronic Transactions Act was passed by Congress to deal with the legality of electronic transactions.   true | false

3. The UCITA is not in line with any of the provisions of the E-Sign Act or the UETA.   true | false

Summary

11.1   The Statutes of Frauds outlines six types of contracts that must be in writing to be enforceable. These include contracts that cannot be completed within one year; contracts transferring real property rights; contracts for the sale of goods of $500 or more; certain contracts entered by executors and administrators; contracts by one party to pay a debt incurred by another party; and contracts in consideration of marriage.

11.2   The legal system has developed certain basic criteria that make the construction and interpretation of written contracts consistent. These four criteria are (1) the standard construction rule, (2) the parol evidence rule, (3) the best evidence rule, and (4) the equal dignities rule.

11.3   Certain formalities are followed in the formation of contracts. Written agreements need not be signed

by both parties. However, any agreement signed by only one party would obligate only that party. Facsimile signatures are allowed on a contract if the contract states that such signatures are valid. Some states have statutes allowing facsimile signatures. Persons who are illiterate usually sign written contracts with an X. Such signatures should be witnessed. Witnesses are not required when parties enter written agreements. However, to avoid misunderstandings, the use of witnesses is advisable. The law provides that some documents must be recorded in a public office for inspection by the public.

11.4   There are problems associated with buying and selling on the Internet. One of these problems involves the difficulty of verifying the identity of the person on the other side of an Internet connection. Another involves the question of how to deal with the fact that electronic transactions do not produce paper documents. In both cases, the law has provided some solutions to these difficulties. Three laws that address these problems include the E-Sign Act, the Uniform Electronic Transactions Act (UETA), and the Uniform Computer Information Transactions Act (UCITA). A fourth act that deals with the problem of identity theft is the Fair and Accurate Credit Transactions Act (FACT).

Key Terms

acknowledgment, 240

antenuptial agreement, 233

best evidence rule, 239

collateral contract, 233

condition precedent, 237

cosigner, 233

cyber-signature, 242

equal dignities rule, 239

equitable estoppel, 231

guarantor, 233

guaranty contract, 233

guaranty of payment, 233

leading objective test, 233

main purpose test, 233

memorandum, 235

obligee, 233

obligor, 233

parol evidence rule, 236

part performance, 231

premarriage agreement, 233

prenuptial agreement, 233

primary objective test, 233

standard construction rule, 236

Statute of Frauds, 229

Uniform Facsimile Signatures of Public Officials Act, 240

Questions for Review and Discussion

1. What are the goals of the Statute of Frauds?
2. What contracts must be in writing under the Statute of Frauds?
3. What information must be in a writing under the Statute of Frauds?
4. What is the standard construction rule?
5. What is the parol evidence rule?
6. What are the exceptions to the parol evidence rule?
7. What is the best evidence rule?
8. What is the equal dignities rule?
9. What are the problems associated with cyber-commerce?
10. What are the latest cyber-commerce statutes?

Cases for Analysis

1. Several identity theft victims filed a series of class action lawsuits against firms that had not made the changes required by the Fair and Accurate Credit Transactions Act (FACT) by the statutory deadline. One of the issues before the court was whether the victims had to demonstrate that the offending company deliberately refused to comply or did so with reckless disregard for the new requirements. Which standard would be the appropriate one in this situation? Explain. Amanda Bronstad, "Suits Multiply over Credit Card Exposure: Cash Registers Displaying Too Many Digits Spark Dozens of Class Actions," *The National Law Journal*, February 19, 2007, p. 4.

2. Harold Perdue entered an individually negotiated employment contract with Nicholas Paynter. Under terms of the contract, Perdue was to work for Paynter as a private investigator in Paynter's newly established firm, known as Eye-Spy Investigations. The employment contract was on a trial basis and was to last for nine months. That nine-month period was set to begin one month after Paynter had set up shop. However, Paynter could not begin his operation until the contractors finished remodeling his office. Johnson Contractors, Ltd., had promised to have the office completed within one to three months. One month after the contract had been finalized, Paynter notified Perdue that he had hired someone else and that his services were no longer needed. Perdue, who had relied on the contract, had turned down several other lucrative offers that had since been filled by other operatives. Moreover, Perdue was now having trouble getting a similar job. Perdue threatened to bring suit against Paynter. Paynter told

Perdue to go ahead and sue. Privately, Paynter believes that he is immune to a lawsuit because, since Johnson Construction had three months to finish remodeling the office, the contract could not have been performed within one year. Perdue argued that, because Johnson could have finished in less than one month, the contract could be performed within a year, and it did not have to be in writing to be enforceable. Who is correct here? Explain.

3. Meng, a vice-president at Boston University, resigned his position to protest what he regarded as the unethical and unprofessional behavior of the university's president, John Silber, in terminating a recently renewed contract with Linkage Corporation. Silber orally promised Meng, as a severance package when he resigned, 14 months of salary and benefits and free tuition for two of his children if either should attend the university. Was the oral promise enforceable? Explain. *Meng v. Trustees of Boston University,* 96-9776 Appeals Court (MA).

4. As part of an employment agreement, Bazzy orally promised to give Hall an option to buy 1,000 shares of company stock at $20 per share. Hall brought suit against the company when it refused to sell the stock to him. What legal argument may Bazzy's company use to refuse to sell the stock to Hall as agreed? *Hall v. Horizon House Microwave, Inc.,* 506 N.E.2d 178 (MA).

5. Anna Wilson was assistant manager of a Montgomery Ward store. When Montgomery Ward announced that it would be closing the store, the manager quit, leaving Wilson in charge. A district manager orally promised Wilson that if she stayed on and assisted in the closing of the store, she would receive a sum of money calculated according to a certain formula. Wilson stayed on and managed the closing of the store (which took two months) in addition to her regular duties. Montgomery

Ward refused to pay her the money, claiming that the oral promise was unenforceable. Was the store correct? Why or why not? *Wilson v. Montgomery Ward,* 610 F. Supp. 1035 (DC IN).

6. Curtis Hendrix orally agreed to compensate Beverly Spertell for services rendered in connection with their living together out of wedlock. Later, when suit was brought to collect the money, Hendrix argued that the oral contract was unenforceable under the Statute of Frauds. Do you agree with Hendrix? Explain. *Spertell v. Hendrix,* 461 N.Y.S.2d 823 (NY).

7. Lawson hired Konves to conduct extensive audits of her 87 boutiques, located throughout the United States. As part of the agreement, Lawson required Konves to spend one week at each boutique. Konves demanded a written agreement before she would agree to Lawson's terms. Why was Konves correct in making this demand?

8. Butler leased a certain piece of property from Wheeler with an option to purchase it at a later date. The agreement was handwritten and consisted of two separate documents, each listing part of the transaction. Butler later attempted to purchase the property but Wheeler refused to sell, claiming that the agreement was unenforceable because it was contained in two documents. Was Wheeler correct? Explain. *Butler v. Lovoll,* 620 P.2d 1251 (NV).

9. Ray's Motor Sales sold a mobile home to Hathaway. Before the written contract was signed, the salesperson told Hathaway that Ray's would take care of any problems that Hathaway might have with the mobile home. This promise was not included in the written document. When Hathaway had problems with the mobile home, he asked Ray's to take care of them. Ray's refused to be of any assistance. Could Hathaway enforce Ray's promise? Explain. *Hathaway v. Ray's Motor Sales,* 247 A.2d 512 (VT).

quick quiz Answers

11-1	11-2	11-3	11-4
1. F	1. F	1. F	1. F
2. F	2. T	2. F	2. F
3. T	3. F	3. F	3. F

Chapter 12

Third Parties, Discharge, and Remedies

THE OPENING CASE Punitive Damages and the
Limits of the Law: *State Farm
Mutual v. Campbell*

When one party breaks the terms of a contract, and the other party sues, the court will do its best to place the parties in as good a position as they would have been had the contract been performed as promised in the first place. In this way contract law differs from other areas of the law, such as criminal law, which generally seeks to punish the wrongdoer and deter the criminal conduct in the future. Contract law also differs from tort law which is designed to compensate the victim, punish the wrongdoer, and deter tortious behavior in the future. One reason for this policy is that people voluntarily assume responsibilities when they make a contract and those responsibilities affect only the parties and not the general public as is the case with criminal law and, at times, tort law.

All of this is fine as far as it goes, but what happens when the breaching party has deliberately undermined the basic intent of contract law by committing fraud not just in the contract at issue, but as a pattern of conduct, perhaps even an official policy, affecting hundreds and thousands of other contracts? This is precisely what happened in *State Farm Mutual v. Campbell*. In that case, the

Campbells had been involved in an automobile accident. They filed their case with State Farm, which refused to settle out of court, despite the desires of the Campbells and the advice of State Farm's own investigators. The original case went to trial and the Campbells lost.

When State Farm refused to pay the full amount of the award, the Campbells sued the insurer for bad faith, fraud, and intentional infliction of emotional distress. The Campbells offered evidence that the refusal to settle was not just fraudulent in relation to their contract, but was, instead, part of a larger pattern of conduct planned and executed by State Farm over a 20-year period against hundreds of policy holders. The conduct involved a national campaign referred to as the Performance, Planning, and Review (PP&R) Policy. Once the jury heard evidence about the systematic execution of the PP&R policy, they awarded the Campbells $145 million in punitive damages. The judge then reduced the punitive damages to $25 million. On appeal the Campbells stressed the fraudulent nature of the PP&R policy and State Farm argued that their conduct in relation to the other contracts should not be used to punish them for their conduct in relation to the contract that they had with the Campbells. The supreme court of Utah agreed with the Campbells and reinstated the $145 million in punitive damages. The case made its way to the United States Supreme Court. As you read the chapter consider the facts in the Campbell case, remember the general principles of contract law, and see if you can predict the Supreme Court's ultimate decision in the case. [See *State Farm Mutual Automobile Ins. Co. v. Campbell,* 538 U.S. 408 (United States Supreme Court).]

Opening Case Questions

1. In what way does the Campbell case against State Farm Mutual appear to be both a contract case and a tort case? Explain

2. Should the evidence brought by the Campbells in relation to State Farm's conduct outside of the contract be considered to determine the measure of damages? Explain.

3. Should the reprehensible conduct of the company be considered in measuring the extent of the damages? Explain.

4. What if the conduct that the Campbell's complained of was perfectly legal in the other states? Should the court punish conduct that is illegal in its home state but is perfectly legal in another state? Why or why not?

5. Should the courts be allowed to punish a corporation that makes a contract in bad faith? Explain.

Learning Objectives

1. Explain the legal rights given to all beneficiaries.
2. Identify the legal rights given to incidental beneficiaries.
3. Explain the assignment of rights and the delegation of duties.
4. Explain the nature of a novation.
5. Relate what constitutes satisfactory performance of a contract.
6. Outline the difference between complete and substantial performance.
7. List the ways that a contract can be discharged by nonperformance.
8. Clarify the concept of anticipatory repudiation.
9. Enumerate the types of damages available in the event of a breach of contract.
10. Contrast specific performance with injunctive relief.

12-1 Contracts and Third Parties

A third party is a person who may in some way be affected by a contract but who is not one of the contracting parties. A third party, also known as an outside party, is at times given benefits from a contract made between two or more other parties. A third party receiving benefits from a contract made by others is known as a third party beneficiary or sometimes simply as a beneficiary to the contract. Although not obligated by the agreement made between those in privity, third parties may have the legal right to enforce the benefits given them by such agreements.

Intended Beneficiaries

A beneficiary in whose favor a contract is made is an intended beneficiary. With exceptions in some states, an intended beneficiary can enforce the contract made by those in privity of contract. Those who are most frequently recognized to be intended beneficiaries and have the right to demand and enforce the benefits promised are creditor beneficiaries, donee beneficiaries, and insurance beneficiaries.

Creditor Beneficiaries A creditor beneficiary is an outside third party to whom one or both contracting parties owe a continuing debt of obligation arising from a contract. Frequently, the obligation results from the failure of the contracting party or parties to pay for goods delivered or services rendered by the third party at some time in the past.

Donee Beneficiaries A third party who provides no consideration for the benefits received and who owes the contracting parties no legal duty is known as a donee beneficiary. However, the contracting parties owe the donee beneficiary the act promised; if it is not forthcoming, the donee beneficiary may bring suit. The consideration that supports this type of agreement is the consideration exchanged by the parties in privity of contract.

Insurance Beneficiaries An individual named as the beneficiary of an insurance policy is usually considered a donee beneficiary. The beneficiary does not have to furnish the insured with consideration to enforce payment of the policy. In some cases, an insurance beneficiary may also be a creditor beneficiary. This situation occurs in consumer or mortgage loans when the creditor requires the debtor to furnish a life-term insurance policy naming the creditor as the beneficiary. The policy will pay the debt if the debtor dies before the loan has been repaid.

Incidental Beneficiaries

An incidental beneficiary is an outside party for whose benefit a contract was not made but who would substantially benefit if the agreement were performed according to its terms and conditions. An incidental beneficiary, in contrast to an intended beneficiary, has no legal grounds for enforcing the contract made by those in privity of contract.

EXAMPLE 12-1: *Faber v. The Brotherhood of Aerospace Workers*

Mark Faber owned a hotel and restaurant in downtown Indianapolis. The Brotherhood of Aerospace Workers (BAW) had a contract with the city for the use of the municipal auditorium for the union's annual convention. One week before the convention, the union announced that it was canceling the meeting. The move was a clear violation of BAW's contract with the city. Faber brought suit against the BAW for damages due to lost business caused by the breach. The court dismissed the case on a motion for summary judgment. The court ruled that Faber was an incidental beneficiary and therefore had no grounds on which to bring the suit against the union.

quick quiz 12-1

1. A third party who provides no consideration and owes no legal duty to the contracting parties is a donee beneficiary.   true | false

2. The principle of privity stopped many judges from establishing third party rights.   true | false

3. Incidental and intended beneficiaries have the same rights.   true | false

12-2 The Law of Assignment

When people enter contracts, they receive certain rights and incur particular duties. It is completely accepted today that, with some exceptions noted subsequently and unless the contract itself provides otherwise, these rights and duties can be transferred to others. An assignment is a transfer of a contract right, and a delegation is a transfer of a contract duty.

Assignment and Delegation

In general, rights are *assigned,* and duties are *delegated.* In most cases, both are governed by the same rules. If A is owed money by B, A may assign to C the right to collect the money. However, if A has agreed to pay B to harvest 200 acres of wheat for a price, B may delegate the duty of harvesting to C. Restrictions against the delegation of duties are presented later in this chapter.

EXAMPLE 12-2: *Wesley, et al. v. Lerro*

Lee Wesley agreed to lay cement on the driveway leading up to Walter Lerro's house for $24,000. Plans and specifications were provided by Lerro. Wesley delegated the duties involved in laying the asphalt to Hanover Construction, Inc., another contractor. Hanover then assigned the right to collect the $24,000 from Lerro to Olsen Construction Supplies, Ltd. Lerro, who did not like the way his job and his money were being bounced all over the tri-county area, refused to pay Olsen. Lerro then called Wesley and ordered him to tear out the driveway because he was insulted by the fact that Wesley thought so little of his job that he had assigned it to Hanover. In hindsight, this choice was probably a poorly thought out decision, because everyone involved in the situation, from Wesley to Hanover to Olsen, sued Lerro, who still ended up paying the original $24,000—and then some.

Parties to Assignment

Three parties are associated with any assignment. Two of the parties are the ones who entered the original agreement. The party who assigns rights or delegates duties is the assignor. The outside third party to whom the assignment is made is the assignee. The remaining party to the original agreement is the obligor.

EXAMPLE 12-3: *From King to Gomez to Walker*

Lisa Gomez owed Roger King $500 for some photography work that King had done for her. At the same time, King owed Ted Walker $500 back rent. King assigned Walker the right to receive the money from Gomez. In this situation, King was the assignor, Walker the assignee, and Gomez the obligor. The following flowchart clearly illustrates these points.

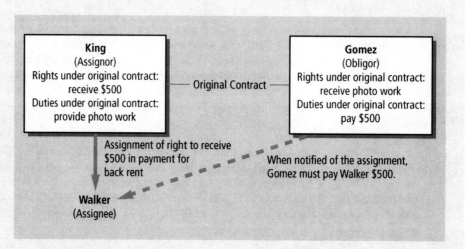

Consideration in Assignment

Consideration is not required in the assignment of a contract. When there is no supporting consideration, however, the assignor may repudiate the assignment at any time prior to its execution. In the previous example, the consideration supporting King's assignment is found in the rental agreement between King and Walker.

In addition, when no consideration is given for an assignment, creditors of the assignor may have the assignment rescinded on the grounds that it is a fraudulent conveyance. A fraudulent conveyance is a transfer of property with the intent to defraud creditors. If the $500 assignment to Walker in Example 12-3 had been a gift instead of payment for back rent, King's creditors could have had the assignment rescinded, because they could rightfully anticipate the money coming from Gomez.

Assignment Methods

To be valid, an assignment must follow certain accepted procedures designed to protect all of the parties. Form of assignment, notice of assignment, and the rights of parties in successive or subsequent assignments must conform to practices established by case law and state statutes.

Form of Assignment
Assignment may be accomplished through written, oral, or implied agreements between the assignor and the assignee. Parties to an assignment must observe the requirement provided by the equal dignities rule discussed in Chapter 11. Under that rule, the law requires that if the agreement by the original parties must be in writing, the assignment also must be in writing.

Notice of Assignment
An assignment is valid at the time it is made. As a measure of protection against subsequent assignments, the assignee should give notice of the assignment to the obligor. Although this obligation falls to the assignee, either party may give notice. Once notice is received, the obligor should deal with the assignee. If notice is not given, it would be normal practice for the obligor to render performance to the original contracting party, the assignor. If due notice has been given and the obligor makes payment to the assignor, the obligor is not excused from making payment to the assignee.

Bryant, Inc.
6225 St. Clair Avenue
Cleveland, OH 44103

June 15, 20 - -

Mr. Carl Newfield
750 Maple Street, Apt. 4-C
Lakewood, Ohio 44117

Dear Mr. Newfield:

You are hereby notified that Pendleton Architects Limited of Euclid,
Ohio, has assigned to Bryant, Inc., all rights to its claim against you
in the amount of $750.

You are further notified to direct all payments to Bryant, Inc., at the
above address to ensure credit for payment.

Sincerely yours,

Norbert Bryant

Norbert Bryant
Vice-President

Figure 12-1 The format used by Bryant, Inc., in the case described in Example
12-4, to notify Newfield of the assignment from Pendleton.

EXAMPLE 12-4: *Bryant, Inc. v. Newfield*

Carl Newfield owed Pendleton Architects Limited $750 as a final payment for architectural work.
Pendleton in turn owed Bryant, Inc., a substantial sum. As partial payment of that amount, Pendleton
assigned Newfield's debt to Bryant. As the assignee in this case, Bryant sent a letter to Newfield indicating that the debt that Newfield owed to Pendleton should now be paid to Bryant, Inc. Figure 12-1

presents a copy of the letter that Bryant sent to Newfield informing him of the assignment. Newfield would now be legally required to adhere to the assignment. When Newfield refused to honor the assignment, Bryant could bring suit against him.

Subsequent Assignments Should the assignor make a subsequent assignment of the same right, the courts must decide which of the two assignees has a superior right and claim against the obligor. A majority of the states hold that the first assignee has a superior right, even if a later assignee was the first to give notice of the assignment to the obligor. A minority of courts hold that whichever assignee was first to give notice of assignment has a superior right and claim to any assigned benefits.

quick quiz 12-2

1. A delegation is the transfer of a contractual right.   true | false

2. The equal dignities axiom has no application in the law of   true | false
   assignment.

3. It is the responsibility of the assignor to give notice of the   true | false
   assignment to the obligor.

About the Law

An assignment, rather than a negotiation, occurs when a check is transferred to a third party without a required endorsement.

12-3 Assignment Rights, Duties, and Restrictions

Rights can be assigned, and duties can be delegated. Although this rule seems simple enough, disputes still arise regarding both assignment and delegation. What is generally in dispute is whether a particular right or duty can be transferred and, if so, what legal effects arise from that transfer.

Rights and Duties of the Assignee

The rights and duties of the assignee are the same as those previously held by the assignor under the original contract. It is fair to say that the assignee "steps into the shoes" of the assignor. Claims the assignor may have had against the obligor now belong to the assignee. Also, defenses the obligor may have had against the assignor's claims may now be used against the assignee.

The assignee's duty in an assignment is to give notice of the assignment to the obligor. The obligor is allowed a reasonable time to seek assurance that an assignment has been truly made. Making the assignment in writing reduces the possibility of fraudulent representation as an assignee.

EXAMPLE 12-5: The Quitter–Stalker Assignment, Part I

Quitter appeared at the payroll department of the Meadville Delivery Company and told the paymaster that one of Meadville's drivers, Stalker, had made an assignment of part of his paycheck to her. Under terms of the assignment, Quitter was to receive $150 of the money that Meadville owed Stalker. Meadville, the obligor, would not have to pay Quitter the $150 until the paymaster had a reasonable amount of time to verify the assignment.

Liabilities and Warranties of the Assignor

The assignor is obligated to any express and implied warranties that serve to protect either the assignee or the obligor. A warranty is a promise, statement, or other representation that a thing has certain qualities.

Warranties to the Assignee The assignor is bound by an implied warranty that the obligor will respect the assignment and make the performance, as required by the original agreement between the assignor and the obligor.

EXAMPLE 12-6: The Quitter–Stalker Assignment, Part II

Suppose, in the Quitter–Stalker assignment, that the Meadville Trucking Company had been either unwilling or unable to pay Quitter the $150. Stalker would be bound by an implied warranty to Quitter that the $150 would be paid. If the assignment were a gift to Quitter, there would be no enforceable warranty in the absence of consideration between the assignor and the assignee.

Warranties to the Obligor If the assignor delegates to an assignee duties owed the obligor, there is an implied warranty that the duties delegated will be carried out in a complete and satisfactory manner.

Restrictions on Assignments

Although most contracts may be assigned, those for personal and professional services may not. The right of assignment may also be restricted by agreement of the original parties to the contract and, in certain cases, by law.

Restrictions on Personal and Professional Service Contracts A party may not delegate duties that are of a personal or professional nature. *Personal*, in this context, means "other than routine." Musicians or artists, for example, could not delegate their services to someone else. They are chosen for their ability or artistic talent. Professional services are those rendered by physicians, lawyers, certified public accountants, ministers, and others. People in these occupations are selected because of their special abilities, and their services could not be delegated to someone else. In contrast, routine services may usually be delegated. These are services performed by electricians, mechanics, woodworkers, plumbers, waitstaff, bankers, publishers, and others whose skills and abilities are judged according to the usual customs and standards of the marketplace.

Professionals, like dentists, are chosen based on their particular skills and abilities and may not delegate their professional duties to another.

Restrictions Imposed by Original Contract Parties to a contract may include a condition that will not allow its assignment. Some courts have held that a restriction against the assignment of a debt owed by the obligor robs the assignor of a property right guaranteed by law and would be contrary to public policy. Other courts have permitted this restrictive condition.

Restrictions Imposed by Law Assignment, in special situations, may be restricted by law or declared void because it is contrary to public policy. Thus, members of the armed services may not assign any part of their pay except to a spouse or family member. Police officers, persons elected or appointed to public office, and others are likewise restricted from making assignment of their pay or of duties that they have been especially chosen to perform.

Novation and Assignment

Sometimes a party to a contract will assign all rights and delegate all duties to a third party (the assignee). Once this happens, the assignee will work directly with the obligor, performing the duties and receiving the benefits. Nevertheless, the assignor will remain in privity of contract with the obligor and be liable to the obligor if the assignee does not perform or performs improperly.

EXAMPLE 12-7: *Superfine Market v. Allgood Canning Company*

Allgood Canning Company entered into a contract to sell 1,000 cases of baked beans to Superfine Market for a specific price. Shortly thereafter, Allgood delegated its duty to ship the beans and assigned its rights to receive the money to Fastway Canning Company. The beans Fastway shipped turned out to be bad. If Superfine were to bring suit for damages, it would have to be brought against Allgood, because that was the company with which it had contracted. There was no privity between Superfine and Fastway.

In contrast, if all three parties agree, the assignor can be released from liability at the time of the assignment, and privity of contract can exist between the assignee and the obligor. Such an arrangement is called a novation, which is a substitution, by mutual agreement, of a new party for one of the original parties to a contract. If, in Example 12-7, Superfine and Fastway had agreed to release Allgood from responsibility under the original contract, a novation would have occurred. Privity of contract then would have been between Superfine and Fastway. Superfine's only recourse upon receiving the bad beans would have been to bring suit against Fastway because, by mutual consent, Allgood had been discharged.

quick quiz 12-3

1. The phrase "assignment of a contract" means the same thing as the phrase "assignment of rights."   true | false

2. Personal and professional duties are just as transferable as all other duties.   true | false

3. Novations have been outlawed under the Restatement of Contracts.   true | false

12-4 Discharge by Performance

Most contracts are discharged by performance, which means that the parties do what they agreed to do under the terms of the contract. When performance occurs, the obligations of the parties end. Sometimes, however, the parties do not perform in a timely or satisfactory manner. At other times, they perform partially but not completely. At still other times, they do not perform at all.

Time for Performance

When the time for performance is not stated in the contract, the contract must be performed within a reasonable time. A reasonable time is the time that may fairly, properly, and conveniently be required to do the task that is to be done, considering attending circumstances. Whether a task is performed within a reasonable time is a question of fact to be decided by the jury in a jury trial or the judge in a nonjury trial.

EXAMPLE 12-8: *Rostow Aviation, Ltd. v. Futuregraphics, Inc.*

Rostow Aviation, Ltd., entered a contract with Futuregraphics, Inc., for the design and implementation of a new Web site for Rostow. The Web site was supposed to be up and operational within 60 days of the making of the contract. Futuregraphics was one week late in the completion of the Web site. Rostow attempted to rescind the agreement, claiming that time was of special importance. The court ruled that it had not been clearly established that time was essential for the completion of the Web site. Because time was not essential to the satisfactory performance of the agreement, Rostow was held to the contract.

A QUESTION OF ETHICS

The court held Rostow to the contract in Example 12-8 even though Futuregraphics was one week late in fulfilling its part of the agreement. Because time really was not essential to the agreement, and because Rostow presumably knew that, was it ethical for Rostow to raise the issue of Futuregraphics' lateness in the first place? If time had been important to the completion of the Web site, did Rostow have a responsibility to raise the issue of time before the contract was finalized? If Futuregraphics knew it was running behind schedule, did it have a duty to notify Rostow and offer some sort of compensation for the breach? Explain your answers.

When the time for performance is stated in the contract but there is nothing to indicate that time is of particular importance, the court will usually allow additional time to perform. When the time for performance is stated in the contract and there is something special about the contract that indicates time is essential, the time for performance will be strictly enforced.

EXAMPLE 12-9: *Carter City School System v. Spectrum Images, Inc.*

Spectrum Images, Inc. entered a contract with the entire Carter City school system for the design, production, and distribution of the yearbooks for each of the system's three high schools. A very strict schedule was developed for each high school yearbook staff, specifying when the manuscript, art, and photos had to be delivered to Spectrum; when the material had to be read and returned; and when the page proofs had to be read, corrected, and returned to Spectrum. The yearbooks were to be delivered to each high school 90 days after Spectrum had received all page proofs so that they would be ready for distribution on the graduation day for each of the high schools. In such a situation, it is clear that time is an important factor in this agreement. Unfortunately, the students at two of the three schools did not return the proofs on time, and the yearbooks were late. This missed deadline caused an extra expense for the city school system, which had to send the yearbooks to students by FedEx because they were no longer on campus to pick up their books personally. When Carter City sued Spectrum, the court ruled that because the students knew that time was of the essence and had not made the scheduled deadline, the city could not complain when Spectrum failed to meet the delivery date.

Similarly, when the phrase "time is of the essence" is included among the terms of a written contract, the time period will be enforced. The phrase makes it clear that the time element is of the utmost importance to the parties. Some contracts use a "best efforts" clause to avoid committing parties to a date but instead committing them to do their best to perform by a certain date.

Satisfactory, Complete, and Substantial Performance

Satisfactory performance exists when either personal taste or objective standards have determined that the contracting parties have performed their contractual duties according to the agreement. Satisfactory performance is either an express or implied condition of every contract. Sales agreements for consumer goods often note this condition by including the words: "money back if not entirely satisfied." In other contracts, satisfaction may be carefully defined according to the expectations of the parties. When there is no express agreement, the law implies that work will be done in a skillful manner and the materials or goods will be free of defects. Ordinarily, the parties may be discharged from a contract only if there has been satisfactory performance. Sometimes, one person will agree to do something to another person's satisfaction. Services rendered in a beauty salon or barbershop, photographs taken at a studio, and portraits painted by an artist fall within this classification. Regardless of the skill and application of the person doing the work, dissatisfied customers may, on the basis of their personal judgment and satisfaction, refuse to make payment.

Complete performance occurs when all the parties fully accomplish every term, condition, and promise to which they agreed. Substantial performance occurs when a party, in good faith, executes all promised terms and conditions with the exception of minor details that do not affect the real intent of their agreement. Complete performance terminates an agreement, freeing the parties of any further obligation. Ordinarily, substantial performance also serves to discharge the agreement but with one difference: A party who correctly complains that the other party's performance has been substantial but not complete has the right to demand reimbursement from the offending party to correct those details that were not performed.

EXAMPLE 12-10: *South Central State College v. McLaughlin Construction, Inc.*

McLaughlin Construction, Inc., was the primary contractor for the construction of a new engineering center for South Central State College. The construction of the center was supposed to be completed within one year, and the doors were to open in time for the fall term. The building was completed by fall, but the architect for McLaughlin had committed an error. Apparently he had failed to take into consideration the stress that would be placed on the floor-to-ceiling windows in the building's lobby.

As a result, several of those floor-to-ceiling windows developed cracks. An inspection by the state engineers demonstrated that the cracks posed no danger to anyone in or near the building. Nevertheless, the cracked windows were quite unsightly, and they leaked heavily when it rained, flooding the lobby. Consequently, the college demanded that the construction company make repairs at its own expense. The company refused, and the college threatened to rescind the entire contract. Instead, cooler heads prevailed, and the college hired another construction firm to make adjustments to the stress so that the floor-to-ceiling windows would be the showpieces they were supposed to be. When the college asked for and was refused reimbursement for the additional expense, it sued McLaughlin. The court held that there had been substantial performance of the original contract. However, because the cracked windows were caused by an error on the part of the McLaughlin architect, the court awarded reimbursement costs to the college.

Conditions and Tender of Performance

Some contracts have conditions or terms that determine the rights and duties of the parties prior to performance, during performance, and following performance. These conditions may be classified as conditions precedent, conditions concurrent, or conditions subsequent. Also, in most situations it is necessary for a nonbreaching party to continue to offer to perform as promised. This is referred to as a tender of performance. It is discussed below at length.

Conditions of Performance A condition precedent is a condition that requires the performance of certain acts or promises before the other party is obligated to pay money or provide any other agreed to consideration. In a *unilateral contract,* the performance of a condition precedent serves as the offeree's acceptance of the offer. In a *bilateral contract,* it is a promise that if not performed leads to either rescission or termination of the entire agreement.

EXAMPLE 12-11: The Pressler Case

Pressler, a third-year law student, signed an agreement to accept a position with a law firm. The members of the firm agreed to hire Pressler on the condition that she receive her law degree and pass the bar examination in their state. Earning the law degree and passing the bar examination are conditions precedent to the performance of the obligation of the law firm in giving Pressler the position.

A condition that requires both parties to perform at the same time is a condition concurrent. A promise to deliver goods supported by the buyer's promise to pay on delivery is a very common condition concurrent. Real estate sales agreements, by custom, usually state that the owner–seller will deliver a good and complete deed to the real property on the buyer's presentation of either cash or a certified check for the amount of the purchase price. Failure of either to do as promised concurrently would be a breach of the express contract condition. A condition subsequent is one in which the parties agree that the contract will be terminated when a prescribed event occurs or does not occur. An agreement between a builder and a client stating that contract performance would terminate if a required building permit were not obtained from the issuing public authority within 60 days after the contract is signed is a condition subsequent. Some warranties included in contracts also illustrate these conditions.

EXAMPLE 12-12: *Graham v. Metcalf*

Luben Metcalf agreed to remodel Trisha Graham's back porch for $15,000. Both parties signed a written agreement. One clause in the agreement stated that Metcalf guaranteed the improvements would be free of defects for 12 months after the work was completed. Graham agreed to pay for the improvements upon completion. Metcalf's guarantee constituted a condition subsequent, that is, a condition that applies after both parties have performed their primary obligations under the contract. When, after only one month, the roof of the porch roof leaked, Graham demanded that Metcalf return and fix the problem. Metcalf repeatedly refused to do anything about the leaky roof. Graham was forced to hire another contractor to correct Metcalf's errors. Graham then successfully sued Metcalf and recovered the cost of the repairs.

Tender of Performance In contract law, tender of performance means to offer to do what one has agreed to do under the terms of the contract. If someone has agreed to sell a parcel of land for $40,000, for example, tender of performance would be offering to give a signed deed to the buyer at the agreed time. Similarly, tender of payment would be presenting the $40,000 to the seller at the agreed time. It is important to make tender even if one knows that the other party is not going to perform the contract. This provision is necessary in some states to test the other party's willingness and ability to perform. If neither party has made tender, the court would hold that a breach of contract has not been established. Thus, neither party would be in a position to bring suit against the other. People who must perform acts (e.g., selling goods, performing services) are excused from performing if they make proper tender and it is rejected. However, people who must pay money are not excused from paying if their tender of payment is rejected. They are merely excused from paying further interest.

quick quiz 12-4

1. Very few contracts are discharged by performance.   true | false

2. A condition precedent is a condition that requires the   true | false
   performance of certain actions before the other party to the
   contract is obligated.

3. Tender of performance means to offer to do what one has   true | false
   agreed to do under the terms of the contract.

12-5 Discharge by Nonperformance

Nonperformance may be defined as failing to fulfill or accomplish a promise, contract, or obligation according to its terms. Sometimes the failure to perform makes a party vulnerable to legal action. However, not every instance of nonperformance results in a legal action. Sometimes, nonperformance results from mutual agreement between the parties. At other times, nonperformance is excused because of conditions that make performance impossible or by operation of law. Nevertheless, under certain circumstances, nonperformance will result in a breach of contract. Discharge by nonperformance often comes about in the following ways:

- Discharge by agreement.
- Discharge by impossibility and by operation of law.
- Discharge by breach of contract.

Discharge by Agreement

Parties to a contract may stipulate the time and conditions for termination and discharge as part of their agreement. They also may subsequently agree not to do what they had originally promised. The latter is the case when there is a mutual rescission of the contract, a waiver of performance by one or more of the parties, a novation, or an accord and satisfaction to liquidate an outstanding debt or obligation.

Termination by Terms of the Contract During contract negotiations, parties may agree to certain terms that provide for automatic termination of the contract. For example, a professional athlete may contract with management that the agreement will be terminated if for any reason the player becomes either physically or mentally incapable of rendering full performance.

Mutual Rescission Contracting parties may, either before or after performance commences, rescind their contract as a result of further negotiation and by their mutual assent. Mutual rescission, in the majority of cases, requires both parties to return to the other any consideration already received or pay for any services or materials already rendered.

Termination by Waiver When a party with the right to complain of the other party's unsatisfactory performance or nonperformance fails to complain, termination by waiver occurs. It is a voluntary relinquishing (waiver) of one's rights to demand performance. A waiver differs from a discharge by mutual rescission in that a waiver entails no obligation by the parties to return any consideration that may have been exchanged up to the moment of rescission. Discharge by waiver, when made, is complete in itself.

Novation By novation, the parties to a contract mutually agree to replace one of the parties with a new party. The former, original party is released from liability under the contract. Novation is discussed in detail earlier in the chapter.

Accord and Satisfaction An accord and satisfaction is a new agreement resulting from a bona fide dispute between the parties as to the terms of their original agreement. The mutual agreement to the new terms is the accord; performance of the accord is the satisfaction—thus, accord and satisfaction. The accord, though agreed to, is not a binding agreement until the satisfaction has been made. The original agreement therefore is not discharged until the performance or satisfaction has been provided as promised.

General Release A general release is a document expressing the intent of a creditor to release a debtor from obligations on an existing and valid debt. A general release terminates a debt and excuses the debtor of any future payment, without the usual requirement that consideration be given in return.

Discharge by Impossibility and by Law

Occasionally, it becomes impossible to perform a contract. For example, when the subject matter of a contract, without the knowledge of the parties, had been destroyed before the contract was entered into, the contract would be discharged. Sometimes a contract that is legal when it is originally entered into by the parties becomes illegal before it is performed. This leads to a discharge by operation of law.

Types and Conditions of Impossibility

Conditions that arise subsequent to the making of a contract may either void the agreement or make it voidable by one of the parties. Discharge through impossibility of performance may, in some situations, be allowed only if the specific and anticipated impossibility has been made a condition to the agreement. When the exact subject matter of an executory contract has been selected by the parties and later is destroyed, the performance obligation is discharged. In contrast, when the contract is not specific in the description or the location of the subject matter, a promisor is not discharged if the subject matter intended for delivery is destroyed. In this case, the promisor is obligated to locate and deliver subject matter of the same kind and quantity that could be secured elsewhere. Any financial losses due to the misfortune must be borne by the promisor.

When the performance of a contract requires actions declared illegal because of existing common law, statute, or public policy, the contract is void from its inception. When the performance of a contract is made illegal through the passing of laws subsequent to the formation of the contract, the contract is likewise declared void, and the parties are discharged. The death, insanity, or disability of a party obligated to perform an act that requires a special talent or skill terminates and discharges an agreement, including promises to perform by musicians, artists, writers, skilled craftspeople, and certain professionals. When promised services are to be performed for the personal benefit of a promisee, the death of the promisee will also terminate the agreement. When the contract relates to services that may be performed by others and do not demand the personal services of the contracting party, performance is not excused through death, insanity, or disability. The guardian of the party involved or the estate of the deceased may be held liable for performance.

Frustration-of-Purpose Doctrine

The frustration-of-purpose doctrine releases a party from a contractual obligation when performing the obligations would be thoroughly impractical and senseless. The doctrine is applied only in those cases in which a party recognizes and understands possible risks and accepts them in contemplation of performance.

EXAMPLE 12-13: *Stewart v. Gaverick*

George Gaverick rented a 50th-floor apartment from Thomas Stewart for the night of December 31. The apartment had a balcony overlooking Times Square in midtown Manhattan. The rental period was for only 24 hours, and the landlord knew that the purpose of the contract was to allow Gaverick an unrestricted view of Times Square for the city's New Year's Eve celebration. Unfortunately, a terrorist alert canceled the entire Times Square celebration that year. Stewart still demanded payment from Gaverick and brought a suit in small claims court to recover the amount due. The referee refused to force Gaverick to pay for the apartment. The referee concluded that, because the apartment was of no use to Gaverick, the purpose of the agreement was frustrated, and Gaverick would not have to pay the rent.

Commercial Impracticability

Although not identical to the frustration-of-purpose doctrine, a related concept is known as commercial impracticability. Under this doctrine, the courts may excuse the nonperformance of one party to a contract because an unforeseen and very severe hardship has arisen that would place an enormous hardship on that party. Commercial impracticability is not the same as impossibility, because the party still can perform the contract. It is just that the performance itself would cause a great deal of adversity. Also with commercial impracticability, the purpose of the contract is not undermined by the unforeseen event, so the frustration-of-purpose doctrine does not apply. Nevertheless, under this relatively modern doctrine, some parties may escape performance if the unforeseen event was truly unforeseen and not in any way the fault of the party seeking an escape from performance.

Operation of Law

The performance of a promised act may be discharged by operation of law. Some law that causes the parties to be discharged from their obligations, such as bankruptcy or the statute of limitations, comes into play in this case. Through the provisions of the Bankruptcy Reform Act, a discharge in bankruptcy from a court will be allowed as a defense against the collection of most, but not all, debts of the bankrupt. Therefore, most contractual obligations to pay money come to an end when a party files for bankruptcy. State statutes providing time limits within which suits may be brought are known as statutes of limitations. Each state sets its own time limits. In general, actions for collection of open accounts (charge accounts) must be brought within 3 to 5 years, written agreements within 10 years, and judgments from 10 to 20 years. Those states requiring a seal on certain contracts have still other limitations and requirements that are much broader than those applied to simple contracts. The time limit for bringing suit for breach of a sales contract is four years under the Uniform Commercial Code. The statute of limitations does not technically void the debt, but it gives the debtor a defense against any demand for collection.

Discharge by Breach of Contract

When there is a breach of contract, the injured party has the right to remedy in court. There are several ways in which a breach may occur.

Deliberate Breach of Contract
A breach of contract results when one of the parties fails to do what was agreed to under the terms of the contract. When time is of the essence, there is a breach if performance is not completed within the time limits agreed to by the parties. A breach also results if the performance has been negligent or unskillful. The services rendered must adhere to the standards of skill, as determined by the custom of the marketplace. Wrongful performance or nonperformance discharges the other party from further obligation and permits that party to bring suit to rescind the contract or recover money to compensate it for any loss sustained. Such compensation is known as *damages*.

Repudiation and Anticipatory Breach
An anticipatory breach occurs when a party to a contract either expresses or clearly implies an intention not to perform the contract, even before being required to act. The repudiation must indicate a deliberate refusal to perform according to the terms of the contract. Breaches of this kind are also called *constructive breaches*. The injured party may either commence suit at the time of the anticipatory breach or await the date agreed to for performance, thus giving the breaching party time to reconsider and begin performance. To succeed in a case based on anticipatory repudiation, the injured party must demonstrate that he or she was ready, willing, and able to comply with the contract but could not do so because of the other party's material breach. Anticipatory breach cannot be used if the only action repudiated was the promise to pay money to another party.

Abandonment of Contractual Obligations Stopping performance once it has begun is called abandonment of contractual obligations. Leaving or deserting a party's obligations discharges the other party from any promises made and permits a suit for damages. A temporary, or short-lived, interruption of performance is not deemed abandonment. To constitute abandonment, the promisor must have inexcusably interrupted performance with the obvious intention of not returning to complete the obligations promised.

---

quick quiz 12-5

1. A general release is a document expressing the intent of a   true | false
   creditor to release a debtor from the obligations of an existing
   and valid debt.

2. With commercial impracticability, the purpose of a contract is   true | false
   undermined by an unforeseen event.

3. Stopping a performance once it has begun is called abandonment   true | false
   of contractual obligations.

12-6 Damages and Equitable Remedies

A breach of contract releases the injured party from any obligations under the contract and gives that party the right to ask a court of law for a remedy. The usual remedy for breach of contract is the payment of damages in the form of money. At times, however, the payment of monetary damages is not enough to satisfy the injured party. In such situations, the injured party will ask the court for rescission, specific performance, or an injunction.

Damages in Contract Law

Damages describe money awarded to parties who have been victimized or suffered injury to their legal rights by others. Damages are of different kinds, and the nature of a claim usually determines what type of damages will apply. In some states, by statute or judicial rule, juries are charged with two decisions: They must decide which party is to be given favorable judgment and determine how much is to be awarded in damages. Appeals to a higher court are allowed when the amount of damages awarded appears to be unreasonably low or excessively high.

Actual or Compensatory Damages
Actual damages are the sum of money equal to the real financial loss suffered by the injured party. Because they are intended to compensate the injured party, actual damages are also called compensatory damages. Thus, damages awarded for nondelivery of promised goods or services would be an amount equal to the difference between the price stated in the contract and what the promisee would have to pay elsewhere. Should the same goods or services be conveniently available elsewhere at the same or at a lower price, no actual loss could be claimed.

Incidental and Consequential Damages
Incidental damages and consequential damages are awarded for losses indirectly but closely attributable to a breach. Incidental damages cover any expenses paid out by the innocent party to prevent further loss. Consequential damages result indirectly from the breach because of special circumstances

that exist with a particular contract. To recover consequential damages, the injured party must show that such losses were foreseeable when the contract was made.

Punitive or Exemplary Damages

Damages in excess of actual losses suffered by the plaintiff awarded as a measure of punishment for the defendant's wrongful acts are punitive damages, also called *exemplary damages*. They are a court-ordered punishment rather than compensation for a known loss. Punitive damages are awarded when a defendant is responsible for abusive and dishonest practices in consumer transactions that are unconscionable and contrary to the public good. Often such abusive and dishonest practices are associated with certain business-related torts, including fraudulent misrepresentation, disparagement, the violation of an implied covenant of fairness and honesty, and intentional interference with an existing contract.

Fraudulent Misrepresentation As noted previously, fraud, or fraudulent misrepresentation, occurs when one party makes false statements or commits some sort of false action that causes another party to rely on those falsehoods then experience and an injury or loss as a result. Because fraud is a deliberate attempt to subvert proper business relationships, the court views it as especially reprehensible, and those that commit fraud will find themselves paying not only compensatory damages, if applicable, but also punitive damages. The idea of punitive damages is to punish the defrauding party to such an extent that he or she will be dissuaded from any future fraudulent conduct. Punitive

THE OPENING CASE *Revisited, Part I*
Punitive Damages and the Limits of the Law:
State Farm Mutual v. Campbell, Round 2

As we learned in the Opening Case at the beginning of this chapter, when one party breaks the terms of a contract and the other party sues, the court will do its best to place the parties in as good a position as they would have been had the contract been performed as promised in the first place. One reason for this policy is that people voluntarily assume responsibilities when they make a contract and those responsibilities affect only the parties and not the general public as is the case with criminal law and, at times, tort law.

As we saw, all of this is fine in most cases, but what happens when the breaching party has deliberately undermined the basic intent of contract law by committing fraud not just in the contract at issue in the case, but as a pattern of conduct, perhaps even an official policy, affecting hundreds and thousands of other contracts? This is exactly what happened in *State Farm Mutual v. Campbell,* the Opening Case at the beginning of Chapter 12. In that case, the Campbells offered evidence that State Farm's refusal to settle their case was not just fraudulent in relation to their contract but was,

instead, part of a larger pattern of conduct planned and executed by State Farm over a 20-year period against hundreds of policyholders. After the jury heard this evidence, they awarded the Campbell's $145 million in punitive damages. The judge then reduced the punitive damages to $25 million.

On appeal the Campbells stressed the fraudulent nature of State Farm's conduct and State Farm, in turn, argued that their conduct in relation to the other contracts should not be used to punish them for their conduct in relation to the contract that they had with Campbells. The Utah Supreme Court agreed with the Campbells and reinstated the $145 million in punitive damages. The case made its way to the United States Supreme Court. The U.S. Supreme Court struck down that portion of the punitive damages that involved conduct unrelated to the Campbell's claim. The Court concluded that awarding punitive damage for conduct unrelated to the claim before the court in the present case violated the basic principles of due process.

damages are also supposed to serve as a deterrent so that other people do not even think about committing fraud. For this reason, punitive damages are also called *exemplary damages*. Exemplary damages are used as an example for other "would-be con artists" who ought to know better than to subvert the law through fraud.

Nominal Damages
Token damages awarded to parties who have experienced an injury to their legal rights but no actual loss are nominal damages. Common law usually awarded six cents to the successful plaintiff when no actual losses were shown. In today's practice, the award is usually one dollar.

Present and Future Damages
Damages may be awarded for present injuries and for others that might reasonably be anticipated in the future. Thus, a party charged with fraud in the sale of a building infested with termites may be held liable for all damages revealed at the time of the suit and for damages that would reasonably be forthcoming as a result of the undisclosed and concealed infestation of the property.

Liquidated Damages
Parties may stipulate (agree) as a condition of their contract to the amount of damages that might be assessed if there is a breach. Damages agreed to in the initial contract are called liquidated damages. Liquidated damages must be realistic and in proportion to the losses that might be reasonably anticipated should there be a breach. When liquidated damages are found to be excessive or unreasonable, a court will disregard them and leave the matter of setting damages to the discretion of a jury.

Damages under *Quantum Meruit*
The doctrine of *quantum meruit* (i.e., as much as one had earned) is important in assessing damages in cases founded on contracts implied in law, or quasi-contracts. Thus, when there has been no express or implied mutual agreement, a court will at times impose an obligation against a party who has been unjustly rewarded at the innocent expense of another. Damages awarded are in an amount considered reasonable in return for the benefits the one party derived through the quasi-contract relationship.

Speculative Damages
Courts do not allow speculative damages. These damages are computed on losses that have not actually been suffered and that cannot be proved; they are damages based entirely on an expectation of losses that might be suffered from a breach. They differ from future damages in that speculative damages are not founded on fact but only on hope or expectation. Their basis is nothing more than a calculated guess as to the gains a party might have received had there not been a breach.

Mitigation of Damages
The injured party has an obligation to do what is reasonably possible to mitigate the damages, that is, to keep damages to a minimum. A party who has been wronged by another's breach must exercise reasonable precautions to prevent the damages from becoming unfairly and unreasonably burdensome to the other party.

Equitable Remedies

When money in the form of damages is not enough to provide a fair and just award to the injured party, the court may grant an equitable remedy. Rather than simply order the breaching party to pay damages, a court issuing an equitable remedy compels the breaching party to perform an act or refrain from performing an act. The two most common equitable remedies are specific performance and injunctive relief.

Specific Performance
A decree of specific performance is a court order calling for the breaching party to do what he or she promised to do under the original contract. The

courts order specific performance only when the subject matter of a contract is unique or rare. The classic example of unique subject matter calling for specific performance is a contract for the sale and transfer of title to land, because each piece of land is unique. However, unique or rare subject matter could also include such items as antiques, family heirlooms, original works of art, and special animals, such as a particular race horse. Obviously, an award of monetary damages would not provide the injured party satisfaction in any of these situations. Contracts for personal services are rarely enforced through specific performance. Demanding that an unwilling party perform promised personal services would be contrary to Amendment 13 of the U.S. Constitution, which prohibits human servitude. A remedy in cases of this kind, however, may be found through injunctive relief.

Injunctive Relief An injunction is an order issued by a court directing that a party do or refrain from doing something. An injunction may be either temporary or permanent. A temporary injunction is issued as a means of delaying further activity in any contested matter until the court determines whether a permanent injunction should be entered or the injunction should be removed entirely. One who disobeys an injunction does so under threat of penalty of contempt of court.

quick quiz 12-6

1. Actual damages are also called compensatory damages.   true | false

2. Punitive damages cover any expenses paid out by the innocent   true | false
   party to prevent further loss.

3. The courts order specific performance only when the subject   true | false
   matter of a contract is unique or rare.

Summary

12.1 Third parties are at times given benefits through a contract made between two other parties. Some contracts are made specifically to benefit a third party. Such a third party is known as a third party beneficiary. Three types of intended beneficiaries include creditor beneficiaries, donee beneficiaries, and insurance beneficiaries. Some third parties benefit from a contract even though the contract was not made for their benefit. These parties are known as incidental beneficiaries.

12.2 The transfer of contract rights to a third party outside of the original agreement is an assignment. In general, rights are assigned, and duties are delegated. However, the rules apply to both transfers in the same way. The party who assigns rights or delegates duties is the assignor. The outside third party to whom the assignment is made is the assignee. The remaining party

to the original agreement is the obligor. The assignee must give notice of assignment to the obligor.

12.3 The rights and duties of the assignee are the same as those held by the assignor under the original agreement. Contracts for personal or professional services cannot be assigned. Assignments also can be limited by agreement. A novation occurs when two contracting parties agree to replace one of the parties with a new party.

12.4 Most contracts are discharged by performance, which means that the parties do what they agreed to do. Unless the parties agree otherwise, satisfactory performance will be determined by objective standards. Substantial performance will discharge the agreement with the right to reimbursement for correcting details that were not completed. Conditions may determine the rights and duties of the parties prior to performance, during performance, and following performance. If neither party makes tender, a breach of contract is not established.

12.5 Nonperformance can discharge contractual obligations. Not every instance of nonperformance results in a breach of contract. Parties can agree to discharge a contractual obligation by terms in the contract, mutual rescission, waiver, novation, accord and satisfaction, or general release. Contractual obligations can also be discharged when it becomes impossible to perform a contract or under the frustration-of-purpose doctrine. These obligations can also be discharged by operation of law under principles of bankruptcy and the statute of limitations.

12.6 An injured party is released from any obligations under the contract following the other party's breach. In addition, the injured party has the right to ask a court of law for a remedy. The usual remedy is the payment of damages in the form of money. When the payment of monetary damages is not enough, the injured party will ask the court for rescission, specific performance, or an injunction.

Key Terms

abandonment of contractual obligations, 264

actual damages, 264

anticipatory breach, 263

assignee, 251

assignment, 251

assignor, 251

beneficiary, 249

commercial impracticability, 262

compensatory damages, 264

complete performance, 260

condition concurrent, 259

condition precedent, 259

condition subsequent, 259

consequential damages, 264

creditor beneficiary, 250

delegation, 251

donee beneficiary, 250

fraud (or fraudulent misrepresentation), 265

fraudulent conveyance, 252

frustration-of-purpose doctrine, 262

general release, 261

incidental beneficiary, 250

incidental damages, 264

injunction, 267

intended beneficiary, 249

liquidated damages, 266

mutual rescission, 261

nominal damages, 266

novation, 256

obligor, 251

outside party, 249

performance, 256

punitive damages, 265

reasonable time, 257

satisfactory performance, 258

specific performance, 266

speculative damages, 266

substantial performance, 258

tender of payment, 260

tender of performance, 260

termination by waiver, 261

third party, 249

third party beneficiary, 249

warranty, 255

Questions for Review and Discussion

1. What are the legal rights given to all beneficiaries?
2. What are the legal rights given to incidental beneficiaries?
3. What is involved in an assignment of rights and a delegation of duties?
4. What is a novation?
5. What constitutes the satisfactory performance of a contract?
6. What is the difference between complete and substantial performance?
7. How can a contract be discharged by nonperformance?
8. What is anticipatory repudiation?
9. What types of damages are available in the event of a breach of contract?
10. What is the difference between specific performance and injunctive relief?

Cases for Analysis

1. Under a divorce decree, Blackston was ordered to pay $600 a month in child support to his former wife. The decree provided that the payments were to be paid to the clerk of the court's office. The clerk of the court assigned the right to receive the payments to the Department of Human Resources. Who was obligated to notify Blackston of the assignment? *Blackston v. State Ex Rel. Blackston*, 585 So.2d 58 (AL).

2. Gary Jones retained the law firm of Irace and Lowry after being injured in a motorcycle accident. Later, Jones required surgery after dislocating his shoulder in an unrelated incident. Having no money to pay the surgeon, Jones signed a letter requesting that the money from the accident settlement be assigned to Dr. Herzog for treatment of a shoulder injury that occurred at a different time. The law firm was notified of the assignment. When the settlement was received by the law firm, Jones instructed the firm to pay the money to him rather than to the surgeon. It did, and the surgeon was never paid. Could Dr. Herzog recover the money owed him from the law firm? Why or why not? *Herzog v. Irace*, 594 A.2d 1106 (ME).

3. Copeland contracted with McDonald's Systems, Inc., for a franchise. Copeland was granted the fast-food outlet franchise for Omaha. McDonald's also gave Copeland first refusal rights for any plans to open other franchise outlets in Omaha. Copeland exercised the right several times, opening several additional outlets. He then sold the franchise to Schupack and assigned to Schupack the right to open new McDonald's outlets in Omaha. When Schupack tried to exercise the first refusal right, McDonald's objected, claiming its relationship with Copeland developed through a special confidence in Copeland's ability to manage and promote its new franchise outlets. Was McDonald's correct? Explain. *Schupack v. McDonald's Systems, Inc.*, 264 N.W.2d 827 (NE).

4. Timbercrest built a house for the Murphys. After occupying the house for a while, the Murphys complained of several problems. Timbercrest fixed the problems, and the Murphys had no further complaints. The Litwins bought the house from the Murphys three years later. When the house was sold, neither the Litwins nor the Murphys were aware of any problems. After living in the house

for two years, the Litwins became aware of several problems. The Litwins then contacted the Murphys and had the Murphys assign them their rights under the original construction agreement with Timbercrest. The Litwins then sued Timbercrest, claiming Timbercrest had breached its contract with the Murphys by not providing them with a house free of defects. Were the Litwins correct? *Litwins v. Timbercrest Estates, Inc.*, 347 N.E.2d 378 (IL).

5. Nolan wrote the song "Tumbling Tumbleweeds" and, in an agreement with Sam Fox Publishing Company, transferred all rights to the song to the company. In return, Nolan was to receive royalties according to terms laid out in the agreement. Sam Fox later assigned all rights and interests in "Tumbling Tumbleweeds" to Williamson Music, Inc. Was it necessary for Sam Fox to obtain Nolan's consent before making the assignment to Williamson? Explain. *Nolan v. Williamson Music, Inc.*, 300 F. Supp. 1311 (S.D. NY).

6. When Kent contracted to have his new house constructed, he specifically noted that the plumbing must be made by Reading manufacturers. After the house had been completed, Kent did an inspection tour during which he discovered that, though much of the plumbing had come from Reading, there were some parts that did not. After making his discovery, Kent demanded that the non-Reading plumbing fixtures be ripped out and replaced with the supplies he had specified in the contract. In addition, Kent refused to pay the contractor until the proper plumbing supplies were added to the house. The contractor brought suit against Kent, arguing that though there were minor deviations from certain specified parts of the contract concerning the plumbing fixtures, he had nevertheless substantially performed his end of the deal. Kent stuck to his strict construction of the contract and labeled the contractor's performance unsatisfactory. He thus claimed to be released from the agreement unless the contractor lived up to every term in the original agreement. Who should prevail in this case? Explain. *Jacob and Young v. Kent*, 129 N.E. 889.

7. Sai Grafio agreed to paint Gerald Weaver's and Katherine Brewer's house for $5,650. Weaver and Brewer paid for the paint job in installments but

stopped payment on the final $1,845 check, claiming that Grafio had breached the contract by doing a poor job. The lower court judge found that the only defect in the paint job was a footprint left on the roof that would cost $50 to repair. How much money, if any, and under what legal theory, did the court allow Grafio to recover for the paint job? *Weaver v. Grafio*, 595 A.2d 983 (DC).

8. Arthur Murray, Inc., and Parker entered a series of contracts under which Arthur Murray agreed to teach Parker how to dance. Under the terms of each agreement, refunds were impossible, and the lessons could not be canceled. After the contracts were entered, Parker suffered a permanent disability that made it physically impossible for him to dance. When Arthur Murray refused to refund any part of Parker's money, he sued to rescind the contracts on grounds of impossibility. Arthur Murray claimed that the non-refund clause must be upheld by the court. Was Arthur Murray correct? Explain. *Parker v. Arthur Murray, Inc.*, 295 N.E.2d 487 (IL).

9. Bob Pagan Ford, Inc., hired Smith to work as a car salesperson in Galveston County. As part of his contract, Smith agreed not to work as an auto salesperson in Galveston County for three years after leaving his employment with Bob Pagan Ford. Smith worked for Bob Pagan for only a few months. He then left and took a sales job with another dealership in Galveston County. Was injunctive relief an appropriate remedy in this case? Explain. *Bob Pagan Ford, Inc., v. Smith*, 638 S.W.2d 176 (TX).

10. Kucha sold a house to Pilder for $75,293. The agreement was in writing, as required by the Statute of Frauds. As part of the contract, Kucha agreed to pay for the remodeling of the sun porch. However, when Kucha found out that it would cost $12,728 to do the remodeling, he refused to sell the property. Pilder sued to compel Kucha to go through with the deal. Kucha argued that under the circumstances the court could not force him to sell under any equitable remedy. Was Kucha correct? Why or why not?

quick quiz Answers

12-1	12-2	12-3	12-4	12-5	12-6
1. T	1. F	1. F	1. F	1. T	1. T
2. T	2. F	2. F	2. T	2. F	2. F
3. F	3. F	3. F	3. T	3. T	3. T

Part 2 Case Study

Murray v. Accounting Center & Tax Services, Inc., et al.
Court of Appeals of Ohio, Sixth District
178 Ohio App. 3d 432 (2008)

Summary

Julie Ray Murray had worked as an accountant for Accounting Center and Tax Services for eight years when her boss, Phillip Roberts, asked her to sign a non-compete agreement. Under the agreement, Murray would be unable to work for any of her former clients for two years after leaving the Accounting Center, unless she got written permission from the firm to do so. Moreover, if she chose to work for such clients without written permission, she would be obligated to pay the Accounting Center an amount set out by the terms of the agreement. The agreement also contained an assignment clause that permitted Accounting Services to transfer the noncompete agreement, should the firm be sold. That is exactly what happened. The firm was sold to Timothy Pinkelman and Murray's noncompete agreement was assigned to him as part of that sale. Despite this, Pinkelman tried to persuade Murray to sign a new noncompete agreement that included a change in her compensation. Under the old system, she was an hourly employee. Under the new system, she would be paid on commission. Murray refused to sign the new non-compete agreement and Pinkelman fired her. Two days later Pinkelman sent a letter to Murray reminding her of the original non-compete agreement and warning her that, should she violate the agreement, she would be subjected to a wide variety of legal consequences, none of them pleasant. Undaunted, Murray worked for the prohibited clients and, as a preemptive strike, brought a lawsuit against the Accounting Center seeking a declaratory judgment that would strike down the noncompete agreement as unfair. The trial court agreed with Murray and the Accounting Center appealed that decision.

The Court's Opinion

Skow, Judge

This is an appeal from a judgment by the Lucas County Court of Common Pleas, granting summary judgment in favor of appellee, Julie Ray Murray, and against appellants, Accounting Center & Tax Services, Inc. and TPAC, Inc. For the reasons that follow, we reverse the judgment of the trial court.

(Note: TPAC, Inc. and Accounting Center &Tax Services, Inc. are one and the same entity, TPAC, Inc. having changed its name to Accounting Center & Tax Services sometime after February 27, 2004. Thus, although the complaint in this case names both TPAC, Inc. and Accounting Center & Tax Services, Inc. as defendants, there is, in fact, just one defendant corporation.) . . .

On January 16, 2007, Murray filed a complaint in this action seeking declaratory judgment. Appellant responded with an answer and counterclaim. The parties subsequently filed cross-motions for summary judgment, and on December 12, 2007, the trial court issued an opinion and judgment entry granting Murray's motion for summary judgment that appellant currently appeals, raising the following assignment of error:

I. "The trial court erred as a matter of law when it found that the non-compete agreement entered into between the plaintiff-appellee and her former employer was not enforceable by defendant-appellant."

An appellate court reviewing a trial court's granting of a summary judgment does so de novo, applying the same standard used by the trial court. *Grafton v. Ohio Edison Co.* (1996), 77 Ohio St. 3d 102, 105, 671 N.E. 2d 241. Civ. R, 56 (C) provides:

"Summary judgment shall be rendered forthwith if the pleadings, depositions, answers to interrogatories, written admissions, affidavits, transcripts of evidence, and written stipulations of fact, if any, timely filed in the action, show that there is no genuine issue as to any material fact and that the moving party is entitled to judgment as a matter of law. No evidence or stipulation may be considered except as stated in this rule. ***."

Summary judgment is proper where (1) no genuine issue as to any material fact remains to be litigated and (2) the moving party is entitled to judgment as a matter of law, and (3) when the evidence is viewed most strongly in favor of the nonmoving party, reasonable minds can come to but one conclusion, a conclusion adverse to the nonmoving party. *Ryberg v. Allstate Ins. Co.* (July 12, 2001), 10th Dist. No. 00AP-1243, 2001 WL 777121, citing *Tokles & Son, Inc. v. Midwestern Indemn. Co.* (1992), 65 Ohio St. 3d 621, 629, 605 N.E. 2d 939.

The moving party bears the initial burden of informing the trial court of the basis for the motion and identifying those portions of the record that demonstrate the absence of a genuine issue of fact as to an essential element of one or more of the nonmoving party's claims. *Dresher v. Burt* (1996), 75 Ohio St. 3d 280, 292, 662 N.E. 2d 264. Once the burden has been satisfied, the nonmoving party has the burden as set forth at Civ. R. 56 (E), to offer specific facts showing a genuine issue for trial Id.

The instant case requires us to determine: (1) whether the 1999 employment-and-noncompete agreement was properly assigned to appellant when it acquired Roberts's business; and if so, (2) whether, and to what extent, the 1999 employment-and-noncompete agreement is enforceable against Murray.

Here, the assignment clause contained within the 1999 employment-and-noncompete agreement expressly provides that the agreement and its provisions are transferable upon the merger or sale of the firm. The agreement (although clearly not the product of any meaningful negotiation) was signed, and apparently assented to, by Murray. In 2004, in conjunction with Roberts's sale of the firm to appellant, the employment-and-noncompete was properly assigned to appellant by way of the assignment-and-assumption agreement executed by Roberts and Pinkelman.

Arguing that there was no valid assignment, Murray points out that she was not notified of the assignment at the time of the 2004 transfer of the business. In making this argument, Murray fails to cite (and this court's research fails to reveal) any authority to support her position that notification to her was required for a valid assignment.

Having found that the 1999 employment-and-noncompete agreement was validly assigned, we must next determine whether, and to what extent, it may be enforced against Murray. In Ohio, reasonable noncompete agreements are enforced, and unreasonable noncompete agreements are enforced to the extent necessary to protect an employer's legitimate interest. *Procter & Gamble Co. v. Stoneham* (2000), 140 Ohio App. 3d 260, 270, 747 N.E. 2d 268. "A covenant restraining an employee from competing with his former employer upon termination of employment is reasonable if the restraint is no greater than is required for the protection of the employer, does not impose undue hardship on the employee, and is not injurious to the public." *Raimonde v. Van Vlerah* (1975), 42 Ohio St. 2d 21, 71 O.O. 2d 12, 235 N.E. 2d 544, paragraph two of the syllabus.

If a covenant not to compete is unreasonable, courts are empowered to modify the terms to create a reasonable covenant between the parties. *Rogers v. Runfola & Assoc., Inc.* (1991), 57 Ohio St. 3d 5, 8, 565 N.E. 2d 540. In so doing the courts should consider the following factors:

"'[T]he absence or presence as to time and space, * * * whether the employee represents the sole contact with the customer; whether the employee is possessed with confidential information or trade secrets; whether the covenant seeks to eliminate competition which would be unfair to the employer or merely seeks to eliminate ordinary competition; whether the covenant seeks to stifle the inherent skill and experience of the employee; whether the benefit to the employer is disproportional to the detriment to the employer; whether the covenant operates as a bar to the employee's sole means of support; whether the employee's talent which the employer seeks to suppress was actually developed during the period of employment; and whether the forbidden employment is merely incidental to the main employment.' ***." Id., quoting *Raimonde*, 42 Ohio St. 2d at 25, 72 O.O. 2d 12, 325 N.E.2d 544.

With these facts in mind, we conclude that the restraints and resulting hardships on Murray do, in fact, exceed that which is reasonable to protect appellant's legitimate business interests. Temporally, Murray is prohibited from working for customers of appellant for a period of 24 months. For 16 years, Murray has supported herself, in whole or in part, by doing tax-preparation work. She has done so by working for employers, such as appellant, and by working on her own. We find that imposing a two-year time restriction is unreasonable and will create an undue hardship on her.

Our inquiry does not end here, however. We must next determine whether some restrictions prohibiting Murray from competing are necessary to protect appellant's business interests. The record reveals that appellant and his predecessor in interest developed a clientele with which Murray had direct contact, on a regular and ongoing basis. Certainly, appellant has a legitimate commercial interest to protect. For this reason, we find appellant's assignment of error well taken.

Balancing the restraints and projected hardships on Murray with appellant's interests, and upon the authority of *Raimonde,* 42 Ohio St. 2d 21, 71, O.O. 2d 12, 325 N.E. 2d 544 and App. R. 12 (B), we modify the 24-month restriction as follows:

Sixty days from the date of this order, Murray shall be prohibited for a period of one year from servicing appellant's clients.

For all of the foregoing reasons, the judgment of the Lucas County Court of Common Pleas is reversed. Appellee is ordered to pay the costs of this appeal pursuant to App. R. 24. Judgment for the clerk's expense incurred in preparation of the record, fees allowed by law, and the fee for filing the appeal is awarded to Lucas County.

Judgment reversed

Handwork and Osowik, J., concur.

Questions for Analysis

1. What is a summary judgment motion? What must be proven for a successful summary judgment motion? Who has the initial burden? What is that burden? What happens when the burden shifts to the other party? What is that party's responsibility at that point? Explain everything here.

2. Who is the assignor in this assignment? Who is the assignee? Who is the obligor? Explain.

3. The court labels the transfer of Murray's employment-and-noncompete agreement from Roberts to Pinkelman as an assignment. Is the court correct or are is the transfer actually a novation? Explain.

4. The court concludes that Roberts had no duty to give notice of the assignment (if it was an assignment) to Murray? Is the court correct here? Explain.

5. As we learned in Chapter 12, the law states that "a party may not delegate duties that are of a personal or professional nature." Is that what happened in this case? Why or why not?

6. Has the assignor transferred any warranties to the assignee in this case? If not, why not? If so, what are they?

7. What are the limits that are placed on Murray in the noncompete agreement?

8. How does the court evaluate these limits? Are they fair or unfair? Do you agree or disagree with the court? Explain.

9. What consideration did Roberts transfer to Murray for her signature on the noncompete agreement? Is this consideration adequate? Explain. What consideration did Pinkelman promise to transfer to Murray for her signature on the noncompete agreement? Would that consideration have been adequate? Why or why not?

10. In general, noncompete agreements like the one in this case are not favored by the law. Why is this so?

Sales and Consumer Protection

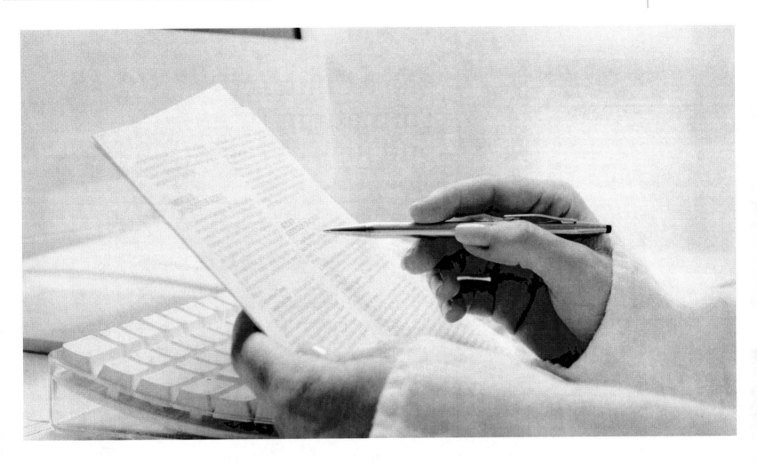

Part Three

Sales and Consumer Protection

Chapter 13

Sales Contracts: Formation, Title, and Risk of Loss

THE OPENING CASE Purchase Orders and the UCC: *XCEL Mold & Machine v. DeVault Indus.*

The Uniform Commercial Code (UCC) governs contracts that are made for the sale or the lease of goods. Goods, as we have seen, are movable tangible objects such as vehicles, electronic devices, and clothing. Many of the rules that are found in the UCC are straightforward, unambiguous expressions of legal principles that have been imbedded in the law for centuries. This simple fact makes the case of *XCEL v. DeVault* relatively easy for the court to solve. The facts in the case play out like this. DeVault Industries manufactures custom built shotguns. XCEL has perfected a wire-cutting process that is ideally suited for the trigger assemblies in the DeVault shotguns. After an initial trial run, during which XCEL successfully produced six trigger assemblies, DeVault sent a purchase order (No. 27) to XCEL for 20 additional units (although there was enough material to produce 60 units), at a total cost of $1,080. XCEL received and accepted purchase order No. 27. Within a few days, however, Mr. Cain, the president of XCEL, phoned Mr. DeVault, the president of DeVault, and told him that XCEL could not manufacture the parts at that price. DeVault remembers the phone call differently, arguing that the two men did not talk price but, instead, discussed the quantity of the order, which was set at 20. However, DeVault did admit that Cain said he needed to produce more than 20 units to cover the set-up costs for that initial 20 units. DeVault told him not to worry because they would later figure out what a fair price would be. XCEL did, in fact, manufacture the units and sent them to DeVault. Once DeVault received the units, they sent a check to XCEL for $1,080. The check included a notation that read, "pymt in full PO#27 60 pcs@18.00 ea." Someone at XCEL cashed the check and deposited the proceeds in an XCEL bank account. Nevertheless, Cain continued to claim that DeVault had not paid the full amount owed under the contract. Later XCEL sent its own check for $1,080 back to DeVault. By this time it was too late. DeVault would no longer listen to Cain and Cain refused to hear DeVault. That was when the lawsuit erupted. So what do you think? Did DeVault and XCEL enter a contract here? If so, when was the offer made? When did the acceptance occur? Did the parties need to put all of this in writing? Consider these questions as you read this chapter on selling and leasing goods. (See *XCEL Mold & Machine v. DeVault Indus.*, 146 Ohio Misc. 2d 32, 2008-Ohio-269.)

Opening Case Questions

1. Is the case of *XCEL v. DeVault* governed by common law or by the Uniform Commercial Code? Explain.

2. Does the contract involved in this case have to be in writing to be enforceable? Explain.

3. When was the offer made here? When was it accepted? When did mutual assent emerge during the flow of events? Explain.

4. Will the court listen to and consider evidence based on the content of the phone conversations? Why or why not?

5. Is the cashed check significant in this case? Why or why not?

Learning Objectives

1. Define the term goods and explain the nature of a sale.
2. Explain how Article 2 of the UCC applies to contractual relationships.
3. Explain the UCC rules that relate to written contracts.
4. Explain the two laws related to cyber-sales contracts.
5. Contrast an auction with reserve with an auction without reserve.
6. Explain title, void title, and voidable title.
7. Determine when title of goods passes from seller to buyer.
8. Decide when the buyer or seller must bear the risk of loss.
9. Compare a sale on approval with a sale or return.
10. Define an insurable interest.

13-1 The Sale and Lease of Goods

In the previous unit we discussed the general principles of contract law as they relate to common law principles regardless of what is being purchased or sold. Now we shift our focus to contracts that involve the sale or the lease of goods. Recall that goods are movable, tangible pieces of property such as vehicles, clothing, and electronic devices. As we saw in Chapter 7, much of the law regarding the sale of goods evolved from the law merchant on the European continent. With the Roman Catholic Church supplying political and social support, with Canon Law providing a moral framework, and with practicality guiding their activities over a 300-year period, the merchants developed a body of active law that was characterized by neutrality, universality, mutuality, involvement, integration, and evolution. The law of sales has gone through many changes over the years. However, throughout all these changes, even those that have integrated advanced cyber-technology into the sales contract, the people responsible for the Uniform Commercial Code (UCC) have attempted to preserve those six basic principles. The UCC, which has been adopted either in whole or in part by every state in the United States, will, therefore, be the focal point of our study of sales law.

UCC 2-105(1) (see pages 959–960)

Sales of Goods

Some medieval version of the 21st century Madison Avenue advertising executive knew exactly what he was doing when he branded the subject matter of every sales contracts as "goods." It would hardly have attracted sales to call them "bads" or to settle on some other mundane label. Nevertheless, as we all know by the time we are old enough to read a

UCC 2-105(2) (see
page 960)

UCC 2-106(2) (see
page 960)

Christmas catalogue, goods are things (other than money, stocks, and bonds) that are tangible, movable, and valuable (to someone). They include toys, candy, growing crops, timber, and minerals if they are to be sold separately from the real property. Office furniture, mobile homes, milk, wedding pictures, electricity, vehicles, computers, waste paper, kerosene, books, clothing, jewelry, horses, soybeans, PDAs, DVDs, and baseball caps are all considered goods. Goods that are not yet in existence or under the control of people are called future goods. They include fish in the sea, minerals in the ground, goods not yet manufactured, and commodities futures. Whenever anyone buys food in a supermarket, gasoline at a gas station, clothing at a shopping mall, a meal at a restaurant, or even a daily newspaper, a sale of goods occurs. In fact, several sales contracts usually occur for a particular item before the item reaches the consumer and sometimes even after it reaches the consumer.

EXAMPLE 13-1: Sales Contracts at Different Levels

The Steven Andrew Corporation manufactures lawn mowers. The company enters into sales contracts with its suppliers every time it purchases parts and materials to make the mowers. In addition, the company enters into sales contracts with wholesalers when it sells the mowers. Similarly, wholesalers enter into sales contracts when they sell the mowers to retailers. In the same manner, retailers enter into sales contracts when they sell the mowers to consumers. Going even further, consumers enter into sales contracts when they sell their second-hand lawn mowers to other private parties. All of these contracts are governed by the UCC.

A gift is not considered a sale because, though title passes, it is not given for a price. Similarly, a bailment (e.g., when an item is left at a store to be sold on consignment) does not meet the definition of a sale because title does not pass between the parties. Article 2 of the UCC applies whenever people buy or sell goods, whether in person, online, over the telephone, or in any other manner. This law applies to sales of goods between private parties and sales of goods by businesspeople or merchants. To determine whether the UCC applies, ask if the contract is a contract for the sale of goods. If the answer is yes, apply the law under the UCC. If the answer is no, apply the common law of contracts. (See Table 13-1).

UCC Article 2 (see
pages 821–842)

Leases of Goods

UCC 2A-101-532 (see
pages 842–862)

The leasing of goods is governed by Article 2A of the Uniform Commercial Code. This article includes leasing of such things as automobiles, trucks, machinery, computers, furniture, electronic equipment, and all types of tools. Many of the rules that are found in the UCC relating to the sale of goods (discussed in the following chapters) also apply to the leasing of goods under Article 2A of the UCC.

Goods and Services

When a contract includes both goods and services, the dominant element of the contract determines whether it is a contract for goods or a contract for services. If the sale of goods is dominant, as when someone purchases a furnace and has it installed, the law under the UCC applies. In contrast, if the performance of services is dominant, as when someone has a furnace repaired and a few new parts are installed, the common law of contracts applies instead.

Table 13-1 Different Laws Apply to Different Transactions

Transaction	Applicable Law
Contract for the sale of real estate	General contract law (sometimes referred to as common law) and real property law
Contract for employment	General contract law and employment law
Sale of goods between two private parties	UCC (Article 2)
Sale of goods by a merchant to a consumer	UCC (Article 2) and state consumer protection laws
Sale of goods between two merchants	UCC (Article 2)
Contract for a mixture of goods and services—consisting mostly of goods	UCC (Article 2)
Contract for a mixture of goods and services—consisting mostly of services	General contract law
Sale of goods over the Internet	UCC (Article 2)
Sale of goods at an auction	UCC (Article 2)
The leasing of goods	UCC (Article 2A)
International sales of goods	United Nations convention on Contracts for the International Sale of Goods (CISG)
Sale of stock on the stock market	UCC (Article 8)
The writing of a check, promissory note, or draft	UCC (Article 3)

quick quiz 13-1

1. A gift is considered a sale.   true | false

2. Money, stocks, and bonds are movable items that are   true | false
    not goods.

3. The dominant element of a contract determines whether it is a   true | false
    sales contract or a services contract.

13-2 Rules for Sales Contracts

The fundamental rules of contract law, discussed in the Contract Law Unit, serve as a foundation for the principles found in the UCC, but the UCC is often more flexible. This flexibility is built into the UCC in order to accommodate the day-to-day reality of the world of sales. The daily operation of the commercial world requires a rapid response to the demands of customers and the needs of suppliers. Unlike real property contracts, which sometimes seem to be moving in slow motion, sales contracts for goods often occur at a moment's notice with little or no preparation. Unlike collective bargaining contracts that require that all the parties agree to each word in each clause of each part of the agreement, purchase orders

UCC 1-203 (see page 820)

UCC 1-205 (see page 820)

UCC 2-204(1)(2) (see page 823)

and invoices often have different terms hidden in the fine print, terms that might contradict one another, but which really do not matter to the actual completion of the contract. Unlike employment contracts, that will not begin until the parties know exactly what is expected of them, a shipment of goods might have to get started before all of the details of a deal are finalized. As we shall see, the UCC handles these realities in an effective and responsible way. In a very real sense, it is the almost universal adherence to the UCC that makes our commercial world work as well as it does. Some of these special rules for sales contracts are covered below.

Good Faith, Course of Dealings, and Usage of Trade

Under the UCC, every contract or duty imposes an obligation of good faith. In other words, the parties to a sales contract must act and deal fairly with each other. When the parties have dealt with each other before, their prior dealings give special meaning to sales contracts. Similarly, usage of trade, that is, any method of dealing that is commonly used in the particular field, is given special meaning. Unless the parties express otherwise, a course of dealings or usage of trade may be used to supplement or qualify the terms of a sales contract.

Formation of a Sales Contract

UCC 2-206(1)(a) (see page 823)

UCC 2-206(1)(b) (see page 823)

UCC 2-106(2) (see page 822)

Contracts may be formed either orally or in writing; however, a writing may be required by the Statute of Frauds for the contract to be enforceable.

A contract may be made in any manner that shows that the parties reached an agreement. It may be oral (with some exceptions) or in writing, or it may be established by the conduct of the parties. An enforceable sales contract may come about even if the exact moment of its making cannot be determined and even though some terms are not completely agreed upon.

Offer and Acceptance   To establish a contract for the sale of goods, unless otherwise indicated by the offeror or the circumstances, the offeree may accept the offer in any manner and by any medium that is reasonable. A contract for the sale of goods comes into existence when the acceptance is sent, as long as the method used to send it is reasonable. Unless the buyer indicates otherwise, an order or other offer to buy goods for prompt shipment may be accepted by either a prompt shipment or a prompt promise to ship. Under this rule, the goods that are shipped may be either conforming or nonconforming goods. Conforming goods are those that are in accordance with the obligations under the contract. Nonconforming goods are those that are not the same as those called for under the contract or that are in some way defective.

Firm Offer   The UCC holds merchants to a higher standard than nonmerchants. A merchant is a person who deals in goods of the kind sold in the ordinary course of business or who otherwise claims to have knowledge or skills peculiar to those goods. Although most rules under the UCC apply to both merchants and nonmerchants alike, some rules apply only to merchants. One such rule involves a firm offer.

No consideration is necessary when a merchant promises in writing to hold an offer

THE OPENING CASE *Revisited, Part 1*
Purchase Orders and the UCC: *XCEL Mold & Machine v. DeVault Indus.*, Round 2

In the Opening Case at the beginning of this chapter we learned that DeVault, a shotgun manufacturer, sent a purchase order (No. 27) to XCEL for 20 trigger-assembly units (although there was enough material to produce 60 units and although XCEL did manufacture 60 units), at a total cost of $1,080. XCEL received and accepted purchase order No. 27. Within a few days, however, Mr. Cain, the president of XCEL, phoned Mr. DeVault, the president of DeVault, and told him that XCEL could not manufacture the parts at that price. DeVault remembers the phone call differently, arguing that the two men did not talk price but, instead, discussed the quantity of the order, which was set at 20. However, DeVault did admit that Cain said he needed to produce more than 20 units to cover the set-up costs for that initial 20 units. DeVault told him not to worry because they would later figure out what a fair price would be. XCEL did, in fact, manufacture all 60 units and sent them to DeVault. Once DeVault received the units, they sent a check to XCEL for $1,080. The check included a notation that read, "pymt in full PO#27 60 pcs@18.00 ea." Someone at XCEL cashed the check and deposited the proceeds in an XCEL bank account. Nevertheless, Cain continued to claim that DeVault had not paid the full amount owed under the contract. He argued that the purchase order was not a valid offer and that the alterations made by phone actually provided the terms for a new contract under which DeVault had agreed to pay $9,000 for the trigger assembly units. The court, using the UCC, had no trouble determining that a contract existed under the terms of the purchase order. As noted above, unless the buyer indicates otherwise, an order or other *offer to buy goods* for *prompt shipment* may be accepted by either a prompt shipment or a prompt promise to ship. The court identified DeVault's purchase order as the *offer to buy goods* and the XCEL's *prompt shipment* of the trigger assemblies as the acceptance. Moreover, since there was no indication that the goods were nonconforming, there could be no successful challenge to the existence of the contract.

open for the sale or lease of goods. Known as a firm offer, the writing must be signed by the merchant, and the time period for holding the offer open may not exceed three months. This rule differs from the general rule of contract law which requires consideration in an option contract.

Open-Price Terms
Another change that the UCC has made is that a contract for the sale of goods may be established even though the price is not settled. Such open-price terms may occur when the parties intend to be bound by a contract but fail to mention the price or decide to set the price later. Under non-UCC law, no contract would come about because the terms are not definite. The UCC allows such a contract to come into existence. If the parties cannot agree on the price at the later date, the UCC requires that the price will be reasonable at the time the goods are delivered.

UCC 2-104(1) (see page 821)

UCC 2-205 (see page 823)

UCC 2-305(1) (see page 825)

Output and Requirements Terms
Sometimes, a seller will agree to sell "all the goods we manufacture" or "all the crops we produce" to a particular buyer. This agreement is known as an output contract. At other times, a buyer will agree to buy "all the oil we need to heat our building" (or some similar requirement) from a particular seller. This agreement is called a requirements contract. Such contracts often were not allowed under common law because the quantity of the goods to be bought or sold was not definite. The UCC allows output and requirements contracts for the sale of goods, as long as the parties deal in good faith and according to *reasonable expectations*.

UCC 2-306 (see page 825)

EXAMPLE 13-2: Unreasonable Expectations

Spencer Oil Co. agreed to sell to Lopaz Manufacturing Co. all the heating oil Lopaz would need during the next year. Spencer knew that Lopaz used about 5,000 gallons of oil each year. During the summer, Lopaz enlarged its building to an extent that it would require 25,000 gallons of heating oil during the next year. Spencer would not be bound to supply that amount of oil to Lopaz because it was far beyond the amount it expected to supply.

UCC 2-207 (see page 823)

Additional Terms in Acceptance

Under the general rules of contract law, an acceptance of an offer must be an absolute, unqualified, unconditional assent to the offer. If the acceptance differs in the slightest from the offer, it is considered a rejection. The UCC changes this rule somewhat. A contract for the sale of goods occurs even though the acceptance states terms that are additional to or different from those offered or agreed upon (unless acceptance is made conditional on assent to the additional terms). The additional terms are treated as proposals for additions to the contract if the parties are not both merchants. If both parties are merchants, the additional terms become part of the contract unless they materially alter it, the other party objects within a reasonable time, or the offer limits acceptance to its terms. This rule is intended to deal with two typical situations. The first is when an agreement has been reached either orally or by informal correspondence between the parties and is followed by one or both of the parties sending formal acknowledgments or memos that contain additional terms not discussed earlier. The second situation in which this rule applies is one in which a fax or letter intended to be the closing or confirmation of an agreement adds further minor suggestions or proposals, such as "ship by Thursday" or "rush."

EXAMPLE 13-3: Additional Terms in Acceptance

Cobb and Sons, Inc., reached an oral agreement with Valley Theatres, Inc., for the sale of an air conditioning system. Later, Cobb put the agreement in writing, signed it, and sent it to Valley for its signature. Valley signed the writing but added additional terms relative to the date of completion of the contract. Because both parties were merchants, the additional terms would become part of the contract unless Cobb objected to them within a reasonable time. Had one of them not been a merchant, the contract would have to come into existence without the additional terms, and the added terms would have been treated as proposals for additions to the contract.

EXAMPLE 13-4: Different Terms in Acceptance

Cal-Cut Pipe and Supply, Inc., offered in writing to sell used pipe to Southern Idaho Pipe and Steel Co., specifying a delivery date. Southern Idaho accepted by sending a check but changed the delivery date. Cal-Cut mailed a confirmation containing the original delivery date with the postscript, "We will work it out." The court held that there was a binding contract between them despite the conflicting delivery terms.

Modification Under the general rules of contract law, if the parties have already entered into a binding contract, a later agreement to change that contract needs consideration to be binding. The UCC has done away with this rule in contracts for the sale of goods. An agreement modifying a contract for the sale of goods needs no consideration to be binding. Any such modification may be oral unless the original agreement is in writing and provides that it may not be modified except by a signed writing. Any such clause in a form supplied by a merchant to a nonmerchant, however, must be separately signed (such as in the margin) by the nonmerchant to be effective.

UCC 2-209(1) (see page 823)

UCC 2-209(2) (see page 824)

quick quiz 13-2

1. Under the UCC, a contract comes into existence when the acceptance is sent if the method used is reasonable.   true | false

2. No consideration is necessary to establish a firm offer when a consumer promises in writing to hold an offer open for the sale or lease of goods.   true | false

3. Under the UCC, a contract for the sale of goods may be established even though the price is not settled.   true | false

13-3 The Form of a Sales Contract

The Uniform Commercial Code also outlines the rules that must be followed in relation to written sales contracts. This is critical because many contracts in the commercial world are written. Today many sales contracts are also made online which has required some fine tuning of the law. As we shall see, however, there are not quite as many changes in the law as one might expect because of the cyber-revolution in sales. This is a testimony to the law of sales which has adopted a set of rules so well adjusted to its subject matter that it can adapt to even the most radical upheavals in the economic world without missing a beat. Some of this flexibility is made possible by the members of the National Conference of Commissioners on Uniform State Laws who have been willing to accommodate the needs of those involved with the new technology

UCC 2-201(1) (see page 822)

The Written Sales Contract

As long as the value of the goods involved in a sales contract do not exceed $500, the contract can oral and still be enforceable. Once the price is $500 or more, however, the contract must be in writing to be enforceable. Also under the UCC, a lease of goods must be in writing if the total payments to be made under the lease are $1,000 or more.

UCC 2A-201(1) (see page 845)

Exceptions to the General Rule There are four exceptions to the requirement that contracts for the sale of goods for $500 or more and the lease of goods for $1,000 or more must be in writing to be enforceable. These exceptions involve the following:

UCC 2-201(2) (see page 822)

1. Oral contracts between merchants in which a confirmation has been received by one party and not objected to by the other party.

2. Specially manufactured goods.

3. Admissions in court.

4. Executed contracts.

THE OPENING CASE Revisited, Part II
Purchase Orders and the UCC: XCEL Mold & Machine v. DeVault Indus., Round 3

In the Opening Case at the beginning of this chapter, you will recall that Mr. DeVault, the president of DeVault Industries, sent a purchase order to XCEL Industries for 20 (later changed to 60) trigger assembly units for DeVault's shotguns at a total cost of $1,080. Within a few days, however, Mr. Cain, the president of XCEL, phoned DeVault and told him that XCEL could not manufacture the parts at that price. At some point in the conversation, DeVault told Cain not to worry because they would later figure out a "fair price" for the units. It seems that Cain believed that this "fair price" would be $9,000. XCEL manufactured the units and sent them to DeVault. Once DeVault received the units, someone in his office sent a check to XCEL for $1,080. The check included a notation that read, "pymt in full PO#27 60 pcs@18.00 ea." In the lawsuit

that followed, Cain argued that the oral modification of the written purchase order for the "fair price" of $9,000 should be upheld by the court. In contrast, DeVault argued that the real agreement was embodied in the purchase order that included the $1,080 price. The court had little problem coming to a conclusion. The court saw the purchase order as a written confirmation of the initial agreement. Under the UCC, after this written confirmation was sent by DeVault and received by XCEL, the only way to countermand that confirmation was to send a written objection. Cain sent no written objection. Instead, he called DeVault to complain about the price. Unfortunately for Cain, that phone conversation changed nothing and the contents of the original purchase order, including the $1,080 price, was seen as the real contract.

Oral Contracts between Merchants An exception to the general rule occurs when there is an oral agreement made between two merchants. If either merchant receives a written confirmation of the oral agreement from the other merchant within a reasonable time and does not object to it in writing within 10 days, the writing is sufficient under the UCC even though it has not been signed by the other party. It is important to understand that this exception applies only to merchants, not to ordinary consumers. The UCC defines a merchant as "a person who deals in goods of the kind" that are the subject matter of the contract at hand. It is also crucial to note that any objection to the original written confirmation must be in writing. If that is not the case then the court will honor the original written confirmation, no matter how loudly and how persuasively the other party objected to the agreement.

Specially Manufactured Goods Another exception occurs when goods are to be specially manufactured for the buyer and are not suitable for sale to others in the ordinary course of the seller's business. If the seller has made either a substantial beginning in manufacturing the goods or commitments to buy them, the oral agreement will be enforceable.

UCC 2-201(3) (see page 822)

EXAMPLE 13-5: Specially Manufactured Goods

Lifetime Windows, Inc., entered into an oral agreement to manufacture 15 oversized windows for Harold Cohen for the price of $6,000. The windows were such an odd shape that no one else would have a need for them. When the windows were manufactured, Cohen refused to take them on the ground that the oral contract was unenforceable. The court held against Cohen, however, and enforced the oral agreement. The windows were specially manufactured and were not suitable for sale to others.

Admissions in Court

If the party against whom enforcement is sought admits in court that an oral contract for the sale of goods was made, the contract will be enforceable. The contract is not enforceable under this exception, however, beyond the quantity of goods admitted.

UCC 2-201(3)(b) (see page 823)

Executed Contracts

When the parties carry out their agreement in a satisfactory manner, the law will not render the transaction unenforceable for want of an agreement in writing. Executed contracts (those that have been carried out) need not be in writing; the writing requirements apply only to contracts that are executory, that is, not yet performed. This provision means that contracts for goods that have been received and accepted need not be in writing. If there has been a part payment or a part delivery, the court will enforce only that portion of the agreement that has been performed.

UCC 2-201(3)(c) (see page 823)

Requirements of Writing

The writing that is required to satisfy the UCC must indicate that a contract for sale has been made between the parties and mention the quantity of goods being sold. It must also be signed by the party against whom enforcement is sought (the defendant). A writing is acceptable even though it omits or incorrectly states an agreed-upon term. However, a contract will not be enforceable beyond the quantity of goods shown in such writing. For that reason, it is necessary to put the quantity of goods to be bought and sold in the written agreement. Although a paper similar to the one shown in Figure 13-1 may be used, an informal note, memorandum, fax, or sales slip will satisfy the writing requirements.

UCC 2-201(1) (see page 822)

Signature Requirements

Under the UCC, a signature includes any symbol made with the intent to authenticate a writing. Thus, in addition to a handwritten signature, the courts have held various kinds of marks, including an X and a typewritten name, qualify as a signature as long as they were written with the intent to be signatures.

UCC 1-201(39) (see page 819)

Cyber-Sales Contracts

Statutes covering the problems associated with cyber-sales contracts have taken many forms over the past decade. One of the problems that required a solution was how to treat an online contract that required a written form. Two acts that have dealt with that problem are the E-Sign Act and the Uniform Electronic Transactions Act (UETA).

The E-Sign Act

Congress passed the E-Sign Act to address some of the difficulties associated with cyber-commerce, especially those that involve the recognition of electronic contracts and electronic signatures. In short, the statute declares that, as long as the parties to a cyber-contract have freely decided to conduct business electronically, the cyber-contract that results will have the same legal effect as a paper contract. The statute makes it clear that the parties to the contract must have some way to store and duplicate a cyber-record of the contract; otherwise, the cyber-record will not be legally sufficient under the act. It is also important to understand that some critical documents are not covered by the act. These include court records, eviction notices, health insurance cancellations, foreclosure notices, prenuptial contracts, and divorce papers. On the other hand, UCC contracts for the sale and lease of goods are included in the E-Sign Act.

The Uniform Electronic Transactions Act (UETA)

The Uniform Electronic Transactions Act (UETA), which was produced by the NCCUSL, is very similar to the E-Sign Act. The UETA promises the same legal parity between electronic records and paper records that is guaranteed by the E-Sign Act. However, the UETA applies only to

---

CONTRACT FOR SALE OF GOODS

AGREEMENT made by and between Ozzie Caldwell (Seller) and Geordi Hasenzahl (Buyer).

It has been agreed between the two parties that:

1. Seller agrees to sell, and Buyer agrees to buy, the following described property: one regulation-size pool table now located at the residence of Ozzie Caldwell, RD #1, Box 118, Ashberry, Kentucky.

2. Buyer agrees to pay Seller the total price of $850.00;

   payable as follows:

   $600.00 deposit herewith

   $250.00 balance by cash or certified check at time of transfer

3. Seller warrants he has full legal title to said property, authority to sell said property, and that said property shall be sold free and clear of all claims by other parties.

4. Said property is sold in "as is" condition. SELLER HEREBY EXCLUDES THE WARRANTY OF MERCHANTABILITY AND FITNESS FOR A PARTICULAR PURPOSE.

5. Parties agree to transfer title on February 7, 20 - -, at RD #1, Box 118, Ashberry, Kentucky, the address of the Seller.

6. This agreement shall be binding on the parties, their successors, assigns, and personal representatives.

7. This writing is intended to represent the entire agreement between the parties.

Signed under seal this nineteenth day of January, 20 - -.

_____
Buyer

_____
Seller

Figure 13-1   With four exceptions, contracts for the sale of goods of $500 or more must be in writing to be enforceable. A formal writing such as this is not necessary to satisfy the writing requirements of the UCC, however.

transactions that involve a business, governmental, or commercial situation. Still, the statute does ensure that, whenever a writing is required under the Statute of Frauds, any electronic signature that results from a cyber-transaction will fulfill that requirement. Under the UETA an electronic signature is defined as "an electronic sound, symbol, or process attached to or logically associated with a record and executed or adopted by a person with the intent to sign the record."

International Law

Interestingly, the trend in other countries is to eliminate the requirement that a sales contract be in writing. Great Britain, for example, after having such a requirement for 277 years, did away with it in 1954. International sales law also has no writing requirements for a sales contract; instead, a sales contract may be proved by any means.

International sales law, called the United Nations Convention on Contracts for the International Sale of Goods (CISG), applies only to sales between businesses whose places of business are in different countries that have adopted the law. It does not apply to sales of goods that are bought for personal, family, or household purposes. Also, the international law does not apply to auction sales; sales of stock, securities, negotiable instruments, or money; sales of ships or aircraft; or sales of electricity. The United States adopted the international sales law in 1988, and by 2007, 70 countries had made it part of their law.

The CISG is similar in many ways to the UCC. It also contains some differences. The CISG governs only the formation of a sales contract and the rights and duties of the parties that arise from it. The CISG is not concerned with the validity of a contract regarding, for example, the sale of illegal drugs, which would be governed by other laws. In addition, the CISG does not apply to the liability of the seller for death or personal injury caused by the goods to any person. In such a case, people would have to look to other laws for a remedy.

Auction Sales and Cyber-Auction Fraud

In an auction sale, the auctioneer presents goods for sale and invites the audience to make offers, which are known as bids. This process is similar to an invitation to trade. Bidders in the crowd respond with their offers. The highest bid (offer) is accepted by the auctioneer, usually by the drop of the gavel, together with the auctioneer's calling out the word *sold*. If, while the gavel is falling, a higher bid comes from those in the crowd, the auctioneer has two options: declare the goods sold or reopen the bidding.

An auction sale is "with reserve" unless the goods are expressly put up without reserve. In an *auction with reserve*, the auctioneer may withdraw the goods at any time before announcing completion of the sale if the highest bid is not high enough. In an *auction without reserve*, after the auctioneer calls for bids on an article or lot, that article or lot cannot be withdrawn unless no bid is made within a reasonable time. In either case, a bidder may retract a bid until the auctioneer's announcement of completion of the sale. A bidder's retraction does not revive any previous bid.

The practice of planting persons in the crowd for the purpose of raising bids by innocent purchasers is not allowed. Except in a forced sale, such as by a sheriff, if a seller (or the seller's agent) makes a bid at an auction without notifying other bidders, a buyer has two options. Under the UCC, a buyer may either avoid the sale or take the goods at the price of the last good-faith bid prior to the completion of the sale. In a forced sale, as when a sheriff auctions property on foreclosure or to satisfy a lien creditor, the owner is allowed to bid on the property being sold.

CISG Articles 1 and 2 (page 863)

CISG Articles 4 and 5 (page 863)

UCC 2-328(2) (see page 829)

UCC 2-328(3) (see page 830)

UCC 2-328(4) (see page 830)

Auctions are frequently used to dispose of unwanted property, satisfy judgments, and to liquidate foreclosed property.

288   Part Three   Sales and Consumer Protection

Auctions on the Internet provide the opportunity to buy and sell goods worldwide as well as locally. An Internet auction (AKA a cyber-auction and an e-auction) can be either person-to person or business-to-person. In person-to-person auctions, sellers offer items directly to consumers. The highest bidder must deal directly with the seller to arrange for payment and delivery. In contrast, operators of business-to-person auctions have control of the items being offered and take charge of payment and delivery of goods bought and sold.

Cyber-auction fraud is alarming. Sometimes sellers don't deliver the goods or deliver something less valuable than they advertised. At other times, sellers don't disclose everything about a product or fail to deliver it when they say they will. The Federal Trade Commission (FTC) provides helpful information about cyber-auctions in its free brochures and on its Web site.

quick quiz 13-3

1. A lease of goods must be in writing if the total payments to be made under the lease are $500 or more.   true | false

2. The E-Sign Act was developed, written, and passed by the U.S. Congress.   true | false

3. The practice of planting persons in the crowd for the purpose of raising bids by innocent purchasers is not allowed.   true | false

13-4 Title, Passage of Title, and Risk of Loss

It is good for us to remember that the law of sales was born within the context of the law merchant and that the law merchant was closely associated with the development of capitalism. Moreover, it is also critical to recall that one of the driving forces behind the growth of capitalism was the Roman Catholic Church which helped provide a rational and moral foundation for the principles and procedures that guided the activities of merchants in the making of their contracts. One of the things that the church insisted upon was that merchants never engage in fraud and always follow a good faith approach to contract development. The problem of determining title to goods, especially determining just when title legitimately passes from one party to another, is a problem that must be solved to ensure the basic fairness of the law of sales. After all, it is not only ownership that passes with title, but also the risk associated with that ownership. [See Harold J. Berman, *Law and Revolution: The Formation of the Western Legal Tradition,* (Cambridge: Harvard UP, 1983), pp. 336–341; and Rodney Stark, *The Victory of Reason: How Christianity Led to Freedom, Capitalism, and Western Science* (New York: Random House, 2005), p. xi. See also Henri Sée, *Modern Capitalism: Its Origin and Evolutions,* trans. Homer B. Vanderblue and Georges F. Doriot (New York: Adelphi Co. 1928), pp. 7–13.]

Valid Title, Void Title, and Voidable Title

Title, or valid title, is the right of ownership to goods. People who own goods have title to them. Sellers sometimes give a bill of sale to a buyer as evidence that the sale took place. A bill of sale is a written statement that provides evidence of the transfer of personal property from one person to another. It does not prove, however, that the seller had perfect title to the goods. The goods may have been stolen, obtained by fraud, purchased from a minor or an incompetent person, or entrusted with the seller by the true owner and sold by mistake. The question that arises in such cases is whether an innocent purchaser for value receives good title to the goods. The answer to this question depends on whether the seller's title to the goods was void or voidable and whether the goods had been entrusted to a merchant.

With the exception of voidable title, buyers of goods acquire whatever title their sellers had to the property. If a seller has void title (no title at all), a buyer of the goods obtains no title to them. The continued sale of the stolen property through several innocent buyers would not in any way defeat the real owner's right to the property. The rights of possession and title of successive buyers of stolen property can never be any better than the rights of the thief, who had no title at all. Of course, innocent purchasers may bring suit against the person from whom stolen goods were purchased for breach of warranty of title.

Anyone who obtains property as a result of another's fraud, misrepresentation, mutual mistake, undue influence, or duress holds only voidable title to the goods. Voidable title means title that may be voided if the injured party elects to do so. This kind of title is also received when goods are bought from a minor or a person who is mentally impaired. Some people refer to voidable title as title that is valid until voided. Anyone with voidable title to goods is able to transfer good title to others. According to the UCC, "A person with voidable title has power to transfer a good title to a good faith purchaser for value."

Entrusting Goods to a Merchant People often entrust goods that belong to them to merchants. For example, they leave their watches with jewelers and their vehicles with the body shop to be repaired. When this occurs, if the merchant sells the goods in the ordinary course of business to a third party who has no knowledge of the real owner's rights, the third party receives good title to them. The original owner who entrusted them to the merchant loses title to the goods altogether but may bring an action against the merchant for money damages caused by the loss. The reason for this rule of law is to give confidence to people who buy in the marketplace. People can be assured that they will receive good title to property (except stolen property) that they buy from a merchant who deals in goods of that kind in the ordinary course of business.

Passage of Title and Risk of Loss

It is not unusual for goods to be stolen, damaged, or destroyed while they are awaiting shipment, are being shipped, or are awaiting pickup after a sales contract has been entered. When something happens to the goods, it becomes necessary to determine who must suffer the loss: the seller or the buyer. The rules for determining the risk of loss are contained in the UCC. Except when goods are to be picked up by the buyer and in a few other cases, whoever has title to the goods bears the risk of loss. Goods must be identified in the contract before title can be transferred to the buyer. Identified goods are specific goods that have been selected as the subject matter of the contract. Once goods are identified, title passes to the buyer when the seller does whatever is required under the contract to deliver the goods. Contracts calling for the seller to deliver the goods are either *shipment contracts* or *destination contracts*.

Shipment Contracts A shipment contract is one in which the seller turns the goods over to a carrier for delivery to the buyer. The seller has no responsibility for seeing that the goods reach their destination. In a shipment contract, both title and risk of loss pass to the buyer when the goods are given to the carrier. Shipment contracts are often designated by the term *f.o.b. [the place of shipment]* (such as f.o.b. Chicago). The abbreviation f.o.b. means "free on board." When goods are sent f.o.b. the place of shipment, they will be delivered free to the place of shipment. The buyer must pay all shipping charges from there to the place of destination. The terms indicate that title to the goods and the risk of loss pass at the point of origin. Delivery to the carrier by the seller and acceptance by the

Table 13-2 Abbreviations

Abbreviation	Meaning
f.o.b. New York	Free on bard to New York (This would be a *shipment contract* if shipped from New York.)
f.o.b. Los Angeles	Free on board to Los Angeles (This would be a *destination contract* if shipped from New York.)
c.o.d.	Collect on delivery
c.i.f.	Cost of goods shipped, insurance, and freight
c.f.	Cost of goods shipped and freight
f.a.s.	Free alongside vessel or at a dock

carrier complete the transfer of both title and risk of loss. Thus, the buyer accepts full responsibility during the transit of the goods. (See Table 13-2.)

Destination Contracts
If the contract requires the seller to deliver goods to a destination, it is called a destination contract. Both title and risk of loss pass to the buyer when the seller tenders the goods at the place of destination. Tender means to offer to turn the goods over to the buyer. Destination contracts are often designated by f.o.b. the place of destination (such as f.o.b. Tampa); goods shipped under such terms belong to the seller until they have been delivered to the destination shown on the contract. Similarly, the risk of loss remains with the seller until the goods are tendered at destination. Tender at destination requires that the goods arrive at the place named in the contract, the buyer is given notice of their arrival, and a reasonable time is allowed for the buyer to pick up the goods from the carrier.

When terms of shipment do not specify shipping point or destination, it is assumed to be a shipment contract. Adding the term c.o.d. (collect on delivery) instructs the carrier to

THE OPENING CASE *Revisited, Part III*
Purchase Orders and the UCC: *XCEL Mold & Machine v. DeVault Indus.*, Round 4

In the Opening Case at the beginning of this chapter we learned that DeVault, a shotgun manufacturer, sent a purchase order to XCEL for trigger-assembly units, at a total cost of $1,080. XCEL received and accepted purchase order No. 27. Within a few days, however, Mr. Cain, the president of XCEL, phoned Mr. DeVault, the president of DeVault, and told him that XCEL could not manufacture the parts at that price. DeVault told him not to worry because they would later figure out what a fair price would be. XCEL did, in fact, manufacture all 60 units and sent them to DeVault. If the order had been a shipment contract, the seller, XCEL, would have turned the trigger-assembly units over to a carrier for delivery to DeVault. The seller, XCEL, would then have no responsibility for seeing that the trigger-assemblies reached DeVault. In a shipment contract, both title and risk of loss pass to the buyer when the goods are given to the carrier. In contrast, if the order had been a destinations contract, then both title and risk of loss would have passed to the buyer, DeVault, when XCEL delivered the trigger-assemblies to DeVault's place of business, which was, of course, the final destination of the shipment.

Table 13-3 Passage of Title and Risk of Loss

Terms of Contract	Title Passes	Risk of Loss Passes
Shipment contract	When goods are delivered to carrier	When goods are delivered to carrier
Destination contract	When goods are tendered at destination	When goods are tendered at destination
No delivery required	When contract is made	*Merchant seller:* When buyer receives goods; *Nonmerchant seller:* When seller tenders goods to buyer
Document of title	When document of title is given to buyer	When document of title is given to buyer
Agreement of the parties	At time and place agreed upon	At time and place agreed upon

retain possession until the carrier has collected the cost of the goods. The term c.i.f. (cost, insurance, and freight) instructs the carrier to collect all charges and fees in one lump sum. This sum includes the cost of goods shipped, insurance, and freight charges to the point of destination. The term c.f. means that insurance is not included in the sum. The term f.a.s. vessel (free alongside vessel) at a named port requires sellers to deliver the goods, at their own risk, alongside the vessel or at a dock designated by the buyer.

No Delivery Required When the contract calls for the buyer to pick up the goods, title passes to the buyer when the contract is made. Risk of loss, however, passes at different times depending on whether the seller is a merchant. If the seller is a merchant, the risk of loss passes when the buyer receives the goods. If the seller is not a merchant, the risk of loss passes to the buyer when the seller tenders the goods to the buyer (See Table 13-3).

Fungible Goods The UCC defines fungible goods as "goods of which any unit is, by nature or usage of trade, the equivalent of any like unit." Wheat, flour, sugar, and liquids of various kinds are examples of fungible goods. They have no important characteristics that identify them as coming from a particular supplier, and they are usually sold by weight or measure. Title to fungible goods may pass without the necessity of separating goods sold from the bulk. Under the UCC, "an undivided share of an identified bulk of fungible goods is sufficiently identified to be sold although the quantity of the bulk is not determined."

EXAMPLE 13-6: Fungible Goods

Logan Trucking Co. owned a large fuel storage tank that was partially filled with diesel fuel. The exact quantity of fuel in the tank was not known. The company was going out of business. Interstate Trucking Co. contracted to buy half of the fuel in the tank, and Union Trucking Co. contracted to buy the other half. Both buyers agreed to send their own trucks to pick up the fuel. Title passed to the buyers when the contract was made even though the exact quantity of each sale was unknown and neither buyer had taken a share of the fuel from the entire lot.

Documents of Title Sometimes, when people buy goods, they receive a document of title to the goods rather than the goods themselves. They then give the document of title to the warehouse or carrier that is holding the goods and receive possession of them. A

document of title is a paper giving the person who possesses it the right to receive the goods named in the document. Bills of lading and warehouse receipts are examples of documents of title. However, an automobile title certificate has not been given the legal status of a document of title, as the term is used in the UCC. When a document of title is used in a sales transaction, both title and risk of loss pass to the buyer when the document is delivered to the buyer.

Agreement of the Parties   The parties may, if they wish, enter into an agreement setting forth the time that title and risk of loss pass from the seller to the buyer. With one exception, title and risk of loss will pass at the time and place agreed upon. If the agreement allows the seller to retain title after the goods are shipped, title will pass to the buyer at the time of shipment, regardless of the agreement, and the seller will have a security interest in the goods rather than title. A security interest gives the seller a right to have the property sold in the event that the buyer fails to pay money owed to the seller.

EXAMPLE 13-7: Security Interest

Raymond agreed to sell Glover her John Deere tractor for $12,000. The agreement called for Glover to pay $3,000 down and the balance in monthly installments for two years. Under the terms of the agreement, title to the tractor would not pass to Glover until the $12,000 was paid in full. Because Raymond delivered the tractor to Glover on the day that the agreement was signed, title passed to Glover at that time, regardless of the terms in the contract. The effect of those terms was to give Raymond a security interest in the tractor for the balance of the money owed to her.

Revesting of Title in Seller   Buyers, after entering into sales contracts, sometimes refuse to accept the goods that are delivered or are otherwise made available to them. In all such cases, title to the goods returns to the seller. This reversion is true whether or not the buyer's rejection of the goods is justified. Similarly, title to goods returns to the seller when the buyer accepts the goods and then for a justifiable reason decides to revoke the acceptance. A justifiable reason for revoking an acceptance would be the discovery of a defect in the goods after having inspected them. When the seller sends goods to the buyer that do not meet the contract requirements and are therefore unacceptable, the risk of loss remains with the seller. For situations in which the buyer accepts the goods but later discovers some defect and rightfully revokes the acceptance, the passage of risk of loss depends on whether the buyer is insured. If the buyer has insurance, that insurance will cover the loss. If there is no insurance, the risk of loss remains with the seller from the beginning. When the buyer breaches the contract with regard to goods that have been the contract, the seller may, to the extent of having no insurance coverage, treat the risk of loss as resting with the buyer.

International Sales   The rules governing international sales are given in the United Nations Convention on Contracts for the International Sale of Goods (CISG). The international law does not address questions dealing with the passage of title because the laws of each country vary considerably. Instead, it leaves such questions to be decided by domestic law. This determination exists because third parties are usually involved in claiming title for themselves, and the laws of each country vary considerably. In contrast, the rules governing the passage of risk of loss are addressed in international law and are quite similar to those found in the UCC. The risk of loss passes to the buyer when the goods are handed over to the first carrier for transmission to the buyer unless the seller agrees to hand them over at a particular place. In that case, the risk of loss passes to the buyer at that time. Sometimes, goods are sold when they are in transit. When this kind of sale occurs (with some exceptions), the risk of loss passes to the buyer when the contract is made. In all other situations, the risk of loss, in general, passes when the buyer takes over the goods. The CISG has several exceptions in the contracts that it covers. It does not apply to goods bought for personal, household, or family use, or to contracts that mainly supply services. Nor does it cover the liability of the seller for death or injury caused by the goods sold.

quick quiz 13-4

1. *Void title* means title that may be voided if the injured party elects to do so.　　　　true | false

2. *Voidable title* means no title at all.　　　　true | false

3. Fungible goods must be separated from the bulk before title to them can pass to a buyer.　　　　true | false

13-5 Sales, Returns, and Insurable Interest

Because of competition and a desire to give satisfaction, goods are sometimes sold with the understanding that they may be returned even though they conform to the contract. Determination of ownership and risk of loss while such goods are in the buyer's possession is sometimes necessary. Sales with the right of return are of two kinds: sale on approval and sale or return.

Sale on Approval

A sale that allows goods to be returned even though they conform to the contract is called a sale on approval when the goods are primarily for the buyer's use. When goods are sold on approval, they remain the property of the seller until the buyer's approval has been expressed. The approval may be indicated by the oral or written consent of the buyer or by the buyer's act of retaining the goods for more than a reasonable time. Using the goods in a reasonable and expected manner on a trial basis does not imply an acceptance. Grossly careless use and a failure to inform the seller of the buyer's intent to return, however, could constitute an acceptance. Goods held by the buyer on approval are not subject to the claims of the buyer's creditors until the buyer decides to accept them. In addition, the risk of loss remains with the seller until the buyer has accepted the goods.

Sale or Return

A sale that allows goods to be returned even though they conform to the contract is called a sale or return when the goods are delivered primarily for resale. When such a sale occurs, the buyer takes title to the goods with the right to revest (reinstate) title in the seller after a specified period or reasonable time. In such cases, the buyer must accept all of the obligations of ownership while retaining possession of the goods. Goods held on sale or return are subject to the claims of the buyer's creditors. While in the buyer's possession, the goods must be cared for and used in a reasonable manner, anticipating their possible return in the same condition as when received, after making allowance for ordinary wear and tear. Also, the goods must be returned at the buyer's risk and expense.

EXAMPLE 13-8: Consignment Contract

Butcher owned a gift shop in which she sold other people's goods on consignment. Hanson delivered a dozen handmade braided rugs to Butcher with the understanding that she would be paid for any that were sold. Any rugs that did not sell after three months would be returned to Hanson. This agreement was a sale or return because the rugs were delivered primarily for resale. Butcher would be required to pay Hanson for any rugs that were damaged, lost, or stolen while in Butcher's possession.

Insurable Interest

People must have an insurable interest in property to be able to place insurance on it. An insurable interest is the financial interest that an insured party has in the insured property. Buyers may place insurance on goods the moment a contract is made and the goods are identified to the contract. At this point, buyers receive an insurable interest in the goods they buy. They obtain an insurable interest even though they might later reject or return the goods to the seller. Notwithstanding the buyer's right to insure the goods, sellers retain an insurable interest in the goods as long as they have title to them.

EXAMPLE 13-9: Dual Insurable Interests

While shopping on vacation in an antique store in Connecticut, Maniff, who lived in Nevada, came upon a Native American totem pole she liked. She decided to buy the totem pole on the condition that the antique dealer would ship it f.o.b. Winnemucca, Nevada. The dealer agreed. Maniff received an insurable interest in the totem pole when it was identified to the contract. At the same time, the dealer retained an insurable interest in it until it was tendered at its destination in Winnemucca. Both Maniff and the antique dealer could insure the totem pole.

---

quick quiz 13-5

1. Goods that are sold on approval are subject to the claims of the buyer's creditors until the buyer decides to accept them.   true | false

2. Goods that are sold on approval remain the property of the seller until the buyer's approval has been expressed.   true | false

3. Goods that are sold on sale or return are not subject to the claims of the buyer's creditors.   true | false

Summary

13.1 The Uniform Commercial Code (UCC), which contains the law of sales, has been adopted, either in whole or in part, by every state in the United States. Article 2 of the UCC applies whenever people buy or sell goods. It applies to transactions between private parties as well as transactions by businesspeople or merchants. Article 2A applies to leases of goods.

13.2 The following rules that are different from general contract law apply to sales contracts:

- A sales contract may be made in any manner that shows that the parties reached an agreement.
- Unless otherwise specified, an offeree may accept an offer in any way that is reasonable, including a prompt shipment of the goods.
- A written promise by a merchant to hold an offer open needs no consideration to be binding.
- A sales contract may be made even though the price is not settled.
- Output and requirements contracts are allowed in sales contracts as long as the parties deal in good faith and according to reasonable expectations.
- A sales contract may result even when an offeree adds different or additional terms from those offered or agreed upon.
- No consideration is necessary to modify a contract for the sale of goods.

13.3 With four exceptions, a contract for the sale of goods for $500 or more and the lease of goods for $1,000 or more must be in writing. The exceptions are oral contracts between merchants in which a confirma-

tion has been received by one party and not objected to by the other party, specially manufactured goods, admissions in court, and executed contracts. The United Nations Convention on Contracts for the International Sale of Goods (CISG) applies to sales between U.S. businesses and foreign businesses.

In an auction sale, offers are made by the people in the audience. The acceptance takes place when the auctioneer bangs the gavel.

13.4 Title to goods can be either valid, void, or voidable. When a merchant sells goods without authority, the purchaser obtains good title. With few exceptions, such as when goods are to be picked up by the buyer, whoever has title to the goods bears the risk of loss. Once goods are identified, title passes to the buyer when the seller does whatever is required under the contract to deliver the goods. Title to fungible goods may pass without the need to separate goods sold from bulk. With a document of title, title and risk of loss pass to the buyer when the document is delivered. Title returns to the seller when the buyer refuses the goods. The risk of loss remains with the seller when the goods do not meet the requirements.

13.5 Goods sold on approval remain the property of the seller until the buyer approves. The seller retains the risk of loss. In a sale or return, the buyer takes title to the goods but is given the right to return the goods to the seller at a later time. The buyer must care for the goods in a reasonable manner and suffer the risk. Buyers have an insurable interest in goods the moment a contract is made and the goods are identified to the contract.

Key Terms

Questions for Review and Discussion

1. What are goods and what is a sale?
2. When does Article 2 of the UCC apply to contractual relationship?
3. What are the UCC rules that relate to written contracts?
4. What are the two laws that relate to cyber-sales contracts and what do they accomplish?
5. What is the difference between an auction with reserve with an auction without reserve?

6. What are valid title, void title, and voidable title?
7. When does the title to goods pass from seller to buyer?
8. When must the buyer and when must the seller bear the risk of loss?
9. What is the difference between a sale on approval and a sale or return?
10. What is an insurable interest?

Cases for Analysis

1. Brenda Brandt had a medical device implanted as part of her treatment for a serious medical condition. A charge for the device was included in the hospital bill. Later, the device was recalled by its manufacturer as substandard. Brandt had suffered serious complications, and the device was removed. She brought suit against the hospital for, among other things, breach of warranty under the Uniform Commercial Code. Was the purchase of the medical device from the hospital covered under the Uniform Commercial Code? Explain. *Brandt v. Boston Scientific Corporation*, Docket No. 93982, Illinois Supreme Court (IL).

2. Alberto Parreira, a lobsterman, contracted in writing to sell Sam Adams 1,000 pounds of fresh lobsters at a particular price during the following season. A few months later, when lobsters became plentiful and the price went down, Adams tried to get out of the contract. He argued that the contract was not enforceable because the lobsters had not yet been caught when the contract was made. Do you agree with Adams? Why or why not?

3. Harnois entered into an oral contract with Neverson to lease a compact computer and a printer for three months for $600. In an attempt to rescind the contract, Harnois claimed that the contract was unenforceable because it was not in writing. Do you agree with Harnois? Why or why not?

4. Carolina Transformer Co., Inc., brought suit against Anderson for several thousand dollars owed it for the purchase of transformers. Anderson testified in court that he had orally negotiated the contract and reached a final agreement with Carolina for the purchase of the transformers. Anderson argued, however, that he was not responsible because under the UCC, a contract for the sale of goods of $500 or more is not enforceable unless it is in writing. Do you agree with Anderson? *Carolina Transformer Co. v. Anderson*, 341 So.2d 1327 (MS).

5. Representatives of a fish marketing association (AIFMA) and a fish company (NEFCO) met at Bristol Bay, Alaska, to negotiate a marketing agreement for the forthcoming fishing season. At this meeting, NEFCO's agent, Gage, signed an agreement that contained the price that was to be paid for the fish and other details about the transaction. It omitted the quantity of fish to be purchased. Later, when suit was brought on the agreement, NEFCO argued that it was unenforceable because the written agreement failed to mention the quantity. Do you agree with NEFCO? Explain. *Alaska Indus Fish Mktg. Assoc. v. New England Fish Co.*, 548 P.2d 348 (WA).

6. Wheel Sports Center entered into a sales contract agreeing to deliver a motorcycle to Ramos for the price of $893. Ramos paid the full price for the motorcycle and immediately had it insured and

registered in his name. However, before it was delivered to Ramos, the motorcycle was stolen from Wheel Sports Center. Who must suffer the loss, Wheel Sports Center or Ramos? Why? *Ramos v. Wheel Sports Center,* 409 N.Y.S.2d 505 (NY).

7. Fanning, who was 17 years old, sold her bicycle to Gerard, an adult, for $75. The next day, Gerard advertised the bicycle for sale in the classified section of a local newspaper and sold it for $150. The person who bought the bicycle was unaware that it had belonged to Fanning. When Fanning discovered what Gerard had done, she attempted to get the bicycle back from the person who bought it, claiming that Gerard had voidable title to the bicycle. Does Fanning have the legal right to the return of the bicycle? Why or why not?

8. Harold Marcus entered into a contract with Corrigan's Yacht Yard & Marine Sales, Inc., to trade in his 34-foot Silverton power boat toward a later model Mainship boat. He delivered his Silverton boat to the yacht yard at the time of the contract in November. The new boat was not to be delivered until the following April. The yacht yard sold the Silverton boat to William Heiselman soon after receiving it. When the yacht yard was unable to deliver the Mainship boat to Marcus in April, Marcus

took back his Silverton boat. Who had title to the boat, Marcus or Heiselman? Explain. *Heiselman v. Marcus,* 488 N.Y.S.2d 571 (NY).

9. Eberhard Manufacturing Company sold goods to Brown Industrial Sales Company without agreeing on who would bear the risk of loss. The contract contained no f.o.b. terms. Eberhard placed the goods on board a common carrier with instructions to deliver them to Brown. The goods were lost in transit. Who suffered the loss, Eberhard or Brown? Why? *Eberhard Mfg. Co. v. Brown,* 232 N.W.2d 378 (MI).

10. Henry Heide, Inc., received a warehouse receipt for 3,200 100-pound bags of sugar that it bought from Olavarria. The corporation withdrew 800 bags of the sugar from the warehouse (where thousands of pounds were stored), but when it returned for the balance, it discovered that the warehouse was padlocked and empty. Some 200,000 pounds of sugar had mysteriously disappeared from it. Henry Heide, Inc., carried insurance for such a loss, but its insurance company refused to pay, claiming that the corporation had no insurable interest in the sugar. Do you agree with the insurance company? Why or why not? *Henry Heide, Inc., v. Atlantic Mut. Ins. Co.,* 363 N.Y.S.2d 515 (NY).

quick quiz Answers

13.1	13.2	13.3	13.4	13.5
1. F	1. T	1. F	1. F	1. F
2. T	2. F	2. T	2. F	2. T
3. T	3. T	3. T	3. F	3. F

Chapter 14

Sales Contracts Rights, Duties, Breach, and Warranties

THE OPENING CASE The Case of the Disappearing Delivery: Ninth Street East, Ltd. v. Harrison

Any contract that involves clothing, even avant-garde clothing, is covered by the Uniform Commercial Code (UCC). Keep in mind, as you read this case that the commissioners who wrote the UCC did their best to protect all the parties involved in a contract, even those who might not deserve that protection. In this case, the plaintiff is a Los Angeles clothing manufacturer and the defendant is a retailer doing business in Westport, Connecticut, as a clothing store named The Rage. The manufacturer received an order from The Rage for a shipment of clothing that amounted to $2,216.00. The clothing was packaged carefully and then turned over to a reputable and dependable shipper named the Denver-Chicago Shipping Company (Denver). Denver gave a bill of lading to the manufacturer and the manufacturer sent along four separate invoices to The Rage. The invoices stated explicitly that the shipment was "F.O.B. Los Angeles," that the shipper was Denver-Chicago, and that the buyer bore the risk of loss. Moreover, the bill of lading stated quite clearly that all shipping charges would be paid by The Rage. At some point along the way between LA and Westport, exactly where is never made clear, Denver handed the shipment off to another trucking firm, this one named the Old Colony Transportation Company of South Dartmouth, Massachusetts. When

the Old Colony truck arrived at The Rage, the driver refused to deliver the goods inside of the store, preferring, instead, to deliver them outside the premises. When the store manager refused to accept the eight cartons of clothing unless they ended up inside the store, the trucker drove off, still in possession of the shipment. The clothing was never seen again. The owner of The Rage sent an immediate letter of protest to the manufacturer, which filed a claim against Denver, which Denver refused to honor. Meanwhile, back in Connecticut, the owner of The Rage continued to demand that the missing shipment be delivered inside the store. Yet, whenever the manufacturer tried to contact the owner, he was unavailable. When the manufacturer finally sued, the owner of The Rage argued that he could not possibly be liable for goods he never received. Instead, he claims that the manufacturer is responsible for the loss of the shipment because he chose an unreliable shipper who apparently ran off with the goods. In turn, the manufacturer argues that, since the risk of loss passed to the retailer when the shipment was delivered to the trucker, and since the retailer refused to accept a shipment that was quite literally on his doorstep, he must pay for the eight cartons of clothing whether he actually received them or not. As you read the chapter, see if you can solve the Case if the Disappearing Delivery or, as they say in Massachusetts, the Mystery of the Missing Merchandise. (See *Ninth Street East, Ltd. v. Harrison,* 259 A.2d 772, 5 Conn.Cir.Ct. 597 (Connecticut Circuit Court, First Circuit).)

Opening Case Questions

1. In the case of *Ninth Street East, Ltd. v. Harrison,* what does the notation "F.O.B. Los Angeles" mean?

2. At what point did the risk of loss pass to the buyer? Explain.

3. The bill of lading in this case noted that the shipment was to be "collect." How does this notation figure into the passage of risk? Explain.

4. Did the truck driver's refusal to deliver the cartons inside the store amount to a refusal to tender performance? Why or why not?

5. Is the shipper's refusal to honor the manufacturer's claim significant in this case? Why or why not?

Learning Objectives

1. Describe what is meant by tender of performance.
2. Outline the rights and duties of sellers and buyers in a sales contract.
3. Explain the doctrine of anticipatory breach.
4. Discuss the seller's and the buyer's remedies in case of a breach.
5. Define the term *statute of limitations.*
6. Describe the three ways in which an express warranty may be created.
7. State the requirements of the Magnuson-Moss Warranty Act.
8. Differentiate among the implied warranties of fitness for a particular purpose, merchantability, and usage of trade.
9. Explain the meaning of a warranty of title.
10. Recognize the ways in which warranties may be excluded.

14-1 Rights and Duties of the Parties

The duties of the parties to a sales contract are simple and straightforward: The seller is obligated to turn the goods over to the buyer, and the buyer is obligated to accept and pay for the goods. In addition, all parties must act in good faith, which means that they must act honestly. The court need not enforce a contract or part of a contract that it finds to be unconscionable. An unconscionable contract is one that gives an unfair advantage to one of the parties. Unequal bargaining power, the absence of a meaningful choice by one party, and unreasonably one-sided terms, when put together, indicate unconscionability. When disputes arise between parties who have dealt together in the past, the court often looks to their past dealings to give meaning to the disputed transaction.

When interpreting the meaning of a contract, the court may also consider any usage of trade, that is, any particular methods of doing business, that are commonly used in that field and the way that the parties have dealt with one another in the past. Although terms that are expressly stated in a contract will usually control the contract's meaning, the parties' past dealings and usage of trade are often considered to supplement or qualify the express terms. Moreover, the UCC establishes a series of rights and duties that are key elements within all sales contracts. Most of these rights and duties are based on common sense and the practicality of commercial world. Others have been uniquely created by the NCUSL to ensure stability in the world of sales. These rights and duties include the tender

UCC 1-205 (see page 820)

of performance, the buyer's rights and duties of upon delivery of improper goods, and the seller's right to cure improper tender.

Tender of Performance

When the seller offers to turn the goods over to the buyer and when the buyer offers to pay for them, tender of performance occurs. It is the offering by the parties to do what they have agreed to do under the terms of the contract. Tender is necessary to test the party's ability and willingness to perform his or her part of the bargain. The seller must make tender of delivery, and the buyer must make tender of payment. If one party fails to make tender and the other breaches the contract, the one not making tender cannot bring suit. To be in a position to bring suit on a sales contract, the seller of goods must make tender of delivery, that is, offer to turn the goods over to the buyer. Failure to make this offer is an excuse for buyers not to perform their part of the bargain.

UCC 2-507 (see page 833)

UCC 2-503(1)(b) (see page 832)

UCC 2-504 (see page 832)

UCC 2-503(4) (see page 832)

Making Proper Tender To make proper tender, the seller must put and hold conforming goods at the buyer's disposition during a reasonable hour of the day. Sometimes goods are in the possession of a warehouse and are to be turned over to the buyer without being moved. When this situation occurs, tender requires that the seller either tender a document of title covering the goods or obtain an acknowledgment by the warehouse of the buyer's right to their possession. In a shipment contract, the seller must put the goods in

THE OPENING CASE Revisited, Part I
The Case of the Disappearing Delivery: Ninth Street East, Ltd. v. Harrison, Round 2

In the Opening Case at the beginning of the chapter, the plaintiff, a Los Angeles clothing manufacturer, received an order from The Rage, a retailer in Connecticut. The clothing was packaged carefully and then released to a reliable and responsible shipping company known as the Denver-Chicago Shipping Company (Denver). Denver gave a *bill of lading* to the manufacturer and the manufacturer sent along *four separate invoices* to The Rage. The invoices stated explicitly that the shipment was *"F.O.B. Los Angeles,"* that the shipper was Denver-Chicago, and that the buyer bore the risk of loss. Moreover, the *bill of lading* stated quite clearly that the order was to be "collect," which meant that all shipping charges would be paid by The Rage. The plaintiff in this case, made all the proper moves and obtained or produced all of the proper paper work as required by the UCC. Therefore, the contract was clearly a *shipping contract*. Moreover, Connecticut court had no difficulty coming to this conclusion. The court simply referred to the official comments of the NCCUSL in explaining UCC

2-503, which note that all transactions carried out under the authority of the UCC are presumed to be shipment contracts unless proven otherwise. This meant that the risk of loss passed to buyer the moment that the clothing was delivered to the trucking company in Los Angeles. More specifically, the court referred to UCC 2-504, which states that it is the responsibility of the seller to "(a) put the goods in the possession of such a carrier and make such a contract for their transportation as may be reasonable having regard to the nature of the goods and other circumstances of the case; and (b) obtain and promptly deliver or tender in due form any document necessary to enable the buyer to obtain possession of the goods or otherwise required by the agreement or by usage of trade; and (c) promptly notify the buyer of the shipment." The seller had done all of this indicating that, if the buyer had any legal case at all, it would have to be levied against the trucking company, which had control of the goods, not the seller who relinquished control in Los Angeles.

the possession of a carrier and contract with that carrier for their transportation. Any necessary documents must be sent to the buyer, who must be promptly notified of the shipment.

Tender of Payment by Buyer

Although the seller is obligated to deliver the goods to the buyer, this obligation stands on the condition that the buyer make tender of payment, unless otherwise agreed. Tender of payment means offering to turn the necessary money over to the seller. Such tender may be made by any means or in any manner that is commonly used in the ordinary course of business. The seller has the right to demand payment in legal tender but must give the buyer a reasonable time to obtain it. Legal tender is money that may be offered legally in satisfaction of a debt and that must be accepted by a creditor when offered. Payment by check is conditional under the UCC. If the check clears, the debt is discharged. If the check is dishonored, the debt is revived. When a contract requires payment before inspection, as when goods are shipped c.o.d., the buyer must pay for them first, even if they turn out to be defective when they are inspected. Of course, if the defect is obvious, the buyer would not have to accept or pay for the goods. Payment by the buyer before inspecting the goods does not constitute an acceptance of them. Upon discovering a defect and notifying the seller, the buyer may use any of the remedies that are mentioned later in the chapter against the seller for breach of contract.

UCC 2-511(1) (see page 833)

UCC 2-511(3) (see page 833)

UCC 2-512 (see page 833)

Buyer's Rights and Duties

Except when goods are shipped c.o.d. or when the contract provides for payment against a document of title, the buyer has the right to inspect the goods before accepting or paying for them. The inspection may take place after the goods arrive at their destination. Expenses of inspection must be borne by the buyer but may be recovered from the seller if the goods do not conform to the contract and are rejected by the buyer. Goods conform to a contract when they are in accordance with the obligations under the contract. When defective goods or goods not of the kind specified in the contract are delivered, the buyer may elect to reject them all, accept them all, or accept any commercial unit or units and reject the rest. A commercial unit is a single whole for the purpose of sale, the division of which impairs its character or value on the market. For example, a commercial unit or a set of articles (e.g., suite of furniture, assortment of sizes). It may be a quantity (e.g., bale, gross, carload) or any other unit treated may be a single article (e.g., a machine) in the marketplace as a single whole item.

UCC 2-513 (see page 834)

UCC 2-106(2) (see page 822)

Failure of the buyer to inspect goods upon delivery results in an acceptance of the goods, even if nonconforming.

Rejection of Goods by the Buyer

A rejection occurs when a buyer refuses to accept delivery of goods tendered. A rejection must be done within a reasonable time after delivery or tender to the buyer. After a rejection, the buyer may not claim ownership of the goods. In addition, the buyer must notify the seller of the particular defect in the goods so as to give the seller an opportunity to correct the defect. If the goods are in the buyer's possession, the buyer must hold them with reasonable care long enough for the seller to remove them.

UCC 2-601 (see page 834)

CISG Article 38 (see page 886)

UCC 2-602 (see page 834)

If the seller gives no instructions within a reasonable time after being notified of the rejection, the buyer may store the goods for the seller, reship them to the seller, or resell them for the seller. In all cases, the buyer is entitled to be reimbursed for expenses. A special duty comes into existence when a buyer who is a merchant rejects goods. Merchant buyers have a duty after the rejection of goods in their possession or control to follow any reasonable instructions received from the seller with respect to the goods. If there are no such instructions, they must make reasonable efforts to sell the goods for the seller if they

THE OPENING CASE *Revisited, Part II*
The Case of the Disappearing Delivery: *Ninth Street East,*
Ltd. v. Harrison, Round 3

In the Opening Case at the beginning of the chapter, the Los Angeles clothing manufacturer appears to have done everything by the book. After receiving an order from The Rage in Connecticut, the manufacturer packaged the clothing in eight cartons and turned those cartons over to a reputable shipper named the Denver-Chicago Shipping Company (Denver). Denver then transferred a bill of lading to the manufacturer and the manufacturer then sent four separate invoices to The Rage. The invoices stated explicitly that the shipment was "F.O.B. Los Angeles," that the shipper was Denver-Chicago, and that the buyer bore the risk of loss. In addition, the bill of lading stated quite clearly that all shipping charges would be paid by The Rage. Later, Denver handed the shipment off to Old Colony Transportation which attempted to deliver the goods to The Rage. At that point, the buyer rejected the ship-

ment because the driver refused to deliver the goods inside of the store. The trucker then drove off, apparently still in possession of the shipment. At first blush, this may seem like a rejection under UCC 2-602 and 2-603, permitting the buyer to walk away from the contract with no liability. This interpretation, however, would be a misreading of the statute. In order for a rejection to be legally correct, the buyer must first notify the seller of the rejection [UCC 2-602 (1)] and then follow the reasonable instructions of the seller in relation to the goods [UCC 603 (1)]. The buyer in this case did neither. First, the buyer continued to demand that the missing shipment be delivered to The Rage, thus negating any claim under UCC 2-602 (1) and (2) the buyer refused to respond to the seller's attempts to contact the store with instructions about the goods, thus violating his duties under UCC 2-603 (1).

UCC 2-604 (see page 835)

are perishable or threaten to decline speedily in value. Merchants who sell rejected goods are entitled to be reimbursed either by the seller or from the proceeds of the sale for reasonable expenses of caring for and selling the goods. They are also entitled to such commission as is usual in the trade or, if none, a reasonable sum not exceeding 10 percent of the proceeds of the sale. A buyer who is not a merchant has no other obligation regarding goods that are rightfully rejected.

UCC 2-603(1) (see page 834)

UCC 2-603(2) (see page 834)

UCC 2-606 (see page 835)

Acceptance of Goods by the Buyer
Once goods have been accepted, they cannot be rejected. Acceptance of goods takes place when the buyer, after a reasonable opportunity to inspect them, does any of the following:

- Signifies to the seller that the goods are conforming, that is, that they are in accordance with the obligations under the contract.
- Signifies to the seller a willingness to take them even though they are not conforming.
- Fails to reject them.
- Performs any act that is inconsistent with the seller's ownership.

UCC 2-607(3) (see page 835)

When the buyer accepts goods and later discovers something wrong with them, the buyer must notify the seller within a reasonable time after the discovery. The failure to give proper notice will prevent the buyer from having recourse against the seller.

UCC 2-608 (see page 835)

Revocation of Acceptance
If a buyer has accepted goods on the assumption that their nonconformity would be corrected by the seller and the seller does not do so, the buyer may revoke the acceptance. This revocation must be made within a reasonable time

after the buyer discovers the nonconformity. A revocation of an acceptance is not effective until the buyer notifies the seller of it. Buyers who revoke an acceptance have the same rights and duties with regard to the goods involved as if they had rejected them.

Seller's Rights and Duties

Sellers may sometimes cure an improper tender or delivery of goods; that is, they may correct the defect that caused the goods to be rejected by the buyer. When the time for performance has not yet expired, the seller has the right to cure the defect and make a proper tender within the contract time. If the time for performance has expired, the seller is allowed to have an additional amount of time to substitute a conforming tender if the seller has reasonable grounds to believe that the goods that were delivered were acceptable. In all cases, sellers have a duty to notify buyers that they are going to cure the improper tender or delivery.

UCC 2-508 (see page 833)

EXAMPLE 14-1: Cure of Improper Tender

Caravan Motel ordered 10 dozen bath towels from samples shown by Fleming Towel Company's representative. The representative made a mistake in writing up the order. As a result, the towels that were delivered were inferior to those shown to Caravan at the time the order was given. Caravan rejected them. Because the Fleming Towel Company had reasonable grounds to believe that Caravan Motel would accept the towels that were delivered, it was allowed additional time to substitute correct towels for the ones that were delivered. When it learned of the rejection, Fleming Towel Company was required to notify the motel that it intended to cure the nonconforming delivery.

The seller does not have the right to cure improper tender when a buyer accepts nonconforming goods, even though the buyer may later sue the seller for breach of contract. The seller has this right only when the buyer either rejects the goods tendered or revokes an acceptance of the goods.

quick quiz 14-1

1. According to the law of sales contracts, all parties must act in good faith, which means they must act honestly.   true | false

2. Tender of performance is the offering by the parties to do what they have agreed to do under the terms of the contract.   true | false

3. Buyers have no right to inspect goods before paying for them when they are shipped c.o.d.   true | false

14-2 Breach of Contract

Breach of contract occurs when one of the parties fails to do what was agreed upon in the contract. When this happens, the other party to the contract has specific remedies available under the UCC. All parties must attempt to mitigate the damages, that is, to keep them as low as possible.

Anticipatory Breach

UCC 2-610 (see page 836)

Sometimes, one of the parties will notify the other party before the time for performance that he or she is not going to conform. This notification is known as *anticipatory breach*. It is a breach committed before there is a present duty to perform the contract. Under older contractual law, the injured party in such a case had to wait until the actual time for performance before bringing suit or taking some other action. It was necessary to wait for the actual time for performance to know for sure that the other party was indeed not going to perform. Under the UCC, when either party repudiates the contract before the time for performance, the injured party may take action immediately if waiting would be unjust or cause a material inconvenience. Any of the remedies for breach of contract are available to the aggrieved party, in addition to the right to suspend his or her own performance.

EXAMPLE 14-2: Anticipatory Breach

The Westwell Construction Company ordered 1000 steel I-beams to be made to order from the Anaconda Steel Corporation for use in a building that Westwell was going to begin building in six months. Anaconda Steel agreed to deliver the I-beams on or before that date. Two months before the delivery date, Anaconda Steel notified Westwell that it would not be able to fill the order. Westwell could treat the contract as having been breached and use any of the buyer's remedies that are available to him under the UCC.

Seller's Remedies

UCC 2-703(a) (see page 837)

When a buyer breaches a sales contract, the seller may select from a number of remedies. Table 14-1 lists six remedies that sellers may employ when the buyer breaches. These remedies include withholding the delivery of goods, stopping the delivery of the goods, reselling the goods, recovering damages, suing for the price of the goods, and simply canceling the contract. Of the six remedies, the last one, cancelling the contract, is the simplest and the most pain-free solution. However, from a financial perspective, it is often the most damaging. On the other hand, the most difficult and time-consuming is initiating a lawsuit. However, if it is handled properly, a lawsuit can be the fairest and the most effective remedy available in the law today.

Table 14-1   Seller's Remedies When the Buyer Breaches
1. Withhold delivery of any goods not yet delivered.
2. If the buyer is insolvent, stop delivery of any goods that are still in the possession of a carrier.
3. Resell any goods that have been rightfully withheld, and then sue the buyer for the difference between the agreed price and the resale price.
4. If the goods cannot be resold, sue the buyer for the difference between the agreed price and the market price.
5. Sue the buyer for the price of any goods that were accepted by the buyer.
6. Cancel the contract.

Withhold or Stop the Delivery of Goods

If the goods have not been delivered, the seller has a right to keep them upon learning of the buyer's breach. If, after shipping the goods, the seller discovers that the buyer is insolvent (unable to pay debts), the seller may have the delivery stopped. This right is known as stoppage in transit and is permitted after goods have been shipped but before they have reached their destination. The seller must give information to the carrier (the transportation company) to satisfy the latter that the buyer is insolvent. In addition, the seller must accept responsibility for any damage suffered by the carrier for not completing the shipment. If the insolvency information is incorrect, both the seller and the carrier could be sued for damages. The seller may also stop delivery of a carload, truckload, planeload, or larger shipments of express or freight when the buyer repudiates or fails to make a payment that is due before delivery or otherwise breaches the contract. If the seller has issued a document of title, the seller can stop delivery only by surrendering the document to the carrier. If the buyer has received the document, delivery of the goods cannot be stopped in transit.

UCC 2-705 (see page 838)

Resell the Goods

The seller may resell the goods or the undelivered balance of them. In the case of unfinished manufactured goods, a seller may either complete the manufacture and resell the finished goods or cease manufacture and resell the unfinished goods for scrap or salvage value. In such cases, the seller must use reasonable commercial judgment to avoid losses. After the sale, the injured party may sue the other for the difference between what the property brought on resale and the price the buyer had agreed to pay in the contract. Resale may be a public or private sale. If it is a private sale, the seller must give the buyer reasonable notice of its intention to resell the goods. If it is a public sale, it must be made at a place that is normally used for public sales, if such a place is available. In addition, if the goods are perishable or threaten to decline in value speedily, the seller must give the buyer reasonable notice of the time and place of resale. A purchaser who buys in good faith at a resale takes the goods free of any rights of the original buyer. Furthermore, the seller is not accountable to the buyer for any profit made on the resale. The seller who chooses to do so may buy the goods at resale.

UCC 2-706(1) (see page 838)

UCC 2-704(2) (see page 838)

UCC 2-706(4)(b) (see page 838)

UCC 2-706(4)(d) (see page 838)

Damages

The seller may retain the merchandise and sue the buyer for either the difference between the contract price and the market price at the time the buyer breached the agreement or the profit (including overhead) that the seller would have made had the contract been performed. In either case, the seller is also entitled to *incidental damages*. These damages are reasonable expenses that indirectly result from the breach, such as expenses incurred in stopping delivery of goods, transporting goods, and caring for goods after the buyer's breach.

UCC 2-708 (see page 839)

UCC 2-710 (see page 839)

Sue for Price

The seller may sue for the price of any goods that the buyer has accepted. Similarly, upon the buyer's breach, the seller may bring suit for the price of goods that cannot be resold at a reasonable price. In addition, the seller may sue the buyer for the price of any *lost* or damaged goods after the risk of their loss has passed to the buyer. In the commercial setting this remedy is sanctioned by the Uniform Commercial Code in UCC 2-709 (1) (a). The seller who sues the buyer for the price must hold for the buyer any goods that are under the seller's control. The goods may be sold, however, at any time resale is possible before the collection of a judgment in the case. The net proceeds of any resale must be credited to the buyer. Any goods that are not resold become the property of the buyer if the buyer pays for them as a result of a court judgment.

UCC 2-709 (see page 839)

Cancel the Contract

The seller can cancel the contract. This cancellation occurs when the seller ends the contract because the other party breached. When cancellation takes place in this manner, the seller may use any of the remedies mentioned for breach of contract.

UCC 2-106 (see page 822)

THE OPENING CASE Revisited, Part III
The Case of the Disappearing Delivery: *Ninth Street East, Ltd. v. Harrison*, Round 4

Recall in the Opening Case at the beginning of the chapter that, when the Old Colony truck arrived at The Rage with eight cartons of clothing, the driver refused to deliver the goods inside of the store, preferring, instead, to leave them outside the premises. When the store manager refused to accept the eight cartons of clothing unless they were placed inside the store, the trucker drove off, still holding the shipment. The shipment was never seen again. The owner of The Rage protested this sorry state of affairs to the manufacturer, which filed a claim against Denver, which Denver did not honor. Back in Connecticut, the owner of The Rage continued to demand that the missing shipment be delivered inside the store. Yet, whenever the manufacturer tried to contact him, he was unavailable. When the manufacturer sued, the owner of The Rage argued that he could not possibly be liable for goods he never received. Instead, he claims that the manufacturer is responsible for the loss of the shipment because he chose an unreliable shipper who apparently absconded with the goods into the night. In turn, the manufacturer argues that, since the risk of loss passed to the retailer when the shipment was delivered to the trucker, and since the retailer refused to accept a shipment that was quite literally on his doorstep, he must pay for the eight cartons of clothing whether he actually received them or not. The court agreed with the manufacturer. To prove its point, the court referred directly to UCC 2-709 which says quite clearly that, "(1) When the buyer fails to pay the price as it becomes due the seller may recover . . . the price (a) * * * of conforming goods lost or damaged within a commercially reasonable time after the risk of their loss has passed to the buyer." (See UCC Section 2- 709 *Ninth Street East, Ltd. v. Harrison*, 259 A.2d 772, 5 Conn.Cir.Ct. 597 (Connecticut Circuit Court, First Circuit).)

Buyer's Remedies

UCC 2-711 (see page 839)

UCC 2-712 (see page 839)

When a seller breaches a sales contract, the buyer may select from a number of remedies. Table 14-2 lists six remedies that buyers may use whenever the seller breaches the sales contract. The first two remedies are relatively clear and straightforward. The buyer either [1] tells the seller that the deal is off or [2] demands a repayment of any money that has already been handed over to the seller as a down payment or some other type of monetary guarantee of performance. If the seller cooperates, there is no need to go any further.

Table 14-2 Buyer's Remedies When the Seller Breaches

1. Cancel the contract.

2. Sue the seller for the return of any money that has been paid.

3. Cover the sale—that is, buy similar goods from someone else and sue the seller for the difference between the agreed price and the cost of the purchase.

4. Sue the seller for the difference between the agreed price and the market price at the time the buyer learned of the breach.

5. If nonconforming goods have been accepted, notify the seller that they do not conform to the contract. Then, if no adjustment is made, sue the seller either for breach of contract or for breach of warranty.

6. When goods are unique or rare, sue for specific performance.

However, if the seller refuses to comply, the buyer has several additional options available. These include cover the sale, sue for breach, keep the goods and seek an adjustment, or, in some rare circumstances, sue for specific performance. Of these four remedies, the last one, suing for specific performance is the most difficult and the least applicable remedy because it can only be used when the subject matter of the sales contract is something unique, such as an original work of art, or when the subject is very rare, as with an antique, a family heirloom, or a vintage automobile. On the other hand, from a financial perspective, it is often a very rewarding process for buyers because, if they are successful, they receive exactly what they bargained for in the original contract.

Cover the Sale or Sue for Breach The buyer may cover the sale, that is, buy similar goods from someone else. The buyer may then sue the seller for the difference between the agreed pice and the cost of the purchase. Cover must be made without unreasonable delay. In the alternative, when a seller breaches a contract by not delivering the goods, the buyer may sue for damages if any were suffered. The measure of damages is the difference between the price that the parties agreed upon and the price of the same goods in the marketplace on the date the buyer learned of the breach. In addition, the buyer may sue for incidental and consequential damages. Damages for breach of contract may be liquidated, that is, agreed upon by the parties when they first enter into the contract. Liquidated damages will be allowed by the court if they are reasonable.

EXAMPLE 14-3: Cover of a Sales Contract

Flamme Bros. contracted to deliver a specific quantity of corn to Farmers' Union Co-op Co., a cooperative grain elevator. When Flamme Bros. failed to deliver the corn, Farmers' Union bought corn from its members over a two-week period. The court held that this purchase was cover of the contract without unreasonable delay. Farmers' Union recovered the difference between the agreed price of the corn from Flamme Bros. and the price it paid to the farmers for the corn it bought. In the alternative, the Farmer's Union could have refrained from purchasing the grain from other suppliers and simply brought a lawsuit against Flamme Brothers for damages. The damages would be measured by the difference between the price that the parties agreed upon and the price of corn in the marketplace on the date the Farmer's Union learned of the breach. In addition, the Farmer's Union may sue for incidental and consequential damages.

Keep Goods and Seek Adjustment When improper goods are delivered, the buyer may keep them and ask the seller for an adjustment. If no adjustment is made, the buyer may sue the seller for either breach of contract or breach of warranty, whichever applies. The amount of the suit would be the difference between the value of the goods contracted for and the value of the goods received. Warranties are discussed in later in this chapter.

EXAMPLE 14-4: Swimsuit Adjustment

The Jacobs Brothers Department chain of Omaha ordered 40 dozen swimsuits from Illumination Encore, Ltd, a clothing manufacturer in Fort Worth. The suits that were delivered were totally different from the samples shown by Illumination's sales rep. Because the Jacobs Brothers needed swimsuits for its spring trade show, Kenneth Jacobs, the CEO of the department chain, decided to keep them. If no adjustment is made by the manufacturer, Illumination Encore, Jacobs can sue the manufacturer for damages (including loss of profits) that were suffered because of the breach of the express warranty that the goods would be the same as the sample.

UCC 2-713 (see page 840)

UCC 2-715 (see page 840)

UCC 2-718(1) (see page 840)

UCC 2-714(2) (see page 840)

UCC 2-716(1) (see page 840)

Sue for Specific Performance

When the goods are unique or rare, the buyer may ask the court to order the seller to do what he or she agreed to do under the contract terms. This request is known as an action for specific performance of the contract. A decree of specific performance, if granted by the court, would require the seller to deliver to the buyer the goods described in the sales agreement. This type of action is permitted only when an award of money will not give the buyer sufficient relief. Contracts for *objets d'art*, rare gems, antiques, and goods described as one-of-a-kind come within the scope of this type of action. Under the UCC, the decree of specific performance may include the payment of the price, damages, or other relief as the court may deem just. Buyers have a right of replevin for goods that have been identified to the contract if, after a reasonable effort, they are unable to buy the goods elsewhere. A writ of replevin is a court action that allows a person entitled to goods to recover them from someone who has them wrongfully.

The Commercial Docket

Commercial cases have become so numerous recently that a few states have taken the extraordinary step of establishing a separate court docket dedicated exclusively to commercial cases. Those commentators who support establishing a commercial docket argue that commercial lawsuits can be handled more effectively if they are assigned to judges who have been trained to manage such cases. For example, the state of Ohio recently inaugurated a Commercial Docket Pilot Project. The goal of the project is to create a docket for commercial lawsuits that will be handled by judges and mediators who have received special education sessions devoted exclusively to commercial law. To implement the system, the chief justice of the Ohio Supreme Court chose five trial courts to lead the way by establishing a commercial docket within their jurisdictions. The chief justice then appointed several commercial docket judges who were assigned to handle every case that fit within the commercial docket in their court. The plan limits the commercial docket to cases that involve disputes among two or more businesses, although the court also handles a long list of similar lawsuits including such things as the formation or dissolution of a business, the rights and duties of business partners, and so on. Once a commercial docket is ready to begin operation, the commercial judge chooses a cadre of mediators, referred to in Ohio as special masters, who are trained to handle commercial lawsuits. The special masters are the first line of defense on the commercial docket. They handle cases and make rulings that are then passed onto the commercial judge for evaluation and approval. The commercial judge can uphold, reject, reverse, or resubmit the case to the special master. (See Ohio Sup. R. Temp. Rules 1.01 to 1.11).

UCC 2-716(3) (see page 840)

UCC 2-725 (see page 842)

Self-Evident Truths: The Science Court v. The Commercial Docket

As noted earlier, a planned court system that is similar to the Ohio commercial docket is the proposed science court. The science court would act as a forum for cases involving scientific and technological disputes. Like commercial docket judges, the science court judges would be trained to deal exclusively with cases of a scientific and technological nature. The science court would focus on disputes involving genetic engineering; nuclear energy research; cyber-contract law; energy law; cloning; engineering, architectural, and technological projects; medical treatments; medical research; environmental law; birth control; health care wills; health care power of attorney disputes; abortion law disputes; intellectual property problems; surrogate parenting and so on. The plan is to use specially trained judges with scientific and technological backgrounds who will be equipped to handle the complexities of today's science related cases. The science court and the commercial court look good on paper, but would they actually work in the real world?

Self-Evident Questions

1. What happens when a sales contract involves the purchase of scientific equipment? Would such a case fall under the jurisdiction of the commercial docket court or the science court?

2. What would we do with a case involving a surrogate parenting contract? Is that a job for the science court or the commercial docket? Explain.

3. Would commercial judges begin to lean toward the best interests of merchants rather than the consumer? Explain.

4. Would science court judges begin to lean toward the best interests of scientists and engineers rather than the public? Explain.

5. There is also the question of equal protection of the law. Does the commercial court violate equal protection by giving special treatment to business people? Explain. Does the science court violate equal protection by giving special treatment to scientists and engineers? Why or why not?

Statute of Limitations

Nearly all lawsuits have a time limit within which a lawsuit must be brought. If the time limit is exceeded, the action is forever barred. In general, an action for breach of a sales contract must be brought within four years after the date of the breach. The parties may, if they wish to do so, provide for a shorter time period, not less than one year, in their sales agreement. They may not, however, agree to a period longer than four years.

LO5

CISG Article 49 (see page 888)

CISG Articles 61–64 (see page 889)

CISG Articles 74–77 (see page 891)

CISG Articles 79 (see page 891)

CISG Articles 81 (see page 891)

CISG Articles 85–88 (see page 892)

quick quiz 14-2

1. If the goods have not been delivered, the seller has a right to keep them upon learning of the buyer's breach.   true | false

2. The seller may sue the buyer for the price of any *lost* or damaged goods after the risk of their loss has passed to the buyer.   true | false

3. When the goods are unique or rare, the buyer may ask the court to order the seller to do what he or she agreed to do under the contract terms.   true | false

14-3 Warranty Protection

Up until now, in this chapter we have focused on the actual sales agreement itself. We have looked at what constitutes performance, what constitutes nonperformance, and what happens when the seller does not deliver the goods, the buyer does not pay for the goods, or the trucking company loses the goods. Now we switch focus. Instead of looking at a contract that has not been performed, we will look at contracts that have been performed—sort of. Have you ever purchased an item that turned out to be damaged or broken when you opened the box? Have you ever paid for something that you wanted for a particular purpose, only to find that it would not do the job? Has a salesperson ever made a statement or a promise about a product that did not come true? Have you ever found an impurity or a foreign substance in food that you bought in a store or ate in a restaurant? The UCC gives you protection in all these situations under its law of warranties. A warranty is another name for a guarantee. Warranties come in all shapes and sizes. Still, in one way or another, all warranties fall into one of three categories: express warranties, implied warranties, and warranties of title.

Express Warranties

An express warranty is an oral or written statement, promise, or other representation about the quality of a product. Express warranties arise in three different ways: by a statement of fact or promise, by a description of the goods, or by a sample or model. In states that have adopted Article 2A of the UCC, express warranties arise when goods are leased in exactly the same way that they arise when goods are sold.

Statement of Fact or Promise
Whenever a seller of goods makes a statement of fact to a buyer about the goods, that seller has created an express warranty. The seller's statement is treated legally as a guarantee that the goods will be as "they were stated to be." *This guarantee exists whether the seller is a merchant or not.* If the goods are not as they were stated to be, the seller has breached an express warranty. An express warranty also occurs when a seller makes a promise about the goods to a buyer. The promise must relate to the goods and be part of the transaction. Manufacturers often include express warranties with the products they sell. They are usually found inside the package containing the product and are sometimes referred to as *guarantees*. Formal words such as *warranty* or *guarantee* do not have to be used to create an express warranty. A seller may not intend to make a warranty, but if the language used by the seller is a statement of fact or a promise about the goods and is part of the transaction, an express warranty is created. Advertisements often contain statements and promises about goods that are express warranties.

Advertising Express Warranties
The Federal Trade Commission has established specific rules for advertising express warranties on goods that are sold in interstate commerce:

- An advertisement stating that a product is warranted must tell you how to get a copy of the warranty before you buy the product.
- Advertisers who use expressions such as "Satisfaction Guaranteed," "Money-Back Guarantee," and "Free Trial Offer" must refund the full purchase price of their product at the purchaser's request. Any conditions, such as those limiting the return of the product, must be stated in the ad.
- Advertisers who warrant products for a lifetime must fully explain the terms of their promises, such as "Good for as long as you own the car."

Warranties are based on statements of fact. Therefore, the opinions of salespersons and their exaggerated and persuasive statements do not create express warranties. Courts have long indulged the temptation of salespersons to use sales puffery to extol their merchandise beyond the point of fact. Buyers must use common sense to recognize the difference between a salesperson's statements of fact from statements that are opinion or puffery. Such statements as "this is the best Hi Def screen on the market" or "this GPS system is a great buy" are examples of sales talk or puffery. They are not express warranties. Such statements as "this car has never been in an accident" or "this desk is made of mahogany' are factual statements that do create an express warranty.

Descriptions, Samples, and Models
Any description of the goods that is made part of the basis of the bargain creates an express warranty that the goods will be as described. It is a common practice of salespeople to show samples of their products to

prospective buyers. When a sample or model becomes part of the basis of the bargain, an express warranty is created. The seller warrants that the goods that will be delivered are the same as the sample or model.

Magnuson-Moss Warranty Act   The federal Magnuson-Moss Warranty Act is designed to prevent deceptive warranty practices and provide consumers with more information about warranties that are made on products they buy. The act applies only when written warranties are made voluntarily for purchases of consumer products. These products are defined as tangible personal property normally used for personal, family, or household purposes. Because it is a federal law, the act affects only warranties on products that are sold in interstate commerce. Under the act, when a written warranty is given to a consumer on goods costing more than $10, the warranty must disclose whether it is a full or a limited warranty. When goods cost more than $15, the written warranty must be made available before the consumer decides to buy the product. The writing must express the terms and conditions of the warranty in simple and readily understood language.

A full warranty is one in which a defective product will be repaired without charge within a reasonable time after a complaint has been made about it. If it cannot be repaired within a reasonable time, the consumer may have either a replacement of the product or a refund of the purchase price. The consumer will not have to do anything unreasonable to get warranty service, such as ship a heavy product to the factory. A full warranty applies to anyone who owns the product during the warranty period, not only the original buyer. A full warranty must also state its duration, for example, a "full one-year warranty."

EXAMPLE 14-5: Full Warranty

Kienitz bought an electric range manufactured by a well-known firm. Attached to the box containing the range were several papers, one of which read as follows: "Full one-year warranty. If your range fails because of a manufacturing defect within one year from the date of original purchase, we will repair the product without charge to you. Parts and service labor are included. Service will be provided in your home in the forty-eight contiguous states, the state of Hawaii, or in the District of Columbia." This paper was a full warranty.

A limited warranty is any written warranty that does not meet all of the requirements for a full warranty. The consumer is not given the absolute, free-of-charge repair or replacement of a defective product, as in the full warranty. Something less than a complete remedy is given to the consumer. Examples of limited warranties are those that cover only parts, not labor; allow only pro rata (divided proportionately) refund or credit in the case of a defect rather than a full refund; require the buyer to return a heavy product to the store for service; or cover only the first purchaser.

Implied Warranties

Under the UCC, an implied warranty is a warranty that is imposed by law rather than by statements, descriptions, or samples given by the seller. It arises independently and outside the contract. The law annexes it, by implication, into the contract that the parties have made. Implied warranties are designed to promote high standards in business and to discourage harsh dealings. There are three types of implied warranties: the implied warranty of merchantability, the implied warranty of fitness for a particular purpose, and the implied warranty that is derived from a course of dealing or usage of trade.

Merchantability One of the most beneficial warranties, from the point of view of a buyer, is the implied warranty of merchantability. This warranty provides that, unless excluded in one of the ways discussed, whenever a merchant sells goods, the merchant warrants that the goods are merchantable, that is, they are reasonably fit for the purpose for which they are sold. For example, merchantability means that a lawnmower will cut grass, a sailboat will not sink, an automatic dishwasher will wash dishes, and so on. This warranty is given when the seller is a merchant with respect to goods of that kind. It is given by manufacturers, wholesalers, and retailers whenever they sell goods to give assurance that products sold by them are fit for the purpose for which the goods are to be used. The warranty of merchantability is not given by someone who is not a merchant. To be merchantable, goods must at least pass without objection in the trade under the contract description; if fungible goods, be of fair average quality; be fit for the ordinary purposes for which such goods are used; be of the same kind, quality, and quantity; be adequately contained, packaged, and labeled as the agreement may require; and be in conformance with any promises or statements of fact made on the container or label. A claim for breach of warranty of merchantability can be made only when a defect exists at the time the goods are purchased.

EXAMPLE 14-6: No Defect at Time of Purchase

Haven Hills Farm purchased a truck tire from Sears, Roebuck. On a trip from Mississippi to Alabama, the tire blew out, causing the truck to turn on its side, destroying 11,862 dozen eggs. At the time of the blowout, the tire was four and one-half months old and had been driven 30,000 miles. Haven Hills claimed that Sears was liable for breach of the implied warranty of merchantability. It argued that Sears sold the tire in a defective condition. In finding in favor of Sears, Roebuck, the court held that there was no evidence of a defect in the tire at the time it left the control of the manufacturer or seller.

Fitness for a Particular Purpose Sometimes buyers will have the seller select goods for them rather than select them themselves. They rely on the seller's knowledge and experience to choose the product after telling the seller of the particular use they have for the goods. This arrangement creates an implied warranty of fitness for a particular purpose. When the buyer relies on the seller's skill and judgment to select the goods, the seller implicitly warrants that the goods will be fit for the purpose for which they are to be used.

Usage of Trade Other implied warranties may arise from the ways in which the parties have dealt in the past or by usage of trade. For example, when a person sells a pedigreed dog, there is an implied warranty that the seller will provide pedigree papers to demonstrate the conformity of the animal to the contract. The reason this implied warranty arises is that providing such papers has become a well-established custom or practice of the trade.

Warranty of Title

Whenever goods are sold, either by a merchant or a private party, the seller warrants that the title being conveyed is good and that the transfer is rightful. This warranty is known as the warranty of title. It includes an implied promise that the goods will be delivered free of any liens (claims of others) about which the buyer has no knowledge. When anyone buys goods that turn out to be stolen, the rightful owner will be entitled to the return of those goods. The innocent purchaser may sue the seller for breach of warranty of title.

When the buyer is aware that the person selling the goods does not personally claim title to them, the warranty of title is not made by the seller. Such is the case, for example, in sheriff's sales and sales by personal representatives of estates. To recover money damages for breach of warranty, buyers of defective goods must notify the seller of the defect within a reasonable time either after the discovery or after the defect should have been discovered. Failure to do so will prevent them from recovering damages for breach of warranty.

Warranty Exclusion

To exclude the implied warranty of merchantability in states that allow it, the word *merchantability* must be used in the disclaimer. If the exclusion is in writing, it must be in large, bold type so that it is conspicuous. To exclude the implied warranty of fitness for a particular purpose, the exclusion must be in writing and also be conspicuous. A common practice in the sale of used cars, lawnmowers, electrical appliances, and similar merchandise is for the seller to stipulate that the goods are being sold as is. The use of expressions such as *as is, with all faults,* and others is another way to exclude implied warranties. However, those words do not exclude express warranties or the warranty of title. Implied warranties may also be excluded under the UCC by having buyers examine the goods. When buyers have examined the goods, the sample, or the model as fully as they desire (or have refused to examine them when given the opportunity), there is no implied warranty as to defects that an examination would have revealed. Under the Magnuson-Moss Warranty Act, any clause purporting to exclude or limit consequential damages for breach of warranty must appear conspicuously on the face of the warranty. Consequential damages are losses that do not flow directly and immediately from an act but only from some of the consequences or results of the act.

EXAMPLE 14-7: Consequential Damages

Souci bought a freezer made by a reputable manufacturer. The freezer carried a full one-year warranty. The following sentence appeared in boldface type on the face of the warranty: "In no event shall this company be liable for consequential damages." Shortly after buying the freezer, Souci filled it with $1,500 worth of meat. Several days later, the freezer stopped working owing to a defect in its manufacture. Under the warranty, the company would have to repair or replace the freezer, but it would not be responsible for the loss of the meat. This loss would be considered consequential damage, which the company had effectively disclaimed.

Privity Not Required

Under earlier law, warranties extended only to the actual buyer of the product, that is, the one with whom the seller had dealt or was in privity of contract. People who were injured by defective products had no remedy against the seller for breach of warranty unless they themselves had purchased the goods. Thus, if children were injured by foreign objects in food that had been bought by their parents, the children could not recover for injuries because they had not purchased the goods. The UCC has abolished the requirement of privity. Instead, it provides three alternatives from which a state may choose. In all of the alternatives, warranties extend to people who would normally be expected to use the goods as well as to those who actually buy them.

Alternative A A seller's warranty, whether express or implied, extends to any natural person who is in the family or household of his buyer or who is a guest in his home if it is reasonable to expect that such person may use, consume, or be affected by the goods and who is injured in person by breach of the warranty. A seller may not exclude or limit the operation of this section.

Alternative B A seller's warranty, whether express or implied, extends to any natural person who may reasonably be expected to use, consume, or be affected by the goods and who is injured in person by breach of the warranty. A seller may not exclude or limit the operation of this section.

Alternative C A seller's warranty, whether express or implied, extends to any person who may reasonably be expected to use, consume, or be affected by the goods and who is injured by breach of the warranty. A seller may not exclude or limit the operation of this section with respect to injury to the person of an individual to whom the warranty extends.

quick quiz 14-3

1. An express warranty is an oral or written statement, promise, or other representation about the quality of a product. true | false

2. An implied warranty is a warranty that is imposed by law rather than by statements, descriptions, or samples given by the seller. true | false

3. A warranty of title mans that the seller warrants that the title for the goods being sold is good and that the transfer is rightful. true | false

Summary

14.1 Sellers and buyers must follow the terms of their contract and act in good faith. Tender of performance is necessary to test the other party's ability and willingness to perform. Tender of delivery requires the seller to make conforming goods available to the buyer at a reasonable hour of the day. Tender of payment may be made by any means that is commonly used in the ordinary course of business. Except when goods are shipped c.o.d. or when the contract provides for payment against a document of title, the buyer has the right to inspect goods before accepting or paying for them. When improper goods are delivered, the buyer may elect to reject all of them, accept all of them, or accept any commercial unit or units and reject the rest. Sellers may cure defects or nonconformities that caused the goods to be rejected by the buyer.

14.2 When a buyer breaches a sales contract, the seller may withhold delivery of any goods not yet delivered, stop goods that are in transit, resell the goods or the undelivered balance of them, retain the goods and bring suit for damages, bring suit for the price of any goods that the buyer has accepted, or cancel the contract. When a seller breaches a sales contract, the buyer may cancel the contract and recover any money paid out, buy similar goods from someone else and sue the seller for the difference in price, sue the seller for damages for nondelivery, keep the goods and deduct the cost of damages from any price still due, or sue for specific performance if the goods are rare or unique.

14.3 Express warranties arise by a statement of fact or promise, by a description of the goods, and by a sample or model. Other warranties may arise from the ways in which parties have dealt in the past. When goods are sold, either by a merchant or a private party, the seller warrants that the title is good and that there are no liens on the goods. Except when express warranties are made, sellers may exclude the warranties of merchantability and fitness for a particular purpose. Such an exclusion must be in writing and conspicuous. The words *as is* and *with all faults* serve to disclaim implied warranties but not the warranty of title. Warranties extend to people who would normally be expected to use the goods as well as to those who actually buy them.

Key Terms

carrier, 305
commercial unit, 302
consequential damages, 313
consumer products, 311
cover, 307
cure, 303
express warranty, 310
full warranty, 311
good faith, 299

implied warranty, 311
insolvent, 305
legal tender, 301
limited warranty, 311
merchant, 312
merchantable goods, 312
sales puffery, 310
shipment contract, 300
stoppage in transit, 305

tender of delivery, 300
tender of payment, 301
tender of performance, 300
unconscionable contract, 299
warranty of fitness for a
particular purpose, 312
warranty of merchantability, 312
warranty of title, 312
writ of replevin, 308

Questions for Review and Discussion

1. What is meant by tender of performance?
2. What are the rights and duties of sellers and buyers in a sales contract?
3. What is the doctrine of anticipatory breach?
4. What are the seller's and the buyer's remedies in case of a breach?
5. What is the statute of limitations?
6. In what three ways can an express warranty be created?
7. What are the requirements of the Magnuson-Moss Warranty Act?
8. What is the nature of each of the following warranties: merchantability, fitness for a particular purpose, and usage of trade?
9. What is meant by warranty of title?
10. How can warranties be excluded?

Cases for Analysis

1. Kathleen Liarkos purchased a used Jaguar XJS automobile from Pine Grove Auto Sales. After experiencing various mechanical problems, she discovered that the vehicle's odometer had been turned back. Liarkos notified the seller that she revoked her acceptance of the vehicle. When is this remedy available to a buyer? *Liarkos v. Mello*, 639 N.E.2d 716 (MA).

2. P&F Construction Corporation ordered 338 door units for an apartment condominium project from Friend Lumber Corporation. The doors were delivered to the job site three weeks after they were ordered. Each door unit came wrapped in clear plastic. Three and one-half months after receiving the door units, P&F Construction notified Friend Lumber that the doors were one-quarter inch off size. P&F refused to pay Friend Lumber the balance due. What rule of law may Friend Lumber use to recover the money owed? *P&F Const. v. Friend Lumber Corp.*, 575 N.E.2d 61 (MA).

3. William Young had cut evergreen boughs and sold them exclusively to Frank's Nursery & Crafts, Inc., for 10 years. Upon receiving a $238,000 order for 360 tons of boughs from Frank's, Young obtained cutting rights from many farmers, repaired his machinery, and made 75 new hand tiers to tie the evergreen bundles. Several months later, Frank's reduced its order to less than $60,000 for about 70 tons of boughs. Young delivered the 70 tons of boughs and sued Frank's for breach of contract. How were Young's damages computed? *Young v. Frank's Nursery & Crafts, Inc.*, 569 N.E.2d 1034 (OH).

4. Herman Googe agreed to buy an automobile from Irene Schleimer. Later, Googe changed his mind and refused to buy the car. Schleimer, without making tender of delivery, brought suit against Googe for breach of contract. Did Schleimer recover damages? Explain. *Schleimer v. Googe*, 377 N.Y.S.2d 591 (NY).

5. Mr. and Mrs. Aldridge bought a motor home from Sportsman Travel Trailer Sales, located in Texas. Two years later, after traveling more than 14,000 miles on trips to Louisiana, Colorado, and California, they attempted to reject the motor home, claiming that it was defective. Could they return the vehicle and recover damages? Explain. *Explorer Motor Home Corp. v. Aldridge,* 541 S.W.2d 851 (TX).

6. DiCintio leased for a three-year period from Adzan Auto Sales a Jeep Grand Cherokee Laredo sport utility vehicle manufactured by DaimlerChrysler. Soon after accepting delivery, the automatic transmission failed to shift gears properly, and then the vehicle started to pull to the left while being driven, after which it began to "idle rough" and stall while stopped at traffic lights. DiCintio took the vehicle to authorized dealers for repairs on six or seven occasions, but the defects persisted. When Adzan Auto Sales refused to terminate the lease or give him another car, DiContio brought suit against DaimlerChrysler for breach of the Magnuson-Moss Warranty Act. Does DiCintio have a cause of action under this law? Explain. *Mark DiCintio v. DaimlerChrysler Corporation, et al,* 768 NE2d 1121 (NY).

7. Lohr bought a mobile home from Larry's Homes. The home was damaged during delivery and never fully set up on Lohr's property. Larry's Homes attempted some repairs, but they were insufficient. An arbitrator found that the intended repairs would not have been enough even if they had been carried out. Lohr took the case to arbitration on the grounds of a breach of the warranty of merchantability

under the UCC. Does the UCC apply to this case? Why or why not? *Lohr v. Larry's Homes of Virginia.* Arbitrated by McCammon Group referred out of Cumberland County Circuit Court (VA).

8. Caswell bought a gas grill to give to his friend, Kile, as a birthday present. The grill exploded the first time it was used due to a factory defect, and Kile was injured. The manufacturer of the grill argued that it was not responsible for Kile's injuries because Kile had not purchased the grill. There was no privity of contract between Kile and the manufacturer. How would you decide?

9. Shaffer ordered a glass of rosé wine at the Victoria Station Restaurant. As he took his first sip of wine, the glass broke in his hand, causing permanent injuries. Shaffer brought suit against the restaurant for breach of warranty of merchantability. The restaurant's position was that because it did not sell the wine glass to Shaffer (only its contents), it was not a merchant with respect to the glass and therefore made no warranty. Do you agree with the restaurant? Why or why not? *Shaffer v. Victoria Station, Inc.,* 588 P.2d 233 (WA).

10. McCoy bought an antique pistol from the Old Fort Trading Post for $1,000. Later, the gun was taken from McCoy by the police when they learned that it was stolen property. The police turned the gun over to the rightful owner. McCoy notified the Old Fort Trading Post of what had happened and asked for the return of his money, but the owner of the business refused to give him a refund. What remedy, if any, did McCoy have against the owner of the trading post? Explain. *Trial v. McCoy,* 553 S.W.2d 199 (TX).

quick quiz Answers

14.1	14.2	14.3
1. T	1. T	1. T
2. T	2. T	2. T
3. T	3. T	3. T

Chapter 15

Product Liability and Consumer Protection

THE OPENING CASE Saving Consumers from Themselves: *Huff v. White Motor Co.*

Whether they admit to it or not, all legal professionals will, from time to time, use the law for social engineering purposes. One example of this social engineering function is found in the doctrine of product liability and one clear example of product liability is seen in the automotive industry. A case on point is *Huff v. White Motor Co.*, a lawsuit that started a trend toward a new standard of automotive product liability. Prior to this case, as strange as it may seem to us today, automotive manufacturers had successfully argued that "the intended purpose of an automobile does not include its participation in collisions." The pre-*Huff* rule stated that automobile makers had no responsibility to design and manufacture cars that would protect passengers and drivers from the effects of an accident. Since *Huff* started the ball rolling three decades ago, the courts and the legislatures have altered this standard and have declared that car manufacturers must now design vehicles that have a high level of "crashworthiness." Moreover, and perhaps more to the point, the crashworthiness standard is not based on warranties or negligence. Instead, the standard is based on strict liability. This means that the consumer in an automotive product liability lawsuit does not have to demonstrate that the manufacturer violated a warranty or behaved negligently. The simple fact that the automobile was unsafe beyond what

would be expected by the ordinary consumer is enough to result in liability. Today the strict liability standard applies to all products not just vehicles. In addition, the standard extends beyond privity and can be used to hold both the manufacturer and the seller liable. Remember, though, that the law is a balancing act. The courts have also ruled, on the opposite end of the spectrum, that the manufacturers of dangerous products are permitted to promote the sale of their products even though they know that the products are dangerous (not unsafe, but dangerous; there is a difference). As long as the product itself is legal, the corporation can advertise and sell the product despite its dangerous nature. Thus, somewhere within the intangible dimension of legal niceties there exists an invisible, largely undetectable line between manufacturing products that are unsafe and selling products that are dangerous. Manufacturing "unsafe products" is wrong; selling "dangerous products" is not. As you read the chapter, see if you can detect just where that line might be drawn. (See *Huff v. White Motor Co.*, 565 F.2d 104 (7th Cir. App. Ct 1977); David Lauter, "Automakers Face Strict Liability," *The National Law Journal* (December 21, 1981), p. 18; and Charles H. Moellenberg, Jr., and Leon F. DeJulius, Jr., "Remove the Tort Liability Muzzle," *The National Law Journal*, (May 10, 2010), p. 34.)

Opening Case Questions

1. Is *Huff v. White Motors Co.* a tort case or a contract case? Explain.

2. What is the difference between a lawsuit based on negligence and one based on strict liability? Explain.

3. Is the "crashworthiness" standard found in sales law or tort law? Explain.

4. What is significant about the fact that the plaintiff in an automotive product liability case does not have to prove privity? Explain.

5. What is the difference between a "dangerous" product and an "unsafe" product? Explain.

Learning Objectives

1. Describe the link between social engineering and the law.
2. Explain the difference between public interest and public policy.
3. Explain the difference between negligence and strict liability.
4. State the purpose of the Consumer Product Safety Act.
5. Explain the enforcement of the Federal Trade Commission Act.
6. Develop a list of unfair or deceptive practices.
7. Identify several FTC rules designed to protect the consumer.
8. Identify the function of the Truth-in-Lending Act.
9. Explain the latest amendments to the Truth-in-Lending Act.
10. Explain the requirements of the Consumer Leasing Act.

15-1 Product Liability

One of the fastest growing areas of consumer law is known as product liability. Under product liability standards, a person harmed by a product's unsafe condition may recover damages from the manufacturer, the seller, or the supplier of the product. Product liability results from the court's willingness to react to social problems and, at times, use the law to engineer social results. Because of the court's flexibility in this regard, product liability suits can now be based on one of two legal theories, negligence or strict liability, both of which are tort actions.

Social Engineering and the Law

The German philosopher Max Weber saw the law as a combination of consensus and coercion. Consensus reveals the norms by which the people of a society live, while coercion clarifies the measures taken against those who violate the consensus. Some parts of the legal community, such as the legislature and the agencies, are designed to proactively shape social policy. Others, like the courts, passively deal with problems on a case-by-case basis. Nevertheless, both levels, active and passive alike, must understand consensus and must use coercion. To do this properly, the courts frequently call upon the doctrine of public policy, a concept of based on the assumption that no one should be permitted to do anything that harms the public interest (See Gerald Turkel, *Law and Society: Critical Approaches* (Boston: Allyn and Bacon, 1996), pp. 8–9.)

Public Interest and Public Policy Public policy is not the same as public interest, although the two terms are very similar. Public interest refers to the idea that certain activities affect the entire social structure and must, therefore, be regulated by the government. Public interest, then, is the equivalent of Weber's social consensus. It is in the best interests of society, for example, to have crime-free neighborhoods. Public policy, in contrast, seeks to implement behavior that promotes the public consensus and eliminates behavior that does not. Thus, any activity that somehow permits, encourages, or compels people to break the law and thus disrupt those crime-free neighborhoods would be against public policy and would, therefore, be outlawed. Public interest, then, is the ideal consensus, and public policy is the coercive social engineering strategy by which that consensus is implemented.

Public Policy and Product Liability It is in the public interest to maintain a social structure that promotes health and safety and thus prevents illness and injury. To engineer this public interest goal, public policy promotes the making of safe products. To coerce this behavior, public policy demands that manufacturers, sellers, and distributors be held responsible for any injuries that result from their products. Therefore, public policy insists that manufacturers, sellers, and distributors compensate any innocent victim who is injured by an unsafe product, regardless of whether that victim purchased, used, or simply got in the way of that unsafe product. To meet the public interest goal of a safe society, the courts have produced two legal strategies, negligence and product liability. Nevertheless, of the two standards, strict liability is more effective in reaching that goal.

Negligence and Product Liability

One legal theory available to people who are injured by faulty products is negligence. Negligence results when an individual fails to exercise the degree of care that a reasonable person would have exercised under the same circumstances. To recover for negligence in a product liability case, the victim must prove: (1) that the manufacturer or seller owed a duty to the victim; (2) that the manufacturer or the seller violated that duty by not following the appropriate standard of care; (3) that the victim suffered an injury because of that careless action; and (4) that the careless action was both the actual and the proximate cause of the victim's injury.

THE OPENING CASE *Revisited, Part I*
Saving Consumers from Themselves: *Huff v. White Motor Co.,* Round 2

Before *Huff v. White Motor Co.,* the Opening Case at the beginning of this chapter, automobile makers had no responsibility to design and manufacture cars that would protect passengers and drivers from the effects of an accident. Looking at the elements that are needed to prove a negligence case, we can see just how powerful this rule was for the manufacturers. Think about it. If automobile makers had *no responsibility to design and manufacture cars that were crashworthy,* then the victim of an unsafe vehicle would be unable to prove even the first element of a negligence action, that is, that the manufacturer had a duty to ensure the safety of the

victim. Seen from this perspective, it's no wonder that automobile makers fought so hard against the new rule.

As noted above, it is difficult for an injured consumer to win a product liability case using negligence. This is true not only because the victim cannot prove the existence of duty, but also because the injured party can rarely demonstrate that the manufacturer was careless. The victim was not present when the goods were made and normally has very little information about the manufacturing process. Consequently, injured parties are often more successful when bringing a suit based on strict liability.

THE OPENING CASE *Revisited, Part II*
Saving Consumers from Themselves: *Huff v. White Motor Co.*, Round 3

After *Huff v. White Motor Co.*, the courts and the legislatures declared that car manufacturers must design vehicles that have a high level of "crashworthiness." More importantly, the crashworthiness standard is not based on warranties or negligence. Instead, the standard is based on strict liability. This means that the consumer in an automotive product liability lawsuit does not have to demonstrate that the manufacturer violated a warranty or behaved negligently. The simple fact that the automobile was unsafe beyond what would be expected by the ordinary consumer is enough to result in liability. Today the strict liability standard applies to all products not just vehicles. In addition, the standard extends beyond privity and can be used to hold both the manufacturer and the seller liable.

Strict Liability and Product Liability

The doctrine of strict liability holds manufacturers or suppliers liable for selling goods that are unsafe, without regard to fault or negligence. The principal consideration under the doctrine of strict liability is the safety of the product, not the conduct of the manufacturer or supplier of the goods. Under this rule, manufacturers have the duty to design reasonably safe products. They must also give proper instructions for the product's use and provide warnings of possible danger. People who are injured or suffer property damage from a defective product may recover from the manufacturer or seller only if they can prove all of the following:

1. The manufacturer or seller sold the product in a defective condition.
2. The manufacturer or seller was engaged in the business of selling the product.
3. The product was unsafe to an unreasonable degree to the user or the consumer.
4. The defective condition was the proximate cause of the injury or damage.
5. The defective condition existed at the time it left the hands of the manufacturer or seller.
6. The consumer sustained physical harm or property damage by use or consumption of the product.

The defective condition may arise through faulty product design, faulty manufacturing, inadequate warning of danger, or improper instructions for the product's use. The manufacturer's and seller's liability extends to all persons who may be injured by the product. Injured bystanders, guests, or others who have no relationship to the product, the seller, or the manufacturer may seek damages caused by defects in the offending product.

Duty to Warn   Sometimes a duty is placed on manufacturers to warn consumers that harm may result from a product. Unavoidably dangerous products may require a warning to inform the consumer of possible harm. If the warning is adequate, consumers may be required to use the product at their own risk. A warning must specify the risk presented by the product and give a reason for the warning. When the danger that is presented by a product is obvious, however, no duty to warn exists because a warning will not reduce the likelihood of injury.

Punitive Damages   In addition to recovering damages to compensate them for their losses, injured parties in strict liability cases sometimes recover punitive damages. These are monetary penalties imposed as a punishment for a wrongdoing.

Self-Evident Truths: Unsafe Products v. Dangerous Products

As we have seen many times throughout this text, the law is a balancing act. We have just examined how the courts have been willing (eager?) to use strict liability to hold manufacturers and distributors liable for injuries caused by unsafe products without any reference to negligence or warranties. Just how far will the courts go in this regard? What is the ultimate limit of strict liability as a coercive strategy of public policy? One answer to this question might be that there is no limit, that dangerous products, period, must be targeted by the law, at all cost no matter what. This is known as a *per se* rule. Literally translated from the Latin, *per se* means "in and of itself" and a rule that labels a product dangerous *per se* would assert that the product is dangerous in and of itself. In other words, such a product cannot be made "safe" because to make it "safe" would remove its basic function and render it useless. The prime target of the suggested "dangerous *per se*" rule has been handguns. However, the rule could apply to any firearm or explosive device (read "bomb"). The argument goes something like this. Handguns other firearms, and explosive devices are dangerous *per se* because their function is to kill. When a manufacturer designs, makes, and sells a handgun any other firearm or explosive device, that manufacturer knows that the product is designed to kill. Moreover, the only way to make a handgun safe is to render it unworkable, which makes it useless, and which, therefore, is not an option. Moreover, there is no social benefit to the firearm or the explosive device that outweighs the potential harm that it can cause. Therefore, when a manufacturer places a firearm or explosive device in circulation, he or she is well aware of its potential (inevitable?) criminal use and, when such an event occurs, that manufacturer must be held strictly liable for the injuries and the harm that results—period. Now there are counterarguments to this position which we will see later in the text. For now, however, consider the "dangerous *per se*" rule and answer the following questions. (See Donald E. Santarelli and Nicholas E. Calio, "Turning the Gun on Tort Law: Aiming at Courts to Take Products Liability to the Limit," *St. Mary's Law Journal* 14:3 (1983), pp. 471–508.)

Self-Evident Questions

1. Is the function of a firearm or explosive device to kill? If you believe that the function is to kill, then, what socially justifiable reason is there for continuing to manufacture them?

2. If you believe that the function is *not* to kill, then what other socially redeeming functions does a firearm or explosive device possess? Explain.

3. Max Weber believes that the law can be used to coerce the members of a society into conforming to the general consensus. Will the "dangerous *per se*" rule eliminate killing and, thus, create crime-free neighborhoods? Explain.

4. The very first element of strict liability is that the plaintiff must prove that the manufacturer or seller sold the product in a defective condition. What is the defective condition of a firearm or explosive device that works exactly as it should? Explain.

5. What other products might be outlawed using the "dangerous *per se*" rule? Explain.

Aircraft Cases and Product Liability Despite the court's willingness to impose strict liability in product liability cases involving automobiles and despite the fact that the doctrine could easily be applied to other products, there has been a curious lack of activity in this area of the law. For example, there has been a reluctance on the part of both the courts and the legislature to apply strict liability, especially as it is expressed in the crashworthiness test, to aviation accident cases. Several reasons may explain the lack of movement in this area. One reason for this apparent inactivity is that aviation crashes are rare, at least when compared to automobile accidents. Another reason may be that most aviation cases are settled out of court before litigation even begins. However, probably the most significant reason is that aviation cases tend to be more complex and difficult than automobile cases. Typically, aviation cases will require a more in-depth understanding of and appreciation for the complexity of aircraft design and operation. It may be that product liability arguments in aviation cases will have to wait for the establishment of a science court, one version of which is discussed at length in this text in "Chapter 4 Alternative Dispute Resolution and in the *Self-Evident Truths* feature in Chapter 14." (See Scott G. Lindvall, "Aircraft Crashworthiness: Should the Courts Set Standards?" *William and Mary Law Review,* 27:2 (1986), pp. 371–408.)

The Consumer Product Safety Act

Product safety has not remained solely within the purview of the courts. Congress has also gotten into the act. In an attempt to protect consumers from dangerous products, Congress passed the Consumer Product Safety Act. The act established the Consumer Product Safety Commission (CPSC) to protect consumers from unreasonable risk or injury from hazardous products. The act covers products or component parts, American-made or imported, that are manufactured or distributed for sale to a consumer for personal use, consumption, or enjoyment. The commission can order the recall of products found to be inherently unsafe and dangerous. It has the authority to impose civil fines for violations of its standards and cease-and-desist orders. Private citizens, acting on their own behalf, may bring suit to establish or enforce a safety rule if the commission fails to act.

quick quiz 15-1

1. Public interest and public policy are the same thing.   true | false

2. Negligence would usually be more effective as a legal theory in a   true | false
   product liability lawsuit than strict liability.

3. In addition to recovering damages to compensate them for their   true | false
   losses, injured parties in strict liability cases sometimes recover
   punitive damages.

15-2 Consumer Protection Laws

Consumer protection laws apply to transactions between business people and consumers. A consumer is someone who buys or leases real estate, goods, or services for personal, family, or household purposes. Thus, people who buy or rent things for personal use from a business are protected by consumer protection laws. However, if they buy the same things from another consumer or for business use, they are not, with some exceptions, protected by consumer protection law. State consumer protection offices provide information and help enforce state consumer protection laws. They sometimes assist consumers with individual problems. Consumer protection offices are located in state and county offices and, in some cities, the mayor's office.

Federal consumer protection law stems from the Federal Trade Commission Act (FTCA), which states that "unfair or deceptive acts or practices in . . . or affecting commerce are hereby declared unlawful." The act defines commerce as "commerce among the several states or with foreign nations or the District of Columbia." Thus, the act applies to businesses that sell real estate, goods, or services in interstate commerce or that somehow affect interstate commerce. Interstate commerce is business activity that touches more than one state. Purely local business activity, which has no out-of-state connections, called intrastate commerce, is not governed by the FTCA.

The Federal Trade Commission

The Federal Trade Commission Act transferred certain powers to the Federal Trade Commission, giving it the authority to oversee and eliminate deceptive and unfair practices in commerce. These powers include:

1. To conduct investigations into the practices of businesses.
2. To investigate possible antitrust violations.
3. To compel interstate businesses to file reports with the commission detailing their operations that fall within the FTC's jurisdiction.
4. To publish the results of the commission's investigation of interstate businesses.
5. To deal with disputes that emerge from the application of FTC regulations.
6. To deal with disputes that emerge from the application of federal antitrust law.
7. To make recommendations to Congress concerning new legislation.

In effect, the commission has become a coercive public policy instrument designed to promote the public interest. In doing so, the FTC must determine when a practice is unfair by balancing the harm that might affect consumers with the overall public good promoted by the activity under scrutiny.

If, after a thorough investigation, the FTC concludes that a violation of the law occurred, it may attempt to obtain voluntary compliance by entering into a consent order with the violating company. A consent order is an order under which the company agrees to stop the disputed practice without necessarily admitting that it violated the law. If an agreement cannot be reached, the FTC may issue a complaint. This action begins a formal hearing before an administrative law judge. If a violation of law is found, a cease-and desist order or other appropriate relief may be issued. Consumers may bring individual or class-action lawsuits against businesses for violating FTC rules. A class-action lawsuit is one that is brought by one or more plaintiffs on behalf of a class of persons. Usually, a suit must be brought within one year after the violation. Alternate dispute resolutions are also available for resolving this type of problem.

Unfair or Deceptive Practices

The FTC Act prohibits unfair or deceptive practices. These practices include fraudulent misrepresentations, sending unordered merchandise, bait-and-switch schemes, and odometer tampering.

Fraudulent Misrepresentation
It is unfair or deceptive for a seller to make a fraudulent misrepresentation, that is, a statement that is designed to mislead the buyer. A misrepresentation usually occurs when the seller misstates facts important to the consumer. Making false statements about the construction, durability, reliability, safety, strength, condition, or life expectancy of a product is a deceptive practice. It is also deceptive to fail to disclose to a buyer any fact that would cause the buyer to walk away from the contract. You may see ads like the following in newspapers and magazines: "Would you like to earn hundreds of dollars a week at home in your leisure time? Many people are supplementing their income in a very easy way. Let us tell you how. . . . " An offer like this may sound very attractive, particularly if you are unable to leave your home to work. Be cautious about work-at-home ads, especially ones that promise large profits in a short period of time. Although some work-at-home plans are legitimate, many are not. Home employment schemes are some of the oldest kinds of classified advertising fraud.

Unordered Merchandise Except for free samples clearly and conspicuously marked as such and merchandise mailed by charitable organizations soliciting contributions, it is a violation of the postal law and the FTCA to send merchandise through the mail to people who did not order it. Similarly, it is illegal to send a bill for such unordered merchandise or to send dunning letters, that is, letters requesting payments. People who receive unordered merchandise through the mail may treat it as a gift. They may keep the merchandise or dispose of it in any manner they see fit without any obligation whatsoever to the sender. In addition, senders of unordered merchandise must attach a statement to the package informing recipients of their right to keep and use the goods.

Bait-and-Switch Schemes A bait-and-switch scheme is an alluring but insincere offer to sell a product or service that the advertiser does not really intend to sell. Its purpose is to switch customers from buying the advertised merchandise to buying something else, usually at a higher price or on a basis more advantageous to the advertiser. There is no question that the FTCA prohibits bait-and-switch schemes. The very nature of the strategy is to trick unwary consumers into purchasing something that they neither want nor need and that is more expensive than the original bait that snagged their interest and pulled them into the store. The statute states quite specifically that: "No advertisement containing an offer to sell a product shall be made when the offer is not a *bona fide* effort to sell the advertised product." Any of the following activities could indicate a bait-and-switch scheme:

- A refusal to show, demonstrate, or sell the product offered in accordance with the terms of the offer.
- A "put-down" of the product by the acts or words of the seller.
- Failing to have available at all outlets listed in the advertisement a sufficient quantity of the advertised product to meet reasonably anticipated demands.
- Refusing to take orders for the advertised product to be delivered within a reasonable period of time.
- Showing a product that is defective, unusable, or impractical for the purpose represented in the advertisement.

Odometer Tampering The federal Odometer Law prohibits people from disconnecting, resetting, or altering the odometer of a motor vehicle in order to hide a vehicle's true mileage. Anyone who sells or gives away a car must provide the new owner with a written statement disclosing the odometer reading at the time of the transfer. If the seller believes that the mileage reading on the odometer is incorrect, the disclosure statement must indicate that the actual mileage is unknown. It is also a violation of the act to obtain a vehicle for resale without acquiring a finalized odometer statement from the seller. An odometer must be set at zero if it is repaired and cannot be adjusted to show the true mileage. In addition, the car owner must attach to the left doorframe a written notice showing the true mileage before the service, repair, or replacement and the date that the odometer was set at zero. It is illegal for anyone to alter or remove any such notice attached to the doorframe of a car.

Trade Regulation Rules

To correct wrongdoings in the marketplace, the FTC has also established trade regulation rules to govern the activities of interstate companies. These rules include the Used Car Rule, the Cooling-Off Rule, the negative option rule, the Mail and Telephone Order Rule, the telemarketing sales rule, and the rules connected with 900 numbers. Other rules are established by the antispam and the antislamming laws.

Used Car Rule

To remedy consumer complaints involving used car sales, the FTC established the Used Car Rule. This rule requires used car dealers to place a Buyer's Guide sticker in the window of each used car they offer for sale. The Buyer's Guide provides the following information:

- A statement that the car is sold *as is* if it is sold with no warranties. (Some states do not allow used cars to be sold as is by car dealers.)
- A statement that the car is sold with implied warranties only if that is the case.
- A statement telling whether the warranty is "full" or "limited" and citing the length of the warranty period if the car is sold with an express warranty. In addition, the guide must list the specific systems that are covered by the warranty and state the percentage of the repair costs that will be paid by the dealer.
- A statement that tells consumers not to rely on spoken promises.
- A suggestion that consumers ask whether they may have the vehicle inspected by their own mechanic either on or off the premises.
- A list of the 14 major systems of an automobile and some of the principal defects that may occur in these systems.
- Whenever the sale of a vehicle will be carried on in Spanish, a Spanish language version of the Buyer's Guide must be placed on the window before the vehicle is marketed.

A dealer is defined as anyone who sells more than five used cars in a 12-month period. The law covers the sale of automobiles, light-duty vans, and light-duty trucks. The Buyer's Guide sticker must be printed in black ink on a white sheet of paper that is at least 11 × 7¼ inches in size. The guide becomes part of the sales contract and overrides any contrary provision that may be in the contract.

Cooling-Off Rule

The FTC has established the Cooling-Off Rule to give consumers an opportunity to change their minds after signing contracts with people who come to their houses. Under this rule, sales of consumer goods or services over $25 made away from the seller's regular place of business, such as at a customer's home, may be canceled within three business days after the sale occurs. This rule requires the seller to give the buyer two copies of a cancellation form, one of which the buyer may send to the seller any time before midnight of the third business day after the contract was signed. The law also applies to consumer product parties given in private homes and to sales made in rented hotel rooms or restaurants. There are, however, several exceptions to the rule. The rule does not apply to:

- Sales that are less than $25.
- Sales that involve items used for something other than personal, household, or family reasons.
- Sales that are entered completely by phone or by mail.
- Sales that begin at the seller's regular place of business and then are simply concluded at the buyer's home.
- Sales that are made under emergency conditions.
- Sales that are involved in the repair or maintenance of personal property.

In addition, the Cooling-Off Rule does not cover insurance, securities, real estate, or craft items sold at fairs, civic centers, schools, or shopping malls. Finally, the rule does not cover vehicle sales when the seller has set up a temporary location away from his or her permanent place of business. Under the laws of some states, such as New York, the three-day right to cancel does not begin until the seller gives the buyer a written notice of the right to cancel. Until such notice is given, the buyer may use any means to notify the seller of the cancellation of the contract.

Negative Option Rule   The negative option rule applies when a consumer subscribes to a magazine, joins a CD club, enrolls in a DVD club, or enters some other plan that sends products on a regular basis. Under such plans, the seller notifies the subscriber about the next selection before that selection is shipped. If the subscriber does nothing, the seller will ship the selection automatically. If the subscriber does not want the selection, he or she must tell the seller not to send the item before an agreed to deadline. The negative option rule does not outlaw such agreements but it does demand that sellers tell subscribers:

- The number of selections they must purchase, if any.
- The circumstances under which they can withdraw their membership.
- The notification process used to opt out of a selection.
- The timing for the return of the negative option cancellation forms.
- The circumstances under which subscribers qualify for credit in a return.
- The technique for determining postage and handling costs.
- The timing of each selection announcement.

The negative option rule does not apply to continuity plans. Under a continuity plan, the seller ships the goods to the subscriber on a regular basis without first sending an announcement of the upcoming delivery. While the negative option rule does not limit the use of such continuity plans, they are regulated by standard consumer protection rules. This means that the seller must notify the subscriber of all terms and conditions in a clear and unambiguous way.

The Mail and Telephone Order Rule   The FTC has established a rule to protect consumers who order goods by mail, telephone, Internet, or fax machine. Under the Mail and Telephone Order Rule (MTOR), sellers must ship orders within the time promised in their advertisements. If no time period is promised, sellers must either ship the order within 30 days or send the consumer an option notice. The option notice informs consumers of any shipping delay and gives them a chance to cancel and receive a refund. Instructions on how to cancel orders must be included in the notice. In addition, the seller must provide a free means for consumers to reply.

Telemarketing Sales Rule   The FTC's Telemarketing Sales Rule is designed to protect consumers from abusive and unscrupulous telemarketers. The rule has established the *Do Not Call Registry* (see Figure 15-1) that makes it easier for consumers to reduce or eliminate unwanted sales calls. Under the Telemarketing Sales Rule:

- It is illegal for a telemarketer to call a consumer if the consumer has asked not to be called.
- Calling times are restricted to the hours between 8:00 A.M. and 9:00 P.M.
- Telemarketers must tell the consumer that it is a sales call, the name of the seller, and what they are selling before they make their pitch. If it is a prize promotion, they must tell the consumer that no purchase or payment is necessary to enter or win.

> **NATIONAL
> DO NOT CALL
> REGISTRY**
>
> Place your telephone number on the National Do Not Call Registry by calling toll-free 1-888-382-1222 (TTY: 1-866-290-4236) or going online to donotcall.gov. Registration is free.
>   Placing your telephone number on the Do Not Call Registry will stop all telemarketing calls except those from political organizations, charities, and people making surveys. You can expect fewer calls within three months of the date you sign up for the registry. Your number will stay in the registry for five years, until it is disconnected, or until you delete it from the registry. You may renew your registration after five years.
>   Telemarketers are required to search the registry every three months and avoid calling any phone numbers that are on the registry.
>   If you receive telemarketing calls after you have registered your telephone number and it has been in the registry for three months, you can file a complaint at donotcall.gov or by calling toll-free 1-888-382-1222 (TTY: 1-866-290-4236). You will need to provide the date of the call and the name or phone number of the company that called you. Telemarketers who disregard this law can be fined up to $11,000 for each call they make.

Figure 15-1 Once your number is registered, how long will it remain in the National Do Not Call Registry?

- It is illegal for telemarketers to misrepresent any information, including facts about their goods or services, earnings potential, profitability, the risk or liquidity of an investment, or the nature of a prize in a prize-promotion scheme.
- Before consumers pay, telemarketers must tell them the total cost of the products or services offered and any restrictions on getting or using them or that a sale is final or nonrefundable.

Consumers who have the slightest doubt about a telephone offer should ask for written information about the product, service, investment opportunity, or charity that is the subject of the call. They should resist high-pressure sales tactics and talk to a family member or friend before responding to the call. Consumers should never give out their bank account or credit card number to anyone who calls them. Similarly, they should never send money by courier, overnight delivery, or wire to anyone who insists on immediate payment.

900-Telephone Number Rules Telemarketers sometimes use 900 telephone numbers as part of their strategy, because the consumer, rather than the seller, pays the phone charge. To combat the abusive use of 900 telephone numbers, the Federal Trade Commission has established a series of 900-Telephone Number Rules. These rules require telemarketers who use 900 numbers to warn callers of the cost of the calls and to give those callers a chance to hang up before being charged. Under the rules, customers are also permitted to ask telephone companies to block all 900-prefix number calls. In addition, the rules require telephone companies to send customers pay-per-call disclosure statements. The FTC also prohibits the use of any prefix other than 900 as a pay-per-call service. Moreover, the FTC will not permit telephone companies to disconnect phone service to customers who refuse to pay for 900-number calls. Finally, the FTC has established a series of rules for resolving billing disputes.

AntiSpam Law The Can Spam Act is an attempt by the federal government to reduce the use of unsolicited commercial e-mail, commonly known as spam, on the Internet. Under the law, unsolicited commercial e-mail messages must be truthful and cannot use misleading subject lines or incorrect return addresses. E-mail containing pornography must be specifically labeled in the subject line. In addition, spammers cannot harvest e-mail addresses from chat rooms and other sites without permission. The rule has also been amended to include messages that are intended for mobile phones, provided that a domain name is used as part of the Internet address. This ban does not include short phone-to-phone messages

AntiSlamming Law   The illegal practice of changing a consumer's telephone service without permission is referred to as slamming. New consumer protection rules created by the Federal Communications Commission (FCC) provide a remedy for consumers who have been slammed. With these rules, the FCC has taken the profit out of slamming and protected consumers from illegal charges.

---

quick quiz 15-2

1. A consumer is someone who buys or leases real estate, goods, or services for personal, family, or household purposes.   true | false

2. The Federal Trade Commission Act transferred certain powers to the Federal Trade Commission, giving it the authority to oversee and eliminate deceptive and unfair practices in commerce.   true | false

3. To correct wrongdoings in the marketplace, the FTC has established trade regulation rules that must be followed by companies that transact business only in intrastate commerce.   true | false

---

15-3 Consumer Credit Laws

Consumers need just as much protection (some experts would argue more protection) in their credit transactions as in their consumer product contracts. Most Americans use credit cards as a matter of course on a daily basis, almost without thinking about it. In addition, the average American makes an installment payment on a car loan (perhaps even two) every month, almost as if it were a civic duty, like paying taxes or voting. Due to this extensive use of credit, Congress has found it necessary to pass federal laws to protect the consumer.

The Federal Truth-in-Lending Act

Because lending institutions and businesses charge different rates of interest to consumers, it often pays to shop around before borrowing money or buying on credit. To help consumers know the truth about the cost of borrowing money, Congress passed the Truth-in-Lending Act. Under this act, lenders must disclose two important things to borrowers: the finance charge (the actual cost of the loan in dollars and cents) and the annual percentage rate (APR) (the true rate of interest of the loan). With this information, consumers can compare the cost of loans from different lenders before deciding from which to borrow. Surprisingly, the APR sometimes turns out to be greater than it would appear at first glance.

Most consumers today rely heavily on credit card transactions. For this reason, Congress has enacted several consumer credit protection laws.

EXAMPLE 15-1: True Rate of Interest

Hana borrowed $100 for one year and agreed to pay a finance charge of $10. If she kept the $100 for the year and at the end of the year paid back the full amount, together with the $10 finance charge, the APR would be 10 percent. If, however, she paid the $110 in 12 monthly installments of $9.17 each, the APR would be 18 percent. The latter rate is higher because during the course of the year, she would have the use, on the average, of only about half of the $100.

Equal Credit Opportunity

The Equal Credit Opportunity Act was passed by Congress, as amendment to the Truth-in-Lending Act, to ensure that all consumers are given an equal chance to receive credit. The law makes it illegal for banks and businesses to discriminate against credit applicants because of their sex, race, marital status, national origin, religion, or age or because they get public assistance income. The law must be followed by anyone who regularly extends credit, including banks, credit unions, finance companies, credit card issuers, and retail stores. Some of the rights to consumers under the act are as follows:

1. People who apply for credit may not be asked to reveal their sex, race, national origin, or religion; whether they are divorced or widowed; their marital status, unless they are applying for a joint account or a secured loan; information about their spouse, except in community property states, unless the spouse is also applying for credit or will use the account; their plans for having or raising children; and whether they receive alimony, child support, or separate maintenance payments if they will not be relying on that income.

2. When deciding to extend credit, creditors must not consider the applicant's sex, marital status, race, national origin, or religion; consider the applicant's age, unless the applicant is a minor or is considered favorably for being over 62; refuse to consider public assistance income in the same manner as other income; and refuse to consider income from part-time employment, pensions, or retirement programs.

3. Applicants may apply for credit under the name given to them at birth, their married name, or a combination of both. They may receive credit without a cosigner if they meet the creditor's standards. In addition, applicants have a right to know within 30 days whether their application for credit has been accepted or rejected. If rejected, they have a right to know the reasons for the rejection within 60 days.

Unauthorized Use of Credit Cards

Sometimes credit cards are lost, stolen, or used by people who have no authority to use them. Under the Truth-in-Lending Act, credit cardholders are not responsible for any unauthorized charges made after the card issuer has been notified of the loss, theft, or possible unauthorized use of the card. Such notice may be given to the card issuer by telephone, letter, or any other means. Even then, credit cardholders are responsible only for the first $50 of any unauthorized charges. Debit cards do not have this built-in protection. The credit cardholder can avoid the $50 liability if the credit card issuer has not included on the card a method to identify the user of the card, such as a signature, a photograph, or other means of identification. Card issuers must notify cardholders in advance of the potential $50 liability. As an amendment to the Truth-in-Lending Act, Congress recently launched the Consumer Financial Protection Bureau, a new federal office that is designed to act as a watchdog in the credit industry.

Fair Credit Reporting

The Fair Credit Reporting Act was passed by Congress to ensure that consumers are treated fairly by credit bureaus and consumer reporting agencies. A consumer has the right to know all information (other than medical information) that is in his or her files. A consumer also has the right to know, in most cases, the source of the information on file. In addition, a consumer has the right to be told the name of anyone who received a credit report in the past year (or two years if the credit report relates to a job application). If errors are found, credit bureaus must investigate and then correct or delete information that is inaccurate, incomplete, or obsolete. If the credit bureau retains information that the consumer believes to be incorrect, the consumer's version of the facts must be inserted in the file. Also, creditors are required to tell consumers the specific reasons for the denial of credit.

Billing, Collecting, and Leasing

Even with all of the consumer protection laws outlined above, there are still a variety of ways in which consumers can be victimized. The last of these areas include billing, collecting, and leasing. In billing, retail stores, credit card companies, and other businesses that extend credit sometimes make billing errors that threaten the reputation and the credit record of innocent consumers. To make it easier for billing errors to be corrected, Congress has passed the Fair Credit Billing Act (FCBA). Improper collection procedures can also hassle innocent consumers. Under the Fair Debt Collection Practices Act, specific rules must be followed by companies that are in the business of collecting debts for others. Finally, consumers who must rent or lease products sometimes find themselves victimized by unscrupulous leasing companies. The Consumer Leasing Act is a federal law requiring leasing companies to inform consumers of all of the terms of a lease of personal property.

The Fair Credit Billing Act
Under the Fair Credit Billing Act (FCBA), when consumers believe an error has been made in a bill, they must notify the creditor within 60 days after the bill was mailed. The notice must identify the consumer and give the account number, the suspected amount of error, and an explanation of why the consumer believes there is an error. The creditor must acknowledge the consumer's notice within 30 days. Then, within 90 days, the creditor must conduct an investigation and either correct the mistake or explain why the bill is believed to be correct. Another provision of the act gives consumers protection when they buy unsatisfactory goods or services with credit cards. If a consumer has a dispute with a credit card purchase, the consumer can disregard the bill for the disputed item and, instead, notify the credit card issuer of the error by telephone. The credit card issuer will put the disputed amount on hold and send the consumer a form to fill out explaining the dispute. The credit card issuer will attempt to resolve the dispute and inform the consumer of the results. Then, if the problem is not corrected and suit is brought by the credit card issuer, the consumer may use as a defense the fact that unsatisfactory goods or services were received. For this law to apply, the initial transaction must have taken place in the consumer's state or within 100 miles of the consumer's mailing address. Creditors may not give cardholders a poor credit rating for exercising their rights under this act.

Under the Fair Debt Collection Practices Act, debt collectors must follow strict guidelines when contacting consumers.

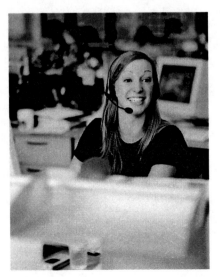

Fair Debt Collection Practices
Under the Fair Debt Collection Practices Act, specific rules must be followed by companies that are in the business of collecting debts for others. Some of these rules are as follows:

1. When trying to locate someone, a debt collector may not communicate by postcard or tell others that the consumer owes money.

2. When the debt collector knows that the consumer is represented by an attorney, the debt collector may communicate only with the attorney.

3. A debt collector may not communicate with the consumer at any unusual or inconvenient time or place. Unless there are circumstances to the contrary, the convenient time for communicating with a consumer is between the hours of 8:00 A.M. and 9:00 P.M.

4. A debt collector may not communicate with the consumer at the consumer's place of employment if the debt collector knows that the employer prohibits such communication.

5. A debt collector may not communicate, in connection with the collection of a debt, with any person other than the consumer, the consumer's attorney, the creditor's attorney, or a consumer reporting agency.

6. If a consumer notifies a debt collector in writing that the consumer refuses to pay the debt or wishes the debt collector to cease further communication, the debt collector must cease communication, except to notify the consumer of a specific action.

7. Debt collectors may not harass consumers or use abusive techniques to collect debts. The use or threatened use of violence or other criminal means to harm the person, property, or reputation of consumers is not allowed. In addition, debt collectors may not use obscene or profane language or publish a list of those who allegedly refuse to pay debts. It is also illegal for a debt collector to cause a telephone to ring or to engage in repeated telephone conversations with the intent to annoy the consumer.

Debt collectors who violate this law may be sued for actual damages, punitive damages, and attorneys' fees.

The Consumer Leasing Act

The Consumer Leasing Act is a federal law requiring leasing companies to inform consumers of all of the terms of a lease of personal property. Consumers can use the information to compare one lease with another or the cost of leasing with the cost of buying the same property. The law applies only to personal property leased by an individual for a period of more than four months for personal, family, or household use. It does not cover daily or weekly rentals, leases for apartments or houses, or leases to anyone for business purposes.

EXAMPLE 15-2: Businesses Not Protected

Guzman decided that her business could be managed much more efficiently if it had a computer. The cost of buying a computer, however, was more than Guzman could afford. She considered leasing one. The Consumer Leasing Act would not apply to Guzman's lease, because the computer was for business rather than personal use. She would be able to make a better decision, however, if she asked the leasing company for the same information the company would be required to provide to a consumer.

The law requires that consumers be given a written statement informing them of the full cost of the lease, including the cost of any necessary licenses, taxes, or other fees. Consumers must be informed of any insurance requirements and penalties for late payment. They must also be told who is responsible for maintaining and servicing the property. In addition, they must be told whether they can buy the property and, if so, when and at what price. The law also places a limit on the amount of a balloon payment (a very large final payment) to no more than three times the average monthly payments. Advertisements of leases are also regulated by law. If an advertisement mentions the amount or number of payments, specifies a particular down payment, or states that no down payment is required; it must also disclose the total of regular payments, the consumer's responsibility at the end of the lease, and whether the consumer may purchase the property.

quick quiz 15-3

1. Under the terms of the Truth-in-Lending Act. Lenders need disclose only things to the finance charge to lenders.   true | false

2. If a credit card or a debit card is lost, the cardholder is responsible only for the first $50 of any unauthorized charges.   true | false

3. Debt collectors who violate the Fair Debt Collection Practices cannot be sued.   true | false

Summary

15.1 Public interest refers to the idea that certain activities affect the entire social structure and must, therefore, be regulated by the government. Public policy, in contrast, seeks to implement behavior that promotes the public consensus and eliminates behavior that does not. Both concepts are inherent within the legal doctrines of product liability. Under the theory of product liability, a buyer or user of a product who is injured because of the product's unsafe or defective condition may recover damages from the manufacturer, the seller, or the supplier of the goods. Product liability suits can now be based on one of two legal theories, negligence or strict liability, both of which are tort actions. Public policy has not remained solely within the purview of the courts. Congress has also entered the product safety arena by establishing the Consumer Product Safety Commission (CPSC) to protect consumers from unreasonable risk or injury from hazardous products.

15.2 The Federal Trade Commission Act gave the Federal Trade Commission (FTC) the authority to oversee and eliminate deceptive and unfair practices in commerce. The FTC and the courts have determined that certain activities are unfair or deceptive. They include fraudulent misrepresentations, sending unordered merchandise, bait-and-switch schemes, and odometer tampering. To correct wrongdoings in

the marketplace, the FTC has also established trade regulation rules to govern the activities of interstate companies. These rules include the used-car rule, the cooling-off rule, the negative-option rule, the mail and telephone order rule, the telemarketing sales rule, and the rules connected with 900 numbers. Other rules are set up by the antispam law and the antislamming law.

15.3 Under the Truth-in-Lending Act, lenders must disclose the true nature of finance charges and the annual percentage rate. The Equal Credit Opportunity Act ensures that all consumers have an equal chance to receive credit. The Fair Credit Reporting Act guarantees fair treatment by credit bureaus and consumer reporting agencies. Under the Truth-in-Lending Act, credit-card holders are not responsible for any unauthorized charges made after the card issuer has been notified of the loss, theft, or possible unauthorized use of the card. The Fair Credit Reporting Act promises that consumers will be treated fairly by credit bureaus and consumer reporting agencies. To make it easier to correct billing errors, Congress has passed the Fair Credit Billing Act (FCBA). Under the Fair Debt Collection Practices Act, specific rules must be followed by companies that are in the business of collecting debts for others. The Consumer Leasing Act requires leasing companies to inform consumers of all of the terms of a lease of personal property.

Key Terms

annual percentage rate (APR), 329	consumer, 323	product liability, 319
bait-and-switch scheme, 325	continuity plan, 327	public interest, 319
balloon payment, 332	Cooling-Off Rule, 326	public policy, 320
Buyer's Guide, 326	dunning letters, 325	strict liability, 321
cancellation form, 326	finance charge, 329	slamming, 329
Can Spam Act, 328	interstate commerce, 323	spam, 328
class-action lawsuit, 324	intrastate commerce, 324	Used Car Rule, 326
commerce, 323	Mail and Telephone Order Rule, 327	
consent order, 324		

Questions for Review and Discussion

1. What is the link between social engineering and the law?
2. What is the difference between the public interest and public policy?
3. What is the difference between negligence and strict liability?
4. What is the purpose of the Consumer Product Safety Act?
5. How is the Federal Trade Commission Act enforced?
6. What are some unfair or deceptive practices?
7. What are the FTC rules designed to protect the consumer?
8. What is the function of the Truth-in-Lending Act?
9. What are some of the latest amendments to the Truth-in-Lending Act?
10. What is required by the Consumer Leasing Act?

Cases for Analysis

1. Paul and Cynthia Vance invited Carl and Jeanne Leichtamer to go for a ride in the Vances's four-wheel drive Jeep at an "off the road" recreation facility called the Hall of Fame Four-Wheel Club. The club had been organized by a Jeep dealer who showed films to club members of Jeeps traveling in hilly country. This activity was coupled with a national advertising program of American Motor Sales Corporation encouraging people to buy Jeeps that could drive up and down steep hills. As the Jeep went up a 33-degree sloped, double-terraced hill, it pitched over from front to back and landed upside-down. The Vances were killed, and the Leichtamers were severely injured. The Jeep was equipped with a factory-installed roll bar attached to the sheet metal that housed the rear wheels. When the vehicle landed upside down, the flat sheet metal gave way, causing the roll bar to move forward and downward 14 inches. The Leichtamers argued that the weakness of the sheet metal housing upon which the roll bar had been attached was the cause of their injuries. The manufacturer claimed that the roll bar was provided solely for side-roll protection, not pitchover, as occurred in this case. Did the Leichtamers recover against the manufacturer on a theory of strict liability? Why or why not? *Leichtamer v. American Motors Corp.*, 424 N.E.2d 568 (OH).

2. Michael P. Babine was injured when he was thrown from an "El Toro" mechanical bull that he rode at a nightclub. The club had placed mattresses around the bull to cushion the fall of riders, but the mattresses were not adequately pushed together. Babine was thrown off during his ride and hit his head on the floor where there was a gap between the mattresses. Before riding the bull, Babine had signed a form releasing the nightclub from liability for injuries sustained from the activity. The mechanical bull had been manufactured for the purpose of being a training device for rodeo cowboys, and it was purchased second-hand by the nightclub. Babine sought to recover damages from the manufacturer under the theory of product liability. Did he succeed? Why or why not? *Babine v. Gilley's Bronco Shop, Inc.*, 488 So.2d 176 (FL).

3. Harriet Glantz lost her job. She was unable to find work for several months and fell behind in the payment of her debts. A debt collector telephoned her at 11:45 P.M., used profanity, and threatened to "take care of her" if she didn't pay the amount owed. Were Glantz's rights violated? Explain.

4. Ingram went to a used car lot in a large city and bought a used car. On his way home from the lot, the car that he had purchased broke down. The engine stopped running altogether. The used car lot refused to fix the car because the salesperson had written "as is" on the sales slip. Ingram had not been informed that the car was sold to him as is. Was a consumer protection law violated? Explain.

5. Prior to his marriage, Edward Garber had been in financial difficulty and had a poor credit rating. His wife, Natalie, applied for a credit card in her family name, fearing that she would be turned down if she used her married name of Garber. She was told that she must use her married name on a credit application. Could Natalie have used her family name when she applied for credit? Explain.

6. Horack bought a used Mustang from a used car lot. The odometer showed that the car had been driven only 30,000 miles. Later, while cleaning her car, Horack found a service receipt showing that the actual mileage on the car a year earlier was 45,000 miles. Was a law violated? Explain.

7. Carboni's MasterCard bill contained several charges that she had not made. Upon investigation, she discovered that her credit card was missing from her wallet. She immediately notified the bank of the lost credit card. The unauthorized charges on the bill that she received amounted to $375. Did Carboni have to pay the full amount of the bill? Explain.

8. Delores Bierlein paid a $200 deposit toward the rental of the Silver Room at Alex's Continental Inn for her wedding reception. Later, Bierlein canceled the reception because her fiancé was transferred from Ohio to New York. The inn refused to refund Bierlein's deposit. The consumer protection law of that state requires suppliers to furnish receipts when they receive deposits. Bierlein was not given a receipt for her $200 deposit. When she sued for the return of the $200, the question arose as to whether this transaction fell within the consumer protection law. Do you think it does? Explain. *Bierlein v. Alex's Continental Inn, Inc.,* 475 N.E.2d 1273 (OH).

9. In response to a radio advertisement, Mr. and Mrs. Lancet telephoned Hollywood Decorators, Inc., and arranged for Mr. Wolff, a company representative, to visit their home. During Wolff's visit, the Lancets signed a contract for interior decoration and paid a $1,000 deposit. Two days later, the Lancets canceled the contract by telephone and asked for the return of their deposit. Twelve days after that, the Lancet's attorney wrote a letter to the company renewing the cancellation. Were they bound by the contract they signed? Why or why not? *Hollywood Decorators, Inc., v. Lancet,* 461 N.Y.S.2d 955 (NY).

10. After receiving an unsuccessful surgical procedure designed to facilitate weight loss, Gatten brought suit against the physician for violation of the state consumer protection law. That law read in part, "unfair methods of competition and deceptive practices in the conduct of any trade or commerce are unlawful." Gatten based her case on statements made to her about her course of treatment and the probable results of that treatment. Does the unsuccessful treatment by a physician fall within the consumer protection law? Explain. *Gatten v. Merzi,* 579 A.2d 974 (PA).

quick quiz Answers

15.1	15.2	15.3
1. F	1. T	1. F
2. F	2. T	2. F
3. T	3. F	3. F

Part 3 Case Study

DiCenzo v. A-Best Products Company Inc.,
Ohio State Supreme Court
120 Ohio St. 3d 149 (2008)

Summary

Joseph DiCenzo worked for Wheeling-Pittsburgh Steel Corporation from the 1950s until 1993. He worked as a tin-line laborer, a tractor operator, a plier, a welding-machine operator, and a tin-line operator. During all of this time, without his knowledge or consent, he was surrounded by asbestos laden insulation products. A good portion of these products originated with George V. Hamilton, Inc. ("Hamilton"), a company which did not manufacture the asbestos filled insulation products but which did, nevertheless, supply many of them to the mill. Several years after leaving the mill, DiCenzo was diagnosed with mesothelioma. He passed away in 1999, as a direct result of this illness, which has been linked to asbestos. DiCenzo's widow joined together with several other plaintiffs in a lawsuit against Hamilton as well as approximately 90 additional defendants. The grounds for the suit included, among several additional claims, failure to warn, breach of warranty, design defects, and product liability, based on the theory of strict liability. Hamilton filed a summary judgment motion demanding a dismissal of the strict liability claim. To support the motion, Hamilton claimed that DiCenzo's strict liability argument could not be applied to Hamilton's pre-1977 behavior because the strict liability standard for product liability had not existed at the time. In fact the standard was not created until 1977 in the case of *Temple v. Wean* 590 Ohio St.2d 317 (1977). Consequently, the strict liability standard could not be applied retrospectively to outlaw conduct that had been perfectly legal at the time it was performed. The lower court agreed and the case was dismissed. The court of appeals, however, disagreed and reversed the lower court's dismissal. The Ohio Supreme Court agreed to hear the case. A good portion of the Ohio Supreme Court's opinion is based on *Chevron Oil Co. v. Huson*, 404 U.S. 97, 92 U.S. 349, 30 L.Ed.2d 296 (1971) a United States Supreme Court case that predates both *Temple* and *DiCenzo*, and that sets the standard for determining when cases are to be viewed as retrospective and when they are to be considered prospective only. To apply the *Chevron* case and to reach the decision that it does, the Ohio State Supreme Court discusses the origin of strict liability as it relates to product liability, as well as the nature of privity and the application of breach of warranty claims.

The Court's Opinion

Lundberg, Stratton, J.

III. Analysis

A. Chevron Oil Co. v. Huson

Because Chevron is central to the dispute before this court, we begin our analysis by examining its holding . . . The court held that the answers to three questions determine whether a decision should be applied prospectively only: (1) does the decision establish a new principle of law that not clearly foreshadowed? (2) does retroactive application of the decision promote or hinder the purpose behind the decision? and (3) does retroactive application of the decision cause an inequitable result? *Chevron Oil,* 404 U.S. at 106–107, 92 S.Ct. 349, 30 L.Ed.2d 296 . . . We now apply the *Chevron Oil* test to determine whether prospective-only application of *Temple* is justified.

1. Nonmanufacturing-Supplier Liability was an Issue of First Impression in *Temple v. Wean.*

(30) Historically, a lack of privity between consumers and manufacturers prevented consumers from recovering damages for a defective product under a breach of warranty claim against the product's manufacturer . . . However, in a series of cases issued from 1958 to 1966; this court gradually relaxed certain long-standing legal rules that made consumer actions against *manufacturers* more viable.

(31) In *Rogers v. Toni Home Permanent Co.* 167 Ohio St. 244, 4 O.O.2d 291. 147 N.E.2d 612, a hair product caused a consumer personal injuries. The consumer filed suit against the manufacturer, alleging negligence, breach of implied warranty, and a breach of express warranty based on the manufacturer's advertisements that the product was safe . . . The issue before then court was whether the consumer could maintain a claim for breach of an express warranty . . . The court recognized that he prevailing view was that privity of contract was required to bring an action alleging the breach of express warranty. However, the court held that the manufacturer's advertisements about its product safety effectively created an express warranty upon which the consumer could rely and that her breach of warranty claim could arise in tort . . . Thus, the court held that a lack of privity did not prevent her claim for breach of an express warranty against the manufacturer for the defective hair product.

(32) In *Inglis,* 3 Ohio St.2d 132, 32 O.O2d 136, 209 N.E.2d 583, the plaintiff succeeded in recovering damages for losses caused by a defectively manufactured automobile under a theory of breach of express warranty. This court affirmed, extending the rule it had announced in *Toni* (permitting express-warranty claim for personal injury to the consumer in *Inglis* for recovery of damages against the manufacturer caused by the defective automobile.)

(33) Finally, in *Lonzrick v. Republic Steel Corp.* (1966), 6 Ohio St.2d 227, 35 O.O.2d 404, 216 N.E.2d 185, the court held that even absent privity, a consumer could maintain a claim of breach of implied warranty against the manufacturer for injuries caused by its defective product.

(34) In *Lonzrick* the plaintiff was injured when steel joists collapsed and fell on him . . . The plaintiff sued the manufacturer of the steel joists in tort based upon a breach of an implied warranty . . . The issue was whether the plaintiff, who was injured by a defective product could maintain an action alleging breach of *implied* warranty based on tort, because unlike in *Toni* and *Inglis,* the manufacturer made no advertised representations about the metal beams. The court held that advertising was not relevant to determining whether a manufacturer should be liable. More critical to the analysis was that by placing the product into the stream of commerce, the manufacturer had implicitly represented the product to be of "good and merchantable quality, fit and safe for the ordinary purposes for which steel joists are used." . . . Thus the court held that the plaintiff could maintain a claim for breach of an implied warranty against the manufacturer based in tort.

(35) Thus, in *Toni, Inglis,* and *Lonzrick,* the court gradually relaxed the long-held legal requirement of privity, held that a breach-of-warranty claim could arise out of tort, and recognized that a claim for breach-of-warranty was viable when the manufacturer did not advertise. The gradual evolution in the products liability law was aimed at making manufacturers more accessible to consumer-product lawsuits. Indeed, it was the lack of a contractual relationship between consumers and manufacturers that spurred the products-liability evolution in the first place . . . These cases epitomized the, "slow, orderly and evolutionary development" of Ohio products-liability law against *manufacturers.*

(36) In contrast, *Temple v. Wean* marked a relatively large step in the further development of the products-liability law in its holding. *"One who sells any product* in a defective condition unreasonably dangerous to the user or consumer or to his property *is subject to liability* for physical harm thereby caused to the ultimate user or consumer, or to his property if

(37) "(a) the seller is engaged in the business of selling such a product, and

(38) "(b) it is expected to and does reach the consumer without substantial change in the condition in which it is sold."

(39) Although plaintiff's evidence in temple failed to prove liability against multiple defendants, the court's analysis makes clear that for the first time, the court defined a rule that allowed *nonmanufacturing* suppliers to be liable for defective products that they sell. We begin our review of the analysis in *Temple* by examining the facts.

(40) Betty Temple was injured by a punch press. Wean United Incorporated manufactured the punch press, which was sold to General Motors Corporation

("G.M."). G.M. in turn sold the punch press to Turner Industries, and Turner sold it to Wean, the plaintiff's employer. After her injury, Temple sued Wean United, as well as the subsequent punch-press vendors, G.M., and Turner.

(41) *Temple* adopted 2 Restatement of the Law 2d, Torts (1965), Section 402A, holding that "a plaintiff must prove that the product was defective at the time it left the seller's hands" for the seller to be held liable . . . However, the evidence showed that the press had been modified *after* it had been sold to the plaintiff's employer and that the modification was the cause of the plaintiff's injury . . . The circumstance "absolved the manufacturer, Wean, and the subsequent vendor G.M., from strict tort liability . . . G.M. was a nonmanufacturing seller of the press.

(42) Thus, *Temple* clearly defined a new rule that nonmanufacturing suppliers of products could be held liable for injuries caused by those products. Prior to *Temple,* no holding form this court had permitted the seller of a product who was not also the manufacturer to be liable for a defective product under breach of warranty theory based in tort absent privity, and none foreshadowed that such a holding was on the horizon. Clearly, *Temple* addressed an issue of first impression that had not been foreshadowed in prior cases.

2. Retroactive Application of temple Neither Promotes Nor Hinders the Purpose Behind the Products-Liability Law.

(43) The second prong of the test in *Chevron Oil* asks whether applying the decision retroactively promotes or hinders the purpose behind the rule stated in the decision . . . We conclude that retroactive application of temple will neither promote nor hinder the purpose behind products liability law.

(44) A primary "purpose of the strict liability doctrine is to induce manufacturers and suppliers to do everything possible to reduce the risk of injury and insure against what risk remains.". . .

(45) Products containing asbestos have not been manufactured or sold for approximately 30 years. The time for making these products safer has come and gone. Thus, retroactively applying temple to nonmanufacturing sellers of asbestos products will not promote the purpose of making those products safer.

(46) Moreover, one of the expressed reasons for the adoption of Section 402A of 2 Restatement of the Law 2d, Torts, in temple was that "there are virtually no distinction between Ohio's "implied warranty in tort' theory and the Restatement version of strict liability in tort and * * * the Restatement formulation, together with its numerous illustrative comments,

greatly facilitates analysis in this area." . . . Again, applying Temple retroactively to impose liability on a nonmanufacturer supplier of asbestos products would neither promote nor impede the purpose of facilitating the analysis of products-liability law.

3. It Would Be Inequitable to Impose *Temple* on Nonmanufacturing Suppliers of Asbestos Products.

(47) As we noted in section I above, *Temple,* which was decided in 1977, marked the first time this court had held that a nonmanufacturing seller of a product could be held liable for injuries caused by a defective product. Thus, nonmanufacturing sellers of asbetstos, such as Hamilton, could not have foreseen that these products, distributed from the 1950s to the 1970s, could decades later result in Hamilton's being liable for injuries caused by that product. Imposing such a potential financial burden on these nonmanufacturing suppliers years after the fact for an obligation that was not foreseeable at the time would result in a great inequity

(48) Thus, the answer to the question posed in *Chevron Oil* collectively indicate that our decision in Temple should be applied prospectively only. Accordingly, we reverse the judgment of the court and reinstate the judgment of the trial court.

Judgment reversed.

O'Connor, O'Donnell, Lanzinger, and Cupp, JJ., concur.
Moyer, C.J., dissents without opinion.
Pfeifer, J. dissents with opinion.

Questions for Analysis

1. What is the difference between an *express* and an *implied* warranty? How are express warranties created in sales law? Explain.

2. How are *implied* warranties created in sales law? What types of implied warranties are recognized in sales law? Explain.

3. The first step in the gradual evolution of the product liability theory involved a modification of *express* warranty. In general how is an express warranty created in sales law? In what way was the warranty made "express" in the case of *Rogers v. Toni Home Permanent?* Explain.

4. How did the case of *Inglis v. Am. Motors Corp.* extend the express warranty claim established by the court in the *Toni* case? Explain.

5. The next step in the development of the product liability theory involved a modification of *implied*

warranty. In general how is an implied warranty created in sales law? Which type of implied warranty is breached in the *Lonzrick* case? Explain.

6. The court notes that *"Temple v. Wean* marked a relatively large step in the further development of the products-liability law." What "relatively large step" was taken by the court in advance in the case of *Temple v. Wean?* Explain.

7. The court decided not to apply the rule created in the case of *Temple v. Wean* restrospectively. What does it mean to apply a rule restrospectively.?

What does it mean to apply a rule prospectively? Explain.

8. The court gives three reasons for not applying the rule created in *Temple v. Wean* retrospectively. What are those three reasons? Explain.

9. What is the public interest promoted by the courts in the line of cases discussed at length in *DiCenzo v. A-Best Products Company Inc.?* Explain.

10. What public policy tactic is at use in the case of *DiCenzo v. A-Best Products Company Inc.?* Explain.

Appendix A The Constitution of the United States

Preamble

We the People of the United States, in Order to form a more perfect Union, establish Justice, insure domestic Tranquility, provide for the common defence, promote the general Welfare, and secure the Blessings of Liberty to ourselves and our Posterity, do ordain and establish this Constitution for the United States of America.

Article I

Section 1. All legislative Powers herein granted shall be vested in a Congress of the United States, which shall consist of a Senate and House of Representatives.

Section 2. [1] The House of Representatives shall be composed of Members chosen every second Year by the People of the several States, and the Electors in each State shall have the Qualifications requisite for Electors of the most numerous Branch of the State Legislature.

[2] No Person shall be a Representative who shall not have attained to the Age of twenty-five Years, and been seven Years a Citizen of the United States, and who shall not, when elected, be an Inhabitant of that State in which he shall be chosen.

[3] Representatives and direct Taxes shall be apportioned among the several States which may be included within this Union, according to their respective Numbers, which shall be determined by adding to the whole Number of free Persons, including those bound to Service for a Term of Years, and excluding Indians not taxed, three fifths of all other Persons. The actual Enumeration shall be made within three Years after the first Meeting of the Congress of the United States, and within every subsequent Term of ten Years, in such Manner as they shall by Law direct. The Number of Representatives shall not exceed one for every thirty Thousand, but each State shall have at Least one Representative; and until such enumeration shall be made, the State of New Hampshire shall be entitled to chuse three, Massachusetts eight, Rhode Island and Providence Plantations one, Connecticut five, New York six, New Jersey four, Pennsylvania eight, Delaware one, Maryland six, Virginia ten, North Carolina five, South Carolina five, and Georgia three.

[4] When vacancies happen in the Representation from any State, the Executive Authority thereof shall issue Writs of Election to fill such Vacancies.

[5] The House of Representatives shall chuse their Speaker and other Officers; and shall have the sole Power of Impeachment.

Section 3. [1] The Senate of the United States shall be composed of two Senators from each State, chosen by the Legislature thereof, for six Years; and each Senator shall have one Vote.

[2] Immediately after they shall be assembled in Consequence of the first Election, they shall be divided as equally as may be into three Classes. The Seats of the Senators of the first Class shall be vacated at the Expiration of the Second Year, of the second Class at the Expiration of the fourth Year, and of the third Class at the Expiration of the sixth Year, so that one third may be chosen every second Year; and if Vacancies happen by Resignation, or otherwise, during the Recess of the Legislature of any State, the Executive thereof may make temporary Appointments until the next Meeting of the Legislature, which shall then fill such Vacancies.

[3] No Person shall be a Senator who shall not have attained to the Age of thirty Years, and been nine Years a Citizen of the United States, and who shall not, when elected, be an Inhabitant of that State for which he shall be chosen.

[4] The Vice President of the United States shall be President of the Senate, but shall have no Vote, unless they be equally divided.

[5] The Senate shall chuse their other Officers, and also a President pro tempore, in the Absence of the Vice President, or when he shall exercise the Office of President of the United States.

[6] The Senate shall have the sole Power to try all Impeachments. When sitting for that Purpose, they shall be on Oath or Affirmation. When the President of the United States is tried, the Chief Justice shall preside: And no Person shall be convicted without the Concurrence of two thirds of the Members present.

[7] Judgment in Cases of Impeachment shall not extend further than to removal from Office, and disqualification to hold and enjoy any Office of honor, Trust, or Profit under the United States: but the Party convicted shall nevertheless be liable and subject to Indictment, Trial, Judgment, and Punishment, according to Law.

Section 4. [1] The Times, Places and Manner of holding elections for Senators and Representatives, shall be prescribed in each State by the Legislature thereof; but the Congress may at any time by Law make or alter such Regulations, except as to the Places of chusing Senators.

[2] The Congress shall assemble at least once in every Year, and such Meeting shall be on the first Monday in December, unless they shall by Law appoint a different Day.

Section 5. [1] Each House shall be the Judge of the Elections, Returns, and Qualifications of its own Members, and a Majority of each shall constitute a Quorum to do Business; but a smaller Number may adjourn from day to day, and may be authorized to compel the Attendance of absent Members, in such Manner, and under such Penalties as each House may provide.

[2] Each House may determine the Rules of its Proceedings, punish its Members for disorderly Behavior, and, with the Concurrence of two thirds, expel a Member.

[3] Each House shall keep a Journal of its Proceedings, and from time to time publish the same, excepting such parts as may in their Judgment require Secrecy; and the Yeas and Nays of the Members of either House on any question shall, at the Desire of one fifth of those Present, be entered on the Journal.

[4] Neither House, during the Session of Congress, shall, without the Consent of the other, adjourn for more than three days, nor to any other Place than that in which the two Houses shall be sitting.

Section 6. **[1]** The Senators and Representatives shall receive a Compensation for their Services, to be ascertained by Law, and paid out of the Treasury of the United States. They shall in all Cases, except Treason, Felony and Breach of the Peace, be privileged from Arrest during their Attendance at the Session of their respective Houses, and in going to and returning from the same; and for any Speech of Debate in either House, they shall not be questioned in any other Place.

[2] No Senator or Representative shall, during the Time for which he was elected, be appointed to any civil Office under the Authority of the United States, which shall have been created, or the Emoluments whereof shall have been increased during such time; and no Person holding any Office under the United States, shall be a Member of either House during his Continuance in Office.

Section 7. **[1]** All Bills for raising Revenue shall originate in the House of Representatives; but the Senate may propose or concur with Amendments as on other Bills.

[2] Every Bill which shall have passed the House of Representatives and the Senate, shall, before it becomes a Law, be presented to the President of the United States; If he approve he shall sign it, but if not he shall return it, with his Objections to the House in which it shall have originated, who shall enter the Objections at large on their Journal, and proceed to reconsider it. If after such Reconsideration two thirds of that House shall agree to pass the Bill, it shall be sent together with the Objections, to the other House, by which it shall likewise be reconsidered, and if approved by two thirds of that House, it shall become a Law. But in all such Cases the Votes of both Houses shall be determined by yeas and Nays, and the Names of the Persons voting for and against the Bill shall be entered on the Journal of each House respectively. If any Bill shall not be returned by the President within ten Days (Sundays excepted) after it shall have been presented to him, the Same shall be a Law, in like Manner as if he had signed it, unless the Congress by their Adjournment prevent its Return in which Case it shall not be a Law.

[3] Every Order, Resolution, or Vote, to Which the Concurrence of the Senate and House of Representatives may be necessary (except on a question of Adjournment) shall be presented to the President of the United States; and before the Same shall take Effect, shall be approved by him, or being disapproved by him, shall be repassed by two thirds of the Senate and House of Representatives, according to the Rules and Limitations prescribed in the Case of a Bill.

Section 8. **[1]** The Congress shall have Power To lay and collect Taxes, Duties, Imposts and Excises, to pay the Debts and provide for the common Defence and general Welfare of the United States; but all Duties, Imposts and Excises shall be uniform throughout the United States;

[2] To borrow money on the credit of the United States;

[3] To regulate Commerce with foreign Nations, and among the several States, and with the Indian Tribes;

[4] To establish an uniform Rule of Naturalization, and uniform laws on the subject of Bankruptcies throughout the United States;

[5] To coin Money, regulate the Value thereof, and of foreign Coin, and fix the Standard of Weights and Measures;

[6] To provide for the Punishment of counterfeiting the Securities and current Coin of the United States;

[7] To Establish Post Offices and Post Roads;

[8] To promote the Progress of Science and useful Arts, by securing for limited Times to Authors and Inventors the exclusive Right to their respective Writings and Discoveries;

[9] To constitute Tribunals inferior to the supreme Court;

[10] To define and punish Piracies and Felonies committed on the high Seas, and Offenses against the Law of Nations;

[11] To declare War, grant Letters of Marque and Reprisal, and make Rules concerning Captures on Land and Water;

[12] To raise and support Armies, but no Appropriation of Money to that Use shall be for a longer Term than two Years;

[13] To provide and maintain a Navy;

[14] To make Rules for the Government and Regulation of the land and naval Forces;

[15] To provide for calling forth the Militia to execute the Laws of the Union, suppress Insurrections and repel Invasions;

[16] To provide for organizing, arming, and disciplining, the Militia, and for governing such Part of them as may be employed in the Service of the United States, reserving to the States respectively, the Appointment of the Officers, and the Authority of training the Militia according to the discipline prescribed by Congress;

[17] To exercise exclusive Legislation in all Cases whatsoever, over such District (not exceeding ten Miles square) as may, by Cession of particular States, and the Acceptance of Congress, become the Seat of the Government of the United States, and to exercise like Authority over all Places purchased by the Consent of the Legislature of the State in which the Same shall be, for the Erection of Forts, Magazines, Arsenals, dock-Yards and other needful Buildings;—And

[18] To make all Laws which shall be necessary and proper for carrying into Execution the foregoing Powers, and all other Powers vested by this Constitution in the Government of the United States, or in any Department or Officer thereof.

Section 9. **[1]** The Migration or Importation of Such Persons as any of the States now existing shall think proper to admit, shall not be prohibited by the Congress prior to the Year one thousand eight hundred and eight, but a Tax or duty may be imposed on such Importation, not exceeding ten dollars for each Person.

[2] The privilege of the Writ of Habeas Corpus shall not be suspended, unless when in Cases of Rebellion or Invasion the public Safety may require it.

[3] No Bill of Attainder or ex post facto Law shall be passed.

[4] No Capitation, or other direct, Tax shall be laid, unless in Proportion to the Census or Enumeration herein before directed to be taken.

[5] No Tax or Duty shall be laid on Articles exported from any State.

[6] No Preference shall be given by any Regulation of Commerce or Revenue to the Ports of one State over those of another: nor shall Vessels bound to, or from, one State be obliged to enter, clear, or pay Duties in another.

[7] No money shall be drawn from the Treasury, but in Consequence of Appropriations made by Law; and a regular Statement and Account of the Receipts and Expenditures of all public Money shall be published from time to time.

[8] No Title of Nobility shall be granted by the United States: And no Person holding any Office of Profit or Trust under them, shall, without the Consent of the Congress, accept of any present, Emolument, Office, or Title, of any kind whatever, from any King, Prince, or foreign State.

Section 10. **[1]** No State shall enter into any Treaty, Alliance, or confederation; grant Letters of Marque and Reprisal; coin Money; emit Bills of Credit; make any Thing but gold and silver Coin a Tender in Payment of Debts; pass any Bill of Attainder, ex post facto Law, or Law impairing the Obligation of Contracts, or grant any Title of Nobility.

[2] No State shall, without the Consent of the Congress, lay any Imposts or Duties on Imports or Exports, except what may be absolutely necessary for executing its inspection Laws: and the net Produce of all Duties and Imposts, laid by any State on Imports or Exports, shall be for the Use of the Treasury of the United States; and all such Laws shall be subject to the Revision and Control of the Congress.

[3] No State shall, without the Consent of Congress, lay any Duty of Tonnage, keep Troops, or Ships of War in time of Peace, enter into any Agreement or Compact with another State, or with a foreign Power, or engage in War, unless actually invaded, or in such imminent Danger as will not admit of delay.

Article II

Section 1. **[1]** The executive Power shall be vested in a President of the United States of America. He shall hold his Office during the Term of four Years, and, together with the Vice President, chosen for the same Term, be elected, as follows:

[2] Each State shall appoint, in such Manner as the Legislature thereof may direct, a Number of Electors, equal to the whole Number of Senators and Representatives to which the State may be entitled in the Congress; but no Senator or Representative, or Person holding an Office of Trust or Profit under the United States, shall be appointed an Elector.

[3] The Electors shall meet in their respective States, and vote by Ballot for two Persons, of whom one at least shall not be an Inhabitant of the same State with themselves. And they shall make a List of all the Persons voted for, and of the Number of Votes for each; which List they shall sign and certify, and transmit sealed to the Seat of the Government of the United States, directed to the President of the Senate. The President of the Senate shall, in the Presence of the Senate and House of Representatives, open all the Certificates, and the Votes shall then be counted. The Person having the greatest Number of Votes shall be the President, if such Number be a Majority of the whole Number of Electors appointed; and if there be more than one who have such Majority, and have an equal Number of Votes, then the House of Representatives shall immediately chuse by Ballot one of them for President; and if no Person have a Majority, then from the five highest on the List the said House shall in like Manner chuse the President. But in chusing the President, the Votes shall be taken by States the Representation from each State having one Vote; A quorum for this Purpose shall consist of a Member or Members from two thirds of the States, and a Majority of all the States shall be necessary to a Choice. In every Case, after the Choice of the President, the Person having the greater Number of Votes of the Electors shall be the Vice President. But if there shall remain two or more who have equal Votes, the Senate shall chuse from them by Ballot the Vice President.

[4] The Congress may determine the Time of chusing the Electors, and the Day on which they shall give their Votes; which Day shall be the same throughout the United States.

[5] No person except a natural born Citizen, or a Citizen of the United States, at the time of the Adoption of this Constitution, shall be eligible to the Office of President; neither shall any Person be eligible to that Office who shall not have attained to the Age of thirty-five Years, and been fourteen Years a Resident within the United States.

[6] In case of the removal of the President from Office, or of his Death, Resignation or Inability to discharge the Powers and Duties of the said Office, the Same shall devolve on the Vice President, and the Congress may by Law provide for the Case of Removal, Death, Resignation or Inability, both of the President and Vice President, declaring what Officer shall then act as President, and such Officer shall act accordingly, until the Disability be removed, or a President shall be elected.

[7] The President shall, at stated Times, receive for his Services, a Compensation, which shall neither be increased nor diminished during the Period for which he shall have been elected, and he shall not receive within that Period any other Emolument from the United States, or any of them.

[8] Before he enter on the Execution of his Office, he shall take the following Oath or Affirmation: "I do solemnly swear (or affirm) that I will faithfully execute the Office of President of the United States, and will to the best of my Ability, preserve, protect, and defend the Constitution of the United States."

Section 2. [1] The President shall be Commander in Chief of the Army and Navy of the United States, and of the militia of the several States, when called into the actual Service of the United States; he may require the Opinion, in writing, of the principal Officer in each of the Executive Departments, upon any subject relating to the Duties of their respective Offices, and he shall have Power to grant Reprieves and Pardons for Offenses against the United States, except in Cases of Impeachment.

[2] He shall have Power, by and with the Advice and Consent of the Senate to make Treaties, provided two thirds of the Senators present concur; and he shall nominate, and by and with the Advice and Consent of the Senate, shall appoint Ambassadors, other public Ministers and Consuls, Judges of the supreme Court, and all other Officers of the United States, whose Appointments are not herein otherwise provided for, and which shall be established by Law; but the Congress may by Law vest the Appointment of such inferior Officers, as they think proper, in the President alone, in the Courts of Law, or in the Heads of Departments.

[3] The President shall have Power to fill up all Vacancies that may happen during the Recess of the Senate, by granting commissions which shall expire at the End of their next Session.

Section 3. He shall from time to time give to the Congress Information of the State of the Union, and recommend to their Consideration such Measures as he shall judge necessary and expedient; he may, on extraordinary Occasions, convene both Houses, or either of them, and in Case of Disagreement between them, with Respect to the Time of Adjournment, he may adjourn them to such Time as he shall think proper; he shall receive Ambassadors and other public Ministers; he shall take Care that the Laws be faithfully executed, and shall commission all the Officers of the United States.

Section 4. The President, Vice President and all civil Officers of the United States, shall be removed from Office on Impeachment for, and Conviction of, Treason, Bribery, or other high Crimes and Misdemeanors.

Article III

Section 1. The judicial Power of the United States, shall be vested in one supreme Court, and in such inferior Courts as the Congress may from time to time ordain and establish. The Judges, both of the supreme and inferior Courts, shall hold their Offices during good Behaviour, and shall, at stated Times, receive for their Services a Compensation, which shall not be diminished during their Continuance in Office.

Section 2. [1] The judicial Power shall extend to all Cases, in Law and Equity, arising under this Constitution, the Laws of the United States, and Treaties made, or which shall be made, under their Authority;—to all Cases affecting Ambassadors, other public Ministers and Consuls;—to all Cases of admiralty and maritime Jurisdiction;—to Controversies to which the United States shall be a Party;—between a State and Citizens of another State; between Citizens of different States;—between Citizens of the same State claiming Lands under the Grants of different States, and between a State, or the Citizens thereof, and foreign States, Citizens or Subjects.

[2] In all Cases affecting Ambassadors, other public Ministers and Consuls, and those in which a State shall be a Party, the supreme Court shall have original Jurisdiction. In all the other Cases before mentioned, the supreme Court shall have appellate Jurisdiction, both as to Law and Fact, with such Exceptions, and under such Regulations as the Congress shall make.

[3] The trial of all Crimes, except in Cases of Impeachment, shall be by Jury; and such Trial shall be held in the State where the said Crimes shall have been committed; but when not committed within any State, the Trial shall be at such Place or Places as the Congress may by Law have directed.

Section 3. [1] Treason against the United States, shall consist only in levying War against them, or, in adhering to their Enemies, giving them Aid and Comfort. No Person shall be convicted of Treason unless on the Testimony of two Witnesses to the same overt Act, or on Confession in open Court.

[2] The Congress shall have Power to declare the Punishment of Treason, but no Attainder of Treason shall work Corruption of Blood, or Forfeiture except during the Life of the Person attainted.

Article IV

Section 1. Full Faith and Credit shall be given in each State to the public Acts, Records, and judicial Proceedings of every other State. And the Congress may by general Laws prescribe the Manner in which such Acts, Records and Proceedings shall be proved, and the Effect thereof.

Section 2. [1] The Citizens of each State shall be entitled to all Privileges and Immunities of Citizens in the several States.

[2] A Person charged in any State with Treason, Felony, or other Crime, who shall flee from Justice, and be found in another State, shall on demand of the executive Authority of the State from which he fled, be delivered up, to be removed to the State having Jurisdiction of the Crime.

[3] No Person held to Service or Labour in one State, under the Laws thereof, escaping into another, shall, in Consequence of any Law or Regulation therein, be discharged from such Service or Labour, but shall be delivered up on Claim of the Party to whom such Service or Labour may be due.

Section 3. **[1]** New States may be admitted by the Congress into this Union; but no new State shall be formed or erected within the Jurisdiction of any other State; nor any State be formed by the Junction of two or more States, or Parts of States, without the Consent of the Legislatures of the States concerned as well as of the Congress.

[2] The Congress shall have Power to dispose of and make all needful Rules and Regulations respecting the Territory or other Property belonging to the United States; and nothing in this Constitution shall be so construed as to Prejudice any Claims of the United States, or of any particular State.

Section 4. The United States shall guarantee to every State in this Union a Republican Form of Government, and shall protect each of them against Invasion; and on Application of the Legislature, or of the Executive (when the Legislature cannot be convened) against domestic Violence.

Article V

The Congress, whenever two thirds of both Houses shall deem it necessary, shall propose Amendments to this Constitution, or, on the Application of the Legislatures of two thirds of the several States, shall call a Convention for proposing Amendments, which, in either case, shall be valid to all Intents and Purposes, as part of this Constitution, when ratified by the Legislatures of three fourths of the several States, or by Conventions in three fourths thereof, as the one or the other Mode of Ratification may be proposed by the Congress; Provided that no Amendment which may be made prior to the Year One thousand eight hundred and eight shall in any Manner affect the first and fourth Clauses in the Ninth Section of the first Article; and that no State, without its Consent, shall be deprived of its equal Suffrage in the Senate.

Article VI

[1] All Debts contracted and Engagements entered into, before the Adoption of this Constitution shall be as valid against the United States under this Constitution, as under the Confederation.

[2] This Constitution, and the Laws of the United States which shall be made in Pursuance thereof; and all Treaties made, or which shall be made, under the Authority of the United States, shall be the supreme Law of the Land; and the Judges in every State shall be bound thereby, any Thing in the Constitution or Laws of any State to the Contrary notwithstanding.

[3] The Senators and Representatives before mentioned, and the Members of the several State Legislatures, and all executive and judicial Officers, both of the United States and of the several States, shall be bound by Oath or Affirmation, to support this Constitution; but no religious Test shall ever be required as a Qualification to any Office or public Trust under the United States.

Article VII

The Ratification of the Conventions of nine States shall be sufficient for the Establishment of this Constitution between the States so ratifying the Same.

Amendments

Articles in addition to, and in amendment of, the Constitution of the United States of America, proposed by Congress, and ratified by the Legislatures of the several States pursuant to the Fifth Article of the original Constitution.

Amendment 1 [1791]

Congress shall make no law respecting an establishment of religion, or prohibiting the free exercise thereof; or abridging the freedom of speech, or of the press; or the right of the people peaceably to assemble, and to petition the Government for a redress of grievances.

Amendment 2 [1791]

A well regulated Militia, being necessary to the security of a free State, the right of the people to keep and bear Arms, shall not be infringed.

Amendment 3 [1791]

No Soldier shall, in time of peace be quartered in any house, without the consent of the Owner, nor in time of war, but in a manner to be prescribed by law.

Amendment 4 [1791]

The right of the people to be secure in their persons, houses, papers, and effects, against unreasonable searches and seizures, shall not be violated, and no Warrants shall issue, but upon probable cause, supported by Oath or affirmation, and particularly describing the place to be searched, and the persons or things to be seized.

Amendment 5 [1791]

No person shall be held to answer for a capital, or other infamous crime, unless on a presentment or indictment of a Grand Jury, except in cases arising in the land or naval forces, or in the Militia, when in actual service in time of War or public danger; nor shall any person be subject for the same offence to be twice put in jeopardy of life or limb; nor shall be compelled in any criminal case to be a witness against himself, nor be deprived of life, liberty, or property, without due process of law; nor shall private property be taken for public use, without just compensation.

Amendment 6 [1791]

In all criminal prosecutions, the accused shall enjoy the right to a speedy and public trial, by an impartial jury of the State and district wherein the crime shall have been committed, which district shall have been previously ascertained by law, and to be informed of the nature and cause of the accusation; to be confronted with the witnesses against him; to have compulsory process for obtaining witnesses in his favor, and to have the Assistance of Counsel for his defence.

Amendment 7 [1791]

In Suits at common law, where the value in controversy shall exceed twenty dollars, the right of trial by jury shall be preserved, and no fact tried by jury, shall be otherwise re-examined in any Court of the United States, than according to the rules of common law.

Amendment 8 [1791]

Excessive bail shall not be required, nor excessive fines imposed, nor cruel and unusual punishments inflicted.

Amendment 9 [1791]

The enumeration in the Constitution, of certain rights, shall not be construed to deny or disparage others retained by the people.

Amendment 10 [1791]

The powers not delegated to the United States by the Constitution, nor prohibited by it to the States, are reserved to the States respectively, or to the people.

Amendment 11 [1798]

The Judicial power of the United States shall not be construed to extend to any suit in law or equity, commenced or prosecuted against one of the United States by Citizens of another State, or by Citizens or Subjects of any Foreign State.

Amendment 12 [1804]

The Electors shall meet in their respective states and vote by ballot for President and Vice President, one of whom, at least, shall not be an inhabitant of the same state with themselves; they shall name in their ballots the person voted for as President, and in distinct ballots the person voted for as Vice President, and they shall make distinct lists of all persons voted for as President, and of all persons voted for as Vice President, and of the number of votes for each, which lists they shall sign and certify, and transmit sealed to the seat of the government of the United States, directed to the President of the Senate;—The President of the Senate shall, in the presence of the Senate and House of Representatives, open all the certificates and the votes shall then be counted;—The person having the greatest number of votes for President, shall be the President, if such number be a majority of the whole number of Electors appointed; and if no person have such majority, then from the persons having the highest numbers not exceeding three on the list of those voted for as President, the House of Representatives shall choose immediately, by ballot, the President. But in choosing the President, the votes shall be taken by states, the representation from each state having one vote; a quorum for this purpose shall consist of a member or members from two thirds of the states, and a majority of all states shall be necessary to a choice. And if the House of Representatives shall not choose a President whenever the right of choice shall devolve upon them before the fourth day of March next following, then the Vice President shall act as President, as in the case of the death or other constitutional disability of the President.—The person having the greatest number of votes as Vice President, shall be the Vice President, if such number be a majority of the whole number of Electors appointed, and if no person have a majority, then from the two highest numbers on the list, the Senate shall choose the Vice President; a quorum for the purpose shall consist of two thirds of the whole number of Senators, and a majority of the whole number shall be necessary to a choice. But no person constitutionally ineligible to the office of President shall be eligible to that of Vice President of the United States.

Amendment 13 [1865]

Section 1. Neither slavery nor involuntary servitude, except as a punishment for crime whereof the party shall have been duly convicted, shall exist within the United States, or any place subject to their jurisdiction.

Section 2. Congress shall have power to enforce this article by appropriate legislation.

Amendment 14 [1868]

Section 1. All persons born or naturalized in the United States, and subject to the jurisdiction thereof, are citizens of the United States and of the State wherein they reside. No State shall make or enforce any law which shall abridge the privileges or immunities of citizens of the United States; nor shall any State deprive any person of life, liberty, or property, without due process of law; nor deny to any person within its jurisdiction the equal protection of the laws.

Section 2. Representatives shall be apportioned among the several States according to their respective numbers, counting the whole number of persons in each State, excluding Indians not taxed. But when the right to vote at any election for the choice of electors for President and Vice President of the United States, Representatives in Congress, the Executive and Judicial officers of a State, or the members of the Legislature thereof, is denied to any of the male inhabitants of such State, being twenty-one years of age, and citizens of the United States, or in any way abridged, except for participation in rebellion, or other crime, the basis of representation therein shall be reduced in the proportion which the number of such male citizens shall bear to the whole number of male citizens twenty-one years of age in such State.

Section 3. No person shall be a Senator or Representative in Congress, or elector of President and Vice President, or hold any office, civil or military, under the United States, or under any State, who having previously taken an oath, as a member of Congress, or as an officer of the United States, or as a member of any State legislature, or as an executive or judicial officer of any State, to support the Constitution of the United States, shall have engaged in insurrection or rebellion against the same, or given aid or comfort to the enemies thereof. But Congress may by a vote of two thirds of each House, remove such disability.

Section 4. The validity of the public debt of the United States, authorized by law, including debts incurred for payment of pensions and bounties for services in suppressing insurrection or rebellion, shall not be questioned. But neither the United States nor any State shall assume or pay any debt or obligation incurred in aid of insurrection or rebellion against the United States, or any claim for the loss or emancipation of any slave; but all such debts, obligations and claims shall be held illegal and void.

Section 5. The Congress shall have power to enforce, by appropriate legislation, the provisions of this article.

Amendment 15 [1870]

Section 1. The right of citizens of the United States to vote shall not be denied or abridged by the United States or by any State on account of race, color, or previous condition of servitude.

Section 2. The Congress shall have power to enforce this article by appropriate legislation.

Amendment 16 [1913]

The Congress shall have power to lay and collect taxes on incomes, from whatever source derived, without apportionment among the several States, and without regard to any census or enumeration.

Amendment 17 [1913]

[1] The Senate of the United States shall be composed of two Senators from each State, elected by the people thereof, for six years; and each Senator shall have one vote. The electors in each State shall have the qualifications requisite for electors of the most numerous branch of the State legislatures.

[2] When vacancies happen in the representation of any State in the Senate, the executive authority of such State shall issue writs of election to fill such vacancies: *Provided,* That the legislature of any State may empower the executive thereof to make temporary appointments until the people fill the vacancies by election as the legislature may direct.

[3] This amendment shall not be so construed as to affect the election or term of any Senator chosen before it becomes valid as part of the Constitution.

Amendment 18 [1919]

Section 1. After one year from the ratification of this article the manufacture, sale, or transportation of intoxicating liquors within, the importation thereof into, or the exportation thereof from the United States and all territory subject to the jurisdiction thereof for beverage purposes is hereby prohibited.

Section 2. The Congress and the several States shall have concurrent power to enforce this article by appropriate legislation.

Section 3. This article shall be inoperative unless it shall have been ratified as an amendment to the Constitution by the legislatures of the several States, as provided in the Constitution, within seven years from the date of the submission hereof to the States by the Congress.

Amendment 19 [1920]

[1] The right of citizens of the United States to vote shall not be denied or abridged by the United States or by any State on account of sex.

[2] Congress shall have power to enforce this article by appropriate legislation.

Amendment 20 [1933]

Section 1. The terms of the President and Vice President shall end at noon on the twentieth day of January, and the terms of Senators and Representatives at noon on the third day of January, of the years in which such terms would have ended if this article had not been ratified; and the terms of their successors shall then begin.

Section 2. The Congress shall assemble at least once in every year, and such meeting shall begin at noon on the third day of January, unless they shall by law appoint a different day.

Section 3. If, at the time fixed for the beginning of the term of the President, the President elect shall have died, the Vice President elect shall become President. If the President shall not have been chosen before the time fixed for the beginning of his term, or if the President elect shall have failed to qualify, then the Vice President elect shall act as President until a President shall have qualified; and the Congress may by law provide for the case wherein neither a President elect nor a Vice President elect shall have qualified, declaring who shall then act as President, or the manner in which one who is to act shall be selected, and such person shall act accordingly until a President or Vice President shall have qualified.

Section 4. The Congress may by law provide for the case of the death of any of the persons from whom the House of Representatives may choose a President whenever the right of choice shall have devolved upon them, and for the case of the death of any of the persons from whom the Senate may choose a Vice President whenever the right of choice shall have devolved upon them.

Section 5. Sections 1 and 2 shall take effect on the fifteenth day of October following the ratification of this article.

Section 6. This article shall be inoperative unless it shall have been ratified as an amendment to the Constitution by the legislatures of three fourths of the several States within seven years from the date of its submission.

Amendment 21 [1933]

Section 1. The eighteenth article of amendment to the Constitution of the United States is hereby repealed.

Section 2. The transportation or importation into any State, Territory, or possession of the United States for delivery or use therein of intoxicating liquors, in violation of the laws therefore, is hereby prohibited.

Section 3. This article shall be inoperative unless it shall have been ratified as an amendment to the Constitution by conventions in the several States, as provided in the Constitution, within seven years from the date of the submission hereof to the States by the Congress.

Amendment 22 [1951]

Section 1. No person shall be elected to the office of the President more than twice, and no person who has held the office of President, or acted as President, for more than two years of a term to which some other person was elected President shall be elected to the office of President more than once. But this Article shall not apply to any person holding the office of President when this Article was proposed by the Congress, and shall not prevent any person who may be holding the office of President, or acting as President, during the term within which this Article becomes operative from holding the office of President or acting as President during the remainder of such term.

Section 2. This article shall be inoperative unless it shall have been ratified as an amendment to the Constitution by the legislatures of three fourths of the several States within seven years from the date of its submission to the States by the Congress.

Amendment 23 [1961]

Section 1. The District constituting the seat of Government of the United States shall appoint in such manner as the Congress may direct:

A number of electors of President and Vice President equal to the whole number of Senators and Representatives in Congress to which the District would be entitled if it were a State, but in no event more than the least populous state;

they shall be in addition to those appointed by the states, but they shall be considered, for the purposes of the election of President and Vice President, to be electors appointed by a state; and they shall meet in the District and perform such duties as provided by the twelfth article of amendment.

Section 2. The Congress shall have power to enforce this article by appropriate legislation.

Amendment 24 [1964]

Section 1. The right of citizens of the United States to vote in any primary or other election for President or Vice President, for electors for President or Vice President, or for Senator or Representative in Congress, shall not be denied or abridged by the United States, or any State by reason of failure to pay any poll tax or other tax.

Section 2. The Congress shall have power to enforce this article by appropriate legislation.

Amendment 25 [1967]

Section 1. In case of the removal of the President from office or of his death or resignation, the Vice President shall become President.

Section 2. Whenever there is a vacancy in the office of the Vice President, the President shall nominate a Vice President who shall take office upon confirmation by a majority vote of both Houses of Congress.

Section 3. Whenever the President transmits to the President pro tempore of the Senate and the Speaker of the House of Representatives his written declaration that he is unable to discharge the powers and duties of his office, and until he transmits to them a written declaration to the contrary, such powers and duties shall be discharged by the Vice President as Acting President.

Section 4. Whenever the Vice President and a majority of either the principal officers of the executive departments or of such other body as Congress may by law provide, transmit to the President pro tempore of the Senate and the Speaker of the House of Representatives their written declaration that the President is unable to discharge the powers and duties of his office, the Vice President shall immediately assume the powers and duties of the office as Acting President.

Thereafter, when the President transmits to the President pro tempore of the Senate and the Speaker of the House of Representatives his written declaration that no inability exists, he shall resume the powers and duties of his office unless the Vice President and a majority of either the principal officers of the executive department or of such other body as Congress may by law provide, transmit within four days to the President pro tempore of the Senate and the Speaker of the House of Representatives their written declaration and the President is unable to discharge the powers and duties of his office. Thereupon Congress shall decide the issue, assembling within forty-eight hours for that purpose if not in session. If the

Congress, within twenty-one days after receipt of the latter written declaration, or, if Congress is not in session, within twenty-one days after Congress is required to assemble, determines by two thirds vote of both Houses that the President is unable to discharge the powers and duties of his office, the Vice President shall continue to discharge the same as Acting President; otherwise, the President shall resume the powers and duties of his office.

Amendment 26 [1971]

Section 1. The right of citizens of the United States, who are eighteen years of age or older, to vote shall not be denied or abridged by the United States or by any State on account of age.

Section 2. The Congress shall have power to enforce this article by appropriate legislation.

Amendment 27 [1992]

No law varying the compensation for the services of Senators and Representatives shall take effect, until an election of Representatives shall have intervened.

Appendix B   Uniform Commercial Code (Articles 1, 2, 2a, and 3)

Article 1: General Provisions

Part 1: Short Title, Construction, Application and Subject Matter of the Act

§1-101. Short Title. This act shall be known and may be cited as Uniform Commercial Code.

§1-102. Purposes; Rules of Construction; Variation by Agreement.

(1) This Act shall be liberally construed and applied to promote its underlying purposes and policies.

(2) Underlying purposes and policies of this Act are

(a) to simplify, clarify and modernize the law governing commercial transactions;

(b) to permit the continued expansion of commercial practices through custom, usage and agreement of the parties;

(c) to make uniform the law among the various jurisdictions.

(3) The effect of provisions of this Act may be varied by agreement, except as otherwise provided in this Act and except that the obligations of good faith, diligence, reasonableness and care prescribed by this Act may not be disclaimed by agreement but the parties may by agreement determine the standards by which the performance of such obligations is to be measured if such standards are not manifestly unreasonable.

(4) The presence in certain provisions of this Act of the words "unless otherwise agreed" or words of similar import does not imply that the effect of other provisions may not be varied by agreement under subsection (3).

(5) In this Act unless the context otherwise requires

(a) words in the singular number include the plural, and in the plural include the singular;

(b) words of the masculine gender include the feminine and the neuter, and when the sense so indicates words of the neuter gender may refer to any gender.

§1-103. Supplementary General Principles of Law Applicable. Unless displaced by the particular provisions of this Act, the principles of law and equity, including the law merchant and the law relative to capacity to contract, principal and agent, estoppel, fraud, misrepresentation, duress, coercion, mistake, bankruptcy or other validating or invalidating cause shall supplement its provisions.

§1-104. Construction Against Implicity Repeal. This Act being a general act intended as a unified coverage of its subject matter, no part of it shall be deemed to be impliedly repealed by subsequent legislation if such construction can reasonably be avoided.

§1-105. Territorial Application of the Act; Parties' Power to Choose Applicable Law.

(1) Except as provided hereafter in this section, when a transaction bears a reasonable relation to this state and also to another state or nation the parties may agree that the law either of this state or of such other state or nation shall govern their rights and duties. Failing such agreement this Act applies to transactions bearing an appropriate relation to this state.

(2) Where one of the following provisions of this Act specifies the applicable law, that provision governs and a contrary agreement is effective only to the extent permitted by the law (including the conflict of laws rules) so specified:

Rights of creditors against sold goods. Section 2-402.

Applicability of the Article on Leases. Sections 2A-105 and 2A-106.

Applicability of the Article on Bank Deposits and Collections. Section 4-102.

Bulk transfers subject to the Article on Bulk Transfers. Section 6-102.

Applicability of the Article on Investment Securities. Section 8-106.

Perfection provisions of the Article on Secured Transactions. Section 9-103.

§1-106. Remedies to Be Liberally Administered.

(1) The remedies provided by this Act shall be liberally administered to the end that the aggrieved party may be put in as good a position as if the other party had fully performed but neither consequential or special nor penal damages may be had except as specifically provided in this Act or by other rule of law.

(2) Any right or obligation declared by this Act is enforceable by action unless the provision declaring it specifies a different and limited effect.

§1-107. Waiver or Renunciation of Claim or Right After Breach. Any claim or right arising out of an alleged breach can be discharged in whole or in part without consideration by a written waiver or renunciation signed and delivered by the aggrieved party.

§1-108. Severability. If any provision or clause of this Act or application thereof to any person or circumstances is held invalid, such invalidity shall not affect other provisions or applications of the Act which can be given effect without the invalid provision or application, and to this end the provisions of this Act are declared to be severable.

§1-109. **Section Captions.** Section captions are parts of this Act.

Part 2: General Definitions and Principles of Interpretation

§1-201. **General Definitions.** Subject to additional definitions contained in the subsequent Articles of this Act which are applicable to specific Articles or Parts thereof, and unless the context otherwise requires, in this Act.

(1) "Action" in the sense of a judicial proceeding includes recoupment, counterclaim, set-off, suit in equity and any other proceedings in which rights are determined.

(2) "Aggrieved party" means a party entitled to resort to a remedy.

(3) "Agreement" means the bargain of the parties in fact as found in their language or by implication from other circumstances including course of dealing or usage of trade or course of performance as provided in this Act (Sections 1-205 and 2-208). Whether an agreement has legal consequences is determined by the provisions of this Act, if applicable; otherwise by the law of contracts (Section 1-103). (Compare "Contract".)

(4) "Bank" means any person engaged in the business of banking.

(5) "Bearer" means the person in possession of an instrument, document of title, or certificated security payable to bearer or indorsed in blank.

(6) "Bill of lading" means a document evidencing the receipt of goods for shipment issued by a person engaged in the business of transporting or forwarding goods, and includes an airbill. "Airbill" means a document serving for air transportation as a bill of lading does for marine or rail transportation, and includes an air consignment note or air waybill.

(7) "Branch" includes a separately incorporated foreign branch of a bank.

(8) "Burden of establishing" a fact means the burden of persuading the triers of fact that the existence of the fact is more probable than its non-existence.

(9) "Buyer in ordinary course of business" means a person who in good faith and without knowledge that the sale to him is in violation of the ownership rights or security interest of a third party in the goods buys in ordinary course from a person in the business of selling goods of that kind but does not include a pawnbroker. All persons who sell minerals or the like (including oil and gas) at wellhead or minehead shall be deemed to be persons in the business of selling goods of that kind. "Buying" may be for cash or by exchange of other property or on secured or unsecured credit and includes receiving goods or documents of title under a pre-existing contract for sale but does not include a transfer in bulk or as security for or in total or partial satisfaction of a money debt.

(10) "Conspicuous": A term or clause is conspicuous when it is so written that a reasonable person against whom it is to operate ought to have noticed it. A printed heading in capitals (as: NON-NEGOTIABLE BILL OF LADING) is conspicuous. Language in the body of a form is "conspicuous" if it is in larger or other contrasting type or color. But in a telegram any stated term is "conspicuous". Whether a term or clause is "conspicuous" or not is for decision by the court.

(11) "Contract" means the total legal obligation which results from the parties' agreement as affected by this Act and any other applicable rules of law. (Compare "Agreement".)

(12) "Creditor" includes a general creditor, a secured creditor, a lien creditor and any representative of creditors, including an assignee for the benefit of creditors, a trustee in bankruptcy, a receiver in equity and an executor or administrator of an insolvent debtor's or assignor's estate.

(13) "Defendant" includes a person in the position of defendant in a cross-action or counterclaim.

(14) "Delivery" with respect to instruments, documents of title, chattel paper or certificated securities means voluntary transfer of possession.

(15) "Document of title" includes bill of lading, dock warrant, dock receipt, warehouse receipt or order for the delivery of goods, and also any other document which in the regular course of business or financing is treated as adequately evidencing that the person in possession of it is entitled to receive, hold and dispose of the document and the goods it covers. To be a document of title a document must purport to be issued by or addressed to a bailee and purport to cover goods in the bailee's possession which are either identified or are fungible portions of an identified mass.

(16) "Fault" means wrongful act, omission or breach.

(17) "Fungible" with respect to goods or securities means goods or securities of which any unit is, by nature or usage of trade, the equivalent of any other like unit. Goods which are not fungible shall be deemed fungible for the purposes of this Act to the extent that under a particular agreement or document unlike units are treated as equivalents.

(18) "Genuine" means free of forgery or counterfeiting.

(19) "Good faith" means honesty in fact in the conduct or transaction concerned.

(20) "Holder" means a person who is in possession of a document of title or a certificated instrument or an investment security drawn, issued or indorsed to him or to his order or to bearer or in blank.

(21) To "honor" is to pay or to accept and pay, or where a credit so engages to purchase or discount a draft complying with the terms of the credit.

(22) "Insolvency proceedings" includes any assignment for the benefit of creditors or other proceedings intended to liquidate or rehabilitate the estate of the person involved.

(23) A person is "insolvent" who either has ceased to pay his debts in the ordinary course of business or cannot pay his debts as they become due or is insolvent within the meaning of the federal bankruptcy law.

(24) "Money" means a medium of exchange authorized or adopted by a domestic or foreign government as part of its currency.

(25) A person has "notice" of a fact when

(a) he has actual knowledge of it; or

(b) he has received a notice or notification of it; or

(c) from all the facts and circumstances known to him at the time in question he has reason to know that it exists.

A person "knows" or has "knowledge" of a fact when he has actual knowledge of it. "Discover" or "learn" or a word or phrase of similar import refers to knowledge rather than to reason to know. The time and circumstances under which a notice or notification may cease to be effective are not determined by this Act.

(26) A person "notifies" or "gives" a notice or notification to another by taking such steps as may be reasonably required to inform the other in ordinary course whether or not such other actually comes to know of it. A person "receives" a notice or notification when

(a) it comes to his attention; or

(b) it is duly delivered at the place of business through which the contract was made or at any other place held out by him as the place for receipt of such communications.

(27) Notice, knowledge or a notice or notification received by an organization is effective for a particular transaction from the time when it is brought to the attention of the individual conducting that transaction, and in any event from the time when it would have been brought to his attention if the organization had exercised due diligence. An organization exercises due diligence if it maintains reasonable routines for communicating significant information to the person conducting the transaction and there is reasonable compliance with the routines. Due diligence does not require an individual acting for the organization to communicate information unless such communication is part of his regular duties or unless he has reason to know of the transaction and that the transaction would be materially affected by the information.

(28) "Organization" includes a corporation, government or governmental subdivision or agency, business trust, estate, trust, partnership or association, two or more persons having a joint or common interest or any other legal or commercial entity.

(29) "Party", as distinct from "third party", means a person who has engaged in a transaction or made an agreement within this Act.

(30) "Person" includes an individual or an organization (See Section 1-102).

(31) "Presumption" or "presumed" means that the trier of fact must find the existence of the fact presumed unless and until evidence is introduced which would support a finding of its non-existence.

(32) "Purchase" includes taking by sale, discount, negotiation, mortgage, pledge, lien, issue or re-issue, gift or any other voluntary transaction creating an interest in property.

(33) "Purchaser" means a person who takes by purchase.

(34) "Remedy" means any remedial right to which an aggrieved party is entitled with or without resort to a tribunal.

(35) "Representative" includes as agent, an officer of a corporation or association, and a trustee, executor or administrator of an estate, or any other person empowered to act for another.

(36) "Rights" includes remedies.

(37) "Security interest" means an interest in personal property or fixtures which secures payment or performance of an obligation. The retention or reservation of title by a seller of goods notwithstanding shipment or delivery to the buyer (Section 2-401) is limited in effect to a reservation of a "security interest". The term also includes any interest of a buyer of accounts or chattel paper which is subject to Article 9. The special property interest of a buyer of goods on identification of those goods to a contract for sale under Section 2-401 is not a "security interest", but a buyer may also acquire a "security interest" by complying with Article 9. Unless a consignment is intended as security, reservation of title thereunder is not a "security interest", but a consignment in any event is subject to the provisions on consignment sales (Section 2-326).

Whether a transaction creates a lease or security interest is determined by the facts of each case; however, a transaction creates a security interest if the consideration the lessee is to pay the lessor for the right to possession and use of the goods is an obligation for the term of the lease not subject to termination by the lessee, and

(a) the original term of the lease is equal to or greater than the remaining economic life of the goods,

(b) the lessee is bound to renew the lease for the remaining economic life of the goods or is bound to become the owner of the goods,

(c) the lessee has an option to renew the lease for the remaining economic life of the goods for no additional consideration or nominal additional consideration upon compliance with the lease agreement, or

(d) the lessee has an option to become the owner of the goods for no additional consideration or nominal additional consideration upon compliance with the lease agreement.

A transaction does not create a security interest merely because it provides that

(a) the present value of the consideration the lessee is obligated to pay the lessor for the right to possession and use of the goods is substantially equal to or is greater than the fair market value of the goods at the time the lease is entered into,

(b) the lessee assumes risk of loss of the goods, or agrees to pay taxes, insurance, filing, recording or registration fees, or service or maintenance costs with respect to the goods,

(c) the lessee has an option to renew the lease or to become the owner of the goods,

(d) the lessee has an option to renew the lease for a fixed rent that is equal to or greater than the reasonably predictable fair market rent for the use of the goods for the term of the renewal at the time the option is to be performed, or

(e) the lessee has an option to become the owner of the goods for a fixed price that is equal to or greater than the reasonably predictable fair market value of the goods at the time the option is to be performed.

For purposes of this subsection (37):

(x) Additional consideration is not nominal if (i) when the option to renew the lease is granted to the lessee the rent is stated to be the fair market rent for the use of the goods for the term of the renewal determined at the time the option is to be performed, or (ii) when the option to become the owner of the goods is granted to the lessee the price is stated to be the fair market value of the goods determined at the time the option is to be performed. Additional consideration is nominal if it is less than the lessee's reasonably predictable cost of performing under the lease agreement if the option is not exercised;

(y) "Reasonably predictable" and "remaining economic life of the goods" are to be determined with reference to the facts and circumstances at the time the transaction is entered into; and

(z) "Present value" means the amount as of a date certain of one or more sums payable in the future, discounted to the date certain. The discount is determined by the interest rate specified by the parties if the rate is not manifestly unreasonable at the time the transaction is entered into; otherwise, the discount is determined by a commercially reasonable rate that takes into account the facts and circumstances of each case at the time the transaction was entered into.

(38) "Send" in connection with any writing or notice means to deposit in the mail or deliver for transmission by any other usual means of communication with postage or cost of transmission provided for and properly addressed and in the case of an instrument to an address specified thereon or otherwise agreed, or if there be none to any address reasonable under the circumstances. The receipt of any writing or notice within the time at which it would have arrived if properly sent has the effect of a proper sending.

(39) "Signed" includes any symbol executed or adopted by a party with present intention to authenticate a writing.

(40) "Surety" includes guarantor.

(41) "Telegram" includes a message transmitted by radio, teletype, cable, any mechanical method of transmission or the like.

(42) "Term" means that portion of an agreement which relates to a particular matter.

(43) "Unauthorized" signature or indorsement means one made without actual, implied or apparent authority and includes a forgery.

(44) "Value". Except as otherwise provided with respect to negotiable instruments and bank collections (Sections 3-303, 4-208 and 4-209) a person gives "value" for rights if he acquires them

(a) in return for a binding commitment to extend credit or for the extension of immediately available credit whether or not drawn upon and whether or not a chargeback is provided for in the event of difficulties in collection; or

(b) as security for or in total or partial satisfaction of a pre-existing claim; or

(c) by accepting delivery pursuant to a pre-existing contract for purchase; or

(d) generally, in return for any consideration sufficient to support a simple contract.

(45) "Warehouse receipt" means a receipt issued by a person engaged in the business of storing goods for hire.

(46) "Written" or "writing" includes printing, typewriting or any other intentional reduction to tangible form. As amended 1962 and 1972.

§1-201. General Definitions *(1977 Amendments).* Subject to additional definitions contained in the subsequent Articles of this Act which are applicable to specific Articles or Parts thereof, and unless the context otherwise requires, in the Act:

* * *

1. (5) "Bearer" means the person in possession of an instrument, document of title or certificated security payable to bearer or indorsed in blank.

* * *

2. (14) "Delivery" with respect to instruments, documents of title chattel paper or certificated securities means voluntary transfer of possession.

* * *

3. (20) "Holder" means a person who is in possession of a document of title or an instrument or a certificated investment security drawn, issued or indorsed to him or his order or to bearer or in blank.

* * *

§1-202. Prima Facie Evidence by Third Party Documents.
A document in due form purporting to be a bill of lading, policy or certificate of insurance, official weigher's or inspector's certificate, consular invoice or any other document authorized or required by the contract to be issued by a third party shall be prima facie evidence of its own authenticity and genuineness and of the facts stated in the document by the third party.

§1-203. Obligation of Good Faith.
Every contract or duty within this Act imposes an obligation of good faith in its performance or enforcement.

§1-204. Time; Reasonable Time; "Seasonably".
(1) Whenever this Act requires any action to be taken within a reasonable time, any time which is not manifestly unreasonable may be fixed by agreement.

(2) What is a reasonable time for taking any action depends on the nature, purpose and circumstances of such action.

(3) An action is taken "seasonably" when it is taken at or within the time agreed or if no time is agreed at or within a reasonable time.

§1-205. Course of Dealing and Usage of Trade.
(1) A course of dealing is a sequence of previous conduct between the parties to a particular transaction which is fairly to be regarded as establishing a common basis of understanding for interpreting their expressions and other conduct.

(2) A usage of trade is any practice or method of dealing having such regularity of observance in a place, vocation or trade as to justify an expectation that it will be observed with respect to the transaction in question. The existence and scope of such a usage are to be proved as facts. If it is established that such a usage is embodied in a written trade code or similar writing the interpretation of the writing is for the court.

(3) A course of dealing between parties and any usage of trade in the vocation or trade in which they are engaged or of which they are or should be aware give particular meaning to and supplement or qualify terms of an agreement.

(4) The express terms of an agreement and an applicable course of dealing or usage of trade shall be construed wherever reasonable as consistent with each other; but when such construction is unreasonable express terms control both course of dealing and usage of trade and course of dealing controls usage of trade.

(5) An applicable usage of trade in the place where any part of performance is to occur shall be used in interpreting the agreement as to that part of the performance.

(6) Evidence of a relevant usage of trade offered by one party is not admissible unless and until he has given the other party such notice as the court finds sufficient to prevent unfair surprise to the latter.

§1-206. Statute of Frauds for Kinds of Personal Property not Otherwise Covered.
(1) Except in the cases described in subsection (2) of this section a contract for the sale of personal property is not enforceable by way of action or defense beyond five thousand dollars in amount or value of remedy unless there is some writing which indicates that a contract for sale has been made between the parties at a defined or stated price, reasonably identifies the subject matter and is signed by the party against whom enforcement is sought or by his authorized agent.

(2) Subsection (1) of this section does not apply to contracts for the sale of goods (Section 2-201) nor of securities (Section 8-319) nor to security agreements (Section 9-203).

§1-207. Performance or Acceptance Under Reservation of Rights.
A party who with explicit reservation of rights performs or promises performance or assents to performance in a manner demanded or offered by the other party does not thereby prejudice the rights reserved. Such words as "without prejudice", "under protest" or the like are sufficient.

§1-208. Option to Accelerate at Will.
A term providing that one party or his successor in interest may accelerate payment or performance or require collateral or additional collateral "at will" or "when he deems himself insecure" or in words of similar import shall be construed to mean that he shall have power to do so only if he in good faith believes that the prospect of payment or performance is impaired. The burden of establishing lack of good faith is on the party against whom the power has been exercised.

§1-209. Subordinated Obligations.
An obligation may be issued as subordinated to payment of another obligation of the person obligated, or a creditor may subordinate his right to payment of an obligation by agreement with either the person obligated or another creditor of the person obligated. Such a subordination does not create a security interest as against either the common debtor or a subordinated creditor. This section shall be construed as declaring the law as it existed prior to the enactment of this section and not as modifying it. Added 1966.

Note: *This new section is proposed as an optional provision to make it clear that a subordination agreement does not create a security interest unless so intended.*

Article 2: Sales

Part 1: Short Title, General Construction and Subject Matter

§2-101. Short Title. This Article shall be known and may be cited as Uniform Commercial Code—Sales.

§2-102. Scope; Certain Security and Other Transactions Excluded from This Article. Unless the context otherwise requires, this Article applies to transactions in goods; it does not apply to any transaction which although in the form of an unconditional contract to sell or present sale is intended to operate only as a security transaction nor does this Article impair or repeal any statute regulating sales to consumers, farmers or other specified classes of buyers.

§2-103. Definitions and Index of Definitions.

(1) In this Article unless the context otherwise requires

   (a) "Buyer" means a person who buys or contracts to buy goods.

   (b) [Reserved.]

   (c) "Receipt" of goods means taking physical possession of them.

   (d) "Seller" means a person who sells or contracts to sell goods.

(2) Other definitions applying to this Article or to specified Parts thereof, and the sections in which they appear are:

   "Acceptance". Section 2-606.

   "Banker's credit". Section 2-325.

   "Between merchants". Section 2-104.

   "Cancellation". Section 2-106(4).

   "Commercial unit". Section 2-105.

   "Confirmed credit". Section 2-325.

   "Conforming to contract". Section 2-106.

   "Contract for sale". Section 2-106.

   "Cover". Section 2-712.

   "Entrusting". Section 2-403.

   "Financing agency". Section 2-104.

   "Future goods". Section 2-105.

   "Goods". Section 2-105.

   "Identification". Section 2-501.

   "Installment contract". Section 2-612.

   "Letter of Credit". Section 2-325.

   "Lot". Section 2-105.

   "Merchant". Section 2-104.

   "Overseas". Section 2-323.

   "Person in position of seller". Section 2-707.

   "Present sale". Section 2-106.

   "Sale". Section 2-106.

   "Sale on approval". Section 2-326.

   "Sale or return". Section 2-326.

   "Termination". Section 2-106.

(3) "Control" as provided in Section 7-106 and the following definitions in other Articles apply to this Article:

   "Check". Section 3-104.

   "Consignee". Section 7-102.

   "Consignor". Section 7-102.

   "Consumer goods". Section 9-102.

   "Dishonor". Section 3-502.

   "Draft". Section 3-104.

(4) In addition Article 1 contains general definitions and principles of construction and interpretation applicable throughout this Article.

§2-104. Definitions: "Merchant"; "Between Merchants"; "Financing Agency".

(1) "Merchant" means a person who deals in goods of the kind or otherwise by his occupation holds himself out as having knowledge or skill peculiar to the practices or goods involved in the transaction or to whom such knowledge or skill may be attributed by his employment of an agent or broker or other intermediary who by his occupation holds himself out as having such knowledge or skill.

(2) "Financing agency" means a bank, finance company or other person who in the ordinary course of business makes advances against goods or documents of title or who by arrangement with either the seller or the buyer intervenes in ordinary course to make or collect payment due or claimed under the contract for sale, as by purchasing or paying the seller's draft or making advances against it or by merely taking it for collection whether or not documents of title accompany or are associated with the draft. "Financing agency" includes also a bank or other person who similarly intervenes between persons who are in the position of seller and buyer in respect to the goods (Section 2–707).

(3) "Between merchants" means in any transaction with respect to which both parties are chargeable with the knowledge or skill of merchants.

§2-105. Definitions: Transferability; "Goods"; "Future" Goods; "Lot"; "Commercial Unit".

(1) "Goods" means all things (including specially manufactured goods) which are movable at the time of identification to the contract for sale other than the money in which the price is to be paid, investment securities (Article 8) and things in action. "Goods" also includes the unborn young of animals and

growing crops and other identified things attached to realty as described in the section on goods to be severed from realty (Section 2–107).

(2) Goods must be both existing and identified before any interest in them can pass. Goods which are not both existing and identified are "future" goods. A purported present sale of future goods or of any interest therein operates as a contract to sell.

(3) There may be a sale of a part interest in existing identified goods.

(4) An undivided share in an identified bulk of fungible goods is sufficiently identified to be sold although the quantity of the bulk is not determined. Any agreed proportion of such a bulk or any quantity thereof agreed upon by number, weight or other measure may to the extent of the seller's interest in the bulk be sold to the buyer who then becomes an owner in common.

(5) "Lot" means a parcel or a single article which is the subject matter of a separate sale or delivery, whether or not it is sufficient to perform the contract.

(6) "Commercial unit" means such a unit of goods as by commercial usage is a single whole for purposes of sale and division of which materially impairs its character or value on the market or in use. A commercial unit may be a single article (as a machine) or a set of articles (as a suite of furniture or an assortment of sizes) or a quantity (as a bale, gross, or carload) or any other unit treated in use or in the relevant market as a single whole.

§2-106. Definitions: "Contract"; "Agreement"; "Contract for Sale"; "Sale"; "Present Sale"; "Conforming" to Contract; "Termination"; "Cancellation".

(1) In this Article unless the context otherwise requires "contract" and "agreement" are limited to those relating to the present or future sale of goods. "Contract for sale" includes both a present sale of goods and a contract to sell goods at a future time. A "sale" consists in the passing of title from the seller to the buyer for a price (Section 2–401). A "present sale" means a sale which is accomplished by the making of the contract.

(2) Goods or conduct including any part of a performance are "conforming" or conform to the contract when they are in accordance with the obligations under the contract.

(3) "Termination" occurs when either party pursuant to a power created by agreement or law puts an end to the contract otherwise than for its breach. On "termination" all obligations which are still executory on both sides are discharged but any right based on prior breach or performance survives.

(4) "Cancellation" occurs when either party puts an end to the contract for breach by the other and its effect is the same as that of "termination" except that the can-

celling party also retains any remedy for breach of the whole contract or any unperformed balance.

§2-107. Goods to Be Severed From Realty: Recording.

(1) A contract for the sale of minerals or the like (including oil and gas) or a structure or its materials to be removed from realty is a contract for the sale of goods within this Article if they are to be severed by the seller but until severance a purported present sale thereof which is not effective as a transfer of an interest in land is effective only as a contract to sell.

(2) A contract for the sale apart from the land of growing crops or other things attached to realty and capable of severance without material harm thereto but not described in subsection (1) or of timber to be cut is a contract for the sale of goods within this Article whether the subject matter is to be severed by the buyer or by the seller even though it forms part of the realty at the time of contracting, and the parties can by identification effect a present sale before severance.

(3) The provisions of this section are subject to any third party rights provided by the law relating to realty records, and the contract for sale may be executed and recorded as a document transferring an interest in land and shall then constitute notice to third parties of the buyer's rights under the contract for sale.

Part 2: Form, Formation and Readjustment of Contract

§2-201. Formal Requirements; Statute of Frauds.

(1) Except as otherwise provided in this section a contract for the sale of goods for the price of $500 or more is not enforceable by way of action or defense unless there is some writing sufficient to indicate that a contract for sale has been made between the parties and signed by the party against whom enforcement is sought or by his authorized agent or broker. A writing is not insufficient because it omits or incorrectly states a term agreed upon but the contract is not enforceable under this paragraph beyond the quantity of goods shown in such writing.

(2) Between merchants if within a reasonable time a writing in confirmation of the contract and sufficient against the sender is received and the party receiving it has reason to know its contents, it satisfies the requirements of subsection (1) against such party unless written notice of objection to its contents is given within 10 days after it is received.

(3) A contract which does not satisfy the requirements of subsection (1) but which is valid in other respects is enforceable

(a) if the goods are to be specially manufactured for the buyer and are not suitable for sale to others in the ordinary course of the seller's business and the seller, before notice of repudiation is received and under circumstances which reasonably indicate that the goods are for the buyer, has made either a substantial beginning of their manufacture or commitments for their procurement; or

(b) if the party against whom enforcement is sought admits in his pleading, testimony or otherwise in court that a contract for sale was made, but the contract is not enforceable under this provision beyond the quantity of goods admitted; or

(c) with respect to goods for which payment has been made and accepted or which have been received and accepted (Sec. 2–606).

§2-202. Final Written Expression: Parol or Extrinsic Evidence. Terms with respect to which the confirmatory memoranda of the parties agree or which are otherwise set forth in a writing intended by the parties as a final expression of their agreement with respect to such terms as are included therein may not be contradicted by evidence of any prior agreement or of a contemporaneous oral agreement but may be explained or supplemented

(a) by course of performance, course of dealing, or usage of trade (Section 1-303); and

(b) by evidence of consistent additional terms unless the court finds the writing to have been intended also as a complete and exclusive statement of the terms of the agreement.

§2-203. Seals Inoperative. The affixing of a seal to a writing evidencing a contract for sale or an offer to buy or sell goods does not constitute the writing a sealed instrument and the law with respect to sealed instruments does not apply to such a contract or offer.

§2-204. Formation in General.

(1) A contract for sale of goods may be made in any manner sufficient to show agreement, including conduct by both parties which recognizes the existence of such a contract.

(2) An agreement sufficient to constitute a contract for sale may be found even though the moment of its making is undetermined.

(3) Even though one or more terms are left open a contract for sale does not fail for indefiniteness if the parties have intended to make a contract and there is a reasonably certain basis for giving an appropriate remedy.

§2-205. Firm Offers. An offer by a merchant to buy or sell goods in a signed writing which by its terms gives assurance that it will be held open is not revocable, for lack of consideration, during the time stated or if no time is stated for a reasonable time, but in no event may such period of irrevocability exceed three months; but any such term of assurance on a form supplied by the offeree must be separately signed by the offeror.

§2-206. Offer and Acceptance in Formation of Contract.

(1) Unless otherwise unambiguously indicated by the language or circumstances

(a) an offer to make a contract shall be construed as inviting acceptance in any manner and by any medium reasonable in the circumstances;

(b) an order or other offer to buy goods for prompt or current shipment shall be construed as inviting acceptance either by a prompt promise to ship or by the prompt or current shipment of conforming or non-conforming goods, but such a shipment of non-conforming goods does not constitute an acceptance if the seller seasonably notifies the buyer that the shipment is offered only as an accommodation to the buyer.

(2) Where the beginning of a requested performance is a reasonable mode of acceptance an offeror who is not notified of acceptance within a reasonable time may treat the offer as having lapsed before acceptance.

§2-207. Additional Terms in Acceptance or Confirmation.

(1) A definite and seasonable expression of acceptance or a written confirmation which is sent within a reasonable time operates as an acceptance even though it states terms additional to or different from those offered or agreed upon, unless acceptance is expressly made conditional on assent to the additional or different terms.

(2) The additional terms are to be construed as proposals for addition to the contract. Between merchants such terms become part of the contract unless:

(a) the offer expressly limits acceptance to the terms of the offer;

(b) they materially alter it; or

(c) notification of objection to them has already been given or is given within a reasonable time after notice of them is received.

(3) Conduct by both parties which recognizes the existence of a contract is sufficient to establish a contract for sale although the writings of the parties do not otherwise establish a contract. In such case the terms of the particular contract consist of those terms on which the writings of the parties agree, together with any supplementary terms incorporated under any other provisions of this Act.

§2-208. [Reserved.]

§2-209. Modification, Rescission and Waiver.

(1) An agreement modifying a contract within this Article needs no consideration to be binding.

(2) A signed agreement which excludes modification or rescission except by a signed writing cannot be otherwise modified or rescinded, but except as between merchants such a requirement on a form supplied by the merchant must be separately signed by the other party.

(3) The requirements of the statute of frauds section of this Article (Section 2–201) must be satisfied if the contract as modified is within its provisions.

(4) Although an attempt at modification or rescission does not satisfy the requirements of subsection (2) or (3) it can operate as a waiver.

(5) A party who has made a waiver affecting an executory portion of the contract may retract the waiver by reasonable notification received by the other party that strict performance will be required of any term waived, unless the retraction would be unjust in view of a material change of position in reliance on the waiver.

§2-210. Delegation of Performance; Assignment of Rights.

(1) A party may perform his duty through a delegate unless otherwise agreed or unless the other party has a substantial interest in having his original promisor perform or control the acts required by the contract. No delegation of performance relieves the party delegating of any duty to perform or any liability for breach.

(2) Except as otherwise provided in Section 9-406, unless otherwise agreed all rights of either seller or buyer can be assigned except where the assignment would materially change the duty of the other party, or increase materially the burden or risk imposed on him by his contract, or impair materially his chance of obtaining return performance. A right to damages for breach of the whole contract or a right arising out of the assignor's due performance of his entire obligation can be assigned despite agreement otherwise.

(3) The creation, attachment, perfection, or enforcement of a security interest in the seller's interest under a contract is not a transfer that materially changes the duty of or increases materially the burden or risk imposed on the buyer or impairs materially the buyer's chance of obtaining return performance within the purview of subsection (2) unless, and then only to the extent that, enforcement actually results in a delegation of material performance of the seller. Even in that event, the creation, attachment, perfection, and enforcement of the security interest remain effective, but (i) the seller is liable to the buyer for damages caused by the delegation to the extent that the damages could not reasonably be prevented by the buyer, and (ii) a court having jurisdiction may grant other appropriate relief, including cancellation of the contract for sale or an injunction against enforcement of the security interest or consummation of the enforcement.

(4) Unless the circumstances indicate the contrary a prohibition of assignment of "the contract" is to be construed as barring only the delegation to the assignee of the assignor's performance.

(5) An assignment of "the contract" or of "all my rights under the contract" or an assignment in similar general terms is an assignment of rights and unless the language or the circumstances (as in an assignment for security) indicate the contrary, it is a delegation of performance of the duties of the assignor and its acceptance by the assignee constitutes a promise by him to perform those duties. This promise is enforceable by either the assignor or the other party to the original contract.

(6) The other party may treat any assignment which delegates performance as creating reasonable grounds for insecurity and may without prejudice to his rights against the assignor demand assurances from the assignee (Section 2–609).

Part 3: General Obligation and Construction of Contract

§2-301. General Obligations of Parties.
The obligation of the seller is to transfer and deliver and that of the buyer is to accept and pay in accordance with the contract.

§2-302. Unconscionable Contract or Clause.

(1) If the court as a matter of law finds the contract or any clause of the contract to have been unconscionable at the time it was made the court may refuse to enforce the contract, or it may enforce the remainder of the contract without the unconscionable clause, or it may so limit the application of any unconscionable clause as to avoid any unconscionable result.

(2) When it is claimed or appears to the court that the contract or any clause thereof may be unconscionable the parties shall be afforded a reasonable opportunity to present evidence as to its commercial setting, purpose and effect to aid the court in making the determination.

§2-303. Allocation or Division of Risks.
Where this Article allocates a risk or a burden as between the parties "unless otherwise agreed", the agreement may not only shift the allocation but may also divide the risk or burden.

§2-304. Price Payable in Money, Goods, Realty, or Otherwise.

(1) The price can be made payable in money or otherwise. If it is payable in whole or in part in goods each party is a seller of the goods which he is to transfer.

(2) Even though all or part of the price is payable in an interest in realty the transfer of the goods and the

seller's obligations with reference to them are subject to this Article, but not the transfer of the interest in realty or the transferor's obligations in connection therewith.

§2-305. Open Price Term.

(1) The parties if they so intend can conclude a contract for sale even though the price is not settled. In such a case the price is a reasonable price at the time for delivery if

(a) nothing is said as to price; or

(b) the price is left to be agreed by the parties and they fail to agree; or

(c) the price is to be fixed in terms of some agreed market or other standard as set or recorded by a third person or agency and it is not so set or recorded.

(2) A price to be fixed by the seller or by the buyer means a price for him to fix in good faith.

(3) When a price left to be fixed otherwise than by agreement of the parties fails to be fixed through fault of one party the other may at his option treat the contract as cancelled or himself fix a reasonable price.

(4) Where, however, the parties intend not to be bound unless the price be fixed or agreed and it is not fixed or agreed there is no contract. In such a case the buyer must return any goods already received or if unable so to do must pay their reasonable value at the time of delivery and the seller must return any portion of the price paid on account.

§2-306. Output, Requirements and Exclusive Dealings.

(1) A term which measures the quantity by the output of the seller or the requirements of the buyer means such actual output or requirements as may occur in good faith, except that no quantity unreasonably disproportionate to any stated estimate or in the absence of a stated estimate to any normal or otherwise comparable prior output or requirements may be tendered or demanded.

(2) A lawful agreement by either the seller or the buyer for exclusive dealing in the kind of goods concerned imposes unless otherwise agreed an obligation by the seller to use best efforts to supply the goods and by the buyer to use best efforts to promote their sale.

§2-307. Delivery in Single Lot or Several Lots.

Unless otherwise agreed all goods called for by a contract for sale must be tendered in a single delivery and payment is due only on such tender but where the circumstances give either party the right to make or demand delivery in lots the price if it can be apportioned may be demanded for each lot.

§2-308. Absence of Specified Place for Delivery.

Unless otherwise agreed

(a) the place for delivery of goods is the seller's place of business or if he has none his residence; but

(b) in a contract for sale of identified goods which to the knowledge of the parties at the time of contracting are in some other place, that place is the place for their delivery; and

(c) documents of title may be delivered through customary banking channels.

§2-309. Absence of Specific Time Provisions; Notice of Termination.

(1) The time for shipment or delivery or any other action under a contract if not provided in this Article or agreed upon shall be a reasonable time.

(2) Where the contract provides for successive performances but is indefinite in duration it is valid for a reasonable time but unless otherwise agreed may be terminated at any time by either party.

(3) Termination of a contract by one party except on the happening of an agreed event requires that reasonable notification be received by the other party and an agreement dispensing with notification is invalid if its operation would be unconscionable.

§2-310. Open Time for Payment or Running of Credit; Authority to Ship Under Reservation.

Unless otherwise agreed

(a) payment is due at the time and place at which the buyer is to receive the goods even though the place of shipment is the place of delivery; and

(b) if the seller is authorized to send the goods he may ship them under reservation, and may tender the documents of title, but the buyer may inspect the goods after their arrival before payment is due unless such inspection is inconsistent with the terms of the contract (Section 2-513); and

(c) if delivery is authorized and made by way of documents of title otherwise than by subsection (b) then payment is due regardless of where the goods are to be received (i) at the time and place at which the buyer is to receive delivery of the tangible documents or (ii) at the time the buyer is to receive delivery of the electronic documents and at the seller's place of business or if none, the seller's residence; and

(d) where the seller is required or authorized to ship the goods on credit the credit period runs from the time of shipment but post-dating the invoice or delaying its dispatch will correspondingly delay the starting of the credit period.

§2-311. Options and Cooperation Respecting Performance.

(1) An agreement for sale which is otherwise sufficiently definite (subsection (3) of Section 2–204) to be a contract is not made invalid by the fact that it leaves particulars of performance to be specified by one of the parties. Any such specification must be made in good faith and within limits set by commercial reasonableness.

(2) Unless otherwise agreed specifications relating to assortment of the goods are at the buyer's option and except as otherwise provided in subsections (1)(c) and (3) of Section 2–319 specifications or arrangements relating to shipment are at the seller's option.

(3) Where such specification would materially affect the other party's performance but is not seasonably made or where one party's cooperation is necessary to the agreed performance of the other but is not seasonably forthcoming, the other party in addition to all other remedies

   (a) is excused for any resulting delay in his own performance; and

   (b) may also either proceed to perform in any reasonable manner or after the time for a material part of his own performance treat the failure to specify or to cooperate as a breach by failure to deliver or accept the goods.

§2-312. Warranty of Title and Against Infringement; Buyer's Obligation against Infringement.

(1) Subject to subsection (2) there is in a contract for sale a warranty by the seller that

   (a) the title conveyed shall be good, and its transfer rightful; and

   (b) the goods shall be delivered free from any security interest or other lien or encumbrance of which the buyer at the time of contracting has no knowledge.

(2) A warranty under subsection (1) will be excluded or modified only by specific language or by circumstances which give the buyer reason to know that the person selling does not claim title in himself or that he is purporting to sell only such right or title as he or a third person may have.

(3) Unless otherwise agreed a seller who is a merchant regularly dealing in goods of the kind warrants that the goods shall be delivered free of the rightful claim of any third person by way of infringement or the like but a buyer who furnishes specifications to the seller must hold the seller harmless against any such claim which arises out of compliance with the specifications.

§2-313. Express Warranties by Affirmation, Promise, Description, Sample.

(1) Express warranties by the seller are created as follows:

   (a) Any affirmation of fact or promise made by the seller to the buyer which relates to the goods and becomes part of the basis of the bargain creates an express warranty that the goods shall conform to the affirmation or promise.

   (b) Any description of the goods which is made part of the basis of the bargain creates an express warranty that the goods shall conform to the description.

   (c) Any sample or model which is made part of the basis of the bargain creates an express warranty that the whole of the goods shall conform to the sample or model.

(2) It is not necessary to the creation of an express warranty that the seller use formal words such as "warrant" or "guarantee" or that he have a specific intention to make a warranty, but an affirmation merely of the value of the goods or a statement purporting to be merely the seller's opinion or commendation of the goods does not create a warranty.

§2-314. Implied Warranty: Merchantability; Usage of Trade.

(1) Unless excluded or modified (Section 2–316), a warranty that the goods shall be merchantable is implied in a contract for their sale if the seller is a merchant with respect to goods of that kind. Under this section the serving for value of food or drink to be consumed either on the premises or elsewhere is a sale.

(2) Goods to be merchantable must be at least such as

   (a) pass without objection in the trade under the contract description; and

   (b) in the case of fungible goods, are of fair average quality within the description; and

   (c) are fit for the ordinary purposes for which such goods are used; and

   (d) run, within the variations permitted by the agreement, of even kind, quality and quantity within each unit and among all units involved; and

   (e) are adequately contained, packaged, and labeled as the agreement may require; and

   (f) conform to the promise or affirmations of fact made on the container or label if any.

(3) Unless excluded or modified (Section 2–316) other implied warranties may arise from course of dealing or usage of trade.

§2-315. Implied Warranty: Fitness for Particular Purpose.
Where the seller at the time of contracting has reason to know any particular purpose for which the goods are required and that the buyer is relying on the seller's skill or judgment to select or furnish suitable goods, there is unless excluded or modified under the next

section an implied warranty that the goods shall be fit for such purpose.

§2-316. Exclusion or Modification of Warranties.

(1) Words or conduct relevant to the creation of an express warranty and words or conduct tending to negate or limit warranty shall be construed wherever reasonable as consistent with each other; but subject to the provisions of this Article on parol or extrinsic evidence (Section 2–202) negation or limitation is inoperative to the extent that such construction is unreasonable.

(2) Subject to subsection (3), to exclude or modify the implied warranty of merchantability or any part of it the language must mention merchantability and in case of a writing must be conspicuous, and to exclude or modify any implied warranty of fitness the exclusion must be by a writing and conspicuous. Language to exclude all implied warranties of fitness is sufficient if it states, for example, that "There are no warranties which extend beyond the description on the face hereof."

(3) Notwithstanding subsection (2)

    (a) unless the circumstances indicate otherwise, all implied warranties are excluded by expressions like "as is", "with all faults" or other language which in common understanding calls the buyer's attention to the exclusion of warranties and makes plain that there is no implied warranty; and

    (b) when the buyer before entering into the contract has examined the goods or the sample or model as fully as he desired or has refused to examine the goods there is no implied warranty with regard to defects which an examination ought in the circumstances to have revealed to him; and

    (c) an implied warranty can also be excluded or modified by course of dealing or course of performance or usage of trade.

(4) Remedies for breach of warranty can be limited in accordance with the provisions of this Article on liquidation or limitation of damages and on contractual modification of remedy (Sections 2–718 and 2–719).

§2-317. Cumulation and Conflict of Warranties Express or Implied.
Warranties whether express or implied shall be construed as consistent with each other and as cumulative, but if such construction is unreasonable the intention of the parties shall determine which warranty is dominant. In ascertaining that intention the following rules apply:

(a) Exact or technical specifications displace an inconsistent sample or model or general language of description.

(b) A sample from an existing bulk displaces inconsistent general language of description.

(c) Express warranties displace inconsistent implied warranties other than an implied warranty of fitness for a particular purpose.

§2-318. Third Party Beneficiaries of Warranties Express or Implied.
Note: *If this Act is introduced in the Congress of the United States this section should be omitted. (States to select one alternative.)*

    Alternative A—A seller's warranty whether express or implied extends to any natural person who is in the family or household of his buyer or who is a guest in his home if it is reasonable to expect that such person may use, consume or be affected by the goods and who is injured in person by breach of the warranty. A seller may not exclude or limit the operation of this section.

    Alternative B—A seller's warranty whether express or implied extends to any natural person who may reasonably be expected to use, consume or be affected by the goods and who is injured in person by breach of the warranty. A seller may not exclude or limit the operation of this section.

    Alternative C—A seller's warranty whether express or implied extends to any person who may reasonably be expected to use, consume or be affected by the goods and who is injured by breach of the warranty. A seller may not exclude or limit the operation of this section with respect to injury to the person of an individual to whom the warranty extends.

§2-319. F.O.B. and F.A.S. Terms.

(1) Unless otherwise agreed the term F.O.B. (which means "free on board") at a named place, even though used only in connection with the stated price, is a delivery term under which

    (a) when the term is F.O.B. the place of shipment, the seller must at that place ship the goods in the manner provided in this Article (Section 2–504) and bear the expense and risk of putting them into the possession of the carrier; or

    (b) when the term is F.O.B. the place of destination, the seller must at his own expense and risk transport the goods to that place and there tender delivery of them in the manner provided in this Article (Section 2–503);

    (c) when under either (a) or (b) the term is also F.O.B. vessel, car or other vehicle, the seller must in addition at his own expense and risk load the goods on board. If the term is F.O.B. vessel the buyer must name the vessel and in an appropriate case the seller must comply with the provisions of this Article on the form of bill of lading (Section 2–323).

(2) Unless otherwise agreed the term F.A.S. vessel (which means "free alongside") at a named port, even though used only in connection with the stated price, is a delivery term under which the seller must

(a) at his own expense and risk deliver the goods alongside the vessel in the manner usual in that port or on a dock designated and provided by the buyer; and

(b) obtain and tender a receipt for the goods in exchange for which the carrier is under a duty to issue a bill of lading.

(3) Unless otherwise agreed in any case falling within subsection (1)(a) or (c) or subsection (2) the buyer must seasonably give any needed instructions for making delivery, including when the term is F.A.S. or F.O.B. the loading berth of the vessel and in an appropriate case its name and sailing date. The seller may treat the failure of needed instructions as a failure of cooperation under this Article (Section 2–311). He may also at his option move the goods in any reasonable manner preparatory to delivery or shipment.

(4) Under the term F.O.B. vessel or F.A.S. unless otherwise agreed the buyer must make payment against tender of the required documents and the seller may not tender nor the buyer demand delivery of the goods in substitution for the documents.

§2-320. C.I.F. and C. & F. Terms.

(1) The term C.I.F. means that the price includes in a lump sum the cost of the goods and the insurance and freight to the named destination. The term C. & F. or C.F. means that the price so includes cost and freight to the named destination.

(2) Unless otherwise agreed and even though used only in connection with the stated price and destination, the term C.I.F. destination or its equivalent requires the seller at his own expense and risk to

(a) put the goods into the possession of a carrier at the port for shipment and obtain a negotiable bill or bills of lading covering the entire transportation to the named destination; and

(b) load the goods and obtain a receipt from the carrier (which may be contained in the bill of lading) showing that the freight has been paid or provided for; and

(c) obtain a policy or certificate of insurance, including any war risk insurance, of a kind and on terms then current at the port of shipment in the usual amount, in the currency of the contract, shown to cover the same goods covered by the bill of lading and providing for payment of loss to the order of the buyer or for the account of whom it may concern; but the seller may add to the price the amount of the premium for any such war risk insurance; and

(d) prepare an invoice of the goods and procure any other documents required to effect shipment or to comply with the contract; and

(e) forward and tender with commercial promptness all the documents in due form and with any indorsement necessary to perfect the buyer's rights.

(3) Unless otherwise agreed the term C. & F. or its equivalent has the same effect and imposes upon the seller the same obligations and risks as a C.I.F. term except the obligation as to insurance.

(4) Under the term C.I.F. or C. & F. unless otherwise agreed the buyer must make payment against tender of the required documents and the seller may not tender nor the buyer demand delivery of the goods in substitution for the documents.

§2-321. C.I.F. or C. & F.: "Net Landed Weights"; "Payment on Arrival"; Warranty of Condition on Arrival. Under a contract containing a term C.I.F. or C. & F.

(1) Where the price is based on or is to be adjusted according to "net landed weights", "delivered weights", "out turn" quantity or quality or the like, unless otherwise agreed the seller must reasonably estimate the price. The payment due on tender of the documents called for by the contract is the amount so estimated, but after final adjustment of the price a settlement must be made with commercial promptness.

(2) An agreement described in subsection (1) or any warranty of quality or condition of the goods on arrival places upon the seller the risk of ordinary deterioration, shrinkage and the like in transportation but has no effect on the place or time of identification to the contract for sale or delivery or on the passing of the risk of loss.

(3) Unless otherwise agreed where the contract provides for payment on or after arrival of the goods the seller must before payment allow such preliminary inspection as is feasible; but if the goods are lost delivery of the documents and payment are due when the goods should have arrived.

§2-322. Delivery "Ex-Ship".

(1) Unless otherwise agreed a term for delivery of goods "ex-ship" (which means from the carrying vessel) or in equivalent language is not restricted to a particular ship and requires delivery from a ship which has reached a place at the named port of destination where goods of the kind are usually discharged.

(2) Under such a term unless otherwise agreed

(a) the seller must discharge all liens arising out of the carriage and furnish the buyer with a direction which puts the carrier under a duty to deliver the goods; and

(b) the risk of loss does not pass to the buyer until the goods leave the ship's tackle or are otherwise properly unloaded.

§2-323. Form of Bill of Lading Required in Overseas Shipment; "Overseas".

(1) Where the contract contemplates overseas shipment and contains a term C.I.F. or C. & F. or F.O.B. vessel, the seller unless otherwise agreed must obtain a negotiable bill of lading stating that the goods have been loaded in board or, in the case of a term C.I.F. or C. & F., received for shipment.

(2) Where in a case within subsection (1) a tangible bill of lading has been issued in a set of parts, unless otherwise agreed if the documents are not to be sent from abroad the buyer may demand tender of the full set; otherwise only one part of the bill of lading need be tendered. Even if the agreement expressly requires a full set

    (a) due tender of a single part is acceptable within the provisions of this Article on cure of improper delivery (subsection (1) of Section 2–508); and

    (b) even though the full set is demanded, if the documents are sent from abroad the person tendering an incomplete set may nevertheless require payment upon furnishing an indemnity which the buyer in good faith deems adequate.

(3) A shipment by water or by air or a contract contemplating such shipment is "overseas" insofar as by usage of trade or agreement it is subject to the commercial, financing or shipping practices characteristic of international deep water commerce.

§2-324. "No Arrival, No Sale" Term.

Under a term "no arrival, no sale" or terms of like meaning, unless otherwise agreed,

    (a) the seller must properly ship conforming goods and if they arrive by any means he must tender them on arrival but he assumes no obligation that the goods will arrive unless he has caused the non-arrival; and

    (b) where without fault of the seller the goods are in part lost or have so deteriorated as no longer to conform to the contract or arrive after the contract time, the buyer may proceed as if there had been casualty to identified goods (Section 2–613).

§2-325. "Letter of Credit" Term; "Confirmed Credit".

(1) Failure of the buyer seasonably to furnish an agreed letter of credit is a breach of the contract for sale.

(2) The delivery to seller of a proper letter of credit suspends the buyer's obligation to pay. If the letter of credit is dishonored, the seller may on seasonable notification to the buyer require payment directly from him.

(3) Unless otherwise agreed the term "letter of credit" or "banker's credit" in a contract for sale means an irrevocable credit issued by a financing agency of good repute and, where the shipment is overseas, of good international repute. The term "confirmed credit" means that the credit must also carry the direct obligation of such an agency which does business in the seller's financial market.

§2-326. Sale on Approval and Sale or Return; Rights of Creditors.

(1) Unless otherwise agreed, if delivered goods may be returned by the buyer even though they conform to the contract, the transaction is

    (a) a "sale on approval" if the goods are delivered primarily for use, and

    (b) a "sale or return" if the goods are delivered primarily for resale.

(2) Goods held on approval are not subject to the claims of the buyer's creditors until acceptance; goods held on sale or return are subject to such claims while in the buyer's possession.

(3) Any "or return" term of a contract for sale is to be treated as a separate contract for sale within the statute of frauds section of this Article (Section 2–201) and as contradicting the sale aspect of the contract within the provisions of this Article on parol or extrinsic evidence (Section 2–202).

§2-327. Special Incidents of Sale on Approval and Sale or Return.

(1) Under a sale on approval unless otherwise agreed

    (a) although the goods are identified to the contract the risk of loss and the title do not pass to the buyer until acceptance; and

    (b) use of the goods consistent with the purpose of trial is not acceptance but failure seasonably to notify the seller of election to return the goods is acceptance, and if the goods conform to the contract acceptance of any part is acceptance of the whole; and

    (c) after due notification of election to return, the return is at the seller's risk and expense but a merchant buyer must follow any reasonable instructions.

(2) Under a sale or return unless otherwise agreed

    (a) the option to return extends to the whole or any commercial unit of the goods while in substantially their original condition, but must be exercised seasonably; and

    (b) the return is at the buyer's risk and expense.

§2-328. Sale by Auction.

(1) In a sale by auction if goods are put up in lots each lot is the subject of a separate sale.

(2) A sale by auction is complete when the auctioneer so announces by the fall of the hammer or in other customary manner. Where a bid is made while the hammer is falling in acceptance of a prior bid the

auctioneer may in his discretion reopen the bidding or declare the goods sold under the bid on which the hammer was falling.

(3) Such a sale is with reserve unless the goods are in explicit terms put up without reserve. In an auction with reserve the auctioneer may withdraw the goods at any time until he announces completion of the sale. In an auction without reserve, after the auctioneer calls for bids on an article or lot, that article or lot cannot be withdrawn unless no bid is made within a reasonable time. In either case a bidder may retract his bid until the auctioneer's announcement of completion of the sale, but a bidder's retraction does not revive any previous bid.

(4) If the auctioneer knowingly receives a bid on the seller's behalf or the seller makes or procures such a bid, and notice has not been given that liberty for such bidding is reserved, the buyer may at his option avoid the sale or take the goods at the price of the last good faith bid prior to the completion of the sale. This subsection shall not apply to any bid at a forced sale.

Part 4: Title, Creditors and Good Faith Purchasers

§2-401. Passing of Title; Reservation for Security; Limited Application of This Section.
Each provision of this Article with regard to the rights, obligations and remedies of the seller, the buyer, purchasers or other third parties applies irrespective of title to the goods except where the provision refers to such title. Insofar as situations are not covered by the other provisions of this Article and matters concerning title become material the following rules apply:

(1) Title to goods cannot pass under a contract for sale prior to their identification to the contract (Section 2–501), and unless otherwise explicitly agreed the buyer acquires by their identification a special property as limited by this Act. Any retention or reservation by the seller of the title (property) in goods shipped or delivered to the buyer is limited in effect to a reservation of a security interest. Subject to these provisions and to the provisions of the Article on Secured Transactions (Article 9), title to goods passes from the seller to the buyer in any manner and on any conditions explicitly agreed on by the parties.

(2) Unless otherwise explicitly agreed title passes to the buyer at the time and place at which the seller completes his performance with reference to the physical delivery of the goods, despite any reservation of a security interest and even though a document of title is to be delivered at a different time or place; and in particular and despite any reservation of a security interest by the bill of lading

(a) if the contract requires or authorizes the seller to send the goods to the buyer but does not require him to deliver them at destination, title passes to the buyer at the time and place of shipment; but

(b) if the contract requires delivery at destination, title passes on tender there.

(3) Unless otherwise explicitly agreed where delivery is to be made without moving the goods,

(a) if the seller is to deliver a tangible document of title, title passes at the time when and the place where he delivers such documents and if the seller is to deliver an electronic document of title, title passes when the seller delivers the document; or

(b) if the goods are at the time of contracting already identified and no documents are to be delivered, title passes at the time and place of contracting.

(4) A rejection or other refusal by the buyer to receive or retain the goods, whether or not justified, or a justified revocation of acceptance revests title to the goods in the seller. Such revesting occurs by operation of law and is not a "sale".

§2-402. Rights of Seller's Creditors Against Sold Goods.

(1) Except as provided in subsections (2) and (3), rights of unsecured creditors of the seller with respect to goods which have been identified to a contract for sale are subject to the buyer's rights to recover the goods under this Article (Sections 2–502 and 2–716).

(2) A creditor of the seller may treat a sale or an identification of goods to a contract for sale as void if as against him a retention of possession by the seller is fraudulent under any rule of law of the state where the goods are situated, except that retention of possession in good faith and current course of trade by a merchant-seller for a commercially reasonable time after a sale or identification is not fraudulent.

(3) Nothing in this Article shall be deemed to impair the rights of creditors of the seller

(a) under the provisions of the Article on Secured Transactions (Article 9); or

(b) where identification to the contract or delivery is made not in current course of trade but in satisfaction of or as security for a pre-existing claim for money, security or the like and is made under circumstances which under any rule of law of the state where the goods are situated would apart from this Article constitute the transaction a fraudulent transfer or voidable preference.

§2-403. Power to Transfer; Good Faith Purchase of Goods; "Entrusting".

(1) A purchaser of goods acquires all title which his transferor had or had power to transfer except that a purchaser of a limited interest acquires rights only to the extent of the interest purchased. A person with voidable title has power to transfer a good title to a good faith purchaser for value. When goods have been delivered under a transaction of purchase the purchaser has such power even though

    (a) the transferor was deceived as to the identity of the purchaser, or

    (b) the delivery was in exchange for a check which is later dishonored, or

    (c) it was agreed that the transaction was to be a "cash sale", or

    (d) the delivery was procured through fraud punishable as larcenous under the criminal law.

(2) Any entrusting of possession of goods to a merchant who deals in goods of that kind gives him power to transfer all rights of the entruster to a buyer in ordinary course of business.

(3) "Entrusting" includes any delivery and any acquiescence in retention of possession regardless of any condition expressed between the parties to the delivery or acquiescence and regardless of whether the procurement of the entrusting or the possessor's disposition of the goods have been such as to be larcenous under the criminal law.

    [Legislative Note: If a state adopts the repealer of Article 6—Bulk Transfers (Alternative A), subsec. (4) should read as follows:]

(4) The rights of other purchasers of goods and of lien creditors are governed by the Articles on Secured Transactions (Article 9) and Documents of Title (Article 7).

    [Legislative Note: If a state adopts Revised Article 6—Bulk Sales (Alternative B), subsec. (4) should read as follows:]

(4) The rights of other purchasers of goods and of lien creditors are governed by the Articles on Secured Transactions (Article 9), Bulk Sales (Article 6) and Documents of Title (Article 7).

    For material relating to the changes made in text in 1988, see section 3 of Alternative A (Repealer of Article 6—Bulk Transfers) and Conforming Amendment to Section 2–403 following end of Alternative B (Revised Article 6—Bulk Sales).

Part 5: Performance

§2-501. Insurable Interest in Goods; Manner of Identification of Goods.

(1) The buyer obtains a special property and an insurable interest in goods by identification of existing goods as goods to which the contract refers even though the goods so identified are non-conforming and he has an option to return or reject them. Such identification can be made at any time and in any manner explicitly agreed to by the parties. In the absence of explicit agreement identification occurs

    (a) when the contract is made if it is for the sale of goods already existing and identified;

    (b) if the contract is for the sale of future goods other than those described in paragraph (c), when goods are shipped, marked or otherwise designated by the seller as goods to which the contract refers;

    (c) when the crops are planted or otherwise become growing crops or the young are conceived if the contract is for the sale of unborn young to be born within twelve months after contracting or for the sale of crops to be harvested within twelve months or the next normal harvest season after contracting whichever is longer.

(2) The seller retains an insurable interest in goods so long as title to or any security interest in the goods remains in him and where the identification is by the seller alone he may until default or insolvency or notification to the buyer that the identification is final substitute other goods for those identified.

(3) Nothing in this section impairs any insurable interest recognized under any other statute or rule of law.

§2-502. Buyer's Right to Goods on Seller's Repudiation, Failure to Deliver, or Insolvency.

(1) Subject to subsections (2) and (3) and even though the goods have not been shipped a buyer who has paid a part or all of the price of goods in which he has a special property under the provisions of the immediately preceding section may on making and keeping good a tender of any unpaid portion of their price recover them from the seller if:

    (a) in the case of goods bought for personal, family, or household purposes, the seller repudiates or fails to deliver as required by the contract; or

    (b) in all cases, the seller becomes insolvent within ten days after receipt of the first installment on their price.

(2) The buyer's right to recover the goods under subsection (1)(a) vests upon acquisition of a special property, even if the seller had not then repudiated or failed to deliver.

(3) If the identification creating his special property has been made by the buyer he acquires the right to recover the goods only if they conform to the contract for sale.

§2-503. Manner of Seller's Tender of Delivery.

(1) Tender of delivery requires that the seller put and hold conforming goods at the buyer's disposition and

give the buyer any notification reasonably necessary to enable him to take delivery. The manner, time and place for tender are determined by the agreement and this Article, and in particular

(a) tender must be at a reasonable hour, and if it is of goods they must be kept available for the period reasonably necessary to enable the buyer to take possession; but

(b) unless otherwise agreed the buyer must furnish facilities reasonably suited to the receipt of the goods.

(2) Where the case is within the next section respecting shipment tender requires that the seller comply with its provisions.

(3) Where the seller is required to deliver at a particular destination tender requires that he comply with subsection (1) and also in any appropriate case tender documents as described in subsections (4) and (5) of this section.

(4) Where goods are in the possession of a bailee and are to be delivered without being moved

(a) tender requires that the seller either tender a negotiable document of title covering such goods or procure acknowledgment by the bailee of the buyer's right to possession of the goods; but

(b) tender to the buyer of a non-negotiable document of title or of a record directing to the bailee to deliver is sufficient tender unless the buyer seasonably objects, and except as otherwise provided in Article 9 receipt by the bailee of notification of the buyer's rights fixes those rights as against the bailee and all third persons; but risk of loss of the goods and of any failure by the bailee to honor the non-negotiable document of title or to obey the direction remains on the seller until the buyer has had a reasonable time to present the document or direction, and a refusal by the bailee to honor the document or to obey the direction defeats the tender.

(5) Where the contract requires the seller to deliver documents

(a) he must tender all such documents in correct form, except as provided in this Article with respect to bills of lading in a set (subsection (2) of Section 2–323); and

(b) tender through customary banking channels is sufficient and dishonor of a draft accompanying or associated with the documents constitutes non-acceptance or rejection.

§2-504. Shipment by Seller.

Where the seller is required or authorized to send the goods to the buyer and the contract does not require him to deliver them at a particular destination, then unless otherwise agreed he must

(a) put the goods in the possession of such a carrier and make such a contract for their transportation as may be reasonable having regard to the nature of the goods and other circumstances of the case; and

(b) obtain and promptly deliver or tender in due form any document necessary to enable the buyer to obtain possession of the goods or otherwise required by the agreement or by usage of trade; and

(c) promptly notify the buyer of the shipment.

Failure to notify the buyer under paragraph (c) or to make a proper contract under paragraph (a) is a ground for rejection only if material delay or loss ensues.

§2-505. Seller's Shipment Under Reservation.

(1) Where the seller has identified goods to the contract by or before shipment:

(a) his procurement of a negotiable bill of lading to his own order or otherwise reserves in him a security interest in the goods. His procurement of the bill to the order of a financing agency or of the buyer indicates in addition only the seller's expectation of transferring that interest to the person named.

(b) a non-negotiable bill of lading to himself or his nominee reserves possession of the goods as security but except in a case of conditional delivery (subsection (2) of Section 2–507) a non-negotiable bill of lading naming the buyer as consignee reserves no security interest even though the seller retains possession or control of the bill of lading.

(2) When shipment by the seller with reservation of a security interest is in violation of the contract for sale it constitutes an improper contract for transportation within the preceding section but impairs neither the rights given to the buyer by shipment and identification of the goods to the contract nor the seller's powers as a holder of a negotiable document of title.

§2-506. Rights of Financing Agency.

(1) A financing agency by paying or purchasing for value a draft which relates to a shipment of goods acquires to the extent of the payment or purchase and in addition to its own rights under the draft and any document of title securing it any rights of the shipper in the goods including the right to stop delivery and the shipper's right to have the draft honored by the buyer.

(2) The right to reimbursement of a financing agency which has in good faith honored or purchased the draft under commitment to or authority from the buyer is not impaired by subsequent discovery of defects with reference to any relevant document which was apparently regular.

§2-507. Effect of Seller's Tender; Delivery on Condition.

(1) Tender of delivery is a condition to the buyer's duty to accept the goods and, unless otherwise agreed, to his duty to pay for them. Tender entitles the seller to acceptance of the goods and to payment according to the contract.

(2) Where payment is due and demanded on the delivery to the buyer of goods or documents of title, his right as against the seller to retain or dispose of them is conditional upon his making the payment due.

§2-508. Cure by Seller of Improper Tender or Delivery; Replacement.

(1) Where any tender or delivery by the seller is rejected because non-conforming and the time for performance has not yet expired, the seller may seasonably notify the buyer of his intention to cure and may then within the contract time make a conforming delivery.

(2) Where the buyer rejects a non-conforming tender which the seller had reasonable grounds to believe would be acceptable with or without money allowance the seller may if he seasonably notifies the buyer have a further reasonable time to substitute a conforming tender.

§2-509. Risk of Loss in the Absence of Breach.

(1) Where the contract requires or authorizes the seller to ship the goods by carrier

    (a) if it does not require him to deliver them at a particular destination, the risk of loss passes to the buyer when the goods are duly delivered to the carrier even though the shipment is under reservation (Section 2–505); but

    (b) if it does require him to deliver them at a particular destination and the goods are there duly tendered while in the possession of the carrier, the risk of loss passes to the buyer when the goods are there duly so tendered as to enable the buyer to take delivery.

(2) Where the goods are held by a bailee to be delivered without being moved, the risk of loss passes to the buyer

    (a) on his receipt of possession or control of a negotiable document of title covering the goods; or

    (b) on acknowledgment by the bailee of the buyer's right to possession of the goods; or

    (c) after his receipt of possession or control of a non-negotiable document of title or other direction to deliver in a record, as provided in subsection (4)(b) of Section 2–503.

(3) In any case not within subsection (1) or (2), the risk of loss passes to the buyer on his receipt of the goods if the seller is a merchant; otherwise the risk passes to the buyer on tender of delivery.

(4) The provisions of this section are subject to contrary agreement of the parties and to the provisions of this Article on sale on approval (Section 2–327) and on effect of breach on risk of loss (Section 2–510).

§2-510. Effect of breach on Risk of Loss.

(1) Where a tender or delivery of goods so fails to conform to the contract as to give a right of rejection the risk of their loss remains on the seller until cure or acceptance.

(2) Where the buyer rightfully revokes acceptance he may to the extent of any deficiency in his effective insurance coverage treat the risk of loss as having rested on the seller from the beginning.

(3) Where the buyer as to conforming goods already identified to the contract for sale repudiates or is otherwise in breach before risk of their loss has passed to him, the seller may to the extent of any deficiency in his effective insurance coverage treat the risk of loss as resting on the buyer for a commercially reasonable time.

§2-511. Tender of Payment by Buyer; Payment by Check.

(1) Unless otherwise agreed tender of payment is a condition to the seller's duty to tender and complete any delivery.

(2) Tender of payment is sufficient when made by any means or in any manner current in the ordinary course of business unless the seller demands payment in legal tender and gives any extension of time reasonably necessary to procure it.

(3) Subject to the provisions of this Act on the effect of an instrument on an obligation (Section 3–310), payment by check is conditional and is defeated as between the parties by dishonor of the check on due presentment.

§2-512. Payment by Buyer before Inspection.

(1) Where the contract requires payment before inspection non-conformity of the goods does not excuse the buyer from so making payment unless

    (a) the non-conformity appears without inspection; or

    (b) despite tender of the required documents the circumstances would justify injunction against honor under this Act (Section 5–109(b)).

(2) Payment pursuant to subsection (1) does not constitute an acceptance of goods or impair the buyer's right to inspect or any of his remedies.

§2-513. Buyer's Right to Inspection of Goods.

(1) Unless otherwise agreed and subject to subsection (3), where goods are tendered or delivered or identified to the contract for sale, the buyer has a right before payment or acceptance to inspect them at any reasonable place and time and in any reasonable manner. When the seller is required or authorized to send the goods to the buyer, the inspection may be after their arrival.

(2) Expenses of inspection must be borne by the buyer but may be recovered from the seller if the goods do not conform and are rejected.

(3) Unless otherwise agreed and subject to the provisions of this Article on C.I.F. contracts (subsection (3) of Section 2–321), the buyer is not entitled to inspect the goods before payment of the price when the contract provides

   (a) for delivery "C.O.D." or on other like terms; or

   (b) for payment against documents of title, except where such payment is due only after the goods are to become available for inspection.

(4) A place or method of inspection fixed by the parties is presumed to be exclusive but unless otherwise expressly agreed it does not postpone identification or shift the place for delivery or for passing the risk of loss. If compliance becomes impossible, inspection shall be as provided in this section unless the place or method fixed was clearly intended as an indispensable condition failure of which avoids the contract.

§2-514. When Documents Deliverable on Acceptance; When on Payment.
Unless otherwise agreed documents against which a draft is drawn are to be delivered to the drawee on acceptance of the draft if it is payable more than three days after presentment; otherwise, only on payment.

§2-515. Preserving Evidence of Goods in Dispute.
In furtherance of the adjustment of any claim or dispute

(a) either party on reasonable notification to the other and for the purpose of ascertaining the facts and preserving evidence has the right to inspect, test and sample the goods including such of them as may be in the possession or control of the other; and

(b) the parties may agree to a third party inspection or survey to determine the conformity or condition of the goods and may agree that the findings shall be binding upon them in any subsequent litigation or adjustment.

Part 6: Breach, Repudiation and Excuse

§2-601. Buyer's Rights on Improper Delivery.
Subject to the provisions of this Article on breach in installment contracts (Section 2–612) and unless otherwise agreed under the sections on contractual limitations of remedy (Sections 2–718 and 2–719), if the goods or the tender of delivery fail in any respect to conform to the contract, the buyer may

(a) reject the whole; or

(b) accept the whole; or

(c) accept any commercial unit or units and reject the rest.

§2-602. Manner and Effect of Rightful Rejection.

(1) Rejection of goods must be within a reasonable time after their delivery or tender. It is ineffective unless the buyer seasonably notifies the seller.

(2) Subject to the provisions of the two following sections on rejected goods (Sections 2–603 and 2–604),

   (a) after rejection any exercise of ownership by the buyer with respect to any commercial unit is wrongful as against the seller; and

   (b) if the buyer has before rejection taken physical possession of goods in which he does not have a security interest under the provisions of this Article (subsection (3) of Section 2–711), he is under a duty after rejection to hold them with reasonable care at the seller's disposition for a time sufficient to permit the seller to remove them; but

   (c) the buyer has no further obligations with regard to goods rightfully rejected.

(3) The seller's rights with respect to goods wrongfully rejected are governed by the provisions of this Article on Seller's remedies in general (Section 2–703).

§2-603. Merchant Buyer's Duties as to Rightfully Rejected Goods.

(1) Subject to any security interest in the buyer (subsection (3) of Section 2–711), when the seller has no agent or place of business at the market of rejection a merchant buyer is under a duty after rejection of goods in his possession or control to follow any reasonable instructions received from the seller with respect to the goods and in the absence of such instructions to make reasonable efforts to sell them for the seller's account if they are perishable or threaten to decline in value speedily. Instructions are not reasonable if on demand indemnity for expenses is not forthcoming.

(2) When the buyer sells goods under subsection (1), he is entitled to reimbursement from the seller or out of the proceeds for reasonable expenses of caring for and selling them, and if the expenses include no selling commission then to such commission as is usual

in the trade or if there is none to a reasonable sum not exceeding ten per cent on the gross proceeds.

(3) In complying with this section the buyer is held only to good faith and good faith conduct hereunder is neither acceptance nor conversion nor the basis of an action for damages.

§2-604. Buyer's Options as to Salvage of Rightfully Rejected Goods. Subject to the provisions of the immediately preceding section on perishables if the seller gives no instructions within a reasonable time after notification of rejection the buyer may store the rejected goods for the seller's account or reship them to him or resell them for the seller's account with reimbursement as provided in the preceding section. Such action is not acceptance or conversion.

§2-605. Waiver of Buyer's Objections by Failure to Particularize.

(1) The buyer's failure to state in connection with rejection a particular defect which is ascertainable by reasonable inspection precludes him from relying on the unstated defect to justify rejection or to establish breach

    (a) where the seller could have cured it if stated seasonably; or

    (b) between merchants when the seller has after rejection made a request in writing for a full and final written statement of all defects on which the buyer proposes to rely.

(2) Payment against documents made without reservation of rights precludes recovery of the payment for defects apparent in the documents.

§2-606. What Constitutes Acceptance of Goods.

(1) Acceptance of goods occurs when the buyer

    (a) after a reasonable opportunity to inspect the goods signifies to the seller that the goods are conforming or that he will take or retain them in spite of their non-conformity; or

    (b) fails to make an effective rejection (subsection (1) of Section 2–602), but such acceptance does not occur until the buyer has had a reasonable opportunity to inspect them; or

    (c) does any act inconsistent with the seller's ownership; but if such act is wrongful as against the seller it is an acceptance only if ratified by him.

(2) Acceptance of a part of any commercial unit is acceptance of that entire unit.

§2-607. Effect of Acceptance; Notice of Breach; Burden of Establishing Breach after Acceptance; Notice of Claim or Litigation to Person Answerable Over.

(1) The buyer must pay at the contract rate for any goods accepted.

(2) Acceptance of goods by the buyer precludes rejection of the goods accepted and if made with knowledge of a non-conformity cannot be revoked because of it unless the acceptance was on the reasonable assumption that the non-conformity would be seasonably cured but acceptance does not of itself impair any other remedy provided by this Article for non-conformity.

(3) Where a tender has been accepted

    (a) the buyer must within a reasonable time after he discovers or should have discovered any breach notify the seller of breach or be barred from any remedy; and

    (b) if the claim is one for infringement or the like (subsection (3) of Section 2–312) and the buyer is sued as a result of such a breach he must so notify the seller within a reasonable time after he receives notice of the litigation or be barred from any remedy over for liability established by the litigation.

(4) The burden is on the buyer to establish any breach with respect to the goods accepted.

(5) Where the buyer is sued for breach of a warranty or other obligation for which his seller is answerable over

    (a) he may give his seller written notice of the litigation. If the notice states that the seller may come in and defend and that if the seller does not do so he will be bound in any action against him by his buyer by any determination of fact common to the two litigations, then unless the seller after seasonable receipt of the notice does come in and defend he is so bound.

    (b) if the claim is one for infringement or the like (subsection (3) of Section 2–312) the original seller may demand in writing that his buyer turn over to him control of the litigation including settlement or else be barred from any remedy over and if he also agrees to bear all expense and to satisfy any adverse judgment, then unless the buyer after seasonable receipt of the demand does turn over control the buyer is so barred.

(6) The provisions of subsections (3), (4) and (5) apply to any obligation of a buyer to hold the seller harmless against infringement or the like (subsection (3) of Section 2–312).

§2-608. Revocation of Acceptance in Whole or in Part.

(1) The buyer may revoke his acceptance of a lot or commercial unit whose non-conformity substantially impairs its value to him if he has accepted it

    (a) on the reasonable assumption that its non-conformity would be cured and it has not been seasonably cured; or

(b) without discovery of such non-conformity if his acceptance was reasonably induced either by the difficulty of discovery before acceptance or by the seller's assurances.

(2) Revocation of acceptance must occur within a reasonable time after the buyer discovers or should have discovered the ground for it and before any substantial change in condition of the goods which is not caused by their own defects. It is not effective until the buyer notifies the seller of it.

(3) A buyer who so revokes has the same rights and duties with regard to the goods involved as if he had rejected them.

§2-609. Right to Adequate Assurance of Performance.

(1) A contract for sale imposes an obligation on each party that the other's expectation of receiving due performance will not be impaired. When reasonable grounds for insecurity arise with respect to the performance of either party the other may in writing demand adequate assurance of due performance and until he receives such assurance may if commercially reasonable suspend any performance for which he has not already received the agreed return.

(2) Between merchants the reasonableness of grounds for insecurity and the adequacy of any assurance offered shall be determined according to commercial standards.

(3) Acceptance of any improper delivery or payment does not prejudice the aggrieved party's right to demand adequate assurance of future performance.

(4) After receipt of a justified demand failure to provide within a reasonable time not exceeding thirty days such assurance of due performance as is adequate under the circumstances of the particular case is a repudiation of the contract.

§2-610. Anticipatory Repudiation. When either party repudiates the contract with respect to a performance not yet due the loss of which will substantially impair the value of the contract to the other, the aggrieved party may

(a) for a commercially reasonable time await performance by the repudiating party; or

(b) resort to any remedy for breach (Section 2–703 or Section 2–711), even though he has notified the repudiating party that he would await the latter's performance and has urged retraction; and

(c) in either case suspend his own performance or proceed in accordance with the provisions of this Article on the seller's right to identify goods to the contract notwithstanding breach or to salvage unfinished goods (Section 2–704).

§2-611. Retraction of Anticipatory Repudiation.

(1) Until the repudiating party's next performance is due he can retract his repudiation unless the aggrieved party has since the repudiation cancelled or materially changed his position or otherwise indicated that he considers the repudiation final.

(2) Retraction may be by any method which clearly indicates to the aggrieved party that the repudiating party intends to perform, but must include any assurance justifiably demanded under the provisions of this Article (Section 2–609).

(3) Retraction reinstates the repudiating party's rights under the contract with due excuse and allowance to the aggrieved party for any delay occasioned by the repudiation.

§2-612. "Installment Contract"; Breach.

(1) An "installment contract" is one which requires or authorizes the delivery of goods in separate lots to be separately accepted, even though the contract contains a clause "each delivery is a separate contract" or its equivalent.

(2) The buyer may reject any installment which is non-conforming if the non-conformity substantially impairs the value of that installment and cannot be cured or if the non-conformity is a defect in the required documents; but if the non-conformity does not fall within subsection (3) and the seller gives adequate assurance of its cure the buyer must accept that installment.

(3) Whenever non-conformity or default with respect to one or more installments substantially impairs the value of the whole contract there is a breach of the whole. But the aggrieved party reinstates the contract if he accepts a non-conforming installment without seasonably notifying of cancellation or if he brings an action with respect only to past installments or demands performance as to future installments.

§2-613. Casualty to Identified Goods. Where the contract requires for its performance goods identified when the contract is made, and the goods suffer casualty without fault of either party before the risk of loss passes to the buyer, or in a proper case under a "no arrival, no sale" term (Section 2-324) then

(a) if the loss is total the contract is avoided; and

(b) if the loss is partial or the goods have so deteriorated as no longer to conform to the contract the buyer may nevertheless demand inspection and at his option either treat the contract as avoided or accept the goods with due allowance from the contract price for the deterioration or the deficiency in quantity but without further right against the seller.

§2-614. Substituted Performance.

(1) Where without fault of either party the agreed berthing, loading, or unloading facilities fail or an agreed type of carrier becomes unavailable or the agreed manner of delivery otherwise becomes commercially impracticable but a commercially reasonable substitute is available, such substitute performance must be tendered and accepted.

(2) If the agreed means or manner of payment fails because of domestic or foreign governmental regulation, the seller may withhold or stop delivery unless the buyer provides a means or manner of payment which is commercially a substantial equivalent. If delivery has already been taken, payment by the means or in the manner provided by the regulation discharges the buyer's obligation unless the regulation is discriminatory, oppressive or predatory.

§2-615. Excuse by Failure of Presupposed Conditions.

Except so far as a seller may have assumed a greater obligation and subject to the preceding section on substituted performance:

(a) Delay in delivery or non-delivery in whole or in part by a seller who complies with paragraphs (b) and (c) is not a breach of his duty under a contract for sale if performance as agreed has been made impracticable by the occurrence of a contingency the non-occurrence of which was a basic assumption on which the contract was made or by compliance in good faith with any applicable foreign or domestic governmental regulation or order whether or not it later proves to be invalid.

(b) Where the causes mentioned in paragraph (a) affect only a part of the seller's capacity to perform, he must allocate production and deliveries among his customers but may at his option include regular customers not then under contract as well as his own requirements for further manufacture. He may so allocate in any manner which is fair and reasonable.

(c) The seller must notify the buyer seasonably that there will be delay or non-delivery and, when allocation is required under paragraph (b), of the estimated quota thus made available for the buyer.

§2-616. Procedure on Notice Claiming Excuse.

(1) Where the buyer receives notification of a material or indefinite delay or an allocation justified under the preceding section he may by written notification to the seller as to any delivery concerned, and where the prospective deficiency substantially impairs the value of the whole contract under the provisions of this Article relating to breach of installment contracts (Section 2–612), then also as to the whole,

(a) terminate and thereby discharge any unexecuted portion of the contract; or

(b) modify the contract by agreeing to take his available quota in substitution.

(2) If after receipt of such notification from the seller the buyer fails so to modify the contract within a reasonable time not exceeding thirty days the contract lapses with respect to any deliveries affected.

(3) The provisions of this section may not be negated by agreement except in so far as the seller has assumed a greater obligation under the preceding section.

Part 7: Remedies

§2-701. Remedies for Breach of Collateral Contracts Not Impaired.
Remedies for breach of any obligation or promise collateral or ancillary to a contract for sale are not impaired by the provisions of this Article.

§2-702. Seller's Remedies on Discovery of Buyer's Insolvency.

(1) Where the seller discovers the buyer to be insolvent he may refuse delivery except for cash including payment for all goods theretofore delivered under the contract, and stop delivery under this Article (Section 2–705).

(2) Where the seller discovers that the buyer has received goods on credit while insolvent he may reclaim the goods upon demand made within ten days after the receipt, but if misrepresentation of solvency has been made to the particular seller in writing within three months before delivery the ten day limitation does not apply. Except as provided in this subsection the seller may not base a right to reclaim goods on the buyer's fraudulent or innocent misrepresentation of solvency or of intent to pay.

(3) The seller's right to reclaim under subsection (2) is subject to the rights of a buyer in ordinary course or other good faith purchaser under this Article (Section 2–403). Successful reclamation of goods excludes all other remedies with respect to them.

§2-703. Seller's Remedies in General.
Where the buyer wrongfully rejects or revokes acceptance of goods or fails to make a payment due on or before delivery or repudiates with respect to a part or the whole, then with respect to any goods directly affected and, if the breach is of the whole contract (Section 2-612), then also with respect to the whole undelivered balance, the aggrieved seller may

(a) withhold delivery of such goods;

(b) stop delivery by any bailee as hereafter provided (Section 2–705);

(c) proceed under the next section respecting goods still unidentified to the contract;

(d) resell and recover damages as hereafter provided (Section 2–706);

(e) recover damages for non-acceptance (Section 2–708) or in a proper case the price (Section 2–709);

(f) cancel.

§2-704. Seller's Right to Identify Goods to the Contract Notwithstanding Breach or to Salvage Unfinished Goods.

(1) An aggrieved seller under the preceding section may

(a) identify to the contract conforming goods not already identified if at the time he learned of the breach they are in his possession or control;

(b) treat as the subject of resale goods which have demonstrably been intended for the particular contract even though those goods are unfinished.

(2) Where the goods are unfinished an aggrieved seller may in the exercise of reasonable commercial judgment for the purposes of avoiding loss and of effective realization either complete the manufacture and wholly identify the goods to the contract or cease manufacture and resell for scrap or salvage value or proceed in any other reasonable manner.

§2-705. Seller's Stoppage of Delivery in Transit or Otherwise.

(1) The seller may stop delivery of goods in the possession of a carrier or other bailee when he discovers the buyer to be insolvent (Section 2–702) and may stop delivery of carload, truckload, planeload or larger shipments of express or freight when the buyer repudiates or fails to make a payment due before delivery or if for any other reason the seller has a right to withhold or reclaim the goods.

(2) As against such buyer the seller may stop delivery until

(a) receipt of the goods by the buyer; or

(b) acknowledgment to the buyer by any bailee of the goods except a carrier that the bailee holds the goods for the buyer; or

(c) such acknowledgment to the buyer by a carrier by reshipment or as warehouseman; or

(d) negotiation to the buyer of any negotiable document of title covering the goods.

(3) (a) To stop delivery the seller must so notify as to enable the bailee by reasonable diligence to prevent delivery of the goods.

(b) After such notification the bailee must hold and deliver the goods according to the directions of the seller but the seller is liable to the bailee for any ensuing charges or damages.

(c) If a negotiable document of title has been issued for goods the bailee is not obliged to obey a notification to stop until surrender of possession or control of the document.

(d) A carrier who has issued a non-negotiable bill of lading is not obliged to obey a notification to stop received from a person other than the consignor.

§2-706. Seller's Resale Including Contract for Resale.

(1) Under the conditions stated in Section 2–703 on seller's remedies, the seller may resell the goods concerned or the undelivered balance thereof. Where the resale is made in good faith and in a commercially reasonable manner the seller may recover the difference between the resale price and the contract price together with any incidental damages allowed under the provisions of this Article (Section 2–710), but less expenses saved in consequence of the buyer's breach.

(2) Except as otherwise provided in subsection (3) or unless otherwise agreed resale may be at public or private sale including sale by way of one or more contracts to sell or of identification to an existing contract of the seller. Sale may be as a unit or in parcels and at any time and place and on any terms but every aspect of the sale including the method, manner, time, place and terms must be commercially reasonable. The resale must be reasonably identified as referring to the broken contract, but it is not necessary that the goods be in existence or that any or all of them have been identified to the contract before the breach.

(3) Where the resale is at private sale the seller must give the buyer reasonable notification of his intention to resell.

(4) Where the resale is at public sale

(a) only identified goods can be sold except where there is a recognized market for a public sale of futures in goods of the kind; and

(b) it must be made at a usual place or market for public sale if one is reasonably available and except in the case of goods which are perishable or threaten to decline in value speedily the seller must give the buyer reasonable notice of the time and place of the resale; and

(c) if the goods are not to be within the view of those attending the sale the notification of sale must state the place where the goods are located and provide for their reasonable inspection by prospective bidders; and

(d) the seller may buy.

(5) A purchaser who buys in good faith at a resale takes the goods free of any rights of the original buyer even though the seller fails to comply with one or more of the requirements of this section.

(6) The seller is not accountable to the buyer for any profit made on any resale. A person in the position of a seller (Section 2–707) or a buyer who has rightfully rejected or justifiably revoked acceptance must account for any excess over the amount of his security interest, as hereinafter defined (subsection (3) of Section 2–711).

§2-707. "Person in the Position of a Seller".

(1) A "person in the position of a seller" includes as against a principal an agent who has paid or become responsible for the price of goods on behalf of his principal or anyone who otherwise holds a security interest or other right in goods similar to that of a seller.

(2) A person in the position of a seller may as provided in this Article withhold or stop delivery (Section 2–705) and resell (Section 2–706) and recover incidental damages (Section 2–710).

§2-708. Seller's Damages for Non-acceptance or Repudiation.

(1) Subject to subsection (2) and to the provisions of this Article with respect to proof of market price (Section 2–723), the measure of damages for non-acceptance or repudiation by the buyer is the difference between the market price at the time and place for tender and the unpaid contract price together with any incidental damages provided in this Article (Section 2–710), but less expenses saved in consequence of the buyer's breach.

(2) If the measure of damages provided in subsection (1) is inadequate to put the seller in as good a position as performance would have done then the measure of damages is the profit (including reasonable overhead) which the seller would have made from full performance by the buyer, together with any incidental damages provided in this Article (Section 2–710), due allowance for costs reasonably incurred and due credit for payments or proceeds of resale.

§2-709. Action for the Price.

(1) When the buyer fails to pay the price as it becomes due the seller may recover, together with any incidental damages under the next section, the price

(a) of goods accepted or of conforming goods lost or damaged within a commercially reasonable time after risk of their loss has passed to the buyer; and

(b) of goods identified to the contract if the seller is unable after reasonable effort to resell them at a reasonable price or the circumstances reasonably indicate that such effort will be unavailing.

(2) Where the seller sues for the price he must hold for the buyer any goods which have been identified to the contract and are still in his control except that if resale becomes possible he may resell them at any time prior to the collection of the judgment. The net proceeds of any such resale must be credited to the buyer and payment of the judgment entitles him to any goods not resold.

(3) After the buyer has wrongfully rejected or revoked acceptance of the goods or has failed to make a payment due or has repudiated (Section 2–610), a seller who is held not entitled to the price under this section shall nevertheless be awarded damages for non-acceptance under the preceding section.

§2-710. Seller's Incidental Damages.
Incidental damages to an aggrieved seller include any commercially reasonable charges, expenses or commissions incurred in stopping delivery, in the transportation, care and custody of goods after the buyer's breach, in connection with return or resale of the goods or otherwise resulting from the breach.

§2-711. Buyer's Remedies in General; Buyer's Security Interest in Rejected Goods.

(1) Where the seller fails to make delivery or repudiates or the buyer rightfully rejects or justifiably revokes acceptance then with respect to any goods involved, and with respect to the whole if the breach goes to the whole contract (Section 2–612), the buyer may cancel and whether or not he has done so may in addition to recovering so much of the price as has been paid

(a) "cover" and have damages under the next section as to all the goods affected whether or not they have been identified to the contract; or

(b) recover damages for non-delivery as provided in this Article (Section 2–713).

(2) Where the seller fails to deliver or repudiates the buyer may also

(a) if the goods have been identified recover them as provided in this Article (Section 2–502); or

(b) in a proper case obtain specific performance or replevy the goods as provided in this Article (Section 2–716).

(3) On rightful rejection or justifiable revocation of acceptance a buyer has a security interest in goods in his possession or control for any payments made on their price and any expenses reasonably incurred in their inspection, receipt, transportation, care and custody and may hold such goods and resell them in like manner as an aggrieved seller (Section 2–706).

§2-712. "Cover"; Buyer's Procurement of Substitute Goods.

(1) After a breach within the preceding section the buyer may "cover" by making in good faith and without unreasonable delay any reasonable purchase of or contract to purchase goods in substitution for those due from the seller.

(2) The buyer may recover from the seller as damages the difference between the cost of cover and the contract price together with any incidental or consequential damages as hereinafter defined (Section 2–715), but less expenses saved in consequence of the seller's breach.

(3) Failure of the buyer to effect cover within this section does not bar him from any other remedy.

§2-713. Buyer's Damages for Non-delivery or Repudiation.

(1) Subject to the provisions of this Article with respect to proof of market price (Section 2–723), the measure of damages for non-delivery or repudiation by the seller is the difference between the market price at the time when the buyer learned of the breach and the contract price together with any incidental and consequential damages provided in this Article (Section 2–715), but less expenses saved in consequence of the seller's breach.

(2) Market price is to be determined as of the place for tender or, in cases of rejection after arrival or revocation of acceptance, as of the place of arrival.

§2-714. Buyer's Damages for Breach in Regard to Accepted Goods.

(1) Where the buyer has accepted goods and given notification (subsection (3) of Section 2–607) he may recover as damages for any non-conformity of tender the loss resulting in the ordinary course of events from the seller's breach as determined in any manner which is reasonable.

(2) The measure of damages for breach of warranty is the difference at the time and place of acceptance between the value of the goods accepted and the value they would have had if they had been as warranted, unless special circumstances show proximate damages of a different amount.

(3) In a proper case any incidental and consequential damages under the next section may also be recovered.

§2-715. Buyer's Incidental and Consequential Damages.

(1) Incidental damages resulting from the seller's breach include expenses reasonably incurred in inspection, receipt, transportation and care and custody of goods rightfully rejected, any commercially reasonable charges, expenses or commissions in connection with effecting cover and any other reasonable expense incident to the delay or other breach.

(2) Consequential damages resulting from the seller's breach include

(a) any loss resulting from general or particular requirements and needs of which the seller at the time of contracting had reason to know and which could not reasonably be prevented by cover or otherwise; and

(b) injury to person or property proximately resulting from any breach of warranty.

§2-716. Buyer's Right to Specific Performance or Replevin.

(1) Specific performance may be decreed where the goods are unique or in other proper circumstances.

(2) The decree for specific performance may include such terms and conditions as to payment of the price, damages, or other relief as the court may deem just.

(3) The buyer has a right of replevin for goods identified to the contract if after reasonable effort he is unable to effect cover for such goods or the circumstances reasonably indicate that such effort will be unavailing or if the goods have been shipped under reservation and satisfaction of the security interest in them has been made or tendered. In the case of goods bought for personal, family, or household purposes, the buyer's right of replevin vests upon acquisition of a special property, even if the seller had not then repudiated or failed to deliver.

§2-717. Deduction of Damages From the Price.

The buyer on notifying the seller of his intention to do so may deduct all or any part of the damages resulting from any breach of the contract from any part of the price still due under the same contract.

§2-718. Liquidation or Limitation of Damages; Deposits.

(1) Damages for breach by either party may be liquidated in the agreement but only at an amount which is reasonable in the light of the anticipated or actual harm caused by the breach, the difficulties of proof of loss, and the inconvenience or nonfeasibility of otherwise obtaining an adequate remedy. A term fixing unreasonably large liquidated damages is void as a penalty.

(2) Where the seller justifiably withholds delivery of goods because of the buyer's breach, the buyer is entitled to restitution of any amount by which the sum of his payments exceeds

(a) the amount to which the seller is entitled by virtue of terms liquidating the seller's damages in accordance with subsection (1), or

(b) in the absence of such terms, twenty per cent of the value of the total performance for which the buyer is obligated under the contract or $500, whichever is smaller.

(3) The buyer's right to restitution under subsection (2) is subject to offset to the extent that the seller establishes

    (a) a right to recover damages under the provisions of this Article other than subsection (1), and

    (b) the amount or value of any benefits received by the buyer directly or indirectly by reason of the contract.

(4) Where a seller has received payment in goods their reasonable value or the proceeds of their resale shall be treated as payments for the purposes of subsection (2); but if the seller has notice of the buyer's breach before reselling goods received in part performance, his resale is subject to the conditions laid down in this Article on resale by an aggrieved seller (Section 2–706).

§2-719. Contractual Modification or Limitation of Remedy.

(1) Subject to the provisions of subsections (2) and (3) of this section and of the preceding section on liquidation and limitation of damages,

    (a) the agreement may provide for remedies in addition to or in substitution for those provided in this Article and may limit or alter the measure of damages recoverable under this Article, as by limiting the buyer's remedies to return of the goods and repayment of the price or to repair and replacement of non-conforming goods or parts; and

    (b) resort to a remedy as provided is optional unless the remedy is expressly agreed to be exclusive, in which case it is the sole remedy.

(2) Where circumstances cause an exclusive or limited remedy to fail of its essential purpose, remedy may be had as provided in this Act.

(3) Consequential damages may be limited or excluded unless the limitation or exclusion is unconscionable. Limitation of consequential damages for injury to the person in the case of consumer goods is prima facie unconscionable but limitation of damages where the loss is commercial is not.

§2-720. Effect of "Cancellation" or "Rescission" on Claims for Antecedent Breach.
Unless the contrary intention clearly appears, expressions of "cancellation" or "rescission" of the contract or the like shall not be construed as a renunciation or discharge of any claim in damages for an antecedent breach.

§2-721. Remedies for Fraud.
Remedies for material misrepresentation or fraud include all remedies available under this Article for non-fraudulent breach. Neither rescission or a claim for rescission of the contract for sale nor rejection or return of the goods shall bar or be deemed inconsistent with a claim for damages or other remedy.

§2-722. Who Can Sue Third Parties for Injury to Goods.
Where a third party so deals with goods which have been identified to a contract for sale as to cause actionable injury to a party to that contract

    (a) a right of action against the third party is in either party to the contract for sale who has title to or a security interest or a special property or an insurable interest in the goods; and if the goods have been destroyed or converted a right of action is also in the party who either bore the risk of loss under the contract for sale or has since the injury assumed that risk as against the other;

    (b) if at the time of the injury the party plaintiff did not bear the risk of loss as against the other party to the contract for sale and there is no arrangement between them for disposition of the recovery, his suit or settlement is, subject to his own interest, as a fiduciary for the other party to the contract;

    (c) either party may with the consent of the other sue for the benefit of whom it may concern.

§2-723. Proof of Market Price: Time and Place.

(1) If an action based on anticipatory repudiation comes to trial before the time for performance with respect to some or all of the goods, any damages based on market price (Section 2–708 or Section 2–713) shall be determined according to the price of such goods prevailing at the time when the aggrieved party learned of the repudiation.

(2) If evidence of a price prevailing at the times or places described in this Article is not readily available the price prevailing within any reasonable time before or after the time described or at any other place which in commercial judgment or under usage of trade would serve as a reasonable substitute for the one described may be used, making any proper allowance for the cost of transporting the goods to or from such other place.

(3) Evidence of a relevant price prevailing at a time or place other than the one described in this Article offered by one party is not admissible unless and until he has given the other party such notice as the court finds sufficient to prevent unfair surprise.

§2-724. Admissibility of Market Quotations.
Whenever the prevailing price or value of any goods regularly bought and sold in any established commodity market is in issue, reports in official publications or trade journals or in newspapers or periodicals of general circulation published as the reports of such market shall be admissible in evidence. The circumstances of the preparation

of such a report may be shown to affect its weight but not its admissibility.

§2-725. Statute of Limitations in Contracts for Sale.

(1) An action for breach of any contract for sale must be commenced within four years after the cause of action has accrued. By the original agreement the parties may reduce the period of limitation to not less than one year but may not extend it.

(2) A cause of action accrues when the breach occurs, regardless of the aggrieved party's lack of knowledge of the breach. A breach of warranty occurs when tender of delivery is made, except that where a warranty explicitly extends to future performance of the goods and discovery of the breach must await the time of such performance the cause of action accrues when the breach is or should have been discovered.

(3) Where an action commenced within the time limited by subsection (1) is so terminated as to leave available a remedy by another action for the same breach such other action may be commenced after the expiration of the time limited and within six months after the termination of the first action unless the termination resulted from voluntary discontinuance or from dismissal for failure or neglect to prosecute.

(4) This section does not alter the law on tolling of the statute of limitations nor does it apply to causes of action which have accrued before this Act becomes effective.

Part 1: General Provisions

§2A-101. Short Title. This Article shall be known and may be cited as the Uniform Commercial Code—Leases.

§2A-102. Scope. This Article applies to any transaction, regardless of form, that creates a lease.

§2A-103. Definitions and Index of Definitions.

(1) In this Article unless the context otherwise requires:

(a) "Buyer in ordinary course of business" means a person who in good faith and without knowledge that the sale to him [or her] is in violation of the ownership rights or security interest or leasehold interest of a third party in the goods buys in ordinary course from a person in the business of selling goods of that kind but does not include a pawnbroker. "Buying" may be for cash or by exchange of other property or on secured or unsecured credit and includes receiving goods or documents of title under a pre-existing contract for sale but does not include a transfer in bulk or as security for or in total or partial satisfaction of a money debt.

(b) "Cancellation" occurs when either party puts an end to the lease contract for default by the other party.

(c) "Commercial unit" means such a unit of goods as by commercial usage is a single whole for purposes of lease and division of which materially impairs its character or value on the market or in use. A commercial unit may be a single article, as a machine, or a set of articles, as a suite of furniture or a line of machinery, or a quantity, as a gross or carload, or any other unit treated in use or in the relevant market as a single whole.

(d) "Conforming" goods or performance under a lease contract means goods or performance that are in accordance with the obligations under the lease contract.

(e) "Consumer lease" means a lease that a lessor regularly engaged in the business of leasing or selling makes to a lessee who is an individual and who takes under the lease primarily for a personal, family, or household purpose [, if the total payments to be made under the lease contract, excluding payments for options to renew or buy, do not exceed $_____].

(f) "Fault" means wrongful act, omission, breach, or default.

(g) "Finance lease" means a lease with respect to which:

(i) the lessor does not select, manufacture, or supply the goods;

(ii) the lessor acquires the goods or the right to possession and use of the goods in connection with the lease; and

(iii) one of the following occurs:

(A) the lessee receives a copy of the contract by which the lessor acquired the goods or the right to possession and use of the goods before signing the lease contract;

(B) the lessee's approval of the contract by which the lessor acquired the goods or the right to possession and use of the goods is a condition to effectiveness of the lease contract;

(C) the lessee, before signing the lease contract, receives an accurate and complete statement designating the promises and warranties, and any disclaimers of warranties, limitations or modifications of remedies, or liquidated damages, including those of a third party, such as the manufacturer of the goods, provided to the lessor by the person supplying the goods in connection with or as part of the contract by which the lessor acquired the goods or the right to possession and use of the goods; or

(D) if the lease is not a consumer lease, the lessor, before the lessee signs the lease contract, informs the lessee in writing (a) of the identity of the person supplying the goods to the lessor, unless the lessee has selected that person and directed the lessor to acquire the goods or the right to possession and use of the goods from that person, (b) that the lessee is entitled under this Article to the promises and warranties, including those of any third party, provided to the lessor by the person supplying the goods in connection with or as part of the contract by which the lessor acquired the goods or the right to possession and use of the goods, and (c) that the lessee may communicate with the person supplying the goods to the lessor and receive an accurate and complete statement of those promises and warranties, including any disclaimers and limitations of them or of remedies.

(h) "Goods" means all things that are movable at the time of identification to the lease contract, or are fixtures (Section 2A–309), but the term does not include money, documents, instruments, accounts, chattel paper, general intangibles, or minerals or the like, including oil and gas, before extraction. The term also includes the unborn young of animals.

(i) "Installment lease contract" means a lease contract that authorizes or requires the delivery of goods in separate lots to be separately accepted, even though the lease contract contains a clause "each delivery is a separate lease" or its equivalent.

(j) "Lease" means a transfer of the right to possession and use of goods for a term in return for consideration, but a sale, including a sale on approval or a sale or return, or retention or creation of a security interest is not a lease. Unless the context clearly indicates otherwise, the term includes a sublease.

(k) "Lease agreement" means the bargain, with respect to the lease, of the lessor and the lessee in fact as found in their language or by implication from other circumstances including course of dealing or usage of trade or course of performance as provided in this Article. Unless the context clearly indicates otherwise, the term includes a sublease agreement.

(l) "Lease contract" means the total legal obligation that results from the lease agreement as affected by this Article and any other applicable rules of law. Unless the context clearly indicates otherwise, the term includes a sublease contract.

(m) "Leasehold interest" means the interest of the lessor or the lessee under a lease contract.

(n) "Lessee" means a person who acquires the right to possession and use of goods under a lease. Unless the context clearly indicates otherwise, the term includes a sublessee.

(o) "Lessee in ordinary course of business" means a person who in good faith and without knowledge that the lease to him [or her] is in violation of the ownership rights or security interest or leasehold interest of a third party in the goods, leases in ordinary course from a person in the business of selling or leasing goods of that kind but does not include a pawnbroker. "Leasing" may be for cash or by exchange of other property or on secured or unsecured credit and includes receiving goods or documents of title under a pre-existing lease contract but does not include a transfer in bulk or as security for or in total or partial satisfaction of a money debt.

(p) "Lessor" means a person who transfers the right to possession and use of goods under a lease. Unless the context clearly indicates otherwise, the term includes a sublessor.

(q) "Lessor's residual interest" means the lessor's interest in the goods after expiration, termination, or cancellation of the lease contract.

(r) "Lien" means a charge against or interest in goods to secure payment of a debt or performance of an obligation, but the term does not include a security interest.

(s) "Lot" means a parcel or a single article that is the subject matter of a separate lease or delivery, whether or not it is sufficient to perform the lease contract.

(t) "Merchant lessee" means a lessee that is a merchant with respect to goods of the kind subject to the lease.

(u) "Present value" means the amount as of a date certain of one or more sums payable in the future, discounted to the date certain. The discount is determined by the interest rate specified by the parties if the rate was not manifestly unreasonable at the time the transaction was entered into; otherwise, the discount is determined by a commercially reasonable rate that takes into account the facts and circumstances of each case at the time the transaction was entered into.

(v) "Purchase" includes taking by sale, lease, mortgage, security interest, pledge, gift, or any other voluntary transaction creating an interest in goods.

(w) "Sublease" means a lease of goods the right to possession and use of which was acquired by the lessor as a lessee under an existing lease.

(x) "Supplier" means a person from whom a lessor buys or leases goods to be leased under a finance lease.

(y) "Supply contract" means a contract under which a lessor buys or leases goods to be leased.

(z) "Termination" occurs when either party pursuant to a power created by agreement or law puts an end to the lease contract otherwise than for default.

(2) Other definitions applying to this Article and the sections in which they appear are:

"Accessions". Section 2A–310(1).

"Construction mortgage". Section 2A–309(1)(d).

"Encumbrance". Section 2A–309(1)(e).

"Fixtures". Section 2A–309(1)(a).

"Fixture filing". Section 2A–309(1)(b).

"Purchase money lease". Section 2A–309(1)(c).

(3) The following definitions in other Articles apply to this Article:

"Account". Section 9–106.

"Between merchants". Section 2–104(3).

"Buyer". Section 2–103(1)(a).

"Chattel paper". Section 9–105(1)(b).

"Consumer goods". Section 9–109(1).

"Document". Section 9–105(1)(f).

"Entrusting". Section 2–403(3).

"General intangibles". Section 9–106.

"Good faith". Section 2–103(1)(b).

"Instrument". Section 9–105(1)(i).

"Merchant". Section 2–104(1).

"Mortgage". Section 9–105(1)(j).

"Pursuant to commitment". Section 9–105(1)(k).

"Receipt". Section 2–103(1)(c).

"Sale". Section 2–106(1).

"Sale on approval". Section 2–326.

"Sale or return". Section 2–326.

"Seller". Section 2–103(1)(d).

(4) In addition Article 1 contains general definitions and principles of construction and interpretation applicable throughout this Article.

§2A-104. Leases Subject to Other Law.

(1) A lease, although subject to this Article, is also subject to any applicable:

(a) certificate of title statute of this State: (list any certificate of title statutes covering automobiles, trailers, mobile homes, boats, farm tractors, and the like);

(b) certificate of title statute of another jurisdiction (Section 2A–105); or

(c) consumer protection statute of this State, or final consumer protection decision of a court of this State existing on the effective date of this Article.

(2) In case of conflict between this Article, other than Sections 2A–105, 2A–304(3), and 2A–305(3), and a statute or decision referred to in subsection (1), the statute or decision controls.

(3) Failure to comply with an applicable law has only the effect specified therein.

§2A-105. Territorial Application of Article to Goods Covered by Certificate of Title.

Subject to the provisions of Sections 2A-304(3) and 2A-305(3), with respect to goods covered by a certificate of title issued under a statute of this State or of another jurisdiction, compliance and the effect of compliance or noncompliance with a certificate of title statute are governed by the law (including the conflict of laws rules) of the jurisdiction issuing the certificate until the earlier of (a) surrender of the certificate, or (b) four months after the goods are removed from that jurisdiction and thereafter until a new certificate of title is issued by another jurisdiction.

§2A-106. Limitation on Power of Parties to Consumer Lease to Choose Applicable Law and Judicial Forum.

(1) If the law chosen by the parties to a consumer lease is that of a jurisdiction other than a jurisdiction in which the lessee resides at the time the lease agreement becomes enforceable or within 30 days thereafter or in which the goods are to be used, the choice is not enforceable.

(2) If the judicial forum chosen by the parties to a consumer lease is a forum that would not otherwise have jurisdiction over the lessee, the choice is not enforceable.

§2A-107. Waiver or Renunciation of Claim or Right After Default.
Any claim or right arising out of an alleged default or breach of warranty may be discharged in whole or in part without consideration by a written waiver or renunciation signed and delivered by the aggrieved party.

§2A-108. Unconscionability.

(1) If the court as a matter of law finds a lease contract or any clause of a lease contract to have been unconscionable at the time it was made the court may refuse to enforce the lease contract, or it may enforce the remainder of the lease contract without the unconscionable clause, or it may so limit the

application of any unconscionable clause as to avoid any unconscionable result.

(2) With respect to a consumer lease, if the court as a matter of law finds that a lease contract or any clause of a lease contract has been induced by unconscionable conduct or that unconscionable conduct has occurred in the collection of a claim arising from a lease contract, the court may grant appropriate relief.

(3) Before making a finding of unconscionability under subsection (1) or (2), the court, on its own motion or that of a party, shall afford the parties a reasonable opportunity to present evidence as to the setting, purpose, and effect of the lease contract or clause thereof, or of the conduct.

(4) In an action in which the lessee claims unconscionability with respect to a consumer lease:

(a) If the court finds unconscionability under subsection (1) or (2), the court shall award reasonable attorney's fees to the lessee.

(b) If the court does not find unconscionability and the lessee claiming unconscionability has brought or maintained an action he [or she] knew to be groundless, the court shall award reasonable attorney's fees to the party against whom the claim is made.

(c) In determining attorney's fees, the amount of the recovery on behalf of the claimant under subsections (1) and (2) is not controlling.

§2A-109. Option to Accelerate at Will.

(1) A term providing that one party or his [or her] successor in interest may accelerate payment or performance or require collateral or additional collateral "at will" or "when he [or she] deems himself [or herself] insecure" or in words of similar import must be construed to mean that he [or she] has power to do so only if he [or she] in good faith believes that the prospect of payment or performance is impaired.

(2) With respect to a consumer lease, the burden of establishing good faith under subsection (1) is on the party who exercised the power; otherwise the burden of establishing lack of good faith is on the party against whom the power has been exercised.

Part 2: Formation and Construction of Lease Contract

§2A-201. Statute of Frauds.

(1) A lease contract is not enforceable by way of action or defense unless:

(a) the total payments to be made under the lease contract, excluding payments for options to renew or buy, are less than $1,000; or

(b) there is a writing, signed by the party against whom enforcement is sought or by that party's

authorized agent, sufficient to indicate that a lease contract has been made between the parties and to describe the goods leased and the lease term.

(2) Any description of leased goods or of the lease term is sufficient and satisfies subsection (1)(b), whether or not it is specific, if it reasonably identifies what is described.

(3) A writing is not insufficient because it omits or incorrectly states a term agreed upon, but the lease contract is not enforceable under subsection (1)(b) beyond the lease term and the quantity of goods shown in the writing.

(4) A lease contract that does not satisfy the requirements of subsection (1), but which is valid in other respects, is enforceable:

(a) if the goods are to be specially manufactured or obtained for the lessee and are not suitable for lease or sale to others in the ordinary course of the lessor's business, and the lessor, before notice of repudiation is received and under circumstances that reasonably indicate that the goods are for the lessee, has made either a substantial beginning of their manufacture or commitments for their procurement;

(b) if the party against whom enforcement is sought admits in that party's pleading, testimony or otherwise in court that a lease contract was made, but the lease contract is not enforceable under this provision beyond the quantity of goods admitted; or

(c) with respect to goods that have been received and accepted by the lessee.

(5) The lease term under a lease contract referred to in subsection (4) is:

(a) if there is a writing signed by the party against whom enforcement is sought or by that party's authorized agent specifying the lease term, the term so specified;

(b) if the party against whom enforcement is sought admits in that party's pleading, testimony, or otherwise in court a lease term, the term so admitted; or

(c) a reasonable lease term.

§2A-202. Final Written Expression: Parol or Extrinsic Evidence.

Terms with respect to which the confirmatory memoranda of the parties agree or which are otherwise set forth in a writing intended by the parties as a final expression of their agreement with respect to such terms as are included therein may not be contradicted by evidence of any prior agreement or of a contemporaneous oral agreement but may be explained or supplemented:

(a) by course of dealing or usage of trade or by course of performance; and

(b) by evidence of consistent additional terms unless the court finds the writing to have been intended also as a complete and exclusive statement of the terms of the agreement.

§2A-203. Seals Inoperative. The affixing of a seal to a writing evidencing a lease contract or an offer to enter into a lease contract does not render the writing a sealed instrument and the law with respect to sealed instruments does not apply to the lease contract or offer.

§2A-204. Formation in General.

(1) A lease contract may be made in any manner sufficient to show agreement, including conduct by both parties which recognizes the existence of a lease contract.

(2) An agreement sufficient to constitute a lease contract may be found although the moment of its making is undetermined.

(3) Although one or more terms are left open, a lease contract does not fail for indefiniteness if the parties have intended to make a lease contract and there is a reasonably certain basis for giving an appropriate remedy.

§2A-205. Firm Offers. An offer by a merchant to lease goods to or from another person in a signed writing that by its terms gives assurance it will be held open is not revocable, for lack of consideration, during the time stated or, if no time is stated, for a reasonable time, but in no event may the period of irrevocability exceed 3 months. Any such term of assurance on a form supplied by the offeree must be separately signed by the offeror.

§2A-206. Offer and Acceptance in Formation of Lease Contract.

(1) Unless otherwise unambiguously indicated by the language or circumstances, an offer to make a lease contract must be construed as inviting acceptance in any manner and by any medium reasonable in the circumstances.

(2) If the beginning of a requested performance is a reasonable mode of acceptance, an offeror who is not notified of acceptance within a reasonable time may treat the offer as having lapsed before acceptance.

§2A-207. Course of Performance or Practical Construction.

(1) If a lease contract involves repeated occasions for performance by either party with knowledge of the nature of the performance and opportunity for objection to it by the other, any course of performance accepted or acquiesced in without objection is relevant to determine the meaning of the lease agreement.

(2) The express terms of a lease agreement and any course of performance, as well as any course of

dealing and usage of trade, must be construed whenever reasonable as consistent with each other; but if that construction is unreasonable, express terms control course of performance, course of performance controls both course of dealing and usage of trade, and course of dealing controls usage of trade.

(3) Subject to the provisions of Section 2A–208 on modification and waiver, course of performance is relevant to show a waiver or modification of any term inconsistent with the course of performance.

§2A-208. Modification, Rescission and Waiver.

(1) An agreement modifying a lease contract needs no consideration to be binding.

(2) A signed lease agreement that excludes modification or rescission except by a signed writing may not be otherwise modified or rescinded, but, except as between merchants, such a requirement on a form supplied by a merchant must be separately signed by the other party.

(3) Although an attempt at modification or rescission does not satisfy the requirements of subsection (2), it may operate as a waiver.

(4) A party who has made a waiver affecting an executory portion of a lease contract may retract the waiver by reasonable notification received by the other party that strict performance will be required of any term waived, unless the retraction would be unjust in view of a material change of position in reliance on the waiver.

§2A-209. Lessee under Finance Lease as Beneficiary of Supply Contract.

(1) The benefit of a supplier's promises to the lessor under the supply contract and of all warranties, whether express or implied, including those of any third party provided in connection with or as part of the supply contract, extends to the lessee to the extent of the lessee's leasehold interest under a finance lease related to the supply contract, but is subject to the terms of the warranty and of the supply contract and all defenses or claims arising therefrom.

(2) The extension of the benefit of a supplier's promises and of warranties to the lessee (Section 2A–209(1)) does not: (i) modify the rights and obligations of the parties to the supply contract, whether arising therefrom or otherwise, or (ii) impose any duty or liability under the supply contract on the lessee.

(3) Any modification or rescission of the supply contract by the supplier and the lessor is effective between the supplier and the lessee unless, before the modification or rescission, the supplier has received notice that the lessee has entered into a finance lease related to the supply contract. If the modification or rescission is effective between the supplier and the lessee,

the lessor is deemed to have assumed, in addition to the obligations of the lessor to the lessee under the lease contract, promises of the supplier to the lessor and warranties that were so modified or rescinded as they existed and were available to the lessee before modification or rescission.

(4) In addition to the extension of the benefit of the supplier's promises and of warranties to the lessee under subsection (1), the lessee retains all rights that the lessee may have against the supplier which arise from an agreement between the lessee and the supplier or under other law.

§2A-210. Express Warranties.

(1) Express warranties by the lessor are created as follows:

(a) Any affirmation of fact or promise made by the lessor to the lessee which relates to the goods and becomes part of the basis of the bargain creates an express warranty that the goods will conform to the affirmation or promise.

(b) Any description of the goods which is made part of the basis of the bargain creates an express warranty that the goods will conform to the description.

(c) Any sample or model that is made part of the basis of the bargain creates an express warranty that the whole of the goods will conform to the sample or model.

(2) It is not necessary to the creation of an express warranty that the lessor use formal words, such as "warrant" or "guarantee," or that the lessor have a specific intention to make a warranty, but an affirmation merely of the value of the goods or a statement purporting to be merely the lessor's opinion or commendation of the goods does not create a warranty.

§2A-211. Warranties against Interference and against Infringement; Lessee's Obligation Against Infringement.

(1) There is in a lease contract a warranty that for the lease term no person holds a claim to or interest in the goods that arose from an act or omission of the lessor, other than a claim by way of infringement or the like, which will interfere with the lessee's enjoyment of its leasehold interest.

(2) Except in a finance lease there is in a lease contract by a lessor who is a merchant regularly dealing in goods of the kind a warranty that the goods are delivered free of the rightful claim of any person by way of infringement or the like.

(3) A lessee who furnishes specifications to a lessor or a supplier shall hold the lessor and the supplier harmless against any claim by way of infringement or the like that arises out of compliance with the specifications.

§2A-212. Implied Warranty of Merchantability.

(1) Except in a finance lease, a warranty that the goods will be merchantable is implied in a lease contract if the lessor is a merchant with respect to goods of that kind.

(2) Goods to be merchantable must be at least such as

(a) pass without objection in the trade under the description in the lease agreement;

(b) in the case of fungible goods, are of fair average quality within the description;

(c) are fit for the ordinary purposes for which goods of that type are used;

(d) run, within the variation permitted by the lease agreement, of even kind, quality, and quantity within each unit and among all units involved;

(e) are adequately contained, packaged, and labeled as the lease agreement may require; and

(f) conform to any promises or affirmations of fact made on the container or label.

(3) Other implied warranties may arise from course of dealing or usage of trade.

§2A-213. Implied Warranty of Fitness for Particular Purpose. Except in a finance lease, if the lessor at the time the lease contract is made has reason to know of any particular purpose for which the goods are required and that the lessee is relying on the lessor's skill or judgment to select or furnish suitable goods, there is in the lease contract an implied warranty that the goods will be fit for that purpose.

§2A-214. Exclusion or Modification of Warranties.

(1) Words or conduct relevant to the creation of an express warranty and words or conduct tending to negate or limit a warranty must be construed wherever reasonable as consistent with each other; but, subject to the provisions of Section 2A–202 on parol or extrinsic evidence, negation or limitation is inoperative to the extent that the construction is unreasonable.

(2) Subject to subsection (3), to exclude or modify the implied warranty of merchantability or any part of it the language must mention "merchantability", be by a writing, and be conspicuous. Subject to subsection (3), to exclude or modify any implied warranty of fitness the exclusion must be by a writing and be conspicuous. Language to exclude all implied warranties of fitness is sufficient if it is in writing, is conspicuous and states, for example, "There is no warranty that the goods will be fit for a particular purpose".

(3) Notwithstanding subsection (2), but subject to subsection (4),

(a) unless the circumstances indicate otherwise, all implied warranties are excluded by expressions like "as is," or "with all faults," or by other language that in common understanding calls the lessee's attention to the exclusion of warranties and makes plain that there is no implied warranty, if in writing and conspicuous;

(b) if the lessee before entering into the lease contract has examined the goods or the sample or model as fully as desired or has refused to examine the goods, there is no implied warranty with regard to defects that an examination ought in the circumstances to have revealed; and

(c) an implied warranty may also be excluded or modified by course of dealing, course of performance, or usage of trade.

(4) To exclude or modify a warranty against interference or against infringement (Section 2A–211) or any part of it, the language must be specific, be by a writing, and be conspicuous, unless the circumstances, including course of performance, course of dealing, or usage of trade, give the lessee reason to know that the goods are being leased subject to a claim or interest of any person.

§2A-215. Cumulation and Conflict of Warranties Express or Implied.
Warranties, whether express or implied, must be construed as consistent with each other and as cumulative, but if that construction is unreasonable, the intention of the parties determines which warranty is dominant. In ascertaining that intention the following rules apply:

(a) Exact or technical specifications displace an inconsistent sample or model or general language of description.

(b) A sample from an existing bulk displaces inconsistent general language of description.

(c) Express warranties displace inconsistent implied warranties other than an implied warranty of fitness for a particular purpose.

§2A-216. Third-Party Beneficiaries of Express and Implied Warranties.
Alternative A—A warranty to or for the benefit of a lessee under this Article, whether express or implied, extends to any natural person who is in the family or household of the lessee or who is a guest in the lessee's home if it is reasonable to expect that such person may use, consume, or be affected by the goods and who is injured in person by breach of the warranty. This section does not displace principles of law and equity that extend a warranty to or for the benefit of a lessee to other persons. The operation of this section may not be excluded, modified, or limited, but an exclusion, modification, or limitation of the warranty, including any with respect to rights and remedies, effective against the lessee is also effective against any beneficiary designated under this section.

Alternative B—A warranty to or for the benefit of a lessee under this Article, whether express or implied, extends to any natural person who may reasonably be expected to use, consume, or be affected by the goods and who is injured in person by breach of the warranty. This section does not displace principles of law and equity that extend a warranty to or for the benefit of a lessee to other persons. The operation of this section may not be excluded, modified, or limited, but an exclusion, modification, or limitation of the warranty, including any with respect to rights and remedies, effective against the lessee is also effective against the beneficiary designated under this section.

Alternative C—A warranty to or for the benefit of a lessee under this Article, whether express or implied, extends to any person who may reasonably be expected to use, consume, or be affected by the goods and who is injured by breach of the warranty. The operation of this section may not be excluded, modified, or limited with respect to injury to the person of an individual to whom the warranty extends, but an exclusion, modification, or limitation of the warranty, including any with respect to rights and remedies, effective against the lessee is also effective against the beneficiary designated under this section.

§2A-217. Identification.
Identification of goods as goods to which a lease contract refers may be made at any time and in any manner explicitly agreed to by the parties. In the absence of explicit agreement, identification occurs:

(a) when the lease contract is made if the lease contract is for a lease of goods that are existing and identified;

(b) when the goods are shipped, marked, or otherwise designated by the lessor as goods to which the lease contract refers, if the lease contract is for a lease of goods that are not existing and identified; or

(c) when the young are conceived, if the lease contract is for a lease of unborn young of animals.

§2A-218. Insurance and Proceeds.
(1) A lessee obtains an insurable interest when existing goods are identified to the lease contract even though the goods identified are nonconforming and the lessee has an option to reject them.

(2) If a lessee has an insurable interest only by reason of the lessor's identification of the goods, the lessor, until default or insolvency or notification to the lessee that identification is final, may substitute other goods for those identified.

(3) Notwithstanding a lessee's insurable interest under subsections (1) and (2), the lessor retains an insurable interest until an option to buy has been exercised by the lessee and risk of loss has passed to the lessee.

(4) Nothing in this section impairs any insurable interest recognized under any other statute or rule of law.

(5) The parties by agreement may determine that one or more parties have an obligation to obtain and pay for insurance covering the goods and by agreement may determine the beneficiary of the proceeds of the insurance.

§2A-219. Risk of Loss.

(1) Except in the case of a finance lease, risk of loss is retained by the lessor and does not pass to the lessee. In the case of a finance lease, risk of loss passes to the lessee.

(2) Subject to the provisions of this Article on the effect of default on risk of loss (Section 2A–220), if risk of loss is to pass to the lessee and the time of passage is not stated, the following rules apply:

    (a) If the lease contract requires or authorizes the goods to be shipped by carrier

        (i) and it does not require delivery at a particular destination, the risk of loss passes to the lessee when the goods are duly delivered to the carrier; but

        (ii) if it does require delivery at a particular destination and the goods are there duly tendered while in the possession of the carrier, the risk of loss passes to the lessee when the goods are there duly so tendered as to enable the lessee to take delivery.

    (b) If the goods are held by a bailee to be delivered without being moved, the risk of loss passes to the lessee on acknowledgment by the bailee of the lessee's right to possession of the goods.

    (c) In any case not within subsection (a) or (b), the risk of loss passes to the lessee on the lessee's receipt of the goods if the lessor, or, in the case of a finance lease, the supplier, is a merchant; otherwise the risk passes to the lessee on tender of delivery.

§2A-220. Effect of Default on Risk of Loss.

(1) Where risk of loss is to pass to the lessee and the time of passage is not stated:

    (a) If a tender or delivery of goods so fails to conform to the lease contract as to give a right of rejection, the risk of their loss remains with the lessor, or, in the case of a finance lease, the supplier, until cure or acceptance.

    (b) If the lessee rightfully revokes acceptance, he [or she], to the extent of any deficiency in his [or her] effective insurance coverage, may treat the risk of loss as having remained with the lessor from the beginning.

(2) Whether or not risk of loss is to pass to the lessee, if the lessee as to conforming goods already identified to a lease contract repudiates or is otherwise in default under the lease contract, the lessor, or, in the case of a finance lease, the supplier, to the extent of any deficiency in his [or her] effective insurance coverage may treat the risk of loss as resting on the lessee for a commercially reasonable time.

§2A-221. Casualty to Identified Goods.
If a lease contract requires goods identified when the lease contract is made, and the goods suffer casualty without fault of the lessee, the lessor or the supplier before delivery, or the goods suffer casualty before risk of loss passes to the lessee pursuant to the lease agreement or Section 2A-219, then:

    (a) if the loss is total, the lease contract is avoided; and

    (b) if the loss is partial or the goods have so deteriorated as to no longer conform to the lease contract, the lessee may nevertheless demand inspection and at his [or her] option either treat the lease contract as avoided or, except in a finance lease that is not a consumer lease, accept the goods with due allowance from the rent payable for the balance of the lease term for the deterioration or the deficiency in quantity but without further right against the lessor.

Part 3: Effect of Lease Contract

§2A-301. Enforceability of Lease Contract.
Except as otherwise provided in this Article, a lease contract is effective and enforceable according to its terms between the parties, against purchasers of the goods and against creditors of the parties.

§2A-302. Title to and Possession of Goods.
Except as otherwise provided in this Article, each provision of this Article applies whether the lessor or a third party has title to the goods, and whether the lessor, the lessee, or a third party has possession of the goods, notwithstanding any statute or rule of law that possession or the absence of possession is fraudulent.

§2A-303. Alienability of Party's Interest Under Lease Contract or of Lessor's Residual Interest in Goods; Delegation of Performance; Transfer of Rights.

(1) As used in this section, "creation of a security interest" includes the sale of a lease contract that is subject to Article 9, Secured Transactions, by reason of Section 9–102(1)(b).

(2) Except as provided in subsections (3) and (4), a provision in a lease agreement which (i) prohibits the voluntary or involuntary transfer, including a transfer by sale, sublease, creation or enforcement of a security interest, or attachment, levy, or other judicial process, of an interest of a party under the lease

contract or of the lessor's residual interest in the goods, or (ii) makes such a transfer an event of default, gives rise to the rights and remedies provided in subsection (5), but a transfer that is prohibited or is an event of default under the lease agreement is otherwise effective.

(3) A provision in a lease agreement which (i) prohibits the creation or enforcement of a security interest in an interest of a party under the lease contract or in the lessor's residual interest in the goods, or (ii) makes such a transfer an event of default, is not enforceable unless, and then only to the extent that, there is an actual transfer by the lessee of the lessee's right of possession or use of the goods in violation of the provision or an actual delegation of a material performance of either party to the lease contract in violation of the provision. Neither the granting nor the enforcement of a security interest in (i) the lessor's interest under the lease contract or (ii) the lessor's residual interest in the goods is a transfer that materially impairs the prospect of obtaining return performance by, materially changes the duty of, or materially increases the burden or risk imposed on, the lessee within the purview of subsection (5) unless, and then only to the extent that, there is an actual delegation of a material performance of the lessor.

(4) A provision in a lease agreement which (i) prohibits a transfer of a right to damages for default with respect to the whole lease contract or of a right to payment arising out of the transferor's due performance of the transferor's entire obligation, or (ii) makes such a transfer an event of default, is not enforceable, and such a transfer is not a transfer that materially impairs the prospect of obtaining return performance by, materially changes the duty of, or materially increases the burden or risk imposed on, the other party to the lease contract within the purview of subsection (5).

(5) Subject to subsections (3) and (4):

(a) if a transfer is made which is made an event of default under a lease agreement, the party to the lease contract not making the transfer, unless that party waives the default or otherwise agrees, has the rights and remedies described in Section 2A–501(2);

(b) if paragraph (a) is not applicable and if a transfer is made that (i) is prohibited under a lease agreement or (ii) materially impairs the prospect of obtaining return performance by, materially changes the duty of, or materially increases the burden or risk imposed on, the other party to the lease contract, unless the party not making the transfer agrees at any time to the transfer in the lease contract or otherwise, then, except as limited by contract, (i) the transferor is liable to the party not making the transfer for damages caused by the transfer to the extent that the damages could not reasonably be prevented by the party not making the transfer and (ii) a court having jurisdiction may grant other appropriate relief, including cancellation of the lease contract or an injunction against the transfer.

(6) A transfer of "the lease" or of "all my rights under the lease", or a transfer in similar general terms, is a transfer of rights and, unless the language or the circumstances, as in a transfer for security, indicate the contrary, the transfer is a delegation of duties by the transferor to the transferee. Acceptance by the transferee constitutes a promise by the transferee to perform those duties. The promise is enforceable by either the transferor or the other party to the lease contract.

(7) Unless otherwise agreed by the lessor and the lessee, a delegation of performance does not relieve the transferor as against the other party of any duty to perform or of any liability for default.

(8) In a consumer lease, to prohibit the transfer of an interest of a party under the lease contract or to make a transfer an event of default, the language must be specific, by a writing, and conspicuous.

§2A-304. Subsequent Lease of Goods by Lessor.

(1) Subject to Section 2A–303, a subsequent lessee from a lessor of goods under an existing lease contract obtains, to the extent of the leasehold interest transferred, the leasehold interest in the goods that the lessor had or had power to transfer, and except as provided in subsection (2) and Section 2A–527(4), takes subject to the existing lease contract. A lessor with voidable title has power to transfer a good leasehold interest to a good faith subsequent lessee for value, but only to the extent set forth in the preceding sentence. If goods have been delivered under a transaction of purchase, the lessor has that power even though:

(a) the lessor's transferor was deceived as to the identity of the lessor;

(b) the delivery was in exchange for a check which is later dishonored;

(c) it was agreed that the transaction was to be a "cash sale"; or

(d) the delivery was procured through fraud punishable as larcenous under the criminal law.

(2) A subsequent lessee in the ordinary course of business from a lessor who is a merchant dealing in goods of that kind to whom the goods were entrusted by the existing lessee of that lessor before the interest of the subsequent lessee became enforceable against that lessor obtains, to the extent of the leasehold interest transferred, all of that lessor's and the existing

lessee's rights to the goods, and takes free of the existing lease contract.

(3) A subsequent lessee from the lessor of goods that are subject to an existing lease contract and are covered by a certificate of title issued under a statute of this State or of another jurisdiction takes no greater rights than those provided both by this section and by the certificate of title statute.

§2A-305. Sale or Sublease of Goods by Lessee.

(1) Subject to the provisions of Section 2A–303, a buyer or sublessee from the lessee of goods under an existing lease contract obtains, to the extent of the interest transferred, the leasehold interest in the goods that the lessee had or had power to transfer, and except as provided in subsection (2) and Section 2A–511(4), takes subject to the existing lease contract. A lessee with a voidable leasehold interest has power to transfer a good leasehold interest to a good faith buyer for value or a good faith sublessee for value, but only to the extent set forth in the preceding sentence. When goods have been delivered under a transaction of lease the lessee has that power even though:

(a) the lessor was deceived as to the identity of the lessee;

(b) the delivery was in exchange for a check which is later dishonored; or

(c) the delivery was procured through fraud punishable as larcenous under the criminal law.

(2) A buyer in the ordinary course of business or a sublessee in the ordinary course of business from a lessee who is a merchant dealing in goods of that kind to whom the goods were entrusted by the lessor obtains, to the extent of the interest transferred, all of the lessor's and lessee's rights to the goods, and takes free of the existing lease contract.

(3) A buyer or sublessee from the lessee of goods that are subject to an existing lease contract and are covered by a certificate of title issued under a statute of this State or of another jurisdiction takes no greater rights than those provided both by this section and by the certificate of title statute.

§2A-306. Priority of Certain Liens Arising by Operation of Law.
If a person in the ordinary course of his [or her] business furnishes services or materials with respect to goods subject to a lease contract, a lien upon those goods in the possession of that person given by statute or rule of law for those materials or services takes priority over any interest of the lessor or lessee under the lease contract or this Article unless the lien is created by statute and the statute provides otherwise or unless the lien is created by rule of law and the rule of law provides otherwise.

§2A-307. Priority of Liens Arising by Attachment or Levy on, Security Interests in, and Other Claims to Goods.

(1) Except as otherwise provided in Section 2A–306, a creditor of a lessee takes subject to the lease contract.

(2) Except as otherwise provided in subsections (3) and (4) and in Sections 2A–306 and 2A–308, a creditor of a lessor takes subject to the lease contract unless:

(a) the creditor holds a lien that attached to the goods before the lease contract became enforceable;

(b) the creditor holds a security interest in the goods and the lessee did not give value and receive delivery of the goods without knowledge of the security interest; or

(c) the creditor holds a security interest in the goods which was perfected (Section 9–303) before the lease contract became enforceable.

(3) A lessee in the ordinary course of business takes the leasehold interest free of a security interest in the goods created by the lessor even though the security interest is perfected (Section 9–303) and the lessee knows of its existence.

(4) A lessee other than a lessee in the ordinary course of business takes the leasehold interest free of a security interest to the extent that it secures future advances made after the secured party acquires knowledge of the lease or more than 45 days after the lease contract becomes enforceable, whichever first occurs, unless the future advances are made pursuant to a commitment entered into without knowledge of the lease and before the expiration of the 45-day period.

§2A-308. Special Rights of Creditors.

(1) A creditor of a lessor in possession of goods subject to a lease contract may treat the lease contract as void if as against the creditor retention of possession by the lessor is fraudulent under any statute or rule of law, but retention of possession in good faith and current course of trade by the lessor for a commercially reasonable time after the lease contract becomes enforceable is not fraudulent.

(2) Nothing in this Article impairs the rights of creditors of a lessor if the lease contract (a) becomes enforceable, not in current course of trade but in satisfaction of or as security for a pre-existing claim for money, security, or the like, and (b) is made under circumstances which under any statute or rule of law apart from this Article would constitute the transaction a fraudulent transfer or voidable preference.

(3) A creditor of a seller may treat a sale or an identification of goods to a contract for sale as void if as against the creditor retention of possession by the seller is fraudulent under any statute or rule of law, but retention of possession of the goods pursuant to a lease contract entered into by the seller as lessee and

the buyer as lessor in connection with the sale or identification of the goods is not fraudulent if the buyer bought for value and in good faith.

§2A-309. Lessor's and Lessee's Rights When Goods Become Fixtures.

(1) In this section:

  (a) goods are "fixtures" when they become so related to particular real estate that an interest in them arises under real estate law;

  (b) a "fixture filing" is the filing, in the office where a mortgage on the real estate would be filed or recorded, of a financing statement covering goods that are or are to become fixtures and conforming to the requirements of Section 9–402(5);

  (c) a lease is a "purchase money lease" unless the lessee has possession or use of the goods or the right to possession or use of the goods before the lease agreement is enforceable;

  (d) a mortgage is a "construction mortgage" to the extent it secures an obligation incurred for the construction of an improvement on land including the acquisition cost of the land, if the recorded writing so indicates; and

  (e) "encumbrance" includes real estate mortgages and other liens on real estate and all other rights in real estate that are not ownership interests.

(2) Under this Article a lease may be of goods that are fixtures or may continue in goods that become fixtures, but no lease exists under this Article of ordinary building materials incorporated into an improvement on land.

(3) This Article does not prevent creation of a lease of fixtures pursuant to real estate law.

(4) The perfected interest of a lessor of fixtures has priority over a conflicting interest of an encumbrancer or owner of the real estate if:

  (a) the lease is a purchase money lease, the conflicting interest of the encumbrancer or owner arises before the goods become fixtures, the interest of the lessor is perfected by a fixture filing before the goods become fixtures or within ten days thereafter, and the lessee has an interest of record in the real estate or is in possession of the real estate; or

  (b) the interest of the lessor is perfected by a fixture filing before the interest of the encumbrancer or owner is of record, the lessor's interest has priority over any conflicting interest of a predecessor in title of the encumbrancer or owner, and the lessee has an interest of record in the real estate or is in possession of the real estate.

(5) The interest of a lessor of fixtures, whether or not perfected, has priority over the conflicting interest of an encumbrancer or owner of the real estate if:

  (a) the fixtures are readily removable factory or office machines, readily removable equipment that is not primarily used or leased for use in the operation of the real estate, or readily removable replacements of domestic appliances that are goods subject to a consumer lease, and before the goods become fixtures the lease contract is enforceable; or

  (b) the conflicting interest is a lien on the real estate obtained by legal or equitable proceedings after the lease contract is enforceable; or

  (c) the encumbrancer or owner has consented in writing to the lease or has disclaimed an interest in the goods as fixtures; or

  (d) the lessee has a right to remove the goods as against the encumbrancer or owner. If the lessee's right to remove terminates, the priority of the interest of the lessor continues for a reasonable time.

(6) Notwithstanding subsection (4)(a) but otherwise subject to subsections (4) and (5), the interest of a lessor of fixtures, including the lessor's residual interest, is subordinate to the conflicting interest of an encumbrancer of the real estate under a construction mortgage recorded before the goods become fixtures if the goods become fixtures before the completion of the construction. To the extent given to refinance a construction mortgage, the conflicting interest of an encumbrancer of the real estate under a mortgage has this priority to the same extent as the encumbrancer of the real estate under the construction mortgage.

(7) In cases not within the preceding subsections, priority between the interest of a lessor of fixtures, including the lessor's residual interest, and the conflicting interest of an encumbrancer or owner of the real estate who is not the lessee is determined by the priority rules governing conflicting interests in real estate.

(8) If the interest of a lessor of fixtures, including the lessor's residual interest, has priority over all conflicting interests of all owners and encumbrancers of the real estate, the lessor or the lessee may (i) on default, expiration, termination, or cancellation of the lease agreement but subject to the agreement and this Article, or (ii) if necessary to enforce other rights and remedies of the lessor or lessee under this Article, remove the goods from the real estate, free and clear of all conflicting interests of all owners and encumbrancers of the real estate, but the lessor or lessee must reimburse any encumbrancer or owner of the real estate who is not the lessee and who has not otherwise agreed for the cost of repair of any physical injury, but not for any diminution in value of the real estate caused by the absence of the goods removed or by any necessity of replacing them. A person entitled to reimbursement may refuse permission to remove until the party seeking removal gives adequate security for the performance of this obligation.

(9) Even though the lease agreement does not create a security interest, the interest of a lessor of fixtures, including the lessor's residual interest, is perfected by filing a financing statement as a fixture filing for leased goods that are or are to become fixtures in accordance with the relevant provisions of the Article on Secured Transactions (Article 9).

§2A-310. Lessor's and Lessee's Rights When Goods Become Accessions.

(1) Goods are "accessions" when they are installed in or affixed to other goods.

(2) The interest of a lessor or a lessee under a lease contract entered into before the goods became accessions is superior to all interests in the whole except as stated in subsection (4).

(3) The interest of a lessor or a lessee under a lease contract entered into at the time or after the goods became accessions is superior to all subsequently acquired interests in the whole except as stated in subsection (4) but is subordinate to interests in the whole existing at the time the lease contract was made unless the holders of such interests in the whole have in writing consented to the lease or disclaimed an interest in the goods as part of the whole.

(4) The interest of a lessor or a lessee under a lease contract described in subsection (2) or (3) is subordinate to the interest of

(a) a buyer in the ordinary course of business or a lessee in the ordinary course of business of any interest in the whole acquired after the goods became accessions; or

(b) a creditor with a security interest in the whole perfected before the lease contract was made to the extent that the creditor makes subsequent advances without knowledge of the lease contract.

(5) When under subsections (2) or (3) and (4) a lessor or a lessee of accessions holds an interest that is superior to all interests in the whole, the lessor or the lessee may (a) on default, expiration, termination, or cancellation of the lease contract by the other party but subject to the provisions of the lease contract and this Article, or (b) if necessary to enforce his [or her] other rights and remedies under this Article, remove the goods from the whole, free and clear of all interests in the whole, but he [or she] must reimburse any holder of an interest in the whole who is not the lessee and who has not otherwise agreed for the cost of repair of any physical injury but not for any diminution in value of the whole caused by the absence of the goods removed or by any necessity for replacing them. A person entitled to reimbursement may refuse permission to remove until the party seeking removal gives adequate security for the performance of this obligation.

§2A-311. Priority Subject to Subordination.
Nothing in this Article prevents subordination by agreement by any person entitled to priority.

Part 4: Performance of Lease Contract: Repudiated, Substituted and Excused

§2A-401. Insecurity: Adequate Assurance of Performance.

(1) A lease contract imposes an obligation on each party that the other's expectation of receiving due performance will not be impaired.

(2) If reasonable grounds for insecurity arise with respect to the performance of either party, the insecure party may demand in writing adequate assurance of due performance. Until the insecure party receives that assurance, if commercially reasonable the insecure party may suspend any performance for which he [or she] has not already received the agreed return.

(3) A repudiation of the lease contract occurs if assurance of due performance adequate under the circumstances of the particular case is not provided to the insecure party within a reasonable time, not to exceed 30 days after receipt of a demand by the other party.

(4) Between merchants, the reasonableness of grounds for insecurity and the adequacy of any assurance offered must be determined according to commercial standards.

(5) Acceptance of any nonconforming delivery or payment does not prejudice the aggrieved party's right to demand adequate assurance of future performance.

§2A-402. Anticipatory Repudiation.
If either party repudiates a lease contract with respect to a performance not yet due under the lease contract, the loss of which performance will substantially impair the value of the lease contract to the other, the aggrieved party may:

(a) for a commercially reasonable time, await retraction of repudiation and performance by the repudiating party;

(b) make demand pursuant to Section 2A–401 and await assurance of future performance adequate under the circumstances of the particular case; or

(c) resort to any right or remedy upon default under the lease contract or this Article, even though the aggrieved party has notified the repudiating party that the aggrieved party would await the repudiating party's performance and assurance and has urged retraction. In addition, whether or not the aggrieved party is pursuing one of the foregoing remedies, the aggrieved party may suspend performance or, if the aggrieved party is the lessor, proceed in accordance with the provisions of this Article on the lessor's right to identify goods to the lease contract notwithstanding default or to salvage unfinished goods (Section 2A–524).

§2A-403. Retraction of Anticipatory Repudiation.

(1) Until the repudiating party's next performance is due, the repudiating party can retract the repudiation unless, since the repudiation, the aggrieved party has cancelled the lease contract or materially changed the aggrieved party's position or otherwise indicated that the aggrieved party considers the repudiation final.

(2) Retraction may be by any method that clearly indicates to the aggrieved party that the repudiating party intends to perform under the lease contract and includes any assurance demanded under Section 2A–401.

(3) Retraction reinstates a repudiating party's rights under a lease contract with due excuse and allowance to the aggrieved party for any delay occasioned by the repudiation.

§2A-404. Substituted Performance.

(1) If without fault of the lessee, the lessor and the supplier, the agreed berthing, loading, or unloading facilities fail or the agreed type of carrier becomes unavailable or the agreed manner of delivery otherwise becomes commercially impracticable, but a commercially reasonable substitute is available, the substitute performance must be tendered and accepted.

(2) If the agreed means or manner of payment fails because of domestic or foreign governmental regulation:

(a) the lessor may withhold or stop delivery or cause the supplier to withhold or stop delivery unless the lessee provides a means or manner of payment that is commercially a substantial equivalent; and

(b) if delivery has already been taken, payment by the means or in the manner provided by the regulation discharges the lessee's obligation unless the regulation is discriminatory, oppressive, or predatory.

§2A-405. Excused Performance. Subject to Section 2A-404 on substituted performance, the following rules apply:

(a) Delay in delivery or nondelivery in whole or in part by a lessor or a supplier who complies with paragraphs (b) and (c) is not a default under the lease contract if performance as agreed has been made impracticable by the occurrence of a contingency the nonoccurrence of which was a basic assumption on which the lease contract was made or by compliance in good faith with any applicable foreign or domestic governmental regulation or order, whether or not the regulation or order later proves to be invalid.

(b) If the causes mentioned in paragraph (a) affect only part of the lessor's or the supplier's capacity to perform, he [or she] shall allocate production and deliveries among his [or her] customers but at his [or her] option may include regular customers not then under contract for sale or lease as well as his [or her] own requirements for further manufacture. He [or she] may so allocate in any manner that is fair and reasonable.

(c) The lessor seasonally shall notify the lessee and in the case of a finance lease the supplier seasonally shall notify the lessor and the lessee, if known, that there will be delay or nondelivery and, if allocation is required under paragraph (b), of the estimated quota thus made available for the lessee.

§2A-406. Procedure on Excused Performance.

(1) If the lessee receives notification of a material or indefinite delay or an allocation justified under Section 2A–405, the lessee may by written notification to the lessor as to any goods involved, and with respect to all of the goods if under an installment lease contract the value of the whole lease contract is substantially impaired (Section 2A–510):

(a) terminate the lease contract (Section 2A–505(2)); or

(b) except in a finance lease that is not a consumer lease, modify the lease contract by accepting the available quota in substitution, with due allowance from the rent payable for the balance of the lease term for the deficiency but without further right against the lessor.

(2) If, after receipt of a notification from the lessor under Section 2A–405, the lessee fails so to modify the lease agreement within a reasonable time not exceeding 30 days, the lease contract lapses with respect to any deliveries affected.

§2A-407. Irrevocable Promises: Finance Leases.

(1) In the case of a finance lease that is not a consumer lease the lessee's promises under the lease contract become irrevocable and independent upon the lessee's acceptance of the goods.

(2) A promise that has become irrevocable and independent under subsection (1):

(a) is effective and enforceable between the parties, and by or against third parties including assignees of the parties; and

(b) is not subject to cancellation, termination, modification, repudiation, excuse, or substitution without the consent of the party to whom the promise runs.

(3) This section does not affect the validity under any other law of a covenant in any lease contract making the lessee's promises irrevocable and independent upon the lessee's acceptance of the goods.

Part 5: Default

A. In General

§2A-501. Default: Procedure.

(1) Whether the lessor or the lessee is in default under a lease contract is determined by the lease agreement and this Article.

(2) If the lessor or the lessee is in default under the lease contract, the party seeking enforcement has rights and remedies as provided in this Article and, except as limited by this Article, as provided in the lease agreement.

(3) If the lessor or the lessee is in default under the lease contract, the party seeking enforcement may reduce the party's claim to judgment, or otherwise enforce the lease contract by self-help or any available judicial procedure or nonjudicial procedure, including administrative proceeding, arbitration, or the like, in accordance with this Article.

(4) Except as otherwise provided in Section 1–106(1) or this Article or the lease agreement, the rights and remedies referred to in subsections (2) and (3) are cumulative.

(5) If the lease agreement covers both real property and goods, the party seeking enforcement may proceed under this Part as to the goods, or under other applicable law as to both the real property and the goods in accordance with that party's rights and remedies in respect of the real property, in which case this Part does not apply.

§2A-502. Notice after Default. Except as otherwise provided in this Article or the lease agreement, the lessor or lessee in default under the lease contract is not entitled to notice of default or notice of enforcement from the other party to the lease agreement.

§2A-503. Modification or Impairment of Rights and Remedies.

(1) Except as otherwise provided in this Article, the lease agreement may include rights and remedies for default in addition to or in substitution for those provided in this Article and may limit or alter the measure of damages recoverable under this Article.

(2) Resort to a remedy provided under this Article or in the lease agreement is optional unless the remedy is expressly agreed to be exclusive. If circumstances cause an exclusive or limited remedy to fail of its essential purpose, or provision for an exclusive remedy is unconscionable, remedy may be had as provided in this Article.

(3) Consequential damages may be liquidated under Section 2A–504, or may otherwise be limited, altered, or excluded unless the limitation, alteration, or exclusion is unconscionable. Limitation, alteration, or exclusion of consequential damages for injury to the person in the case of consumer goods is prima facie unconscionable but limitation, alteration, or exclusion of damages where the loss is commercial is not prima facie unconscionable.

(4) Rights and remedies on default by the lessor or the lessee with respect to any obligation or promise collateral or ancillary to the lease contract are not impaired by this Article.

§2A-504. Liquidation of Damages.

(1) Damages payable by either party for default, or any other act or omission, including indemnity for loss or diminution of anticipated tax benefits or loss or damage to lessor's residual interest, may be liquidated in the lease agreement but only at an amount or by a formula that is reasonable in light of the then anticipated harm caused by the default or other act or omission.

(2) If the lease agreement provides for liquidation of damages, and such provision does not comply with subsection (1), or such provision is an exclusive or limited remedy that circumstances cause to fail of its essential purpose, remedy may be had as provided in this Article.

(3) If the lessor justifiably withholds or stops delivery of goods because of the lessee's default or insolvency (Section 2A–525 or 2A–526), the lessee is entitled to restitution of any amount by which the sum of his [or her] payments exceeds:

    (a) the amount to which the lessor is entitled by virtue of terms liquidating the lessor's damages in accordance with subsection (1); or

    (b) in the absence of those terms, 20 percent of the then present value of the total rent the lessee was obligated to pay for the balance of the lease term, or, in the case of a consumer lease, the lesser of such amount or $500.

(4) A lessee's right to restitution under subsection (3) is subject to offset to the extent the lessor establishes:

    (a) a right to recover damages under the provisions of this Article other than subsection (1); and

    (b) the amount or value of any benefits received by the lessee directly or indirectly by reason of the lease contract.

§2A-505. Cancellation and Termination and Effect of Cancellation, Termination, Rescission, or Fraud on Rights and Remedies.

(1) On cancellation of the lease contract, all obligations that are still executory on both sides are discharged, but any right based on prior default or performance

survives, and the cancelling party also retains any remedy for default of the whole lease contract or any unperformed balance.

(2) On termination of the lease contract, all obligations that are still executory on both sides are discharged but any right based on prior default or performance survives.

(3) Unless the contrary intention clearly appears, expressions of "cancellation," "rescission," or the like of the lease contract may not be construed as a renunciation or discharge of any claim in damages for an antecedent default.

(4) Rights and remedies for material misrepresentation or fraud include all rights and remedies available under this Article for default.

(5) Neither rescission nor a claim for rescission of the lease contract nor rejection or return of the goods may bar or be deemed inconsistent with a claim for damages or other right or remedy.

§2A-506. Statute of Limitations.

(1) An action for default under a lease contract, including breach of warranty or indemnity, must be commenced within 4 years after the cause of action accrued. By the original lease contract the parties may reduce the period of limitation to not less than one year.

(2) A cause of action for default accrues when the act or omission on which the default or breach of warranty is based is or should have been discovered by the aggrieved party, or when the default occurs, whichever is later. A cause of action for indemnity accrues when the act or omission on which the claim for indemnity is based is or should have been discovered by the indemnified party, whichever is later.

(3) If an action commenced within the time limited by subsection (1) is so terminated as to leave available a remedy by another action for the same default or breach of warranty or indemnity, the other action may be commenced after the expiration of the time limited and within 6 months after the termination of the first action unless the termination resulted from voluntary discontinuance or from dismissal for failure or neglect to prosecute.

(4) This section does not alter the law on tolling of the statute of limitations nor does it apply to causes of action that have accrued before this Article becomes effective.

§2A-507. Proof of Market Rent: Time and Place.

(1) Damages based on market rent (Section 2A–519 or 2A–528) are determined according to the rent for the use of the goods concerned for a lease term identical to the remaining lease term of the original lease agreement and prevailing at the times specified in Sections 2A–519 and 2A–528.

(2) If evidence of rent for the use of the goods concerned for a lease term identical to the remaining lease term of the original lease agreement and prevailing at the times or places described in this Article is not readily available, the rent prevailing within any reasonable time before or after the time described or at any other place or for a different lease term which in commercial judgment or under usage of trade would serve as a reasonable substitute for the one described may be used, making any proper allowance for the difference, including the cost of transporting the goods to or from the other place.

(3) Evidence of a relevant rent prevailing at a time or place or for a lease term other than the one described in this Article offered by one party is not admissible unless and until he [or she] has given the other party notice the court finds sufficient to prevent unfair surprise.

(4) If the prevailing rent or value of any goods regularly leased in any established market is in issue, reports in official publications or trade journals or in newspapers or periodicals of general circulation published as the reports of that market are admissible in evidence. The circumstances of the preparation of the report may be shown to affect its weight but not its admissibility.

B. Default by Lessor

§2A-508. Lessee's Remedies.

(1) If a lessor fails to deliver the goods in conformity to the lease contract (Section 2A–509) or repudiates the lease contract (Section 2A–402), or a lessee rightfully rejects the goods (Section 2A–509) or justifiably revokes acceptance of the goods (Section 2A–517), then with respect to any goods involved, and with respect to all of the goods if under an installment lease contract the value of the whole lease contract is substantially impaired (Section 2A–510), the lessor is in default under the lease contract and the lessee may:

(a) cancel the lease contract (Section 2A–505(1));

(b) recover so much of the rent and security as has been paid and is just under the circumstances;

(c) cover and recover damages as to all goods affected whether or not they have been identified to the lease contract (Sections 2A–518 and 2A–520), or recover damages for nondelivery (Sections 2A–519 and 2A–520);

(d) exercise any other rights or pursue any other remedies provided in the lease contract.

(2) If a lessor fails to deliver the goods in conformity to the lease contract or repudiates the lease contract, the lessee may also:

(a) if the goods have been identified, recover them (Section 2A–522); or

(b) in a proper case, obtain specific performance or replevy the goods (Section 2A–521).

(3) If a lessor is otherwise in default under a lease contract, the lessee may exercise the rights and pursue the remedies provided in the lease contract, which may include a right to cancel the lease, and in Section 2A–519(3).

(4) If a lessor has breached a warranty, whether express or implied, the lessee may recover damages (Section 2A–519(4)).

(5) On rightful rejection or justifiable revocation of acceptance, a lessee has a security interest in goods in the lessee's possession or control for any rent and security that has been paid and any expenses reasonably incurred in their inspection, receipt, transportation, and care and custody and may hold those goods and dispose of them in good faith and in a commercially reasonable manner, subject to Section 2A–527(5).

(6) Subject to the provisions of Section 2A–407, a lessee, on notifying the lessor of the lessee's intention to do so, may deduct all or any part of the damages resulting from any default under the lease contract from any part of the rent still due under the same lease contract.

§2A-509. Lessee's Rights on Improper Delivery; Rightful Rejection.

(1) Subject to the provisions of Section 2A–510 on default in installment lease contracts, if the goods or the tender or delivery fail in any respect to conform to the lease contract, the lessee may reject or accept the goods or accept any commercial unit or units and reject the rest of the goods.

(2) Rejection of goods is ineffective unless it is within a reasonable time after tender or delivery of the goods and the lessee seasonably notifies the lessor.

§2A-510. Installment Lease Contracts: Rejection and Default.

(1) Under an installment lease contract a lessee may reject any delivery that is nonconforming if the nonconformity substantially impairs the value of that delivery and cannot be cured or the nonconformity is a defect in the required documents; but if the nonconformity does not fall within subsection (2) and the lessor or the supplier gives adequate assurance of its cure, the lessee must accept that delivery.

(2) Whenever nonconformity or default with respect to one or more deliveries substantially impairs the value of the installment lease contract as a whole there is a default with respect to the whole. But, the aggrieved party reinstates the installment lease contract as a whole if the aggrieved party accepts a nonconforming delivery without seasonably notifying of cancellation or brings an action with respect only to past deliveries or demands performance as to future deliveries.

§2A-511. Merchant Lessee's Duties as to Rightfully Rejected Goods.

(1) Subject to any security interest of a lessee (Section 2A–508(5)), if a lessor or a supplier has no agent or place of business at the market of rejection, a merchant lessee, after rejection of goods in his [or her] possession or control, shall follow any reasonable instructions received from the lessor or the supplier with respect to the goods. In the absence of those instructions, a merchant lessee shall make reasonable efforts to sell, lease, or otherwise dispose of the goods for the lessor's account if they threaten to decline in value speedily. Instructions are not reasonable if on demand indemnity for expenses is not forthcoming.

(2) If a merchant lessee (subsection (1)) or any other lessee (Section 2A–512) disposes of goods, he [or she] is entitled to reimbursement either from the lessor or the supplier or out of the proceeds for reasonable expenses of caring for and disposing of the goods and, if the expenses include no disposition commission, to such commission as is usual in the trade, or if there is none, to a reasonable sum not exceeding 10 percent of the gross proceeds.

(3) In complying with this section or Section 2A–512, the lessee is held only to good faith. Good faith conduct hereunder is neither acceptance or conversion nor the basis of an action for damages.

(4) A purchaser who purchases in good faith from a lessee pursuant to this section or Section 2A–512 takes the goods free of any rights of the lessor and the supplier even though the lessee fails to comply with one or more of the requirements of this Article.

§2A-512. Lessee's Duties as to Rightfully Rejected Goods.

(1) Except as otherwise provided with respect to goods that threaten to decline in value speedily (Section 2A–511) and subject to any security interest of a lessee (Section 2A–508(5)):

(a) the lessee, after rejection of goods in the lessee's possession, shall hold them with reasonable care at the lessor's or the supplier's disposition for a reasonable time after the lessee's seasonable notification of rejection;

(b) if the lessor or the supplier gives no instructions within a reasonable time after notification of rejection, the lessee may store the rejected goods for the lessor's or the supplier's account or ship them to the lessor or the supplier or dispose of them for the lessor's or the supplier's account with reimbursement in the manner provided in Section 2A–511; but

(c) the lessee has no further obligations with regard to goods rightfully rejected.

(2) Action by the lessee pursuant to subsection (1) is not acceptance or conversion.

§2A-513. Cure by Lessor of Improper Tender or Delivery; Replacement.

(1) If any tender or delivery by the lessor or the supplier is rejected because nonconforming and the time for performance has not yet expired, the lessor or the supplier may seasonably notify the lessee of the lessor's or the supplier's intention to cure and may then make a conforming delivery within the time provided in the lease contract.

(2) If the lessee rejects a nonconforming tender that the lessor or the supplier had reasonable grounds to believe would be acceptable with or without money allowance, the lessor or the supplier may have a further reasonable time to substitute a conforming tender if he [or she] seasonably notifies the lessee.

§2A-514. Waiver of Lessee's Objections.

(1) In rejecting goods, a lessee's failure to state a particular defect that is ascertainable by reasonable inspection precludes the lessee from relying on the defect to justify rejection or to establish default:

   (a) if, stated seasonably, the lessor or the supplier could have cured it (Section 2A–513); or

   (b) between merchants if the lessor or the supplier after rejection has made a request in writing for a full and final written statement of all defects on which the lessee proposes to rely.

(2) A lessee's failure to reserve rights when paying rent or other consideration against documents precludes recovery of the payment for defects apparent on the face of the documents.

§2A-515. Acceptance of Goods.

(1) Acceptance of goods occurs after the lessee has had a reasonable opportunity to inspect the goods and

   (a) the lessee signifies or acts with respect to the goods in a manner that signifies to the lessor or the supplier that the goods are conforming or that the lessee will take or retain them in spite of their nonconformity; or

   (b) the lessee fails to make an effective rejection of the goods (Section 2A–509(2)).

(2) Acceptance of a part of any commercial unit is acceptance of that entire unit.

§2A-516. Effect of Acceptance of Goods; Notice of Default; Burden of Establishing Default After Acceptance; Notice of Claim or Litigation to Person Answerable Over.

(1) A lessee must pay rent for any goods accepted in accordance with the lease contract, with due allowance for goods rightfully rejected or not delivered.

(2) A lessee's acceptance of goods precludes rejection of the goods accepted. In the case of a finance lease, if made with knowledge of a nonconformity, acceptance cannot be revoked because of it. In any other case, if made with knowledge of a nonconformity, acceptance cannot be revoked because of it unless the acceptance was on the reasonable assumption that the nonconformity would be seasonably cured. Acceptance does not of itself impair any other remedy provided by this Article or the lease agreement for nonconformity.

(3) If a tender has been accepted:

   (a) within a reasonable time after the lessee discovers or should have discovered any default, the lessee shall notify the lessor and the supplier, if any, or be barred from any remedy against the party not notified;

   (b) except in the case of a consumer lease, within a reasonable time after the lessee receives notice of litigation for infringement or the like (Section 2A–211) the lessee shall notify the lessor or be barred from any remedy over for liability established by the litigation; and

   (c) the burden is on the lessee to establish any default.

(4) If a lessee is sued for breach of a warranty or other obligation for which a lessor or a supplier is answerable over the following apply:

   (a) The lessee may give the lessor or the supplier, or both, written notice of the litigation. If the notice states that the person notified may come in and defend and that if the person notified does not do so that person will be bound in any action against that person by the lessee by any determination of fact common to the two litigations, then unless the person notified after seasonable receipt of the notice does come in and defend that person is so bound.

   (b) The lessor or the supplier may demand in writing that the lessee turn over control of the litigation including settlement if the claim is one for infringement or the like (Section 2A–211) or else be barred from any remedy over. If the demand states that the lessor or the supplier agrees to bear all expense and to satisfy any adverse judgment, then unless the lessee after seasonable receipt of the demand does turn over control the lessee is so barred.

(5) Subsections (3) and (4) apply to any obligation of a lessee to hold the lessor or the supplier harmless against infringement or the like (Section 2A–211).

§2A-517. Revocation of Acceptance of Goods.

(1) A lessee may revoke acceptance of a lot or commercial unit whose nonconformity substantially impairs its value to the lessee if the lessee has accepted it:

(a) except in the case of a finance lease, on the reasonable assumption that its nonconformity would be cured and it has not been seasonably cured; or

(b) without discovery of the nonconformity if the lessee's acceptance was reasonably induced either by the lessor's assurances or, except in the case of a finance lease, by the difficulty of discovery before acceptance.

(2) Except in the case of a finance lease that is not a consumer lease, a lessee may revoke acceptance of a lot or commercial unit if the lessor defaults under the lease contract and the default substantially impairs the value of that lot or commercial unit to the lessee.

(3) If the lease agreement so provides, the lessee may revoke acceptance of a lot or commercial unit because of other defaults by the lessor.

(4) Revocation of acceptance must occur within a reasonable time after the lessee discovers or should have discovered the ground for it and before any substantial change in condition of the goods which is not caused by the nonconformity. Revocation is not effective until the lessee notifies the lessor.

(5) A lessee who so revokes has the same rights and duties with regard to the goods involved as if the lessee had rejected them.

§2A-518. Cover; Substitute Goods.

(1) After a default by a lessor under the lease contract of the type described in Section 2A–508(1), or, if agreed, after other default by the lessor, the lessee may cover by making any purchase or lease of or contract to purchase or lease goods in substitution for those due from the lessor.

(2) Except as otherwise provided with respect to damages liquidated in the lease agreement (Section 2A–504) or otherwise determined pursuant to agreement of the parties (Sections 1–102(3) and 2A–503), if a lessee's cover is by a lease agreement substantially similar to the original lease agreement and the new lease agreement is made in good faith and in a commercially reasonable manner, the lessee may recover from the lessor as damages (i) the present value, as of the date of the commencement of the term of the new lease agreement, of the rent under the new lease agreement applicable to that period of the new lease term which is comparable to the then remaining term of the original lease agreement minus the present value as of the same date of the total rent for the then remaining lease term of the original lease agreement, and (ii) any incidental or consequential damages, less expenses saved in consequence of the lessor's default.

(3) If a lessee's cover is by lease agreement that for any reason does not qualify for treatment under subsection (2), or is by purchase or otherwise, the lessee may recover from the lessor as if the lessee had elected not to cover and Section 2A–519 governs.

§2A-519. Lessee's Damages for Non-delivery, Repudiation, Default, and Breach of Warranty in Regard to Accepted Goods.

(1) Except as otherwise provided with respect to damages liquidated in the lease agreement (Section 2A–504) or otherwise determined pursuant to agreement of the parties (Sections 1–102(3) and 2A–503), if a lessee elects not to cover or a lessee elects to cover and the cover is by lease agreement that for any reason does not qualify for treatment under Section 2A–518(2), or is by purchase or otherwise, the measure of damages for non-delivery or repudiation by the lessor or for rejection or revocation of acceptance by the lessee is the present value, as of the date of the default, of the then market rent minus the present value as of the same date of the original rent, computed for the remaining lease term of the original lease agreement, together with incidental and consequential damages, less expenses saved in consequence of the lessor's default.

(2) Market rent is to be determined as of the place for tender or, in cases of rejection after arrival or revocation of acceptance, as of the place of arrival.

(3) Except as otherwise agreed, if the lessee has accepted goods and given notification (Section 2A–516(3)), the measure of damages for non-conforming tender or delivery or other default by a lessor is the loss resulting in the ordinary course of events from the lessor's default as determined in any manner that is reasonable together with incidental and consequential damages, less expenses saved in consequence of the lessor's default.

(4) Except as otherwise agreed, the measure of damages for breach of warranty is the present value at the time and place of acceptance of the difference between the value of the use of the goods accepted and the value if they had been as warranted for the lease term, unless special circumstances show proximate damages of a different amount, together with incidental and consequential damages, less expenses saved in consequence of the lessor's default or breach of warranty.

§2A-520. Lessee's Incidental and Consequential Damages.

(1) Incidental damages resulting from a lessor's default include expenses reasonably incurred in inspection, receipt, transportation, and care and custody of goods rightfully rejected or goods the acceptance of which is justifiably revoked, any commercially reasonable charges, expenses or commissions in connection with effecting cover, and any other reasonable expense incident to the default.

(2) Consequential damages resulting from a lessor's default include:

(a) any loss resulting from general or particular requirements and needs of which the lessor at the time of contracting had reason to know and which could not reasonably be prevented by cover or otherwise; and

(b) injury to person or property proximately resulting from any breach of warranty.

§2A-521. Lessee's Right to Specific Performance or Replevin.

(1) Specific performance may be decreed if the goods are unique or in other proper circumstances.

(2) A decree for specific performance may include any terms and conditions as to payment of the rent, damages, or other relief that the court deems just.

(3) A lessee has a right of replevin, detinue, sequestration, claim and delivery, or the like for goods identified to the lease contract if after reasonable effort the lessee is unable to effect cover for those goods or the circumstances reasonably indicate that the effort will be unavailing.

§2A-522. Lessee's Right to Goods on Lessor's Insolvency.

(1) Subject to subsection (2) and even though the goods have not been shipped, a lessee who has paid a part or all of the rent and security for goods identified to a lease contract (Section 2A–217) on making and keeping good a tender of any unpaid portion of the rent and security due under the lease contract may recover the goods identified from the lessor if the lessor becomes insolvent within 10 days after receipt of the first installment of rent and security.

(2) A lessee acquires the right to recover goods identified to a lease contract only if they conform to the lease contract.

C. Default by Lessee

§2A-523. Lessor's Remedies.

(1) If a lessee wrongfully rejects or revokes acceptance of goods or fails to make a payment when due or repudiates with respect to a part or the whole, then, with respect to any goods involved, and with respect to all of the goods if under an installment lease contract the value of the whole lease contract is substantially impaired (Section 2A–510), the lessee is in default under the lease contract and the lessor may:

(a) cancel the lease contract (Section 2A–505(1));

(b) proceed respecting goods not identified to the lease contract (Section 2A–524);

(c) withhold delivery of the goods and take possession of goods previously delivered (Section 2A–525);

(d) stop delivery of the goods by any bailee (Section 2A–526);

(e) dispose of the goods and recover damages (Section 2A–527), or retain the goods and recover

damages (Section 2A–528), or in a proper case recover rent (Section 2A–529);

(f) exercise any other rights or pursue any other remedies provided in the lease contract.

(2) If a lessor does not fully exercise a right or obtain a remedy to which the lessor is entitled under subsection (1), the lessor may recover the loss resulting in the ordinary course of events from the lessee's default as determined in any reasonable manner, together with incidental damages, less expenses saved in consequence of the lessee's default.

(3) If a lessee is otherwise in default under a lease contract, the lessor may exercise the rights and pursue the remedies provided in the lease contract, which may include a right to cancel the lease. In addition, unless otherwise provided in the lease contract:

(a) if the default substantially impairs the value of the lease contract to the lessor, the lessor may exercise the rights and pursue the remedies provided in subsections (1) or (2); or

(b) if the default does not substantially impair the value of the lease contract to the lessor, the lessor may recover as provided in subsection (2).

§2A-524. Lessor's Right to Identify Goods to Lease Contract.

(1) After default by the lessee under the lease contract of the type described in Section 2A–523(1) or 2A–523(3)(a) or, if agreed, after other default by the lessee, the lessor may:

(a) identify to the lease contract conforming goods not already identified if at the time the lessor learned of the default they were in the lessor's or the supplier's possession or control; and

(b) dispose of goods (Section 2A–527(1)) that demonstrably have been intended for the particular lease contract even though those goods are unfinished.

(2) If the goods are unfinished, in the exercise of reasonable commercial judgment for the purposes of avoiding loss and of effective realization, an aggrieved lessor or the supplier may either complete manufacture and wholly identify the goods to the lease contract or cease manufacture and lease, sell, or otherwise dispose of the goods for scrap or salvage value or proceed in any other reasonable manner.

§2A-525. Lessor's Right to Possession of Goods.

(1) If a lessor discovers the lessee to be insolvent, the lessor may refuse to deliver the goods.

(2) After a default by the lessee under the lease contract of the type described in Section 2A–523(1) or 2A–523(3)(a) or, if agreed, after other default by the lessee, the lessor has the right to take possession of the goods. If the lease contract so provides, the lessor

may require the lessee to assemble the goods and make them available to the lessor at a place to be designated by the lessor which is reasonably convenient to both parties. Without removal, the lessor may render unusable any goods employed in trade or business, and may dispose of goods on the lessee's premises (Section 2A–527).

(3) The lessor may proceed under subsection (2) without judicial process if it can be done without breach of the peace or the lessor may proceed by action.

§2A-526. Lessor's Stoppage of Delivery in Transit or Otherwise.

(1) A lessor may stop delivery of goods in the possession of a carrier or other bailee if the lessor discovers the lessee to be insolvent and may stop delivery of carload, truckload, planeload, or larger shipments of express or freight if the lessee repudiates or fails to make a payment due before delivery, whether for rent, security or otherwise under the lease contract, or for any other reason the lessor has a right to withhold or take possession of the goods.

(2) In pursuing its remedies under subsection (1), the lessor may stop delivery until

   (a) receipt of the goods by the lessee;

   (b) acknowledgment to the lessee by any bailee of the goods, except a carrier, that the bailee holds the goods for the lessee; or

   (c) such an acknowledgment to the lessee by a carrier via reshipment or as warehouseman.

(3) (a) To stop delivery, a lessor shall so notify as to enable the bailee by reasonable diligence to prevent delivery of the goods.

   (b) After notification, the bailee shall hold and deliver the goods according to the directions of the lessor, but the lessor is liable to the bailee for any ensuing charges or damages.

   (c) A carrier who has issued a nonnegotiable bill of lading is not obliged to obey a notification to stop received from a person other than the consignor.

§2A-527. Lessor's Rights to Dispose of Goods.

(1) After a default by a lessee under the lease contract of the type described in Section 2A–523(1) or 2A–523(3)(a) or after the lessor refuses to deliver or takes possession of goods (Section 2A–525 or 2A–526), or, if agreed, after other default by a lessee, the lessor may dispose of the goods concerned or the undelivered balance thereof by lease, sale, or otherwise.

(2) Except as otherwise provided with respect to damages liquidated in the lease agreement (Section 2A–504) or otherwise determined pursuant to agreement of the parties (Sections 1–102(3) and 2A–503), if the disposition is by lease agreement substantially

similar to the original lease agreement and the new lease agreement is made in good faith and in a commercially reasonable manner, the lessor may recover from the lessee as damages (i) accrued and unpaid rent as of the date of the commencement of the term of the new lease agreement, (ii) the present value, as of the same date, of the total rent for the then remaining lease term of the original lease agreement minus the present value, as of the same date, of the rent under the new lease agreement applicable to that period of the new lease term which is comparable to the then remaining term of the original lease agreement, and (iii) any incidental damages allowed under Section 2A–530, less expenses saved in consequence of the lessee's default.

(3) If the lessor's disposition is by lease agreement that for any reason does not qualify for treatment under subsection (2), or is by sale or otherwise, the lessor may recover from the lessee as if the lessor had elected not to dispose of the goods and Section 2A–528 governs.

(4) A subsequent buyer or lessee who buys or leases from the lessor in good faith for value as a result of a disposition under this section takes the goods free of the original lease contract and any rights of the original lessee even though the lessor fails to comply with one or more of the requirements of this Article.

(5) The lessor is not accountable to the lessee for any profit made on any disposition. A lessee who has rightfully rejected or justifiably revoked acceptance shall account to the lessor for any excess over the amount of the lessee's security interest (Section 2A–508(5)).

§2A-528. Lessor's Damages for Non-acceptance, Failure to Pay, Repudiation, or Other Default.

(1) Except as otherwise provided with respect to damages liquidated in the lease agreement (Section 2A–504) or otherwise determined pursuant to agreement of the parties (Sections 1–102(3) and 2A–503), if a lessor elects to retain the goods or a lessor elects to dispose of the goods and the disposition is by lease agreement that for any reason does not qualify for treatment under Section 2A–527(2), or is by sale or otherwise, the lessor may recover from the lessee as damages for a default of the type described in Section 2A–523(1) or 2A–523(3)(a), or, if agreed, for other default of the lessee, (i) accrued and unpaid rent as of the date of default if the lessee has never taken possession of the goods, or, if the lessee has taken possession of the goods, as of the date the lessor repossesses the goods or an earlier date on which the lessee makes a tender of the goods to the lessor, (ii) the present value as of the date determined under clause (i) of the total rent for the then remaining lease

term of the original lease agreement minus the present value as of the same date of the market rent at the place where the goods are located computed for the same lease term, and (iii) any incidental damages allowed under Section 2A–530, less expenses saved in consequence of the lessee's default.

(2) If the measure of damages provided in subsection (1) is inadequate to put a lessor in as good a position as performance would have, the measure of damages is the present value of the profit, including reasonable overhead, the lessor would have made from full performance by the lessee, together with any incidental damages allowed under Section 2A–530, due allowance for costs reasonably incurred and due credit for payments or proceeds of disposition.

§2A-529. Lessor's Action for the Rent.

(1) After default by the lessee under the lease contract of the type described in Section 2A–523(1) or 2A–523(3)(a) or, if agreed, after other default by the lessee, if the lessor complies with subsection (2), the lessor may recover from the lessee as damages:

(a) for goods accepted by the lessee and not repossessed by or tendered to the lessor, and for conforming goods lost or damaged within a commercially reasonable time after risk of loss passes to the lessee (Section 2A–219), (i) accrued and unpaid rent as of the date of entry of judgment in favor of the lessor, (ii) the present value as of the same date of the rent for the then remaining lease term of the lease agreement, and (iii) any incidental damages allowed under Section 2A–530, less expenses saved in consequence of the lessee's default; and

(b) for goods identified to the lease contract if the lessor is unable after reasonable effort to dispose of them at a reasonable price or the circumstances reasonably indicate that effort will be unavailing, (i) accrued and unpaid rent as of the date of entry of judgment in favor of the lessor, (ii) the present value as of the same date of the rent for the then remaining lease term of the lease agreement, and (iii) any incidental damages allowed under Section 2A–530, less expenses saved in consequence of the lessee's default.

(2) Except as provided in subsection (3), the lessor shall hold for the lessee for the remaining lease term of the lease agreement any goods that have been identified to the lease contract and are in the lessor's control.

(3) The lessor may dispose of the goods at any time before collection of the judgment for damages obtained pursuant to subsection (1). If the disposition is before the end of the remaining lease term of the lease agreement, the lessor's recovery against the lessee for damages is governed by Section 2A–527 or Section

2A–528, and the lessor will cause an appropriate credit to be provided against a judgment for damages to the extent that the amount of the judgment exceeds the recovery available pursuant to Section 2A–527 or 2A–528.

(4) Payment of the judgment for damages obtained pursuant to subsection (1) entitles the lessee to the use and possession of the goods not then disposed of for the remaining lease term of and in accordance with the lease agreement.

(5) After default by the lessee under the lease contract of the type described in Section 2A–523(1) or Section 2A–523(3)(a) or, if agreed, after other default by the lessee, a lessor who is held not entitled to rent under this section must nevertheless be awarded damages for non-acceptance under Section 2A–527 or Section 2A–528.

§2A-530. Lessor's Incidental Damages.

Incidental damages to an aggrieved lessor include any commercially reasonable charges, expenses, or commissions incurred in stopping delivery, in the transportation, care and custody of goods after the lessee's default, in connection with return or disposition of the goods, or otherwise resulting from the default.

§2A-531. Standing to Sue Third Parties for Injury to Goods.

(1) If a third party so deals with goods that have been identified to a lease contract as to cause actionable injury to a party to the lease contract (a) the lessor has a right of action against the third party, and (b) the lessee also has a right of action against the third party if the lessee:

(i) has a security interest in the goods;

(ii) has an insurable interest in the goods; or

(iii) bears the risk of loss under the lease contract or has since the injury assumed that risk as against the lessor and the goods have been converted or destroyed.

(2) If at the time of the injury the party plaintiff did not bear the risk of loss as against the other party to the lease contract and there is no arrangement between them for disposition of the recovery, his [or her] suit or settlement, subject to his [or her] own interest, is as a fiduciary for the other party to the lease contract.

(3) Either party with the consent of the other may sue for the benefit of whom it may concern.

§2A-532. Lessor's Rights to Residual Interest.

In addition to any other recovery permitted by this Article or other law, the lessor may recover from the lessee an amount that will fully compensate the lessor for any loss of or damage to the lessor's residual interest in the goods caused by the default of the lessee.

Article 3: Negotiable Instruments (Revised 1990)

Part 1: General Provisions and Definitions

§3-101. Short Title.— This Article may be cited as Uniform Commercial Code—Negotiable Instruments.

§3-102. Subject Matter.—

(a) This Article applies to negotiable instruments. It does not apply to money, to payment orders governed by Article 4A, or to securities governed by Article 8.

(b) If there is conflict between this Article and Article 4 or 9, Articles 4 and 9 govern.

(c) Regulations of the Board of Governors of the Federal Reserve System and operating circulars of the Federal Reserve Banks supersede any inconsistent provision of this Article to the extent of the inconsistency.

Note: The previous version of Article 3, Commercial Paper, is found in the Instructor's Resource Guide. You may wish to photocopy it for your students' use.

§3-103. Definitions.—

(a) In this Article:

    (1) "Acceptor" means a drawee who has accepted a draft.

    (2) "Drawee" means a person ordered in a draft to make payment.

    (3) "Drawer" means a person who signs or is identified in a draft as a person ordering payment.

    (4) "Good faith" means honesty in fact and the observance of reasonable commercial standards of fair dealing.

    (5) "Maker" means a person who signs or is identified in a note as a person undertaking to pay.

    (6) "Order" means a written instruction to pay money signed by the person giving the instruction. The instruction may be addressed to any person, including the person giving the instruction, or to one or more persons jointly or in the alternative but not in succession. An authorization to pay is not an order unless the person authorized to pay is also instructed to pay.

    (7) "Ordinary care" in the case of a person engaged in business means observance of reasonable commercial standards, prevailing in the area in which the person is located, with respect to the business in which the person is engaged. In the case of a bank that takes an instrument for processing for collection or payment by automated means, reasonable commercial standards do not require the bank to examine the instrument if the failure to examine does not violate the bank's prescribed procedures and the bank's procedures do not vary unreasonably from general banking usage not disapproved by this Article or Article 4.

    (8) "Party" means a party to an instrument.

    (9) "Promise" means a written undertaking to pay money signed by the person undertaking to pay. An acknowledgment of an obligation by the obligor is not a promise unless the obligor also undertakes to pay the obligation.

    (10) "Prove" with respect to a fact means to meet the burden of establishing the fact (Section 1-201(8)).

    (11) "Remitter" means a person who purchases an instrument from its issuer if the instrument is payable to an identified person other than the purchaser.

(b) Other definitions applying to this Article and the sections in which they appear are:

"Acceptance"	Section 3-409
"Accommodated party"	Section 3-419
"Accommodation party"	Section 3-419
"Alteration"	Section 3-407
"Anomalous indorsement"	Section 3-205
"Blank indorsement"	Section 3-205
"Cashier's check"	Section 3-104
"Certificate of deposit"	Section 3-104
"Certified check"	Section 3-409
"Check"	Section 3-104
"Consideration"	Section 3-303
"Draft"	Section 3-104
"Holder in due course"	Section 3-302
"Incomplete instrument"	Section 3-115
"Indorsement"	Section 3-204
"Indorser"	Section 3-204
"Instrument"	Section 3-104
"Issue"	Section 3-105
"Issuer"	Section 3-105
"Negotiable instrument"	Section 3-104
"Negotiation"	Section 3-201
"Note"	Section 3-104
"Payable at a definite time"	Section 3-108
"Payable on demand"	Section 3-108
"Payable to bearer"	Section 3-109
"Payable to order"	Section 3-109
"Payment"	Section 3-602
"Person entitled to enforce"	Section 3-301
"Presentment"	Section 3-501
"Reacquisition"	Section 3-207

"Special indorsement"	Section 3-205
"Teller's check"	Section 3-104
"Transfer of instrument"	Section 3-203
"Traveler's check"	Section 3-104
"Value"	Section 3-303

(c) The following definitions in other Articles apply to this Article:

"Bank"	Section 4-105
"Banking day"	Section 4-104
"Clearinghouse"	Section 4-104
"Collecting bank"	Section 4-105
"Depositary bank"	Section 4-105
"Documentary draft"	Section 4-104
"Intermediary bank"	Section 4-105
"Item"	Section 4-104
"Payor bank"	Section 4-105
"Suspends payments"	Section 4-104

(d) In addition, Article 1 contains general definitions and principles of construction and interpretation applicable throughout this Article.

§3-104. Negotiable Instrument.—

(a) Except as provided in subsections (c) and (d), "negotiable instrument" means an unconditional promise or order to pay a fixed amount of money, with or without interest or other charges described in the promise or order, if it:

   (1) is payable to bearer or to order at the time it is issued or first comes into possession of a holder;

   (2) is payable on demand or at a definite time; and

   (3) does not state any other undertaking or instruction by the person promising or ordering payment to do any act in addition to the payment of money, but the promise or order may contain (i) an undertaking or power to give, maintain, or protect collateral to secure payment, (ii) an authorization or power to the holder to confess judgment or realize on or dispose of collateral, or (iii) a waiver of the benefit of any law intended for the advantage or protection of an obligor.

(b) "Instrument" means a negotiable instrument.

(c) An order that meets all of the requirements of subsection (a), except paragraph (1), and otherwise falls within the definition of "check" in subsection (f) is a negotiable instrument and a check.

(d) A promise or order other than a check is not an instrument if, at the time it is issued or first comes into possession of a holder, it contains a conspicuous statement, however expressed, to the effect that the promise or order is not negotiable or is not an instrument governed by this Article.

(e) An instrument is a "note" if it is a promise and is a "draft" if it is an order. If an instrument falls within the definition of both "note" and "draft", a person entitled to enforce the instrument may treat it as either.

(f) "Check" means (i) a draft, other than a documentary draft, payable on demand and drawn on a bank or (ii) a cashier's check or teller's check. An instrument may be a check even though it is described on its face by another term, such as "money order".

(g) "Cashier's check" means a draft with respect to which the drawer and drawee are the same bank or branches of the same bank.

(h) "Teller's check" means a draft drawn by a bank (i) on another bank, or (ii) payable at or through a bank.

(i) "Traveler's check" means an instrument that (i) is payable on demand, (ii) is drawn on or payable at or through a bank, (iii) is designated by the term "traveler's check" or by a substantially similar term, and (iv) requires, as a condition to payment, a countersignature by a person whose specimen signature appears on the instrument.

(j) "Certificate of deposit" means an instrument containing an acknowledgment by a bank that a sum of money has been received by the bank and a promise by the bank to repay the sum of money. A certificate of deposit is a note of the bank.

§3-105. Issue of Instrument.—

(a) "Issue" means the first delivery of an instrument by the maker or drawer, whether to a holder or nonholder, for the purpose of giving rights on the instrument to any person.

(b) An unissued instrument, or an unissued incomplete instrument that is completed, is binding on the maker or drawer, but nonissuance is a defense. An instrument that is conditionally issued or is issued for a special purpose is binding on the maker or drawer, but failure of the condition or special purpose to be fulfilled is a defense.

(c) "Issuer" applies to issued and unissued instruments and means a maker or drawer of an instrument.

§3-106. Unconditional Promise or Order.—

(a) Except as provided in this section, for the purposes of Section 3-104(a), a promise or order is unconditional unless it states (i) an express condition to payment, (ii) that the promise or order is subject to or governed by another writing, or (iii) that rights or obligations with respect to the promise or order are stated in another writing. A reference to another writing does not of itself make the promise or order conditional.

(b) A promise or order is not made conditional (i) by a reference to another writing for a statement of rights with respect to collateral, prepayment, or acceleration, or (ii) because payment is limited to resort to a particular fund or source.

(c) If a promise or order requires, as a condition to payment, a countersignature by a person whose specimen signature appears on the promise or order, the condition does not make the promise or order conditional for the purposes of Section 3-104(a). If the person whose specimen signature appears on an instrument fails to countersign the instrument, the failure to countersign is a defense to the obligation of the issuer, but the failure does not prevent a transferee of the instrument from becoming a holder of the instrument.

(d) If a promise or order at the time it is issued or first comes into possession of a holder contains a statement, required by applicable statutory or administrative law, to the effect that the rights of a holder or transferee are subject to claims or defenses that the issuer could assert the original payee, the promise or order is not thereby made conditional for the purposes of Section 3-104(a); but if the promise or order is an instrument, there cannot be a holder in due course of the instrument.

§3-107. Instrument Payable in Foreign Money.—

Unless the instrument otherwise provides, an instrument that states the amount payable in foreign money may be paid in the foreign money or in an equivalent amount in dollars calculated by using the current bank-offered spot rate at the place of payment for the purchase of dollars on the day on which the instrument is paid.

§3-108. Payable on Demand or at Definite Time.—

(a) A promise or order is "payable on demand" if it (i) states that it is payable on demand or at sight, or otherwise indicates that it is payable at the will of the holder, or (ii) does not state any time of payment.

(b) A promise or order is "payable at a definite time" if it is payable on elapse of a definite period of time after sight or acceptance or at a fixed date or dates or at a time or times readily ascertainable at the time the promise or order is issued, subject to rights of (i) prepayment, (ii) acceleration, (iii) extension at the option of the holder, or (iv) extension to a further definite time at the option of the maker or acceptor or automatically upon or after a specified act or event.

(c) If an instrument, payable at a fixed date, is also payable upon demand made before the fixed date, the instrument is payable on demand until the fixed date and, if demand for payment is not made before that date, becomes payable at a definite time on the fixed date.

§3-109. Payable to Bearer or to Order.—

(a) A promise or order is payable to bearer if it:

(1) states that it is payable to bearer or to the order of bearer or otherwise indicates that the person in possession of the promise or order is entitled to payment;

(2) does not state a payee; or

(3) states that it is payable to or to the order of cash or otherwise indicates that it is not payable to an identified person.

(b) A promise or order that is not payable to bearer is payable to order if it is payable (i) to the order of an identified person or (ii) to an identified person or order. A promise or order that is payable to order is payable to the identified person.

(c) An instrument payable to bearer may become payable to an identified person if it is specially indorsed pursuant to Section 3-205(a). An instrument payable to an identified person may become payable to bearer if it is indorsed in blank pursuant to Section 3-205(b).

§3-110. Identification of Person to Whom Instrument is Payable.—

(a) The person to whom an instrument is initially payable is determined by the intent of the person, whether or not authorized, signing as, or in the name or behalf of, the issuer of the instrument. The instrument is payable to the person intended by the signer even if that person is identified in the instrument by a name or other identification that is not that of the intended person. If more than one person signs in the name or behalf of the issuer of an instrument and all the signers do not intend the same person as payee, the instrument is payable to any person intended by one or more of the signers.

(b) If the signature of the issuer of an instrument is made by automated means, such as a check-writing machine, the payee of the instrument is determined by the intent of the person who supplied the name or identification of the payee, whether or not authorized to do so.

(c) A person to whom an instrument is payable may be identified in any way, including by name, identifying number, office, or account number. For the purpose of determining the holder of an instrument, the following rules apply:

(1) If an instrument is payable to an account and the account is identified only by number, the instrument is payable to the person to whom the account is payable. If an instrument is payable to an account identified by number and by the name of a person, the instrument is payable to the named person, whether or not that person is the owner of the account identified by number.

(2) If an instrument is payable to:

(i) a trust, an estate, or a person described as trustee or representative of a trust or estate, the instrument is payable to the trustee, the representative, or a successor of either, whether or not the beneficiary or estate is also named;

(ii) a person described as agent or similar representative of a named or identified person, the instrument is payable to the represented person, the representative, or a successor of the representative;

(iii) a fund or organization that is not a legal entity, the instrument is payable to a representative of the members of the fund or organization; or

(iv) an office or to a person described as holding an office, the instrument is payable to the named person, the incumbent of the office, or a successor to the incumbent.

(d) If an instrument is payable to two or more persons alternatively, it is payable to any of them and may be negotiated, discharged, or enforced by any or all of them in possession of the instrument. If an instrument is payable to two or more persons not alternatively, it is payable to all of them and may be negotiated, discharged, or enforced only by all of them. If an instrument payable to two or more persons is ambiguous as to whether it is payable to the persons alternatively, the instrument is payable to the persons alternatively.

§3-111. Place of Payment.—

Except as otherwise provided for items in Article 4, an instrument is payable at the place of payment stated in the instrument. If no place of payment is stated, an instrument is payable at the address of the drawee or maker stated in the instrument. If no address is stated, the place of payment is the place of business of the drawee or maker. If a drawee or maker has more than one place of business, the place of payment is any place of business of the drawee or maker chosen by the person entitled to enforce the instrument. If the drawee or maker has no place of business, the place of payment is the residence of the drawee or maker.

§3-112. Interest.—

(a) Unless otherwise provided in the instrument, (i) an instrument is not payable with interest, and (ii) interest on an interest-bearing instrument is payable from the date of the instrument.

(b) Interest may be stated in an instrument as a fixed or variable amount of money or it may be expressed as a fixed or variable rate or rates. The amount or rate of interest may be stated or described in the instrument in any manner and may require reference to information not contained in the instrument. If an instrument provides for interest, but the amount of interest payable cannot be ascertained from the description, interest is payable at the judgment rate in effect at the place of payment of the instrument and at the time interest first accrues.

§3-113. Date of Instrument.—

(a) An instrument may be antedated or postdated. The date stated determines the time of payment if the instrument is payable at a fixed period after date. Except as provided in Section 4-401(c), an instrument payable on demand is not payable before the date of the instrument.

(b) If an instrument is undated, its date is the date of its issue or, in the case of an unissued instrument, the date it first comes into possession of a holder.

§3-114. Contradictory Terms of Instrument.—

If an instrument contains contradictory terms, typewritten terms prevail over printed terms, handwritten terms prevail over both, and words prevail over numbers.

§3-115. Incomplete Instrument.—

(a) "Incomplete instrument" means a signed writing, whether or not issued by the signer, the contents of which show at the time of signing that it is incomplete but that the signer intended it to be completed by the addition of words or numbers.

(b) Subject to subsection (c), if an incomplete instrument is an instrument under Section 3-104, it may be enforced according to its terms if it is not completed, or according to its terms as augmented by completion. If an incomplete instrument is not an instrument under Section 3-104, but, after completion, the requirements of Section 3-104 are met, the instrument may be enforced according to its terms as augmented by completion.

(c) If words or numbers are added to an incomplete instrument without authority of the signer, there is an alteration of the incomplete instrument under Section 3-407.

(d) The burden of establishing that words or numbers were added to an incomplete instrument without authority of the signer is on the person asserting the lack of authority.

§3-116. Joint and Several Liability; Contribution.—

(a) Except as otherwise provided in the instrument, two or more persons who have the same liability on an instrument as makers, drawers, acceptors, indorsers who indorse as joint payees, or anomalous indorsers are jointly and severally liable in the capacity in which they sign.

(b) Except as provided in Section 3-419(e) or by agreement of the affected parties, a party having joint and several liability who pays the instrument is entitled to receive from any party having the same joint and several liability contribution in accordance with applicable law.

(c) Discharge of one party having joint and several liability by a person entitled to enforce the instrument does not affect the right under subsection (b) of a party having the same joint and several liability to receive contribution from the party discharged.

§3-117. Other Agreements Affecting Instrument.

Subject to applicable law regarding exclusion of proof of contemporaneous or previous agreements, the obligation of a party to an instrument to pay the instrument may be modified, supplemented, or nullified by a separate agreement of the obligor and a person entitled to enforce the instrument, if the instrument is issued or the obligation is incurred in reliance on the agreement or as part of the same transaction giving rise to the agreement. To the extent an obligation is modified, supplemented, or nullified by an agreement under this section, the agreement is a defense to the obligation.

§3-118. Statute of Limitations.

(a) Except as provided in subsection (e), an action to enforce the obligation of a party to pay a note payable at a definite time must be commenced within six years after the due date or dates stated in the note or, if a due date is accelerated, within six years after the accelerated due date.

(b) Except as provided in subsection (d) or (e), if demand for payment is made to the maker of a note payable on demand, an action to enforce the obligation of a party to pay the note must be commenced within six years after the demand. If no demand for payment is made to the maker, an action to enforce the note is barred if neither principal nor interest on the note has been paid for a continuous period of 10 years.

(c) Except as provided in subsection (d), an action to enforce the obligation of a party to an unaccepted draft to pay the draft must be commenced within three years after dishonor of the draft or 10 years after the date of the draft, whichever period expires first.

(d) An action to enforce the obligation of the acceptor of a certified check or the issuer of a teller's check, cashier's check, or traveler's check must be commenced within three years after demand for payment is made to the acceptor or issuer, as the case may be.

(e) An action to enforce the obligation of a party to a certificate of deposit to pay the instrument must be commenced within six years after demand for payment is made to the maker, but if the instrument states a due date and the maker is not required to pay before that date, the six-year period begins when a demand for payment is in effect and the due date has passed.

(f) An action to enforce the obligation of a party to pay an accepted draft, other than a certified check, must be commenced (i) within six years after the due date or dates stated in the draft or acceptance if the obligation of the acceptor is payable at a definite time, or (ii) within six years after the date of the acceptance if the obligation of the acceptor is payable on demand.

(g) Unless governed by other law regarding claims for indemnity or contribution, an action (i) for conversion of an instrument, for money had and received, or like action based on conversion, (ii) for breach of warranty, or (iii) to enforce an obligation, duty, or right arising under this Article and not governed by this section must be commenced within three years after the [cause of action] accrues.

§3-119. Notice of Right to Defend Action.

In an action for breach of an obligation for which a third person is answerable over pursuant to this Article or Article 4, the defendant may give the third person written notice of the litigation, and the person notified may then give similar notice to any other person who is answerable over. If the notice states (i) that the person notified may come in and defend and (ii) that failure to do so will bind the person notified in an action later brought by the person giving the notice as to any determination of fact common to the two litigations, the person notified is so bound unless after reasonable receipt of the notice the person notified does come in and defend.

Part 2: Negotiation, Transfer, and Indorsement

§3-201. Negotiation.

(a) "Negotiation" means a transfer of possession, whether voluntary or involuntary, of an instrument by a person other than the issuer to a person who thereby becomes its holder.

(b) Except for negotiation by a remitter, if an instrument is payable to an identified person, negotiation requires transfer of possession of the instrument and its indorsement by the holder. If an instrument is payable to bearer, it may be negotiated by transfer of possession alone.

§3-202. Negotiation Subject to Rescission.

(a) Negotiation is effective even if obtained (i) from an infant, a corporation exceeding its powers, or a person without capacity, (ii) by fraud, duress, or mistake, or (iii) in breach of duty or as part of an illegal transaction.

(b) To the extent permitted by other law, negotiation may be rescinded or may be subject to other remedies, but those remedies may not be asserted against a subsequent holder in due course or a person paying the instrument in good faith and without knowledge of facts that are a basis for rescission or other remedy.

§3-203. Transfer of Instrument; Rights Acquired by Transfer.

(a) An instrument is transferred when it is delivered by a person other than its issuer for the purpose of giving to the person receiving delivery the right to enforce the instrument.

(b) Transfer of an instrument, whether or not the transfer is a negotiation, vests in the transferee any right of the transferor to enforce the instrument, including any right as a holder in due course, but the transferee cannot acquire rights of a holder in due course by a transfer, directly or indirectly, from a holder in due course if the transferee engaged in fraud or illegality affecting the instrument.

(c) Unless otherwise agreed, if an instrument is transferred for value and the transferee does not become a holder because of lack of indorsement by the transferor, the transferee has a specially enforceable right to the unqualified indorsement of the transferor, but negotiation of the instrument does not occur until the indorsement is made.

(d) If a transferor purports to transfer less than the entire instrument, negotiation of the instrument does not occur. The transferee obtains no rights under this Article, and has only the rights of a partial assignee.

§3-204. Indorsement.—

(a) "Indorsement" means a signature, other than that of a signer as maker, drawer, or acceptor, that alone or accompanied by other words is made on an instrument for the purpose of (i) negotiating the instrument, (ii) restricting payment of the instrument, or (iii) incurring indorser's liability on the instrument, but regardless of the intent of the signer, a signature and its accompanying words is an indorsement unless the accompanying words, terms of the instrument, place of the signature, or other circumstances unambiguously indicate that the signature was made for a purpose other than indorsement. For the purpose of determining whether a signature is made on an instrument, a paper affixed to the instrument is a part of the instrument.

(b) "Indorser" means a person who makes an indorsement.

(c) For the purpose of determining whether the transferee of an instrument is a holder, an indorsement that transfers a security interest in the instrument is effective as an unqualified indorsement of the instrument.

(d) If an instrument is payable to a holder under a name that is not the name of the holder, indorsement may be made by the holder in the name stated in the instrument or in the holder's name or both, but signature in both names may be required by a person paying or taking the instrument for value or collection.

§3-205. Special Indorsement; Blank Indorsement; Anomalous Indorsement.—

(a) If an indorsement is made by the holder of an instrument, whether payable to an identified person or payable to bearer, and the indorsement identifies a person to whom it makes the instrument payable, it is a "special indorsement". When specially indorsed, an instrument becomes payable to the identified person and may be negotiated only by the indorsement of that person. The principles stated in Section 3-110 apply to special indorsements.

(b) If an indorsement is made by the holder of an instrument and it is not a special indorsement, it is a "blank indorsement". When indorsed in blank, an instrument becomes payable to bearer and may be negotiated by transfer of possession alone until specially indorsed.

(c) The holder may convert a blank indorsement that consists only of a signature into a special indorsement by writing, above the signature of the indorser, words identifying the person to whom the instrument is made payable.

(d) "Anomalous indorsement" means an indorsement made by a person who is not the holder of the instrument. An anomalous indorsement does not affect the manner in which the instrument may be negotiated.

§3-206. Restrictive Indorsement.—

(a) An indorsement limiting payment to a particular person or otherwise prohibiting further transfer or negotiation of the instrument is not effective to prevent further transfer or negotiation of the instrument.

(b) An indorsement stating a condition to the right of the indorsee to receive payment does not affect the right of the indorsee to enforce the instrument. A person paying the instrument or taking it for value or collection may disregard the condition, and the rights and liabilities of that person are not affected by whether the condition has been fulfilled.

(c) If an instrument bears an indorsement (i) described in Section 4-201(b), or (ii) in blank or to a particular bank using the words "for deposit", "for collection", or other words indicating a purpose of having the instrument collected by a bank for the indorser or for a particular account, the following rules apply:

(1) A person, other than a bank, who purchases the instrument when so indorsed converts the instrument unless the amount paid for the instrument is received by the indorser or applied consistently with the indorsement.

(2) A depositary bank that purchases the instrument or takes it for collection when so indorsed converts the instrument unless the amount paid by the bank with respect to the instrument is received by the indorser or applied consistently with the indorsement.

(3) A payor bank that is also the depositary bank or that takes the instrument for immediate payment over the counter from a person other than a collecting bank converts the instrument unless the proceeds of the instrument are received by the indorser or applied consistently with the indorsement.

(4) Except as otherwise provided in paragraph (3), a payor bank or intermediary bank may disregard the indorsement and is not liable if the proceeds of the instrument are not received by the indorser or applied consistently with the indorsement.

(d) Except for an indorsement covered by subsection (c), if an instrument bears an indorsement using words to the effect that payment is to be made to the indorsee as agent, trustee, or other fiduciary for the benefit of the indorser or another person, the following rules apply:

(1) Unless there is notice of breach of fiduciary duty as provided in Section 3-307, a person who purchases the instrument from the indorsee or takes the instrument from the indorsee for collection or payment may pay the proceeds of payment or the value given for the instrument to the indorsee without regard to whether the indorsee violates a fiduciary duty to the indorser.

(2) A subsequent transferee of the instrument or person who pays the instrument is neither given notice nor otherwise affected by the restriction in the indorsement unless the transferee or payor knows that the fiduciary dealt with the instrument or its proceeds in breach of fiduciary duty.

(e) The presence on an instrument of an indorsement to which this section applies does not prevent a purchaser of the instrument from becoming a holder in due course of the instrument unless the purchaser is a converter under subsection (c) or has notice or knowledge of breach of fiduciary duty as stated in subsection (d).

(f) In an action to enforce the obligation of a party to pay the instrument, the obligor has a defense if payment would violate an indorsement to which this section applies and the payment is not permitted by this section.

§3-207. Reacquisition.—
Reacquisition of an instrument occurs if it is transferred to a former holder, by negotiation or otherwise. A former holder who reacquires the instrument may cancel indorsements made after the reacquirer first became a holder of the instrument. If the cancellation causes the instrument to be payable to the reacquirer or to bearer, the reacquirer may negotiate the instrument. An indorser whose indorsement is canceled is discharged, and the discharge is effective against any subsequent holder.

Part 3: Enforcement of Instruments

§3-301. Person Entitled to Enforce Instrument.—
"Person entitled to enforce" an instrument means (i) the holder of the instrument, (ii) a nonholder in possession of the instrument who has the rights of a holder, or (iii) a person not in possession of the instrument who is entitled to enforce the instrument pursuant to Section 3-309 or 3-418(d). A person may be a person entitled to enforce the instrument even though the person is not the owner of the instrument or is in wrongful possession of the instrument.

§3-302. Holder in Due Course.—

(a) Subject to subsection (c) and Section 3106(d), "holder in due course" means the holder of an instrument if:

(1) the instrument when issued or negotiated to the holder does not bear such apparent evidence of forgery or alteration or is not otherwise so irregular or incomplete as to call into question its authenticity; and

(2) the holder took the instrument (i) for value, (ii) in good faith, (iii) without notice that the instrument is overdue or has been dishonored or that there is an uncured default with respect to payment of another instrument issued as part of the same series, (iv) without notice that the instrument contains an unauthorized signature or has been altered, (v) without notice of any claim to the instrument described in Section 3-306, and (vi) without notice that any party has a defense or claim in recoupment described in Section 3-305(a).

(b) Notice of discharge of a party, other than discharge in an insolvency proceeding, is not notice of a defense under subsection (a), but discharge is effective against a person who became a holder in due course with notice of the discharge. Public filing or recording of a document does not of itself constitute notice of a defense, claim in recoupment, or claim to the instrument.

(c) Except to the extent a transferor or predecessor in interest has rights as a holder in due course, a person does not acquire rights of a holder in due course of an instrument taken (i) by legal process or by purchase in an execution, bankruptcy, or creditor's sale or similar proceeding, (ii) by purchase as part of a bulk transaction not in ordinary course of business of the transferor, or (iii) as the successor in interest to an estate or other organization.

(d) If, under Section 3-303(a)(1), the promise of performance that is the consideration for an instrument has been partially performed, the holder may assert rights as a holder in due course of the instrument only to the fraction of the amount payable under the instrument equal to the value of the partial performance divided by the value of the promised performance.

(e) If (i) the person entitled to enforce an instrument has only a security interest in the instrument and (ii) the person obliged to pay the instrument has a defense, claim in recoupment, or claim to the instrument that may be asserted against the person who granted the security interest, the person entitled to enforce the instrument may assert rights as a holder in due course only to an amount payable under the instrument which, at the time of enforcement of the instrument, does not exceed the amount of the unpaid obligation secured.

(f) To be effective, notice must be received at a time and in a manner that gives a reasonable opportunity to act on it.

(g) This section is subject to any law limiting status as a holder in due course in particular classes of transactions.

§3-303. Value and Consideration.—

(a) An instrument is issued or transferred for value if:

(1) the instrument is issued or transferred for a promise of performance, to the extent the promise has been performed;

(2) the transferee acquires a security interest or other lien in the instrument other than a lien obtained by judicial proceeding;

(3) the instrument is issued or transferred as payment of, or as security for, an antecedent claim against any person, whether or not the claim is due;

(4) the instrument is issued or transferred in exchange for a negotiable instrument; or

(5) the instrument is issued or transferred in exchange for the incurring of an irrevocable obligation to a third party by the person taking the instrument.

(b) "Consideration" means any consideration sufficient to support a simple contract. The drawer or maker of an instrument has a defense if the instrument is issued without consideration. If an instrument is issued for a promise of performance, the issuer has a defense to the extent performance of the promise is due and the promise has not been performed. If an instrument is issued for value as stated in subsection (a), the instrument is also issued for consideration.

§3-304. Overdue Instrument.—

(a) An instrument payable on demand becomes overdue at the earliest of the following times:

(1) on the day after the day demand for payment is duly made;

(2) if the instrument is a check, 90 days after its date; or

(3) if the instrument is not a check, when the instrument has been outstanding for a period of time after its date which is unreasonably long under the circumstances of the particular case in light of the nature of the instrument and usage of the trade.

(b) With respect to an instrument payable at a definite time the following rules apply:

(1) If the principal is payable in installments and a due date has not been accelerated, the instrument becomes overdue upon default under the instrument for nonpayment of an installment, and the instrument remains overdue until the default is cured.

(2) If the principal is not payable in installments and the due date has not been accelerated, the instrument becomes overdue on the day after the due date.

(3) If a due date with respect to principal has been accelerated, the instrument becomes overdue on the day after the accelerated due date.

(c) Unless the due date of principal has been accelerated, an instrument does not become overdue if there is default in payment of interest but no default in payment of principal.

§3-305. Defenses and Claims in Recoupment.—

(a) Except as stated in subsection (b), the right to enforce the obligation of a party to pay an instrument is subject to the following:

(1) a defense of the obligor based on (i) infancy of the obligor to the extent it is a defense to a simple contract, (ii) duress, lack of legal capacity, or illegality of the transaction which, under other law, nullifies the obligation of the obligor, (iii) fraud that induced the obligor to sign the instrument with neither knowledge nor reasonable opportunity to learn of its character or its essential terms, or (iv) discharge of the obligor in insolvency proceedings;

(2) defense of the obligor stated in another section of this Article or a defense of the obligor that would be available if the person entitled to enforce the instrument were enforcing a right to payment under a simple contract; and

(3) a claim in recoupment of the obligor against the original payee of the instrument if the claim arose from the transaction that gave rise to the instrument; but the claim of the obligor may be asserted against a transferee of the instrument only to reduce the amount owing on the instrument at the time the action is brought.

(b) The right of a holder in due course to enforce the obligation of a party to pay the instrument is subject to defenses of the obligor stated in subsection (a)(1), but is not subject to defenses of the obligor stated in subsection (a)(2) or claims in recoupment stated in subsection (a)(3) against a person other than the holder.

(c) Except as stated in subsection (d), in an action to enforce the obligation of a party to pay the instrument, the obligor may not assert against the person entitled to enforce the instrument a defense, claim in recoupment, or claim to the instrument (Section 3-306) of another person, but the other person's claim to the instrument may be asserted by the obligor if the other person is joined in the action and personally asserts the claim against the person entitled to enforce the instrument. An obligor is not obliged to pay the instrument if the person seeking enforcement of the instrument does not have rights of a holder in due course and the obligor proves that the instrument is a lost or stolen instrument.

(d) In an action to enforce the obligation of an accommodation party to pay an instrument, the accommodation party may assert against the person entitled to enforce the instrument any defense or claim in recoupment under subsection (a) that the accommodated party could assert against the person entitled to enforce the instrument, except the defenses of discharge in insolvency proceedings, infancy, and lack of legal capacity.

§3-306. Claims to an Instrument.— A person taking an instrument, other than a person having rights of a holder in due course, is subject to a claim of a property or possessory right in the instrument or its proceeds, including a claim to rescind a negotiation and to recover the instrument or its proceeds. A person having rights of a holder in due course takes free of the claim to the instrument.

§3-307. Notice of Breach of Fiduciary Duty.—

(a) In this section:

(1) "Fiduciary" means an agent, trustee, partner, corporate officer or director, or other representative owing a fiduciary duty with respect to an instrument.

(2) "Represented person" means the principal, beneficiary, partnership, corporation, or other person to whom the duty stated in paragraph (1) is owed.

(b) If (i) an instrument is taken from a fiduciary for payment or collection or for value, (ii) the taker has knowledge of the fiduciary status of the fiduciary, and (iii) the represented person makes a claim to the instrument or its proceeds on the basis that the transaction of the fiduciary is a breach of fiduciary duty, the following rules apply:

(1) Notice of breach of fiduciary duty by the fiduciary is notice of the claim of the represented person.

(2) In the case of an instrument payable to the represented person or the fiduciary as such, the taker has notice of the breach of fiduciary duty if the instrument is (i) taken in payment of or as security for a debt known by the taker to be the personal debt of the fiduciary, (ii) taken in a transaction known by the taker to be for the personal benefit of the fiduciary, or (iii) deposited to an account other than an account of the fiduciary, as such, or an account of the represented person.

(3) If an instrument is issued by the represented person or the fiduciary as such, and made payable to the fiduciary personally, the taker does not have notice of the breach of fiduciary duty unless the taker knows of the breach of fiduciary duty.

(4) If an instrument is issued by the represented person or the fiduciary as such, to the taker as payee, the taker has notice of the breach of fiduciary duty if the instrument is (i) taken in payment of or as security for a debt known by the taker to be the personal debt of the fiduciary, (ii) taken in a transaction known by the taker to be for the personal benefit of the fiduciary, or (iii) deposited to an account other than an account of the fiduciary, as such, or an account of the represented person.

§3-308. Proof of Signatures and Status as Holder in Due Course.—

(a) In an action with respect to an instrument, the authenticity of, and authority to make, each signature on the instrument is admitted unless specifically denied in the pleadings. If the validity of a signature is denied in the pleadings, the burden of establishing validity is on the person claiming validity, but the signature is presumed to be authentic and authorized unless the action is to enforce the liability of the purported signer and the signer is dead or incompetent at the time of trial of the issue of validity of the signature. If an action to enforce the instrument is brought against a person as the undisclosed principal of a person who signed the instrument as a party to the instrument, the plaintiff has the burden of establishing that the defendant is liable on the instrument as a represented person under Section 3-402(a).

(b) If the validity of signatures is admitted or proved and there is compliance with subsection (a), a plaintiff producing the instrument is entitled to payment if the plaintiff proves entitlement to enforce the instrument under Section 3-301, unless the defendant proves a defense or claim in recoupment. If a defense or claim in recoupment is proved, the right to payment of the plaintiff is subject to the defense or claim, except to the extent the plaintiff proves that the plaintiff has rights of a holder in due course which are not subject to the defense or claim.

§3-309. Enforcement of Lost, Destroyed, or Stolen Instrument.—

(a) A person not in possession of an instrument is entitled to enforce the instrument if (i) the person was in possession of the instrument and entitled to enforce it when loss of possession occurred, (ii) the loss of possession was not the result of a transfer by the person or a lawful seizure, and (iii) the person cannot reasonably obtain possession of the instrument because the instrument was destroyed, its whereabouts cannot be determined, or it is in the wrongful possession of an unknown person or a person that cannot be found or is not amenable to service of process.

(b) A person seeking enforcement of an instrument under subsection (a) must prove the terms of the instrument and the person's right to enforce the instrument. If that proof is made, Section 3-308 applies to the case as if the person seeking enforcement had produced the instrument. The court may not enter judgment in favor of the person seeking enforcement unless it finds that the person required to pay the instrument is adequately protected against loss that might occur by reason of a claim by another person to enforce the instrument. Adequate protection may be provided by any reasonable means.

§3-310. Effect of Instrument on Obligation for Which Taken.—

(a) Unless otherwise agreed, if a certified check, cashier's check, or teller's check is taken for an obligation, the obligation is discharged to the same extent discharge would result if an amount of money equal to the amount of the instrument were taken in payment of the obligation. Discharge of the obligation does not affect any liability that the obligor may have as an indorser of the instrument.

(b) Unless otherwise agreed and except as provided in subsection (a), if a note or an uncertified check is taken for an obligation, the obligation is suspended to the same extent the obligation would be discharged if an amount of money equal to the amount of the instrument were taken, and the following rules apply:

(1) In the case of an uncertified check, suspension of the obligation continues until dishonor of the check or until it is paid or certified. Payment or certification of the check results in discharge of the obligation to the extent of the amount of the check.

(2) In the case of a note, suspension of the obligation continues until dishonor of the note or until it is paid. Payment of the note results in discharge of the obligation to the extent of the payment.

(3) Except as provided in paragraph (4), if the check or note is dishonored and the obligee of the obligation for which the instrument was taken is the person entitled to enforce the instrument, the obligee may enforce either the instrument or the obligation. In the case of an instrument of a third person which is negotiated to the obligee by the obligor, discharge of the obligor on the instrument also discharges the obligation.

(4) If the person entitled to enforce the instrument taken for an obligation is a person other than the obligee, the obligee may not enforce the obligation to the extent the obligation is suspended. If the obligee is the person entitled to enforce the instrument but no longer has possession of it because it was lost, stolen, or destroyed, the obligation may not be enforced to the extent of the amount payable on the instrument, and to that extent the obligee's rights against the obligor are limited to enforcement of the instrument.

(c) If an instrument other than one described in subsection (a) or (b) is taken for an obligation, the effect is (i) that stated in subsection (a) if the instrument is one on which a bank is liable as maker or acceptor, or (ii) that stated in subsection (b) in any other case.

§3-311. Accord and Satisfaction by Use of Instrument.—

(a) If a person against whom a claim is asserted proves that (i) that person in good faith tendered an instrument to the claimant as full satisfaction of the claim, (ii) the amount of the claim was unliquidated or subject to a bona fide dispute, and (iii) the claimant obtained payment of the instrument, the following subsections apply.

(b) Unless subsection (c) applies, the claim is discharged if the person against whom the claim is asserted proves that the instrument or an accompanying written communication contained a conspicuous statement to the effect that the instrument was tendered as full satisfaction of the claim.

(c) Subject to subsection (d), a claim is not discharged under subsection (b) if either of the following applies:

(1) The claimant, if an organization, proves that (i) within a reasonable time before the tender, the claimant sent a conspicuous statement to the person against whom the claim is asserted that communications concerning disputed debts, including an instrument tendered as full satisfaction of a debt, are to be sent to a designated person, office, or place, and (ii) the instrument or accompanying communication was not received by that designated person, office, or place.

(2) The claimant, whether or not an organization, proves that within 90 days after payment of the instrument, the claimant tendered repayment of the amount of the instrument to the person against whom the claim is asserted. This paragraph does not apply if the claimant is an organization that sent a statement complying with paragraph (1)(i).

(d) A claim is discharged if the person against whom the claim is asserted proves that within a reasonable time before collection of the instrument was initiated, the claimant, or an agent of the claimant having direct responsibility with respect to the disputed obligation, knew that the instrument was tendered in full satisfaction of the claim.

§3-312. Lost, Destroyed, or Stolen Cashier's Check, Teller's Check, or Certified Check.—

(a) In this section:

    (1) "Check" means a cashier's check, teller's check, or certified check.

    (2) "Claimant" means a person who claims the right to receive the amount of a cashier's check, teller's check, or certified check that was lost, destroyed, or stolen.

    (3) "Declaration of loss" means a written statement, made under penalty of perjury, to the effect that (i) the declarer lost possession of a check, (ii) the declarer is the drawer or payee of the check, in the case of a certified check, or the remitter or payee of the check, in the case of a cashier's check or teller's check, (iii) the loss of possession was not the result of a transfer by the declarer or a lawful seizure, and (iv) the declarer cannot reasonably obtain possession of the check because the check was destroyed, its whereabouts cannot be determined, or it is in the wrongful possession of an unknown person or a person that cannot be found or is not amenable to service of process.

    (4) "Obligated bank" means the issuer of a cashier's check or teller's check or the acceptor of a certified check.

(b) A claimant may assert a claim to the amount of a check by a communication to the obligated bank describing the check with reasonable certainty and requesting payment of the amount of the check, if (i) the claimant is the drawer or payee of a certified check or the remitter or payee of a cashier's check or teller's check, (ii) the communication contains or is accompanied by a declaration of loss of the claimant with respect to the check, (iii) the communication is received at a time and in a manner affording the bank a reasonable time to act on it before the check is paid, and (iv) the claimant provides reasonable identification if requested by the obligated bank. Delivery of a declaration of loss is a warranty of the truth of the statements made in the declaration. If a claim is asserted in compliance with this subsection, the following rules apply:

    (1) The claim becomes enforceable at the later of (i) the time the claim is asserted, or (ii) the 90th day following the date of the check, in the case of a cashier's check or teller's check, or the 90th day following the date of the acceptance, in the case of a certified check.

    (2) Until the claim becomes enforceable, it has no legal effect and the obligated bank may pay the check or, in the case of a teller's check, may permit the drawee to pay the check. Payment to a person entitled to enforce the check discharges all liability of the obligated bank with respect to the check.

    (3) If the claim becomes enforceable before the check is presented for payment, the obligated bank is not obliged to pay the check.

    (4) When the claim becomes enforceable, the obligated bank becomes obliged to pay the amount of the check to the claimant if payment of the check has not been made to a person entitled to enforce the check. Subject to Section 4-302(a)(1), payment to the claimant discharges all liability of the obligated bank with respect to the check.

(c) If the obligated bank pays the amount of a check to a claimant under subsection (b)(4) and the check is presented for payment by a person having rights of a holder in due course, the claimant is obliged to (i) refund the payment to the obligated bank if the check is paid, or (ii) pay the amount of the check to the person having rights of a holder in due course if the check is dishonored.

(d) If a claimant has the right to assert a claim under subsection (b) and is also a person entitled to enforce a cashier's check, teller's check, or certified check which is lost, destroyed, or stolen, the claimant may assert rights with respect to the check either under this section or Section 3-309.

Part 4: Liability of Parties

§3-401. Signature.—

(a) A person is not liable on an instrument unless (i) the person signed the instrument, or (ii) the person is represented by an agent or representative who signed the instrument and the signature is binding on the represented person under Section 3-402.

(b) A signature may be made (i) manually or by means of a device or machine, and (ii) by the use of any name, including a trade or assumed name, or by a word, mark, or symbol executed or adopted by a person with present intention to authenticate a writing.

§3-402. Signature by Representative.—

(a) If a person acting, or purporting to act, as a representative signs an instrument by signing either the name of the represented person or the name of the signer, the represented person is bound by the signature to the same extent the represented person would be bound if the signature were on a simple contract. If the represented person is bound, the signature of the representative is the "authorized signature of the represented person" and the represented person is liable on the instrument, whether or not identified in the instrument.

(b) If a representative signs the name of the representative to an instrument and the signature is an authorized signature of the represented person, the following rules apply:

(1) If the form of the signature shows unambiguously that the signature is made on behalf of the represented person who is identified in the instrument, the representative is not liable on the instrument.

(2) Subject to subsection (c), if (i) the form of the signature does not show unambiguously that the signature is made in a representative capacity or (ii) the represented person is not identified in the instrument, the representative is liable on the instrument to a holder in due course that took the instrument without notice that the representative was not intended to be liable on the instrument. With respect to any other person, the representative is liable on the instrument unless the representative proves that the original parties did not intend the representative to be liable on the instrument.

(c) If a representative signs the name of the representative as drawer of a check without indication of the representative status and the check is payable from an account of the represented person who is identified on the check, the signer is not liable on the check if the signature is an authorized signature of the represented person.

§3-403. Unauthorized Signature.—

(a) Unless otherwise provided in this Article or Article 4, an unauthorized signature is ineffective except as the signature of the unauthorized signer in favor of a person who in good faith pays the instrument or takes it for value. An unauthorized signature may be ratified for all purposes of this Article.

(b) If the signature of more than one person is required to constitute the authorized signature of an organization, the signature of the organization is unauthorized if one of the required signatures is lacking.

(c) The civil or criminal liability of a person who makes an unauthorized signature is not affected by any provision of this Article which makes the unauthorized signature effective for the purposes of this Article.

§3-404. Impostors; Fictitious Payees.—

(a) If an impostor, by use of the mails or otherwise, induces the issuer of an instrument to issue the instrument to the impostor, or to a person acting in concert with the impostor, by impersonating the payee of the instrument or a person authorized to act for the payee, an indorsement of the instrument by any person in the name of the payee is effective as the indorsement of the payee in favor of a person who, in good faith, pays the instrument or takes it for value or for collection.

(b) If (i) a person whose intent determines to whom an instrument is payable (Section 3-110(a) or (b)) does not intend the person identified as payee to have any interest in the instrument, or (ii) the person identified as payee of an instrument is a fictitious person, the following rules apply until the instrument is negotiated by special indorsement:

(1) Any person in possession of the instrument is its holder.

(2) An indorsement by any person in the name of the payee stated in the instrument is effective as the indorsement of the payee in favor of a person who, in good faith, pays the instrument or takes it for value or for collection.

(c) Under subsection (a) or (b), an indorsement is made in the name of a payee if (i) it is made in a name substantially similar to that of the payee or (ii) the instrument, whether or not indorsed, is deposited in a depositary bank to an account in a name substantially similar to that of the payee.

(d) With respect to an instrument to which subsection (a) or (b) applies, if a person paying the instrument or taking it for value or for collection fails to exercise ordinary care in paying or taking the instrument and that failure substantially contributes to loss resulting from payment of the instrument, the person bearing the loss may recover from the person failing to exercise ordinary care to the extent the failure to exercise ordinary care contributed to the loss.

§3-405. Employer's Responsibility for Fraudulent Indorsement by Employee.—

(a) In this section

(1) "Employee" includes an independent contractor and employee of an independent contractor retained by the employer.

(2) "Fraudulent indorsement" means (i) in the case of an instrument payable to the employer, a forged indorsement purporting to be that of the employer, or (ii) in the case of an instrument with respect to which the employer is the issuer, a forged indorsement purporting to be that of the person identified as payee.

(3) "Responsibility" with respect to instruments means authority (i) to sign or indorse instruments on behalf of the employer, (ii) to process instruments received by the employer for bookkeeping purposes, for deposit to an account, or for other disposition, (iii) to prepare or process instruments for issue in the name of the employer, (iv) to supply information determining the names or addresses of payees of instruments to be issued in the name of the employer, (v) to control the disposition of instruments to be issued in the name of the employer, or (vi) to act otherwise with respect to instruments in a responsible capacity. "Responsibility" does not include authority that merely

allows an employee to have access to instruments or blank or incomplete instrument forms that are being stored or transported or are part of incoming or outgoing mail, or similar access.

(b) For the purpose of determining the rights and liabilities of a person who, in good faith, pays an instrument or takes it for value or for collection, if an employer entrusted an employee with responsibility with respect to the instrument and the employee or a person acting in concert with the employee makes a fraudulent indorsement of the instrument, the indorsement is effective as the indorsement of the person to whom the instrument is payable if it is made in the name of that person. If the person paying the instrument or taking it for value or for collection fails to exercise ordinary care in paying or taking the instrument and that failure substantially contributes to loss resulting from the fraud, the person bearing the loss may recover from the person failing to exercise ordinary care to the extent the failure to exercise ordinary care contributed to the loss.

(c) Under subsection (b), an indorsement is made in the name of the person to whom an instrument is payable if (i) it is made in a name substantially similar to the name of that person or (ii) the instrument, whether or not indorsed, is deposited in a depositary bank to an account in a name substantially similar to the name of that person.

§3-406. Negligence Contributing to Forged Signature or Alteration of Instrument.—

(a) A person whose failure to exercise ordinary care substantially contributes to an alteration of an instrument or to the making of a forged signature on an instrument is precluded from asserting the alteration or the forgery against a person who, in good faith, pays the instrument or takes it for value or for collection.

(b) Under subsection (a), if the person asserting the preclusion fails to exercise ordinary care in paying or taking the instrument and that failure substantially contributes to loss, the loss is allocated between the person precluded and the person asserting the preclusion according to the extent to which the failure of each to exercise ordinary care contributed to the loss.

(c) Under subsection (a), the burden of proving failure to exercise ordinary care is on the person asserting the preclusion. Under subsection (b), the burden of proving failure to exercise ordinary care is on the person precluded.

§3-407. Alteration.—

(a) "Alteration" means (i) an unauthorized change in an instrument that purports to modify in any respect the obligation of a party, or (ii) an unauthorized addition of words or numbers or other change to an incomplete instrument relating to the obligation of a party.

(b) Except as provided in subsection (c), an alteration fraudulently made discharges a party whose obligation is affected by the alteration unless that party assents or is precluded from asserting the alteration. No other alteration discharges a party, and the instrument may be enforced according to its original terms.

(c) A payor bank or drawee paying a fraudulently altered instrument or a person taking it for value, in good faith and without notice of the alteration, may enforce rights with respect to the instrument (i) according to its original terms, or (ii) in the case of an incomplete instrument altered by unauthorized completion, according to its terms as completed.

§3-408. Drawee Not Liable on Unaccepted Draft.—
A check or other draft does not of itself operate as an assignment of funds in the hands of the drawee available for its payment, and the drawee is not liable on the instrument until the drawee accepts it.

§3-409. Acceptance of Draft; Certified Check.—

(a) "Acceptance" means the drawee's signed agreement to pay a draft as presented. It must be written on the draft and may consist of the drawee's signature alone. Acceptance may be made at any time and becomes effective when notification pursuant to instructions is given or the accepted draft is delivered for the purpose of giving rights on the acceptance to any person.

(b) A draft may be accepted although it has not been signed by the drawer, is otherwise incomplete, is overdue, or has been dishonored.

(c) If a draft is payable at a fixed period after sight and the acceptor fails to date the acceptance, the holder may complete the acceptance by supplying a date in good faith.

(d) "Certified check" means a check accepted by the bank on which it is drawn. Acceptance may be made as stated in subsection (a) or by a writing on the check which indicates that the check is certified. The drawee of a check has no obligation to certify the check, and refusal to certify is not dishonor of the check.

§3-410. Acceptance Varying Draft.—

(a) If the terms of a drawee's acceptance vary from the terms of the draft as presented, the holder may refuse the acceptance and treat the draft as dishonored. In that case, the drawee may cancel the acceptance.

(b) The terms of a draft are not varied by an acceptance to pay at a particular bank or place in the United States, unless the acceptance states that the draft is to be paid only at that bank or place.

(c) If the holder assents to an acceptance varying the terms of a draft, the obligation of each drawer and indorser that does not expressly assent to the acceptance is discharged.

§3-411. Refusal to Pay Cashier's Checks, Teller's Checks, and Certified Checks.—

(a) In this section, "obligated bank" means the acceptor of a certified check or the issuer of a cashier's check or teller's check bought from the issuer.

(b) If the obligated bank wrongfully (i) refuses to pay a cashier's check or certified check, (ii) stops payment of a teller's check, or (iii) refuses to pay a dishonored teller's check, the person asserting the right to enforce the check is entitled to compensation for expenses and loss of interest resulting from the nonpayment and may recover consequential damages if the obligated bank refuses to pay after receiving notice of particular circumstances giving rise to the damages.

(c) Expenses or consequential damages under subsection (b) are not recoverable if the refusal of the obligated bank to pay occurs because (i) the bank suspends payments, (ii) the obligated bank asserts a claim or defense of the bank that it has reasonable grounds to believe is available against the person entitled to enforce the instrument, (iii) the obligated bank has a reasonable doubt whether the person demanding payment is the person entitled to enforce the instrument, or (iv) payment is prohibited by law.

§3-412. Obligation of Issuer of Note or Cashier's Check.—

The issuer of a note or cashier's check or other draft drawn on the drawer is obliged to pay the instrument (i) according to its terms at the time it was issued or, if not issued, at the time it first came into possession of a holder, or (ii) if the issuer signed an incomplete instrument, according to its terms when completed, to the extent stated in Sections 3-115 and 3-407. The obligation is owed to a person entitled to enforce the instrument or to an indorser who paid the instrument under Section 3-415.

§3-413. Obligation of Acceptor.—

(a) The acceptor of a draft is obliged to pay the draft (i) according to its terms at the time it was accepted, even though the acceptance states that the draft is payable "as originally drawn" or equivalent terms, (ii) if the acceptance varies the terms of the draft, according to the terms of the draft as varied, or (iii) if the acceptance is of a draft that is an incomplete instrument, according to its terms when completed, to the extent stated in Sections 3-115 and 3-407. The obligation is owed to a person entitled to enforce the draft or to the drawer or an indorser who paid the draft under Section 3-414 or 3-415.

(b) If the certification of a check or other acceptance of a draft states the amount certified or accepted, the obligation of the acceptor is that amount. If (i) the certification or acceptance does not state an amount, (ii) the amount of the instrument is subsequently raised, and (iii) the instrument is then negotiated to a

holder in due course, the obligation of the acceptor is the amount of the instrument at the time it was taken by the holder in due course.

§3-414. Obligation of Drawer.—

(a) This section does not apply to cashier's checks or other drafts drawn on the drawer.

(b) If an unaccepted draft is dishonored, the drawer is obliged to pay the draft (i) according to its terms at the time it was issued or, if not issued, at the time it first came into possession of a holder, or (ii) if the drawer signed an incomplete instrument, according to its terms when completed, to the extent stated in Sections 3-115 and 3-407. The obligation is owed to a person entitled to enforce the draft or to an indorser who paid the draft under Section 3-415.

(c) If a draft is accepted by a bank, the drawer is discharged, regardless of when or by whom acceptance was obtained.

(d) If a draft is accepted and the acceptor is not a bank, the obligation of the drawer to pay the draft if the draft is dishonored by the acceptor is the same as the obligation of an indorser under Section 3-415(a) and (c).

(e) If a draft states that it is drawn "without recourse" or otherwise disclaims liability of the drawer to pay the draft, the drawer is not liable under subsection (b) to pay the draft if the draft is not a check. A disclaimer of the liability stated in subsection (b) is not effective if the draft is a check.

(f) If (i) a check is not presented for payment or given to a depositary bank for collection within 30 days after its date, (ii) the drawee suspends payments after expiration of the 30-day period without paying the check, and (iii) because of the suspension of payments, the drawer is deprived of funds maintained with the drawee to cover payment of the check, the drawer to the extent deprived of funds may discharge its obligation to pay the check by assigning to the person entitled to enforce the check the rights of the drawer against the drawee with respect to the funds.

§3-415. Obligation of Indorser.—

(a) Subject to subsections (b), (c), and (d) and to Section 3-419(d), if an instrument is dishonored, an indorser is obliged to pay the amount due on the instrument (i) according to the terms of the instrument at the time it was indorsed, or (ii) if the indorser indorsed an incomplete instrument, according to its terms when completed, to the extent stated in Sections 3-115 and 3-407. The obligation of the indorser is owed to a person entitled to enforce the instrument or to a subsequent indorser who paid the instrument under this section.

(b) If an indorsement states that it is made "without recourse" or otherwise disclaims liability of the indorser, the indorser is not liable under subsection (a) to pay the instrument.

(c) If notice of dishonor of an instrument is required by Section 3-503 and notice of dishonor complying with that section is not given to an indorser, the liability of the indorser under subsection (a) is discharged.

(d) If a draft is accepted by a bank after an indorsement is made, the liability of the indorser under subsection (a) is discharged.

(e) If an indorser of a check is liable under subsection (a) and the check is not presented for payment, or given to a depositary bank for collection, within 30 days after the day the indorsement was made, the liability of the indorser under subsection (a) is discharged.

§3-416. Transfer Warranties.—

(a) A person who transfers an instrument for consideration warrants to the transferee and, if the transfer is by indorsement, to any subsequent transferee that:

    (1) the warrantor is a person entitled to enforce the instrument;

    (2) all signatures on the instrument are authentic and authorized;

    (3) the instrument has not been altered;

    (4) the instrument is not subject to a defense or claim in recoupment of any party which can be asserted against the warrantor; and

    (5) the warrantor has no knowledge of any insolvency proceeding commenced with respect to the maker or acceptor or, in the case of an unaccepted draft, the drawer.

(b) A person to whom the warranties under subsection (a) are made and who took the instrument in good faith may recover from the warrantor as damages for breach of warranty an amount equal to the loss suffered as a result of the breach, but not more than the amount of the instrument plus expenses and loss of interest incurred as a result of the breach.

(c) The warranties stated in subsection (a) cannot be disclaimed with respect to checks. Unless notice of a claim for breach of warranty is given to the warrantor within 30 days after the claimant has reason to know of the breach and the identity of the warrantor, the liability of the warrantor under subsection (b) is discharged to the extent of any loss caused by the delay in giving notice of the claim.

(d) A [cause of action] for breach of warranty under this section accrues when the claimant has reason to know of the breach.

§3-417. Presentment Warranties.—

(a) If an unaccepted draft is presented to the drawee for payment or acceptance and the drawee pays or accepts the draft, (i) the person obtaining payment or acceptance, at the time of presentment, and (ii) a previous transferor of the draft, at the time of transfer, warrant to the drawee making payment or accepting the draft in good faith that:

    (1) the warrantor is, or was, at the time the warrantor transferred the draft, a person entitled to enforce the draft or authorized to obtain payment or acceptance of the draft on behalf of a person entitled to enforce the draft;

    (2) the draft has not been altered; and

    (3) the warrantor has no knowledge that the signature of the drawer of the draft is unauthorized.

(b) A drawee making payment may recover from any warrantor damages for breach of warranty equal to the amount paid by the drawee less the amount the drawee received or is entitled to receive from the drawer because of the payment. In addition, the drawee is entitled to compensation for expenses and loss of interest resulting from the breach. The right of the drawee to recover damages under this subsection is not affected by any failure of the drawee to exercise ordinary care in making payment. If the drawee accepts the draft, breach of warranty is a defense to the obligation of the acceptor. If the acceptor makes payment with respect to the draft, the acceptor is entitled to recover from any warrantor for breach of warranty the amounts stated in this subsection.

(c) If a drawee asserts a claim for breach of warranty under subsection (a) based on an unauthorized indorsement of the draft or an alteration of the draft, the warrantor may defend by proving that the indorsement is effective under Section 3-404 or 3-405 or the drawer is precluded under Section 3-406 or 4-406 from asserting against the drawee the unauthorized indorsement or alteration.

(d) If (i) a dishonored draft is presented for payment to the drawer or an indorser or (ii) any other instrument is presented for payment to a party obliged to pay the instrument, and (iii) payment is received, the following rules apply:

    (1) The person obtaining payment and a prior transferor of the instrument warrant to the person making payment in good faith that the warrantor is, or was, at the time the warrantor transferred the instrument, a person entitled to enforce the instrument or authorized to obtain payment on behalf of a person entitled to enforce the instrument.

    (2) The person making payment may recover from any warrantor for breach of warranty an amount equal to the amount paid plus expenses and loss of interest resulting from the breach.

(e) The warranties stated in subsections (a) and (d) cannot be disclaimed with respect to checks. Unless notice of a claim for breach of warranty is given to the warrantor within 30 days after the claimant has reason to know of the breach and the identity of the warrantor, the liability of the warrantor under subsection (b) or (d) is discharged to the extent of any loss caused by the delay in giving notice of the claim.

(f) A [cause of action] for breach of warranty under this section accrues when the claimant has reason to know of the breach.

§3-418. Payment or Acceptance by Mistake.—

(a) Except as provided in subsection (c), if the drawee of a draft pays or accepts the draft and the drawee acted on the mistaken belief that (i) payment of the draft had not been stopped pursuant to Section 4-403 or (ii) the signature of the drawer of the draft was authorized, the drawee may recover the amount of the draft from the person to whom or for whose benefit payment was made or, in the case of acceptance, may revoke the acceptance. Rights of the drawee under this subsection are not affected by failure of the drawee to exercise ordinary care in paying or accepting the draft.

(b) Except as provided in subsection (c), if an instrument has been paid or accepted by mistake and the case is not covered by subsection (a), the person paying or accepting may, to the extent permitted by the law governing mistake and restitution, (i) recover the payment from the person to whom or for whose benefit payment was made or (ii) in the case of acceptance, may revoke the acceptance.

(c) The remedies provided by subsection (a) or (b) may not be asserted against a person who took the instrument in good faith and for value or who in good faith changed position in reliance on the payment or acceptance. This subsection does not limit remedies provided by Section 3-417 or 4-407.

(d) Notwithstanding Section 4-215, if an instrument is paid or accepted by mistake and the payor or acceptor recovers payment or revokes acceptance under subsection (a) or (b), the instrument is deemed not to have been paid or accepted and is treated as dishonored, and the person from whom payment is recovered has rights as a person entitled to enforce the dishonored instrument.

§3-419. Instruments Signed for Accommodation.—

(a) If an instrument is issued for value given for the benefit of a party to the instrument ("accommodated party") and another party to the instrument ("An accommodation party") signs the instrument for the purpose of incurring liability on the instrument without being a direct beneficiary of the value given for the instrument, the instrument is signed by the accommodation party "for accommodation".

(b) An accommodation party may sign the instrument as maker, drawer, acceptor, or indorser and, subject to subsection (d), is obliged to pay the instrument in the capacity in which the accommodation party signs.

The obligation of an accommodation party may be enforced notwithstanding any statute of frauds and whether or not the accommodation party receives consideration for the accommodation.

(c) A person signing an instrument is presumed to be an accommodation party and there is notice that the instrument is signed for accommodation if the signature is an anomalous indorsement or is accompanied by words indicating that the signer is acting as surety or guarantor with respect to the obligation of another party to the instrument. Except as provided in Section 3-605, the obligation of an accommodation party to pay the instrument is not affected by the fact that the person enforcing the obligation had notice when the instrument was taken by that person that the accommodation party signed the instrument for accommodation.

(d) If the signature of a party to an instrument is accompanied by words indicating unambiguously that the party is guaranteeing collection rather than payment of the obligation of another party to the instrument, the signer is obliged to pay the amount due on the instrument to a person entitled to enforce the instrument only if (i) execution of judgment against the other party has been returned unsatisfied, (ii) the other party is insolvent or in an insolvency proceeding, (iii) the other party cannot be served with process, or (iv) it is otherwise apparent that payment cannot be obtained from the other party.

(e) An accommodation party who pays the instrument is entitled to reimbursement from the accommodated party and is entitled to enforce the instrument against the accommodated party. An accommodated party who pays the instrument has no right of recourse against, and is not entitled to contribution from, an accommodation party.

§3-420. Conversion of Instrument.—

(a) The law applicable to conversion of personal property applies to instruments. An instrument is also converted if it is taken by transfer, other than a negotiation, from a person not entitled to enforce the instrument or a bank makes or obtains payment with respect to the instrument for a person not entitled to enforce the instrument or receive payment. An action for conversion of an instrument may not be brought by (i) the issuer or acceptor of the instrument or (ii) a payee or indorsee who did not receive delivery of the instrument either directly or through delivery to an agent or a co-payee.

(b) In an action under subsection (a), the measure of liability is presumed to be the amount payable on the instrument, but recovery may not exceed the amount of the plaintiff's interest in the instrument.

(c) A representative, other than a depositary bank, who has in good faith dealt with an instrument or its proceeds on behalf of one who was not the person entitled to enforce the instrument is not liable in conversion to that person beyond the amount of any proceeds that it has not paid out.

Part 5: Dishonor

§3-501. Presentment.—

(a) "Presentment" means a demand made by or on behalf of a person entitled to enforce an instrument (i) to pay the instrument made to the drawee or a party obliged to pay the instrument or, in the case of a note or accepted draft payable at a bank, to the bank, or (ii) to accept a draft made to the drawee.

(b) The following rules are subject to Article 4, agreement of the parties, and clearing-house rules and the like:

  (1) Presentment may be made at the place of payment of the instrument and must be made at the place of payment if the instrument is payable at a bank in the United States; may be made by any commercially reasonable means, including an oral, written, or electronic communication; is effective when the demand for payment or acceptance is received by the person to whom presentment is made; and is effective if made to any one of two or more makers, acceptors, drawees, or other payors.

  (2) Upon demand of the person to whom presentment is made, the person making presentment must (i) exhibit the instrument, (ii) give reasonable identification and, if presentment is made on behalf of another person, reasonable evidence of authority to do so, and (iii) sign a receipt on the instrument for any payment made or surrender the instrument if full payment is made.

  (3) Without dishonoring the instrument, the party to whom presentment is made may (i) return the instrument for lack of a necessary indorsement, or (ii) refuse payment or acceptance for failure of the presentment to comply with the terms of the instrument, an agreement of the parties, or other applicable law or rule.

  (4) The party to whom presentment is made may treat presentment as occurring on the next business day after the day of presentment if the party to whom presentment is made has established a cut-off hour not earlier than 2 p.m for the receipt and processing of instruments presented for payment or acceptance and presentment is made after the cut-off hour.

§3-502. Dishonor.—

(a) Dishonor of a note is governed by the following rules:

  (1) If the note is payable on demand, the note is dishonored if presentment is duly made to the maker and the note is not paid on the day of presentment.

  (2) If the note is not payable on demand and is payable at or through a bank or the terms of the note require presentment, the note is dishonored if presentment is duly made and the note is not paid on the day it becomes payable or the day of presentment, whichever is later.

  (3) If the note is not payable on demand and paragraph (2) does not apply, the note is dishonored if it is not paid on the day it becomes payable.

(b) Dishonor of an unaccepted draft other than a documentary draft is governed by the following rules:

  (1) If a check is duly presented for payment to the payor bank otherwise than for immediate payment over the counter, the check is dishonored if the payor bank makes timely return of the check or sends timely notice of dishonor or nonpayment under Section 4-301 or 4-302, or becomes accountable for the amount of the check under Section 4-302.

  (2) If a draft is payable on demand and paragraph (1) does not apply, the draft is dishonored if presentment for payment is duly made to the drawee and the draft is not paid on the day of presentment.

  (3) If a draft is payable on a date stated in the draft, the draft is dishonored if (i) presentment for payment is duly made to the drawee and payment is not made on the day the draft becomes payable or the day of presentment, whichever is later, or (ii) presentment for acceptance is duly made before the day the draft becomes payable and the draft is not accepted on the day of presentment.

  (4) If a draft is payable on elapse of a period of time after sight or acceptance, the draft is dishonored if presentment for acceptance is duly made and the draft is not accepted on the day of presentment.

(c) Dishonor of an unaccepted documentary draft occurs according to the rules stated in subsection (b)(2), (3), and (4), except that payment or acceptance may be delayed without dishonor until no later than the close of the third business day of the drawee following the day on which payment or acceptance is required by those paragraphs.

(d) Dishonor of an accepted draft is governed by the following rules:

  (1) If the draft is payable on demand, the draft is dishonored if presentment for payment is duly made to the acceptor and the draft is not paid on the day of presentment.

  (2) If the draft is not payable on demand, the draft is dishonored if presentment for payment is duly made to the acceptor and payment is not made on the day it becomes payable or the day of presentment, whichever is later.

(e) In any case in which presentment is otherwise required for dishonor under this section and presentment is excused under Section 3-504, dishonor occurs without presentment if the instrument is not duly accepted or paid.

(f) If a draft is dishonored because timely acceptance of the draft was not made and the person entitled to demand acceptance consents to a late acceptance, from the time of acceptance the draft is treated as never having been dishonored.

§3-503. Notice of Dishonor.—

(a) The obligation of an indorser stated in Section 3-415(a) and the obligation of a drawer stated in Section 3-414(d) may not be enforced unless (i) the indorser or drawer is given notice of dishonor of the instrument complying with this section or (ii) notice of dishonor is excused under Section 3-504(b).

(b) Notice of dishonor may be given by any person; may be given by any commercially reasonable means, including an oral, written, or electronic communication; and is sufficient if it reasonably identifies the instrument and indicates that the instrument has been dishonored or has not been paid or accepted. Return of an instrument given to a bank for collection is sufficient notice of dishonor.

(c) Subject to Section 3-504(c), with respect to an instrument taken for collection by a collecting bank, notice of dishonor must be given (i) by the bank before midnight of the next banking day following the banking day on which the bank receives notice of dishonor of the instrument, or (ii) by any other person within 30 days following the day on which the person receives notice of dishonor. With respect to any other instrument, notice of dishonor must be given within 30 days following the day on which dishonor occurs.

§3-504. Excused Presentment and Notice of Dishonor.—

(a) Presentment for payment or acceptance of an instrument is excused if (i) the person entitled to present the instrument cannot with reasonable diligence make presentment, (ii) the maker or acceptor has repudiated an obligation to pay the instrument or is dead or in insolvency proceedings, (iii) by the terms of the instrument presentment is not necessary to enforce the obligation of indorsers or the drawer, (iv) the drawer or indorser whose obligation is being enforced has waived presentment or otherwise has no reason to expect or right to require that the instrument be paid or accepted, or (v) the drawer instructed the drawee not to pay or accept the draft or the drawee was not obligated to the drawer to pay the draft.

(b) Notice of dishonor is excused if (i) by the terms of the instrument notice of dishonor is not necessary to enforce the obligation of a party to pay the instrument, or (ii) the party whose obligation is being enforced waived notice of dishonor. A waiver of presentment is also a waiver of notice of dishonor.

(c) Delay in giving notice of dishonor is excused if the delay was caused by circumstances beyond the control of the person giving the notice and the person giving the notice exercised reasonable diligence after the cause of the delay ceased to operate.

§3-505. Evidence of Dishonor.—

(a) The following are admissible as evidence and create a presumption of dishonor and of any notice of dishonor stated:

(1) a document regular in form as provided in subsection (b) which purports to be a protest;

(2) a purported stamp or writing of the drawee, payor bank, or presenting bank on or accompanying the instrument stating that acceptance or payment has been refused unless reasons for the refusal are stated and the reasons are not consistent with dishonor;

(3) a book or record of the drawee, payor bank, or collecting bank, kept in the usual course of business which shows dishonor, even if there is no evidence of who made the entry.

(b) A protest is a certificate of dishonor made by a United States consul or vice consul, or a notary public or other person authorized to administer oaths by the law of the place where dishonor occurs. It may be made upon information satisfactory to that person. The protest must identify the instrument and certify either that presentment has been made or, if not made, the reason why it was not made, and that the instrument has been dishonored by nonacceptance or nonpayment. The protest may also certify that notice of dishonor has been given to some or all parties.

Part 6: Discharge and Payment

§3-601. Discharge and Effect of Discharge.—

(a) The obligation of a party to pay the instrument is discharged as stated in this Article or by an act or agreement with the party which would discharge an obligation to pay money under a simple contract.

(b) Discharge of the obligation of a party is not effective against a person acquiring rights of a holder in due course of the instrument without notice of the discharge.

§3-602. Payment.—

(a) Subject to subsection (b), an instrument is paid to the extent payment is made (i) by or on behalf of a party obliged to pay the instrument, and (ii) to a person entitled to enforce the instrument. To the extent of the payment, the obligation of the party obliged to pay the instrument is discharged even though payment is made with knowledge of a claim to the instrument under Section 3-306 by another person.

(b) The obligation of a party to pay the instrument is not discharged under subsection (a) if:

(1) a claim to the instrument under Section 3-306 is enforceable against the party receiving payment and (i) payment is made with knowledge by the payor that payment is prohibited by injunction or similar process of a court of competent jurisdiction, or (ii) in the case of an instrument other than a cashier's check, teller's check, or certified check, the party making payment accepted, from the person having a claim to the instrument, indemnity against loss resulting from refusal to pay the person entitled to enforce the instrument; or

(2) the person making payment knows that the instrument is a stolen instrument and pays a person it knows is in wrongful possession of the instrument.

§3-603. Tender of Payment.—

(a) If tender of payment of an obligation to pay an instrument is made to a person entitled to enforce the instrument, the effect of tender is governed by principles of law applicable to tender of payment under a simple contract.

(b) If tender of payment of an obligation to pay an instrument is made to a person entitled to enforce the instrument and the tender is refused,. . . .

§3-604. Discharge by Cancellation or Renunciation.—

(a) A person entitled to enforce an instrument, with or without consideration, may discharge the obligation of a party to pay the instrument (i) by an intentional voluntary act, such as surrender of the instrument to the party, destruction, mutilation, or cancellation of the instrument, cancellation or striking out of the party's signature, or the addition of words to the instrument indicating discharge, or (ii) by agreeing not to sue or otherwise renouncing rights against the party by a signed writing.

(b) Cancellation or striking out of an indorsement pursuant to subsection (a) does not affect the status and rights of a party derived from the indorsement.

§3-605. Discharge of Indorsers and Accommodation Parties.—

(a) In this section, the term "indorser" includes a drawer having the obligation described in Section 3-414(d).

(b) Discharge, under Section 3-604, of the obligation of a party to pay an instrument does not discharge the obligation of an indorser or accommodation party having a right of recourse against the discharged party.

(c) If a person entitled to enforce an instrument agrees, with or without consideration, to an extension of the due date of the obligation of a party to pay the instrument, the extension discharges an indorser or accommodation party having a right of recourse against the party whose obligation is extended to the extent the indorser or accommodation party proves that the extension caused loss to the indorser or accommodation party with respect to the right of recourse.

(d) If a person entitled to enforce an instrument agrees, with or without consideration, to a material modification of the obligation of a party other than an extension of the due date, the modification discharges the obligation of an indorser or accommodation party having a right of recourse against the person whose obligation is modified to the extent the modification causes loss to the indorser or accommodation party with respect to the right of recourse. The loss suffered by the indorser or accommodation party as a result of the modification is equal to the amount of the right of recourse unless the person enforcing the instrument proves that no loss was caused by the modification or that the loss caused by the modification was an amount less than the amount of the right of recourse.

(e) If the obligation of a party to pay an instrument is secured by an interest in collateral and a person entitled to enforce the instrument impairs the value of the interest in collateral, the obligation of an indorser or accommodation party having a right of recourse against the obligor is discharged to the extent of the impairment. The value of an interest in collateral is impaired to the extent (i) the value of the interest is reduced to an amount less than the amount of the right of recourse of the party asserting discharge, or (ii) the reduction in value of the interest causes an increase in the amount by which the amount of the right of recourse exceeds the value of the interest. The burden of proving impairment is on the party asserting discharge.

(f) If the obligation of a party is secured by an interest in collateral not provided by an accommodation party and a person entitled to enforce the instrument impairs the value of the interest in collateral, the obligation of any party who is jointly and severally liable with respect to the secured obligation is discharged to the extent the impairment causes the party asserting discharge to pay more than that party would have been obliged to pay, taking into account rights of contribution, if impairment had not occurred. If the party asserting discharge is an accommodation party not entitled to discharge under subsection (e), the party is deemed to have a right to contribution based on joint and several liability rather than a right to reimbursement. The burden of proving impairment is on the party asserting discharge.

(g) Under subsection (e) or (f), impairing value of an interest in collateral includes (i) failure to obtain or maintain perfection or recordation of the interest in collateral, (ii) release of collateral without substitution of collateral of equal value, (iii) failure to perform a duty to preserve the value of collateral owed, under Article 9 or other law, to a debtor or surety or other person secondarily liable, or (iv) failure to comply with applicable law in disposing of collateral.

(h) An accommodation party is not discharged under subsection (c), (d), or (e) unless the person entitled to enforce the instrument knows of the accommodation or has notice under Section 3-419(c) that the instrument was signed for accommodation.

(i) A party is not discharged under this section if (i) the party asserting discharge consents to the event or conduct that is the basis of the discharge, or (ii) the instrument or a separate agreement of the party provides for waiver of discharge under this section either specifically or by general language indicating that parties waive defenses based on suretyship or impairment of collateral.

Appendix C

United Nations Convention on Contracts for the International Sale of Goods

THE STATES PARTIES TO THIS CONVENTION,

BEARING IN MIND the broad objectives in the resolutions adopted by the sixth special session of the General Assembly of the United Nations on the establishment of a New International Economic Order,

CONSIDERING that the development of international trade on the basis of equality and mutual benefit is an important element in promoting friendly relations among States,

BEING OF THE OPINION that the adoption of uniform rules which govern contracts for the international sale of goods and take into account the different social, economic and legal systems would contribute to the removal of legal barriers in international trade and promote the development of international trade,

HAVE AGREED as follows:

Part I Sphere of Application and General Provisions

Chapter I Sphere of Application

Article 1

(1) This Convention applies to contracts of sale of goods between parties whose places of business are in different States:

  (a) when the States are Contracting States; or

  (b) when the rules of private international law lead to the application of the law of a Contracting State. [Pursuant to the reservation permitted by Article 95, the United States has excluded applicability of the Convention under this subparagraph.]

(2) The fact that the parties have their places of business in different States is to be disregarded whenever this fact does not appear either from the contract or from any dealings between, or from information disclosed by, the parties at any time before or at the conclusion of the contract.

(3) Neither the nationality of the parties nor the civil or commercial character of the parties or of the contract is to be taken into consideration in determining the application of this Convention.

Article 2 This Convention does not apply to sales:

(a) of goods bought for personal, family or household use, unless the seller, at any time before or at the conclusion of the contract, neither knew nor ought to have known that the goods were bought for any such use;

(b) by auction;

(c) on execution or otherwise by authority of law;

(d) of stocks, shares, investment securities, negotiable instruments or money;

(e) of ships, vessels, hovercraft or aircraft;

(f) of electricity.

Article 3

(1) Contracts for the supply of goods to be manufactured or produced are to be considered sales unless the party who orders the goods undertakes to supply a substantial part of the materials necessary for such manufacture or production.

(2) This Convention does not apply to contracts in which the preponderant part of the obligations of the party who furnishes the goods consists in the supply of labour or other services.

Article 4 This Convention governs only the formation of the contract of sale and the rights and obligations of the seller and the buyer arising from such a contract. In particular, except as otherwise expressly provided in this Convention, it is not concerned with:

(a) the validity of the contract or of any of its provisions or of any usage;

(b) the effect which the contract may have on the property in the goods sold.

Article 5 This Convention does not apply to the liability of the seller for death or personal injury caused by the goods to any person.

Article 6 The parties may exclude the application of this Convention or, subject to Article 12, derogate from or vary the effect of any of its provisions.

Chapter II General Provisions

Article 7

(1) In the interpretation of this Convention, regard is to be had to its international character and to the need to promote uniformity in its application and the observance of good faith in international trade.

(2) Questions concerning matters governed by this Convention which are not expressly settled in it are to be settled in conformity with the general principles on which it is based or, in the absence of such principles, in conformity with the law applicable by virtue of the rules of private international law.

Article 8

(1) For the purposes of this Convention statements made by and other conduct of a party are to be interpreted according to his intent where the other party knew or could not have been unaware what that intent was.

(2) If the preceding paragraph is not applicable, statements made by and other conduct of a party are to be interpreted according to the understanding that a reasonable person of the same kind as the other party would have had in the same circumstances.

(3) In determining the intent of a party or the understanding a reasonable person would have had, due consideration is to be given to all relevant circumstances of the case including the negotiations, any practices which the parties have established between themselves, usages and any subsequent conduct of the parities.

Article 9

(1) The parties are bound by any usage to which they have agreed and by any practices which they have established between themselves.

(2) The parties are considered, unless otherwise agreed, to have impliedly made applicable to their contract or its formation a usage of which the parties know or ought to have known and which in international trade is widely known to, and regularly observed by, parties to contracts of the type involved in the particular trade concerned.

Article 10 For the purposes of this Convention:

(a) if a party has more than one place of business, the place of business is that which has the closest relationship to the contract and its performance, having regard to the circumstances known to or contemplated by the parties at any time before or at the conclusion of the contract;

(b) if a party does not have a place of business, reference is to be made to his habitual residence.

Article 11 A contract of sale need not be concluded in or evidenced by writing and is not subject to any other requirement as to form. It may be proved by any means, including witnesses.

Article 12 Any provision of Article 11, Article 29 or Part II of this Convention that allows a contract of sale or its modification or termination by agreement or any offer, acceptance or other indication of intention to be made in any form other than in writing does not apply where any party has his place of business in a Contracting State which has made a declaration under Article 96 of this Convention. The parties may not derogate from or vary the effect of this article.

Article 13 For the purposes of this Convention "writing" includes telegram and telex.

Part II Formation of the Contract

Article 14

(1) A proposal for concluding a contract addressed to one or more specific persons constitutes an offer if it

is sufficiently definite and indicates the intention of the offeror to be bound in case of acceptance. A proposal is sufficiently definite if it indicates the goods and expressly or implicitly fixes or makes provision for determining the quantity and the price.

(2) A proposal other than one addressed to one or more specific persons is to be considered merely as an invitation to make offers, unless the contrary is clearly indicated by the person making the proposal.

Article 15

(1) An offer becomes effective when it reaches the offeree.

(2) An offer, even if it is irrevocable, may be withdrawn if the withdrawal reaches the offeree before or at the same time as the offer.

Article 16

(1) Until a contract is concluded an offer may be revoked if the revocation reaches the offeree before he has dispatched an acceptance.

(2) However, an offer cannot be revoked:
   (a) if it indicates, whether by stating a fixed time for acceptance or otherwise, that it is irrevocable; or
   (b) if it was reasonable for the offeree to rely on the offer as being irrevocable and the offeree has acted in reliance on the offer.

Article 17 An offer, even if it is irrevocable, is terminated when a rejection reaches the offeror.

Article 18

(1) A statement made by or other conduct of the offeree indicating assent to an offer is an acceptance. Silence or inactivity does not in itself amount to acceptance.

(2) An acceptance of an offer becomes effective at the moment the indication of assent reaches the offeror. An acceptance is not effective if the indication of assent does not reach the offeror within the time he has fixed or, if no time is fixed, within a reasonable time, due account being taken of the circumstances of the transaction, including the rapidity of the means of communication employed by the offeror. An oral offer must be accepted immediately unless the circumstances indicate otherwise.

(3) However, if, by virtue of the offer or as a result of practices which the parties have established between themselves or of usage, the offeree may indicate assent by performing an act, such as one relating to the dispatch of the goods or payment of the price, without notice to the offeror, the acceptance is effective at the moment the act is performed, provided that the act is performed within the period of time laid down in the preceding paragraph.

Article 19

(1) A reply to an offer which purports to be an acceptance but contains additions, limitations or other modifications is a rejection of the offer and constitutes a counter-offer.

(2) However, a reply to an offer which purports to be an acceptance but contains additional or different terms which do not materially alter the terms of the offer constitutes an acceptance, unless the offeror, without undue delay, objects orally to the discrepancy or dispatches a notice to that effect. If he does not so object, the terms of the contract are the terms of the offer with the modifications contained in the acceptance.

(3) Additional or different terms relating, among other things, to the price, payment, quality and quantity of the goods, place and time of delivery, extent of one party's liability to the other or the settlement of disputes are considered to alter the terms of the offer materially.

Article 20

(1) A period of time for acceptance fixed by the offeror in a telegram or a letter begins to run from the moment the telegram is handed in for dispatch or from the date shown on the letter or, if on such date is shown, from the date shown on the envelope. A period of time for acceptance fixed by the offeror by telephone, telex or other means of instantaneous communication, begins to run from the moment that the offer reaches the offeree.

(2) Official holidays or non-business days occurring during the period for acceptance are included in calculating the period. However, if a notice of acceptance cannot be delivered at the address of the offeror on the last day of the period because that day falls on an official holiday or a non-business day at the place of business of the offeror, the period is extended until the first business day which follows.

Artcle 21

(1) A late acceptance is nevertheless effective as an acceptance if without delay the offeror orally so informs the offeree or dispatches a notice to that effect.

(2) If a letter or other writing containing a late acceptance shows that it has been sent in such circumstances that if its transmission had been normal it would have reached the offeror in due time, the late acceptance is effective as an acceptance unless, without delay, the offeror orally informs the offeree that he considers his offer as having lapsed or dispatches a notice to that effect.

Article 22 An acceptance may be withdrawn if the withdrawal reaches the offeror before or at the same time as the acceptance would have become effective.

Article 23 A contract is concluded at the moment when an acceptance of an offer becomes effective in accordance with the provisions of this Convention.

Article 24 For the purposes of this Part of the Convention, an offer, declaration of acceptance or any other indication of intention "reaches" the addressee when it is made orally to him or delivered by any other means to him personally, to his place of business or mailing address or, if he does not have a place of business or mailing address, to his habitual residence.

Part III Sale of Goods

Chapter I General Provisions

Article 25 A breach of contract committed by one of the parties is fundamental if it results in such detriment to the other party as substantially to deprive him of what he is entitled to expect under the contract, unless the party in breach did not foresee and a reasonable person of the same kind in the same circumstances would not have foreseen such a result.

Article 26 A declaration of avoidance of the contract is effective only if made by notice to the other party.

Article 27 Unless otherwise expressly provided in this Part of the Convention, if any notice, request or other communication is given or made by a party in accordance with this Part and by means appropriate in the circumstances, a delay or error in the transmission of the communication or its failure to arrive does not deprive that party of the right to rely on the communication.

Article 28 If, in accordance with the provisions of this Convention, one party is entitled to require performance of any obligation by the other party, a court is not bound to enter a judgment for specific performance unless the court would do so under its own law in respect of similar contracts of sale not governed by this Convention.

Article 29

(1) A contact may be modified or terminated by the mere agreement of the parties.

(2) A contact in writing which contains a provision requiring any modification or termination by agreement to be in writing may not be otherwise modified or terminated by agreement. However, a party may be precluded by his conduct from asserting such a provision to the extent that the other party has relied on that conduct.

Chapter II Obligations of the Seller

Article 30 The seller must deliver the goods, hand over any documents relating to them and transfer the property in the goods, as required by the contract and this Convetion.

Section I. Delivery of the goods and handing over of documents

Article 31 If the seller is not bound to deliver the goods at any other particular place, his obligation to deliver consists:

(a) if the contract of sale involves carriage of the goods— in handing the goods over to the first carrier for transmission to the buyer;

(b) if, in cases not within the preceding subparagraph, the contract relates to specific goods, or unidentified goods to be drawn from a specific stock or to be manufactured or produced, and at the time of the conclusion of the contract the parties knew that the goods were at, or were to be manufactured or produced at, a particular place—in placing the goods at the buyer's disposal at the place;

(c) in other cases—in placing the goods at the buyer's disposal at the place where the seller had his place of business at the time of the conclusion of the contract.

Article 32

(1) If the seller, in accordance with the contract or this Convention, hands the goods over to a carrier and if the goods are not clearly identified to the contract by markings on the goods, by shipping documents or otherwise, the seller must give the buyer notice of the consignment specifying the goods.

(2) If the seller is bound to arrange for carriage of the goods, he must make such contracts as are necessary for carriage to the place fixed by means of transportation appropriate in the circumstances and according to the usual terms for such transportation.

(3) If the seller is not bound to effect insurance in respect of the carriage of the goods, he must, at the buyer's request, provide him with all available information necessary to enable him to effect such insurance.

Article 33 The seller must deliver the goods:

(a) if a date is fixed by or determinable from the contract, on that date;

(b) if a period of time is fixed by or determinable from the contract, at any time within that period unless circumstances indicate that the buyer is to choose a date; or

(c) in any other case, within a reasonable time after the conclusion of the contract.

Article 34 If the seller is bound to hand over documents relating to the goods, he must hand them over at the time and place and in the form required by the contract. If the seller has handed over documents before that time, he may, up to that time, cure any lack of conformity in the documents, if the exercise of this right does not cause the buyer unreasonable inconvenience or unreasonable expense. However, the buyer retains any right to claim damages as provided for in this Convention.

Section II. Conformity of the goods and third party claims

Article 35

(1) The seller must deliver goods which are of the quantity, quality and description required by the contract and which are contained or packaged in the manner required by the contract.

(2) Except where the parties have agreed otherwise, the goods do not conform with the contract unless they:

  (a) are fit for the purposes for which goods of the same description would ordinarily be used;

  (b) are fit for any particular purpose expressly or impliedly made known to the seller at the time of the conclusion of the contract, except where the circumstances show that the buyer did not rely, or that it was unreasonable for him to rely, on the seller's skill and judgment;

  (c) possess the qualities of goods which the seller has held out to the buyer as a sample or model;

  (d) are contained or packaged in the manner usual for such goods or, where there is no such manner, in a manner adequate to preserve and protect the goods.

(3) The seller is not liable under subparagraphs (a) to (d) of the preceding paragraph for any lack of conformity of the preceding paragraph for any lack of conformity of the goods if at the time of the conclusion of the contract the buyer knew or could not have been unaware of such lack of conformity.

Article 36

(1) The seller is liable in accordance with the contract and this Convention for any lack of conformity which exists at the time when the risk passes to the buyer, even though the lack of conformity becomes apparent only after that time.

(2) The seller is also liable for any lack of conformity which occurs after the time indicated in the preceding paragraph and which is due to a breach of any of his obligations, including a breach of any guarantee that for a period of time the goods will remain fit for their ordinary purpose or for some particular purpose or will retain specified qualities or characteristics.

Article 37 If the seller has delivered goods before the date for delivery, he may, up to that date, deliver any missing part or make up any deficiency in the quantity of the goods delivered, or deliver goods in replacement of any non-conforming goods delivered or remedy any lack of conformity in the goods delivered, provided that the exercise of this right does not cause the buyer unreasonable inconvenience or unreasonable expense. However, the buyer retains any right to claim damages as provided for in this Convention.

Article 38

(1) The buyer must examine the goods, or cause them to be examined, within as short a period as is practicable in the circumstances.

(2) If the contract involves carriage of the goods, examination may be deferred until after the goods have arrived at their destination.

(3) If the goods are redirected in transit or redispatched by the buyer without a reasonable opportunity for examination by him and at the time of the conclusion of the contract the seller knew or ought to have known of the possibility of such redirection or redispatch, examination may be deferred until after the goods have arrived at the new destination.

Article 39

(1) The buyer loses the right to rely on a lack of conformity of the goods if he does not give notice to the seller specifying the nature of the lack of conformity within a reasonable time after he has discovered it or ought to have discovered it.

(2) In any event, the buyer loses the right to rely on a lack of conformity of the goods if he does not give the seller notice thereof at the latest within a period of two years from the date on which the goods were actually handed over to the buyer, unless this time-limit is inconsistent with a contractual period of guarantee.

Article 40 The seller is not entitled to rely on the provisions of Articles 38 and 39 if the lack of conformity relates to facts of which he knew or could not have been unaware and which he did not disclose to the buyer.

Article 41 The seller must deliver goods which are free from any right or claim of a third party, unless the buyer agreed to take the goods subject to that right or claim. However, if such right or claim is based on industrial property or other intellectual property, the seller's obligation is governed by Article 42.

Article 42

(1) The seller must deliver goods which are free from any right or claim of a third party based on industrial property or other intellectual property, of which at the time of the conclusion of the contract the seller knew or could not have been unaware, provided that the right or claim is based on industrial property or other intellectual property:

    (a) under the law of the State where the goods will be resold or otherwise used, if it was contemplated by the parties at the time of the conclusion of the contract that the goods would be resold or otherwise used in that State; or

    (b) in any other case, under the law of the State where the buyer has his place of business.

(2) The obligation of the seller under the preceding paragraph does not extend to cases where:

    (a) at the time of the conclusion of the contract the buyer knew or could not have been unaware of the right or claim; or

    (b) the right or claim results from the seller's compliance with technical drawings, designs, formulae or other such specifications furnished by the buyer.

Article 43

(1) The buyer loses the right to rely on the provisions of Article 41 or Article 42 if he does not give notice to the seller specifying the nature of the right or claim of the third party within a reasonable time after he has become aware or ought to have become aware of the right or claim.

(2) The seller is not entitled to rely on the provisions of the preceding paragraph if he knew of the right or claim of the third party and the nature of it.

Article 44 Notwithstanding the provisions of paragraph (1) of Article 39 and paragraph (1) of Article 43, the buyer may reduce the price in accordance with Article 50 or claim damages, except for loss of profit, if he has a reasonable excuse for his failure to give the required notice.

Section III. Remedies for breach of contract by the seller

Article 45

(1) If the seller fails to perform any of his obligations under the contract or this Convention, the buyer may:

    (a) exercise the rights provided in Articles 46 to 52;

    (b) claim damages as provided in Articles 74 to 77.

(2) The buyer is not deprived of any right he may have to claim damages by exercising his right to other remedies.

(3) No period of grace may be granted to the seller by a court or arbitral tribunal when the buyer resorts to a remedy for breach of contract.

Article 46

(1) The buyer may require performance by the seller of his obligations unless the buyer has resorted to a remedy which is inconsistent with this requirement.

(2) If the goods do not conform with the contract, the buyer may require delivery of substitute goods only if the lack of conformity constitutes a fundamental breach of contract and a request for substitute goods is made either in conjunction with notice given under Article 39 or within a reasonable time thereafter.

(3) If the goods do not conform with the contract, the buyer may require the seller to remedy the lack of conformity by repair, unless this is unreasonable having regard to all the circumstances. A request for repair must be made either in conjunction with notice given under Article 39 or within a reasonable time thereafter.

Article 47

(1) The buyer may fix an additional period of time of reasonable length for performance by the seller of his obligations.

(2) Unless the buyer has received notice from the seller that he will not perform within the period so fixed, the buyer may not, during that period, resort to any remedy for breach of contract. However, the buyer is not deprived thereby of any right he may have to claim damages for delay in performance.

Article 48

(1) Subject to Article 49, the seller may, even after the date for delivery, remedy at his own expense any failure to perform his obligations, if he can do so without unreasonable delay and without causing the buyer unreasonable inconvenience or uncertainty of reimbursement by the seller of expenses advanced by the buyer. However, the buyer retains any right to claim damages as provided for in this Convention.

(2) If the seller requests the buyer to make known whether he will accept performance and the buyer does not comply with the request within a reasonable time, the seller may perform within the time indicated in his request. The buyer may not, during that period of time, resort to any remedy which is inconsistent with performance by the seller.

(3) A notice by the seller that he will perform within a specified period of time is assumed to include a request, under the preceding paragraph, that the buyer make known his decision.

(4) A request or notice by the seller under paragraph (2) or (3) of this article is not effective unless received by the buyer.

Article 49

(1) The buyer may declare the contract avoided:
  (a) if the failure by the seller to perform any of his obligations under the contract or this Convention amounts to a fundamental breach of contract; or
  (b) in case of non-delivery, if the seller does not deliver the goods within the additional period of time fixed by the buyer in accordance with paragraph (1) of Article 47 or declares that he will not deliver within the period so fixed.

(2) However, in cases where the seller has delivered the goods, the buyer loses the right to declare the contract avoided unless he does so:
  (a) in respect of late delivery, within a resonable time after he has become aware that delivery has been made;
  (b) in respect of any breach other than late delivery, within a reasonable time:
    (i) after he knew or ought to have known of the breach;
    (ii) after the expiration of any additional period of time fixed by the buyer in accordance with paragraph (1) of Article 47, or after the seller

has declared that he will not perform his obligations within such an additional period; or
    (iii) after the expiration of any additional period of time indicated by the seller in accordance with paragraph (2) of Article 48, or after the buyer has declared that he will not accept performance.

Article 50
If the goods do not conform with the contract and whether or not the price has already been paid, the buyer may reduce the price in the same proportion as the value that the goods actually delivered had at the time of the delivery bears to the value that conforming goods would have had at that time. However, if the seller remedies any failure to perform his obligations in accordance with Article 37 or Article 48 or if the buyer refuses to accept performance by the seller in accordance with those articles, the buyer may not reduce the price.

Article 51

(1) If the seller delivers only a part of the goods or if only a part of the goods delivered is in conformity with the contract, Articles 46 to 50 apply in respect of the part which is missing or which does not conform.

(2) The buyer may declare the contract avoided in its entirety only if the failure to make delivery completely or in conformity with the contract amounts to a fundamental breach of the contract.

Article 52

(1) If the seller delivers the goods before the date fixed, the buyer may take delivery or refuse to take delivery.

(2) If the seller delivers a quantity of goods greater than that provided for in the contract, the buyer may take delivery or refuse to take delivery of the excess quantity. If the buyer takes delivery of all or part of the excess quantity, he must pay for it at the contract rate.

Chapter III Obligations of the Buyer

Article 53 The buyer must pay the price for the goods and take delivery of them as required by the contract and this Convention.

Section I. Payment of the price

Article 54 The buyer's obligation to pay the price includes taking such steps and complying with such formalities as may be required under the contract or any laws and regulations to enable payment to be made.

Article 55 Where a contract has been validly concluded but does not expressly or implicitly fix or make provision for determining the price, the parties are considered, in the absence of any indication to the contrary, to have impliedly made reference to the price generally charged at the time of the conclusion of the contract for such goods sold under comparable circumstances in the trade concerned.

Article 56 If the price is fixed according to the weight of the goods, in case of doubt it is to be determined by the net weight.

Article 57

(1) If the buyer is not bound to pay the price at any other particular place, he must pay it to the seller:

    (a) at the seller's place of business; or

    (b) if the payment is to be made against the handing over of the goods or of documents, at the place where the handing over takes place.

(2) The seller must bear any increase in the expenses incidental to payment which is caused by a change in his place of business subsequent to the conclusion of the contract.

Article 58

(1) If the buyer is not bound to pay the price at any other specific time, he must pay it when the seller places either the goods or documents controlling their disposition at the buyer's disposal in accordance with the contract and this Convention. The seller may make such payment a condition for handling over the goods or documents.

(2) If the contract involves carriage of the goods, the seller may dispatch the goods on terms whereby the goods, or documents controlling their disposition, will not be handed over to the buyer except against payment of the price.

(3) The buyer is not bound to pay the price until he has had an opportunity to examine the goods, unless the procedures for delivery or payment agreed upon by the parties are inconsistent with his having such an opportunity.

Article 59 The buyer must pay the price on the date fixed by or determinable from the contract and this Convention without the need for any request or compliance with any formality on the part of the seller.

Section II. Taking delivery

Article 60 The buyer's obligation to take delivery consists:

(a) in doing all the acts which could reasonably be expected of him in order to enable the seller to make delivery; and

(b) in taking over the goods.

Section III. Remedies for breach of contract by the buyer

Article 61

(1) If the buyer fails to perform any of his obligations under the contract or this Convention, the seller may:

    (a) exercise the rights provided in Articles 62 to 65;

    (b) claim damages as provided in Articles 74 to 77.

(2) The seller is not deprived of any right he may have to claim damages by exercising his right to other remedies.

(3) No period of grace may be granted to the buyer by a court or arbitral tribunal when the seller resorts to a remedy for breach of contract.

Article 62 The seller may require the buyer to pay the price, take delivery or perform his other obligations, unless the seller has resorted to a remedy which is inconsistent with this requirement.

Article 63

(1) The seller may fix an additional period of time of reasonable length for performance by the buyer of his obligations.

(2) Unless the seller has received notice from the buyer that he will not perform within the period so fixed, the seller may not, during that period, resort to any remedy for breach of contract. However, the seller is not deprived thereby of any right he may have to claim damages for delay in performance.

Article 64

(1) The seller may declare the contract avoided:

    (a) if the failure by the buyer to perform any of his obligations under the contract or this Convention amounts to a fundamental breach of contract; or

    (b) if the buyer does not, within the additional period of time fixed by the seller in accordance with paragraph (1) of Article 63, perform his obligation to pay the price or take delivery of the goods, or if he declares that he will not do so within the period so fixed.

(2) However, in cases where the buyer has paid the price, the seller loses the right to declare the contract avoided unless he does so:

    (a) in respect of late performance by the buyer, before the seller has become aware that performance has been rendered; or

    (b) in respect of any breach other than late performance by the buyer, within a reasonable time:

        (i) after the seller knew or ought to have known of the breach; or

        (ii) after the expiration of any additional period of time fixed by the seller in accordance with paragraph (1) of Article 63, or after the buyer has declared that he will not perform his obligations within such an additional period.

Article 65

(1) If under the contract the buyer is to specify the form, measurement or other features of the goods and he fails to make such specification either on the date agreed upon or within a reasonable time after receipt of a request from the seller, the seller may, without

prejudice to any other rights he may have, make the specification himself in accordance with the requirements of the buyer that may be known to him.

(2) If the seller makes the specification himself, he must inform the buyer of the details thereof and must fix a reasonable time within which the buyer may make a different specification. If, after receipt of such a communication, the buyer fails to do so within the time so fixed, the specification made by the seller is binding.

Chapter IV Passing of Risk

Article 66 Loss of or damage to the goods after the risk has passed to the buyer does not discharge him from his obligation to pay the price, unless the loss or damage is due to an act or omission of the seller.

Article 67

(1) If the contract of sale involves carriage of the goods and the seller is not bound to hand them over at a particular place, the risk passes to the buyer when the goods are handed over to the first carrier for transmission to the buyer in accordance with the contract of sale. If the seller is bound to hand the goods over to a carrier at a particular place, the risk does not pass to the buyer until the goods are handed over to the carrier at that place. The fact that the seller is authorized to retain documents controlling the disposition of the goods does not affect the passage of the risk.

(2) Nevertheless, the risk does not pass to the buyer until the goods are clearly identified to the contract, whether by markings on the goods, by shipping documents, by notice given to the buyer or otherwise.

Article 68 The risk in respect of goods sold in transit passes to the buyer from the time of the conclusion of the contract. However, if the circumstances so indicate, the risk is assumed by the buyer from the time the goods were handed over to the carrier who issued the documents embodying the contract of carriage. Nevertheless, if at the time of the conclusion of the contract of sale the seller knew or ought to have known that the goods had been lost or damaged and did not disclose this to the buyer, the loss or damage is at the risk of the seller.

Article 69

(1) In cases not within Article 67 and 68, the risk passes to the buyer when he takes over the goods or, if he does not do so in due time, from the time when the goods are placed at his disposal and he commits a breach of contract by failing to take delivery.

(2) However, if the buyer is bound to take over the goods at a place other than a place of business of the seller, the risk passes when delivery is due and the buyer is aware of the fact that the goods are placed at his disposal at that place.

(3) If the contract relates to goods not then identified, the goods are considered not to be placed at the disposal of the buyer until they are clearly identified to the contract.

Article 70 If the seller has committed a fundamental breach of contract, Articles 67, 68 and 69 do not impair the remedies available to the buyer on account of the breach.

Chapter V Provisions Common to the Obligations of the Seller and of the Buyer

Section 1. Anticipatory breach and installment contracts

Article 71

(1) A party may suspend the performance of his obligations if, after the conclusion of the contract, it becomes apparent that the other party will not perform a substantial part of his obligations as a result of:

(a) a serious deficiency in his ability to perform or in his creditworthiness; or

(b) his conduct in preparing to perform or in performing the contract.

(2) If the seller has already dispatched the goods before the grounds described in the preceding paragraph become evident, he may prevent the handing over of the goods to the buyer even though the buyer holds a document which entitles him to obtain them. The present paragraph relates only to the rights in the goods as between the buyer and the seller.

(3) A party suspending performance, whether before or after dispatch of the goods, must immediately give notice of the suspension to the other party and must continue with performance if the other party provides adequate assurance of his performance.

Article 72

(1) If prior to the date for performance of the contract it is clear that one of the parties will commit a fundamental breach of contract, the other party may declare the contract avoided.

(2) If time allows, the party intending to declare the contract avoided must give reasonable notice to the other party in order to permit him to provide adequate assurance of his performance.

(3) The requirements of the preceding paragraph do not apply if the other party has declared that he will not perform his obligations.

Article 73

(1) In the case of a contract for delivery of goods by installments, if the failure of one party to perform any of his obligations in respect of any installment constitutes a fundamental breach of contract with respect to that installment, the other party may declare the contract avoided with respect to that installment.

(2) If one party's failure to perform any of his obligations in respect of any installment gives the other party good grounds to conclude that a fundamental breach of contract will occur with respect to future installments, he may declare the contract avoided for the future, provided that he does so within a reasonable time.

(3) A buyer who declares the contract avoided in respect of any delivery may, at the same time, declare it avoided in respect of deliveries already made or of future deliveries if, by reason of their interdependence, those deliveries could not be used for the purpose contemplated by the parties at the time of the conclusion of the contract.

Section II. Damages

Article 74 Damages for breach of contract by one party consist of a sum equal to the loss, including loss of profit, suffered by the other party as a consequence of the breach. Such damages may not exceed the loss which the party in breach foresaw or ought to have foreseen at the time of the conclusion of the contract, in the light of the facts and matters of which he then knew or ought to have known, as a possible consequence of the breach of contract.

Article 75 If the contract is avoided and if, in a reasonable manner and within a reasonable time after avoidance, the buyer has bought goods in replacement or the seller has resold the goods, the party claiming damages may recover the difference between the contract price and the price in the substitute transaction as well as any further damages recoverable under Article 74.

Article 76

(1) If the contract is avoided and there is a current price for the goods, the party claiming damages may, if he has not made a purchase or resale under Article 75, recover the difference between the price fixed by the contract and the current price at the time of avoidance as well as any further damages recoverable under Article 74. If, however, the party claiming damages has avoided the contract after taking over the goods, the current price at the time of such taking over shall be applied instead of the current price at the time of avoidance.

(2) For the purposes of the preceding paragraph, the current price is the price prevailing at the place where delivery of the goods should have been made or, if there is no current price at that place, the price at such other place as serves as a reasonable substitute, making due allowance for differences in the cost of transporting the goods.

Article 77 A party who relies on a breach of contract must take such measures as are reasonable in the circumstances to mitigate the loss, including loss of profit, resulting from the breach. If he fails to take such measures, the

party in breach may claim a reduction in the damages in the amount by which the loss should have been mitigated.

Section III. Interest

Article 78 If a party fails to pay the price or any other sum that is in arrears, the other party is entitled to interest on it, without prejudice to any claim for damages recoverable under Article 74.

Section IV. Exemptions

Article 79

(1) A party is not liable for a failure to perform any of his obligations if he proves that the failure was due to an impediment beyond his control and that he could not reasonably be expected to have taken the impediment into account at the time of the conclusion of the contract or to have avoided or overcome it or its consequences.

(2) If the party's failure is due to the failure by a third person whom he has engaged to perform the whole or a part of the contract, that party is exempt from liability only if:

(a) he is exempt under the preceding paragraph; and

(b) the person whom he has so engaged would be so exempt if the provisions of that paragraph were applied to him.

(3) The exemption provided by this article has effect for the period during which the impediment exists.

(4) The party who fails to perform must give notice to the other party of the impediment and its effect on his ability to perform. If the notice is not received by the other party within a reasonable time after the party who fails to perform knew or ought to have known of the impediment, he is liable for damages resulting from such non-receipt.

(5) Nothing in this article prevents either party from exercising any right other than to claim damages under this Convention.

Article 80 A party may not rely on a failure of the other party to perform, to the extent that such failure was caused by the first party's act or omission.

Section V. Effects of avoidance

Article 81

(1) Avoidance of the contract releases both parties from their obligations under it, subject to any damages which may be due. Avoidance does not affect any provision of the contract for the settlement of disputes or any other provision of the contract governing the rights and obligations of the parties consequent upon the avoidance of the contract.

(2) A party who has performed the contract either wholly or in part may claim restitution from the other party

of whatever the first party has supplied or paid under the contract. If both parties are bound to make restitution, they must do so concurrently.

Article 82

(1) The buyer loses the right to declare the contract avoided or to require the seller to deliver substitute goods if it is impossible for him to make restitution of the goods substantially in the condition in which he received them.

(2) The preceding paragraph does not apply:

(a) if the impossibility of making restitution of the goods or of making restitution of the goods substantially in the condition in which the buyer received them is not due to his act or omission;

(b) if the goods or part of the goods have perished or deteriorated as a result of the examination provided for in Article 38; or

(c) if the goods or part of the goods have been sold in the normal course of business or have been consumed or transformed by the buyer in the course of normal use before he discovered or ought to have discovered the lack of conformity.

Article 83

A buyer who has lost the right to declare the contract avoided or to require the seller to deliver substitute goods in accordance with Article 82 retains all other remedies under the contract and this Convention.

Article 84

(1) If the seller is bound to refund the price, he must also pay interest on it, from the date on which the price was paid.

(2) The buyer must account to the seller for all benefits which he has derived from the goods or part of them:

(a) if he must make restitution of the goods or part of them; or

(b) if it is impossible for him to make restitution of all or part of the goods or to make restitution of all or part of the goods substantially in the condition in which he received them, but he has nevertheless declared the contract avoided or required the seller to deliver substitute goods.

Section VI. Preservation of the goods

Article 85

If the buyer is in delay in taking delivery of the goods or, where payment of the price and delivery of the goods are to be made concurrently, if he fails to pay the price, and the seller is either in possession of the goods or otherwise able to control their disposition, the seller must take such steps as are reasonable in the circumstances to preserve them. He is entitled to retain them until he has been reimbursed his reasonable expenses by the buyer.

Article 86

(1) If the buyer has received the goods and intends to exercise any right under the contract or this Convention to reject them, he must take such steps to preserve them as are reasonable in the circumstances. He is entitled to retain them until he has been reimbursed his reasonable expenses by the seller.

(2) If goods dispatched to the buyer have been placed at his disposal at their destination and he exercises the right to reject them, he must take possession of them on behalf of the seller, provided that this can be done without payment of the price and without unreasonable inconvenience or unreasonable expense. This provision does not apply if the seller or a person authorized to take charge of the goods on his behalf is present at the destination. If the buyer takes possession of the goods under this paragraph, his rights and obligations are governed by the preceding paragraph.

Article 87

A party who is bound to take steps to preserve the goods may deposit them in a warehouse of a third person at the expense of the other party provided that the expense incurred is not unreasonable.

Article 88

(1) A party who is bound to preserve the goods in accordance with Article 85 or 86 may sell them by any appropriate means if there has been an unreasonable delay by the other party in taking possession of the goods or in taking them back or in paying the price or the cost of preservation, provided that reasonable notice of the intention to sell has been given to the other party.

(2) If the goods are subject to rapid deterioration or their preservation would involve unreasonable expense, a party who is bound to preserve the goods in accordance with Article 85 or 86 must take reasonable measures to sell them. To the extent possible he must give notice to the other party of his intention to sell.

(3) A party selling the goods has the right to retain out of the proceeds of sale an amount equal to the reasonable expenses of preserving the goods and of selling them. He must account to the other party for the balance.

Part IV Final Provisions

Article 89

The Secretary-General of the United Nations is hereby designated as the depositary for this Convention.

Article 90

This Convention does not prevail over any international agreement which has already been or may be entered into and which contains provisions concerning the matters governed by this Convention, provided that the parties have their places of business in States parties to such agreement.

Article 91

(1) This Convention is open for signature at the concluding meeting of the United Nations Conference on Contracts for the International Sale of Goods and will remain open for signature by all States at the Headquarters of the United Nations, New York, until 30 September 1981.

(2) This Convention is subject to ratification, acceptance or approval by the signatory States.

(3) This Convention is open for accession by all States which are not signatory States as from the date it is open for signature.

(4) Instruments of ratification, acceptance, approval and accession are to be deposited with the Secretary-General of the United Nations.

Article 92

(1) A Contracting State may declare at the time of signature, ratification, acceptance, approval or accession that it will not be bound by Part II of this Convention or that it will not be bound by Part III of this Convention.

(2) A Contracting State which makes a declaration in accordance with the preceding paragraph in respect of Part II or Part III of this Convention is not to be considered a Contracting State within paragraph (1) of Article 1 of this Convention in respect of matters governed by the Part to which the declaration applies.

Article 93

(1) If a Contracting State has two or more territorial units in which, according to its constitution, different systems of law are applicable in relation to the matters dealt with in this Convention, it may, at the time of signature, ratification, acceptance, approval or accession, declare that this Convention is to extend to all its territorial units or only to one or more of them, and may amend its declaration by submitting another declaration at any time.

(2) These declarations are to be notified to the depositary and are to state expressly the territorial units to which the Convention extends.

(3) If, by virtue of a declaration under this article, this Convention extends to one or more but not all of the territorial units of a Contracting State, and if the place of business of a party is located in that State, this place of business, for the purposes of this Convention, is considered not to be in a Contracting State, unless it is in a territorial unit to which the Convention extends.

(4) If a Contracting State makes no declaration under paragraph (1) of this article, the Convention is to extend to all territorial units of that State.

Article 94

(1) Two or more Contracting States which have the same or closely related legal rules on matters governed by this Convention may at any time declare that the Convention is not to apply to contracts of sale or to their formation where the parties have their places of business in those States. Such declarations may be made jointly or by reciprocal unilateral declarations.

(2) A Contracting State which has the same or closely related legal rules on matters governed by this Convention as one or more non-Contracting States may at any time declare that the Convention is not to apply to contracts of sale or to their formation where the parties have their places of business in those States.

(3) If a State which is the object of a declaration under the preceding paragraph subsequently becomes a Contracting State, the declaration made will, as from the date on which the Convention enters into force in respect of the new Contracting State, have the effect of a declaration made under paragraph (1), provided that the new Contracting State joins in such declaration or makes a reciprocal unilateral declaration.

Article 95
Any State may declare at the time of the deposit of its instrument of ratification, acceptance, approval or accession that it will not be bound by subparagraph (1)(b) of Article 1 of this Convention. [The United States has made such reservation.]

Article 96
A Contracting State whose legislation requires contracts of sale to be concluded in or evidenced by writing may at any time make a declaration in accordance with Article 12 that any provision of Article 11, Article 29, or Part II of this Convention, that allows a contract of sale or its modification or termination by agreement or any offer, acceptance, or other indication of intention to be made in any form other than in writing, does not apply where any party has his place of business in that State.

Article 97

(1) Declarations made under this Convention at the time of signature are subject to confirmation upon ratification, acceptance or approval.

(2) Declarations and confirmations of declarations are to be in writing and be formally notified to the depositary.

(3) A declaration takes effect simultaneously with the entry into force of this Convention in respect of the State concerned. However, a declaration of which the depositary receives formal notification after such entry into force takes effect on the first day of the month following the expiration of six months after the date of its receipt by the depositary. Reciprocal unilateral declarations under Article 94 take effect on the first day of the month following the expiration of six months after the receipt of the latest declaration by the depositary.

(4) Any State which makes a declaration under this Convention may withdraw it at any time by a formal notification in writing addressed to the depositary. Such withdrawal is to take effect on the first day of the

month following the expiration of six months after the date of the receipt of the notification by the depositary.

(5) A withdrawal of a declaration made under Article 94 renders inoperative, as from the date on which the withdrawal takes effect, any reciprocal declaration made by another State under that article.

Article 98 No reservations are permitted except those expressly authorized in this Convention.

Article 99

(1) This Convention enters into force, subject to the provisions of paragraph (6) of this article, on the first day of the month following the expiration of twelve months after the date of deposit of the tenth instrument of ratification, acceptance, approval or accession, including an instrument which contains a declaration made under Article 92.

(2) When a State ratifies, accepts, approves or accedes to this Convention after the deposit of the tenth instrument of ratification, acceptance, approval or accession, this Convention, with the exception of the Part excluded, enters into force in respect of that State, subject to the provisions of paragraph (6) of this article, on the first day of the month following the expiration of twelve months after the date of the deposit of its instrument of ratification, acceptance, approval or accession.

(3) A State which ratifies, accepts, approves or accedes to this Convention and is a party to either or both the Convention relating to a Uniform Law on the Formation of Contracts for the International Sale of Goods done at The Hague on 1 July 1964 (1964 Hague Formation Convention) and the Convention relating to a Uniform Law on the International Sale of Goods done at The Hague on 1 July 1964 (1964 Hague Sales Convention) shall at the same time denounce, as the case may be, either or both the 1964 Hague Sales Convention and the 1964 Hague Formation Convention by notifying the Government of the Netherlands to that effect.

(4) A State party to the 1964 Hague Sales Convention which ratifies, accepts, approves or accedes to the present Convention and declares or has declared under Article 92 that it will not be bound by Part II of this Convention shall at the time of ratification, acceptance, approval or accession denounce the 1964 Hague Sales Convention by notifying the Government of the Netherlands to that effect.

(5) A State party to the 1964 Hague Formation Convention which ratifies, accepts, approves or accedes to the present Convention and declares or has declared under Article 92 that it will not be bound by Part III of this Convention shall at the time of ratification, acceptance, approval or accession denounce the 1964 Hague Formation Convention by notifying the Government of the Netherlands to that effect.

(6) For the purpose of this article, ratifications, acceptances, approvals and accessions in respect of this Convention by States parties to the 1964 Hague Formation Convention or to the 1964 Hague Sales Convention shall not be effective until such denunciations as may be required on the part of those States in respect of the latter two Conventions have themselves become effective. The depositary of this Convention shall consult with the Government of the Netherlands, as the depositary of the 1964 Conventions, so as to ensure necessary co-ordination in this respect.

Article 100

(1) This Convention applies to the formation of a contract only when the proposal for concluding the contract is made on or after the date when the Convention enters into force in respect of the Contracting States referred to in subparagraph (1)(a) or the Contracting States referred to in subparagraph (1)(b) of Article 1.

(2) This Convention applies only to contracts concluded on or after the date when the Convention enters into force in respect of the Contracting States referred to in subparagraph (1)(a) or the Contracting State referred to in subparagraph (1)(b) of Article 1.

Article 101

(1) A Contracting State may denounce this Convention, or Part II or Part III of the Convention, by a formal notification in writing addressed to the depositary.

(2) The denunciation takes effect on the first day of the month following the expiration of twelve months after the notification is received by the depositary. Where a longer period for the denunciation to take effect is specified in the notification, the denunciation takes effect upon the expiration of such longer period after the notification is received by the depositary.

DONE at Vienna, this day of eleventh day of April, one thousand nine hundred and eighty, in a single original, of which the Arabic, Chinese, English, French, Russian and Spanish texts are equally authentic.

IN WITNESS WHEREOF the undersigned plenipotentiaries, being duly authorized by their respective Governments, have signed this Convention.

Glossary

abandoned In contract law, the condition that exists when a minor has left home and given up all rights to parental support.

abandoned property Property that has been discarded by the owner without the intent to reclaim ownership of it. Courts require clear and convincing evidence of both the desertion by the owner and the owner's intent never to return.

abandonment of contractual obligations The situation that exists when a party to a contract stops performance once it has begun.

abuse of discretion The determination that the judge in the lower court has misused his or her authority.

abuse of process The use of a legal procedure for a purpose other than that for which it is legitimately intended.

acceleration A provision in a mortgage agreement that allows the mortgagee to demand the entire balance due when the mortgagor misses a single installment payment.

acceptance A promise or act on the part of an offeree indicating a willingness to be bound by the terms and conditions contained in an offer. Also, the acknowledgment of the drawee that binds the drawee to the terms of a draft.

acceptor A drawee of a draft who has promised to honor the draft as presented by signing it on its face.

accommodation party A person who signs an instrument in any capacity for the purpose of lending his or her name to another party to the instrument. That person then assumes the same liability as the marker.

accord The implied or expressed acceptance of less than what the creditor billed the debtor.

accord and satisfaction An agreement (accord) whereby a creditor accepts as full payment an amount that is less than the amount due.

accountant A professional who can plan, direct, and evaluate a client's financial affairs.

accounting A statement detailing the financial transactions of a business and the status of its assets.

acknowledgment The official recognition by a notary public that another's signature was made by that party's free will. The acknowledgment is accomplished when the notary has signed the document and added the official seal to it.

active data Data in a computer system that are actually being used at the present time.

active fraud A false statement made or an action actually taken by one party with the intent to deceive a second party and thus lead that second party into a deceptively based agreement.

activist agencies Agencies that use their regulatory powers to advance social agendas that are technically outside their legislative authority.

actual authority rule A rule that states a manager may be liable for exceeding his or her authority if the corporation is harmed as a result.

actual cause In tort law, the relationship between the unreasonable conduct and the injury to the innocent party, whether the injury was or was not foreseeable. Actual cause is also referred to as cause-in-fact.

actual damages A sum of money equal to the real financial loss suffered by an injured party. Also called *compensatory damages.*

actual eviction An eviction in which the tenant is physically deprived of the leasehold.

actual malice The legal test used by the courts to determine defamation against a public official or a public figure. The actual malice test requires the public official or public figure to prove not only that the statement was false, negative, and communicated to a third party, but also that it was made with the knowledge that it was false or with a reckless disregard for its truth or falsity.

actual malice test A defense against libel cases that states public officials must prove not only that the statement was false, negative, and communicated to a third party, but was also made with actual malice.

add-on coverage In insurance law, optional coverage, such as personal injury insurance, that allows a driver to receive payments without having to determine fault.

adhesion contract A contract drawn by one party that must be accepted on a take-it-or-leave-it basis.

adjustable rate mortgage (ARM) In property law, a variable or changing rate of interest in a mortgage agreement that fluctuates based on the index (the bank's prime rate or the Federal Reserve's discount rate, and so on) to which the mortgage is tied.

administrative law That body of law, including decrees and legal decisions, generated by administrative agencies.

administrator (male); administratrix (female) A person appointed by the court to do the work of an executor if none is named in a will or if the executor either refuses to perform or is incapable of performing the duties.

admiralty court In the historical development of the law merchant, a local court established by a coastal city, usually in Italy, to handle commercial disputes regarding goods carried as cargo by ships docked at the city's port.

ADR contract clause A clause that specifies that the parties to the agreement have promised to use an alternative dispute resolution technique when a disagreement arises rather than litigating the issue.

advance directives Written statement in which people gives instructions for their future medical care.

adversarial system The system on which the American legal process is built. An orderly and aggressive way to settle disputes in which attorneys for each side attempt to persuade a judge or jury of the veracity of his or her case.

adverse opinion An auditor's opinion that states that deviations from generally accepted accounting principles are so serious that an unqualified opinion is impossible and a qualified opinion is not justified.

adverse possession Title to real property obtained by taking actual possession of the property openly, notoriously, exclusively, under a claim of right, and continuously for a period of time set by state statute.

affirmance See *ratification*.

affirmative action A policy designed to reduce the effects of past discrimination.

affirmative defense A set of circumstances that indicates that a defendant should not be held liable, even if the plaintiff proves all of the facts in a complaint.

agency A legal agreement between two persons, whereby one is designated the agent of the other.

agency coupled with an interest An irrevocable agency agreement in which the agent is given an interest in the subject matter of the agency. Also called *irrevocable agency*.

agent A person authorized to act on behalf of another and subject to the other's control in dealing with third parties.

aggravated arson In criminal law, using fire or explosives to create a substantial risk of harm to an individual or an occupied structure, often also including the hiring of another person to carry out the offense.

aggravated burglary In criminal law, gaining unlawful entry to an occupied building by using a deadly weapon, inflicting actual harm, attempting to harm, or threatening to harm, with the intent to commit a crime.

aggravated murder In criminal law, killing someone with premeditation or with prior calculation and design, or while committing a serious felony such as rape, robbery, or kidnapping.

aggravated robbery In criminal law, attempting to commit or actually committing theft using a deadly weapon or a dangerous ordnance, or doing the same by inflicting harm on the victim.

aggregate theory A theory in partnership law that holds that a partnership is actually a conglomeration of the partners rather than a separate legal person with its own legal identity.

agreements in restraint of trade Agreements that remove competition, deny to the public the services it would otherwise have, or result in higher prices and hardship.

algorithm A series of mathematical steps that, if followed properly, will reach a desired goal.

alien corporation A corporation that though incorporated in a foreign country does business in the United States.

allonge A strip of paper attached to a negotiable instrument for the writing of indorsements.

alter ego In corporate law, a subsidiary corporation set up by a parent corporation to do the bidding of the original parent corporation.

alternative dispute resolution (ADR) A process that occurs whenever individuals attempt to resolve a disagreement by stepping outside the usual adversarial system and applying creative settlement techniques, many of which have fact finding and the discovery of truth as their goal.

alternative payment system A computer based payment system such as Pay-Pal that is not card dependent.

American Law Institute (ALI) test A test under which a criminal defendant will be judged not guilty by reason of insanity "as a result of mental disease or defect he lacks substantial capacity either to appreciate the criminality of his conduct or to conform his conduct to the requirements of the law."

annual percentage rate (APR) The true rate of interest on a loan.

annuity A guaranteed retirement income.

anomalous indorsement An indorsement made by an accommodation party.

answer A defendant's official response to a complaint.

antenuptial agreement In contract law, a written agreement between two people planning marriage, who agree in writing to change the property rights they possess by law.

anticipatory breach A breach that occurs when a party to a contract either expresses or clearly implies an intention not to perform the contract even before being required to act. Also called *constructive breach*.

Antitrust Procedures and Penalty Act In federal antitrust law, a federal statute that regulates the Department of Justice's antitrust consent decrees.

apparent authority An accountability doctrine whereby a principal, by virtue of words or actions, leads a third party to believe that an agent has authority but no such authority was intended. Also called *ostensible authority* and *agency by estoppel*.

appeal The referral of a case to a higher court for review.

appeal bond The payment of a set sum of money into a protected account to secure the payment of that money to the plaintiff should the defendant be defeated.

appellate jurisdiction The power of a court to review a case for errors.

arbitration The process by which an outside party settles a dispute between two other parties.

arbitrator The third party in the arbitration procedure whose job is to settle the dispute.

arraignment A formal court proceeding during which the defendant, after hearing the indictment or information read, pleads either guilty or not guilty.

arson The willful or malicious act of causing the burning of another's property.

Articles of Confederation The first constitution of the United States; replaced by the U.S. Constitution in 1787.

articles of incorporation A written application to a state for permission to incorporate.

articles of organization The written application to the state for permission to form a limited liability company.

articles of partnership A written agreement that establishes a partnership.

assault An attempt to commit a battery.

asset acquisition The purchase of all the property of a corporation by another corporation.

assign To transfer property by sale, mortgage, pledge, or otherwise.

asset-backed securities In property law, lending money by establishing a security interest in goods such as cars, furniture, boats, and so on.

assignee A person to whom an assignment is made.

assignment The transfer of a contract right from one person to another.

assignor A person who assigns rights or delegates duties under an assignment.

associative corporativism The process of doing business as a self-governing business association, that is, as a corporation. Also known as *corporativism*.

assume the mortgage An agreement whereby the buyer of real property already mortgaged agrees to pay the mortgage.

assumption of the risk A defense against negligence that states the victim voluntarily exposed him- or herself to a known risk.

ATM card A card used together with a personal identification number (PIN) to gain access to an automatic teller machine (ATM).

attachment The act of taking a person's property and bringing it into the custody of law.

attorney-client privilege The guarantee that information that passes between clients and attorneys remains secret.

auction A sale that is open to the public, during which potential buyers compete for the right to purchase certain items by placing higher and higher bids until the highest bid is reached and the auctioneer accepts on behalf of the seller

auction with reserve An auction at which the auctioneer has the right to withdraw goods and not sell them if acceptable bids are not made.

auction without reserve An auction at which the auctioneer cannot withdraw goods unless no bid is made within a reasonable time.

audit An examination of the financial records of an organization to determine whether those records are a fair representation of the actual financial health of the institution.

Auditing Standards Board A group of experts established by the American Institute of Certified Public Accountants (AICPA) to set up auditing standards.

auditor The accountant who examines the financial records of an organization to determine whether those records are a fair representation of the actual financial health of the institution.

authenticate (*a*) to sign; or (*b*) with the intent to sign a record, otherwise to execute or adopt an electronic symbol, sound, message, or process referring to, attached to, included in, or logically associated or linked with, that record.

automatic stay A self-operating postponement of collection proceedings against a debtor who has filed a petition for bankruptcy.

automatic suspension A court order that stops a debtor's creditors from making any further moves to collect the money that the debtor owes them.

back-up data Data associated with a computer system that have been duplicated for safekeeping at another location.

bailee The person to whom personal property is transferred under a contract of bailment.

bailment The transfer of possession and control of personal property to another with the intent that the same property will be returned later.

bailment by necessity A bailment that arises when a customer must give up possession of property for the benefit of both parties; for example, when one purchases a suit or dress and is required to give up possession of one's own property while being fitted.

bailment for the sole benefit of the bailee A bailment in which the bailee receives all the benefits of the transaction.

bailment for the sole benefit of the bailor A bailment in which the bailor receives all the benefits of the transaction.

bailor The person who transfers personal property under a contract of bailment.

bait-and-switch confidence game An illegal promotional practice in which a seller attracts consumers by promoting a product (bait) that he or she does not intend to sell and then directs the consumers' attention to a higher-priced product (switch).

balloon payment A large final payment on a mortgage that has relatively low fixed payments during the life of the mortgage.

balloon-payment mortgage A mortgage that has relatively low fixed payments during the life of the mortgage followed by one large final (balloon) payment.

bank draft A check drawn by one bank on another bank in which it has funds on deposit in favor of a third person, the payee. Also called *teller's check*.

bankruptcy The legal process by which the assets of a debtor are sold to pay off creditors so that the debtor can make a fresh start financially.

bankruptcy trustee A person appointed by the court who is charged with the responsibility of liquidating the assets of the debtor for the benefit of all interested parties.

bargain-and-sale deed A deed that transfers title to real property but contains no warranties. This type of deed is not valid without consideration.

bargained-for exchange In reference to agreements, when a promise is made in exchange for another promise, in exchange for an act, or in exchange for a forbearance to act.

bargaining unit Employees joined together for the purpose of collective bargaining.

battered spouse syndrome A defense to criminal liability available to defendants if they can prove that they believed the only way to escape death or severe bodily injury was to use force against their tormentors.

battery The unlawful touching of another person.

bearer A person who is in possession of a negotiable instrument that is payable to the "bearer" or "cash" or that has been indorsed in blank.

bearer paper An instrument payable to bearer or cash that may be negotiated by delivery only.

beneficiary A third party receiving benefits from a contract made between two other parties. Also, the person named in an insurance policy to receive benefits paid by the insurer in event of a claim.

bequest Personal property left in a will. Also called *legacy*.

best evidence rule The legal rule that holds that the courts generally accept into evidence only the original of a writing, not a copy.

best-price rule Rules that prohibit suitors from offering different prices to different shareholders during a tender offer process.

bilateral contract A contract in which both parties make promises.

bilateral mistake In contract law, a mistake made by both parties to a contract. Bilateral mistake allows rescission by either party. Also called *mutual mistake*.

bill of exchange See *draft*.

bill of lading A document evidencing the receipt of goods for shipment and issued by a person engaged in the business of transporting or forwarding goods.

bill of sale A written statement evidencing the transfer of personal property from one person to another.

binder An oral or a written memorandum of an agreement for insurance intended to provide temporary insurance coverage until the policy is formally accepted.

binding precedent A previous case that a particular court must follow.

blank indorsement An indorsement made by a signature alone, with no particular indorsee, written on a negotiable instrument.

blue laws State statutes and local ordinances that regulate the making and performing of contracts on Sunday.

bodily injury liability insurance A type of automobile insurance that covers the risk of bodily injury or death to pedestrians and to the occupants of other cars arising from the negligent operation of the insured's motor vehicle.

bond A certificate of indebtedness that obligates a government or corporation to pay the bondholder a fixed rate of interest on the principal at regular intervals and to pay the principal on a stated maturity date. Also, a promise by the executor or administrator (and the sureties, if any) of a will to pay the amount of the bond to the probate court if the duties of the position are not faithfully performed.

bot A type of cyberagent that searches cyberspace for the lowest price in a contract, sifts through the net for the best accommodations, hunts cyberspace for the most economical plan, or spontaneously responds to a bidding process. Also known as *robot, shopping bot, cyberbot,* and *e-bot.*

boycott A concerted refusal to have dealings with someone to force the acceptance of certain conditions.

breach of contract The failure of one of the parties to a contract to do what was previously agreed upon.

breaking and entering In criminal law, using force, deceit, or cunning to trespass into an unoccupied building with the intent to commit a felony.

bribery The act of offering, giving, receiving, or soliciting something of value to influence official action or the discharge of a public duty.

bright-line test Test used by the courts that establishes violations of the best-price rule occur only during the actual tender offer.

bulk transfer Any transfer of a major party of the materials, supplies, merchandise, or other inventory of an enterprise that is not in the ordinary course of the transferor's business.

burglary The break-in of a dwelling or building for the purpose of carrying out a felony.

business compulsion See *economic duress.*

business judgment rule The rule that a corporate manager's decisions will not be interfered with by a court as long as the decision was made with due care, is in good faith, is lawful, and is in the best interest of the corporation.

business system Until recently, business systems were considered unpatentable because they were not a "process, machine, or composition of matter." Recently, however, some computerized business systems have been patented if they consist of some nonobvious, new, and useful feature not known or understood before the invention of this system.

buyer in the ordinary course of business A person who in good faith and without knowledge that the sale is in violation of ownership rights or security interests of a third party buys goods in ordinary course from a person in the business of selling goods of that kind, not including a pawnbroker.

Buyer's Guide A window sticker that is required by the Federal Trade Commission Act to be placed in the window of each used car offered for sale by a used car dealer. The sticker discloses the warranties that are made with the sale of the car and other consumer protection information.

bylaws Rules that guide a corporation's day-to-day internal affairs. Also known as regulations.

c.f. Cost and freight. Terms instructing a carrier to collect the cost of goods shipped and freight charges.

c.i.f. Cost, insurance, and freight. Terms instructing a carrier to collect the cost of goods shipped, insurance, and freight charges.

c.o.d. Cash on delivery. Instructs a carrier to retain goods until he or she has collected the costs of the goods.

Can Spam Act A federal law designed to reduce the use of unsolicited email, commonly known as spam, on the Internet.

cancellation form Under the Federal Trade Commission's Cooling-Off Rule, a document that can be filled out to terminate an order for consumer goods or services made at the buyer's home for consumer goods or services valued at $25 or more.

capacity In contract law, the legal ability to enter into a contractual relationship.

capital The money and property that a business needs to operate.

capital contribution The sum contributed by a business partner as a permanent investment in the business. It is then considered to be the property of the partnership.

carrier A business that undertakes to transport persons, goods, or both.

case in chief The collection of evidence that will prove a plaintiff's version of case to a jury.

case trustee A person appointed by a bankruptcy court to meet with creditors and report whether the case should proceed.

cash dividend Dividend paid to shareholders in the form of cash.

cashier's check A check drawn by a bank upon its own funds.

cause in fact In tort law, the relationship between the unreasonable conduct and the injury to the innocent party, whether the injury was or was not foreseeable. Cause in fact is also referred to as actual cause.

certificate of authority A document that grants a foreign corporation permission to do business within another state.

certificate of deposit (CD) An acknowledgment by a bank of the receipt of money and a promise to pay the money back on the due date, usually with interest.

certificate of incorporation A corporation's official authorization to do business in a state. Also called *charter* or *corporate charter*.

certification authority (CA) It is the job of the CA to provide businesses with digital signatures and to make certain that those signatures are kept current.

certified check A check that has been marked, or certified, by the bank on which it was drawn, guaranteeing payment to the holder.

certified public accountant (CPA) An accountant who has met certain age, character, education, experience, and testing requirements.

chattels Property that has substance and that can be touched.

check A draft drawn on a bank and payable on demand.

Check 21 Act A law that makes check clearing much quicker by the use of a *substitute check* in place of the original check for electronic check processing.

chemical abuse The use of drugs or alcohol to such an extent that a person's judgment is impaired or his or her physical body is harmed.

chemical dependency The state a person reaches when she or he can no longer function normally without regularly consuming drugs or alcohol.

chose in action Evidence of the right to property but not the property itself.

civil litigation The process of bringing a case to court to enforce a right.

civilization A group of people in a series of different nation-states that share certain common characteristics, including history, language, religion, traditions, beliefs, and sometimes blood.

class-action lawsuit A lawsuit that is brought by one or more plaintiffs on behalf of a class of persons.

Clean Air Act In environmental law, a federal statute designed to limit pollution from vehicles and from stationary sources such factories and manufacturing centers.

Clean Water Act In environmental law, a federal statute that sets requirements for limiting the pollution of the nation's water sources according to a schedule, based on the most effective technology currently available.

clearly erroneous standard The determination that the decision made in the lower court was undeniably wrong, given the facts and evidence in the case.

click-on acceptance A method of acceptance used in Internet contracts in which a party manifests acceptance by clicking on an icon on the computer screen that states that he or she agrees to the terms of the contract.

close corporation A corporation whose shares of stock and managerial control are closely held by fewer than 50 shareholders (often members of the same family) or by one person.

close-end credit Credit that is extended only for a specific amount of money, such as to buy a car or other expensive item.

closed shop A place of employment in which the employer, by agreement, hires only union members in good standing.

code A compilation of all the statutes of a particular state or of the federal government.

Code of Federal Regulations (CFR) Annual listing of finalized federal rules and regulations.

Code of Professional Ethics A set of rules established by the American Institute of Certified Public Accountants that outlines rules that govern the ethical conduct of accountants.

codicil A formal document used to supplement or change an existing will.

coinsurance An insurance policy provision under which the insurer and the insured share costs, after the deductible is met, according to a specific formula.

collateral The property that is subject to a security interest.

collateral contract In contract law, a contract by which one party agrees to pay the debt of another party if that party fails to meet that obligation.

collecting bank Any bank handling an item for collection except the payor bank.

collective bargaining A good faith meeting between representatives of employees and employers to discuss the terms and conditions of employment.

collective bargaining agreement A contract negotiated by an employer and a labor union that covers all issues related to employment.

collision insurance A type of automobile insurance that protects the insured against any loss arising from damage to the insured's automobile caused by accidental collision with another object or with any part of the roadbed.

comaker A person obligated, along with at least one other person, as a payor on a promissory note.

commerce Trade among the several states or between any foreign country and any state or territory.

commerce clause The clause in the U.S. Constitution that gives the federal government the power to regulate business among the states.

commercial impracticability A doctrine under which the courts may excuse the performance of one party to a contract because an unforeseen and very severe hardship has arisen that would place an enormous amount of hardship on that party.

commercial unit A single whole for the purpose of sale, the division of which impairs its character or value on the market, such as a set of furniture.

commingled Mixed together, as in goods stored at a warehouse or funds in a bank account.

common carrier A company that transports goods or persons for compensation and offers its facilities to the general public without discrimination. Compare *contract carrier.*

common law The body of recorded decisions that courts refer to and rely upon when making later legal decisions.

common stock The most usual type of corporate stock. It carries with it all the risks of the business and does not guarantee its holder the right to profits.

community property Property that is acquired by the personal effects of either spouse during marriage and which, by law, belongs to both spouses equally.

comparative negligence A form of contributory negligence that requires the court to assign damages according to the degree of fault of each party.

compelling interest The inescapable, overriding interest that the government of a nation or state has in a particular issue, such as the state or the nation's interest in the lives of its own citizens, which the government cannot ignore, and which it must pursue and protect at

the risk of losing its legitimacy as the proper governing body of that state or nation.

compensatory damages See *actual damages.*

competent authority The requirement that just war may be declared and run only by legitimately recognized nation-states.

competitive impact statement (CIS) In antitrust law, a decree that clarifies any potential antitrust problems inherent within a corporate expansion and the solutions to those problems.

complaint A legal document filed by a plaintiff to begin a lawsuit. The complaint sets forth the names of the parties, the facts in the case, the alleged legal violations by the defendant, and the relief sought by the plaintiff.

complete performance In contract law, the situation that exists when both parties to a contract have fully accomplished every term, condition, and promise to which they agreed.

comprehensive coverage A type of automobile insurance that provides protection against loss when the insured's car is damaged or destroyed by fire, lightning, flood, hail, windstorm, riot, vandalism, or theft.

computer firmware Computer software that is written to be used with only one type or brand of computer.

computer hardware The actual device known as a computer and its components, including the keyboard, screen, disk drive, and printer.

computer information Information in a form directly capable of being processed or used by, or obtained from or through, a computer.

computer package The combination of the computer hardware and the computer software when sold together.

computer program The instructions that tell the computer hardware what to do and when to do it.

computer software The card, tape, disk, or silicon chip that contains the computer program.

concealment In insurance, the intentional withholding of a fact that would be of material importance to the insurer's decision to issue a policy. In contract law, the intentional withholding of a material fact that the other party relies upon and which results in financial harm to the innocent party. See also *passive fraud.*

condemnation See *eminent domain.*

condition concurrent A condition in a contract that requires both parties to perform at the same time.

902   Glossary

condition precedent In contract law, an act or promise that must take place or be fulfilled before the other party is obligated to perform his or her part of the agreement.

condition subsequent A condition in a contract in which the parties agree that the contract will be terminated depending on a prescribed event occurring or not occurring.

conditional indorsement An indorsement that makes the rights of the indorsee subject to the happening of a certain event or condition.

confidential relationship A relationship of trust and dependence between persons in a continued relationship, as between doctor and patient, between parent and child, or between a caretaker and a dependent person.

confirmation In bankruptcy law, the official approval of a reorganization plan.

conforming goods Goods that are in accordance with the obligations under the contract.

conglomerate expansion The joining of two companies that were not in competition with each other either because they dealt in different products or services or because they operated in different geographical areas.

consensual A freely given agreement to act.

consent decree Agreements created by the Department of Justice to help parties negotiate a legal merger.

consent order Under the Federal Trade Commission Act, an order under which a company agrees to stop a disputed practice without necessarily admitting that the practice violated the law.

consequential damages Losses that do not flow directly and immediately from an act but only from some of the consequences or results of the act.

consideration In contract law, the mutual promise to exchange benefits and detriments between parties.

consignee One to whom goods are entrusted under a *consignment contract* for the purpose of selling those goods.

consignment contract A type of mutual benefit bailment in which the *consignor* entrusts goods to the *consignee* for the purpose of selling them.

consignor One who entrusts goods under a *consignment contract* to a *consignee* for the purpose of selling them.

consolidation The joining of two corporations.

conspiracy The crime that occurs when people get together with others to talk about, plan, or agree to the commission of a crime.

constitution The basic law of a nation or state.

constitutional law That body of law that involves a constitution and its interpretation.

construction loan A loan for the building of a home that permits staggered payments that fall due at various stages in the building process.

constructive discharge Discriminatory action whereby an employee is demoted to a job with less pay, authority, or poorer working conditions than the job that person previously held or is subjected to supervisory harassment.

constructive eviction An eviction that occurs by the act of the landlord depriving the tenant of something of a substantial nature that was called for under the lease.

consumer Someone who buys or leases real estate, goods, or services for personal, family, or household purposes.

consumer goods Goods normally used for personal, family, or household purposes.

consumer products Tangible personal property normally used for personal, family, or household purposes.

continuity of existence A concept promoted by the Revised Uniform Partnership Act that permits a partnership to continue to operate as an entity even after individual partners are no longer associated with it.

continuity plan In sales law, an arrangement by which the seller of goods ships the goods to the subscriber on a regular basis without first sending an announcement of the upcoming delivery.

contract An agreement based on mutual promises between two or more competent parties to do or to refrain from doing some particular thing that is neither illegal nor impossible. The agreement results in an obligation or a duty that can be enforced in a court of law.

contract carrier A company that transports goods or persons for compensation only for those people with whom it desires to do business. Compare *common carrier.*

contract for sale Either a present sale of goods or a contract to sell goods at a future time.

contract of record A special type of formal contract usually confirmed by a court with an accompanying judgment issued in favor of one of the parties.

contributory copyright infringement A violation of copyright law in which one party provides a way for a second party to violate the copyright protection granted to the third party even though the first party never violates the copyright himself or herself.

contributory negligence A legal defense that involves the failure of an injured party to be careful enough to ensure personal safety.

control test In tort law and in agency law, the test within the doctrine of *respondeat superior* which asks that we determine the degree of control or right to control that the hiring person had over the hired person in order to determine liability.

controlled company A corporation that has more than half its voting power concentrated in one person or a small group of persons, who always vote together.

Convention on Contracts for the International Sale of Goods (CISG) A United Nations treaty designed to govern commercial transactions between parties whose places of business are in different countries.

conventional mortgage A mortgage that involves no government backing by either insurance or guarantee.

conversion The wrongful exercise of dominion and control over another's personal property.

conveyance in trust A trust in which the settlor conveys away the legal title to a trustee to hold for the benefit of either the settlor or another as beneficiary.

Cooling-Off Rule A Federal Trade Commission rule under which sales of consumer goods or services over $25 made away from the seller's regular place of business may be canceled within three business days after the sale occurs.

Copenhagen Accord An agreement made under the auspices of the UN Framework Conference on Climate Change and entered by five nations, including China, the United States, and India, to reduce greenhouse gases and to provide $30 billion annually to help developing nations balance sustainable development with environmental protection.

copyright A right granted to an author, composer, photographer, or artist to exclusively publish and sell an artistic or literary work for the life of the author plus 70 years.

corporate democracy See *shareholder democracy.*

corporate opportunity doctrine A principle that states corporate managers cannot take a business opportunity for themselves if they know their corporation would be interested in that opportunity.

corporate raid An unfriendly takeover, designed to dismantle the target corporation.

corporate raider An unfriendly suitor that intends to dismantle the target corporation after obtaining it.

corporate shell A subsidiary corporation set up as a mere instrumentality of a parent corporation.

corporation A legal entity (or a legal person) created by either a state or federal statute authorizing individuals to operate an enterprise.

corporation by estoppel The doctrine by which parties who have benefited by dealing with a business as though it were a corporation—though in law it is not—cannot deny its existence as a corporation. Similarly, individuals who have acted as if they were a corporation would not be able to deny that the corporation existed.

corporativism In corporate law, the process of doing business as a self-governing business association, that is, as a corporation.

cost-benefit thinking A system of thought that focuses on the consequences to one person or institution and then weighs the cost against the benefits of performing the action under scrutiny.

cost of repair rule The principle that states that an architect or contractor may have to reimburse a client for any extra money spent by the client to correct an error initially made by the architect or contractor.

cost-plus contract A contract in which the price is determined by the cost of labor and materials plus an agreed percentage markup.

cotenancy The quality or state of more than one owner of a single property.

cotenants Two or more persons who own real property together.

counteroffer A response to an offer in which the terms and conditions of the original offer are changed.

courts Judicial tribunals that meet in a regular place and apply the law in an attempt to settle disputes by weighing the arguments presented by advocates for each party.

cover Buying similar goods from someone else when a seller breaches a contract.

creditor beneficiary A third party to whom one or both contracting parties owe a continuing debt of obligation arising from a contract.

crime An offense against the public at large punishable by the official governing body of a nation or state.

criminal simulation In criminal law, the altering or falsifying of art objects, antiques, photos, films, recordings, manuscripts, and/or antiquities with the intent to defraud.

cross-appeal An appeal filed by a party that has prevailed at trial.

cross-examination The questioning of witnesses by an opposing attorney.

cumulative voting A system of voting for corporate directors that is designed to benefit minority shareholders by allowing shareholders to multiply their voting shares by the number of directors to be elected.

cure The correction of a defect in goods that caused the goods to be rejected by a buyer.

current market price contract An agreement in which the prices are determined with reference to the market price of the goods on a specified date.

curtesy Under common law, the right that a widower had, if children of the marriage were born alive, to a life estate in all real property owned by the wife during the marriage.

cyber-agent (AKA electronic agent and e-agent) A computer program that acts without human intervention to begin an activity, to answer cybermessages, to deliver or accept cybermail, or to enter cybercontracts.

cyber-bulletin board An electronic message board.

cyber-commerce Involves transacting business by any one of several types of electronic communication, from debit card purchases to buying and selling goods on the Internet.

cyber-consumer Someone who buys something on the Internet.

cyber-contract A contract involving the sale or licensing of information in a digital format.

cybercrime Any criminal act that includes a computer.

cyber-defamation The communication of false and destructive information about an individual through the use of a computer or other electronic device.

cyber-discovery A search for evidence using a computer. Also called *cyberspace discovery*.

cyber-disparagement In tort law, disparagement committed using a computer system.

cyber-evidence Any and all types of computer-generated data.

cyber-germ warfare Using viruses to attack a computer system.

cyber-invasion of privacy The unwelcome intrusion into private matters initiated or maintained by a computer.

cyber-jurisdiction The authority of a court to hear a case based on Internet-related transactions.

cyber-pirate Someone who registers a trademark or trademarks as a domain name with little or no intention of actually using the domain name in the hope that the

actual holders of the trademark will buy the domain name for enormous sums.

cyber-principal A principal who places authority in the hands of a cyberagent.

cyber-signature An electronic sound or process attached to or logically associated with a record and executed or adopted by a person with the intent to sign a record.

cyber-spoiler See *cyber-pirate*.

cyber-spoofing Falsely adopting the identity of another computer user or creating a false identity on a computer Web site to commit fraud.

cyber-spyware (AKA cyber-snoopware) A program which, once it is installed in a computer, can keep a record of the keyboarding patterns established by the computer user.

cybers-stalking Targeting an individual for exploitation using that person's computer connections.

cyber-terrorism Using a computer to disrupt or destroy one of the critical elements of the nation's electronic infrastructure.

cybertort The invasion, distortion, theft, falsification, misuse, destruction, or financial exploitation of information stored in a computer.

cyber-trespass Gaining access to a computer with the intent to commit a crime.

cyber-vandalism Attacking a computer system so that a Web site is completely destroyed or paralyzed.

damage cap A limit on the amount of money that juries can award in certain types of tort law cases.

damages Money recovered by a party in a court action to compensate that party for injury or loss.

database The compilation of information in a form that can be understood and used by a computer.

de facto **corporation** A corporation defectively incorporated in good faith that exists in fact though not in law.

de jure **corporation** A corporation whose existence is the result of incorporators having fully or substantially complied with the relevant corporation statutes.

debit card A card used to electronically subtract money from a bank account to pay for goods or services.

debtor in possession A debtor who continues to operate his or her business after filing for bankruptcy.

declaration of trust A trust in which the settlor holds the legal title to the property as trustee for the benefit of some other person (the beneficiary) to whom the settlor now conveys the equitable title.

deductible An amount of any loss that is to be paid by the insured.

deed of trust A formal written instrument that transfers legal ownership of real property to a third party while the mortgagor remains on the property. The third party holds certain rights to that property as security for the mortgagor's creditors.

defamation The intentional tort that occurs when a false statement is communicated to others that harms a person's good name or reputation.

defective agreement An apparent contract in which mutual assent has been destroyed, thus rendering the alleged contract void.

defective condition A condition that makes a product unreasonably dangerous to the consumer, user, or property. See *product liability*.

defendant The person against whom a lawsuit is brought and from whom recovery is sought.

defense of others A defense to criminal liability to defendants if they can show they used force to rescue another person who was the victim of an apparent attack. The rescuer must have good reason to believe the victim was in danger of severe bodily injury or death.

del credere agent (del·KREH·de·reh) A factor who guarantees the credit of a third party to a principal and guarantees the solvency of the purchaser and the performance of the contract.

delegation The transfer of a contractual duty.

demand note A promissory note that is payable whenever the payee demands payment.

demurrage charge A fee charged by a carrier for the storage of goods still remaining in its possession beyond the time allowed for unloading by the cosignee.

demurrer A motion for dismissal of a case on the grounds that a plaintiff has failed to state a claim for which relief can be granted.

depositary bank The first bank to which an item is transferred for collection; the depositary bank may also be the payor bank.

deposition An oral question-and-answer session conducted under oath during which an attorney questions parties or witnesses from the opposition in a lawsuit.

dereliction of duty In criminal law, an activity that involves a law enforcement officer's failure to carry out his or her lawful duties.

derivative suit A lawsuit brought by shareholders on behalf of the corporation.

descriptive theory A system of ethical thought that describes the values at work within a social system.

descriptive threshold In insurance law, a guideline that determines when a victim can bring a lawsuit for injuries that result from an auto accident.

destination contract A contract under which the seller is required to deliver goods to a place of destination. The title and risk of loss remain with the seller until the goods reach the place of destination.

devise Real property that is left in a will. In states that have adopted the Uniform Probate Code, the term refers to both real and personal property.

devisee One who receives the real property under a will. In states that have adopted the Uniform Probate Code, the term refers to a person who receives a gift of either real or personal property under a will.

devolution When courts redefine a right and transfer the power and the obligation to enforce that right from a higher legal authority to a lower one.

digital information contract A contract involving the sale or licensing of information in a digital format.

Digital Millennium Copyright Act (DMCA) A law that makes it illegal to use technological means to bypass or override programs designed to prevent access to a copyrighted work.

digital signature An encoded message that appears at the end of a contract created online.

direct examination The questioning of witnesses by the lawyer who has called them.

direct suit A suit brought by shareholders who have been deprived of a right that belongs to them as shareholders.

disability Any physical or mental impairment that substantially limits one or more of the major life activities.

disaffirm In contract law, to indicate by a statement or act an intent not to live up to the terms of the contract.

disclaimer In employment law, a statement that regardless of provisions or policies in an employment handbook and regardless of oral promises to the contrary, an employment-at-will situation still exists between an employer and its employees. In the accounting profession, a statement declaring that an auditor has decided not to give any opinion on a firm's financial records.

disclaimer of general partner status A document filed with the appropriate state office when a limited partner has been incorrectly named as a general partner.

disclosed principal The person known by a third party to be the principal of an agent.

discounting System by which a bank will buy an instrument at a price below its face amount with the aim of ultimately collecting the face amount.

discovery The process by which parties to a civil suit search for information relevant to the case.

dishonor To refuse to accept or pay a negotiable instrument when it is presented.

disparagement In tort law, any false statement made to others that questions the legal ownership or raises doubts as to the quality of merchandise.

disparate impact A type of discrimination in an employer's policy that seems neutral on the surface but has an unequal or unfair impact on members of one or more of the protected classes.

disparate treatment Intentional discrimination against an individual or group belonging to a protected class. The protected classes are sex, race, color, religion, and national origin.

disposable income The amount of money left from a person's income, after subtracting certain allowable deductions.

Dispute Settlement Board (DSB) See *Dispute Settlement Understanding.*

Dispute Settlement Understanding (DSU) A series of measures administered by an international Dispute Settlement Board that are designed to improve the way trading quarrels are handled.

disputed amount Consideration on which parties to a contract never agree.

dissociation A process authorized under the Revised Uniform Partnership Act that takes place whenever a partner is no longer associated with the running of the partnership firm.

dissolution A change in the relation of partners caused by any partner ceasing to be associated in the carrying on of the business.

diversity cases Federal lawsuits that are between persons from different states, between citizens of the United States and a foreign government, or between citizens of the United States and citizens of a foreign nation. Diversity cases must involve an amount over $75,000.

dividends Net profits, or surplus, set aside for shareholders.

Division for Science and Technology A United Nations agency created to coordinate activities regarding international cooperation in the sharing of science and technology for economic development.

document of title A paper that serves as evidence that the person holding the paper has title to the goods mentioned in the document.

Dodd-Frank Wall Street and Consumer Protection Act An act passed by Congress to deal with the 21st century financial crisis.

domain name The Internet address of a business, institution, or individual.

domain name dispute A disagreement that arises when an individual or organization has registered a domain name that is actually the protected trademark of a business or institution.

domestic bill of exchange A draft that is drawn and payable in the United States.

domestic corporation A corporation created by or organized under the laws of the state where it is operating.

domestic violence statute State laws that outlaw physical violence directed at any family member.

dominant tenement The property to which the right or privilege of an easement attaches.

donee One to whom a gift is given.

donee beneficiary A third party who provides no consideration for the benefits received and who owes the contracting parties no legal duty.

donor One who gives a gift.

double indemnity An optional provision in life insurance policies that provides that the insurer will pay double the amount due to a beneficiary if the insured dies from accidental causes.

double jeopardy In criminal procedure, the possibility of being tried twice for the same crime.

dower By common law, the vested rights of the wife to a one-third lifetime interest in the real property owned by her spouse. Compare *curtesy.*

draft A written order by which the party creating it orders another party to pay money to a third party. Also called *bill of exchange.*

drawee The party named in a draft who is ordered to pay the money to the payee.

drawer The party who draws a draft, that is, the party who orders that the money be paid.

drug trafficking The unauthorized manufacture or distribution of any controlled substance or the possession of such a substance with the intention of manufacturing or distributing it illegally.

dummy corporation A corporation that is set up as a mere instrumentality of a parent corporation. Also called *corporate shell* and *empty shell.*

dunning letter A letter representing payment for goods.

durable power of attorney A document that authorizes an agent to act on another's behalf, with the power either surviving incapacity or becoming effective upon incapacity.

duress An action by one party that forces another party to do what need not be done otherwise.

duty An obligation placed on individuals because of the law.

duty of due diligence A duty that says that corporate managers when acting on behalf of the corporation must act (1) in good faith; (2) using the same level of care that an ordinarily prudent person would use in a comparable situation, and (3) in the reasonable belief that the best interests of the corporation are being met.

duty of loyalty A duty that states managers must place the corporation's interests above their own.

duty of obedience Managers' duty to ensure their exercise of authority is not excessive and does not harm the corporation.

e-911 location identifier system An electronic chip located in a mobile phone that sends out a signal that is designed to ensure that EMS personnel can locate people who are unable or unwilling to reveal their location when making an emergency call.

early neutral evaluation (ENE) A process similar to that of a settlement hearing, which may result in a final decision or be used to help shape the final decision.

easement The right to use the land of another for a particular purpose.

easement by prescription An easement that is obtained by passing over another's property without permission openly and continuously for a period of time set by state statute (20 years in many states).

e-check (sometimes called *electronic check conversion*) A system in which funds are electronically transferred from a customer's checking account, eliminating the need to process a paper check.

e-commerce Involves transacting business by any one of several types of electronic communication, from debit card purchases to buying and selling goods on the Internet.

economic compensatory damages Damages that are directly quantifiable, including damages awarded for lost wages, medical expenses, and expenses incurred in the repair or replacement of property.

economic duress Threats of a business nature that force another party without real consent to enter a commercial agreement. Also called *business compulsion.*

Economic Espionage Act Legislation that outlines criminal sanctions for the theft of trade secrets and the use of fraud to obtain trade secrets.

economic reality test In agency law, a test used by the court in vicarious liability to determine whether a worker is a servant or an independent contractor.

Economic Security Council (ESC) A single, unified international agency under the management of the United Nations that would monitor the economic activities of member nations.

e-consumer Someone who buys something on the Internet.

ejectment The common law name given to the lawsuit brought by a landlord to have a tenant evicted from the premises.

elective share See *forced share.*

electronic contracts Contracts made using computers, either via e-mail or the Internet, or that involve computer-related products, such as databases and software.

electronic data interchange (EDI) An electronic process used to negotiate contracts.

electronic fund transfer (EFT) A method of banking that uses computers and electronic technology as a substitute for checks and other banking methods.

electronic or jurisdiction The authority of a court to hear a case based on Internet-related transactions.

electronically stored information (ESI) Computerized evidence.

emancipated In contract law, the condition that exists when minors are no longer under the control of their parents and are responsible for their contracts.

embezzlement The act of wrongfully taking property entrusted into one's care.

eminent domain The right of federal, state, and local governments, or other public bodies, to take private lands, with compensation to their owners, for public use. Also called *condemnation.*

emotional duress Acts or threats that create emotional distress and lead a person into a contract against his or her will.

employment-at-will A doctrine followed by most jurisdictions in the United States that says an employer can dismiss an employee at any time for any reason.

employment contacts   In employment law, an enforceable agreement between the hiring party (the employer) and the hired party (the employee).

end user   A purchaser who is not involved in the production or assembly of the product.

endowment insurance   Insurance protection that combines life insurance and investment so that if the insured outlives the time period of the policy, the face value is paid to the beneficiary.

entity theory   A theory in partnership law that holds that a partnership is actually a separate legal person with its own legal identity.

entrapment   A defense to criminal liability that claims that a previously law-abiding citizen was induced to commit a crime by a law enforcement officer.

equal dignities rule   The legal rule that provides that when a party appoints an agent to negotiate an agreement that must be in writing, the appointment of the agent must also be in writing.

equipment   Goods that are used or bought for use primarily in business.

equitable estoppel   See *part performance.*

equitable remedy   The requirement that a party do something or refrain from doing something, beyond the payment of money.

equity financing   The issuing and selling of shares of stock to raise capital.

equity of redemption   A mortgagor's right to pay off the mortgage in full, including interest.

espionage   The gathering or transmitting of information pertaining to the national defense of a nation for the political or military use of any foreign nation.

estate in fee simple   An estate in which the owner owns the land for life with the right to use it or dispose of it freely.

estoppel   A legal bar to denying acts, statements, or promises.

ethic of responsibility   The ethical principle that says that the first duty of governmental leaders is to protect their own people and their own nation-states.

ethic of ultimate ends   The ethical principle that holds that, since people can never know the final consequences of their actions, they must always act to promote benevolence, that is, to do good and to avoid evil.

ethical relativism   A system of ethical thought that says there is no objective or absolute standard of right and wrong.

ethics   Rules of conduct that transcend legal rules, telling people how to act when the law does not.

EU Data Protection Directive   A decree issued by the European Union (EU) that prevents European companies from sharing ESI with countries that do not provide the same level of protection for the ESI as the EU.

EU E-Privacy Directive   A decree issued by the European Union (EU) that guarantees EU citizens a high level of privacy for electronically stored information.

euro   The European Union's common currency.

European Central Bank (ECB)   The bank was established by provisions within the Maastricht Treaty and is the central hub of the European System of Central Banks.

European System of Central Banks (ESCB)   A system of banks including the European Central Bank and the National Central Banks.

European Union (EU)   A group of countries in Europe that have joined together to formulate a common European economic policy, minimize trade barriers, and introduce a common currency with the goal of making the EU a major global competitor.

eviction   An act of the landlord that deprives the tenant of the enjoyment of the premises.

exculpatory agreement   A clause that says one of the parties to a contract, generally the one who wrote the contract, is not liable for any economic loss or physical injury, even if that party caused the loss or injury.

exculpatory clause   A clause in a contract that releases a party from liability for his or her wrongful acts. These clauses are not favored by law.

executed contract   A contract whose terms have been completely and satisfactorily carried out by both parties.

executor (male); executrix (female)   The party named in a will to carry out the terms of the will.

executory contract   A contract that has not yet been fully performed by the parties.

exempt property   Property of a decedent that passes to the surviving spouse or children and is beyond the reach of creditors.

express authority   An agent's authority that the principal voluntarily and specifically sets forth as oral or written instructions in an agency agreement.

express contract A contract in which both parties accept mutual obligations through either oral discussion or written communication.

express warranty An oral or written statement, promise, or other representation about the quality of a product.

extant data Data that are difficult to retrieve because they are hidden within a computer system.

extortion The act of taking another's property with consent when such consent is coerced by threat to injure a victim's person, property, or reputation.

f.a.s vessel Free alongside vessel. Indicates that the seller must deliver goods, at the seller's own risk, alongside the vessel or at a dock designated by the buyer.

f.o.b. Free on board.

f.o.b. the place of destination Terms indicating that goods will be delivered free to the place of destination.

f.o.b. the place of shipment Terms indicating that goods will be delivered free to the place of shipment.

factor A special agent who is employed to sell merchandise consigned for that purpose.

failure of consideration A personal defense that may be used by a maker or drawer of a negotiable instrument when the party with whom the maker dealt breaches the contract by not furnishing the agreed consideration.

fair court Historically in the Middle Ages in Europe, a court set up at a festival (a fair) to handle disputes between merchants at that festival (fair).

fairness rule The rule that requires managers to be fair to the corporation when they personally benefit from their business decisions.

false imprisonment An intentional tort involving the unjustified confinement or detention of a person.

family allowance An amount of money taken from a decedent's estate and given to the family to meet its immediate needs while the estate is being probated.

family farmer Under Chapter 12 of the Bankruptcy Code, a farmer who receives more than half the total income from the farm. In addition, to qualify as a family farmer, 80 percent of the farmer's debt must result from farm expenses.

farm products Crops, livestock, or supplies used or produced in farming operations.

fault-based insurance An automobile insurance policy that will measure liability in an automobile accident by the degree of fault that can be assigned to each driver using negligence principles.

featherbedding Requiring an employer, usually by a union, to keep unneeded employees, to pay employees for not working, or to assign more employees to a given job than are needed.

federal question A matter that involves the U.S. Constitution, a federal statute or statutes, or a treaty; handled by federal district courts.

Federal Register Publication that produces a daily compilation of new regulations issued by federal administrative agencies.

felony A crime punishable by death or by imprisonment in a federal or state prison for a term exceeding one year.

fiduciary A person who acts in a position of trust or confidence.

fiduciary relationship A relationship based on trust such as exists between an attorney and a client, an agent and a principal, a guardian and a ward, a trustee and a beneficiary, or a director and a corporation.

field warehousing The practice of using goods that are stored in a warehouse as security for a loan.

finance charge The actual cost of a loan in dollars and cents.

firm offer A rule that no consideration is necessary when a merchant agrees in writing to hold an offer open for the sale of goods.

first degree murder In criminal law, killing someone with premeditation or with prior calculation and design, or while committing a serious felony such as rape, robbery, or kidnapping.

fixture An article of personal property physically attached to real property in such a way that an interest arises in it under real estate law.

flexible-rate mortgage A mortgage that has a rate of interest that changes according to fluctuations in the index to which it is tied. Also called *variable-rate mortgage*.

floater policy A policy that insures property that cannot be covered by specific insurance because the property is constantly changing in either value or location.

floating lien A provision, placed by the creditor, in a security agreement that a security interest of the creditor also applies to goods the debtor acquires at a later time.

forbearance The act of refraining from doing (or promising not to do) something that a person has a legal right to do.

forced share The portion of a decedent's estate assured to the family by state statute.

foreclosure The right of a mortgagee to apply to a court to have property sold when the mortgagor defaults or fails to perform some agreement in the mortgage.

foreign corporation A corporation created by or organized under the laws of a state other than the one in which it is operating.

foreign draft See *international bill of exchange*.

forgery The false making or alteration of a writing with the intent to defraud.

formal contract Under common law, a contract that is written; signed, witnessed, and placed under the seal of the parties; and delivered.

formalist theory A theory of legal interpretation under which the court will look to see if certain elements (offer, acceptance, mutual assent, consideration, capacity, and legality) exist before concluding whether or not the parties in a lawsuit have actually entered a legally binding contract.

forum shopping The process of locating a jurisdiction that has a friendly track record for the type of lawsuit that is about to be filed.

fraud A wrongful statement, action, or concealment pertinent to the subject matter of a contract knowingly made to damage the other party.

fraud in the inception Fraud that occurs when one party tricks another into a contract by lying to the innocent party about the actual nature of the contract.

fraud in the inducement Fraud that occurs when one party tricks another into a contract by lying about the terms of the agreement to get the innocent party to enter the contract under false pretenses.

fraudulent conveyance A transfer of property with the intent to defraud creditors.

fraudulent misrepresentation A wrongful statement, action, or concealment, pertinent to the subject matter of a contract, that is knowingly made to damage the other party.

friendly suitor See *white knight*.

frustration-of-purpose doctrine In contract law, the doctrine that releases a party from a contractual obligation when performing the obligations would be thoroughly impractical and senseless.

full warranty A warranty under which a defective product will be repaired or replaced without charge within a reasonable time after a complaint has been made about it.

fungible goods Goods of which any unit is, by nature or usage of trade, the equivalent of any like unit; wheat, flour, sugar, and liquids of various kinds are examples.

future goods Goods that are not yet in existence or under the control of people; they include fish in the sea, minerals in the ground, goods not yet manufactured, and commodities futures.

general agent A person who is given broad authority to act on behalf of the principal in conducting the bulk of the principal's business activities on a daily basis.

General Agreement on Tariffs and Trade (GATT) A nonstatic agreement among the principal trading countries to reduce or eliminate tariffs and to promote free trade on a global basis.

General Assembly The member nations of the United Nations.

general consent Consent that arises automatically when a patient enters a hospital for routine tests and procedures needed for diagnosis and treatment.

general jurisdiction The power of a court to hear any type of case.

general partner A partner who takes an active part in running a partnership and has unlimited liability for the firm's debts.

general release A document expressing the intent of a creditor to release a debtor from obligations to an existing and valid debt.

general warranty deed A deed that contains express warranties under which a grantor guarantees property to be free of encumbrances created by the grantor or by others who had title previously. Also called *full covenant* and *warranty deed*.

general welfare clause Article I, Section 8, Clause 1 of the U.S. Constitution which reads in part that Congress is empowered to "lay and collect taxes, Duties, Imposts, and Excises, to pay the Debts and provide for the common defense and general welfare of the United States."

generally accepted accounting principles (GAAP) Rules established by the Financial Accounting Standards Board (FASB) that outline the procedures that accountants use in accumulating financial data and in preparing financial statements.

generally accepted auditing standards (GAAS) Standards set up by the Auditing Standards Board of the American Institute of Certified Public Accountants (AICPA) that measure the quality of the performance of the auditing procedures.

Genetic Information Nondiscrimination Act (GINA) A law passed by Congress that makes it unlawful for employers or insurance companies to make decisions based on genetic information acquired by genetic testing.

Geneva Conventions International meetings that attempted to deal with many of the contemporary complications brought on by the nature of warfare in the twentieth century.

gift in *causa mortis* (in·KAWS·ah·MORE·tes) A gift given during one's lifetime in contemplation of death from a known cause.

gift *inter vivos* (IN·ter·VY·vose) A gift between the living. For an exchange to be valid, the donor must intend to make a gift, the gift must be delivered to the donee, and the donee must accept it.

good faith Honesty in fact and observance of reasonable commercial standards of fair dealings in the trade.

goods All things (other than money, stocks, and bonds) that are movable.

goodwill The expected continuance of public patronage of a business.

governmental control A theory of corporate control based on the belief that because corporate decision making impacts upon more individuals and groups than just shareholders and managers, those decisions should be made by a group of corporate outsiders, usually government officials. Also called *state control.*

graduated-payment mortgage A mortgage that has a fixed interest rate during the life of the mortgage; however, the monthly payments made by the mortgagor increase over the term of the loan.

grantee A person to whom title to real property is transferred in a deed.

grantor A person who transfers title to real property in a deed.

gratuitous agency An agency relationship that emerges from an agreement that is not a contract.

gratuitous agent An agent who is not under contract and, thus, performs his or her duties without payment.

gratuitous bailment A bailment for the sole benefit of either the bailor or the bailee, in which the other party receives no consideration for benefits bestowed.

greenmail A strategy used to shake off a bidder's hostile suit by offering to buy, at significantly higher cost, the portion of stock already owned by the bidder who is trying to take over the company.

grievance procedure A procedure that allows employees to appeal any decision an employer makes that employees feel violates just cause.

gross negligence Very great negligence.

guaranteed insurability An optional provision in an insurance contract that allows the insured to pay an extra premium initially in exchange for a guaranteed option to buy more insurance at certain specified times later on with no questions asked and no medical examination required.

guarantor The promisor.

guaranty contract In contract law, a contract by which one party agrees to pay the debt of another party if that party fails to meet that obligation.

guaranty of payment A promise to pay another's bills or to settle wrongful acts if that party does not settle them personally.

health care proxy A written statement authorizing an agent to make health care decisions for another in the event of incapacity.

Health Insurance Portability and Accountability Act (HIPAA) Legislation that guarantees patients the right to see their medical records and those of their underage children.

heir One who inherits property either under a will or through someone's dying without a will.

holder A person who is in possession of a negotiable instrument that is issued or indorsed to that person's order or to bearer.

holder in due course A holder who has taken a negotiable instrument for value, in good faith, without notice that it is overdue or has been dishonored and without notice of any defenses against it or claim to it.

holder in due course rule A rule adopted by the FTC that states that holders of consumer credit contracts who are holders in due course are subject to all claims and defenses that the buyer could use against the seller, including personal defenses.

Home Affordable Modification Program (HAMP) A program set up by the Department of the Treasury to support the efforts of homeowners who, though in default, wish to continue to make payments on their mortgages

home equity loan A line of credit made available to home-owners based on the value of the property over and above any existing mortgages.

homeowner's policy A type of insurance that gives protection for all types of losses and liabilities related to home ownership. Items covered include losses from fire, windstorm, burglary, vandalism, and injuries suffered by others while on the property.

homestead exemption A provision in the Bankruptcy Code that allows debtors to exclude a statutory amount of equity in the debtor's place of residence and in property used as a burial ground when filing for bankruptcy.

homicide The killing of one human being by another.

horizontal expansion The joining of companies involved in the same business.

hostile bidder See *unfriendly suitor*.

hot-cargo contract An agreement whereby an employer voluntarily agrees with a union not to handle, use, or deal in nonunion-produced goods for another employer.

identified goods Specific goods that are selected as the subject matter of a contract.

identity theft Using a computer to steal confidential information to clean out a person's bank account, to run up credit card debt, to divert cash transfers, and to disrupt the financial and personal life of the victim.

illegal agreement In contract law, a void agreement to do something that violates the law.

illusory promise A promise that does not obligate the promisor to anything.

implied authority The authority of an agent to perform acts that are necessary or customary to carry out expressly authorized duties.

impaired classes Creditors who receive less than the full value of their claims in bankruptcy proceedings.

implied contract A contract created by the actions or gestures of the parties involved in the transaction.

implied covenant An implied promise in any employment relationship that the employer and the employee will be fair with each other.

implied warranty A warranty that is imposed by law rather than by statements, descriptions, or samples given by the seller.

implied-in-fact contract A contract implied by direct or indirect acts of the parties.

implied-in-law contract A remedy imposed by a court in a situation in which the parties did not create a written, oral, or implied-in-fact agreement but one party has unfairly benefited at the innocent expense of another. Also called *quasi-contract*.

in pari delicto (in pah·ree de·LIK·toh) In equal fault. A contract relationship when both parties to an illegal agreement are equally wrong, in the knowledge of the operation and effect of their contract.

inactive data Data in a computer system that are not being used at the present time but that can be easily retrieved.

incidental beneficiary A third party for whose benefit a contract was not made but who would substantially benefit if the agreement were performed according to its terms and conditions.

incidental damages Damages awarded for losses indirectly, but closely, attributed to a breach to cover any expenses paid out by an innocent party to prevent further loss.

incorporators The people who actually sign the articles of incorporation to start a corporation.

indemnification Payment for loss or damage suffered.

indemnify To compensate for loss or damage or insure against future loss or damage.

independent contractor One who contracts to do a job and who retains complete control over the methods employed to obtain completion.

independent directors Directors who have no family members employed by the corporation, who are not themselves employed by the corporation, or, if they were once employed by the corporation, have not been on staff for at least three years.

independent director control A theory of corporate control that states that the best way to make certain that corporate decisions are made in the best interests of the corporation is to make sure that the decision makers themselves are not affected by the decisions.

indictment A set of formal charges against a defendant issued by a grand jury.

individual justice Justice that is meted out to the people on a case-by-case basis.

indorsee A person to whom a draft, note, or other negotiable instrument is transferred by indorsement.

indorsement in full See *special indorsement*.

indorser A person who indorses a negotiable instrument.

infliction of emotional distress The intentional tort that allows those injured emotionally by the wrongful acts of others to recover damages even without the accompanying physical injury.

informal contract An oral or written contract that is not under a seal or is not a contract of record. Also called *simple contract*.

information A set of formal charges against a defendant drawn up and issued by the prosecutor or district attorney.

informed consent Written consent given by patients for diagnostic tests or treatments that will involve danger or pain after being told about the procedure and the risks involved.

in-house attorney A member of the officer corps of a business who is instructed in his or her duties by a supervisor.

injunction A court order preventing someone from performing a particular act.

inland marine insurance An insurance contract that covers goods that are moved by land carriers such as rail, truck, and airplane.

innkeeper An operator of a hotel, motel, or inn that holds itself out to the public as being ready to accommodate travelers, strangers, and transient guests.

inside information Material, nonpublic, factual data that can be used to buy or sell securities at a profit.

insider trading Using inside information to either cheat the corporation or take unfair advantage of corporate outsiders.

insider trading rule A rule of corporate governance that states that when managers possess important inside information, they are obligated to reveal that information before trading on it themselves.

insolvent Inability of a business entity to pay its debts as they become due in the usual course of business.

installment note A promissory note in which the principal together with interest on the unpaid balance is payable in installments at specified times.

insurable interest The financial interest that a policyholder has in the person or property that is insured.

insurance A contract whereby one party pays premiums to another party who undertakes to pay compensation for losses resulting from risks or perils specified in the contract.

insured A party that is protected by an insurer against losses caused by the risks specified in an insurance policy.

insurer A party that accepts the risk of loss in return for a premium (payment of money) and agrees to compensate the insured against a specified loss.

integral-part test A finding that any type of price enhancement violates the best-price rule.

intended beneficiary A third party in whose favor a contract is made.

intentional or reckless infliction of emotional distress A tort involving someone who intentionally or recklessly causes another to undergo emotional or mental suffering.

interest-only mortgage In property law, a mortgage in which the borrower pays only the interest for a period of time, usually one to three years, as set by the agreement.

interference with a contract The international tort that results when a person, out of ill will, entices a contractual party into breaking the contract.

interlocking directorates In antitrust law, a situation that occurs when individuals serve as two corporations that are competitors.

intermediary bank Any bank to which an item is transferred in the course of collection except the depositary or payor bank.

international arbitration agreement A pledge to use arbitration if parties find themselves in disagreement about enforcement rights under an original contract.

international bill of exchange A draft that is drawn in one country but is payable in another. Also called *foreign draft*.

International Court of Justice (ICJ) One of the principal vehicles for the establishment of international law and justice.

International Criminal Court (ICC) International court that presides over trials involving genocide, war crimes, and other human rights violations.

International Law Commission A thirty-four-member panel of judges who seek to codify international law in as objective a manner as possible.

International Monetary Fund (IMF) A nongovernmental organization that is designed to help financially strapped nations to secure loans that will help them engage in programs of sustainable economic growth and development.

international terrorism Acts transcending national boundaries that violate a state's criminal laws and are intended to intimidate that country's civilians or influence the policy or conduct of the government.

interrogatories Written questions to be answered in writing under oath by the opposite party in a lawsuit.

interstate commerce Business activities that touch more than one state.

interstate shipment A shipment that goes beyond the borders of the state in which it originated.

intestacy The quality or state of one who dies without having prepared a valid will.

intestate Having died without leaving a valid will. Compare *testate*.

intestate succession The process by which property passes to others when people die without a will.

intimidation In criminal law, threats of harm to the person or the property of a public servant, a party official, or a witness, with the intent to coerce that person into violating his or her duty under the law.

intrastate commerce Business activities that have no out-of-state connections.

intrastate shipment A shipment that is entirely within a single state.

invasion of privacy The intentional tort that occurs when one person unreasonably denies another person the right to be left alone.

inventory Goods held for sale or lease, or raw materials used or consumed in a business.

invitation to trade An announcement published for the purpose of creating interest and attracting a response by many people.

involuntary bailment A bailment arising from the leaving of personal property in the possession of a bailee through an act of God, accident, or other uncontrolled phenomenon.

involuntary manslaughter In criminal law, the unlawful killing of another human being caused by negligence.

irresistible impulse test Under this rule, criminal defendants are judged not guilty by reason of insanity if, at the time of the action in question, they suffered from a mental disease that either prevented them from knowing right from wrong or compelled them to commit the criminal act.

irrevocable offer A rule that no consideration is necessary when a merchant agrees in writing to hold an offer open for the sale of goods. Also called *firm offer*.

issue Descendants (children, grandchildren, great-grandchildren).

issuer Either a maker or a drawer of an instrument.

joint tenants Two or more persons who own property where the right of any deceased owner is automatically transferred to other surviving owners.

joint tenants with the right of survivorship See *joint tenants*.

judicial review The process by which a court determines the constitutionality of various legislative statutes, administrative regulations, and executive actions.

judicial–economic system The interaction of the legal system and the economic system so as to become, in effect, a single system.

junior mortgage A mortgage subject to a prior mortgage.

junk bonds Bonds with high risk but also a high rate of return.

junk science The distorted, exaggerated, misapplied, or misrepresented use of scientific evidence.

jurisdiction The authority of a court to hear and decide cases.

juriscience In the development of the law, the point at which science, technology, and the law intersect.

just cause A criterion under the just war theory, which states that to be morally permissible, a war must be waged only for honorable motives.

just war theory A theory for determining when a war can be considered legally and morally correct.

kidnapping The unlawful abduction of an individual against that individual's will.

knowledge In criminal law, the awareness that a particular result will probably occur.

labor union An organization that acts on behalf of all employees in negotiations with the employer regarding terms of their employment.

laches The equitable doctrine that a delay or failure to assert a right or claim at the proper time, which causes a disadvantage to the adverse party, is a bar to recovery.

lack of consideration A personal defense that may be used by a maker or drawer of a negotiable instrument when no consideration existed in the underlying contract for which the instrument was issued.

landlord A person who owns real property and who rents or leases it to someone else. Also called *lessor*.

larceny The act of taking and carrying away the personal property of another without the right to do so.

larceny by false pretenses The taking of someone's money or property by intentionally deceiving that person.

last resort A criterion under the just war theory that states that a war must be waged only as a final course of action.

last will and testament A formal document that governs the transfer of property at death.

law A set of rules created by the governing body of a society to maintain harmony, stability, and justice in that society.

law merchant In England, the commercial law developed by merchants who needed a set of rules to govern their business transactions.

leading objective test In contract law, a test applied by the court to determine the real purpose of a guaranty contract.

lease A contract granting the use of certain real property to another for a specified period in return for the payment of rent.

lease option A contract that permits a party to lease real property while holding an option to purchase that property.

leasehold estate The creation of an ownership interest in the tenant. An interest in real estate that is held under a lease. Also called *tenancy*.

legal detriment In contract law, doing (or promising to do) something that one has a legal right not to do, giving up (or promising to give up) something that one has a legal right to keep, or refraining from doing (or promising not to do) something that one has a legal right to do.

legal imperialism American insistence that all disputes be resolved under American law.

legal tender Money that may be offered legally in satisfaction of a debt and that must be accepted by a creditor when offered.

legatee One who receives personal property in a will.

lessee See *tenant*.

lessor See *landlord*.

leveraged buyout The purchase of a controlling portion of the stock in a corporation by a group of shareholders, usually officers and directors of the company.

lex mercatoria In England, the commercial law developed by merchants who needed a set of rules to govern their business transactions.

liability The legal responsibility of an individual for his or her actions.

liable Legally responsible.

libel Any false statement that harms another person's good name or reputation made in a permanent form, such as movies, writing, and videotape, and communicated to others.

license A grant of permission to do a particular thing, to exercise a certain privilege, to carry on a particular business, or to pursue a certain occupation; an agreement that gives no property right or interest in land but merely allows the licensee to do certain acts that would otherwise be a trespass; a privilege granted by a state or city upon payment of a fee, which is not a contract and may be revoked for cause, conferring authority to perform a designated task, such as operating a motor vehicle.

licensing agreement An agreement in which one party is given permission from another party to do a particular thing in exchange for consideration.

lien A claim that one has against the property of another.

life estate An estate in which the owner owns real property for his or her life or for the life of another.

life insurance An insurance contract that provides monetary compensation for losses suffered by another's death.

limited defense See *personal defense.*

limited liability Status that specifies that an individual's liability will not go beyond his or her original investment.

limited liability company (LLC) A business organization that borrows elements from a partnership and a corporation. LLCs may come into existence only through following the steps laid out in the state code.

limited partner A partner who does not take part in the management of a firm and whose liability does not extend beyond his or her investment.

limited partnership A partnership formed by two or more persons having one or more general partners and one or more limited partners.

limited-payment life insurance Insurance that provides that the payment will stop after a stated length of time—usually 10, 20, or 30 years.

limited warranty A warranty that does not meet all of the requirements of a full warranty.

lingering apparent authority Apparent authority that stays with an agent if the principal has terminated the agent but has failed to give proper notice to third parties entitled to such notice.

liquidated damages Damages agreed to by the parties to a contract in the event of a breach.

liquidation The conversion of property into cash.

litigant A person involved in litigation.

living trust A trust that comes into existence while the person who establishes it is alive. Also called *inter vivos trust.*

living will A document in which individuals can indicate their desire not to be kept alive by artificial means if there is no hope for recovery.

local option The practice in a state of eliminating uniform statewide laws regulating Sunday activities and allowing the local counties, cities, towns, and villages to adopt their own special Sunday ordinances.

locality rule A means to judge a health care provider's actions on the basis of how other health care professionals in the same community would have acted in the same situation.

lockup agreement A contract between a target corporation and a white knight, giving the knight an option to buy valuable property should a hostile bidder gain control of the target corporation.

locus sigilli The place of the seal. The abbreviation L.S. is often used in place of the seal itself on formal written contracts.

lodger A person who has the use of property without actual or exclusive possession of it.

M'Naughten Rule The oldest test for insanity whereby a criminal defendant is declared not guilty by reason of insanity if, at the time of the criminal act, he or she suffered from a mental disease that prevented him or her from understanding the nature of the act and that the act was wrong.

Maastricht Treaty The outcome of a conference held in Maastricht, the Netherlands. The objectives of the treaty were to create a general European economic policy as well as a foreign policy acceptable to all member states.

Mail Order and Telephone Order Rule The Federal Trade Commission rule that states that sellers must ship orders within the time promised in their advertisements.

main purpose test In contract law, a test applied by the court to determine the real purpose of a guaranty contract.

majority A term used to describe persons who have reached the legal age of adulthood.

maker A person obligated as the payor on a promissory note. See also *comaker.*

malicious prosecution Bringing false criminal charges against an innocent victim.

malpractice Occurs when a professional accountant, health care professional, or attorney—fails to meet his or her duty of care.

managerial control A theory of corporate management that favors insulating managers from shareholders by limiting the shareholders' power to vote and by making it difficult for the shareholder to sue managers.

master An outdated term signifying an individual who has the right to control the physical conduct of a servant or employee.

material fact An essential or important fact; a fact of substance.

means test Three steps used to qualify someone for Chapter 7 bankruptcy.

med-arb A form of ADR that combines the best aspects of both mediation and arbitration. The parties first submit to a mediation session. If the matter cannot be settled, it moves to an arbitration hearing.

mediation The process by which an outside party attempts to help two other parties settle their differences.

mediator The third party in mediation whose job is to convince the contending parties to adjust or settle their dispute.

Medicaid A healthcare plan for low-income people that is administered by state governments but funded by both state and federal funds.

medical payments insurance A type of automobile insurance that pays for medical (and sometimes funeral) expenses resulting from bodily injuries to anyone occupying the policyholder's car at the time of an accident.

Medicare A federally funded health insurance program for people 65 years and over who are eligible for Social Security.

memorandum A written agreement containing the terms of an agreement, an identification of the subject matter of the agreement, the consideration promised, the names and identities of the parties to the agreement, and the signature of the party charged to the agreement.

mercantile law In England, the commercial law developed by merchants who needed a set of rules to govern their business transactions.

merchant A person who deals in goods of the kind sold in the ordinary course of business or who otherwise claims to have knowledge or skills peculiar to those goods.

merger The acquisition of one corporation by another.

metadata In computer jargon, data that is used to record information about other computer data.

midnight deadline The deadline by which banks must settle or return checks or be responsible for paying them. If the payor bank is not the depository bank, it must settle for an item by midnight of the banking day of receipt. If the payor bank is also the depository bank, the deadline is midnight of the next banking day following the banking day on which it receives the relevant item.

military caregiver leave A provision under the Family Medical Leave Act (FMLA) which states that an employer must give an employee up to 26 weeks of leave time in a 12-month period to care for a family member who has sustained a serious illness or injury which occurred because of military service.

minimum contacts The doctrine of minimum contacts identifies the fewest number of contacts that will permit a court to exercise personal jurisdiction over an out-of-state defendant.

minority A term used to describe persons who have not reached the legal age of adulthood.

mirror image rule In contract law, the rule that an acceptance must duplicate the terms in the offer.

misdemeanor A crime less serious than a felony that is generally punishable by a prison sentence of not more than one year.

misrepresentation In contract law, a false statement innocently made by one party to a contract with no intent to deceive. Also, in insurance, giving false answers to questions in an insurance application that materially affect the risk undertaken by the insurer.

misuse of legal procedure Bringing legal action without probable cause and with malice.

mitigation A principle that states an innocent party cannot take advantage by deliberately raising the level of damages that the other party will have to pay as a consequence of a breach.

monetary threshold In insurance law, a guideline to determine when a victim can bring a lawsuit for injuries that result from an auto accident.

money order A type of draft that may be purchased from banks, post offices, telegraph companies, and express companies as a substitute for a check.

monopoly The exclusive control of a market by a business enterprise.

morals Values that govern society's attitude toward right and wrong.

mortgage A transfer of an interest in property for the purpose of creating a security for a debt.

mortgagee The party who lends money and takes back a mortgage as security for the loan.

mortgagor The party who borrows money and gives a mortgage to the lender or mortgagee as security for the loan.

most favored nation principle A principle that states that the World Trade Organization nations must apply the same privileges, advantages, and benefits to all other member nations in relation to similar imports.

mutual assent In contract law, the state of mind that exists between an offeror and an offeree once a valid offer has been accepted and once the parties know what the terms are and have agreed to be bound by them. Also known as "a meeting of the minds."

mutual-benefit bailment A bailment in which both the bailor and the bailee receive some benefit.

mutual mistake See *bilateral mistake.*

mutual recession A condition in which both parties to a contract agree to rescind the contract and return to the other any consideration already received or pay for any services or materials already rendered.

mutuum (MYOO·choo·um) A loan of goods with the intention that the goods may be used and later replaced with an equal amount of different goods.

National Central Banks (NCB) Part of the European System of Central Banks, the NCBs are located within the member nations of the EU.

national rule A rule that allows a court to judge a health care provider's degree of care by determining how the same procedure is performed on a national basis.

national standard A rule that allows a court to judge a health care provider's degree of care by determining how the same procedure is performed on a national basis.

national treatment principle A principle that states that the World Trade Organization nations must apply the same standards to imports that they apply to domestic goods.

nation-states Sovereign divisions that govern a recognized area of land on a map, may raise money within their borders, and have a responsibility to provide for their citizens.

natural law theory A system of ethical thought that sees an unbreakable link joining the law and morality.

navigable airspace The space above 1,000 feet over populated areas and above 500 feet over water and unpopulated areas.

necessaries Goods and services that are essential to a minor's health and welfare.

necessary and proper clause In constitutional law, Article I, Section 8, Clause 18, of the U.S. Constitution, which says that Congress has the power "(T)o make all Laws which shall be necessary and proper for carrying into Execution the foregoing Powers, and all other Powers vested by this Constitution in the Government of the United States, or any Department or Officer thereof."

negative rights theory In ethics, the theory that says that rights are human inventions created to escape moral law.

negligence The failure to use that amount of care that a reasonably prudent person would have used under the same circumstances and conditions.

negligent credentialing Occurs if a hospital has retained a physician that the governing body of the hospital knew or should have known was incompetent.

negligent hiring The proprietor's liability for the hiring of an incompetent contractor who consequently harms an innocent third party while performing the hired-for work.

negligent retention The failure of a proprietor to dismiss an incompetent contractor after the proprietor has learned of the contractor's incompetence.

negotiable instrument A written document that is signed by the maker or drawer and that contains an unconditional promise or order to pay a certain sum of money on delivery or at a definite time to the bearer or to order.

negotiated rule making Occurs when an agency that is about to create a new rule or revise existing rules enters into a cooperative process by which all parties affected by the rule have a chance to shape the final form that the rule will take.

negotiation The transfer of a negotiable instrument in such form that the transferee becomes a holder.

new world order A set of initial conditions that describes how nation-states relate to one another on a global scale.

next of kin Those who are most nearly related by blood.

NINJA loan A loan that has been negotiated by a borrower with "no income, no job, and no assets."

No Electronic Theft Act (NET Act) A federal law that grants limited immunity to persons who duplicate copyrighted works on the Internet, as long as those users do not profit from the copying process.

no-fault insurance A type of automobile insurance that allows drivers to collect damages and medical expenses from their own insurance carriers regardless of who is at fault in an accident.

nominal damages Token damages awarded to parties who have experienced an injury to their legal rights but no actual loss.

nonconforming goods Goods that are not the same as those called for under a contract or that are in some way defective.

nonconforming uses Uses of land permitted to continue even though newly enacted zoning laws no longer permit similar uses.

nondelegable duty A duty that the proprietor cannot delegate, or pass off, to another party.

nondisclosure See *passive fraud*.

nondisclosure agreement An agreement that requires employees to promise that, should they leave their employment with their present employer, they will not reveal any confidential trade secrets that they may learn at their current job.

noneconomic compensatory damages Damages that result from injuries that are intangible and, therefore, not directly quantifiable. Examples include damages resulting from pain and suffering, mental anguish, and loss of companionship.

non-governmental organization (NGO) An organization that functions beyond the boundaries of any one governmental body.

North American Free Trade Agreement (NAFTA) A trading coalition that includes the United States, Canada, and Mexico

note A written promise by one party to pay money to another party. Also called *promissory note*.

novation The substitution, by mutual agreement, of another party for one of the original parties to a contract.

object code A computer program after it has been translated by the computer into a language that only the computer can comprehend.

obligee In contract law, the party to whom another party owes an obligation.

obligor In contract law, the party who is obligated to deliver on a promise or to undertake some act.

obstruction of justice In criminal law, an activity designed to prevent the discovery, apprehension, arrest, prosecution, conviction, or punishment of a criminal defendant.

obvious-to-try standard A patent challenge that asserts anyone of ordinary skill could see the invention was obvious to try, which makes the invention not be patentable.

ocean marine insurance A type of insurance that covers ships at sea.

offer In contract law, a proposal made by one party to another indicating a willingness to enter into a contract.

offeree In contract law, the person to whom an offer is made.

offeror In contract law, the person who makes the offer.

Office of Investor Advocate Subtitle A of Title XI of the Dodd-Frank Act creates a new agency, referred to as the Office of Investor Advocate (OIA), the purpose of which is to help make the work of broker-dealers and investment advisors (IAs) more transparent.

Oil Pollution Act A federal law designed to encourage companies that ship, drill for, and store oil to develop and use the most up-to-date equipment and the most effective safety measures possible.

open-end credit Credit that can be increased by the debtor, up to a limit set by the creditor, by continuing to purchase goods on credit.

open-price terms A contract for the sale of goods that is established even though the price is not settled.

operating agreement An agreement containing various rights, provisions, and powers that aid in establishing the bylaws of an LLC.

option In contract law, the giving of consideration to support an offeror's promise to hold an offer open for a stated or reasonable length of time. Also called *option contract.*

order bill of lading A negotiable bill of lading.

order for relief In bankruptcy law, a court's command that the liquidation begin.

order paper A negotiable instrument that is payable to someone's order.

ordinary life insurance See *straight life insurance.*

ordinary negligence Failure to use that amount of care that a reasonable person would use under the same circumstance.

original jurisdiction The authority of a court to hear a case when it is first brought to court.

ostensible authority Occurs when a hospital leads a patient to believe that a physician with staff privileges is an employee of the hospital.

output contract An agreement in which a seller agrees to sell "all the goods we manufacture" or "all the crops we produce" to a particular buyer. See also *requirements contract.*

outside party See *third party.*

overdraft A payment by a bank on behalf of a customer for more than the customer has on deposit.

paper data Data in a computer system that have been printed out in a hard copy for storage or filing in a conventional way.

par value The value that is placed on the shares of stock at incorporation.

parol evidence rule The rule that states that evidence of oral statements made before signing a written agreement is usually not admissible in court to change or to contradict the terms of a written agreement.

part performance An exception to the rule that contracts for the sale of land must be in writing. It applies when a person relies on an owner's oral promise to sell real estate and then makes improvements on the property or changes his or her position in an important way. Also called *equitable estoppel.*

partially disclosed principal A person, in a transaction conducted by an agent, whose existence is known to the third party but whose specific identify is unknown.

participation loan A loan in which the borrower will transfer certain ownership or equity rights to the lender in exchange for a lower interest rate or a lower down payment.

partnering A process that establishes supportive relationships among the parties to a contract to head off disputes before they occur.

partnership An association of two or more persons to carry on a business for profit.

partnership at will A partnership in which any partner may leave without liability.

partnership by estoppel A partnership that occurs when someone says or does something that leads a third party to reasonably believe that a partnership exists.

passenger A person who enters the premises of a carrier with the intention of buying a ticket for a trip. One continues to be a passenger as long as the trip continues.

passing bad checks In criminal law, issuing or transferring a check or other negotiable instrument knowing it will be dishonored and with the intent to defraud.

passive fraud A failure to reveal some material fact about the subject matter of a contract that one party is obligated to reveal to the other party and that intentionally deceives that second party, leading him or her into a damaging contract. Also called *concealment* and *nondisclosure.*

past consideration A promise to give another something of value in return for goods or services rendered and delivered in the past.

patent A grant from the government that gives an inventor the exclusive right to make, use, and sell an invention for a period set by Congress.

pawn See *pledge.*

payee The party named in a note or draft to whom payment is to be made.

payor bank A bank by which an item is payable as drawn or accepted. It includes a drawee bank.

per se violation In antitrust law, a restraint of trade practice so serious that it is prohibited whether or not it actually harms anyone.

perfected The state of a security interest when the secured party has done everything that the law requires to give the secured party greater rights to the goods than others have.

performance In contract law, the situation that exists when the parties to a contract have done what they had agreed to do.

periodic tenancy A leasehold estate, or tenancy, that continues for successive periods until one of the parties terminates it by giving notice to the other party.

perjury In criminal law, making false statements under oath.

personal defense In negotiable-instruments law, a defense that can be used against a holder but not against a holder in due course of a negotiable instrument. Also called *limited defense*.

personal injury protection (PIP) Automobile insurance which places limitations on the insured's ability to sue other drivers but allows drivers to collect damages and medical expenses from their own insurance carriers, regardless of who is at fault in an accident.

personal jurisdiction A court's authority over the parties to a lawsuit.

personal property Everything that can be owned other than real estate.

personal representative Executors and administrators of wills in states that have adopted the Uniform Probate Code.

persuasive precedent A previous case that a court is free to follow or to ignore.

phishing A cyberspoofing method that involves sending out phony e-mails that solicit buyers and, in the process, obtaining credit card information, account numbers, passwords, and the like.

physical duress Violence or the threat of violence against an individual or that person's family, household, or property that is so serious that it forces a person into a contract against his or her will.

picketing The placement of persons for observation, patrol, and demonstration at the site of employment as part of employee pressure on an employer to meet a demand.

pie powder court Historically in the Middle Ages in Europe, a court set up at a festival to handle disputes between merchants at that festival.

pierce the corporate veil The doctrine holding shareholders of a corporation personally liable when they have used the corporation as a facade to defraud or commit some other misdeed.

plaintiff The person who begins a lawsuit by filing a complaint in the appropriate trial court of general jurisdiction.

pledge The giving up of personal property as security for performance of an act or repayment of a debt.

pledgee A person to whom property is given as security for a loan.

pledgor A person who gives property to another as security for a loan.

plenary review The process by which appellate courts determine if lower courts have made errors of law.

police power A state's authority to restrict private rights to promote and maintain public health, safety, welfare, and morals.

policy The contract of insurance.

pooling agreement An agreement made by shareholders whereby they promise to vote the same way on a particular issue. Also called *shareholder agreements* and *voting agreements*.

Population Commission (PC) A group that was created under the auspices of the UN Economic and Social Council to investigate demographic concerns and to consult with the ECOSOC on a variety of population issues.

positive law theory In ethics, the theory that says that laws originate from an outside source that emerges within society.

post-appellate procedures The process of taking a case that has been rejected or dismissed by a domestic court to an international organization, such as the Inter-American Commission on Human Rights of the Organization of American States.

precedent A model case that a court can follow when facing a similar situation.

preemption The process by which the courts decide that a federal statute must take precedence over a state statute.

preemptive right A shareholder's right to purchase a proportionate share of every new offering of stock by the corporation.

preemptive war A conflict waged when one nation attacks a sovereign nation to stop that nation from engaging in activities that the attacking nation has decided are against its national interests.

preexisting duty An obligation that a party is already bound to by law or by some other agreement. The party may not use this as consideration in a new contract.

preferred stock A class of stock that carries with it the right to receive payment of dividends and/or the distribution of assets on the dissolution of the corporation before other classes of stock receive their payments.

preliminary hearing A court procedure during which the judge decides whether probable cause exists to continue holding a defendant for a crime.

premarriage agreement In contract law, an agreement between two people planning marriage and who agree in writing to change the property rights they possess by law.

premeditated murder In criminal law, killing someone with prior calculation and design, or while committing a serious felony such as rape, robbery or kidnapping.

premium The consideration paid by the insured to the insurer for insurance protection.

prenuptial agreement An agreement between two people who are planning marriage and who agree to change the property rights they possess by law in a marriage.

prescriptive theory A system of ethical thought that describes how to come up with the values at work within a social system.

presenting bank Any bank presenting an item except a payor bank.

presentment A demand for acceptance or payment of a negotiable instrument made upon the maker, acceptor, or drawee by or on behalf of the holder of the instrument.

preventative war A war waged to prevent another nation-state from reaching a point that it would be capable of attacking the first nation.

prima facie evidence (PRY·mah FAY·shee) Evidence that is legally sufficient to prove a fact in the absence of evidence to the contrary.

primary committee In bankruptcy law, a committee of creditors set up to work with a debtor in drawing up a reorganization plan.

principal A person who authorizes an agent to act on her or his behalf and subject to her or his control.

principal objective The main goal that the parties to a contract hoped to meet by entering the contract in the first place.

primary objective test A rule that states a writing is not needed for enforcement if the promise to pay another party's debt is made to obtain a gain for the guarantor.

principle of honorable surrender A criterion under a modern version of the just war theory that requires a victor to accept the surrender of the enemy and to treat the defeated combatants with dignity and respect.

principle of repentance A criterion under a modern version of the just war theory that calls for a genuine expression of remorse for the death and destruction caused by war.

principle of restoration A criterion under a modern version of the just war theory that requires a victor in a conflict to act responsibly in rebuilding the defeated nation's physical environment, economy, and governmental structure.

prior art All relevant technical knowledge about the field to which the invention belongs.

private carriers Companies, not in the transportation business, that operate their own trucks and other vehicles to transport their own goods.

private civil trial Trials run according to the same rules of procedure and evidence as trials run under the official auspices of the court. In a private trial, the parties can hold the trial when and where they choose, and they can choose the judge. Lengthy civil cases are well-suited to this approach.

private corporation A corporation formed by private persons to accomplish a task best undertaken by an entity that can raise large amounts of capital quickly or that can grant the protection of limited liability.

private information Reports on personal matters, family matters, sexual habits, employment records, medical data, and financial records. Also called *private-private* information.

private warehouser A warehouser whose warehouse is not for general public use.

privity In contract law, the relationship that exists between two parties to a contract giving each a recognized interest in the subject matter of the contract so that they are bound to that contract.

probability of success A criterion under the just war theory that states that a war must be waged only when there is a reasonable chance of success.

probate To settle the estate of a decedent under the supervision of a court.

product liability A law that imposes liability on the manufacturer and the seller of a product produced and sold in a defective condition.

professional An individual who can perform a highly specialized task because of special abilities, education, experience, and knowledge.

promissory estoppel The legal doctrine that restricts an offeror from revoking an offer under certain conditions, even though consideration has not been promised to bind the agreement. To be effective, promissory estoppel requires that the offeror know, or be presumed to know, that the offeree might otherwise make a definite and decided change of position in contemplation of promises contained in the offer.

promoters The people who do the day-to-day work involved in creating a corporation.

property damage liability insurance A type of automobile insurance that provides protection when other people bring claims or lawsuits against the insured for damaging property such as a car, a fence, or a tree.

proportionality A criterion under the just war theory that states that the good advanced by the war must exceed the negative consequences of entering the conflict.

proprietor An owner, as of a business. The party for which an independent contractor works.

prosecutor An attorney that represents the government in a criminal procedure.

prospectus A document published by a corporation explaining, in simplified fashion for potential investors, the details of a stock issuance and the business making the offer.

protective war A war aimed at providing aid and assistance to innocent civilians who are being victimized by the military of their own nation-state.

protest A certificate of dishonor that states that a draft was presented for acceptance or payment and was dishonored.

provisional Not final.

proximate cause In tort law, the connection between the unreasonable conduct and the resulting harm. Proximate cause is determined by asking whether the harm that resulted from the conduct was foreseeable at the time of the original negligent act.

proxy The authority given to one shareholder to cast another shareholder's votes.

proxy contest A struggle between two factions in a corporation, usually management and a group of dissident shareholders, to obtain the votes of the other shareholders.

proxy solicitation The process by which one shareholder asks another for his or her voting right.

proxy statement A document that communicates information about the identity of a solicitor, the reason for a solicitation, and all other crucial information that shareholders need to make an informed decision about a proxy.

public accountant (PA) An accountant who works for a variety of clients but who is not certified.

Public Company Accounting Oversight Board A regulatory agency that is charged with the task of making certain that correct, unbiased, and comprehensive data finds their way to potential investors, so that they can make informed decisions about investment opportunities.

public corporation A corporation created by the federal, state, or local government for governmental purposes. Also, a large private corporation that generally sells its stock to the public at large.

public interest The idea that certain activities affect the entire social structure and must, therefore, be regulated by the government.

public offer An offer made through the public media but intended for only one person whose identity or address is unknown to the offeror.

public policy The general legal principle that says no one should be allowed to do anything that tends to injure the public at large.

public warehouser A warehouser who owns a warehouse where any member of the public who is willing to pay the regular charge may store goods.

pump and dump scheme A scheme designed to lure unsuspecting investors into the trap of investing in what is essentially an empty shell, that is, a poorly financed corporation that appears to be more valuable than it really is.

punitive damages Damages in excess of actual losses suffered by the plaintiff awarded as a measure of punishment for the defendant's wrongful acts. Also called *exemplary damages*.

purchase money security interest A security interest that arises when someone lends money to a consumer and then takes a security interest in the goods that the consumer buys.

purpose In criminal law, the intent to cause the result that does, in fact, occur.

qualified indorsement An indorsement in which words, such as "without recourse," have been added to the signature to limit the liability of the indorser.

qualified opinion An opinion issued by an auditor saying that, as of a given date, the books of a firm represent its financial health; however, the auditor may qualify the opinion either because the firm is facing some uncertainty that might affect the company in the future or because the firm has deviated from generally accepted accounting principles (GAAP) in some minor way.

qualifying exigency leave Leave time that is granted to employees permitting them to use as much as 20 weeks to take care of certain nonmedical emergencies during the time that a spouse, child, or parent is on active duty in the military

quasi-contract See *implied-in-law contract.*

quasi-public corporation A corporation that is privately organized for profit but also provides a service upon which the public is dependent.

quasi-RPM arrangement An agreement that occurs when a manufacturer lets retailers know the price that it expects to see on an item and declines to sell that item to any retailer that does not list the item at that price.

quid pro quo **sexual harassment** A supervisor's unwelcome advancement or suggestion to a subordinate to trade sexual favors for preferential treatment.

quiet enjoyment The right of a tenant to the undisturbed possession of the property that he or she is renting.

quitclaim deed A deed that transfers to the buyer only the interest that the seller may have in a property and that contains no warranties.

racial profiling The act of targeting a person for criminal investigation primarily because of racial or ethnic characteristics.

ratification The principal's approval of an unauthorized act performed by an agent or by one who has no authority to act as an agent. Also, an approval of a contract made by a minor after reaching maturity.

rational ethics A system of ethical thought that uses reason as the basis for making ethical judgments.

real defense In negotiable-instruments law, any defense that can be used against everyone, including holders in due course. Also called *absolute defense* and *universal defense.*

real estate The ground and everything permanently attached to it including land, buildings, and growing trees and shrubs; the air space above the land is also included.

real property The ground and everything permanently attached to it including land, buildings, and growing trees and shrubs; the air space above the land is also included.

reasonable accommodation The quality of accommodation that allows a disabled worker to accomplish essential functions in the workplace without imposing undue hardship on the employer.

reasonable care The degree of care that a reasonably prudent person would have used under the same circumstances and conditions.

reasonable time In contract law, the time that may fairly, properly, and conveniently be required to do the task that is to be done, with regard to attending circumstances.

rebuttable presumption A disputable presumption that a defending party has the right to attack.

rebuttal The presentation of evidence to discredit the evidence by the opposition and to reestablish the credibility of his or her own evidence.

recklessness In criminal law, a perverse disregard for a known risk of a negative result.

registered limited liability partnership (RLLP or LLP) A general partnership in which partners are not jointly or severally liable for partnership liabilities caused by the act or omission of another partner or employee unless the partner had supervision over the other partner or employee.

registration statement A statement required by the Securities and Exchange Commission to indicate details about a business selling securities.

reg-neg See *negotiated rule making.*

regulations Rules made by the regulatory agencies of the federal and/or state governments.

regulatory justice A fair and balanced interpretation of the law that evolves from and is consistent with previous law.

rehabilitate In contract law, the process of compensating an innocent party for losses that result from a breach of contract.

rejection The express or implied refusal by an offeree to accept an offer.

release In contract law, a promise made by one party agreeing not to sue a second party.

remainder estate A future interest in property when title is to pass to someone other than the grantor or grantor's heirs at the expiration of a life estate.

remitting bank Any payor or intermediary bank remitting for an item.

removal A request to a U.S. District Court to accept a case that was first filed in a state court.

renter's insurance An insurance policy that protects tenants against loss of personal property, against liability for a visitor's personal injury, and against liability for negligent destruction of the rented premises.

renunciation A legal act by which a person abandons a right acquired, but without transferring it to another.

reorganization In bankruptcy law, a plan created by a qualified debtor that alters his or her repayment schedule and allows the debtor to stay in business.

request for admission A request made to secure a statement from a party that a particular fact is true or that a document or set of documents is genuine.

request for physical or mental examination A request for a party to undergo a physical or a mental examination.

request for real evidence A discovery device that asks the opposing party in a lawsuit to produce papers, records, accounts, correspondence, photographs, or other tangible evidence including ESI.

requirements contract An agreement in which one party agrees to purchase all of his or her requirements of a particular product from another party. See also *output contract.*

rescission A remedy in contract law that returns both parties to a contract back to their original positions before the contract was entered into.

reserve funds Earnings from a business that are held in reserve.

resisting arrest In criminal law, interfering with the lawful arrest of a criminal defendant.

respondeat superior (re·SPOND·ee·yat se·PEER·ee·or) The legal doctrine that imposes liability on employers and makes them pay for torts committed by their employees within the scope of the employer's business. Literally translated, it means "Let the master respond."

restraint of trade A limitation on the full exercise of doing business with others.

restrictive covenant A promise by an employee in an employment contract not to work for anyone else in the same field of employment for a specified time period within a particular geographical area.

restrictive employment covenant A promise by an employee in an employment contract not to work for anyone else in the same field of employment for a specified time period within a particular geographical area.

restrictive indorsement An indorsement in which words have been added to the signature of the indorser that specify the purpose of the indorsement or the use to be made of the commercial paper, such as "for deposit only."

reverse discrimination A practice designed to eliminate discrimination against a protected class but that has the opposite effect on members of another protected class.

reverse mortgage A type of loan that allows home owners, over the age of 62, to convert some of the equity in their home into cash while retaining ownership of their home.

reversion estate A future interest in property when title is to return to the grantor or grantor's heirs upon expiration of a life estate.

Revised Uniform Partnership Act (RUPA) The latest partnership statute written by the National Conference of Commissioners on Uniform State Laws.

revocation The calling back of an offer by the offeror.

revolving charge account A charge account with an outstanding balance at all times.

right intention A criterion under the just war theory that states that a war must be waged only if the combatant has the correct objective.

right of way See *easement.*

right-to-work laws State laws that prohibit labor-management agreements requiring union membership as a condition of getting or keeping a job.

riparian owners People who own land along the bank of a river or stream. They have certain rights and duties with respect to the water that flows over, under, and beside their land.

robbery The act of taking personal property from the possession of another against that person's will and under threat to do great bodily harm or damage.

royalty In intellectual property law, the consideration paid to an author or an inventor for permission to use the intellectual property of that author or inventor.

RPM agreement The agreement between a retailer and a manufacturer that the retailer will sell certain products at a price set by the manufacturer.

rule of contemporary ownership The rule that holds that shareholders must own stock at the time of the injury and at the time of the lawsuit if they wish to begin a derivative suit.

rule-of-reason standard In antitrust law, a doctrine that holds that a court should stop certain practices only if they are an unreasonable restriction of competition.

S corporation A corporation in which shareholders have agreed to have the profits (or losses) of the corporation taxed directly to them rather than to the corporation.

Safe Harbor Principles Principles of electronically stored information (ESI) protection established by the Department of Commerce that, if followed by American companies, will qualify them for commerce with the EU.

sale A contract in which ownership of goods is transferred by the seller to the buyer for a price.

sale on approval A conditional sale that becomes absolute only if the buyer approves or is satisfied with the article being sold.

sale or return A sale in which the buyer takes title to goods with the right to revest title in the seller after a specified period or reasonable time.

sales puffery Persuasive words or exaggerated arguments made by salespeople to induce customers to buy their product. As long as such comments are reserved to opinion and do not misstate facts, they are not actionable as fraud, even if they turn out to be grossly in error. Also called *puffery*.

salvage A reward given to persons who voluntarily assist a sinking ship to recover its cargo from peril or loss.

salvor A person who salvages. The law of salvage gives the salvor the right to compensation for assisting a foundering vessel.

same state locality rule A means to judge a health care provider's actions on the basis of the standard of care used in the same state in which that provider practices.

Sarbanes-Oxley Act Legislation that places an affirmative duty on the directors of publicly traded corporations to monitor whether they are conforming to all legal requirements.

satisfaction The agreed-to settlement as contained in an accord.

satisfactory performance In contract law, the situation that exists when either personal taste or objective standards determine the contracting parties have performed their contractual duties according to the agreement.

science court A proposed court that would act as a forum for disputes involving scientific and technological controversies.

scope of authority The range of acts done while performing agency duties. Also called *scope of employment*.

scope of employment See *scope of authority*.

screen display The audiovisual configuration that appears on the screen of the computer monitor.

seal A mark or impression placed on a written contract indicating that the instrument was executed and accepted in a formal manner.

second degree murder In criminal law, the purposeful killing of another human being without premeditation.

second mortgage See *junior mortgage*.

secondary boycott Conspiracy in which a union places pressure on a neutral customer or supplier with whom the union has no dispute in order to cause the neutral entity to cease doing business with the employer with whom the union has a dispute.

second-level domain (SLD) name Indicates the actual name, trade name, or other identifying mark of the institution, organization, or business using the domain name.

secret partner A partner whose identity and existence are not known outside of the firm but who can participate in the management of the firm.

Secretariat The administrative bureaucracy of the United Nations.

Secretary-General of the United Nations The chief administrator of the United Nations.

secured loan A loan in which creditors have something of value, usually called collateral, from which they can be paid if the debtor does not pay.

secured party A lender or seller who holds a security interest.

securitization The process of bundling securities and then selling them to big investors.

security In secured transactions, the assurance that a creditor will be paid back for any money loaned or credit extended to a debtor. In corporate law, a money investment that expects a return solely because of another person's efforts.

security agreement A written agreement that creates a security interest.

security-based swaps According to the SEC, these are "swaps based on (1) a single security, (2) a loan, (3) a narrow-based group or index of securities, or (4) events relating to a single issuer or issuers of securities in a narrow-based security index."

Security Council The United Nations body that deals with international crises.

security interest A creditor's right to use collateral to recover a debt.

self-defense A defense to criminal liability available to defendants if they can demonstrate (1) that they did not start the altercation, (2) that they had good reason to believe they were in danger of death or severe bodily injury, and (3) that they used only enough force to repel the attack.

servant An outdated term signifying a person employed to perform services in the affairs of another and who, with respect to the physical conduct in the performance of the service, is subject to the other's right to control.

service of process The act of giving the summons and the complaint to a defendant.

servient tenement The property through which an easement is created or through which it extends.

settlement week An ADR technique in which the court clears its docket of all business except settlement hearings.

severalty The quality or state of sole ownership of a single property.

sexual harassment A type of sexual discrimination.

shares Portions of a corporation that may be owned by the various shareholders.

shareholder democracy A theory of corporate management that favors making management more responsive to shareholders by giving shareholders greater voting power and by making it easier for shareholders to sue managers.

shareholder of record A person to whom stock has been transferred and whose name has been entered on the corporate books as the owner of that stock. Shareholders of record are entitled to vote, receive dividends, and enjoy all other privileges of being a shareholder.

shareholder proposal A suggestion submitted by a shareholder about a broad company policy or procedure.

shareholder resolution In corporate law, a suggestion about a broad company policy or procedure submitted by a shareholder.

shareholders Persons who own units of ownership interest called shares of stock in a corporation. Also called *stockholders*.

shelter provision A provision whereby a holder who receives an instrument from a holder in due course acquires the rights of the holder in due course even though he or she does not qualify as a holder in due course.

shipment contract A contract under which a seller turns goods over to a carrier for delivery to a buyer. Both the title and risk of loss pass to the buyer when the goods are given to the carrier.

shoplifting The act of stealing goods from a store.

sight draft A draft that is payable as soon as it is presented to the drawee for payment.

silent partner A partner who does not participate in the day-to-day business of the firm.

similar locality rule The rule that allows a court to judge a health care provider's degree of care by determining how the same procedure is performed at another hospital located in a similar locality.

similar practitioner rule A means to judge a health care provider's actions according to whether that provider is a general practitioner or a specialist.

situational ethics A system of ethical thought that argues that each of us can judge a person's ethical decisions only by initially placing ourselves in that person's position.

slamming The illegal practice of changing a consumer's telephone service without permission.

slander Any false statement that harms a person's good name or reputation made in a temporary form, such as speech, and communicated to others.

slight negligence The failure to use that degree of care that persons of extraordinary prudence and foresight are accustomed to use.

social contract theory In ethics, a theory that says that right and wrong are measured by the obligations imposed on each individual by an implied agreement among individuals within a given social system.

social media policy (SMP) In employment law, a set of rules written by an employer telling employees what they can and cannot do when using electronic communication devices, formats, Web sites, and other electronic messaging techniques, such as blogs, text messages, tweets, skype transmissions, and e-mails.

software contract A contract involving the sale or licensing of information in a digital format.

sole proprietorship A business formed by the sole proprietor. It is the easiest business organization to form.

source code A set of instructions that tells the computer what to do or how to perform a particular task.

source code escrow agreement An agreement in which the computer source code is deposited with a third party. Once the agreement is made, the code can be released only by following precisely outlined procedures and usually only if both the buyer and seller agree to the release.

sovereign immunity The somewhat discredited doctrine preventing a lawsuit against government authority without the government's consent.

spam Unsolicited e-mail.

special agent A person who is authorized to conduct only a particular transaction or to perform only a specified act for a principal.

special indorsement An indorsement made by first writing on the back of a negotiable instrument an order to pay a specified person and then signing the instrument. Also called *indorsement in full*.

special interest group control A corporate control theory that is based on the fact that because corporate decision making impacts special interest groups, those groups should participate in that decision-making process.

special jurisdiction The power of a court to hear only certain kinds of cases.

special warranty deed A deed containing express warranties under which the grantor guarantees that no defects arose in the title during the time that he or she owned the property.

specific performance A decree from a court ordering a contracting party to carry out the promises made in a contract.

speculative damages Damage computed on losses that have not actually been suffered and that cannot be proved; they are based entirely on an expectation of losses that might be suffered from a breach; the courts do not allow speculative damages.

staff privileges When a hospital grants physicians, who are not employed by the hospital, the privilege to treat their patients at that hospital.

stale check A check that is presented for payment more than six months after its date.

standard construction rule A theory of legal interpretation under which the court will determine the principal objective of the parties in the making of the contract.

staple court Historically in Europe in the Middle Ages, courts charged with the responsibility for cases involving a set type of goods or a set commodity (a staple).

state control A theory of corporate management that is based on the belief that because corporate decision making impacts upon more individuals and groups than just the shareholders and the managers, those corporate decisions should be made by an impartial group of corporate outsiders, usually government officials.

statute A law passed by a legislature.

Statute of Frauds A law requiring certain contracts to be in writing to be enforceable.

statute of repose An absolute time limit for bringing a cause of action regardless of when the cause of action accrues, such as a certain number of years after a defective product has been sold to an injured customer.

statutes of limitations State laws that restrict the time within which a party is allowed to bring legal action against another.

statutory agent An individual who is designated to receive service of process when a lawsuit is filed against a corporation or an LLC.

statutory interpretation The process by which courts analyze aspects of a statute that are unclear or ambiguous or that were not anticipated at the time the legislature passed the statute.

stock acquisition The purchase of enough of the voting stock of a corporation to allow the buyer to control the corporation. Also called *takeover*.

stock certificate Written evidence of ownership of a unit of interest in a corporation.

stock dividends Dividends paid to shareholders in the form of shares of capital stock.

stoppage in transit A right of the seller, upon learning that the buyer is insolvent, to have the delivery of goods stopped before they reach their destination.

straight bill of lading A bill of lading that does not contain words of negotiability.

straight life insurance Insurance that requires the payment of premiums throughout the life of the insured and pays the beneficiary the face value of the policy upon the insured's death.

strict liability The doctrine under which people may be liable for injuries to others whether or not they have been negligent or committed an international tort. Also called *absolute liability*.

strike A stoppage of work by employees as a means of enforcing a demand made on their employers.

subjective ethics An ethical theory that holds that there are no objective or absolute standards of right and wrong.

subject matter jurisdiction The power of a court to hear a particular type of case.

subject to the mortgage An agreement whereby the seller of real property that is already mortgaged agrees to continue paying the mortgage payments.

sublease A lease given by a lessee to a third person conveying the same interest for a shorter term than the period for which the lessee is holding it. Also called *underlease*.

subordinate To place in a lower order.

subordinated mortgage A mortgage that is reduced in priority to a person holding a second mortgage.

subordination agreement An agreement made by holders of first mortgages to allow their mortgage to be reduced in priority to a person holding a second mortgage.

subrogation The right of one party to substitute itself for another party.

substantial performance In contract law, the situation that results when a party to a contract, in good faith, executes all the promised terms and conditions of the contract with the exception of minor details that do not affect the real intent of their agreement.

substantial similarity test A test to determine whether a work has violated a copyrighted work's integrity by determining whether the two are so like one another that an ordinary reasonable observer would have no recourse other than to conclude that the second was copied from the first.

substitute check A paper reproduction of both sides of an original check that can be processed electronically.

substitute transportation insurance Insurance that reimburses the insured up to specific limits for transportation costs while a car is undergoing covered repairs.

sui generis A law unto itself. An area of the law that has developed its own independent self-contained rules.

suitor A corporation or individual who offers to purchase the voting stock of a corporation with the objective of taking over the corporation.

summary judgment motion A motion that asks a court for an immediate judgment for the party filing the motion because both parties agree on the facts in the case and because under law the party who introduced the motion is entitled to a favorable judgment.

summary jury trial A shortened version of a trial conducted in less than a day before a jury. The jury's verdict is advisory only.

surety One who stands behind executors or administrators and becomes responsible for their wrongdoing.

surplus Funds that remain after a partnership has been dissolved and all other debts and prior obligations have been settled.

surrebuttal A reply to the defendant's rebuttal.

survival statute A state law that allows a lawsuit to be brought even if both the plaintiff and the defendant are deceased.

takeover bid In corporate law, the offer to buy the voting stock of a corporation.

tampering with evidence In criminal law, altering, destroying, or removing any piece of evidence with the intent to somehow lessen the probative value of that evidence.

target In corporate law, a corporation that is the object of a takeover bid.

target corporation The object of a tender offer.

targeted shareholder agreement An agreement by which a suitor negotiates a deal with certain shareholders to provide them with employment-related deals that supplement the price they will receive for selling their stock.

tariff-based principle A principle that states that the only way that World Trade Organization nations can regulate the imports of other nations is through tariffs.

TARP A federal program (Troubled Asset Relief Program) that is designed to allow the government to buy troubled assets that resulted from the securitization epidemic.

taxable costs In procedural law, litigation costs that are charged to the losing party.

taxable expenses Legal expenses, such as those involved in filing a case and issuing subpoenas.

teaching, suggestion, or motivation test, or TSM standard A traditional test that requires patent challengers to demonstrate that the innovation would have been obvious to any one exposed to the same teaching session, the same off-hand suggestion, or the same motivation as the inventor had been exposed to.

teller's check See *bank draft.*

temporary public figures People who are placed against their will into the public view by some event beyond their control.

tenancy An interest in real estate that is held under a lease. Also called *leasehold estate.*

tenancy at sufferance A leasehold estate, or tenancy, that arises when a tenant wrongfully remains in possession of the premise after his or her tenancy has expired.

tenancy at will A leasehold estate, or tenancy, that continues for as long as both parties desire.

tenancy by entirety Ownership by husband and wife, considered by the law as one, with full ownership surviving to the living spouse on the death of the other.

tenancy for years A leasehold estate, or tenancy, for a fixed period of time.

tenancy from year to year See *periodic tenancy.*

tenancy in partnership Ownership in which each person has an interest in partnership property and is co-owner of such property.

tenant A person to whom real property is rented or leased. Also called *lessee.*

tenants in common Owners of an undivided interest in property, with each owner's rights going to his or her heirs upon death rather than to the surviving cotenants.

tender To offer to turn goods over to a buyer.

tender of delivery An offer by the seller of goods to turn the goods over to the buyer.

tender of payment An offer by the buyer of goods to turn the money over to the seller.

tender of performance An offer to do what one has agreed to do under the terms of a contract.

tender offer A public offer by a suitor to buy voting stock.

term insurance Insurance that is issued for a particular period, usually five or ten years.

term partnership A partnership that is set up to run for a set time period or in order to accomplish a task of some sort.

termination by waiver The situation that exists when a party to a contract with the right to complain of the other party's unsatisfactory performance or nonperformance fails to complain.

testamentary trust A trust that is created by a will.

testate Having made a valid will. Compare *intestate.*

testator (male); testatrix (female) A person who makes a will.

theft In criminal law, knowingly taking or obtaining control over the property of another without consent, using deceit, threats, or coercion.

theft in office In criminal law, an offense that involves the use of a governmental official's governmental or party power to obtain unlawful control over governmental or party property or services.

third party In contract law, a person who may, in some way, be affected by a contract but who is not one of the contracting parties. Also called *outside party.*

third-party beneficiary In contract law, a party who is not involved in an original contract but who, nevertheless, benefits from that contract.

time-based threshold In insurance law, a threshold ascertained by measuring the time that the victim has been incapacitated.

time draft A draft that is not payable until the lapse of a particular time period stated on the draft.

threshold guidelines In insurance law, guidelines that determine when victims can bring a lawsuit for injuries that result from an auto accident.

tippees People who receive inside information about corporate stock without being involved in any business need to obtain that information.

title The right of ownership to goods. Also, a subdivision of a code containing all the statutes that deal with a particular area of law.

top-level domain (TLD) name The portion of the domain name that identifies the addressee's zone, for example, .com, .org, or .edu.

tort A private wrong that injures another person's physical well-being, property, or reputation.

tortfeasor A person who commits a tort.

tortious bailee Any party unlawfully in possession of another's personal property.

towing and labor insurance Insurance that reimburses up to specified limits for towing and labor charges whenever a car breaks down, whether or not an accident is involved.

trade acceptance A draft used by a seller of goods to receive payment and also to extend credit. It is often used in combination with a bill of lading.

trade fixtures Items of personal property brought upon the land by a tenant that are necessary to carry on the trade or business to which the premises will be devoted. Contrary to the general rule, trade fixtures remain the personal property of the tenant and are removable at the expiration of the terms of occupancy.

trade secrets A plan, process, or device that is used in a business and is known only to employees who need to know the secret to carry out their jobs.

trademark Any word, name, symbol, or device adopted and used by a manufacturer or merchant to identify goods and distinguish them from those manufactured or sold by others.

transactions in computer information A contract whose subject matter entails the acquisition, development, or distribution of computer information.

transient A person who accepts the service of a hotel or other public accommodation without any obligation to remain a specified length of time.

transnational organizations or transnats Nongovernmental organizations that have neither earned status nor demonstrated the ability, or even willingness, to be accountable for their actions on the world stage.

traveler's check A draft purchased from a bank or express company and signed by the purchaser at the time of cashing as a precaution against forgery.

treason The levying of war against the United States, or the giving of aid and comfort to the nation's enemies.

true locality rule A means to judge a health care provider's actions on the basis of the standard of care used in the exact same locality or community.

trust A legal device by which property is held by one person for the benefit of another.

trustee A person who is entrusted with the management and control of another's property or the rights associated with that property.

Tunney or Antitrust Procedures and Penalties Act The federal statute that regulates the Justice Department's antitrust consent decrees.

tying agreement In antitrust law, an illegal practice that occurs when one party refuses to sell a given product unless the buyer also purchases another product tied to the first product.

UN Commission on International Trade Law (UNCITRAL) The UN organization charged with the task of organizing and integrating international law in relation to international trade.

UN Convention on Contracts for the International Sale of Goods (CISG) International agreement governing sales of goods between businesses located in different countries.

unconscionable contract A contract that is so one-sided that it is oppressive and gives unfair advantage to one of the parties.

unconscionable Ridiculously inadequate.

underinsured-motorist insurance Insurance that provides protection against the risk of being injured by an underinsured motorist.

underlease See *sublease*.

undisclosed principal A person, in a transaction conducted by an agent, whose existence and identity are unknown to the third party.

undisputed amount An amount upon which the parties to a contract have mutually agreed.

undue hardship The amount of inconvenience beyond that which is required of an employer who seeks to provide reasonable accommodation for a disabled worker.

undue influence The use of excessive pressure by the dominant member of a confidential relationship to convince the weaker party to enter a contract that greatly benefits the dominant party.

unenforceable contract A contract that cannot be upheld by a court because of some rule of law.

unfair labor practices Improper employment practices by either an employer or a union.

unfriendly buyer A buyer of a corporation who intends to change management and shake up the corporation after its takeover.

unfriendly suitor A suitor of a corporation who intends to change management and shake up the corporation after its takeover.

Uniform Commercial Code (UCC) A unified set of statutes designated to govern almost all commercial transactions.

Uniform Computer Information Transactions Act A statute that establishes standards for digital information contracts.

Uniform Durable Power of Attorney Act (UDPA) Legislation that states a person may appoint an "attorney in fact" by signing a written durable power of attorney.

Uniform Electronic Transactions Act (UETA) A model code that declares that if the parties to a contract have voluntarily agreed to transact business electronically, then the cyber-contract that results will be just as legally acceptable as a paper contract.

Uniform Facsimile Signatures of Public Officials Act A law that allows use of facsimile signatures of public officials when certain requirements are followed.

Uniform Partnership Act (UPA) The original partnership statute written by the National Conference of Commissioners on Uniform State Laws.

Uniform Power of Attorney Act A unified set of statutes designed to govern all aspects of the durable power of attorney agency relationship.

Uniform Trade Secrets Act Legislation written by the NCCUSL to define a trade secret, describe transgressions, and provide for both damages and injunctive relief when there has been a trade secret infringement.

unilateral contract An agreement in which one party makes a promise to do something in return for an act of some sort.

unilateral mistake In contract law, a mistake made by only one of the contracting parties. Unilateral mistake does not offer sufficient grounds for recession or renegotiation.

unimpaired class In bankruptcy law, a group of creditors whose collection rights are not impaired by a reorganization plan.

uninsured-motorist insurance A type of automobile insurance that provides protection against the risk of being injured by a motorist who does not have insurance.

union shop A place of employment where nonunion workers may be employed for a trial period of not more than 30 days, after which the nonunion workers must join the union or be discharged.

United Nations Commission on International Trade (UNCITRAL) A fraternity of 36 countries that seeks to cultivate the organization and integration of international law in relation to international trade.

United States Antitrust Modernization Committee A congressional think tank designed to examine antitrust law and report recommendations on how to modernize the law.

United States Code (USC) A compilation of all the statutes passed by Congress.

United States Sentencing Commission The commission that issues rules regarding federal courts' discretion in issuing punishments for crimes.

universal defense See *real defense.*

universal life insurance A form of straight life insurance that allows the policy owner flexibility in choosing and changing terms of the policy.

unlawful detainer A legal proceeding that provides landlords with a quick method of evicting a tenant. Also called *summary process, summary ejectment, forcible entry and detainer,* and *dispossessory warrant proceedings.*

unqualified opinion An opinion issued by an auditor that indicates that the financial records of a firm are an accurate reflection of the firm's financial status.

unsecured loan A loan in which creditors have nothing of value that they can repossess and sell in order to recover the money owed to them by the debtor.

Uruguay Round Agreements (URA) The eighth round of GATT talks, lasting from 1986 to 1993, out of which the World Trade Organization and the Dispute Settlement Understanding were created.

usage of trade Any method of dealing that is commonly used in the particular field.

Used Car Rule A rule established by the Federal Trade Commission requiring used car dealers to place a sticker, called a *Buyer's Guide,* in the window of each used car they offer for sale. The sticker provides consumer protection information.

usury The practice of charging more than the amount of interest allowed by law.

utilitarianism A system of ethical thought that focuses on the consequences of an action.

utility thinking A system of thought that focuses the consequences to one person or institution and then weighs the cost against the benefits of performing the action under scrutiny.

uttering The crime of offering a forged instrument to another person, knowing it to be forged.

valid contract A contract that is legally binding and fully enforceable by the court.

values A standard for determining what things hold central importance.

vandalism The act of willfully or maliciously causing damage to property.

variable-rate mortgage See *flexible-rate mortgage.*

variance An exemption that permits a use that differs from those allowed under the existing zoning law.

verdict A finding of fact by the jury in a court case; the jury's decision.

vertical expansion The joining of two companies that were in a customer–supplier relationship.

vicarious liability The concept of laying responsibility or blame upon one person for the actions of another.

victim's rights In criminal law, a series of rights created by the legislature for innocent people who have been victimized by crime.

video conference A conference that uses a televised connection to permit any number of people at widely diverse locations to discuss the details of a case.

void contract A contract that has no legal effect whatsoever.

void title No title at all.

voidable contract A contract that may be voided or canceled by one of the parties.

voidable title Title that may be voided if one of the parties elects to do so.

voluntary manslaughter In criminal law, a killing that results when a criminal defendant is in a state of extreme fright, terror, anger, or blind rage.

voting trust An agreement among shareholders to transfer their voting rights to a trustee.

waiver The voluntary surrender of some right, claim, or privilege.

waiver of premium An optional provision in an insurance contract that excuses the insured from paying premiums if the insured becomes disabled.

warehouse A building or structure in which any goods, but particularly wares or merchandise, are stored.

warehouser A person engaged in the business of storing goods for hire.

warehouse receipt A receipt issued by a person engaged in the business of storing goods for hire.

warehouser's lien The right of a warehouser to retain possession of goods stored in the warehouse until the satisfaction of the charges imposed on them.

warranty A promise, statement, or other representation that an item has certain qualities; also, an insured's promise to abide by restrictions, especially those written into an insurance policy. Also, an obligation imposed by law that an item will have certain qualities. Warranties made by means of a statement or other affirmation of fact are called *express warranties*; those imposed by law are *implied warranties*.

warranty of fitness for a particular purpose An implied warranty that goods will be fit for a particular purpose. This warranty is given by the seller to the buyer of goods whenever the seller has reason to know of any particular purpose for which the goods are needed and the buyer relies on the seller's skill and judgment to select the goods.

warranty of habitability The landlord warrants that the premises are fit for human habitation.

warranty of merchantability An implied warranty that goods are fit for the ordinary purpose for which such goods are used. Unless excluded, this warranty is always given by a merchant who sells goods in the ordinary course of business.

warranty of title A warranty given by a seller to a buyer of goods that states that the title being conveyed is good and that the transfer is rightful.

waste Substantial damage to premises that significantly decreases the value of the property.

Web conference A conference that is carried out online via the Internet using personal computers to permit any number of people at widely diverse locations to discuss the details of a case.

Westphalia system As outlined in the Treaty of Westphalia, a theory that describes nation-states as the primary international actors.

white knight A post-offer technique where a target company invites another suitor to outbid a hostile bidder. The second suitor agrees that it will retain the existing management.

whole life insurance See *straight life insurance*.

widow's allowance See *family allowance*.

will A legal document, not valid until the testator's death, expressing the testator's intent in distribution of all real and personal property.

work product privilege The guarantee that all notes, recordings, research documents, Q&As, voice mails, faxes, e-mails, computer records, memos, letters, flash drives, disks, DVDs, CDs, and so on that are prepared in anticipation of litigation remain confidential.

workers' compensation Worker protection provided for by state statutes that compensates covered workers or their dependents for injury, disease, or death that occurs on the job or as a result of it.

workplace harassment In employment law, misconduct in the workplace that results from quid pro quo sexual harassment or the creation of a hostile work environment

World Bank A nongovernmental organization that works exclusively with the poorest nations in the international community to help them secure loans.

World Intellectual Property Organization (WIPO) A division of the United Nations that supported the development of two international treaties designed to deal with electronic copyright problems.

World Intellectual Property Organization Copyright Treaty A treaty that guarantees copyright holders can use the Internet to post their works with full copyright protection.

World Intellectual Property Organization Phonograms Treaty A treaty that gives copyright holders the right to copy, publish, and distribute their works in any way.

World Trade Organization (WTO) A corporate nucleus for the management of international trade relationships.

worldwide organization Any international institution that transcends and unites nation-states in a common purpose on a global basis. Established worldwide organizations include diplomatic institutions such as the United Nations, legal organizations such as the International Criminal Court, and economic institutions such as the World Bank.

writ of certiorari An order from the U.S. Supreme Court to a lower court to deliver the records of a case to the Supreme Court for review.

writ of execution A court order directing the sheriff of a county to sell the property of a losing defendant to satisfy the judgment against that defendant.

writ of replevin A court order requiring a defendant to turn goods over to a plaintiff because the plaintiff has the right to immediate possession of the goods.

wrongful civil proceedings Filing a false civil lawsuit.

wrongful death statute A law that allows third parties affected by a death to bring a lawsuit only if the death is caused by the negligence or intentional conduct of the defendant.

wrongful discharge Exceptions to employment-at-will that give employees legal ground for lawsuits against employers who have dismissed them unfairly.

yellow-dog contract An agreement whereby an employer requires, as a condition of employment, that an employee promises not to join a union.

zoning law A local regulation or ordinance that restricts certain areas to specific uses; for example, areas zoned for residential, commercial, agricultural, industrial, or other uses.

Photo Credits

Case Index

936   Case Index

Hilt Truck Lanes, Inc., v. Riggins, 422
Hodges v. City of St. Louis, 137
Hollywood Decorators, Inc. v. Lancet, 335
Hong Kong Importers, Inc. v. American
    Express Co., 396–397
Huff v. White Motor Co., 318, 320–321

Ignazio v. Clear Channel, 226
Illinois Controls, Inc., v. Langham, 578
In Matter of Estate of Peters, 701–702
In re Al Zuni Trading, Inc., 421
In re American Medical Response of
    Connecticut, Inc., 494–496, 515
In re Dubuque, 462
In re Estate of Elmer, 696
In re Estate of Flicker, 700
In re Estate of Jung, 701
In re Estate of Norris, 393
In re Estate of Nuss, 558
In re Iwahashi, 772
In re Landrin, 462
In re: Lisa A. Bloch, Debtor Plaintiff v.
    Windham Professionals, et. al.,
    Defendants, 465–467
In re Manchester Lakes Association, 462
In the Matter of Rahl, 462
In the Matter of U.S. Truck Co., Inc., 462–463
Industrial Mach., Inc., v. Creative Displays,
    Inc., 677
Inglis v. Am. Motors Corp., 338

J&K Computer Systems, Inc., v. Parrish, 771
Jackson v. Jackson, 601
Jacob and Young v. Kent, 269
J.E.B. Stewart v. Citizens and Southern
    National Bank, 165
Jessica Ruth Gonzales v. The United States
    of America, 84

Kelo v. City of New London, 654, 666, 772
Kirby v. Bergfield, 375
Klinicki v. Lundgren, 601
Koedding v. N.B. West Contracting Co.,
    Inc., 208
Kruse v. Coos Head Timber Co., 226

Lamas v. Baldwin, 578
Lauretig v. Pierce, 237
Leake v. Cain, 137
LeBlanc v. Stevenson, 65
Leeper v. Pennsylvania Higher Education
    Assistance Agency, 462
Leftkowitz v. Great Minneapolis Surplus
    Store, 188
Leichtamer v. American Motors Corp., 334
Lewis v. S.L.&E., Inc., 601
Liarkos v. Mello, 315
Litwins v. Timbercrest Estates, Inc., 269
Lohr v. Larry's Homes of Virginia, 316
Lonchyna v. Brown, Secretary of
    Defense, 226
Lonzrick v. Republic Steel Corp., 338

Manor Bldg. Corp. v. Manor Complex
    Assocs., 395
Mark DiCintio v. DaimlerChrysler
    Corporation, et al., 316
Marrama v. Citizens Bank, 461
Massachusetts v. Mellon, 704
Matter of Estate of Bolton, 375
Matter of Estate of Dejmal, 696
Matter of Estate of Mikeska, 700
Matter of Estate of Royal, 700
Matter of Marriage of Rutherford, 375
McAndrew v. Mularchuk, 491
McConnell v. Federal Election Comm'n, 141
Meade v. Cedarapids, Inc., 517–518
Melling v. Los Alamos Inn and Suites,
    634, 643–644
Meng v. Trustees of Boston University, 247
Mers v. Dispatch Printing, 207
Miranda v. Arizona, 67
Mitchell v. State Farm Mutual Automobile
    Insurance Co., 225
Montalbano and Friends v. Scranton Bank
    and Trust, 362–364
Montana Association of Underwriters v.
    Department of Administration and
    MBI, 578
Morrison v. Australian National Bank, 50
Morrison v. Thoelke, 188
Murray v. Accounting Center & Tax
    Services, Inc., et al., 271–273
Myers v. Forest City Enterprises, Inc., 138
Myers v. Terminix, 227

Naquin v. Air Engineered Systems and
    Services, Inc., 601
Natare v. D.S.I. Duraplastec Systems, Inc., 74
Nat'l Bank v. Refrigerated Transp., 374
Natural Resources Defense Council, Inc. v.
    Train, 745
New York Central and Hudson River
    Railroad v. United States, 111
New York Times Co. v. Sullivan, 137
Newsome v. Tibbs, 222
Nicastro v. McIntyre, 48
Nicklesworth v. Marblehead Properties, 231
Ninth Street East, Ltd. v. Harrison,
    298–300, 302, 306
NLRB v. Exchange Parts Co., 535
NLRB v. Savair Mfg. Co., 536
Nolan v. Williamson Music, Inc., 269
Northridge Bank v. Lakeshore Com. Fin.
    Corp., 442–443

Office of Disciplinary Counsel v.
    Lloyd, 492
O'Keefe v. Lee Calan Imports, 188
Osborn v. Brown, 677

P&F Const. v. Friend Lumber Corp., 315
Pacific Diamond Co. v. Superior Ct., 651
Pagiarulo v. National Shawmut Bank, 651
Painter v. Graley, 519

Parker v. Arthur Murray, Inc., 270
People v. Roberts, 112
Planned Parenthood v. Casey, 689–690, 750
Pottschmidt v. Thomas J. Klosterman,
    M.D., Inc., 577
Preston v. First Bank of Marietta, 442
Procter and Gamble Co. v. Stoneham, 272
Proprietors of the Charles River Bridge v.
    Proprietors of the Warren Bridge, 165

Quality Motors v. Hays, 225–226

Ralo, Inc., v. Jack Graham, Inc., 677
Ramoinde v. Van Vlerah, 272
Ramos v. Wheel Sports Center, 296–297
R.A.V. v. St. Paul, 112
Republic Aviation Corp. v. NLRB, 535
Reynolds v. Sims, 65
Rice v. The City of St. Louis, 519
Richard Diaz, et al. v. International
    Longshoremen's and Warehousemen's
    Union, Local 13, 535
R.J. Enstrom Corporation v. Interceptor
    Corporation, 627
Robinson v. Kleinfeld, 542, 547–548
Roe v. Wade, 689–690, 750, 756
Rogers v. Rogers, 700
Rogers v. Runfola 7 Assoc., Inc., 272
Rogers v. Toni Home Permanent Co., 338
Rome v. Flower Memorial Hospital, 43
Rostow Aviation, Ltd. v. Futuregraphics,
    Inc., 257
Rothenbeucher v. Tockstein, 188–189
R.R. v. M.H. and Another, 210, 217, 221
Russell v. Russell, 676
Russell v. United Missionary Baptist
    Church, 600
Rux v. Republic of Sudan, 65
Ryberg v. Allstate Ins. Co., 272

Schaeffer v. Cavallero, 651
Schleimer v. Googe, 315
Schupack v. McDonald's Systems, Inc., 269
Scott v. Purser Truck Sales, Inc., 651–652
Scott v. Ross, Workman, Simpson, and the
    Cult Awareness Network, 470, 480–481
Searle v. Allstate Life Insurance, 421
Securities and Exchange Commission v.
    Arthur Young and Company, 727
Securities and Exchange Commission v.
    W.J. Howey Co., 626
Security State Bank v. McCoy, 558
Seier v. Peek, 208
Shaffer v. Victoria Station, Inc., 316
Silkwood v. Kerr-McGee Corporation, 42
Simon v. Simon, 676
Smathers v. Smathers, 360–361
Smith v. VanGorkon, 601
Sorrell v. Young, 189
South Central State College v. McLaughlin
    Construction, Inc., 258–259
Spence v. Huffman, 578

Subject Index

21st century financial crisis and, 433–435
UCC and, 437, 440
Security agreement, 437–438
Security deposits, 670
Security interest, 425
Security-based swap, 610
Sée, Henri, 148–150, 152
Self-defense, 108–109
Semco, Inc., 771
Senior partners, 551
Separation of powers, 29–30
September 11, 2001 attacks, 646–647,
648, 774, 776, 784, 787
Serious intent, 170, 171
Servant, 116, 472
Service of process, 54
Services as consideration, 195
Servient tenement, 657
Settlement week, 79
Settlor, 692
Seventh Circuit Court of Appeals, 604
Severalty, 635, 660
Sexual harassment, 509
Shareholder voting control, 586–588
cumulative voting, 587, 588
nomination of directors, 591–592
pooling agreements, 587, 591
proxy voting, 587–589
shareholder proposals, 587, 589–591
Shareholder Vote on Executive
Compensation Act, 206
unanimous voting restrictions, 592
voting trusts, 587, 591
Shareholders, 565, 583
dividends, 565, 574, 597–598
rights of, 597–598
shareholder democracy, 586, 611
shareholder lawsuits, 587, 592–593
shareholder of record, 598
shareholder proposals, 587, 589–591
shareholder resolutions, 589
targeted shareholder agreements, 619, 620
Shelter provision, 365
Sherman Antitrust Act, 111, 522, 604, 609,
612–614
Shin, Joongok, 699
Shipment contracts, 289–290, 300–301
Shipwrecks, 636–637
Shopping bot, 203, 488
Sievers, Allen M., 552
Sight drafts, 344, 345
Signature requirements
cyber-signatures, 242, 285, 287
negotiable instruments and, 349–350,
357, 369, 370–371, 379
wills and, 683
written contracts and, 239–241, 242, 285
Silber, John, 247
Silence as acceptance of offers, 176–177
Silent partners, 551
Silkwood, Karen, 42
Similar locality rule, 721

Similar practitioner rule, 721–722
Simple contracts, 162
Simpson, Charles, 470
Simpson, O.J., 88
Singapore, 83–84
Sinic Civilization, 778
Situational ethics, 8
Sixth Amendment, 62
S.L.&E., Inc., 601
Slamming, 329
Slander, 119–120
Slight care, 640
Slight negligence, 639
Smallpox, 740
Smishing, 102–103
Smith, Adam, 376, 380, 383, 387,
526, 527
Smith, Anna Nicole, 444, 446, 455
Smith, Douglas, 84
Smith, Scott, 699
Social contract theory, 8–9
Social engineering, 319
Social media policies, 494–496, 513–515
social media policy (SMP), 514
Social responsibility, 15
advantages of, 17–19
traditional corporate culture and, 15–17
Social Security, 414, 451, 504
Social Security Act of 1935, 504–505
Soft power, 734
Software. *See* Computer software programs
Sole proprietorships, 543–544
Somalia, 785
Soundness of mind, 681, 685–686
Sousa, Dawnmarie, 494–496
South Carolina, 530
South Central State College, 258–259
South Dakota, 530
South Korea, 749, 798
Sovereign immunity, 477–478
Sovereignty, 776
Soviet Union, 779, 784
Spain, 661, 798
Spam, 105, 328–329
Spear phishing, 102
Special agents, 479
Special felonies, 90
Special Flood Hazard Areas (SFHAs), 410
Special indorsements, 354
Special interest group control, 584
Special jurisdiction, 46
Special mission, 505
Special warranty deed, 663–664
Specially manufactured goods, 284
Specific performance, 58, 156, 266–267
Specifically foreseen third parties, 711, 712
Speculative damages, 266
Spelling Entertainment Group, 519
Spendthrift trust, 693
Sperry Ford, 225
Spertell, Beverly, 247
Spirit and letter of the law, 26

Spoofing, 102
Sportsman Travel Trailer Sales, 316
Spray trust, 694
Sprinkling trust, 694
S.S. Christos, 781
St. Louis Post-Despatch, 136
Staff privileges, at hospitals, 724
Stale checks, 378
Stalking, 102
Standard construction rule, 159, 236
Staple courts, 151
Stare decisis, 38, 141, 142
Stark, Rodney, 148
State Bank of Lehi, 442
State Bank of Wapello, 375
State constitutions, 33
State exemptions in bankruptcy, 452
State Farm Mutual Automobile Insurance
Company, 248–249, 265, 422
State Intermediate Appellate Courts, 51–52
State police power, 34–35, 89, 607, 706,
714–715, 734
State regulatory power, 607
State Security Bank, 558
State supreme courts, 52
State trial courts, 51
States rights, 31, 33
Statute of Frauds, 158–160, 229
case study, 146, 158–159, 228, 234, 244
contracts required in writing and, 229–235
elements of written contract, 234–235
signature requirements, 239
Statutes of limitations, 133, 200, 263, 309
Statutes of repose, 133
Statutory agent, 569
Statutory interpretation, 39
Statutory law, 35–37
codes and titles, 36
contract law and, 154, 219–220
cyber-law statutes, 37, 104–105,
178–180, 243–245, 391, 488
statutory interpretation, 39
Uniform Commercial Code (UCC), 37
uniform laws, 36, 37
Statutory liability, 476, 712–713
Stern Electronics, Inc., 772
Stevenson, William, 65
Stewart, Alexis, 726
Stewart, Martha, 726–727
Stigler, George, 615
Stock acquisition, 616–618
Stock certificate, 574
Stock dividends, 565, 574, 597–598
Stock transfers, 598
Stokes, Ethel, 375
Stolen property, 638, 644
Stoppage in transit, 305
Stopping performance, 264
Straight life insurance, 406
Strategic Air Command (SAC), 784
Stream of commerce test, 48,
59, 60